BOHEMIANS

BOHEMIANS

A Graphic History

Edited by Paul Buhle and David Berger
with Luisa Cetti

Introduction by Paul Buhle

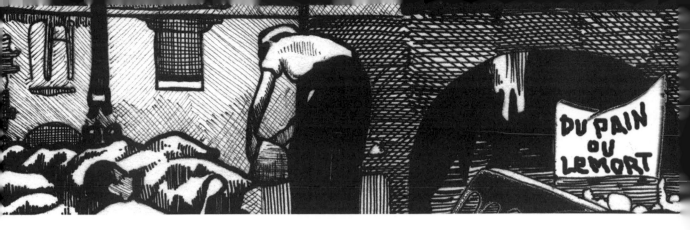

First published by Verso 2014
In the collection © Verso 2014
Contributions © The contributors 2014
Introduction © Paul Buhle 2014

1 3 5 7 9 10 8 6 4 2

Verso
UK: 6 Meard Street, London W1F 0EG
US: 20 Jay Street, Suite 1010, Brooklyn, NY 11201
www.versobooks.com

Verso is the imprint of New Left Books

ISBN-13: 978-1-78168-261-6
eISBN-13: 978-1-78168-262-3 (US)
eISBN-13: 978-1-78168-641-6 (UK)

British Library Cataloguing in Publication Data
A catalogue record for this book is available from the British Library.

Library of Congress Cataloging-in-Publication Data

Bohemians : a Graphic Anthology / edited by Paul Buhle and David Berger.
    pages cm
  ISBN 978-1-78168-261-6 (pbk.)
1. Bohemianism in literature. 2. Counterculture—United States—Comic books,
strips, etc. 3. Bohemianism—United States—Comic books, strips, etc. 4. Graphic
novels. I. Buhle, Paul, 1944– II. Berger, David, 1944–
  PN56.B63B64 2014
  809'.933552—dc23
                2013047893

Typeset in Bernhard Modern by Sean Ford, Brooklyn, NY
Printed in the US by Maple Press

In memory of Spain Rodriguez,
a great artist, a great influence

Contents

Introduction

Paul Buhle

Bohemians have occupied a semi-subversive status in modern society without being, in any consistent way, political-minded or even organized. The danger that they pose for the fretful of every generation since the 1850s is also the secret of their lasting appeal, in particular, to the disaffected and the young. They seem to lead the feckless or merely naïve, and especially artistic-minded youth, toward rack and ruin, morally if not physically. They disregard existing laws, especially those connecting love and marriage. They belong to no clear or certain social class, yet they continue to be the transgressive class.

Their origin, more specifically their naming, has become part of their larger mystery or aura. The real Bohemia, a geographical, ethnic and religious entity destined to become part of the modern Czech Republic, was misidentified by mid–nineteenth-century French journalists as the source of the Roma population and culture. The Roma ("Gypsies" until their near-extermination by Hitler) had already been identified on stage and in literature with Romanticism or at least with some vision of a carefree, musical, traveling folk, swarthy-skinned and wonderful to behold.

Through a double or triple misunderstanding, then, "Bohemians" (we prefer "bohemians") emerged as an individual or group identity contrary to the hard-working, if triumphant, bourgeoisie, dull of taste or imagination but large of bankbook. Political rebels associated with working-class movements seemed the natural allies of men and women of middling origins dedicated to art and the transformation of social conditions, emphatically including the conditions of their own lives. This connection may have been a further misunderstanding, but if so, one of the most fruitful misunderstandings of all.

The anticipated working-class revolution did not happen in Western Europe or the U.S., where modernization of all kinds nevertheless flowered, and was seen as detrimental to moral and artistic traditions. Discontent, including moral disdain for the cruelties, hypocrisies and sheer ugliness of the new industrial–urban order, prompted the opening of alternative outlets for expressions of unrest. Rebellious artists, proletarian autodidacts, and what a later century would call "liberated women" articulated what many others felt. Artistic experimentation, in part a response to the tedium experienced in the lives of the comfortable classes, thus inspired an audience for bohemianism that has never disappeared.

This comic-art volume specifically connects bohemians in their earliest incarnations with the twisted threads of 1850s Paris and Henri Murger's novel *Scènes de la vie de bohème*. Landlords beware, but what made that original set of young people unique was their devotion to art, to love, and to each other, rather than to

respectability and social advance. What made them important beyond themselves was their presence as a cultural phenomenon: European intellectuals and the well-off middle classes, realizing the new pleasures of not-yet-named "vacation," came from across Europe and beyond to see these odd creatures in their lair, the Parisian Left (and eventually also the Right) Bank.

There, avowed bohemians continued to make history for decades as artists, writers, and as the subjects of endless cultural productions in every possible venue. By joining themselves sympathetically to the labor strikes of the 1910s and later to the assorted social causes of industrial unionism, the Popular Front, the wartime antifascist Resistance and the antiwar student uprisings of 1968, they contributed significantly to left-wing movements. It was never quite clear how much any sector of the modern political Left, from Karl Marx onward, appreciated their efforts. The bohemians habitually shunned discipline alongside movements that demanded discipline, and they put an often unseemly face upon respectable working-class causes. Just as bad, altogether too often they flitted off at the first signs of danger or disillusionment. They were artists after all, or thought of themselves as artists first, rather than as political revolutionaries.

By the 1910s, many urban areas across the planet had their imitators and homegrown bohemian types—

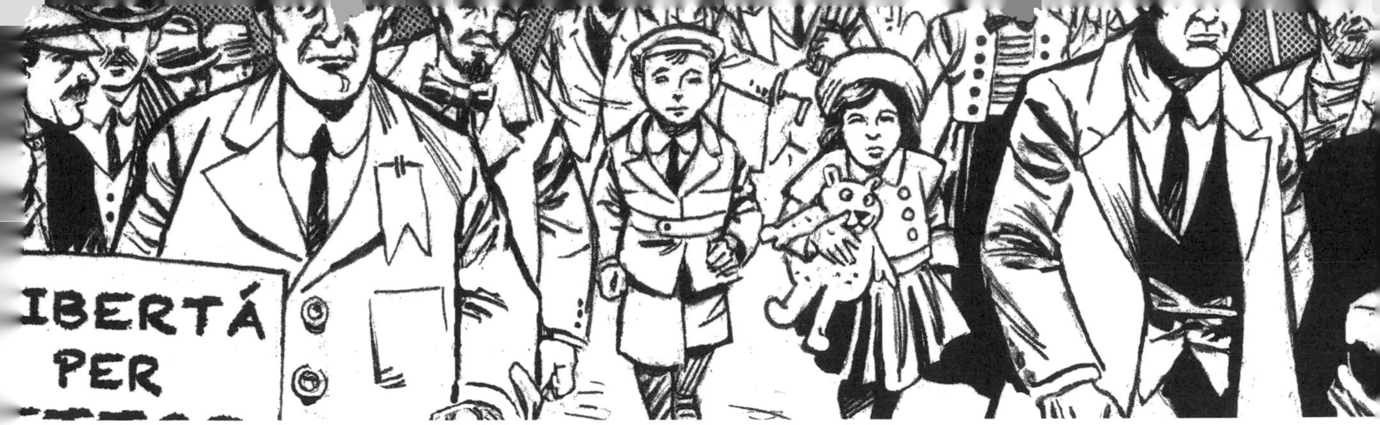
IBERTÁ
PER

disproving the old adage that "bohemia exists only in Paris." None, not even in Paris, were quite so famous or influential as the extended neighborhood of Greenwich Village in New York City. Along with Harlem, which blossomed just a little later, Greenwich Village held the attention of the most powerful publicity machine in the world, and operated as a magnet drawing artists, thrill-seekers and certain kinds of job seekers to the apparent center of the action. Modern dance was being invented no further away than Coney Island, with the "touch" dancing of teenagers who loved the types of jazz played by dance hall orchestras, and who "petted" on benches in the public parks outside. Bohemianism was not only for the elite. In Manhattan, Ashcan Art took shape alongside the introduction of Abstractionism at the Armory Show of 1913. This event was notably almost a decade before the Museum of Modern Art (MoMA) opened. By that time, experimental art had become both respectable and quite a bit less dangerous.

From here, the story becomes more complicated in many ways. We have chosen, in this volume, to tell mainly the U.S. side of the bohemian saga, not only for the sake of coherence, but also because the racial role in bohemianism becomes crucial (rather than a sidebar, as it served in Paris) during the twentieth century. The narrative is complicated, of course, in many ways, and the emergence of the "free woman," the determinedly undaunted version of the late nineteenth-century's New Woman, added more than spice. Businessmen bedding down young, poor women in any variety of settings, whether through formal prostitution or by mistress-keeping, has never resembled bohemianism or even "free love" (someone has to pay the cost, and venereal disease often takes a wide toll). The real Free Love can only occur among equals, and for that matter, can be homosexual or bisexual as well as heterosexual.

Bohemia certainly does not end in 1950 but we stop there—with an occasional glance at a post-1950 personal career and an additional look backward from two noteworthy denizens of decaying 1970s Cleveland, Harvey Pekar and Robert Crumb. Afterward, the world changes too fast to be encompassed by our volume. The Beat Generation and the public attention that it continues to draw is already a different story (told in part in the comic-art volume *The Beats*, scripted largely by Harvey Pekar), and the "massification" of a bohemian-like counterculture in the late 1960s and after would require an entirely different approach.

It is worth saying that today's comic art, as seen in the examples at hand, is heir to the best traditions of rebellious artistic expression. Late nineteenth-century matrons hearing about the excitement on the continent aspired to sit nude for a painter, so as to capture their bodies and their souls on canvas. A decade later, painters in New York City drew distinctly vernacular images of the bustling Manhattan streets, an act as provocative in that time and place as respectable American women going naked for a painting. The artists of the *Masses* magazine, as we will see, were arrested and put on trial for their political (that is to say, antiwar) sympathies, their magazine rudely suppressed by a purportedly liberal Woodrow Wilson administration. Dada, as an art form, came out of a rejection of the war makers' claims to grand ideals, but also a rejection of "pretty" art in favor of a collage-style rearrangement of fragments from the existing world in objects, paper, wood and other materials.

At some time here, and not only in the U.S., popular artistic phenomena resembling modern comics also came into being; though not especially rebellious in any political sense, they were funny and occasionally keenly satirical of existing mores. Notwithstanding a handful of brilliant comic-strip artists' efforts over several generations, socially subversive comics were fairly few in number until the appearance of *Mad* in 1952, with its covert but deeply Bronx-Jewish assaults upon postwar politics and commercialism. Comic art was then reinvented as well as politicized in the "Underground Comix" of the 1960s–70s, and reinvented once more in sections of the "Alternative Comics" of the 1980s through to the present. Some of the older artists included here are themselves part of the story of the comics that shook off respectability (and the expectation of corporate-level salaries with benefits). The late Spain Rodriguez would, undoubtedly, be the single most outstanding example of the bohemian in his generation at work in comic art. *Bohemians* is, in all, a first effort to tackle bohemianism in comic form.

Bohemia itself is supposed to have disappeared, at least several times, as high rents came to formerly low-rent neighborhoods where its denizens dwelled. Yet somehow, it persists, or rather irregularly reappears. Not only in the U.S. or Europe of course, but by now, almost everywhere.

Chapter One

Bohemians and Utopians

The origins of bohemia in the artist studios and the streets of 1850s Paris cannot be easily separated from the city's long history of utopian experiments in collective and cooperative living, nor from the political upheavals that occurred there from 1789 and 1830 to 1848. The desired leap out of the social conditions and relations of the present was ever the dream of a minority and never the dream of the ruling caste of society, even when the dreamers themselves were dissident members of that caste.

What makes modern bohemianism different is the nexus of a new art and sexual expression. Art without patrons (or customers) may be near impossible, even for willing garret-dwellers. But art without restraints belongs first of all to the nineteenth century, with vital earlier exceptions (Bruegel and Goya come to mind) to the contrary. Even the celibate, presumably sex-sublimating Shakers invented a new art, as the simplicity of Shaker design in many areas from furniture to clothing continues to inspire admiration. The desire to live an artistic life, not just for an individual few but with a community of like-minded people, was here to stay.

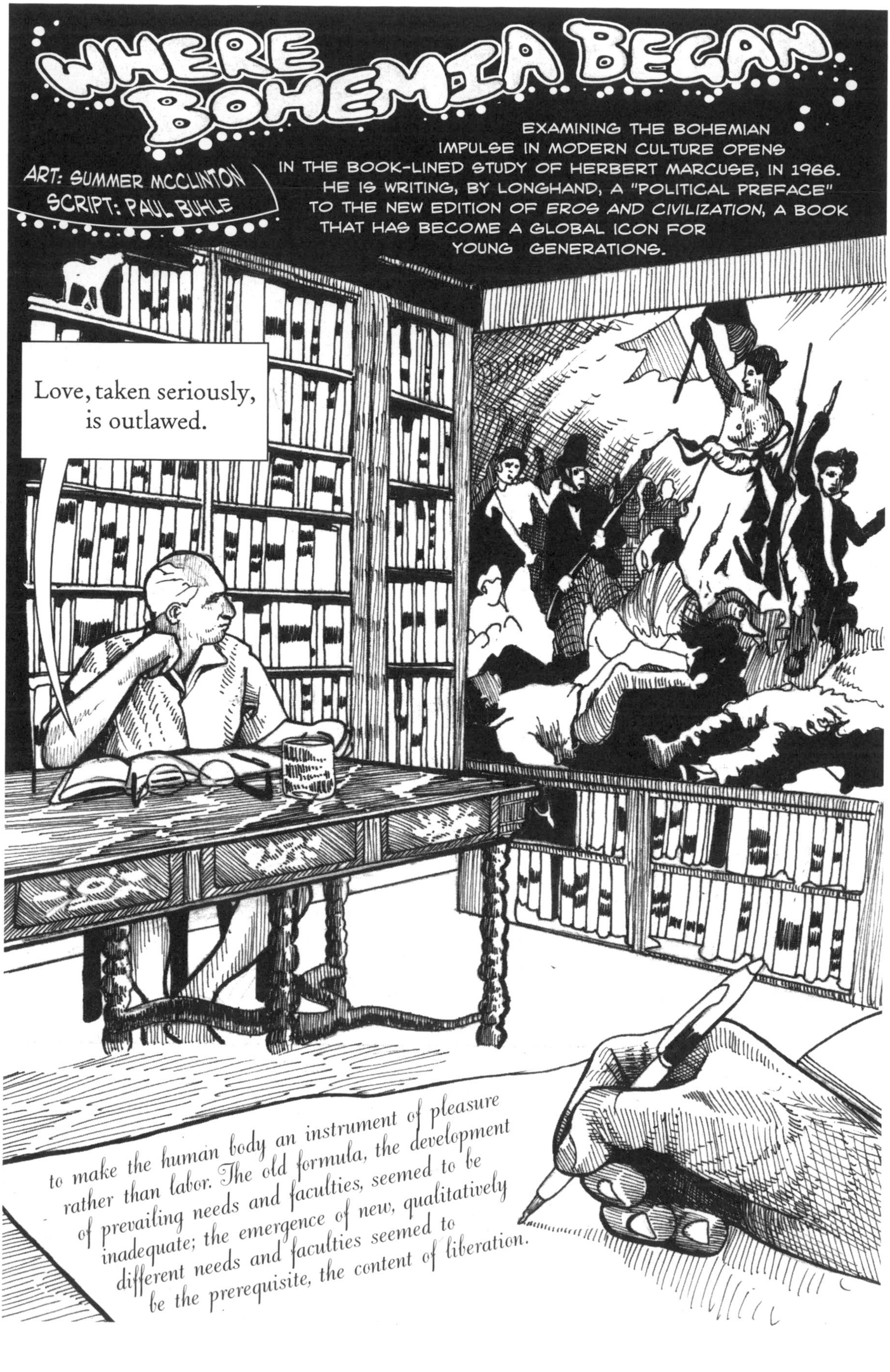
WHERE BOHEMIA BEGAN
ART: SUMMER MCCLINTON
SCRIPT: PAUL BUHLE
EXAMINING THE BOHEMIAN IMPULSE IN MODERN CULTURE OPENS IN THE BOOK-LINED STUDY OF HERBERT MARCUSE, IN 1966. HE IS WRITING, BY LONGHAND, A "POLITICAL PREFACE" TO THE NEW EDITION OF EROS AND CIVILIZATION, A BOOK THAT HAS BECOME A GLOBAL ICON FOR YOUNG GENERATIONS.
Love, taken seriously, is outlawed.
to make the human body an instrument of pleasure rather than labor. The old formula, the development of prevailing needs and faculties, seemed to be inadequate; the emergence of new, qualitatively different needs and faculties seemed to be the prerequisite, the content of liberation.

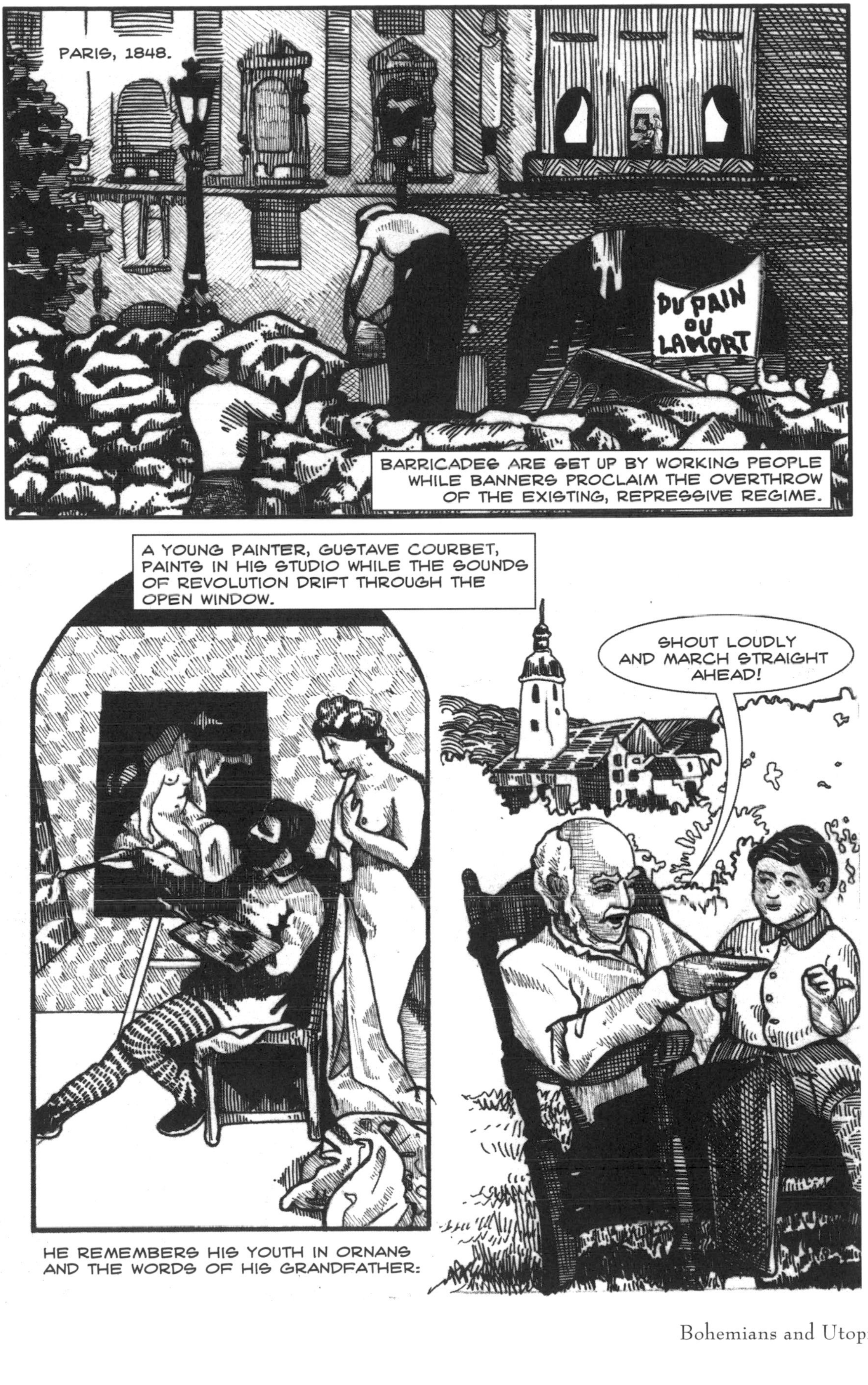
PARIS, 1848.
DU PAIN OU LAMORT
BARRICADES ARE SET UP BY WORKING PEOPLE WHILE BANNERS PROCLAIM THE OVERTHROW OF THE EXISTING, REPRESSIVE REGIME.
A YOUNG PAINTER, GUSTAVE COURBET, PAINTS IN HIS STUDIO WHILE THE SOUNDS OF REVOLUTION DRIFT THROUGH THE OPEN WINDOW.
HE REMEMBERS HIS YOUTH IN ORNANS AND THE WORDS OF HIS GRANDFATHER:
SHOUT LOUDLY AND MARCH STRAIGHT AHEAD!

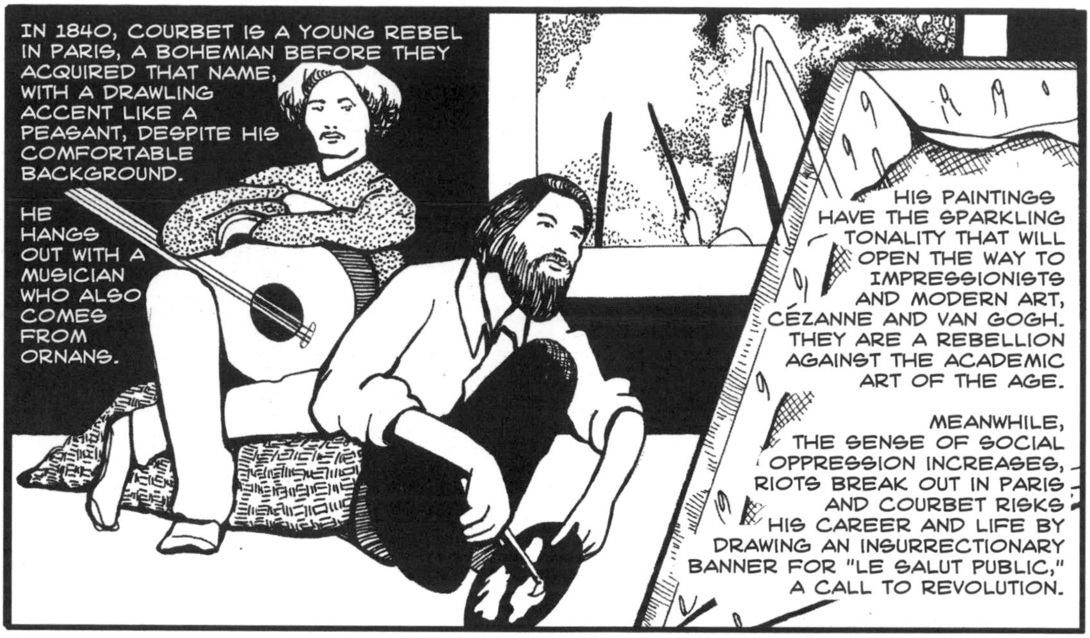
IN 1840, COURBET IS A YOUNG REBEL IN PARIS, A BOHEMIAN BEFORE THEY ACQUIRED THAT NAME, WITH A DRAWLING ACCENT LIKE A PEASANT, DESPITE HIS COMFORTABLE BACKGROUND.
HE HANGS OUT WITH A MUSICIAN WHO ALSO COMES FROM ORNANS.
HIS PAINTINGS HAVE THE SPARKLING TONALITY THAT WILL OPEN THE WAY TO IMPRESSIONISTS AND MODERN ART, CÉZANNE AND VAN GOGH. THEY ARE A REBELLION AGAINST THE ACADEMIC ART OF THE AGE.
MEANWHILE, THE SENSE OF SOCIAL OPPRESSION INCREASES, RIOTS BREAK OUT IN PARIS AND COURBET RISKS HIS CAREER AND LIFE BY DRAWING AN INSURRECTIONARY BANNER FOR "LE SALUT PUBLIC," A CALL TO REVOLUTION.

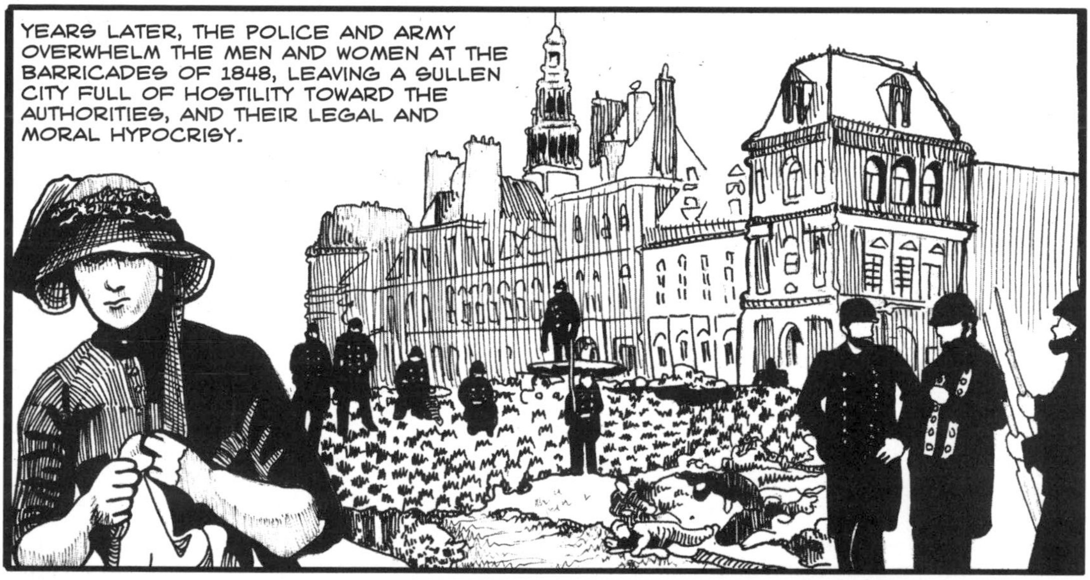
YEARS LATER, THE POLICE AND ARMY OVERWHELM THE MEN AND WOMEN AT THE BARRICADES OF 1848, LEAVING A SULLEN CITY FULL OF HOSTILITY TOWARD THE AUTHORITIES, AND THEIR LEGAL AND MORAL HYPOCRISY.

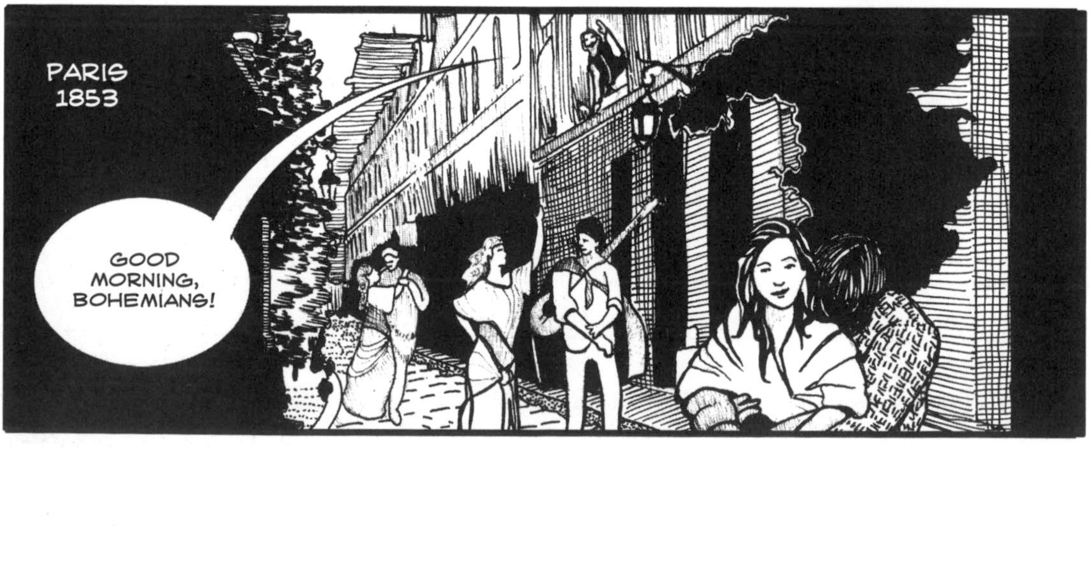
PARIS 1853
GOOD MORNING, BOHEMIANS!

ARTIST: Lisa Lyons

THE UNITARY HOUSEHOLD

SCRIPT: LUISA CETTI

Utopianism had one grand last stand before the Civil War began. **Edward Underhill** founded the Unitary Household in a New York brownstone with the family of **Marx Edgeworth Lazarus**, author of **Love vs. Marriage**, the "first free love bible," beautiful **Julia Branch**, and various other reformers, artists, journalists, feminists, and Spiritualists.

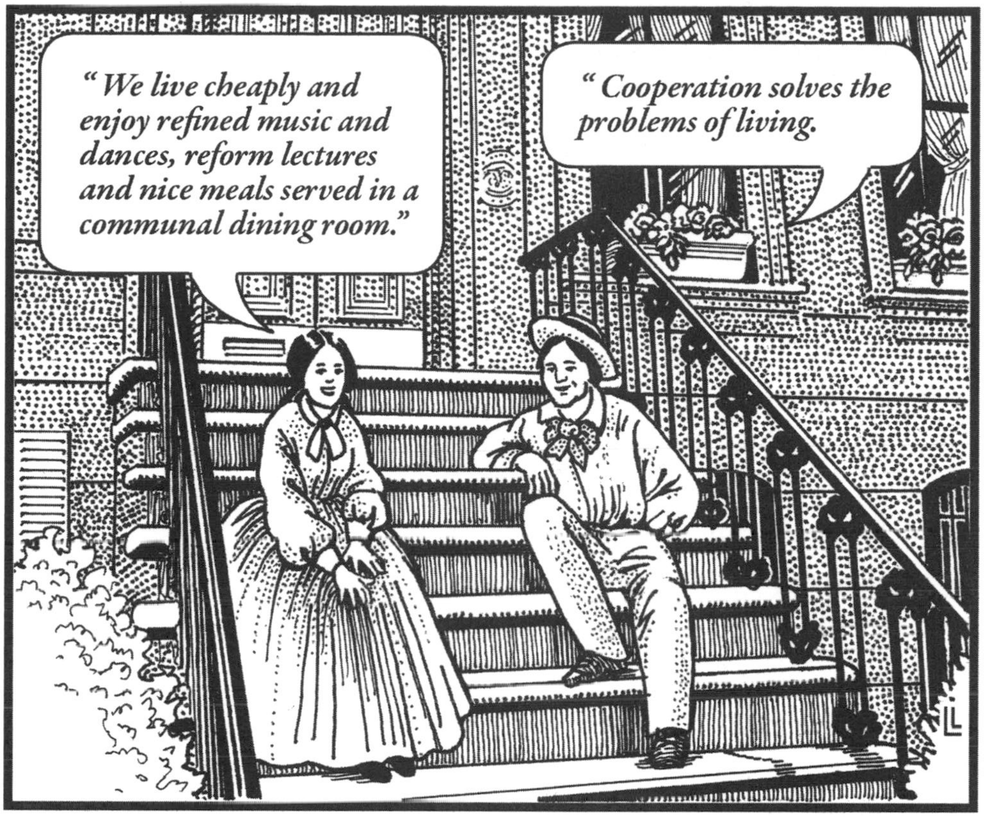

"We live cheaply and enjoy refined music and dances, reform lectures and nice meals served in a communal dining room."
"Cooperation solves the problems of living.
LL

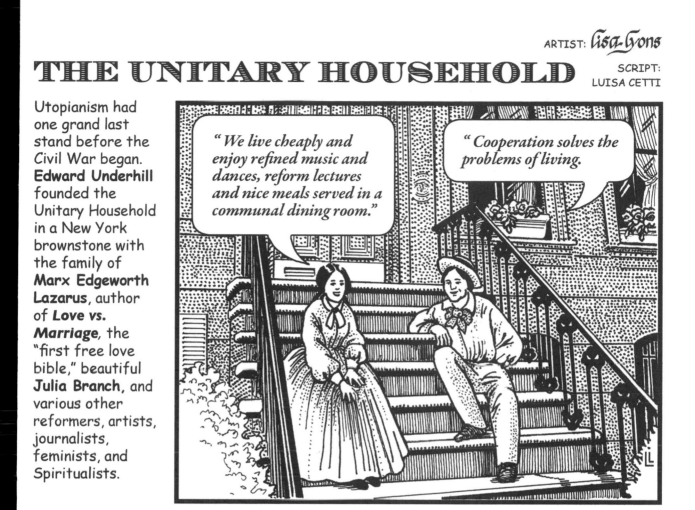

Domestic chores were assigned to paid servants, and both men and women of the Unitary Household were free to follow their "passional attractions" — and define free love.

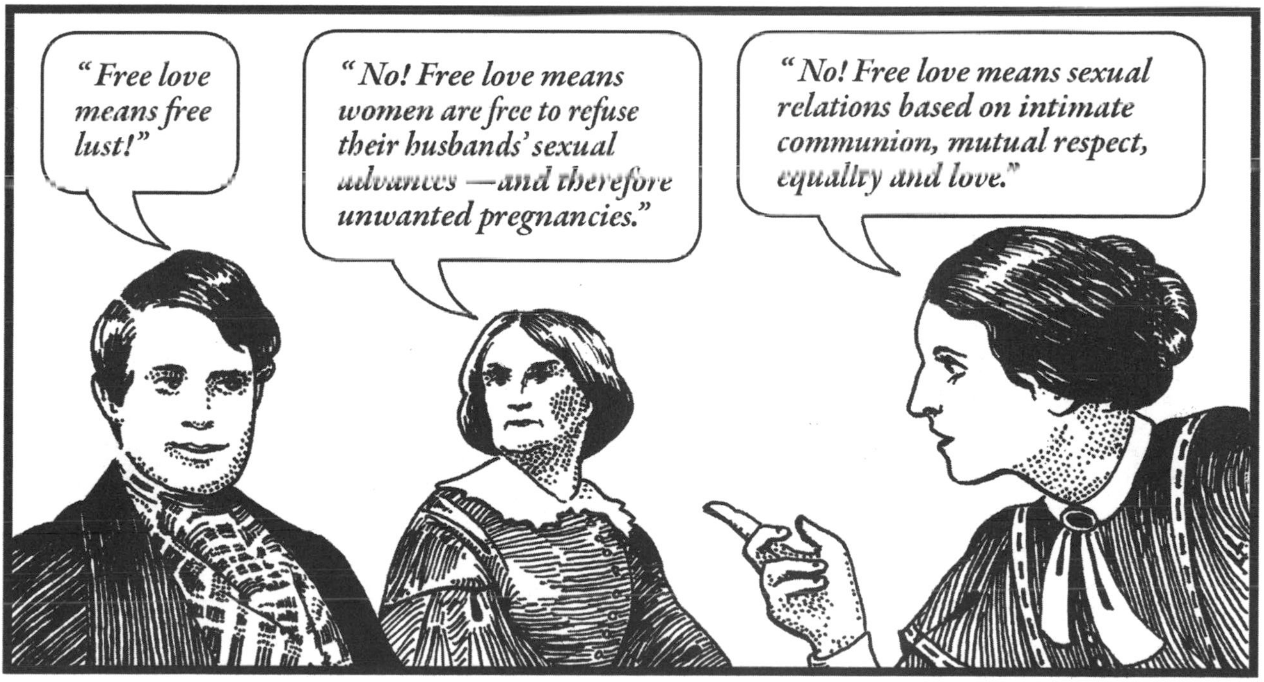

"Free love means free lust!"
"No! Free love means women are free to refuse their husbands' sexual advances —and therefore unwanted pregnancies."
"No! Free love means sexual relations based on intimate communion, mutual respect, equality and love."

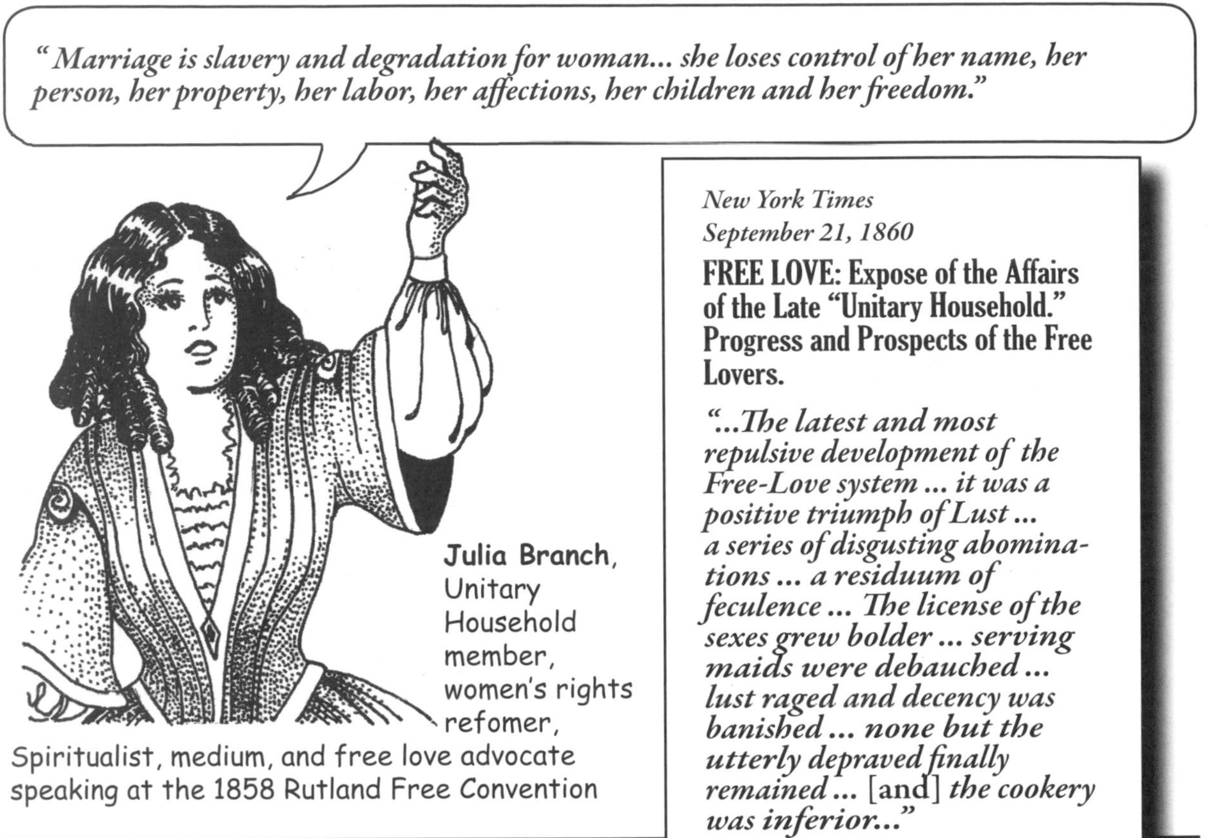
"Marriage is slavery and degradation for woman... she loses control of her name, her person, her property, her labor, her affections, her children and her freedom."

Julia Branch, Unitary Household member, women's rights refomer, Spiritualist, medium, and free love advocate speaking at the 1858 Rutland Free Convention

New York Times
September 21, 1860

FREE LOVE: Expose of the Affairs of the Late "Unitary Household." Progress and Prospects of the Free Lovers.

"...The latest and most repulsive development of the Free-Love system ... it was a positive triumph of Lust ... a series of disgusting abominations ... a residuum of feculence ... The license of the sexes grew bolder ... serving maids were debauched ... lust raged and decency was banished ... none but the utterly depraved finally remained ... [and] the cookery was inferior..."

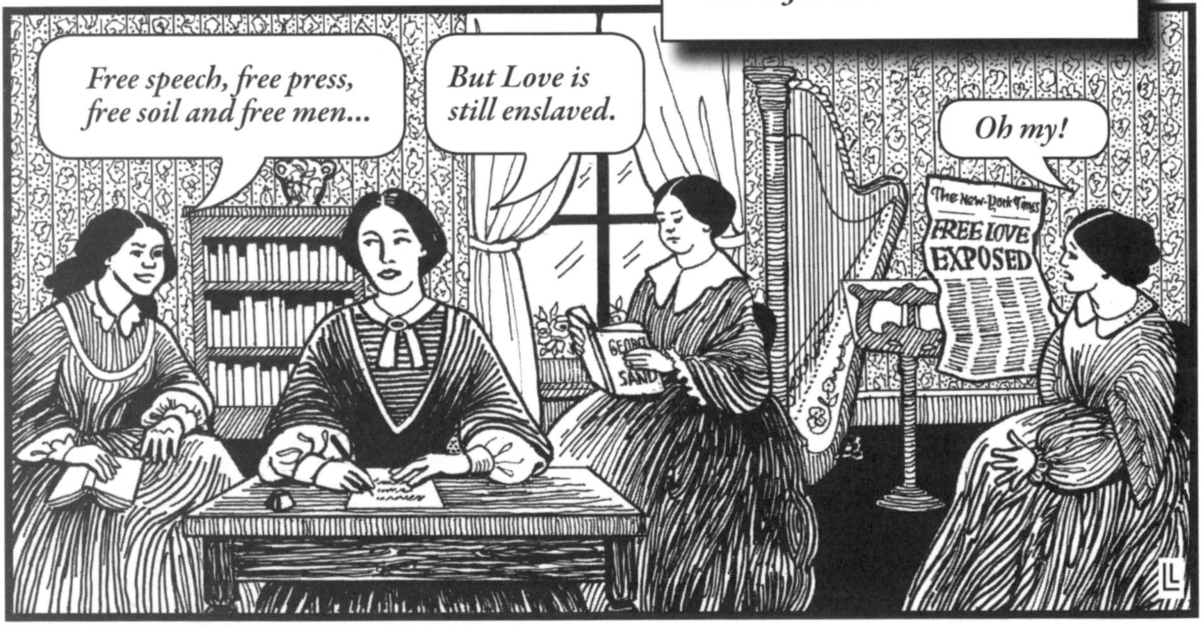
Free speech, free press, free soil and free men...
But Love is still enslaved.
Oh my!
The New-York Times
FREE LOVE EXPOSED
GEORGE SAND

The comfortable life at a moderate price (plus servants) offered by the Unitary Household was far from the communal efforts in the farms, shops and kitchens of Brook Farm and North American Phalanx. Attacked viciously in the press, the Unitary Household lasted only two years, from 1858 to 1860.

ARTIST: Lisa Lyons

THE FREE LOVE LEAGUE

SCRIPT: DAVID BERGER

The Free Love League, which met in Taylor's Saloon and Hotel, an elegant downtown venue often used for socialist and spiritualist meetings, was still more daring.

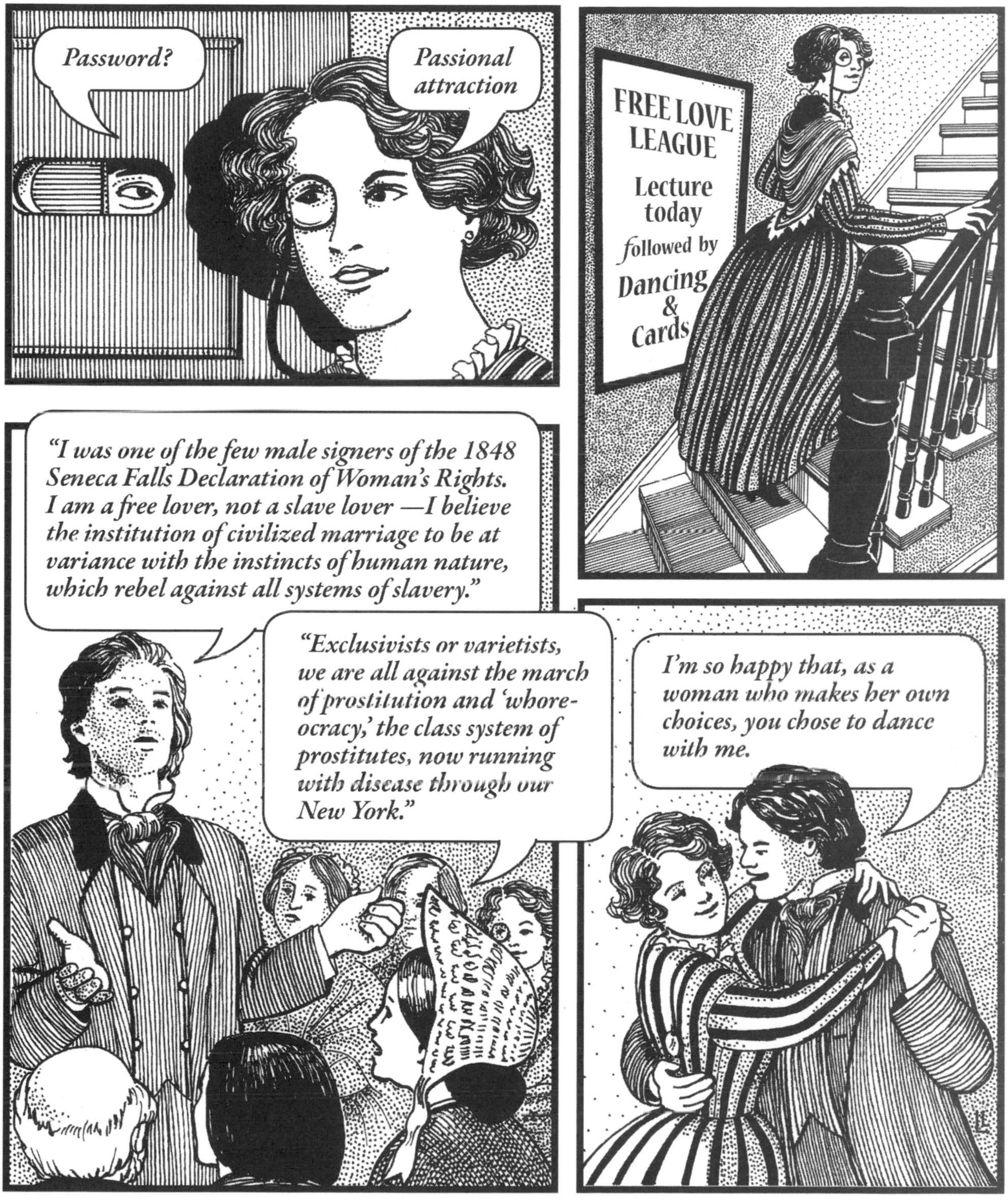

Password?
Passional attraction
FREE LOVE LEAGUE Lecture today followed by Dancing & Cards
"I was one of the few male signers of the 1848 Seneca Falls Declaration of Woman's Rights. I am a free lover, not a slave lover —I believe the institution of civilized marriage to be at variance with the instincts of human nature, which rebel against all systems of slavery."
"Exclusivists or varietists, we are all against the march of prostitution and 'whore-ocracy,' the class system of prostitutes, now running with disease through our New York."
I'm so happy that, as a woman who makes her own choices, you chose to dance with me.

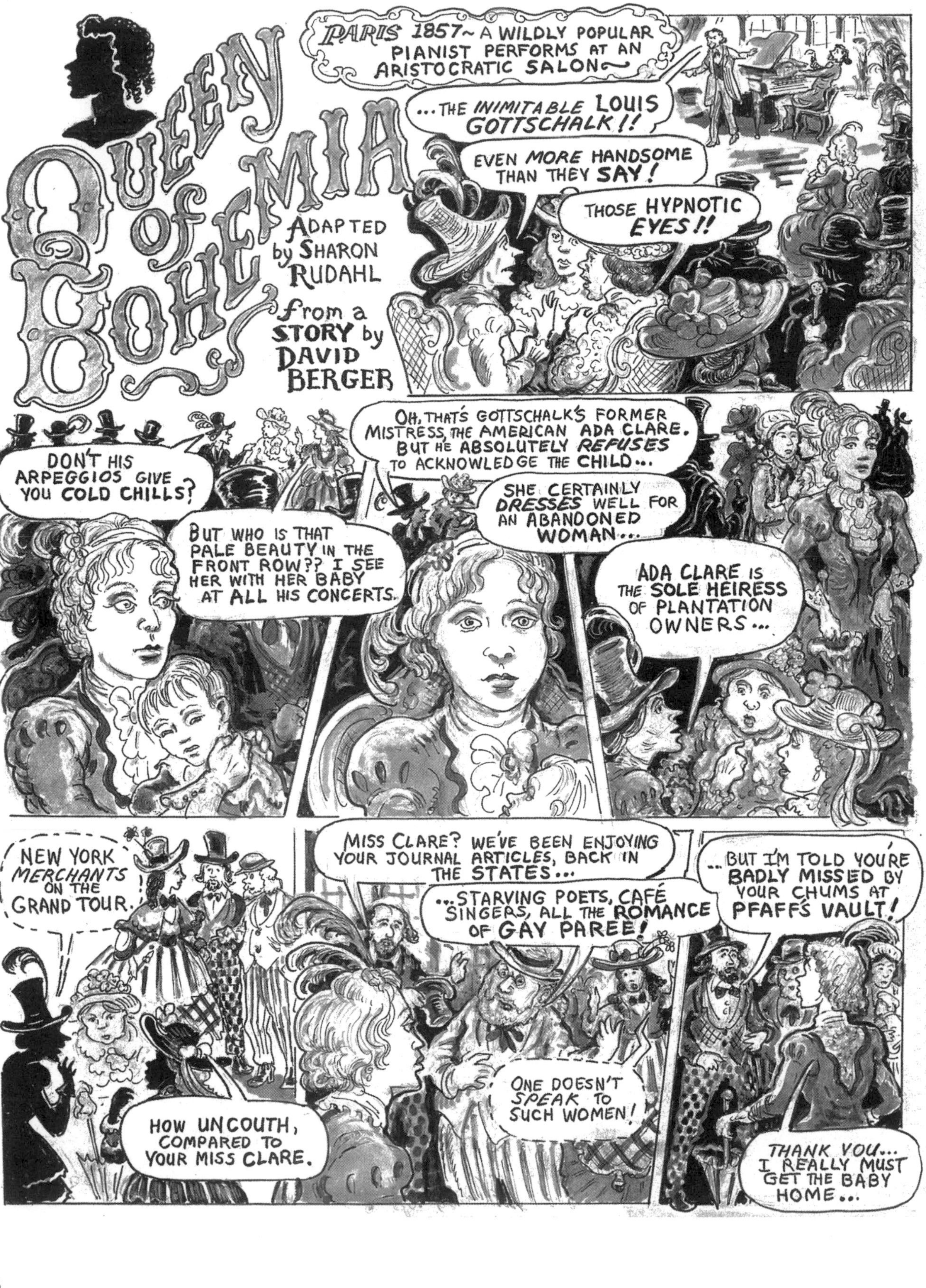

QUEEN of BOHEMIA
ADAPTED by SHARON RUDAHL
from a STORY by DAVID BERGER
PARIS 1857~ A WILDLY POPULAR PIANIST PERFORMS AT AN ARISTOCRATIC SALON~
...THE INIMITABLE LOUIS GOTTSCHALK!!
EVEN MORE HANDSOME THAN THEY SAY!
THOSE HYPNOTIC EYES!!
DON'T HIS ARPEGGIOS GIVE YOU COLD CHILLS?
BUT WHO IS THAT PALE BEAUTY IN THE FRONT ROW?? I SEE HER WITH HER BABY AT ALL HIS CONCERTS.
OH, THAT'S GOTTSCHALK'S FORMER MISTRESS, THE AMERICAN ADA CLARE. BUT HE ABSOLUTELY REFUSES TO ACKNOWLEDGE THE CHILD...
SHE CERTAINLY DRESSES WELL FOR AN ABANDONED WOMAN...
ADA CLARE IS THE SOLE HEIRESS OF PLANTATION OWNERS...
NEW YORK MERCHANTS ON THE GRAND TOUR.
HOW UNCOUTH, COMPARED TO YOUR MISS CLARE.
MISS CLARE? WE'VE BEEN ENJOYING YOUR JOURNAL ARTICLES, BACK IN THE STATES...
...STARVING POETS, CAFÉ SINGERS, ALL THE ROMANCE OF GAY PAREE!
ONE DOESN'T SPEAK TO SUCH WOMEN!
...BUT I'M TOLD YOU'RE BADLY MISSED BY YOUR CHUMS AT PFAFF'S VAULT!
THANK YOU... I REALLY MUST GET THE BABY HOME...

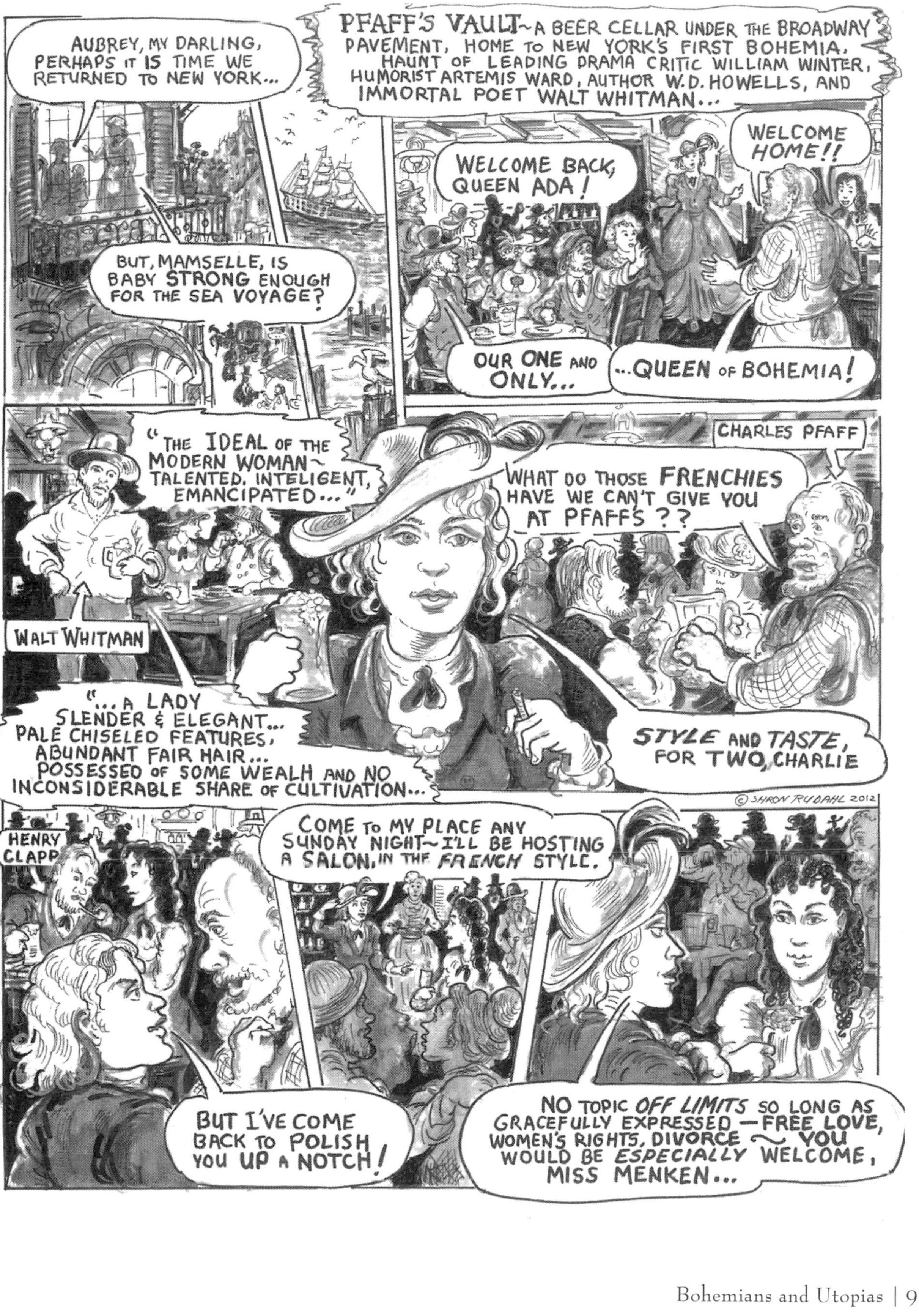
AUBREY, MY DARLING, PERHAPS IT IS TIME WE RETURNED TO NEW YORK...
BUT, MAMSELLE, IS BABY STRONG ENOUGH FOR THE SEA VOYAGE?
PFAFF'S VAULT~A BEER CELLAR UNDER THE BROADWAY PAVEMENT, HOME TO NEW YORK'S FIRST BOHEMIA, HAUNT OF LEADING DRAMA CRITIC WILLIAM WINTER, HUMORIST ARTEMIS WARD, AUTHOR W.D. HOWELLS, AND IMMORTAL POET WALT WHITMAN...
WELCOME BACK, QUEEN ADA!
WELCOME HOME!!
OUR ONE AND ONLY...
...QUEEN OF BOHEMIA!
"THE IDEAL OF THE MODERN WOMAN~ TALENTED, INTELIGENT, EMANCIPATED..."
WALT WHITMAN
"...A LADY SLENDER & ELEGANT... PALE CHISELED FEATURES, ABUNDANT FAIR HAIR... POSSESSED OF SOME WEALH AND NO INCONSIDERABLE SHARE OF CULTIVATION..."
CHARLES PFAFF
WHAT DO THOSE FRENCHIES HAVE WE CAN'T GIVE YOU AT PFAFF'S??
STYLE AND TASTE, FOR TWO, CHARLIE
© SHRON RUDAHL 2012
HENRY CLAPP
COME TO MY PLACE ANY SUNDAY NIGHT~I'LL BE HOSTING A SALON, IN THE FRENCH STYLE.
BUT I'VE COME BACK TO POLISH YOU UP A NOTCH!
NO TOPIC OFF LIMITS SO LONG AS GRACEFULLY EXPRESSED—FREE LOVE, WOMEN'S RIGHTS, DIVORCE ~ YOU WOULD BE ESPECIALLY WELCOME, MISS MENKEN...

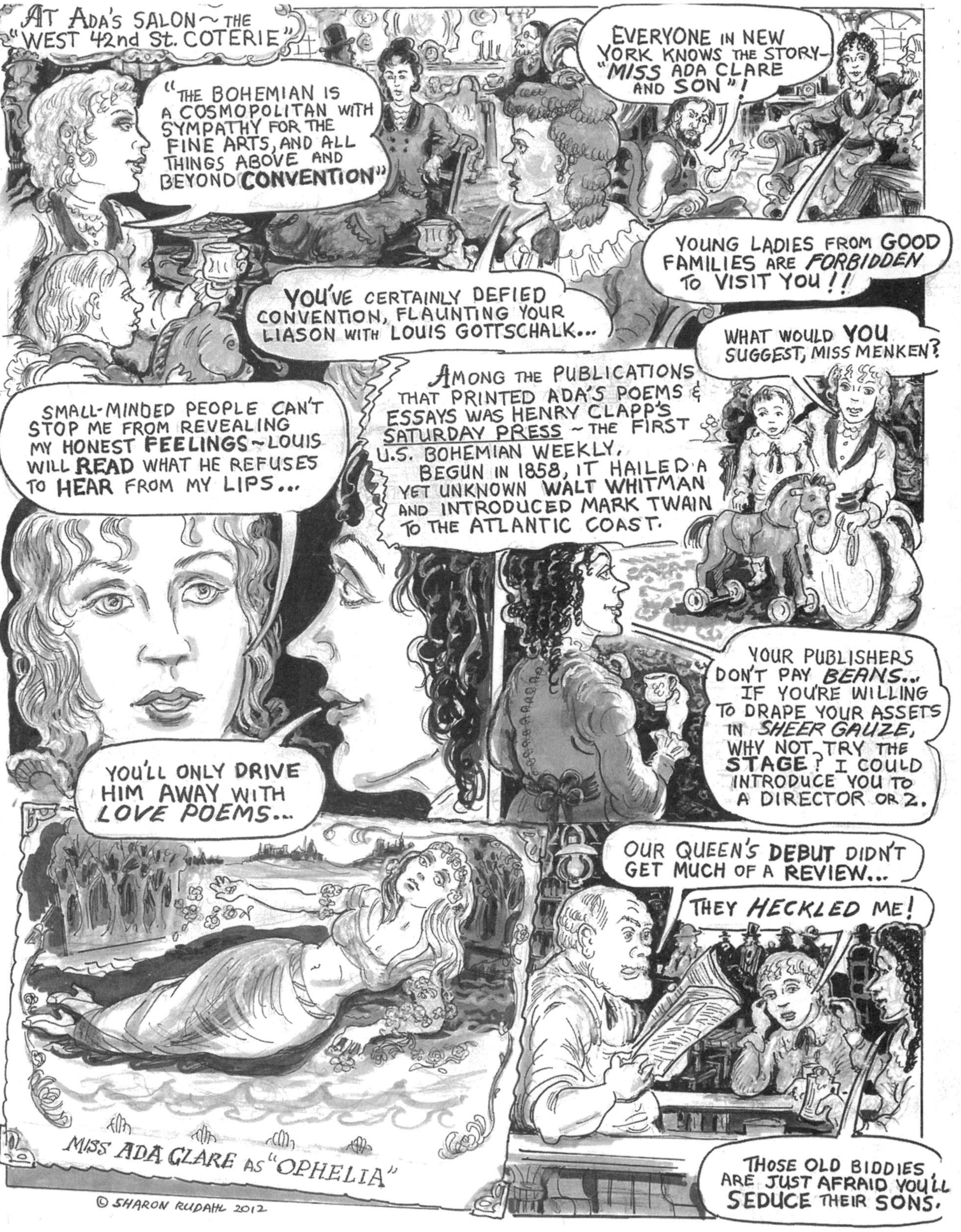

AT ADA'S SALON ~ THE "WEST 42nd St. COTERIE"
"THE BOHEMIAN IS A COSMOPOLITAN WITH SYMPATHY FOR THE FINE ARTS, AND ALL THINGS ABOVE AND BEYOND CONVENTION"
EVERYONE IN NEW YORK KNOWS THE STORY- "MISS ADA CLARE AND SON"!
YOUNG LADIES FROM GOOD FAMILIES ARE FORBIDDEN TO VISIT YOU!!
YOU'VE CERTAINLY DEFIED CONVENTION, FLAUNTING YOUR LIASON WITH LOUIS GOTTSCHALK...
WHAT WOULD YOU SUGGEST, MISS MENKEN?
SMALL-MINDED PEOPLE CAN'T STOP ME FROM REVEALING MY HONEST FEELINGS ~ LOUIS WILL READ WHAT HE REFUSES TO HEAR FROM MY LIPS...
AMONG THE PUBLICATIONS THAT PRINTED ADA'S POEMS & ESSAYS WAS HENRY CLAPP'S SATURDAY PRESS ~ THE FIRST U.S. BOHEMIAN WEEKLY. BEGUN IN 1858, IT HAILED A YET UNKNOWN WALT WHITMAN AND INTRODUCED MARK TWAIN TO THE ATLANTIC COAST.
YOUR PUBLISHERS DON'T PAY BEANS... IF YOU'RE WILLING TO DRAPE YOUR ASSETS IN SHEER GAUZE, WHY NOT TRY THE STAGE? I COULD INTRODUCE YOU TO A DIRECTOR OR 2.
YOU'LL ONLY DRIVE HIM AWAY WITH LOVE POEMS...
OUR QUEEN'S DEBUT DIDN'T GET MUCH OF A REVIEW...
THEY HECKLED ME!
MISS ADA CLARE AS "OPHELIA"
THOSE OLD BIDDIES ARE JUST AFRAID YOU'LL SEDUCE THEIR SONS.
© SHARON RUDAHL 2012

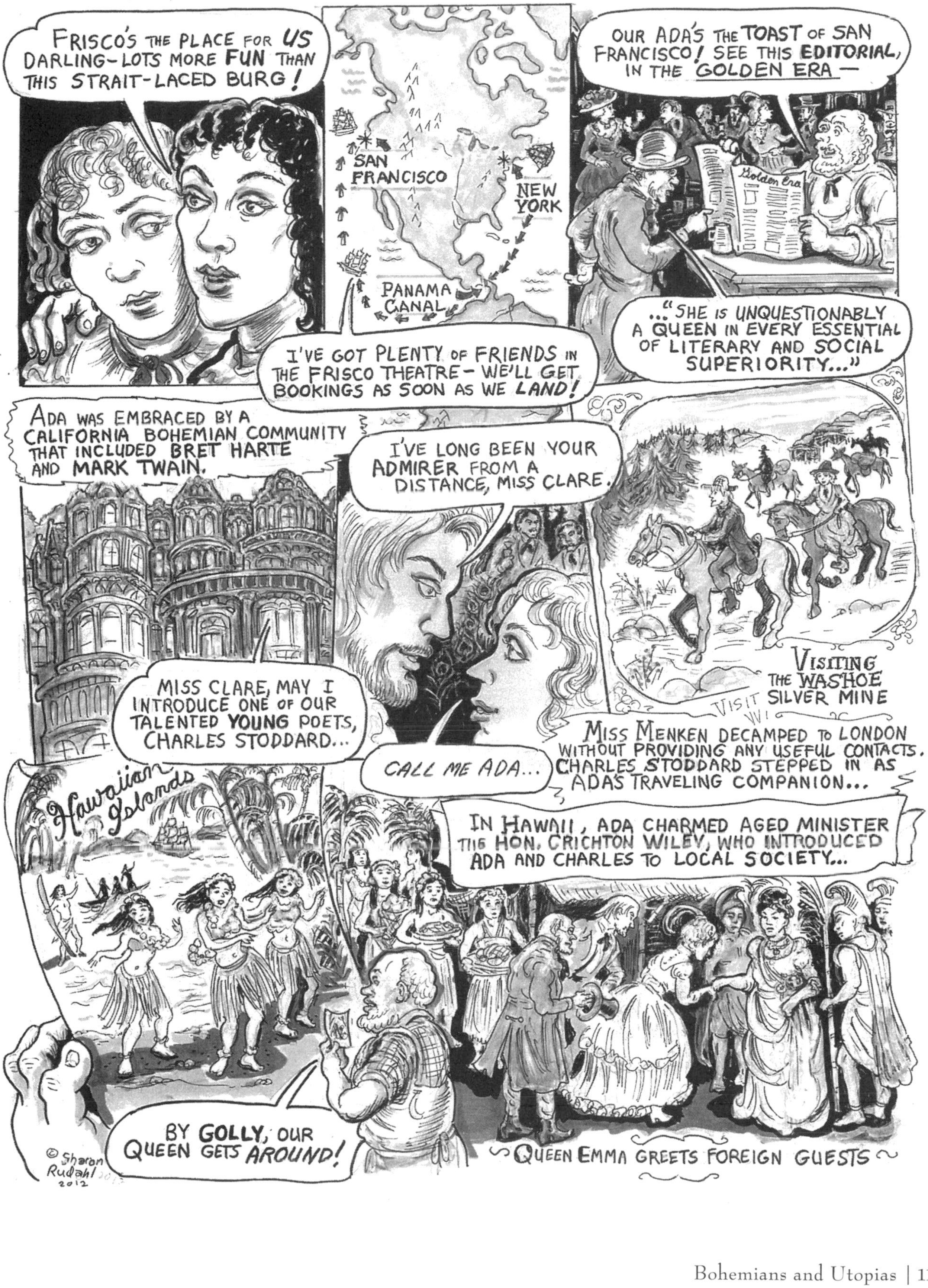
FRISCO'S THE PLACE FOR US DARLING- LOTS MORE FUN THAN THIS STRAIT-LACED BURG!
SAN FRANCISCO
NEW YORK
PANAMA CANAL
I'VE GOT PLENTY OF FRIENDS IN THE FRISCO THEATRE- WE'LL GET BOOKINGS AS SOON AS WE LAND!
OUR ADA'S THE TOAST OF SAN FRANCISCO! SEE THIS EDITORIAL, IN THE GOLDEN ERA—
Golden Era
..."SHE IS UNQUESTIONABLY A QUEEN IN EVERY ESSENTIAL OF LITERARY AND SOCIAL SUPERIORITY..."
ADA WAS EMBRACED BY A CALIFORNIA BOHEMIAN COMMUNITY THAT INCLUDED BRET HARTE AND MARK TWAIN.
MISS CLARE, MAY I INTRODUCE ONE OF OUR TALENTED YOUNG POETS, CHARLES STODDARD...
I'VE LONG BEEN YOUR ADMIRER FROM A DISTANCE, MISS CLARE.
CALL ME ADA...
VISITING THE WASHOE SILVER MINE
VISIT VI!
MISS MENKEN DECAMPED TO LONDON WITHOUT PROVIDING ANY USEFUL CONTACTS. CHARLES STODDARD STEPPED IN AS ADA'S TRAVELING COMPANION...
Hawaiian Islands
IN HAWAII, ADA CHARMED AGED MINISTER THE HON. CRICHTON WILEY, WHO INTRODUCED ADA AND CHARLES TO LOCAL SOCIETY...
BY GOLLY, OUR QUEEN GETS AROUND!
QUEEN EMMA GREETS FOREIGN GUESTS
© Sharon Rudahl 2012

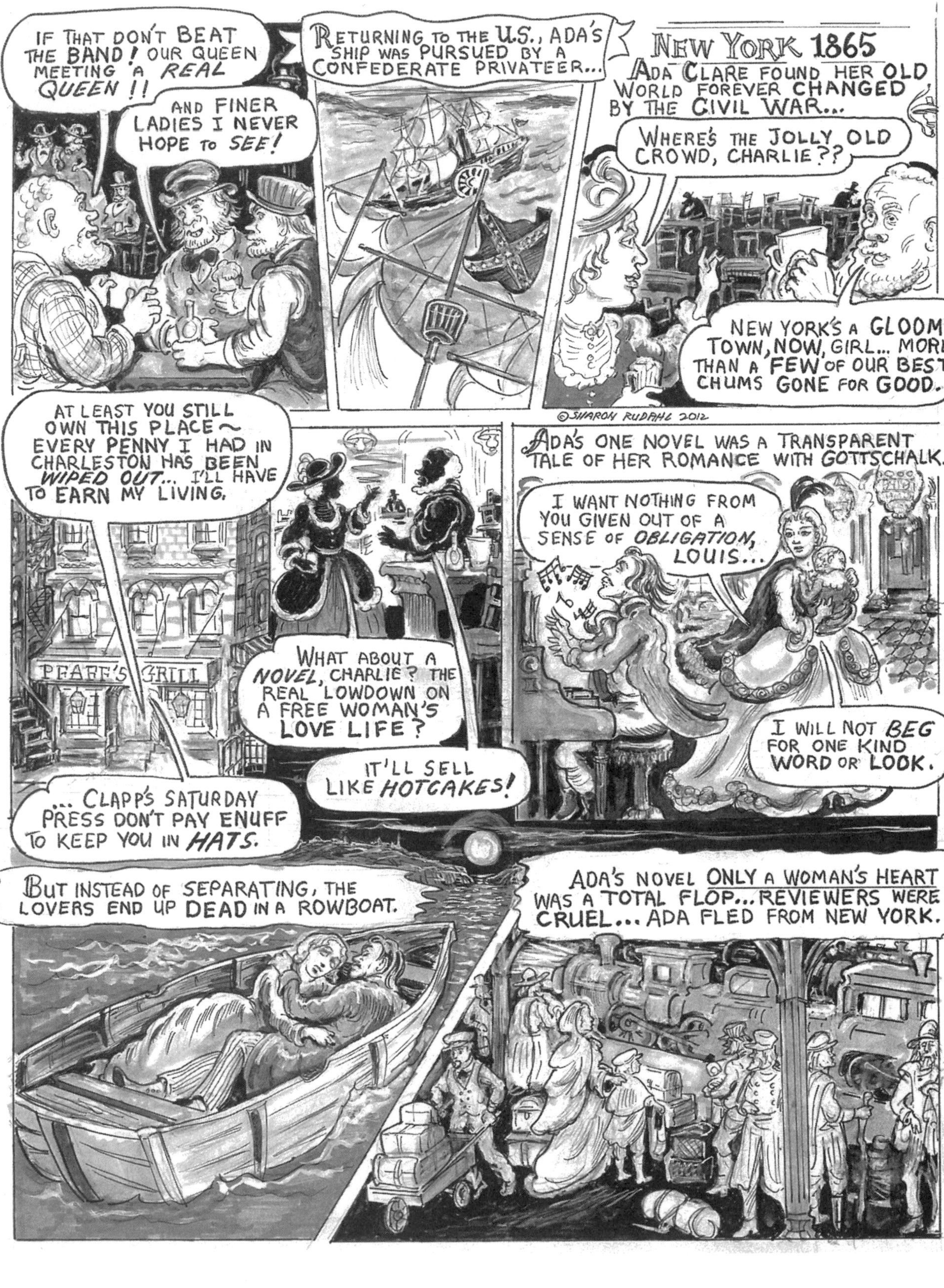

IF THAT DON'T BEAT THE BAND! OUR QUEEN MEETING A REAL QUEEN!!
AND FINER LADIES I NEVER HOPE TO SEE!
RETURNING TO THE U.S., ADA'S SHIP WAS PURSUED BY A CONFEDERATE PRIVATEER...
NEW YORK 1865
ADA CLARE FOUND HER OLD WORLD FOREVER CHANGED BY THE CIVIL WAR...
WHERE'S THE JOLLY OLD CROWD, CHARLIE??
NEW YORK'S A GLOOMY TOWN, NOW, GIRL... MORE THAN A FEW OF OUR BEST CHUMS GONE FOR GOOD.
©SHARON RUDAHL 2012
AT LEAST YOU STILL OWN THIS PLACE ~ EVERY PENNY I HAD IN CHARLESTON HAS BEEN WIPED OUT... I'LL HAVE TO EARN MY LIVING.
PFAFF'S GRILL
... CLAPP'S SATURDAY PRESS DON'T PAY ENUFF TO KEEP YOU IN HATS.
WHAT ABOUT A NOVEL, CHARLIE? THE REAL LOWDOWN ON A FREE WOMAN'S LOVE LIFE?
IT'LL SELL LIKE HOTCAKES!
ADA'S ONE NOVEL WAS A TRANSPARENT TALE OF HER ROMANCE WITH GOTTSCHALK.
I WANT NOTHING FROM YOU GIVEN OUT OF A SENSE OF OBLIGATION, LOUIS...
I WILL NOT BEG FOR ONE KIND WORD OR LOOK.
BUT INSTEAD OF SEPARATING, THE LOVERS END UP DEAD IN A ROWBOAT.
ADA'S NOVEL ONLY A WOMAN'S HEART WAS A TOTAL FLOP... REVIEWERS WERE CRUEL... ADA FLED FROM NEW YORK.

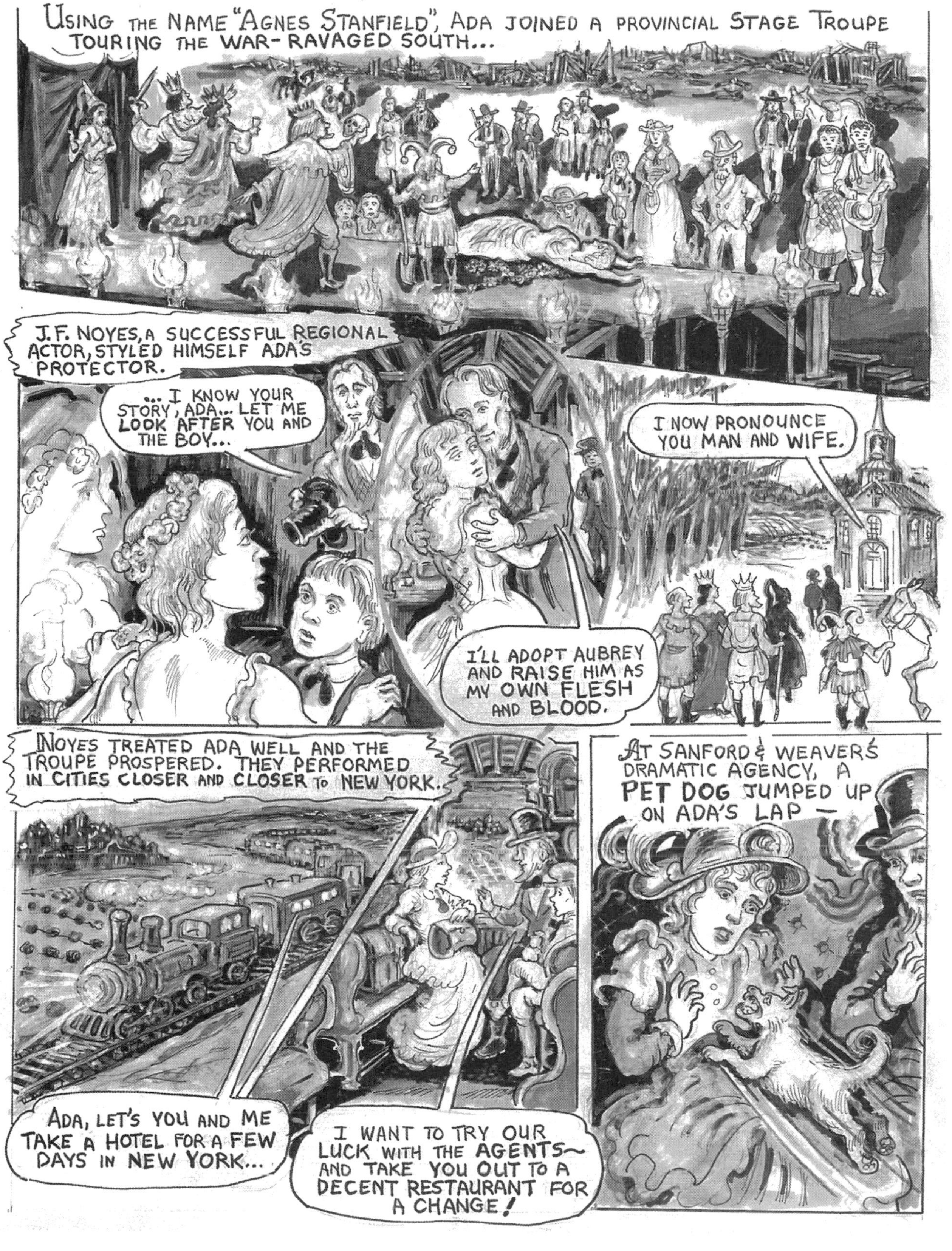
USING THE NAME "AGNES STANFIELD", ADA JOINED A PROVINCIAL STAGE TROUPE TOURING THE WAR-RAVAGED SOUTH...
J.F. NOYES, A SUCCESSFUL REGIONAL ACTOR, STYLED HIMSELF ADA'S PROTECTOR.
... I KNOW YOUR STORY, ADA... LET ME LOOK AFTER YOU AND THE BOY...
I'LL ADOPT AUBREY AND RAISE HIM AS MY OWN FLESH AND BLOOD.
I NOW PRONOUNCE YOU MAN AND WIFE.
NOYES TREATED ADA WELL AND THE TROUPE PROSPERED. THEY PERFORMED IN CITIES CLOSER AND CLOSER TO NEW YORK.
ADA, LET'S YOU AND ME TAKE A HOTEL FOR A FEW DAYS IN NEW YORK...
I WANT TO TRY OUR LUCK WITH THE AGENTS~ AND TAKE YOU OUT TO A DECENT RESTAURANT FOR A CHANGE!
AT SANFORD & WEAVER'S DRAMATIC AGENCY, A PET DOG JUMPED UP ON ADA'S LAP —

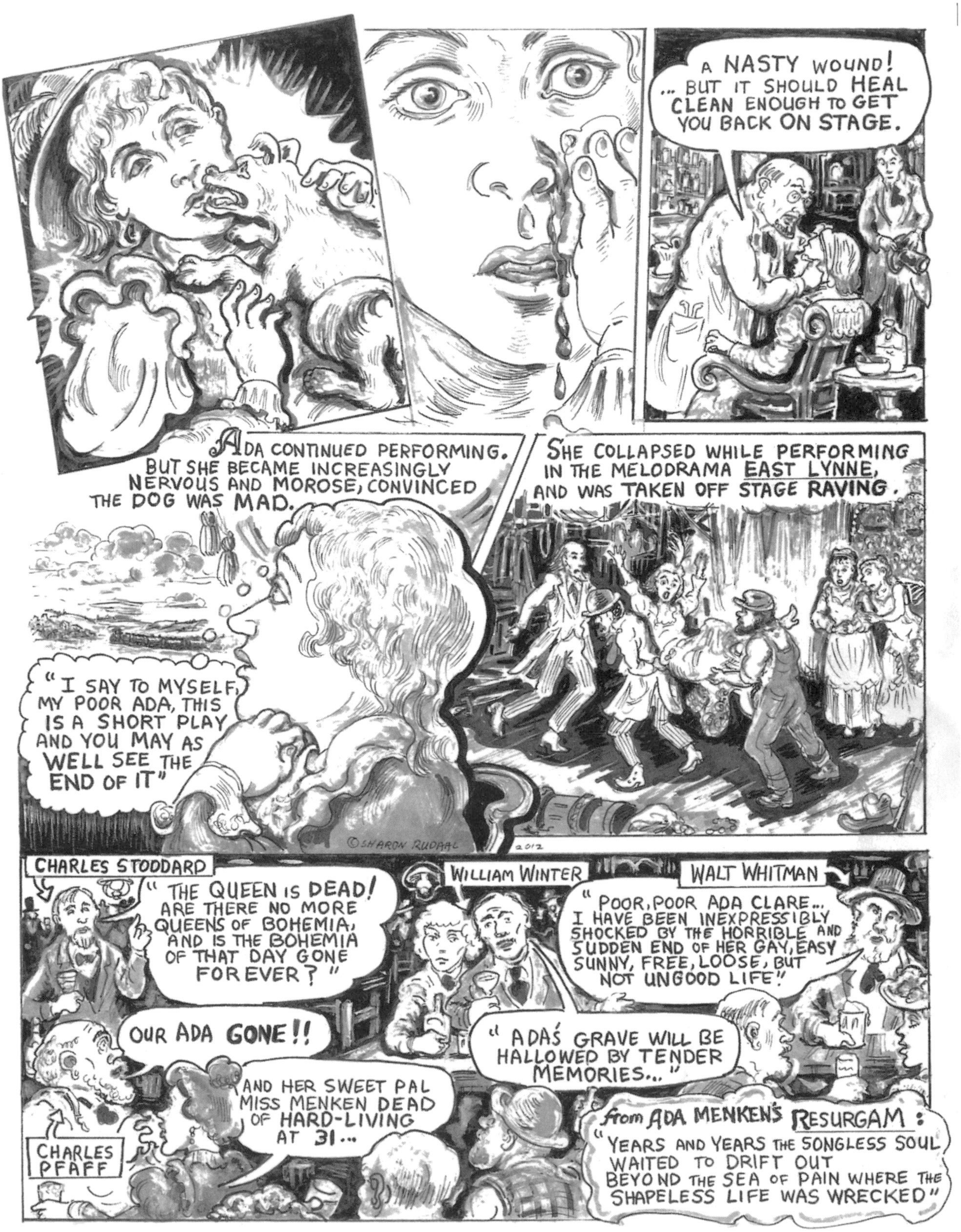
A NASTY WOUND! ... BUT IT SHOULD HEAL CLEAN ENOUGH TO GET YOU BACK ON STAGE.
ADA CONTINUED PERFORMING. BUT SHE BECAME INCREASINGLY NERVOUS AND MOROSE, CONVINCED THE DOG WAS MAD.
"I SAY TO MYSELF, MY POOR ADA, THIS IS A SHORT PLAY AND YOU MAY AS WELL SEE THE END OF IT"
©SHARON RUDAHL
SHE COLLAPSED WHILE PERFORMING IN THE MELODRAMA EAST LYNNE, AND WAS TAKEN OFF STAGE RAVING.
2012
CHARLES STODDARD
"THE QUEEN IS DEAD! ARE THERE NO MORE QUEENS OF BOHEMIA, AND IS THE BOHEMIA OF THAT DAY GONE FOREVER?"
WILLIAM WINTER
WALT WHITMAN
"POOR, POOR ADA CLARE... I HAVE BEEN INEXPRESSIBLY SHOCKED BY THE HORRIBLE AND SUDDEN END OF HER GAY, EASY SUNNY, FREE, LOOSE, BUT NOT UNGOOD LIFE!"
OUR ADA GONE!!
"ADA'S GRAVE WILL BE HALLOWED BY TENDER MEMORIES..."
AND HER SWEET PAL MISS MENKEN DEAD OF HARD-LIVING AT 31...
CHARLES PFAFF
from ADA MENKEN'S RESURGAM:
"YEARS AND YEARS THE SONGLESS SOUL WAITED TO DRIFT OUT BEYOND THE SEA OF PAIN WHERE THE SHAPELESS LIFE WAS WRECKED"

Chapter Two

Walt Whitman

The Great Gray (or Gay) Poet, rightly considered by later critics to be American society's foremost bohemian among those of his own day, may still be usefully considered, for our purposes, as also inhabiting a poetic world of his own making.

Whitman, like dress reformers or even, in a certain way, Abraham Lincoln, could see in "Americanism," despite all the racial and gender strictures of the contemporary U.S., a potential utopia-in-the-making. The country appeared open to all prospects, including for Whitman a quiet homosexuality as well as an improved version of urban civilization. New York City approached, if it had not yet become, a new Paris.

Even though mistaken about so much in economics and social life, Whitman was right in the poetry that contained and exemplified his sweeping vision.

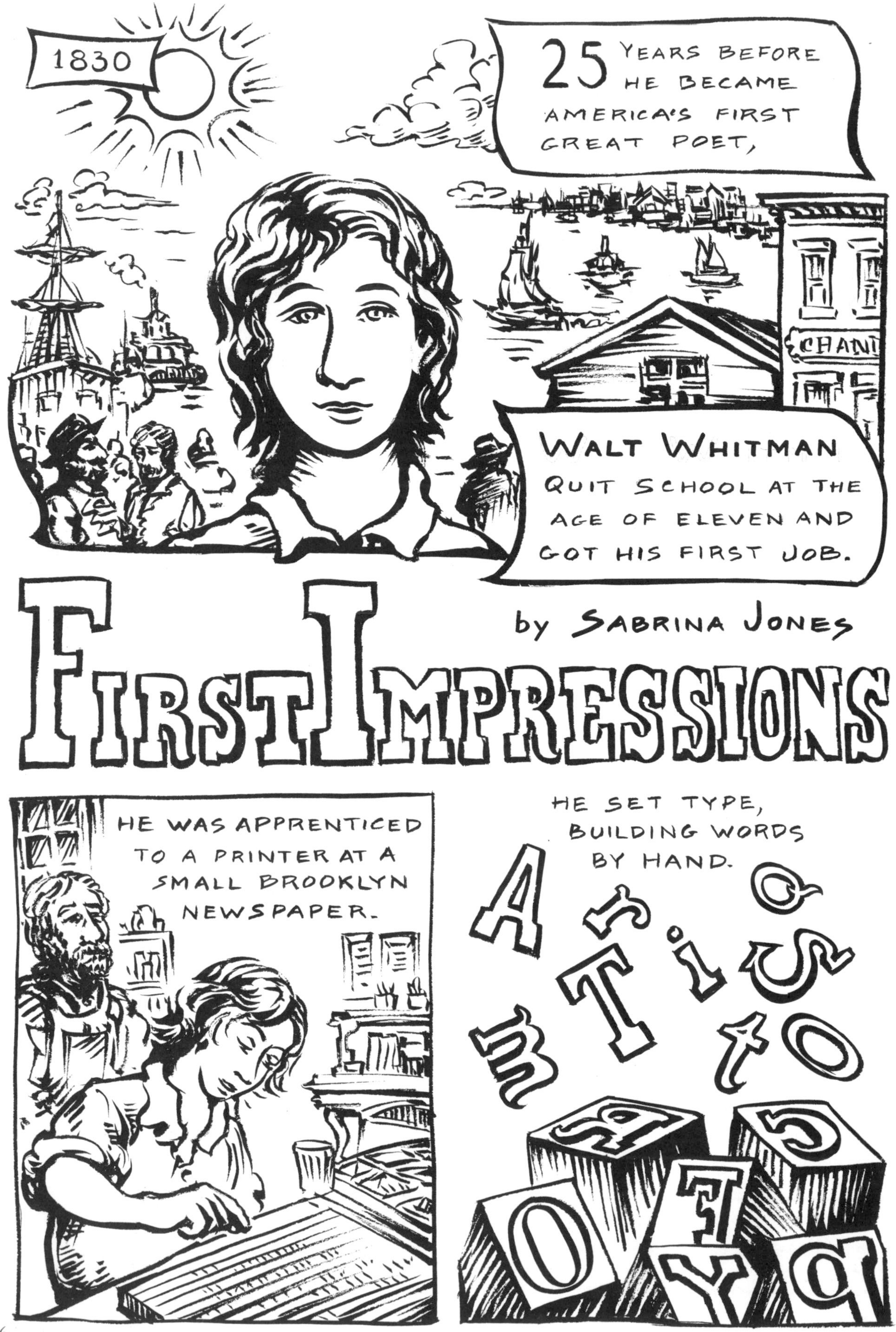
1830
25 YEARS BEFORE HE BECAME AMERICA'S FIRST GREAT POET,
WALT WHITMAN QUIT SCHOOL AT THE AGE OF ELEVEN AND GOT HIS FIRST JOB.
FIRST IMPRESSIONS
by SABRINA JONES
HE WAS APPRENTICED TO A PRINTER AT A SMALL BROOKLYN NEWSPAPER.
HE SET TYPE, BUILDING WORDS BY HAND.

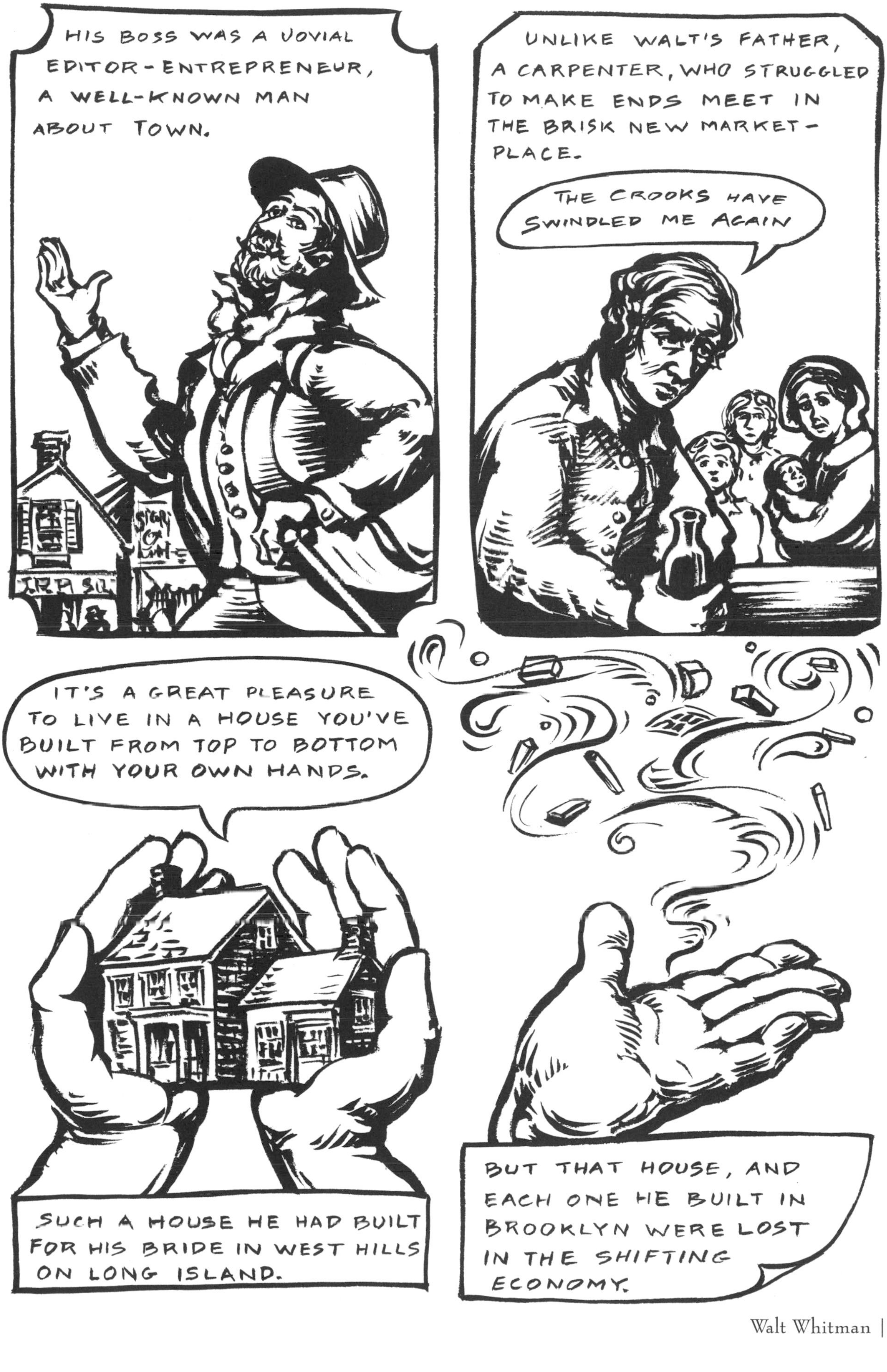
HIS BOSS WAS A JOVIAL EDITOR-ENTREPRENEUR, A WELL-KNOWN MAN ABOUT TOWN.
UNLIKE WALT'S FATHER, A CARPENTER, WHO STRUGGLED TO MAKE ENDS MEET IN THE BRISK NEW MARKET-PLACE.
THE CROOKS HAVE SWINDLED ME AGAIN
IT'S A GREAT PLEASURE TO LIVE IN A HOUSE YOU'VE BUILT FROM TOP TO BOTTOM WITH YOUR OWN HANDS.
SUCH A HOUSE HE HAD BUILT FOR HIS BRIDE IN WEST HILLS ON LONG ISLAND.
BUT THAT HOUSE, AND EACH ONE HE BUILT IN BROOKLYN WERE LOST IN THE SHIFTING ECONOMY.

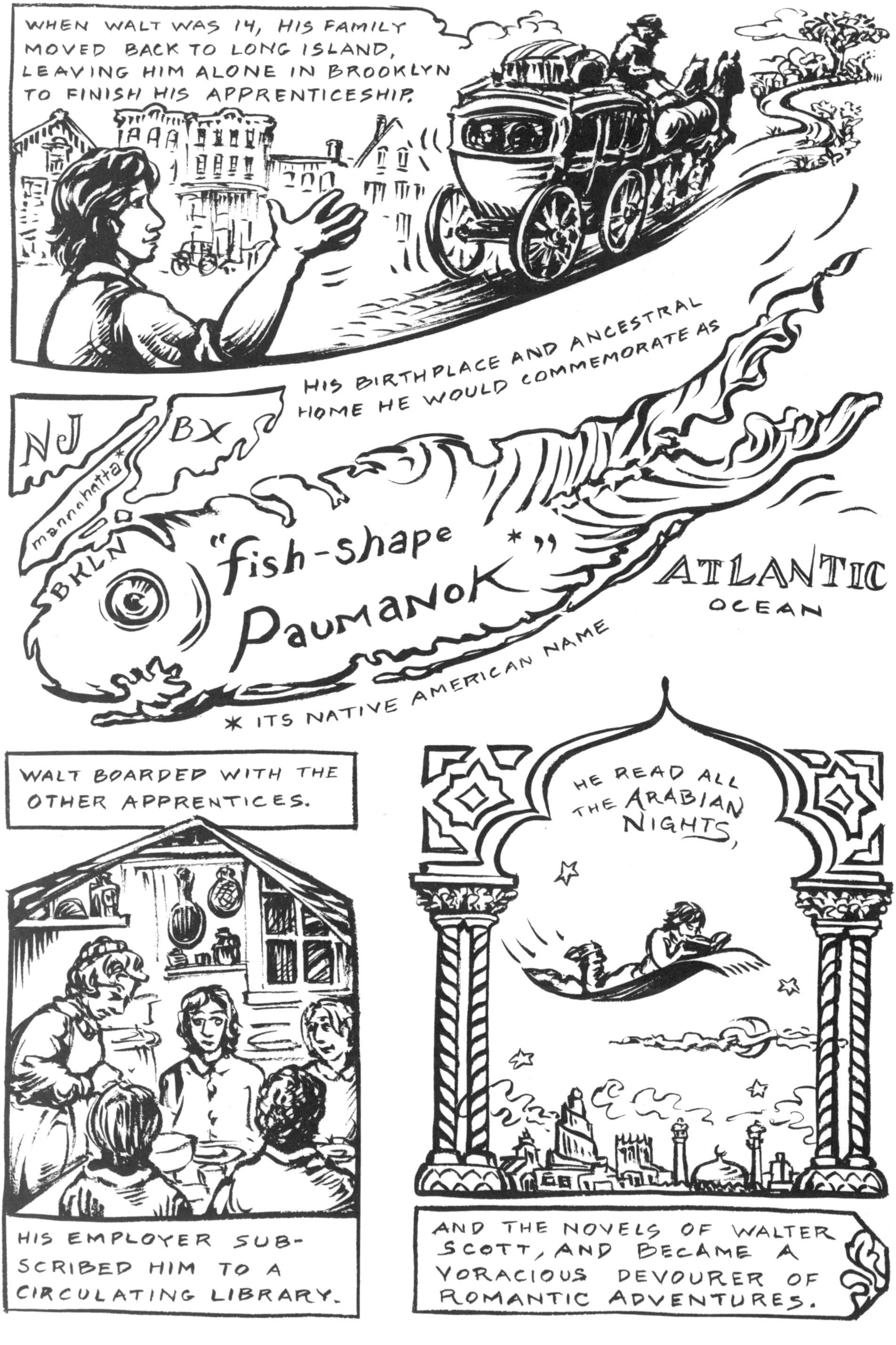
WHEN WALT WAS 14, HIS FAMILY MOVED BACK TO LONG ISLAND, LEAVING HIM ALONE IN BROOKLYN TO FINISH HIS APPRENTICESHIP.
HIS BIRTHPLACE AND ANCESTRAL HOME HE WOULD COMMEMORATE AS
NJ
BX
mannahatta*
BKLN
"fish-shape Paumanok*"
ATLANTIC OCEAN
* ITS NATIVE AMERICAN NAME
WALT BOARDED WITH THE OTHER APPRENTICES.
HIS EMPLOYER SUBSCRIBED HIM TO A CIRCULATING LIBRARY.
HE READ ALL THE ARABIAN NIGHTS,
AND THE NOVELS OF WALTER SCOTT, AND BECAME A VORACIOUS DEVOURER OF ROMANTIC ADVENTURES.

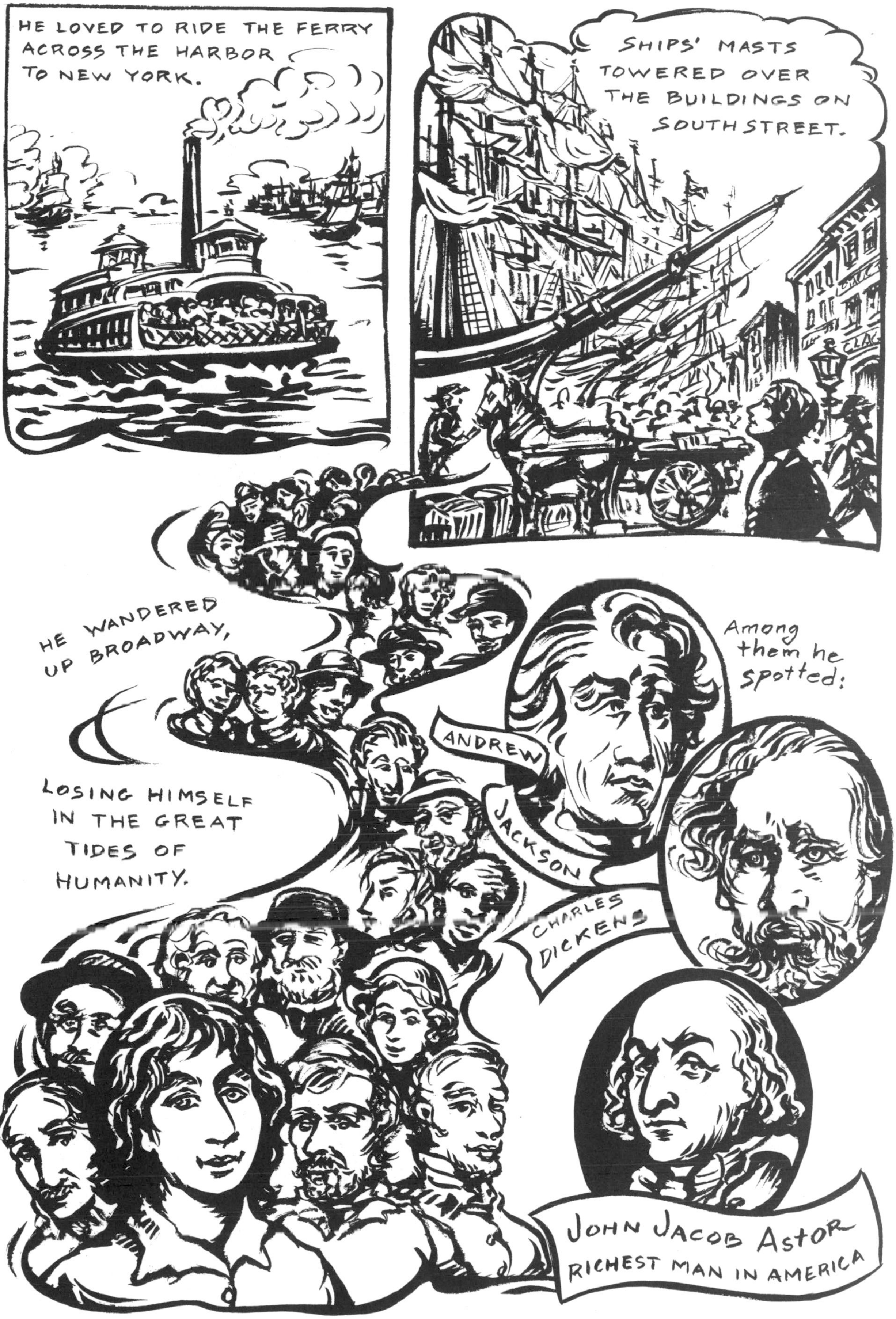
HE LOVED TO RIDE THE FERRY ACROSS THE HARBOR TO NEW YORK.
SHIPS' MASTS TOWERED OVER THE BUILDINGS ON SOUTH STREET.
HE WANDERED UP BROADWAY,
LOSING HIMSELF IN THE GREAT TIDES OF HUMANITY.
Among them he spotted:
ANDREW JACKSON
CHARLES DICKENS
JOHN JACOB ASTOR
RICHEST MAN IN AMERICA

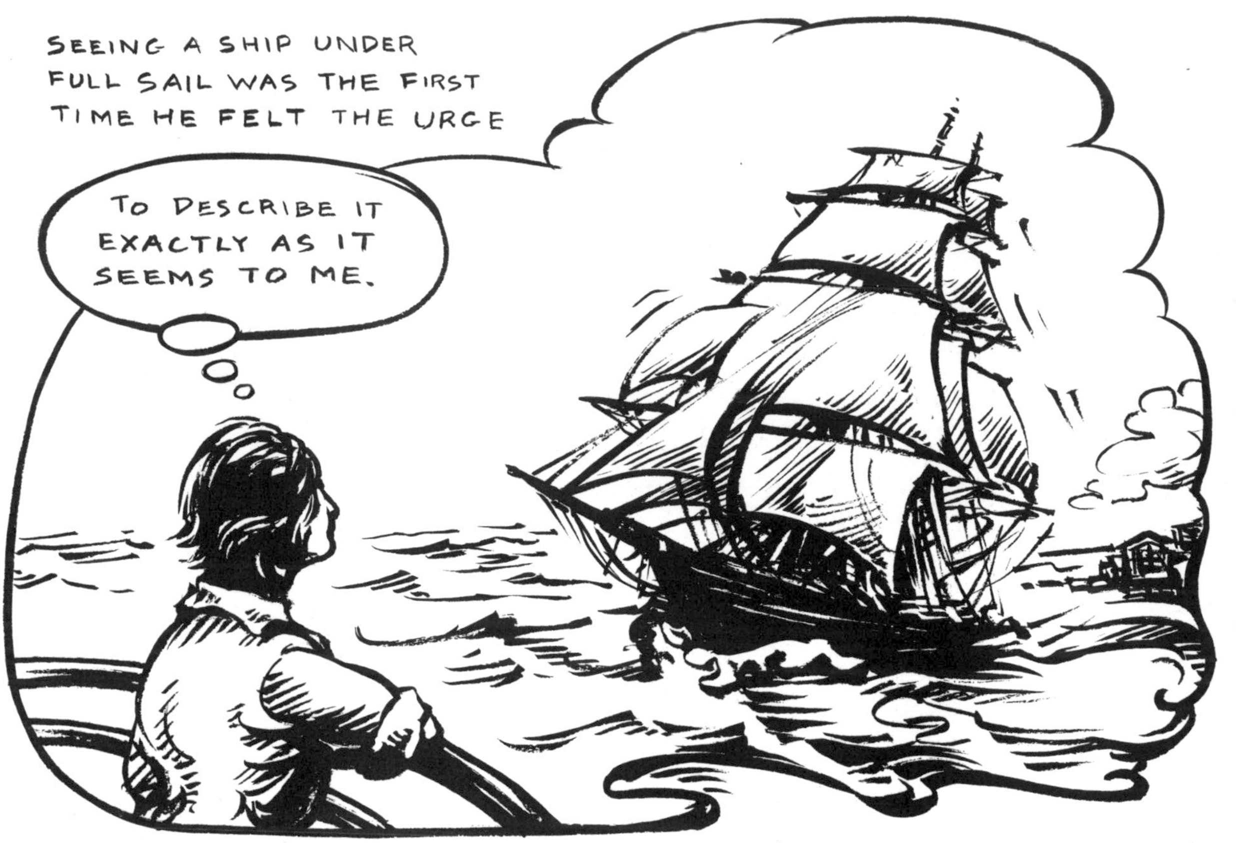
SEEING A SHIP UNDER FULL SAIL WAS THE FIRST TIME HE FELT THE URGE
TO DESCRIBE IT EXACTLY AS IT SEEMS TO ME.

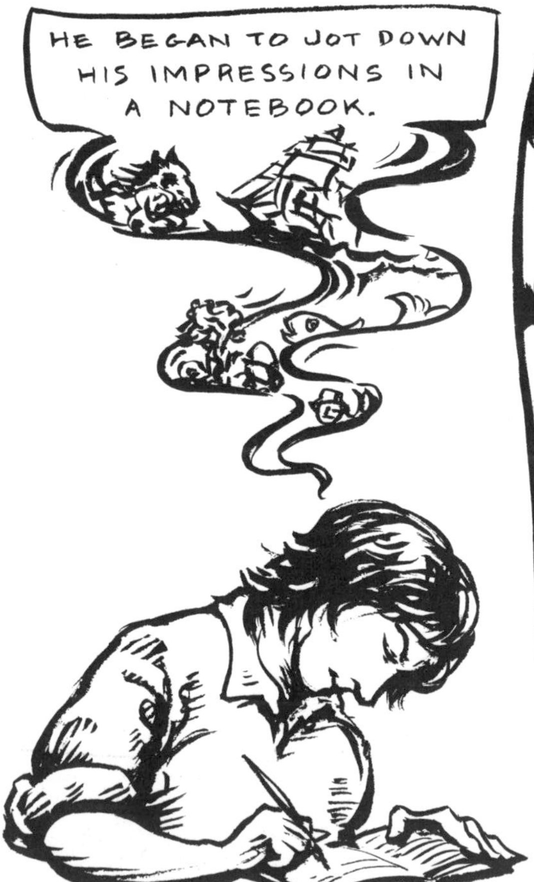
HE BEGAN TO JOT DOWN HIS IMPRESSIONS IN A NOTEBOOK.

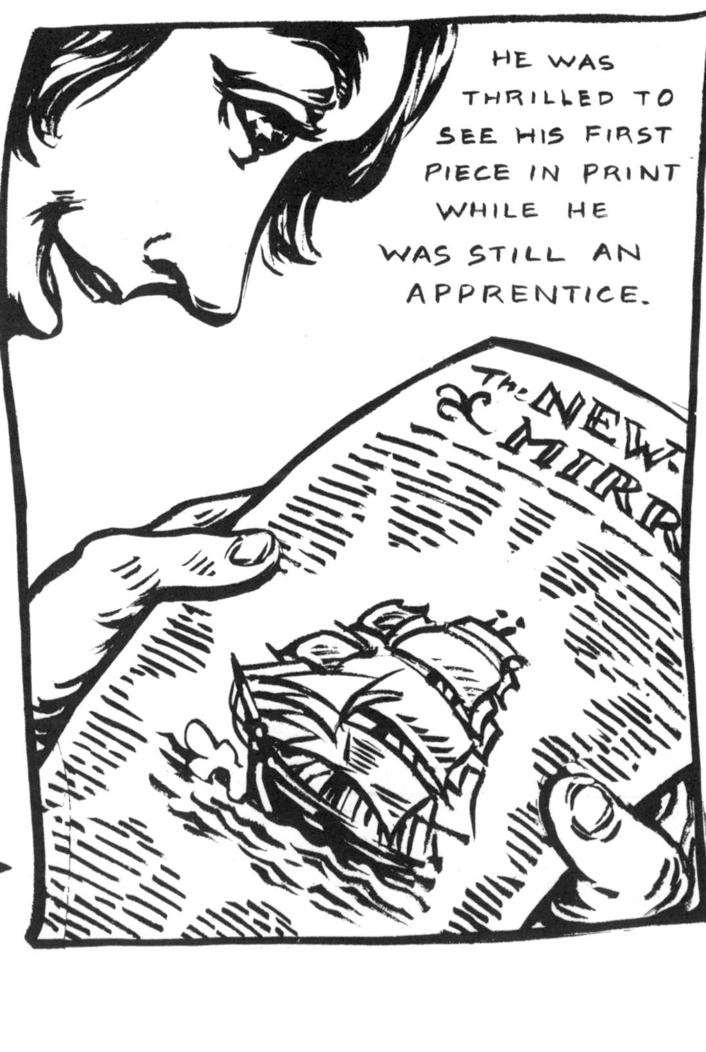
HE WAS THRILLED TO SEE HIS FIRST PIECE IN PRINT WHILE HE WAS STILL AN APPRENTICE.
The NEW MIRR

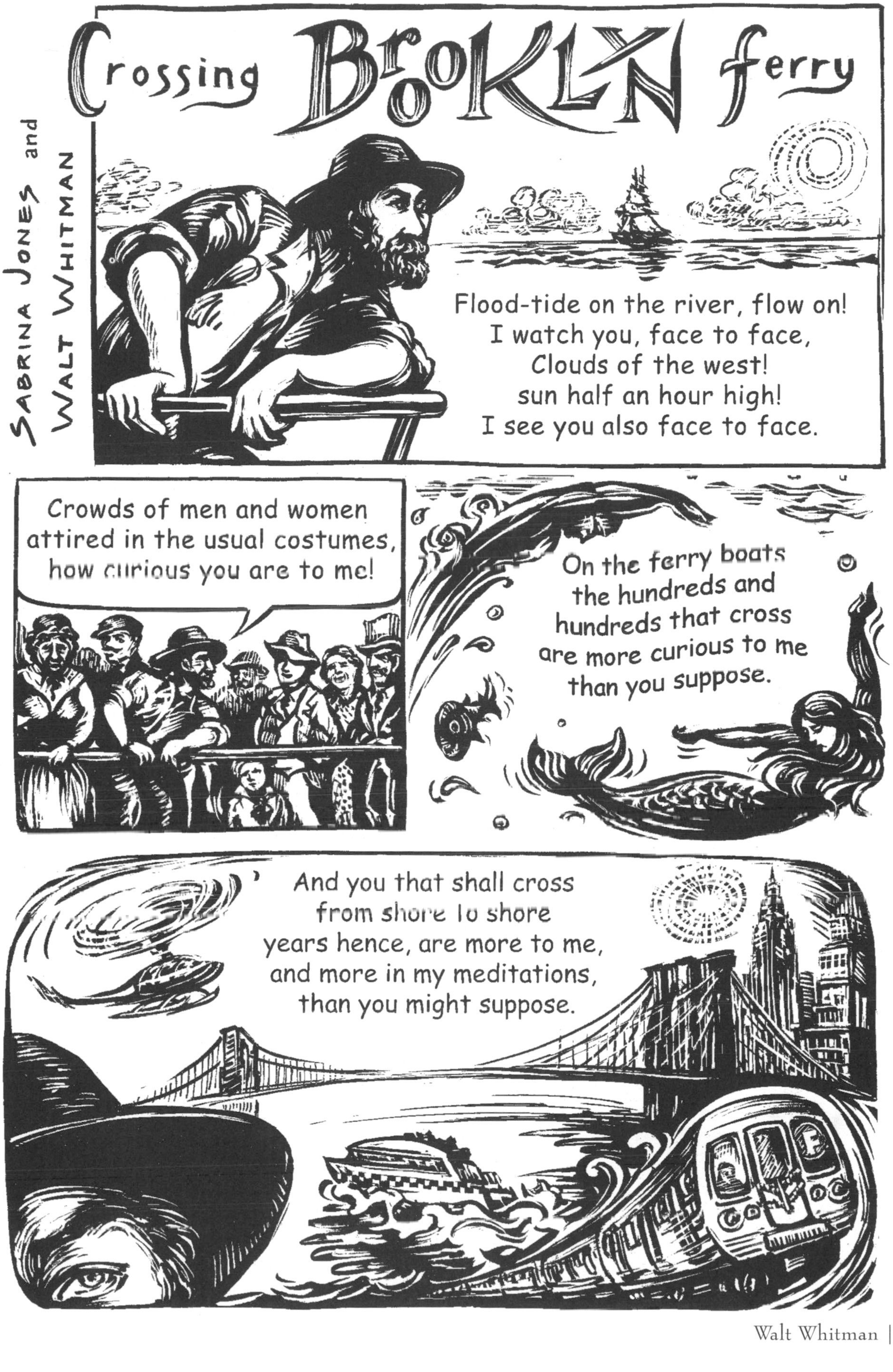
Crossing Brooklyn ferry
Sabrina Jones and Walt Whitman
Flood-tide on the river, flow on! I watch you, face to face, Clouds of the west! sun half an hour high! I see you also face to face.
Crowds of men and women attired in the usual costumes, how curious you are to me!
On the ferry boats the hundreds and hundreds that cross are more curious to me than you suppose.
And you that shall cross from shore to shore years hence, are more to me, and more in my meditations, than you might suppose.

Others will enter the gates
of the ferry, and cross
from shore to shore,
Others will watch
the run of the flood-tide,
A hundred years hence,
or ever so many hundred
years hence,

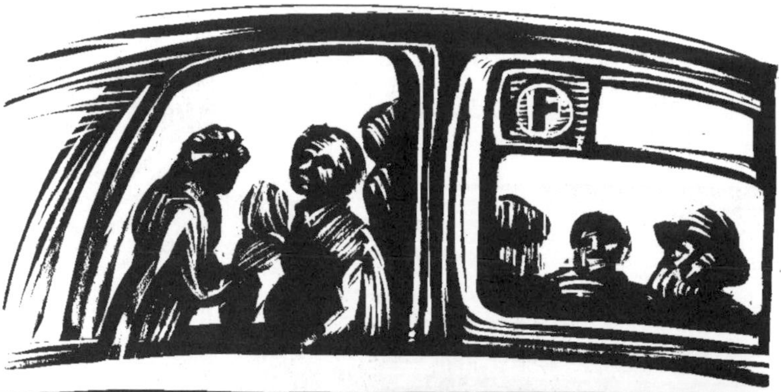
F

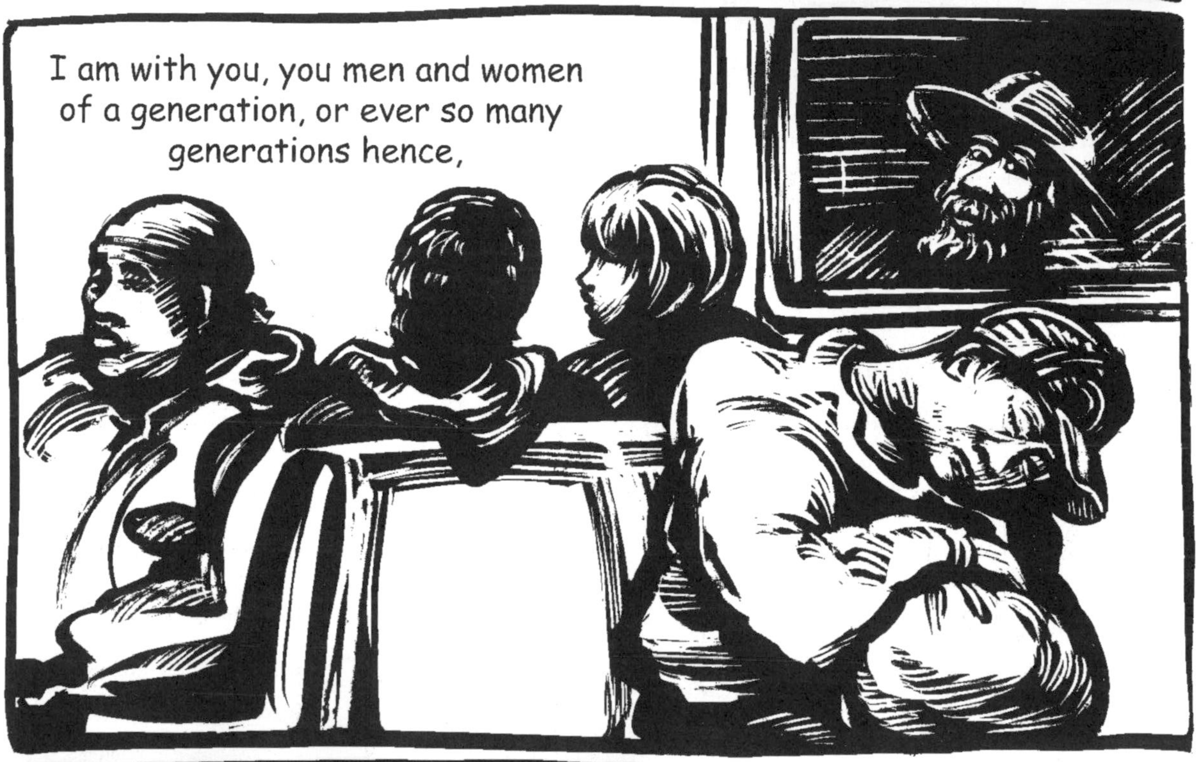
I am with you, you men and women
of a generation, or ever so many
generations hence,

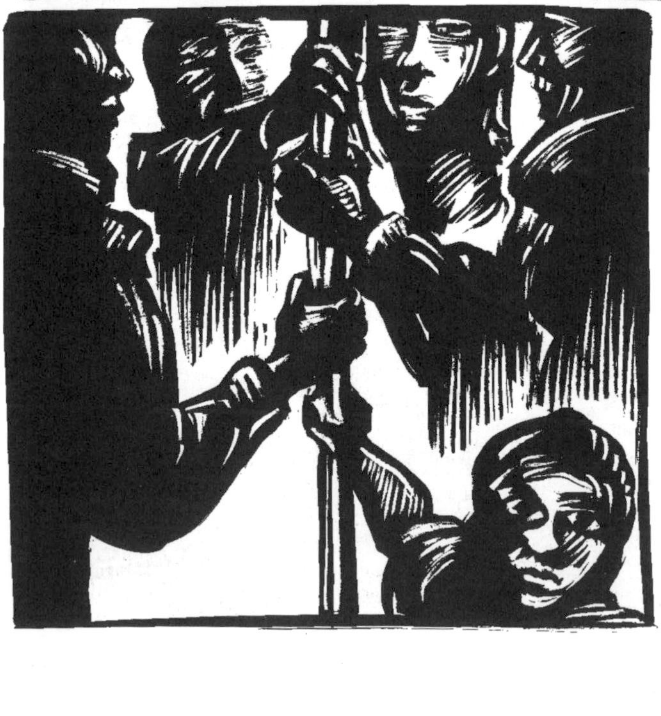

Just as any of you
is one of a living crowd,
I was one of a crowd,

Just as you are
refreshed by the
gladness of the river,
and the bright flow,
I was refreshed,

Just as you stand
and lean on the rail,
yet hurry with the
swift current,
I stood, yet was hurried.

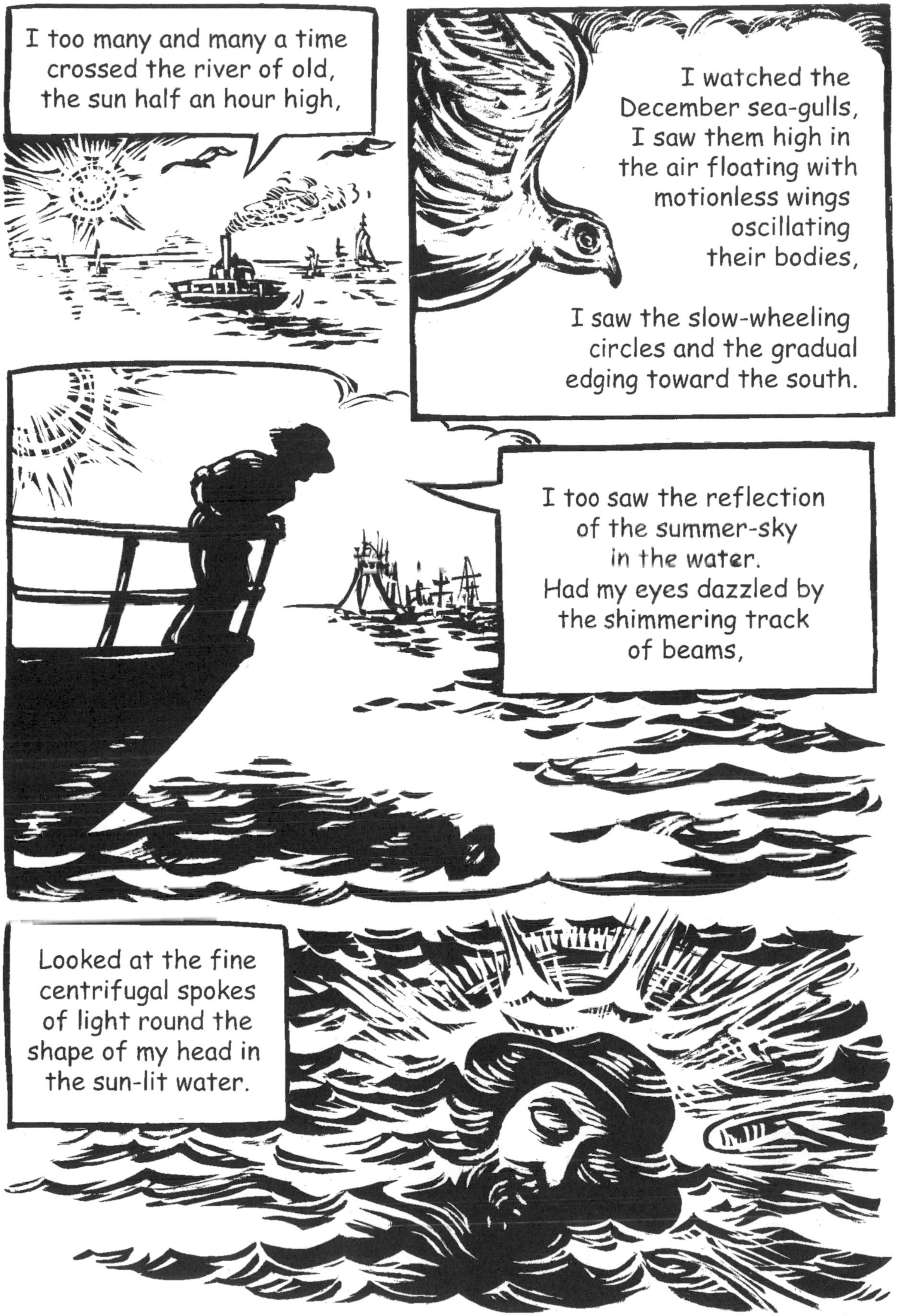
I too many and many a time crossed the river of old, the sun half an hour high,
I watched the December sea-gulls, I saw them high in the air floating with motionless wings oscillating their bodies,
I saw the slow-wheeling circles and the gradual edging toward the south.
I too saw the reflection of the summer-sky in the water. Had my eyes dazzled by the shimmering track of beams,
Looked at the fine centrifugal spokes of light round the shape of my head in the sun-lit water.

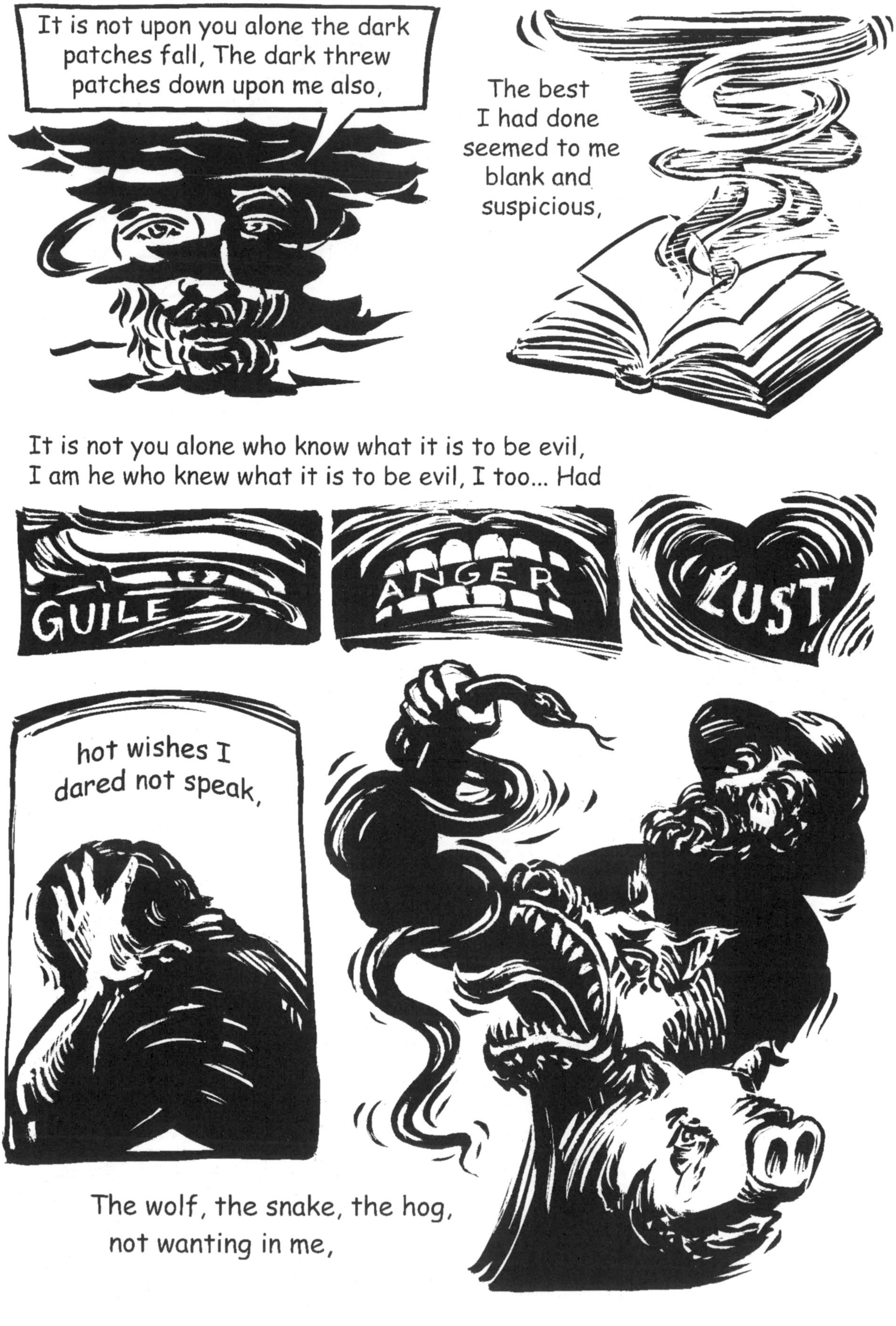
It is not upon you alone the dark patches fall, The dark threw patches down upon me also,
The best I had done seemed to me blank and suspicious,
It is not you alone who know what it is to be evil, I am he who knew what it is to be evil, I too... Had
GUILE
ANGER
LUST
hot wishes I dared not speak,
The wolf, the snake, the hog, not wanting in me,

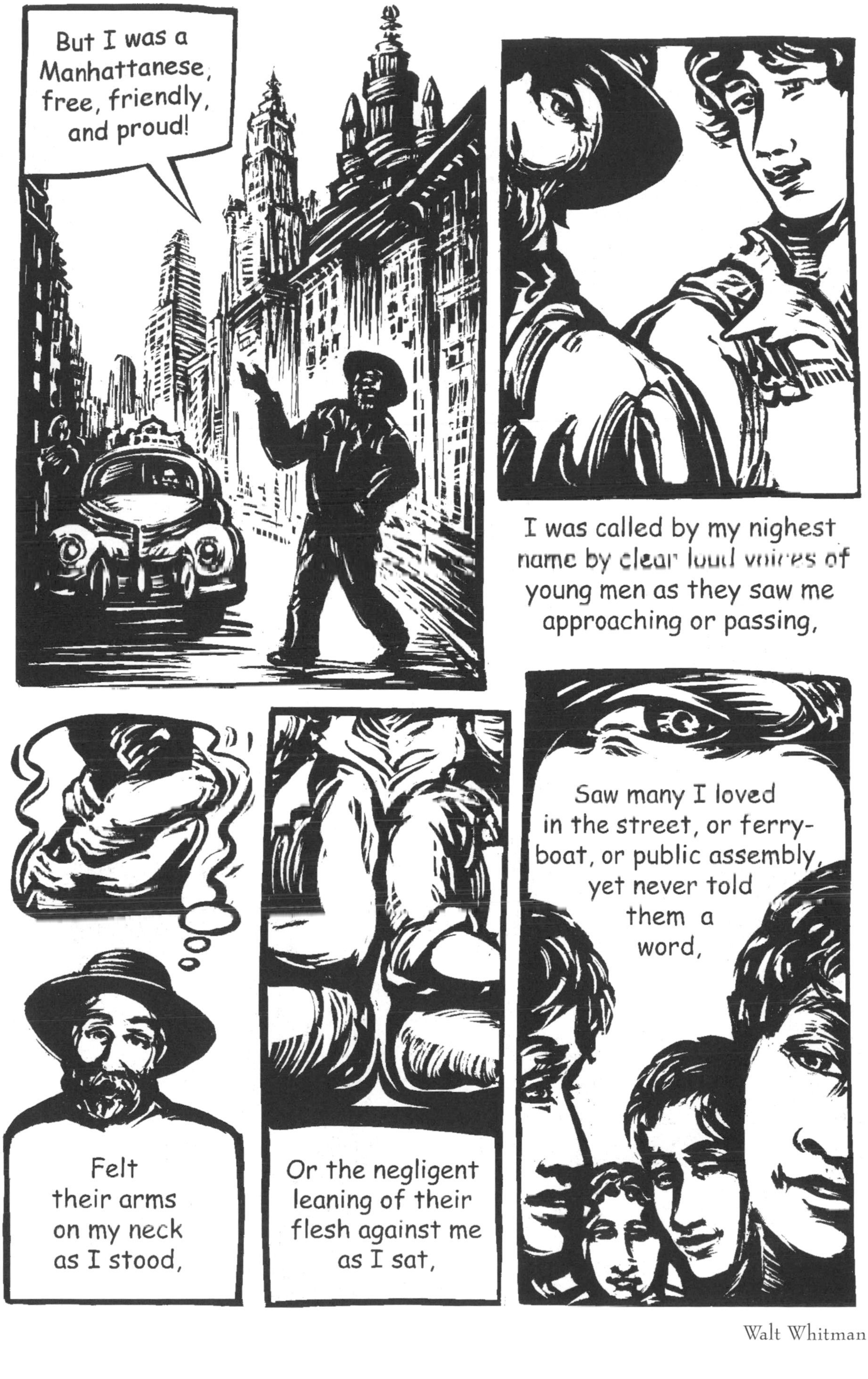
But I was a Manhattanese, free, friendly, and proud!
I was called by my nighest name by clear loud voices of young men as they saw me approaching or passing,
Felt their arms on my neck as I stood,
Or the negligent leaning of their flesh against me as I sat,
Saw many I loved in the street, or ferry-boat, or public assembly, yet never told them a word,

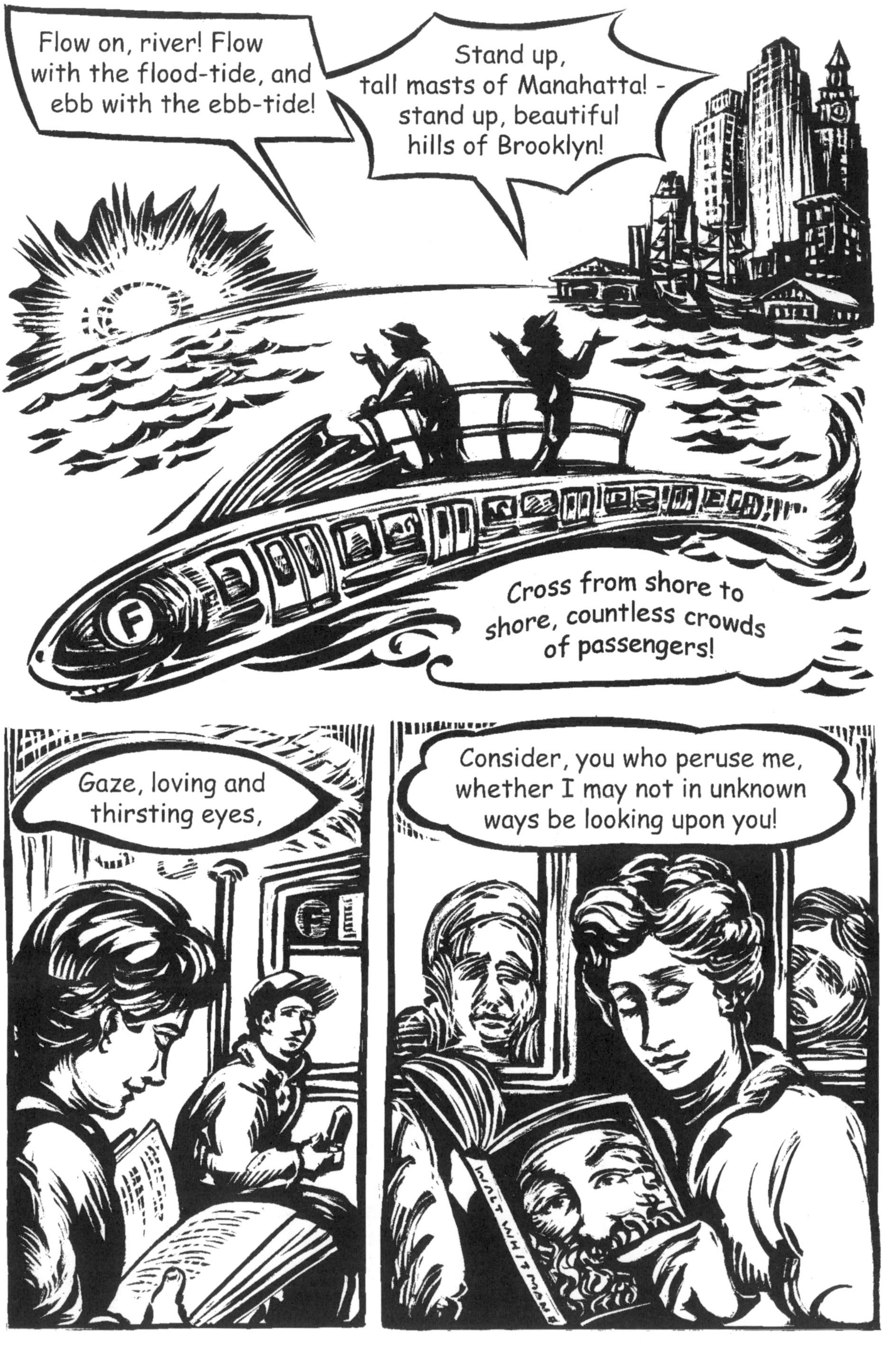
Flow on, river! Flow with the flood-tide, and ebb with the ebb-tide!
Stand up, tall masts of Manahatta! - stand up, beautiful hills of Brooklyn!
Cross from shore to shore, countless crowds of passengers!
Gaze, loving and thirsting eyes,
Consider, you who peruse me, whether I may not in unknown ways be looking upon you!
WALT WHITMAN

Chapter Three

Victorian Bohemia

The grim realities of the Civil War banished utopianism, more or less, as did rapid industrialization, growing immigrant populations, and an urban life of filthy factories and depressed neighborhoods. Williams Morris, so admired by Oscar Wilde, described these developments accurately as a great failure of modern civilization at large.

On the other hand, labor and socialist movements were growing in Europe, with new hopes for sweeping social transformation. Immigrants ranging from German, Jewish, Finnish, and Italian, to genuine ethnic "Bohemians" (Czechs) arrived in the U.S. with their own bohemian communities intact, some practicing free love without marriage. These immigrant communities created theater, poetry and other avant-garde cultural attractions in their adopted neighborhoods and native languages.

Meanwhile, sections of a rising American middle class, introduced to ideas of "vacations" and the "new woman" with her independent-mindedness, themselves wished to become "bohemian," as they understood or misunderstood the term. Overnight, definitions already ambiguous grew still more confused, as in Bohemian Grove, north of San Francisco, where the bourgeoisie frolicked with available women of lower classes in something not so different from pay-for-sex, itself a flourishing industry amid the newly sprawling cities. Who was the real American bohemian, redefined since the pre–Civil War days? A good question and one not easily answered.

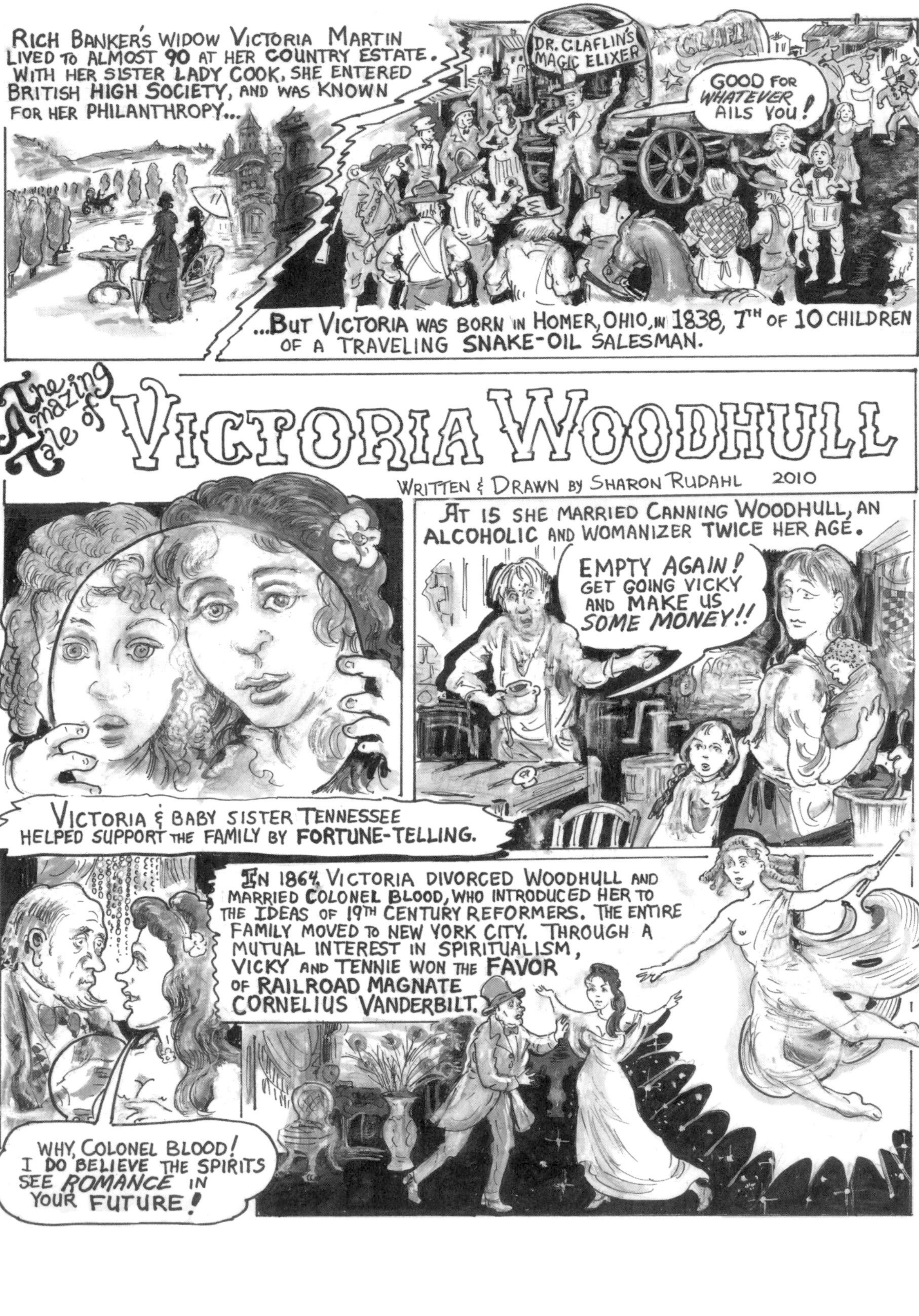
RICH BANKER'S WIDOW VICTORIA MARTIN LIVED TO ALMOST 90 AT HER COUNTRY ESTATE. WITH HER SISTER LADY COOK, SHE ENTERED BRITISH HIGH SOCIETY, AND WAS KNOWN FOR HER PHILANTHROPY...
DR. CLAFLIN'S MAGIC ELIXER
GOOD FOR WHATEVER AILS YOU!
...BUT VICTORIA WAS BORN IN HOMER, OHIO, IN 1838, 7TH OF 10 CHILDREN OF A TRAVELING SNAKE-OIL SALESMAN.
The Amazing Tale of VICTORIA WOODHULL
WRITTEN & DRAWN BY SHARON RUDAHL 2010
AT 15 SHE MARRIED CANNING WOODHULL, AN ALCOHOLIC AND WOMANIZER TWICE HER AGE.
EMPTY AGAIN! GET GOING VICKY AND MAKE US SOME MONEY!!
VICTORIA & BABY SISTER TENNESSEE HELPED SUPPORT THE FAMILY BY FORTUNE-TELLING.
IN 1864 VICTORIA DIVORCED WOODHULL AND MARRIED COLONEL BLOOD, WHO INTRODUCED HER TO THE IDEAS OF 19TH CENTURY REFORMERS. THE ENTIRE FAMILY MOVED TO NEW YORK CITY. THROUGH A MUTUAL INTEREST IN SPIRITUALISM, VICKY AND TENNIE WON THE FAVOR OF RAILROAD MAGNATE CORNELIUS VANDERBILT.
WHY, COLONEL BLOOD! I DO BELIEVE THE SPIRITS SEE ROMANCE IN YOUR FUTURE!

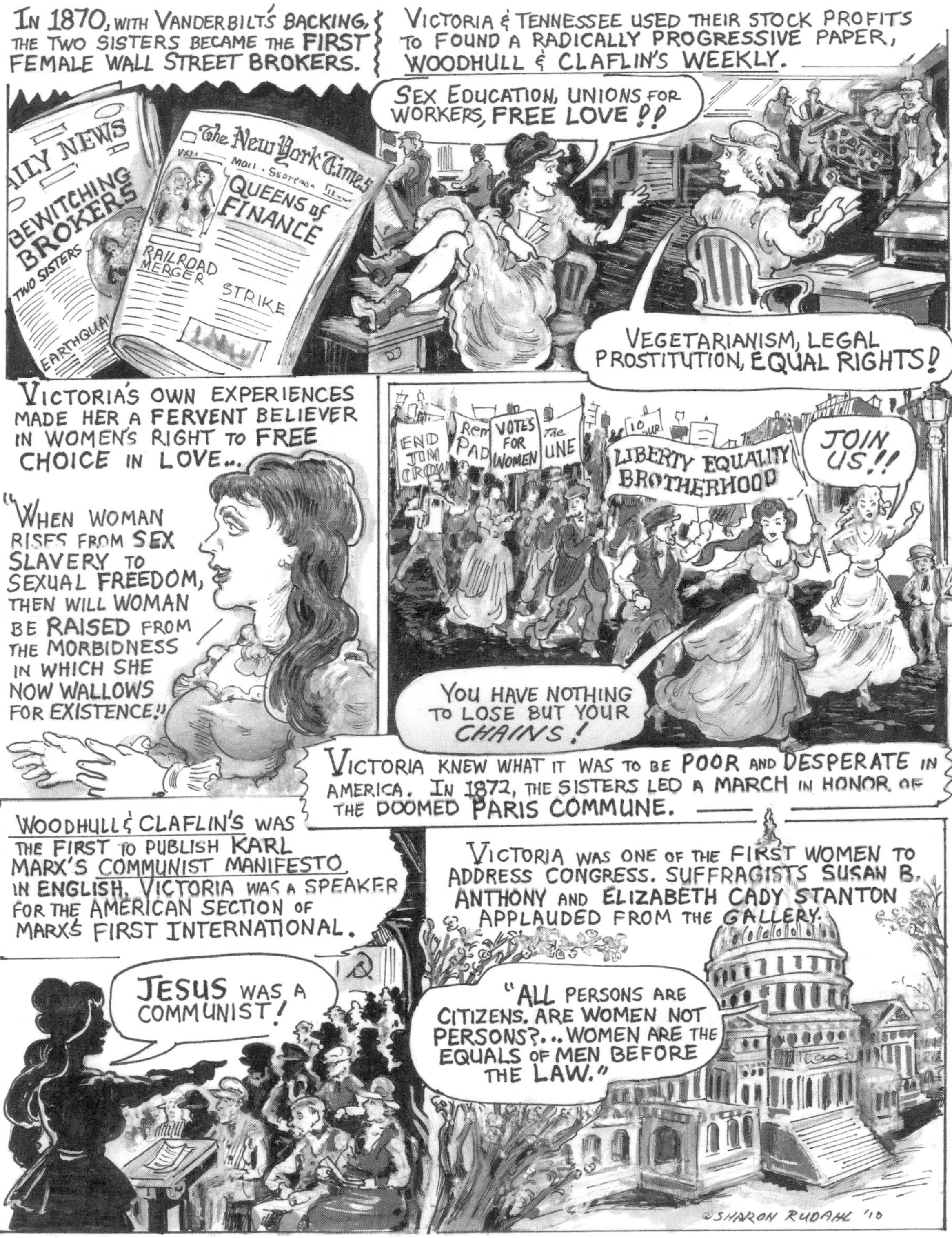
IN 1870, WITH VANDERBILT'S BACKING, THE TWO SISTERS BECAME THE FIRST FEMALE WALL STREET BROKERS.
VICTORIA & TENNESSEE USED THEIR STOCK PROFITS TO FOUND A RADICALLY PROGRESSIVE PAPER, WOODHULL & CLAFLIN'S WEEKLY.
AILY NEWS
BEWITCHING BROKERS
TWO SISTERS
EARTHQUAK
The New York Times
QUEENS of FINANCE
RAILROAD MERGER
STRIKE
SEX EDUCATION, UNIONS FOR WORKERS, FREE LOVE!!
VEGETARIANISM, LEGAL PROSTITUTION, EQUAL RIGHTS!
VICTORIA'S OWN EXPERIENCES MADE HER A FERVENT BELIEVER IN WOMEN'S RIGHT TO FREE CHOICE IN LOVE...
"WHEN WOMAN RISES FROM SEX SLAVERY TO SEXUAL FREEDOM, THEN WILL WOMAN BE RAISED FROM THE MORBIDNESS IN WHICH SHE NOW WALLOWS FOR EXISTENCE."
END JIM CROW
VOTES FOR WOMEN
LIBERTY EQUALITY BROTHERHOOD
JOIN US!!
YOU HAVE NOTHING TO LOSE BUT YOUR CHAINS!
VICTORIA KNEW WHAT IT WAS TO BE POOR AND DESPERATE IN AMERICA. IN 1872, THE SISTERS LED A MARCH IN HONOR OF THE DOOMED PARIS COMMUNE.
WOODHULL & CLAFLIN'S WAS THE FIRST TO PUBLISH KARL MARX'S COMMUNIST MANIFESTO IN ENGLISH. VICTORIA WAS A SPEAKER FOR THE AMERICAN SECTION OF MARX'S FIRST INTERNATIONAL.
JESUS WAS A COMMUNIST!
VICTORIA WAS ONE OF THE FIRST WOMEN TO ADDRESS CONGRESS. SUFFRAGISTS SUSAN B. ANTHONY AND ELIZABETH CADY STANTON APPLAUDED FROM THE GALLERY.
"ALL PERSONS ARE CITIZENS. ARE WOMEN NOT PERSONS?...WOMEN ARE THE EQUALS OF MEN BEFORE THE LAW."
©SHARON RUDAHL '10

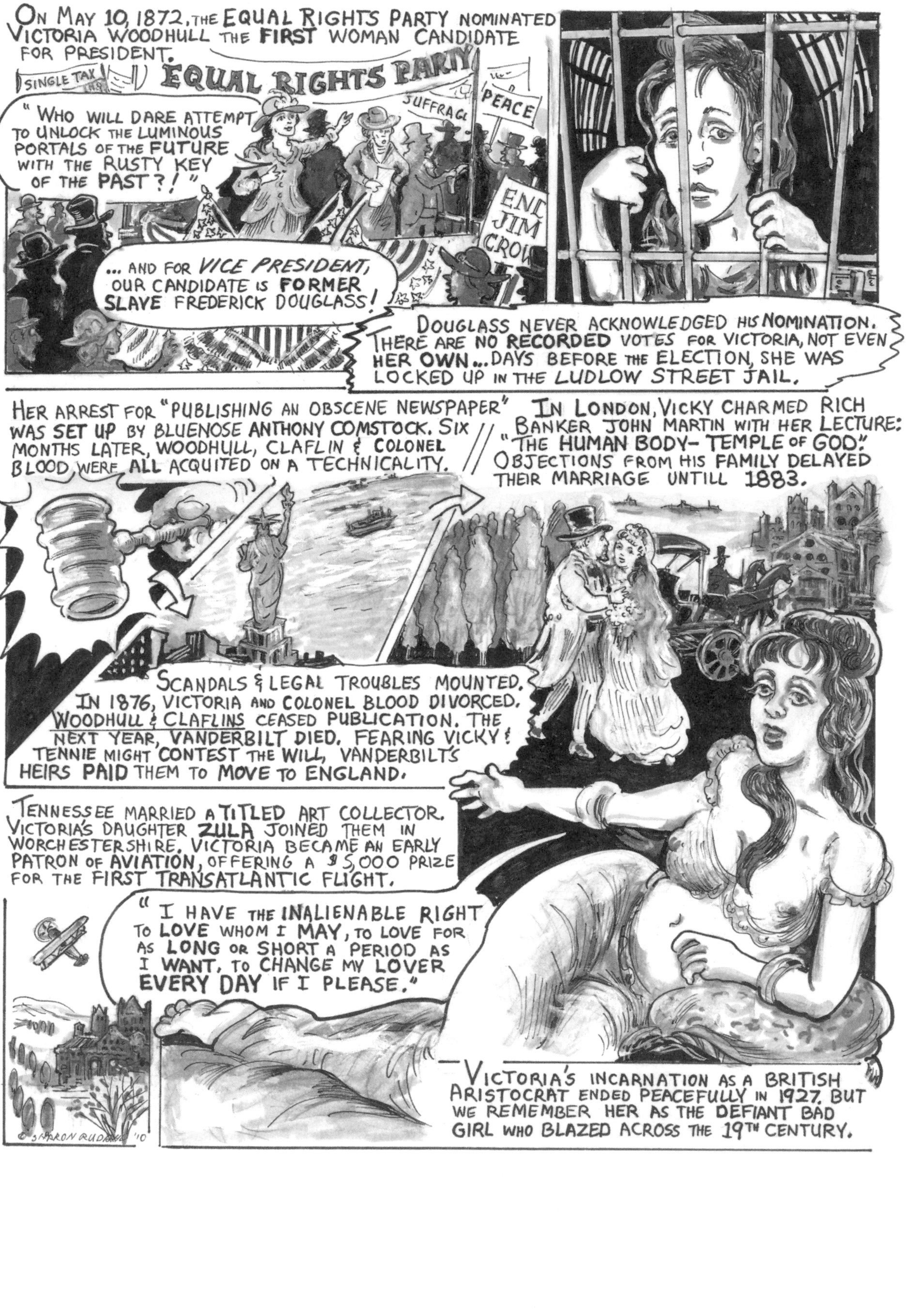

ON MAY 10, 1872, THE EQUAL RIGHTS PARTY NOMINATED VICTORIA WOODHULL THE FIRST WOMAN CANDIDATE FOR PRESIDENT.
SINGLE TAX
EQUAL RIGHTS PARTY
SUFFRAGE
PEACE
"WHO WILL DARE ATTEMPT TO UNLOCK THE LUMINOUS PORTALS OF THE FUTURE WITH THE RUSTY KEY OF THE PAST?!"
END JIM CROW
... AND FOR VICE PRESIDENT, OUR CANDIDATE IS FORMER SLAVE FREDERICK DOUGLASS!
DOUGLASS NEVER ACKNOWLEDGED HIS NOMINATION. THERE ARE NO RECORDED VOTES FOR VICTORIA, NOT EVEN HER OWN... DAYS BEFORE THE ELECTION, SHE WAS LOCKED UP IN THE LUDLOW STREET JAIL.
HER ARREST FOR "PUBLISHING AN OBSCENE NEWSPAPER" WAS SET UP BY BLUENOSE ANTHONY COMSTOCK. SIX MONTHS LATER, WOODHULL, CLAFLIN & COLONEL BLOOD WERE ALL ACQUITED ON A TECHNICALITY.
IN LONDON, VICKY CHARMED RICH BANKER JOHN MARTIN WITH HER LECTURE: "THE HUMAN BODY- TEMPLE OF GOD." OBJECTIONS FROM HIS FAMILY DELAYED THEIR MARRIAGE UNTILL 1883.
SCANDALS & LEGAL TROUBLES MOUNTED. IN 1876, VICTORIA AND COLONEL BLOOD DIVORCED. WOODHULL & CLAFLINS CEASED PUBLICATION. THE NEXT YEAR, VANDERBILT DIED. FEARING VICKY & TENNIE MIGHT CONTEST THE WILL, VANDERBILT'S HEIRS PAID THEM TO MOVE TO ENGLAND.
TENNESSEE MARRIED A TITLED ART COLLECTOR. VICTORIA'S DAUGHTER ZULA JOINED THEM IN WORCHESTERSHIRE. VICTORIA BECAME AN EARLY PATRON OF AVIATION, OFFERING A $5,000 PRIZE FOR THE FIRST TRANSATLANTIC FLIGHT.
"I HAVE THE INALIENABLE RIGHT TO LOVE WHOM I MAY, TO LOVE FOR AS LONG OR SHORT A PERIOD AS I WANT, TO CHANGE MY LOVER EVERY DAY IF I PLEASE."
VICTORIA'S INCARNATION AS A BRITISH ARISTOCRAT ENDED PEACEFULLY IN 1927, BUT WE REMEMBER HER AS THE DEFIANT BAD GIRL WHO BLAZED ACROSS THE 19TH CENTURY.
© SHARON RUDAHL '10

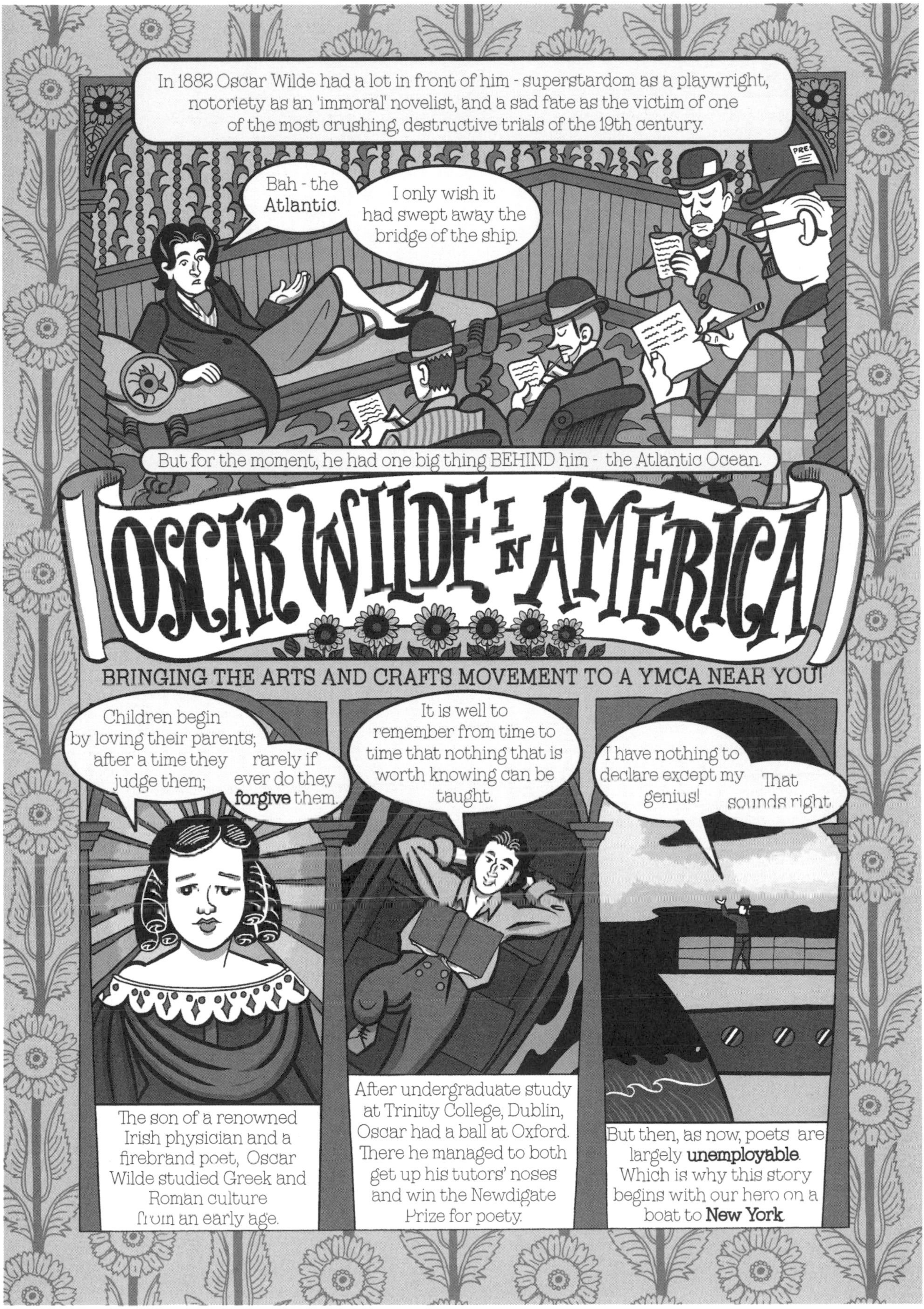
In 1882 Oscar Wilde had a lot in front of him - superstardom as a playwright, notoriety as an 'immoral' novelist, and a sad fate as the victim of one of the most crushing, destructive trials of the 19th century.
Bah - the Atlantic.
I only wish it had swept away the bridge of the ship.
But for the moment, he had one big thing BEHIND him - the Atlantic Ocean.
OSCAR WILDE IN AMERICA
BRINGING THE ARTS AND CRAFTS MOVEMENT TO A YMCA NEAR YOU!
Children begin by loving their parents; after a time they judge them;
rarely if ever do they forgive them.
The son of a renowned Irish physician and a firebrand poet, Oscar Wilde studied Greek and Roman culture from an early age.
It is well to remember from time to time that nothing that is worth knowing can be taught.
After undergraduate study at Trinity College, Dublin, Oscar had a ball at Oxford. There he managed to both get up his tutors' noses and win the Newdigate Prize for poety.
I have nothing to declare except my genius!
That sounds right
But then, as now, poets are largely unemployable. Which is why this story begins with our hero on a boat to New York

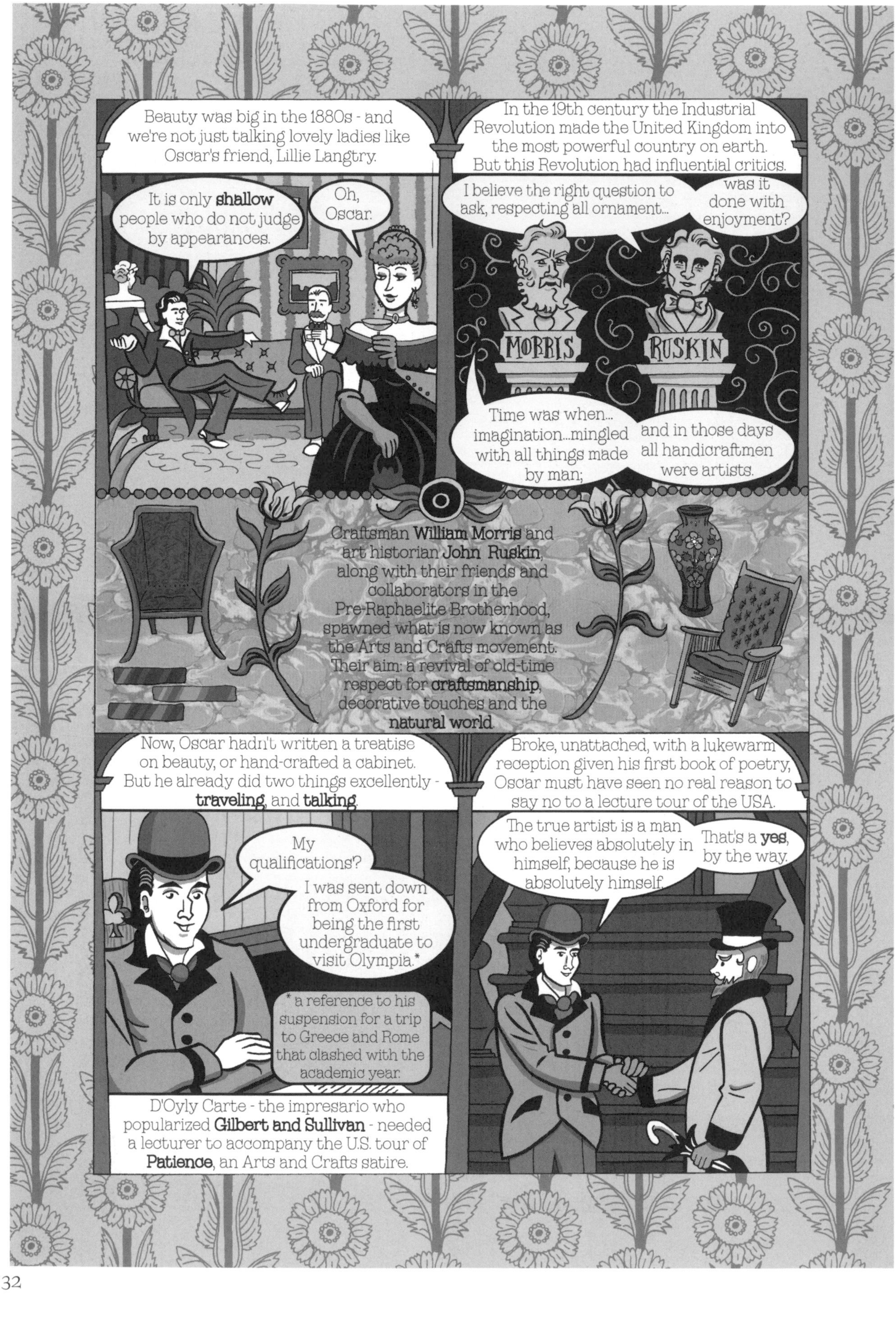

Beauty was big in the 1880s - and we're not just talking lovely ladies like Oscar's friend, Lillie Langtry.
It is only **shallow** people who do not judge by appearances.
Oh, Oscar.
In the 19th century the Industrial Revolution made the United Kingdom into the most powerful country on earth. But this Revolution had influential critics.
I believe the right question to ask, respecting all ornament...
was it done with enjoyment?
MORRIS
RUSKIN
Time was when... imagination...mingled with all things made by man;
and in those days all handicraftmen were artists.
Craftsman **William Morris** and art historian **John Ruskin**, along with their friends and collaborators in the Pre-Raphaelite Brotherhood, spawned what is now known as the Arts and Crafts movement. Their aim: a revival of old-time respect for **craftsmanship**, decorative touches and the **natural world**.
Now, Oscar hadn't written a treatise on beauty, or hand-crafted a cabinet. But he already did two things excellently - **traveling**, and **talking**.
My qualifications?
I was sent down from Oxford for being the first undergraduate to visit Olympia.*
* a reference to his suspension for a trip to Greece and Rome that clashed with the academic year.
D'Oyly Carte - the impresario who popularized **Gilbert and Sullivan** - needed a lecturer to accompany the U.S. tour of **Patience**, an Arts and Crafts satire.
Broke, unattached, with a lukewarm reception given his first book of poetry, Oscar must have seen no real reason to say no to a lecture tour of the USA.
The true artist is a man who believes absolutely in himself, because he is absolutely himself.
That's a **yes**, by the way.

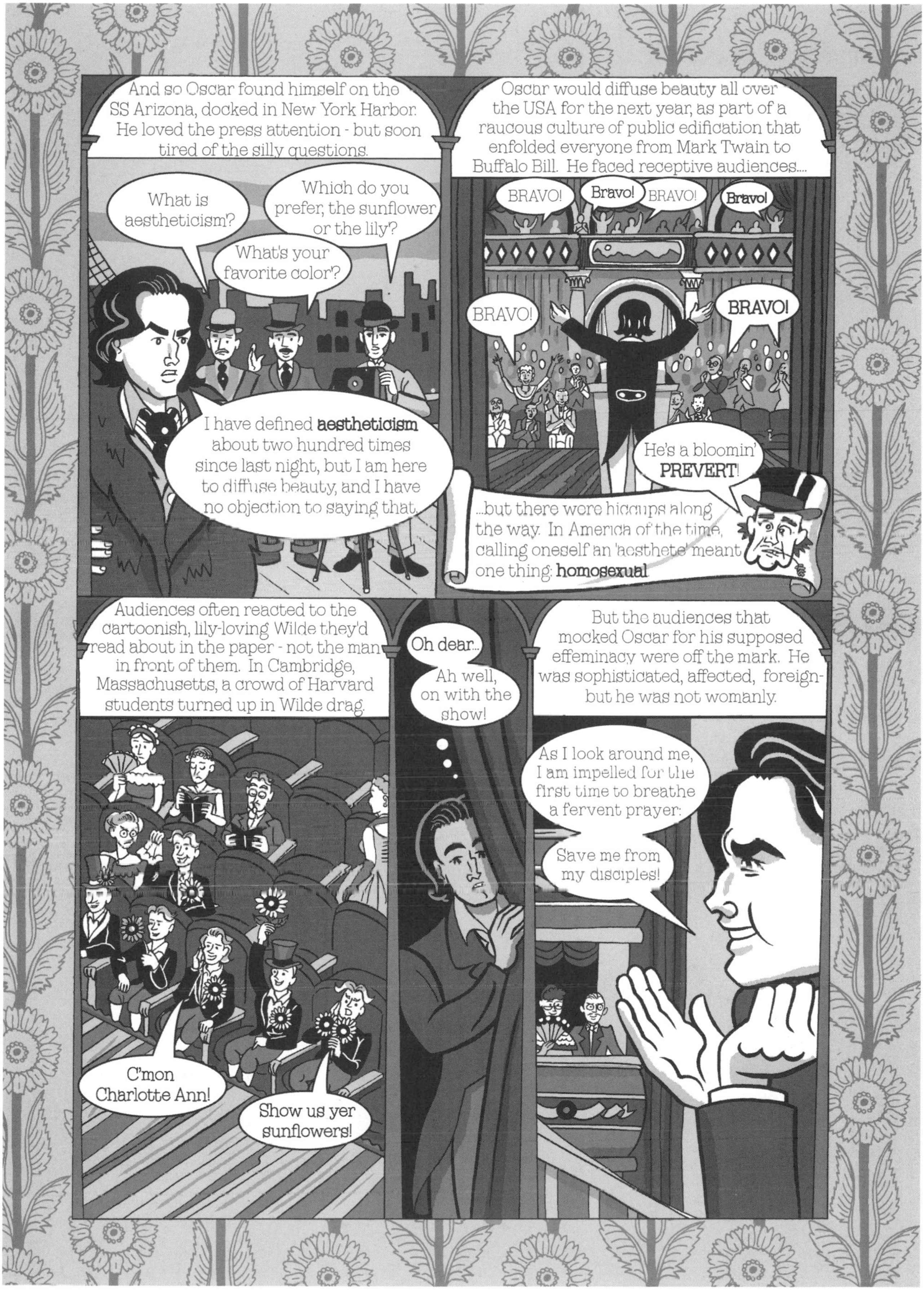

And so Oscar found himself on the SS Arizona, docked in New York Harbor. He loved the press attention - but soon tired of the silly questions.
What is aestheticism?
Which do you prefer, the sunflower or the lily?
What's your favorite color?
I have defined **aestheticism** about two hundred times since last night, but I am here to diffuse beauty, and I have no objection to saying that.
Oscar would diffuse beauty all over the USA for the next year, as part of a raucous culture of public edification that enfolded everyone from Mark Twain to Buffalo Bill. He faced receptive audiences....
BRAVO!
Bravo!
BRAVO!
Bravo!
BRAVO!
BRAVO!
He's a bloomin' PREVERT!
...but there were hiccups along the way. In America of the time, calling oneself an 'aesthete' meant one thing: **homosexual**
Audiences often reacted to the cartoonish, lily-loving Wilde they'd read about in the paper - not the man in front of them. In Cambridge, Massachusetts, a crowd of Harvard students turned up in Wilde drag.
C'mon Charlotte Ann!
Show us yer sunflowers!
Oh dear...
Ah well, on with the show!
But the audiences that mocked Oscar for his supposed effeminacy were off the mark. He was sophisticated, affected, foreign- but he was not womanly.
As I look around me, I am impelled for the first time to breathe a fervent prayer:
Save me from my disciples!

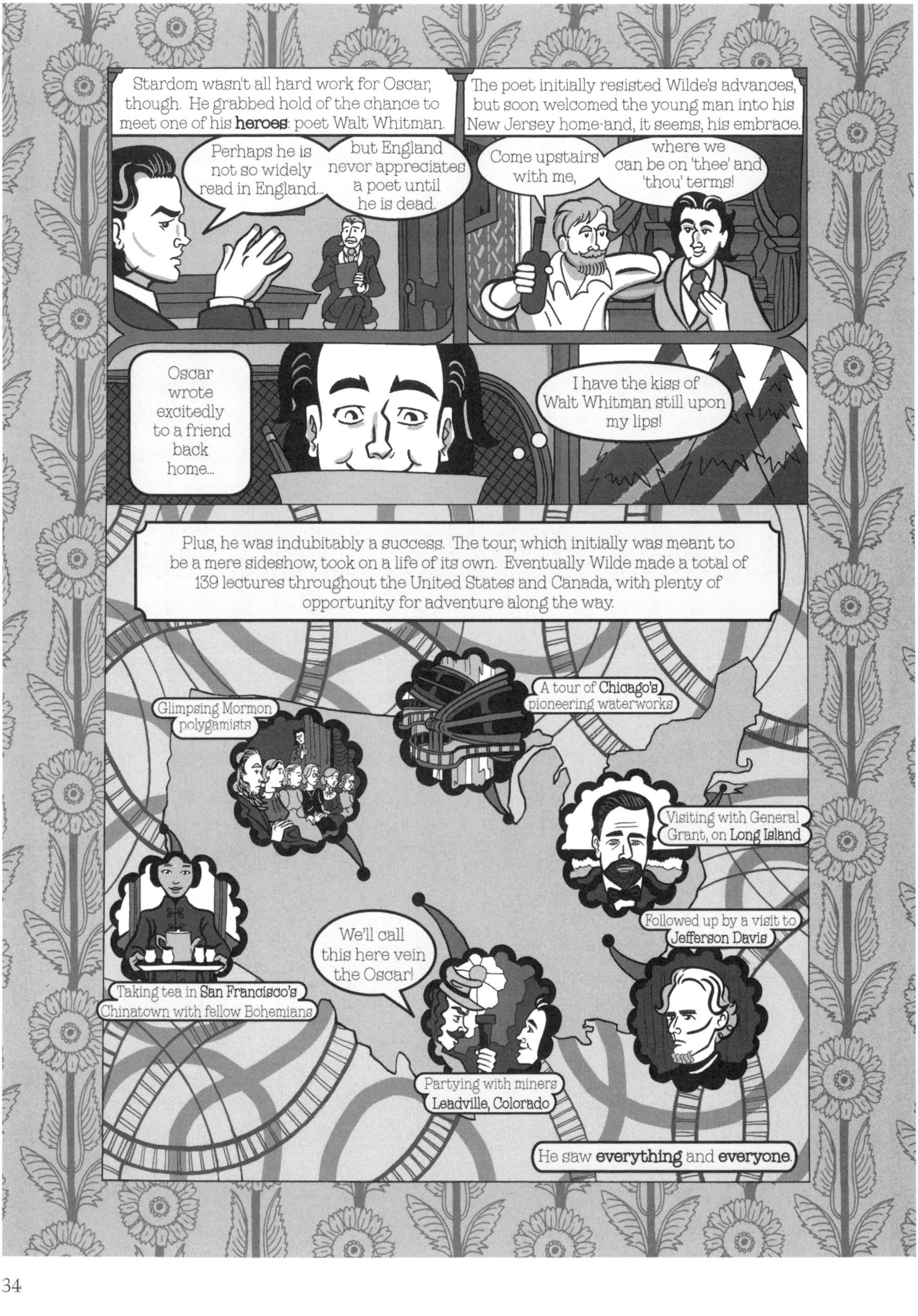
Stardom wasn't all hard work for Oscar, though. He grabbed hold of the chance to meet one of his **heroes**: poet Walt Whitman.
Perhaps he is not so widely read in England...
but England never appreciates a poet until he is dead.
The poet initially resisted Wilde's advances, but soon welcomed the young man into his New Jersey home-and, it seems, his embrace.
Come upstairs with me,
where we can be on 'thee' and 'thou' terms!
Oscar wrote excitedly to a friend back home...
I have the kiss of Walt Whitman still upon my lips!
Plus, he was indubitably a success. The tour, which initially was meant to be a mere sideshow, took on a life of its own. Eventually Wilde made a total of 139 lectures throughout the United States and Canada, with plenty of opportunity for adventure along the way.
Glimpsing Mormon polygamists
A tour of **Chicago's** pioneering waterworks
Visiting with General Grant, on **Long Island**
Followed up by a visit to **Jefferson Davis**
Taking tea in **San Francisco's** Chinatown with fellow Bohemians
We'll call this here vein the Oscar!
Partying with miners **Leadville, Colorado**
He saw **everything** and **everyone**.

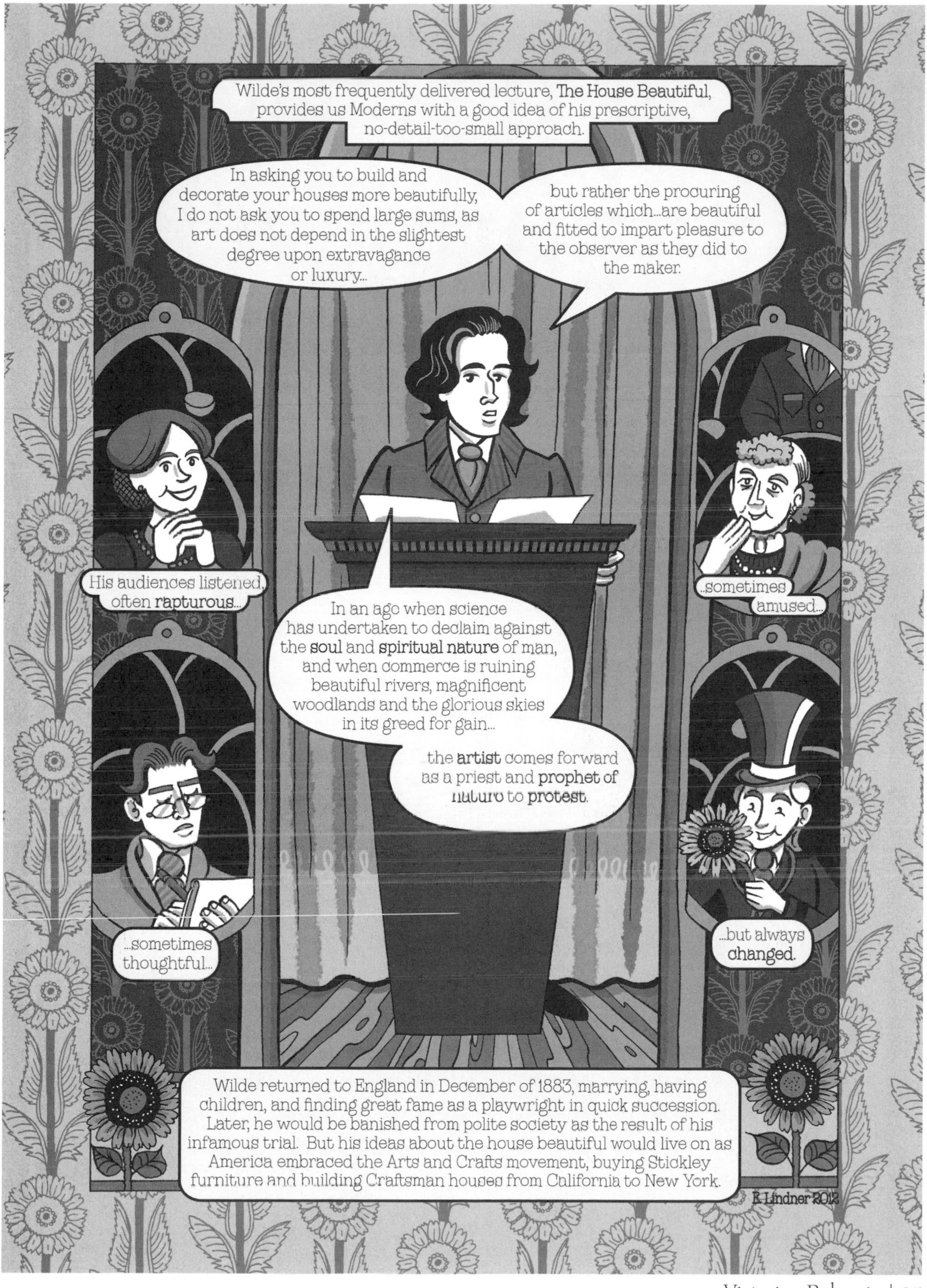

Wilde's most frequently delivered lecture, The House Beautiful, provides us Moderns with a good idea of his prescriptive, no-detail-too-small approach.
In asking you to build and decorate your houses more beautifully, I do not ask you to spend large sums, as art does not depend in the slightest degree upon extravagance or luxury...
but rather the procuring of articles which...are beautiful and fitted to impart pleasure to the observer as they did to the maker.
His audiences listened, often rapturous...
...sometimes amused...
In an age when science has undertaken to declaim against the soul and spiritual nature of man, and when commerce is ruining beautiful rivers, magnificent woodlands and the glorious skies in its greed for gain...
...the artist comes forward as a priest and prophet of nature to protest.
...sometimes thoughtful...
...but always changed.
Wilde returned to England in December of 1883, marrying, having children, and finding great fame as a playwright in quick succession. Later, he would be banished from polite society as the result of his infamous trial. But his ideas about the house beautiful would live on as America embraced the Arts and Crafts movement, buying Stickley furniture and building Craftsman houses from California to New York.
B. Lindner 2012

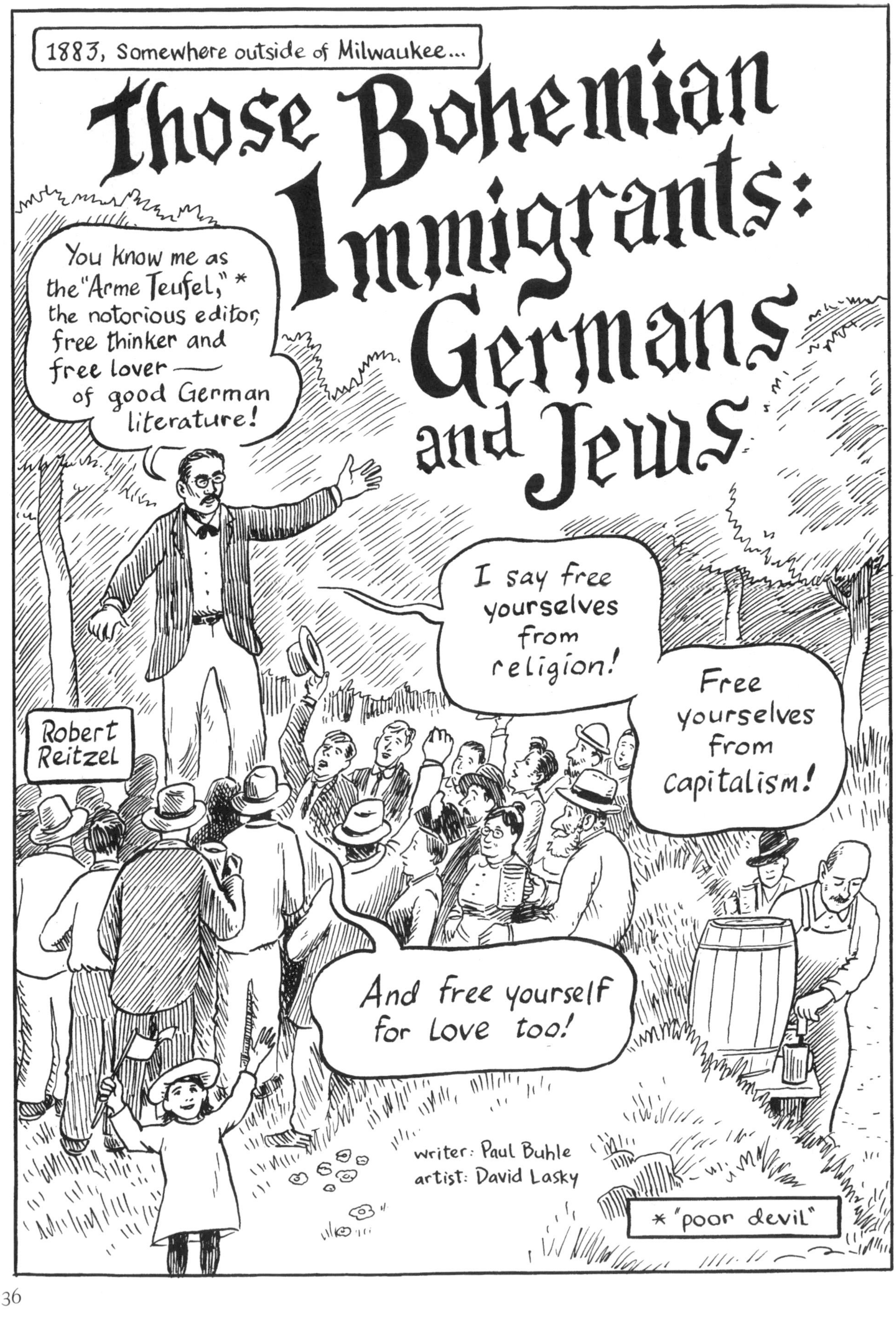

1883, Somewhere outside of Milwaukee...
Those Bohemian Immigrants: Germans and Jews
You know me as the "Arme Teufel," * the notorious editor, free thinker and free lover — of good German literature!
Robert Reitzel
I say free yourselves from religion!
Free yourselves from capitalism!
And free yourself for love too!
writer: Paul Buhle
artist: David Lasky
* "poor devil"

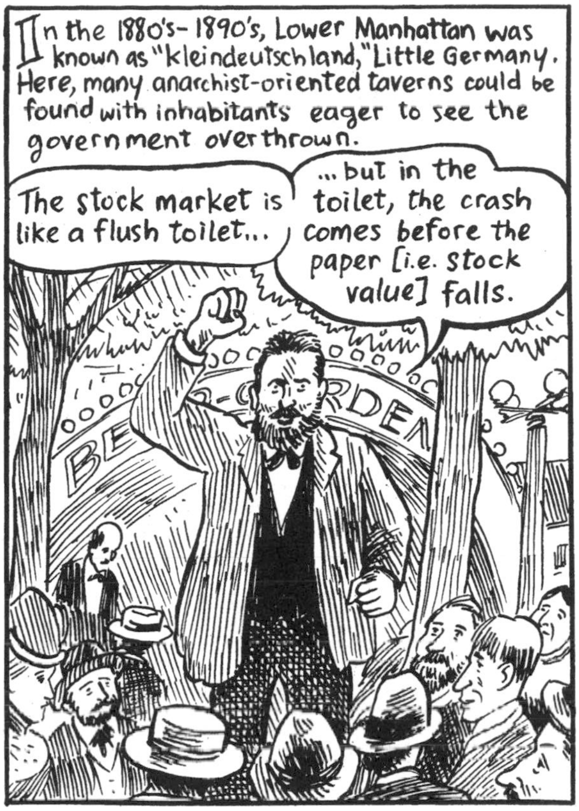
In the 1880's-1890's, Lower Manhattan was known as "kleindeutschland," "Little Germany. Here, many anarchist-oriented taverns could be found with inhabitants eager to see the government overthrown.
The stock market is like a flush toilet...
...but in the toilet, the crash comes before the paper [i.e. stock value] falls.

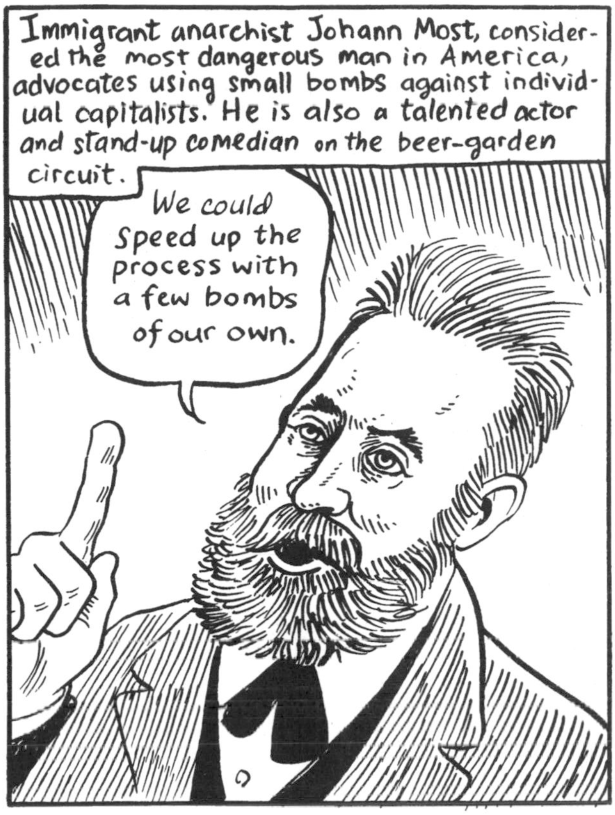
Immigrant anarchist Johann Most, considered the most dangerous man in America, advocates using small bombs against individual capitalists. He is also a talented actor and stand-up comedian on the beer-garden circuit.
We could speed up the process with a few bombs of our own.

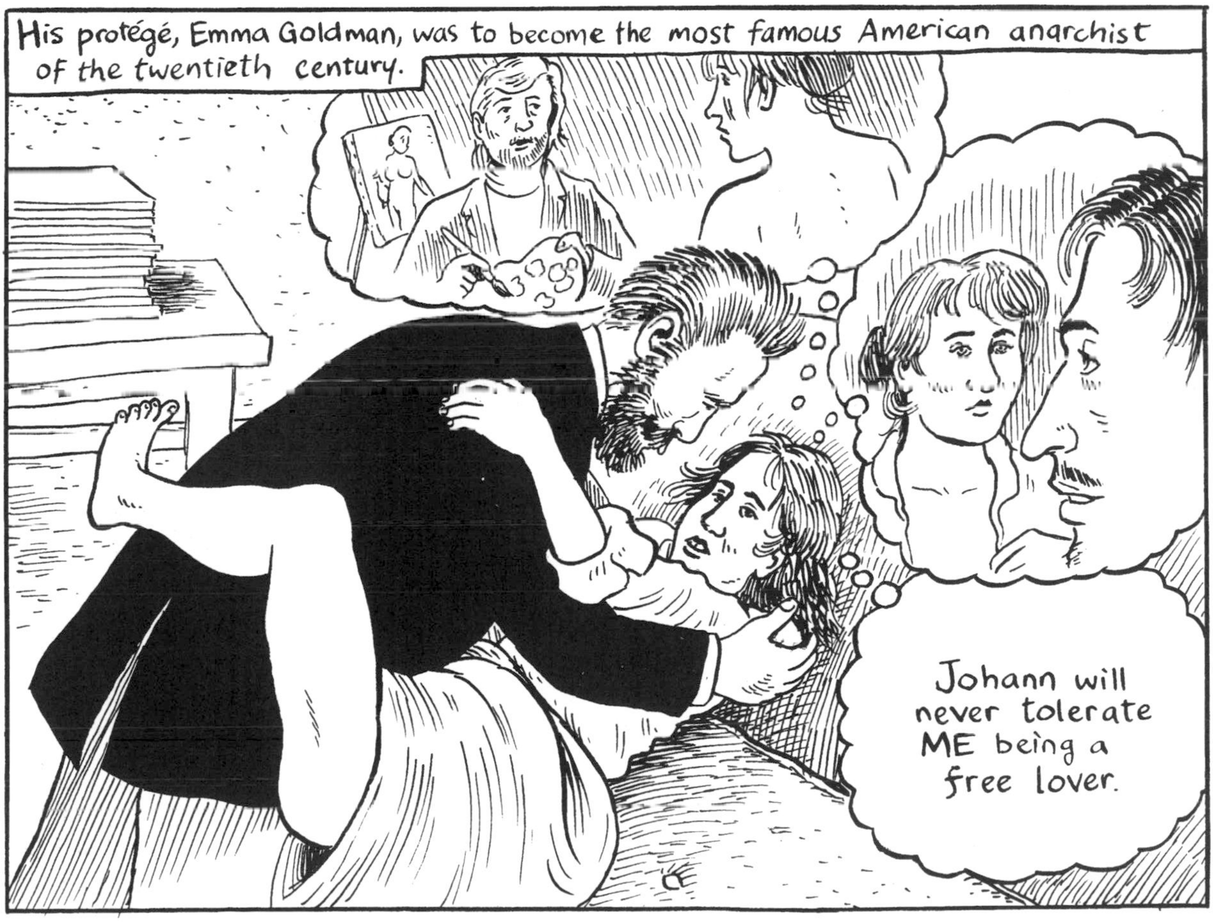
His protégé, Emma Goldman, was to become the most famous American anarchist of the twentieth century.
Johann will never tolerate ME being a free lover.

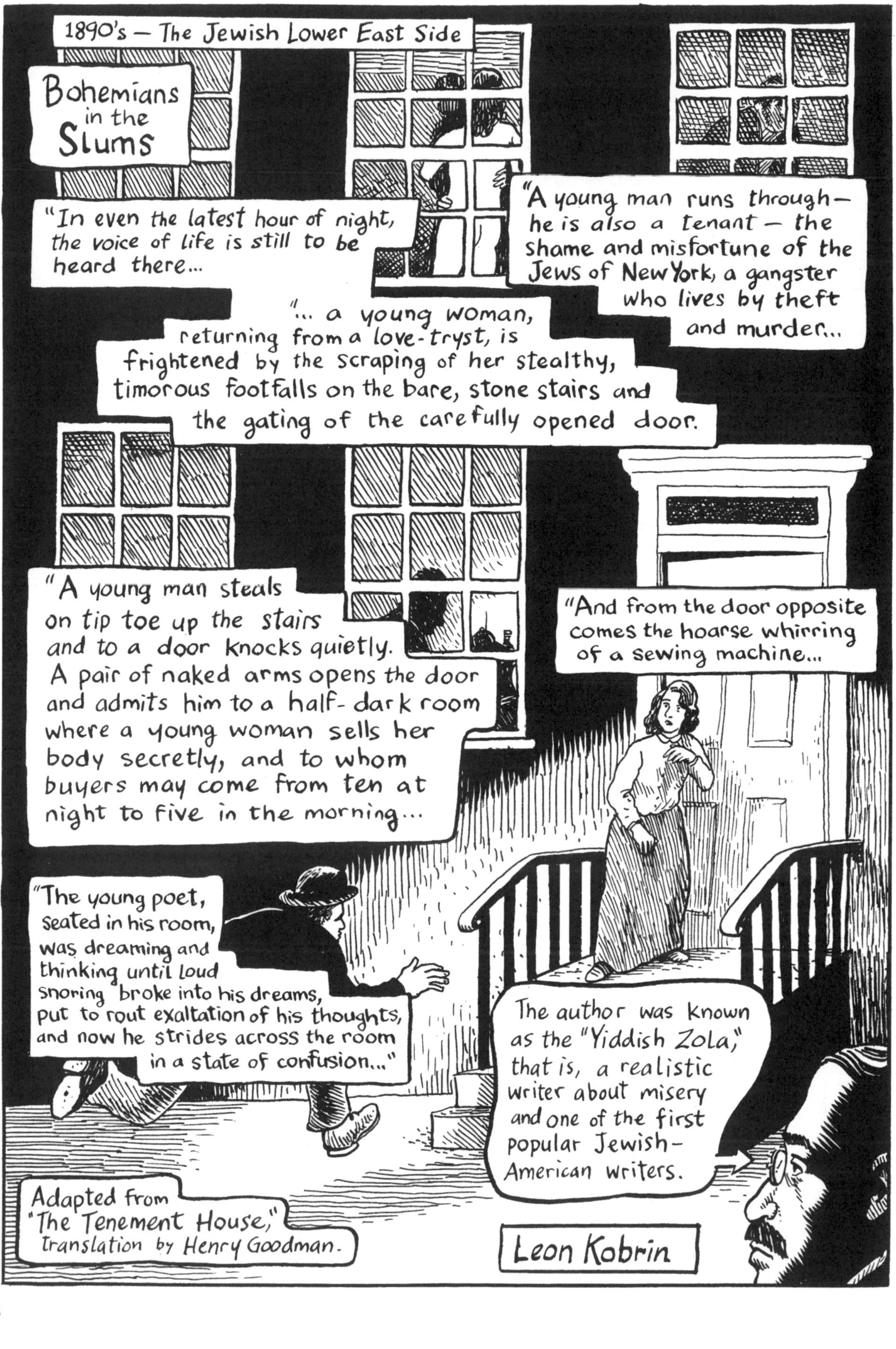
1890's — The Jewish Lower East Side
Bohemians in the Slums
"In even the latest hour of night, the voice of life is still to be heard there...
"A young man runs through— he is also a tenant — the shame and misfortune of the Jews of New York, a gangster who lives by theft and murder...
"... a young woman, returning from a love-tryst, is frightened by the scraping of her stealthy, timorous footfalls on the bare, stone stairs and the gating of the carefully opened door.
"A young man steals on tip toe up the stairs and to a door knocks quietly. A pair of naked arms opens the door and admits him to a half-dark room where a young woman sells her body secretly, and to whom buyers may come from ten at night to five in the morning...
"And from the door opposite comes the hoarse whirring of a sewing machine...
"The young poet, seated in his room, was dreaming and thinking until loud snoring broke into his dreams, put to rout exaltation of his thoughts, and now he strides across the room in a state of confusion..."
The author was known as the "Yiddish Zola," that is, a realistic writer about misery and one of the first popular Jewish-American writers.
Adapted from "The Tenement House," translation by Henry Goodman.
Leon Kobrin

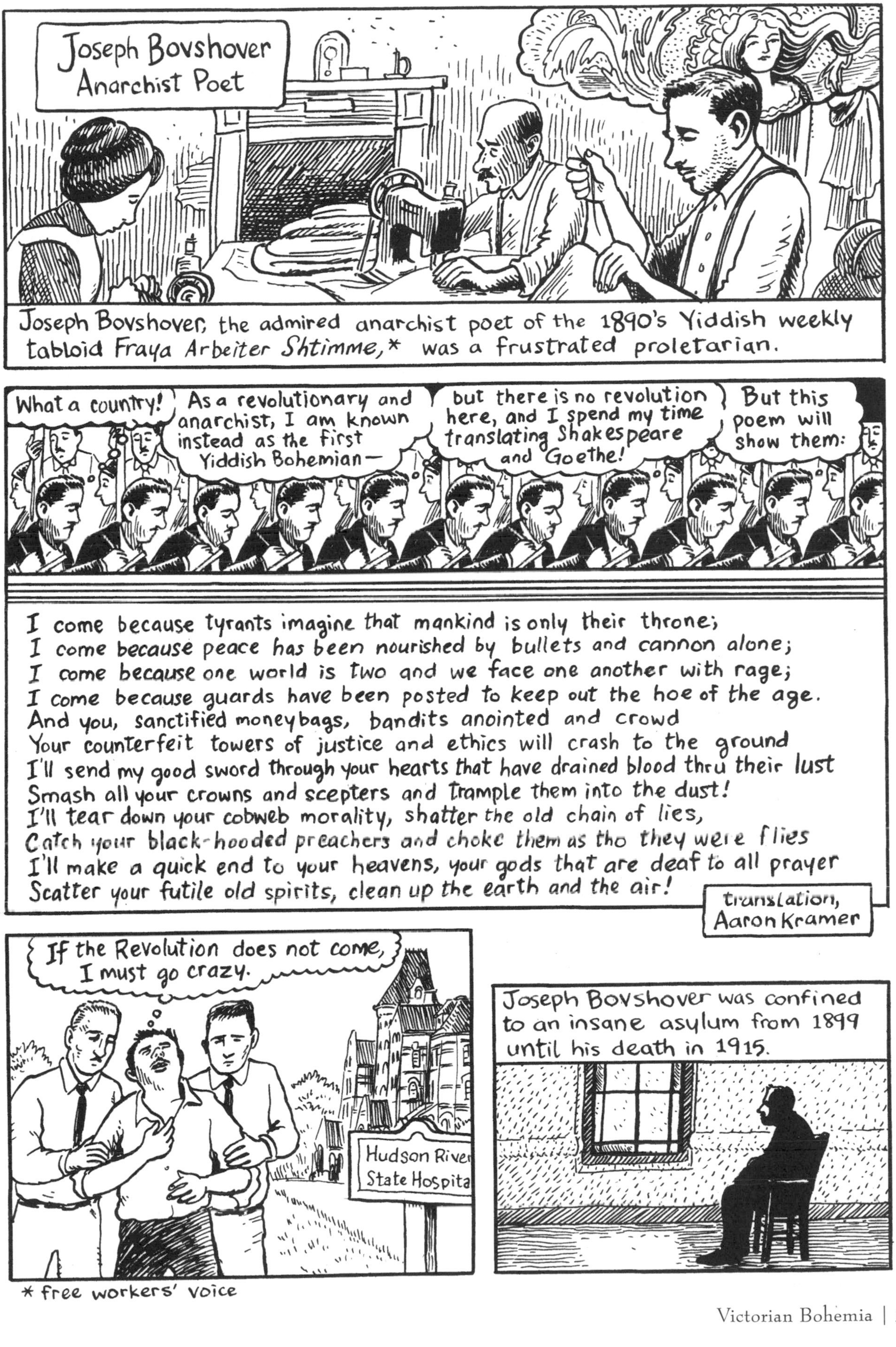
Joseph Bovshover
Anarchist Poet
Joseph Bovshover, the admired anarchist poet of the 1890's Yiddish weekly tabloid Fraya Arbeiter Shtimme,* was a frustrated proletarian.
What a country!
As a revolutionary and anarchist, I am known instead as the first Yiddish Bohemian—
but there is no revolution here, and I spend my time translating Shakespeare and Goethe!
But this poem will show them:
I come because tyrants imagine that mankind is only their throne;
I come because peace has been nourished by bullets and cannon alone;
I come because one world is two and we face one another with rage;
I come because guards have been posted to keep out the hoe of the age.
And you, sanctified moneybags, bandits anointed and crowd
Your counterfeit towers of justice and ethics will crash to the ground
I'll send my good sword through your hearts that have drained blood thru their lust
Smash all your crowns and scepters and trample them into the dust!
I'll tear down your cobweb morality, shatter the old chain of lies,
Catch your black-hooded preachers and choke them as tho they were flies
I'll make a quick end to your heavens, your gods that are deaf to all prayer
Scatter your futile old spirits, clean up the earth and the air!
translation, Aaron Kramer
If the Revolution does not come, I must go crazy.
Hudson River State Hospita
Joseph Bovshover was confined to an insane asylum from 1899 until his death in 1915.

* free workers' voice

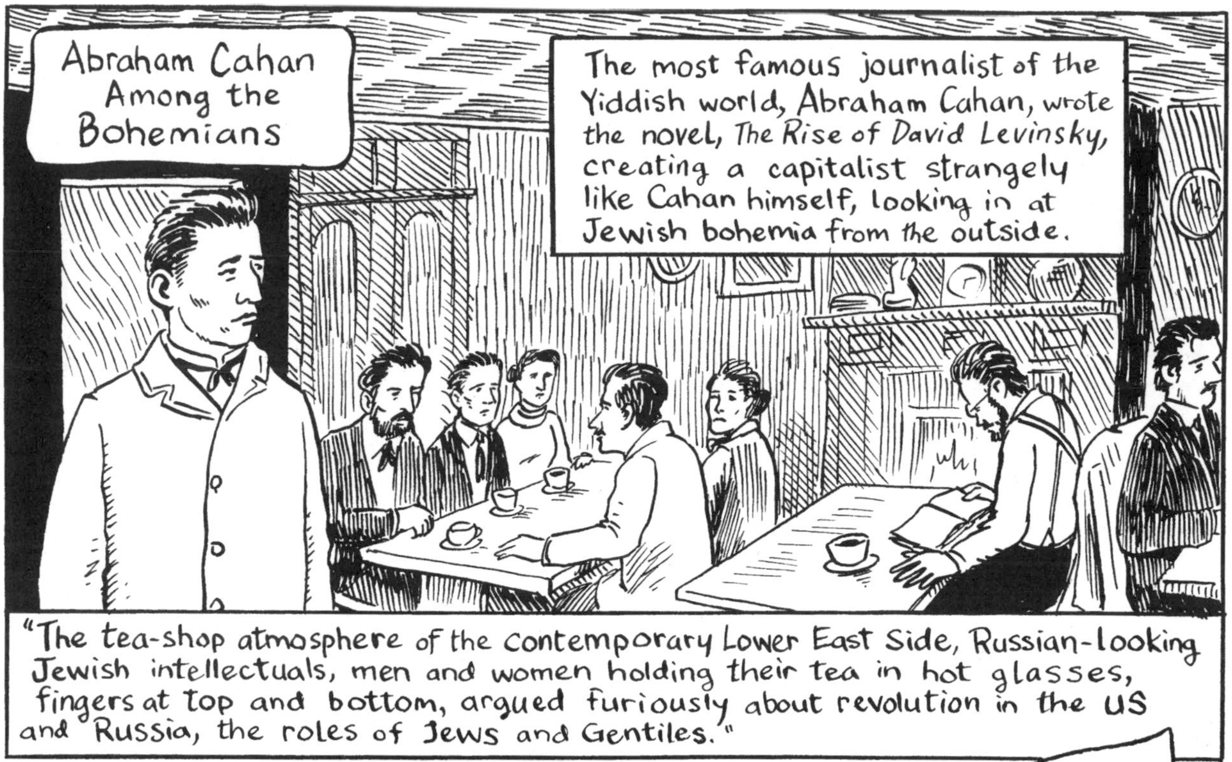
Abraham Cahan Among the Bohemians
The most famous journalist of the Yiddish world, Abraham Cahan, wrote the novel, *The Rise of David Levinsky,* creating a capitalist strangely like Cahan himself, looking in at Jewish bohemia from the outside.
"The tea-shop atmosphere of the contemporary Lower East Side, Russian-looking Jewish intellectuals, men and women holding their tea in hot glasses, fingers at top and bottom, argued furiously about revolution in the US and Russia, the roles of Jews and Gentiles."

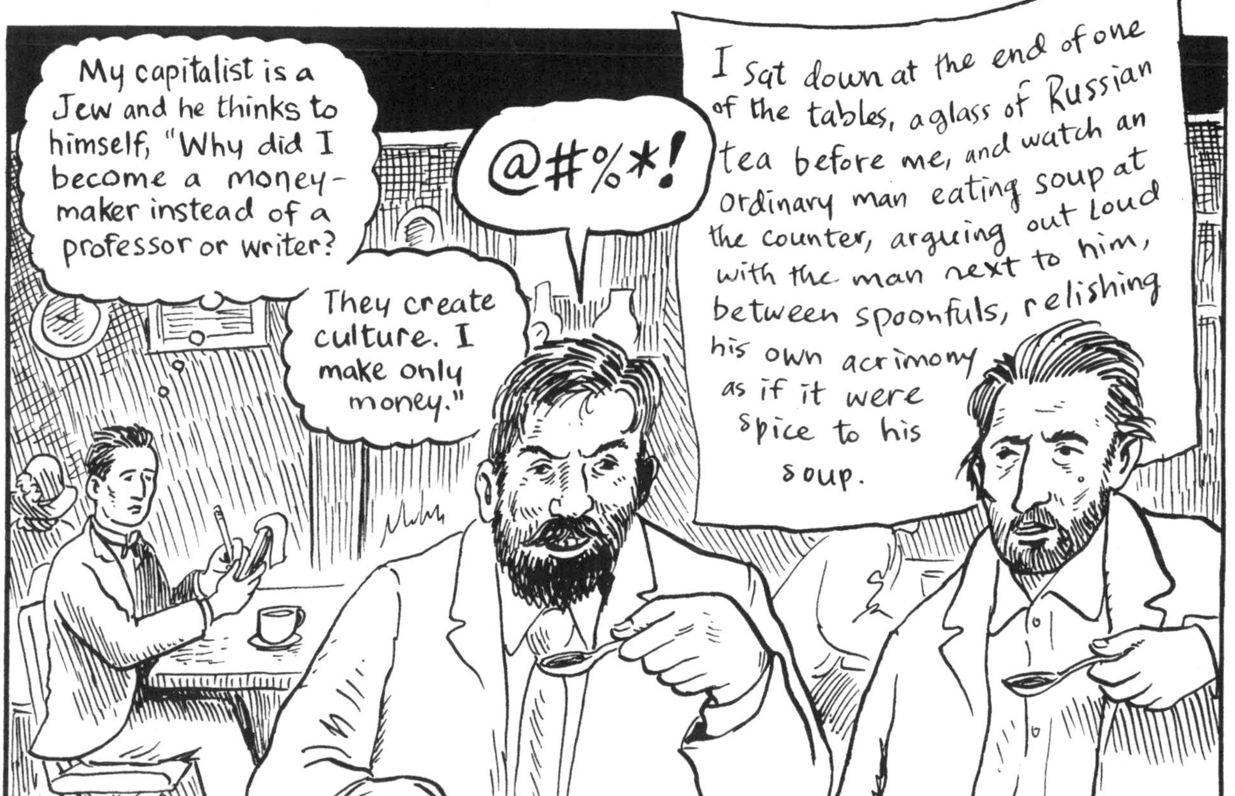
My capitalist is a Jew and he thinks to himself, "Why did I become a money-maker instead of a professor or writer?
They create culture. I make only money."
@#%*!
I sat down at the end of one of the tables, a glass of Russian tea before me, and watch an ordinary man eating soup at the counter, arguing out loud with the man next to him, between spoonfuls, relishing his own acrimony as if it were spice to his soup.

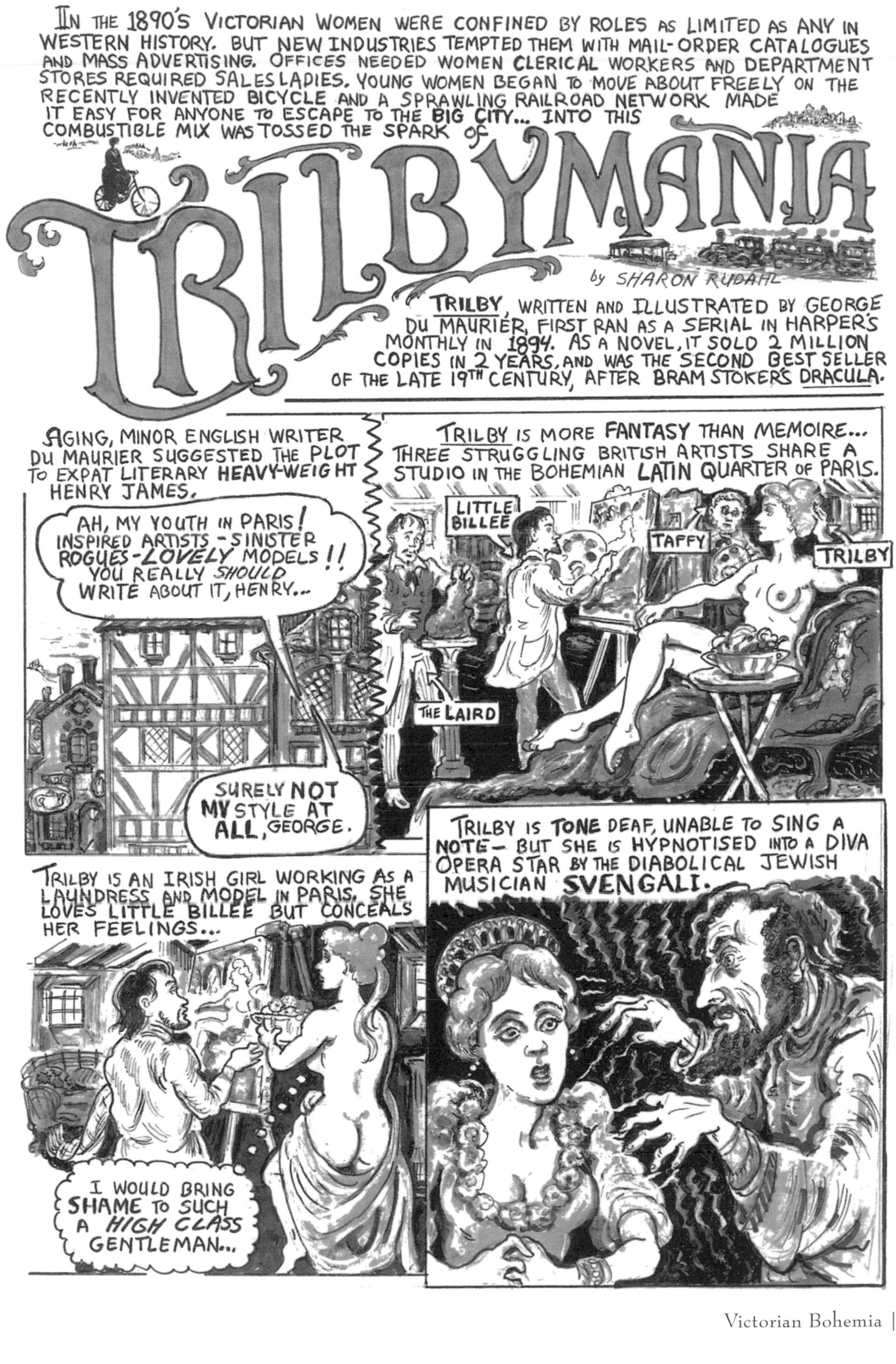

IN THE 1890'S VICTORIAN WOMEN WERE CONFINED BY ROLES AS LIMITED AS ANY IN WESTERN HISTORY. BUT NEW INDUSTRIES TEMPTED THEM WITH MAIL-ORDER CATALOGUES AND MASS ADVERTISING. OFFICES NEEDED WOMEN CLERICAL WORKERS AND DEPARTMENT STORES REQUIRED SALESLADIES. YOUNG WOMEN BEGAN TO MOVE ABOUT FREELY ON THE RECENTLY INVENTED BICYCLE AND A SPRAWLING RAILROAD NETWORK MADE IT EASY FOR ANYONE TO ESCAPE TO THE BIG CITY... INTO THIS COMBUSTIBLE MIX WAS TOSSED THE SPARK OF
TRILBYMANIA
by SHARON RUDAHL
TRILBY, WRITTEN AND ILLUSTRATED BY GEORGE DU MAURIER, FIRST RAN AS A SERIAL IN HARPER'S MONTHLY IN 1894. AS A NOVEL, IT SOLD 2 MILLION COPIES IN 2 YEARS, AND WAS THE SECOND BEST SELLER OF THE LATE 19TH CENTURY, AFTER BRAM STOKER'S DRACULA.
AGING, MINOR ENGLISH WRITER DU MAURIER SUGGESTED THE PLOT TO EXPAT LITERARY HEAVY-WEIGHT HENRY JAMES.
AH, MY YOUTH IN PARIS! INSPIRED ARTISTS - SINISTER ROGUES - LOVELY MODELS!! YOU REALLY SHOULD WRITE ABOUT IT, HENRY...
SURELY NOT MY STYLE AT ALL, GEORGE.
TRILBY IS MORE FANTASY THAN MEMOIRE... THREE STRUGGLING BRITISH ARTISTS SHARE A STUDIO IN THE BOHEMIAN LATIN QUARTER OF PARIS.
LITTLE BILLEE
TAFFY
TRILBY
THE LAIRD
TRILBY IS AN IRISH GIRL WORKING AS A LAUNDRESS AND MODEL IN PARIS. SHE LOVES LITTLE BILLEE BUT CONCEALS HER FEELINGS...
I WOULD BRING SHAME TO SUCH A HIGH CLASS GENTLEMAN...
TRILBY IS TONE DEAF, UNABLE TO SING A NOTE - BUT SHE IS HYPNOTISED INTO A DIVA OPERA STAR BY THE DIABOLICAL JEWISH MUSICIAN SVENGALI.

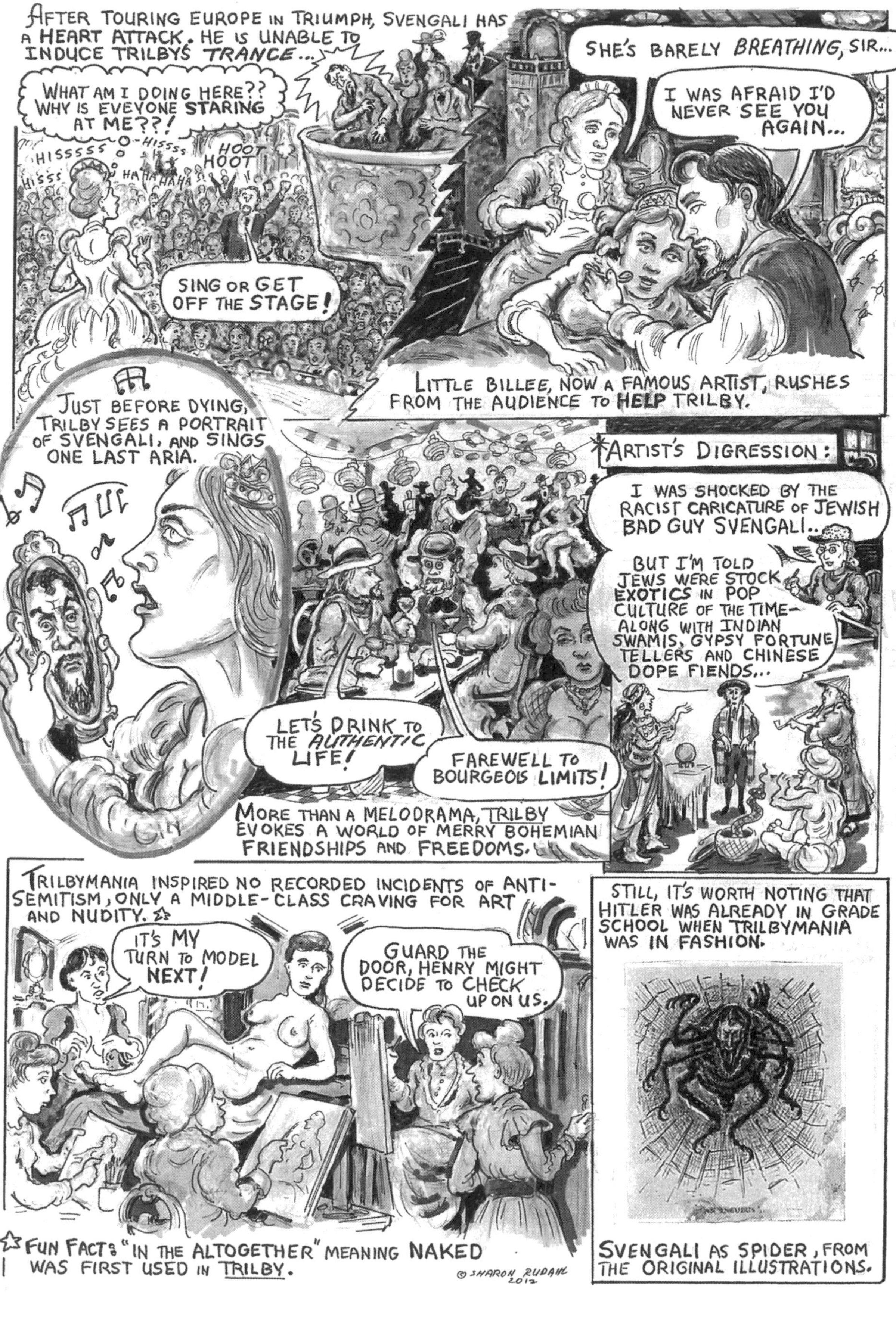

AFTER TOURING EUROPE IN TRIUMPH, SVENGALI HAS A HEART ATTACK. HE IS UNABLE TO INDUCE TRILBY'S TRANCE...
WHAT AM I DOING HERE?? WHY IS EVEYONE STARING AT ME??!
HISSSSS O-HISSSS HISSS HAHAHAHA HOOT HOOT
SING OR GET OFF THE STAGE!
SHE'S BARELY BREATHING, SIR...
I WAS AFRAID I'D NEVER SEE YOU AGAIN...
LITTLE BILLEE, NOW A FAMOUS ARTIST, RUSHES FROM THE AUDIENCE TO HELP TRILBY.
JUST BEFORE DYING, TRILBY SEES A PORTRAIT OF SVENGALI, AND SINGS ONE LAST ARIA.
LET'S DRINK TO THE AUTHENTIC LIFE!
FAREWELL TO BOURGEOIS LIMITS!
MORE THAN A MELODRAMA, TRILBY EVOKES A WORLD OF MERRY BOHEMIAN FRIENDSHIPS AND FREEDOMS.
*ARTIST'S DIGRESSION:
I WAS SHOCKED BY THE RACIST CARICATURE OF JEWISH BAD GUY SVENGALI..
BUT I'M TOLD JEWS WERE STOCK EXOTICS IN POP CULTURE OF THE TIME-ALONG WITH INDIAN SWAMIS, GYPSY FORTUNE TELLERS AND CHINESE DOPE FIENDS...
TRILBYMANIA INSPIRED NO RECORDED INCIDENTS OF ANTI-SEMITISM, ONLY A MIDDLE-CLASS CRAVING FOR ART AND NUDITY. ☆
IT'S MY TURN TO MODEL NEXT!
GUARD THE DOOR, HENRY MIGHT DECIDE TO CHECK UP ON US.
☆ FUN FACT: "IN THE ALTOGETHER" MEANING NAKED WAS FIRST USED IN TRILBY.
© SHARON RUDAHL 2012
STILL, IT'S WORTH NOTING THAT HITLER WAS ALREADY IN GRADE SCHOOL WHEN TRILBYMANIA WAS IN FASHION.
SVENGALI AS SPIDER, FROM THE ORIGINAL ILLUSTRATIONS.

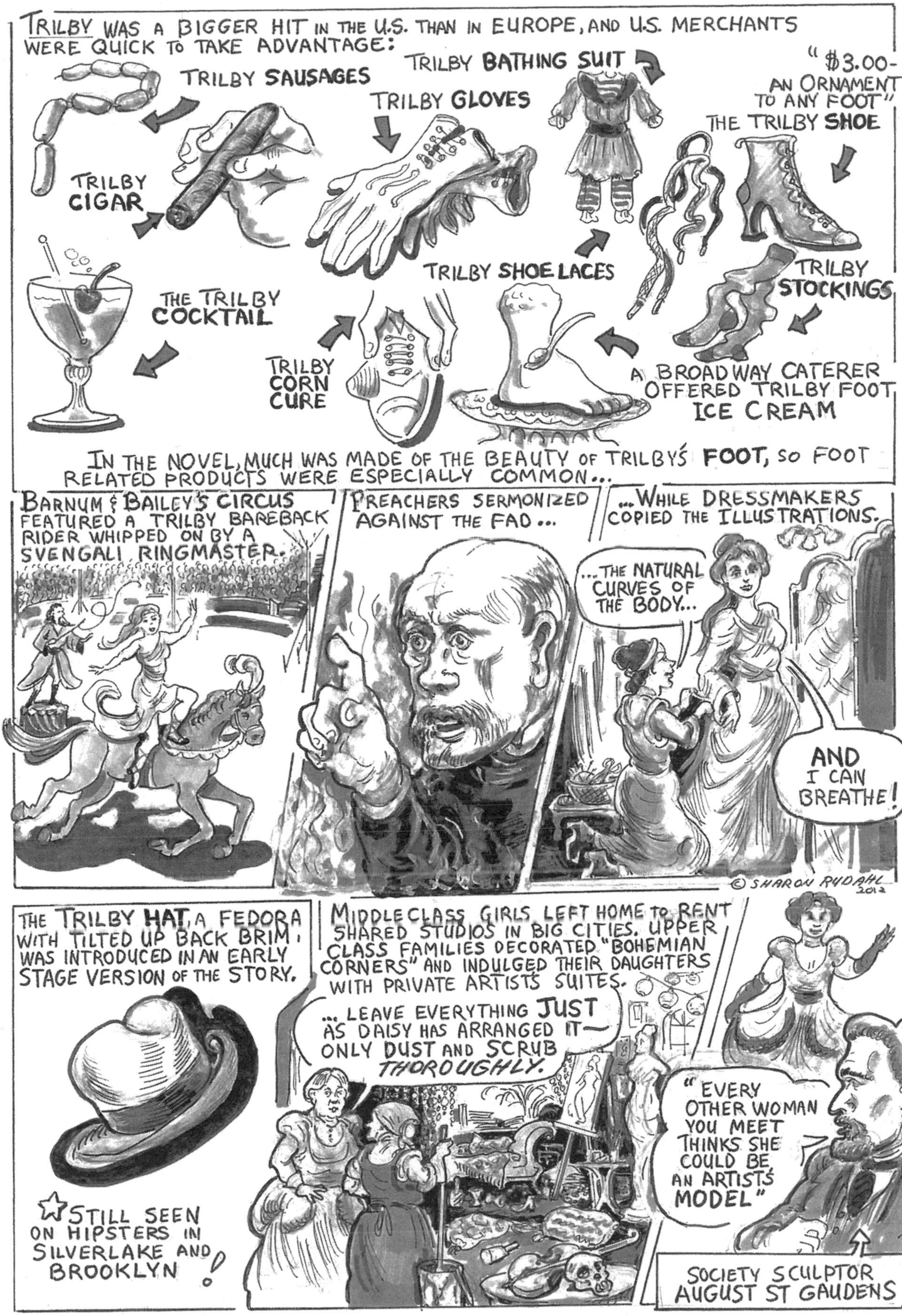
TRILBY WAS A BIGGER HIT IN THE U.S. THAN IN EUROPE, AND U.S. MERCHANTS WERE QUICK TO TAKE ADVANTAGE:
TRILBY SAUSAGES
TRILBY CIGAR
TRILBY GLOVES
TRILBY BATHING SUIT
"$3.00- AN ORNAMENT TO ANY FOOT"
THE TRILBY SHOE
TRILBY SHOE LACES
TRILBY STOCKINGS
THE TRILBY COCKTAIL
TRILBY CORN CURE
A BROADWAY CATERER OFFERED TRILBY FOOT ICE CREAM
IN THE NOVEL, MUCH WAS MADE OF THE BEAUTY OF TRILBY'S FOOT, SO FOOT RELATED PRODUCTS WERE ESPECIALLY COMMON...
BARNUM & BAILEY'S CIRCUS FEATURED A TRILBY BAREBACK RIDER WHIPPED ON BY A SVENGALI RINGMASTER.
PREACHERS SERMONIZED AGAINST THE FAD...
...WHILE DRESSMAKERS COPIED THE ILLUSTRATIONS.
...THE NATURAL CURVES OF THE BODY...
AND I CAN BREATHE!
© SHARON RUDAHL 2012
THE TRILBY HAT, A FEDORA WITH TILTED UP BACK BRIM, WAS INTRODUCED IN AN EARLY STAGE VERSION OF THE STORY.
STILL SEEN ON HIPSTERS IN SILVERLAKE AND BROOKLYN!
MIDDLECLASS GIRLS LEFT HOME TO RENT SHARED STUDIOS IN BIG CITIES. UPPER CLASS FAMILIES DECORATED "BOHEMIAN CORNERS" AND INDULGED THEIR DAUGHTERS WITH PRIVATE ARTISTS SUITES.
...LEAVE EVERYTHING JUST AS DAISY HAS ARRANGED IT— ONLY DUST AND SCRUB THOROUGHLY.
"EVERY OTHER WOMAN YOU MEET THINKS SHE COULD BE AN ARTIST'S MODEL"
SOCIETY SCULPTOR AUGUST ST GAUDENS

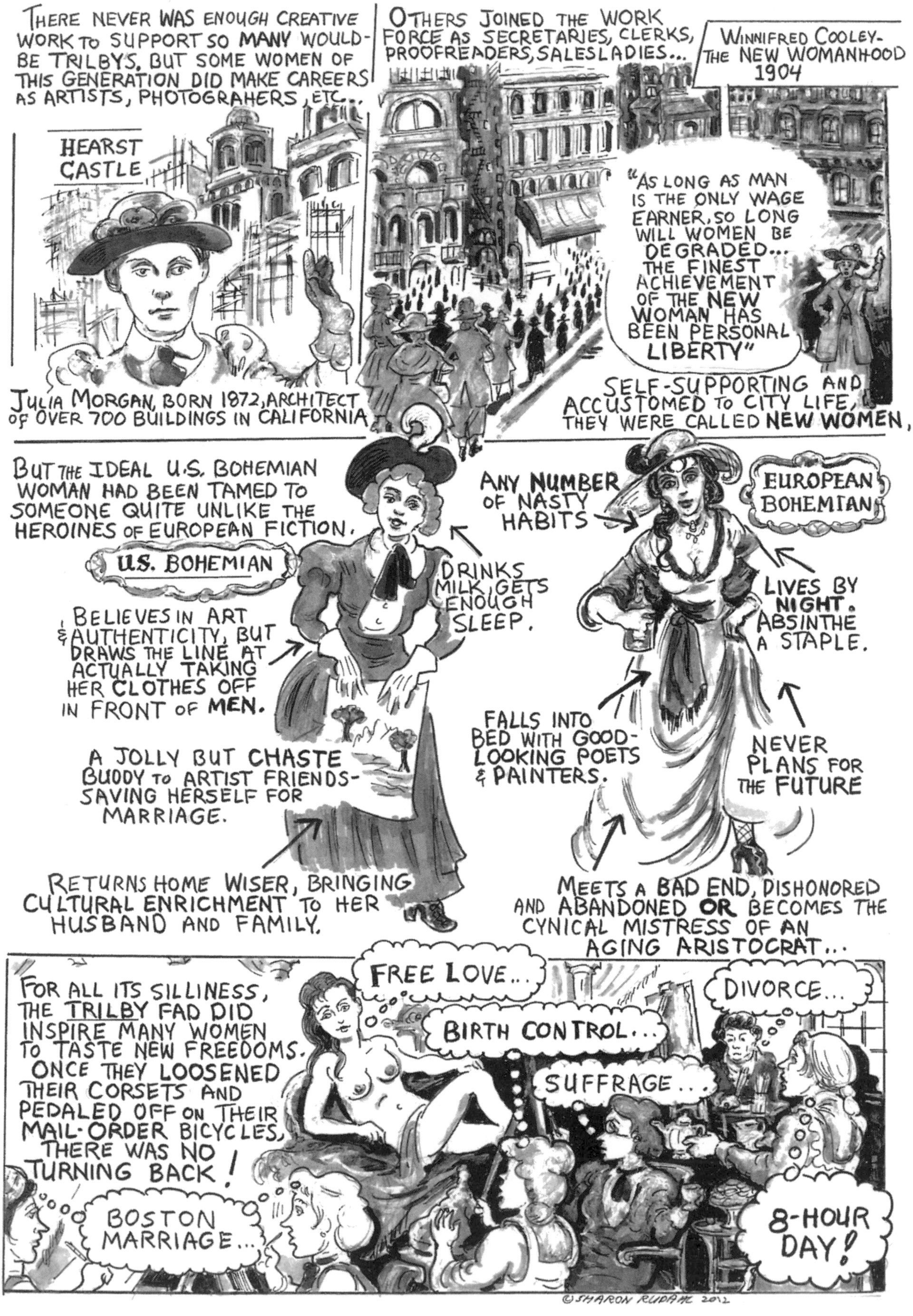
THERE NEVER WAS ENOUGH CREATIVE WORK TO SUPPORT SO MANY WOULD-BE TRILBYS, BUT SOME WOMEN OF THIS GENERATION DID MAKE CAREERS AS ARTISTS, PHOTOGRAHERS, ETC...
HEARST CASTLE
JULIA MORGAN, BORN 1872, ARCHITECT OF OVER 700 BUILDINGS IN CALIFORNIA
OTHERS JOINED THE WORK FORCE AS SECRETARIES, CLERKS, PROOFREADERS, SALESLADIES...
WINNIFRED COOLEY - THE NEW WOMANHOOD 1904
"AS LONG AS MAN IS THE ONLY WAGE EARNER, SO LONG WILL WOMEN BE DEGRADED... THE FINEST ACHIEVEMENT OF THE NEW WOMAN HAS BEEN PERSONAL LIBERTY"
SELF-SUPPORTING AND ACCUSTOMED TO CITY LIFE, THEY WERE CALLED NEW WOMEN,
BUT THE IDEAL U.S. BOHEMIAN WOMAN HAD BEEN TAMED TO SOMEONE QUITE UNLIKE THE HEROINES OF EUROPEAN FICTION.
U.S. BOHEMIAN
DRINKS MILK, GETS ENOUGH SLEEP.
BELIEVES IN ART & AUTHENTICITY, BUT DRAWS THE LINE AT ACTUALLY TAKING HER CLOTHES OFF IN FRONT OF MEN.
A JOLLY BUT CHASTE BUDDY TO ARTIST FRIENDS - SAVING HERSELF FOR MARRIAGE.
RETURNS HOME WISER, BRINGING CULTURAL ENRICHMENT TO HER HUSBAND AND FAMILY.
ANY NUMBER OF NASTY HABITS
EUROPEAN BOHEMIAN
LIVES BY NIGHT. ABSINTHE A STAPLE.
FALLS INTO BED WITH GOOD-LOOKING POETS & PAINTERS.
NEVER PLANS FOR THE FUTURE
MEETS A BAD END, DISHONORED AND ABANDONED OR BECOMES THE CYNICAL MISTRESS OF AN AGING ARISTOCRAT...
FOR ALL ITS SILLINESS, THE TRILBY FAD DID INSPIRE MANY WOMEN TO TASTE NEW FREEDOMS. ONCE THEY LOOSENED THEIR CORSETS AND PEDALED OFF ON THEIR MAIL-ORDER BICYCLES, THERE WAS NO TURNING BACK!
FREE LOVE...
BIRTH CONTROL...
DIVORCE...
SUFFRAGE...
BOSTON MARRIAGE...
8-HOUR DAY!
©SHARON RUDAHL 2012

Chapter Four

Village Days

Greenwich Village in the 1910s: the site of the world's most famous, alluring bohemia, thanks to the emergence of Manhattan as a financial and publishing center of global capitalism, also to the widespread sense that prudish, backward America had "discovered" bohemianism at last. Bohemia flourished not only in the English language neighborhoods: Little Italy, with its coffee houses and tavern restaurants also blossomed with mixtures of artists and revolutionaries, and like the Jewish Lower East Side, had its emissaries and followers.

Free love went from idiosyncratic, individual behavior to lively popular practice, soon spreading to the flapper settings and college campuses of the 1920s. Along with radical bohemians embracing labor strikes and foreign revolutions, there also came a full-throttle middle-class consumer-style bohemianism, a phase of youthful flings before serious family life. These "bohemians" flocked to avant-garde exhibitions and modern dance performances and bought paintings, lithographs and photographs, helping the real bohemians pay the rent and get public attention—and precipitating the rent hikes in heretofore low-rate zones. The further invasion of bohemian neighborhoods, prompted by the creation of new subway stops, lay ahead, with the assorted disillusionments. For the 1910s, among the idealists, such a bourgeois outcome of their excitement was unimaginable.

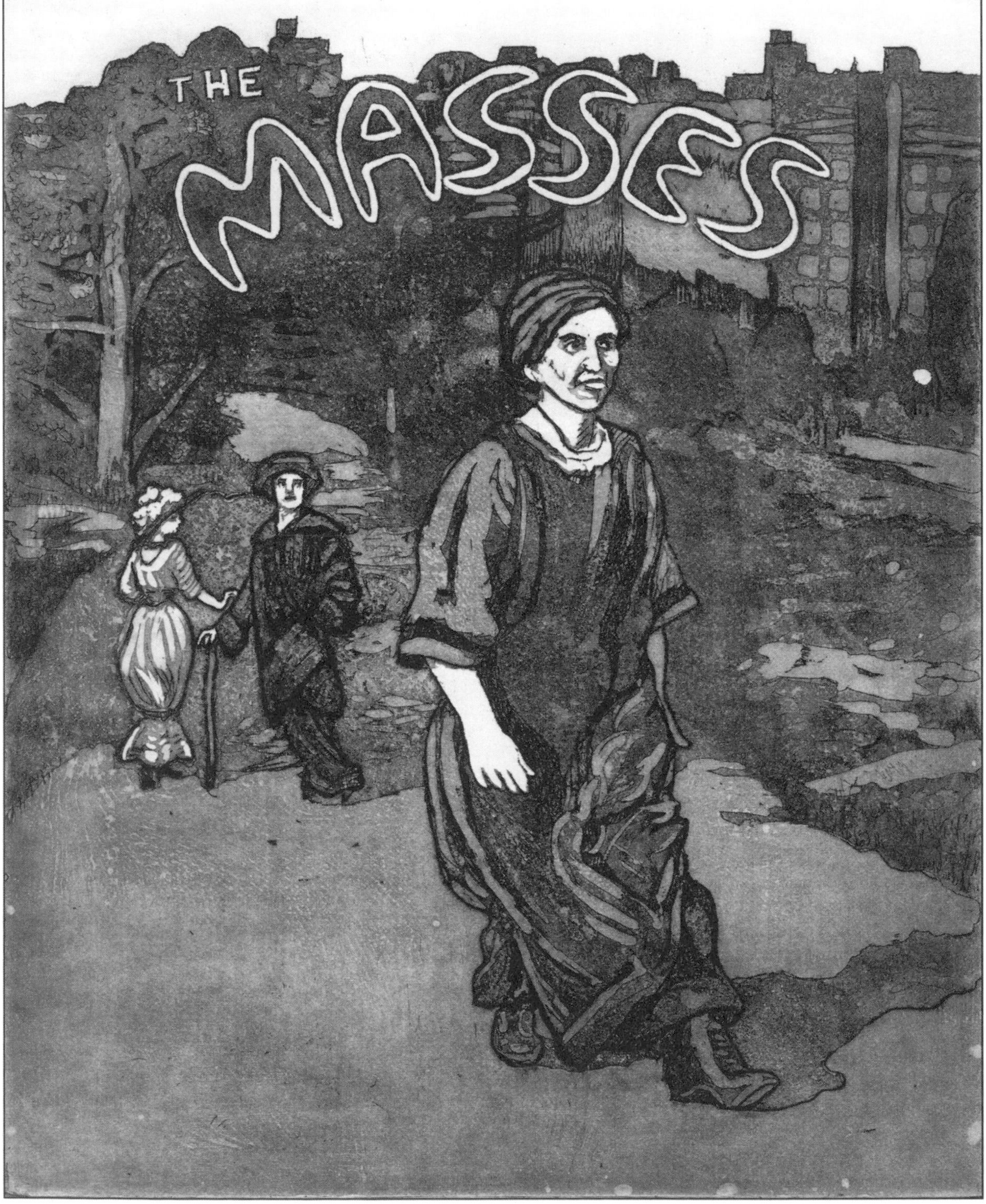
THE
MASSES

Henrietta Rodman: Making Strides

In 1912 the contributors of *The Masses*, a bankrupt socialist periodical, formed a collective to give the magazine new life and a new direction. Its journalists and artists were opinionated, radical, sexually liberated, loud and often drunk. They lived in the seedy low-rent district called Greenwich Village. They wanted something that their day jobs couldn't provide. They wanted their best work to be published, not censored.

Today *The Masses* is barely remembered, yet the magazine was an influential voice at the center of a circle whose daring intellectual achievements ushered in the modern era of American culture.

This tribute, humbly offered, is an attempt to recreate a "lost" *Masses* issue, recalling its fascinating history and the people, both famous and obscure, who inhabited its world. Some of the art was created using intaglio aquatint, a medium favored by Ashcan artists. Some was executed in pen and ink, and some in crayon, miming the look of Daumier's lithographs, an effect made popular by *The Masses*.

The original magazine was produced via rotogravure, using photo-etched cylinders–the state-of-the-art printing technology of a century ago.

Rebecca Migdal, November 2012

The
MASSES

THIS Magazine is Owned and Published Cooperatively by its Editors. It has no Dividends to Pay, and nobody is trying to make Money out of it. A Revolutionary and not a Reform Magazine; a Magazine with a Sense of Humor and no Respect for the Respectable; Frank; Arrogant; Impertinent; Searching for the True Causes; a Magazine Directed against Rigidity and Dogma wherever it is found; Printing what is too Naked or True for a Money-Making Press; a Magazine whose final Policy is to do as it Pleases and Conciliate Nobody, not even its Readers—A Free Magazine.

EDITOR
Max Eastman

MANAGING EDITOR
Floyd Dell

CONTRIBUTING EDITORS

ART	LITERATURE
Arthur Young	John Reed
K. R. Chamberlain	Louis Untermeyer
Maurice Becker	Howard Brubaker
Cornelia Barns	Mary Heaton Vorse
George Bellows	Max Eastman
H. J. Glintenkamp	Arthur Bullard
Stuart Davis	Wm. English Walling
Glenn O. Coleman	Floyd Dell
G. S. Sparks	Frank Bohn

BUSINESS MANAGER
John Lyons

SUBSCRIPTION RATES
Yearly, $1.00. Half Yearly, 50 Cents. Foreign, $1.25 Yearly. Rates on bundle orders and to newsdealers on application

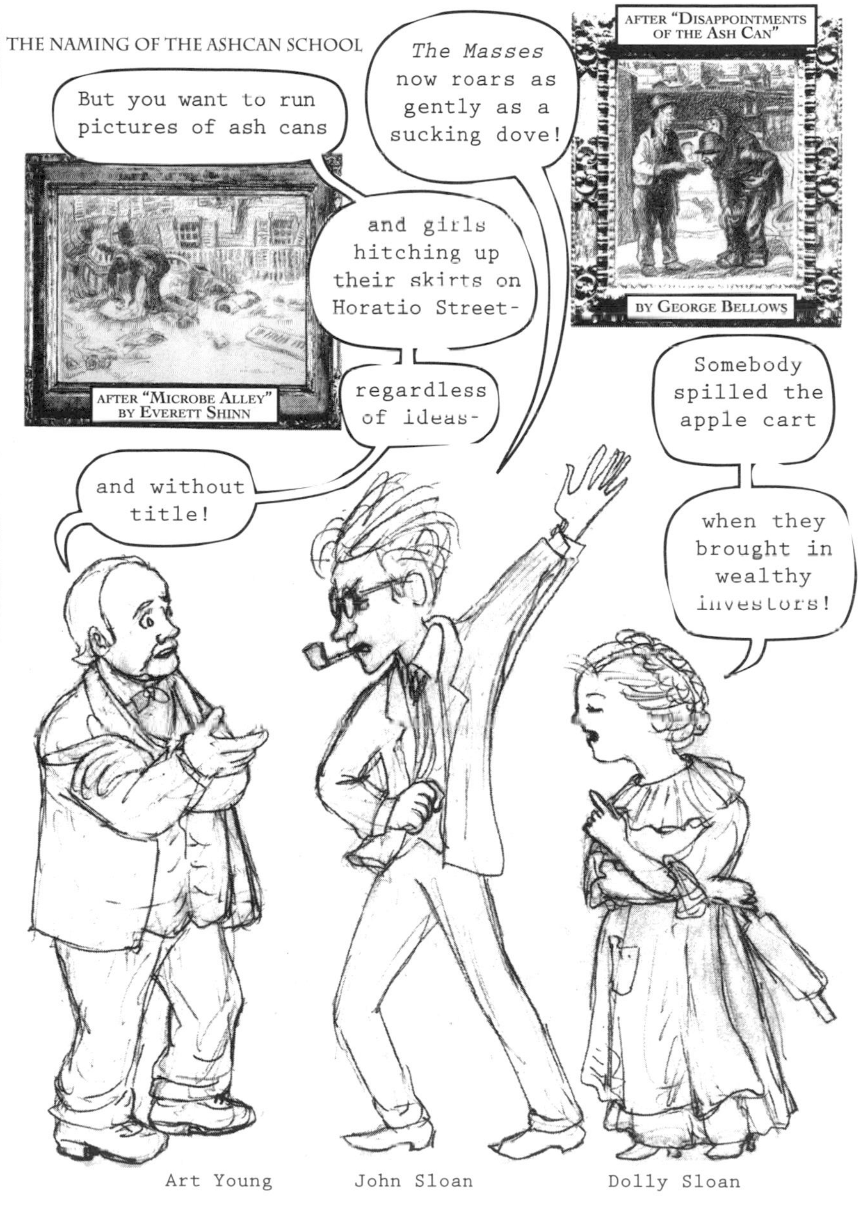
THE NAMING OF THE ASHCAN SCHOOL
But you want to run pictures of ash cans
AFTER "MICROBE ALLEY" BY EVERETT SHINN
and girls hitching up their skirts on Horatio Street-
regardless of ideas-
and without title!
The Masses now roars as gently as a sucking dove!
AFTER "DISAPPOINTMENTS OF THE ASH CAN"
BY GEORGE BELLOWS
Somebody spilled the apple cart
when they brought in wealthy investors!
Art Young
John Sloan
Dolly Sloan

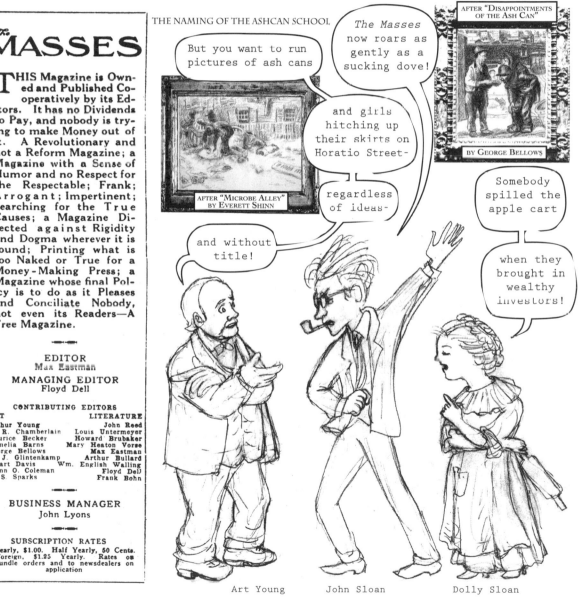

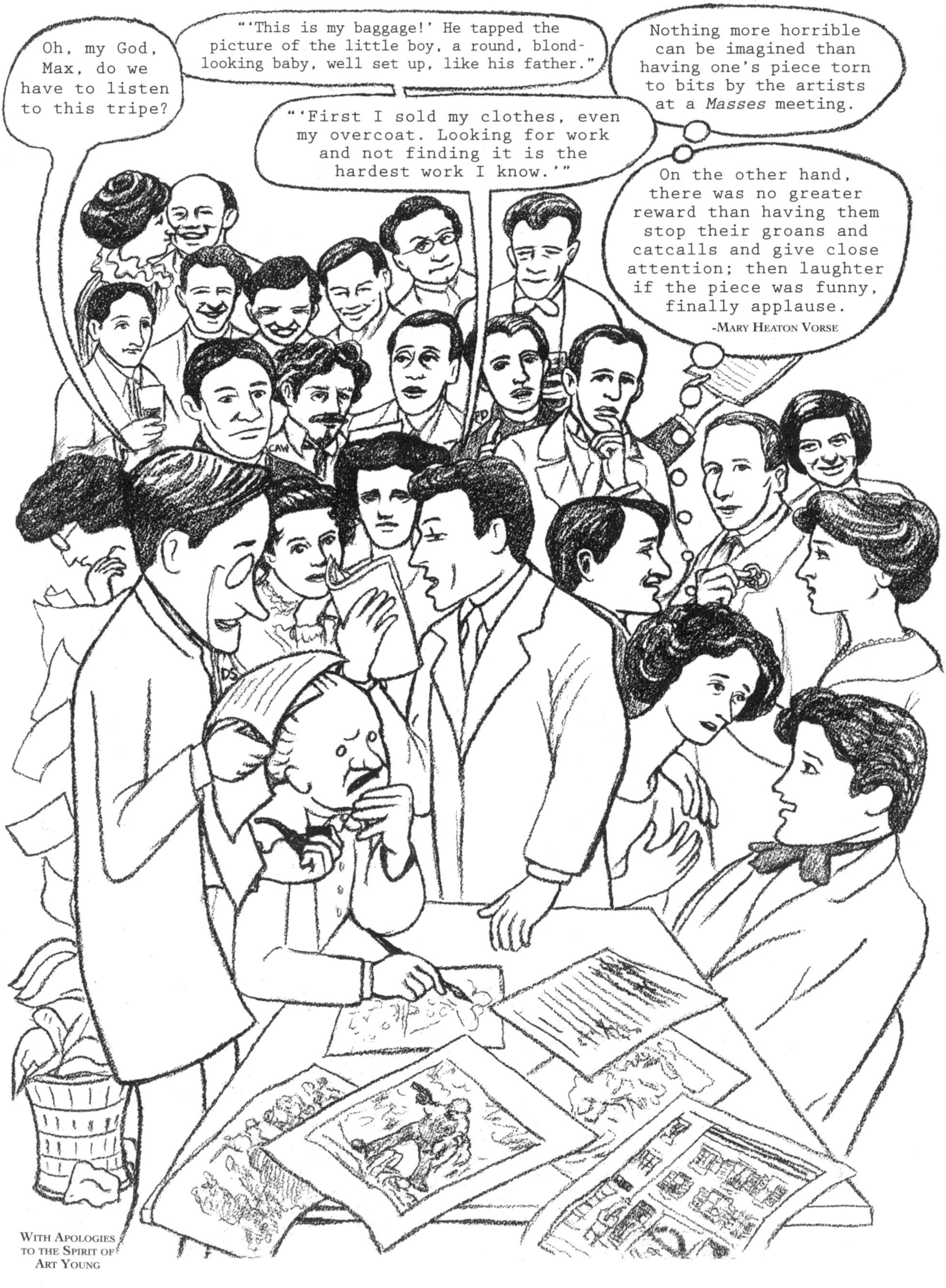
Oh, my God, Max, do we have to listen to this tripe?
"'This is my baggage!' He tapped the picture of the little boy, a round, blond-looking baby, well set up, like his father."
"'First I sold my clothes, even my overcoat. Looking for work and not finding it is the hardest work I know.'"
Nothing more horrible can be imagined than having one's piece torn to bits by the artists at a *Masses* meeting.
On the other hand, there was no greater reward than having them stop their groans and catcalls and give close attention; then laughter if the piece was funny, finally applause.
-Mary Heaton Vorse
With Apologies to the Spirit of Art Young

1. Cornelia Barnes
Illustrator

2. Robert Minor
Illustrator

3. Louis Untermeyer
Poet, Editor
Co-founded
The Seven Arts

4. Kenneth Russell Chamberlain
Illustrator

5. Maurice Becker
Illustrator

6. Harry Kemp
Poet, Author

7. Boardman Robinson
Illustrator

8. Stuart Davis
Illustrator, Painter
(Ashcan School)

9. Henry Glintenkamp
Illustrator, Painter
(Ashcan School)

10. Charles Allen Winter
Illustrator, Painter

11. Glenn O. Coleman
Illustrator, Painter
(Ashcan School)

12. Floyd Dell
Managing Editor of
The Masses, Author,
Playwright

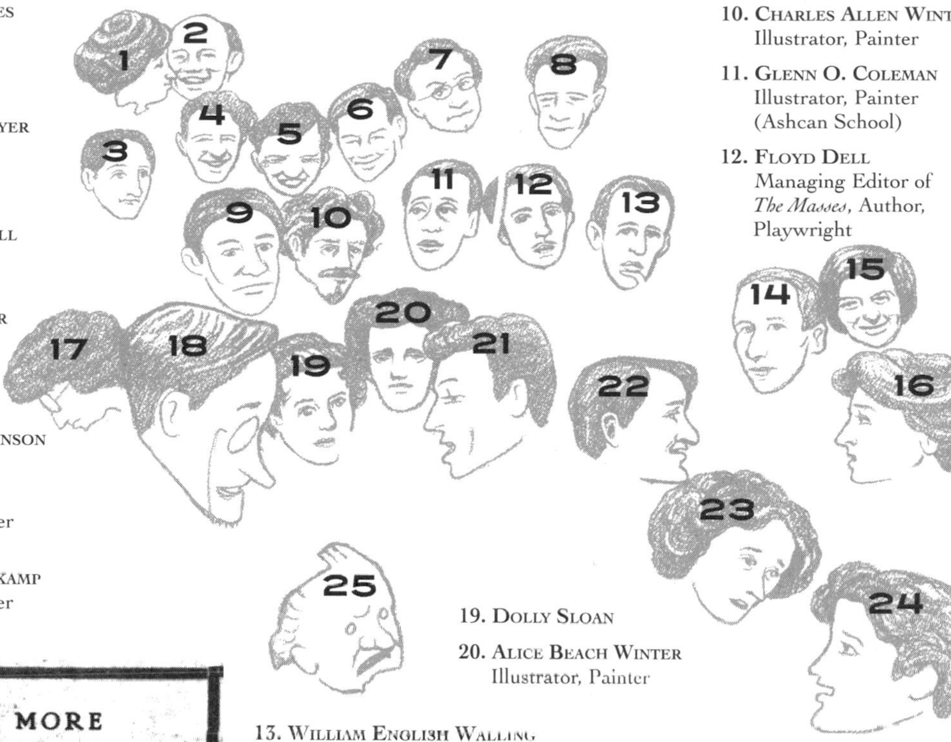
1
2
3
4
5
6
7
8
9
10
11
12
13
14
15
16
17
18
19
20
21
22
23
24
25

13. William English Walling
Journalist, Labor Organizer,
Founding Chairman of
the NAACP

14. George Bellows
Illustrator, Painter
(Ashcan School)

15. Mabel Dodge Luhan*
Masses Editor

16. Crystal Eastman*

17. Ida Rauh*

18. John Sloan
Illustrator, Painter
(Ashcan School)

19. Dolly Sloan

20. Alice Beach Winter
Illustrator, Painter

21. Max Eastman
Editor-in-Chief of
The Masses

22. Joe O'Brien
Journalist, Activist

23. Mary Heaton Vorse*
Masses Editor

24. John "Jack" Reed
Journalist, Activist,
Author, *Masses* Editor

25. Art Young
Illustrator, *Masses* Editor

**More on the following pages*

ONE MORE

—"Will no one catch a Bacillus potent enough to down the epidemic of simpering femininity that is devastating the land through the medium of magazine covers? Some weeks ago an effort in this direction by our sane contemporary, The Masses, took the form of a deliciously clever cover design ("Gee, Mag, Think of Us Bein' on a Magazine Cover!", June issue) which . . . has so far done nothing to check the plague of pink and white imbecility which continues to smirk and ogle and pout. . . . It is in the hope that a second application may prove more efficacious that we are reprinting The Masses cartoon."

Oliver Herford in *Harper's Weekly*.

ONE LESS

Dear Sirs:

Some one who evidently is possessed of more *money* than *brains* has been sending me for the last three months the Socialist magazine called The Masses. I do not want it and I notify you now to stop it. I am not in favor of Socialism at all, and if I have done anything to cause anyone to think that I am, I'm sincerely sorry, for I certainly do not want to be a stumbling block to any one. I stand for *God* and *Country, Christianity* and *Patriotism, and* for *Law* and *Order*. Yours truly,

Mrs. J. A. Johnston,
48 Wadsworth St., Buffalo, N. Y.

P. S.—Three Cheers for "The Star-Spangled Banner."

"The most important work on psychoanalysis since Freud"

PSYCHOLOGY OF THE UNCONSCIOUS

By DR. C. G. JUNG

of the University of Zurich

This great work on psycho-analysis, the exploration of the unconscious mind, the latest and most far-reaching development of psychology, has now been translated by

DR. BEATRICE HINKLE

of the Neurological Dept. of Cornell University Medical School and of the Post Graduate Medical School of New York.

"This remarkable book does for psychology what the theory of evolution did for biology; and promises an equally profound change in the thought of mankind."—*President G. Stanley Hall, Clark University.*

"To me, it is that blend long sought for, the really modern ideal of the artist; namely, the fusion of Science and Art—of truth presented in a quickening manner."—*James Oppenheim, author of "Songs for the New Age," etc.*

Large 8 vo. Illustrated. Price $4.00 net.

At Masses Book Shop and All Booksellers

MOFFAT, YARD & COMPANY, PUBLISHERS NEW YORK

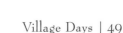

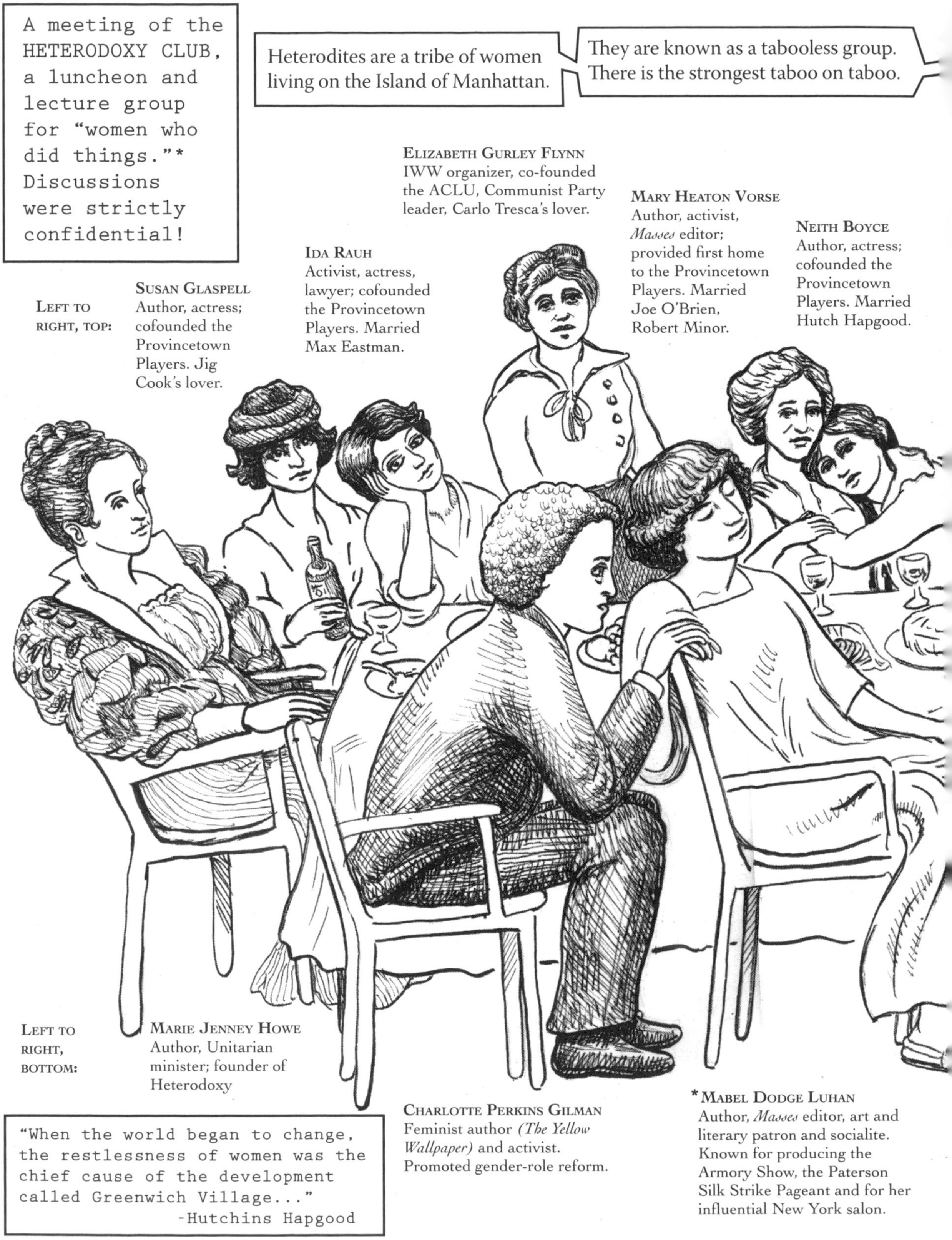
A meeting of the HETERODOXY CLUB, a luncheon and lecture group for "women who did things."* Discussions were strictly confidential!
Heterodites are a tribe of women living on the Island of Manhattan.
They are known as a tabooless group. There is the strongest taboo on taboo.
LEFT TO RIGHT, TOP:
SUSAN GLASPELL Author, actress; cofounded the Provincetown Players. Jig Cook's lover.
IDA RAUH Activist, actress, lawyer; cofounded the Provincetown Players. Married Max Eastman.
ELIZABETH GURLEY FLYNN IWW organizer, co-founded the ACLU, Communist Party leader, Carlo Tresca's lover.
MARY HEATON VORSE Author, activist, *Masses* editor; provided first home to the Provincetown Players. Married Joe O'Brien, Robert Minor.
NEITH BOYCE Author, actress; cofounded the Provincetown Players. Married Hutch Hapgood.
LEFT TO RIGHT, BOTTOM:
MARIE JENNEY HOWE Author, Unitarian minister; founder of Heterodoxy
CHARLOTTE PERKINS GILMAN Feminist author *(The Yellow Wallpaper)* and activist. Promoted gender-role reform.
*MABEL DODGE LUHAN Author, *Masses* editor, art and literary patron and socialite. Known for producing the Armory Show, the Paterson Silk Strike Pageant and for her influential New York salon.
"When the world began to change, the restlessness of women was the chief cause of the development called Greenwich Village..." -Hutchins Hapgood

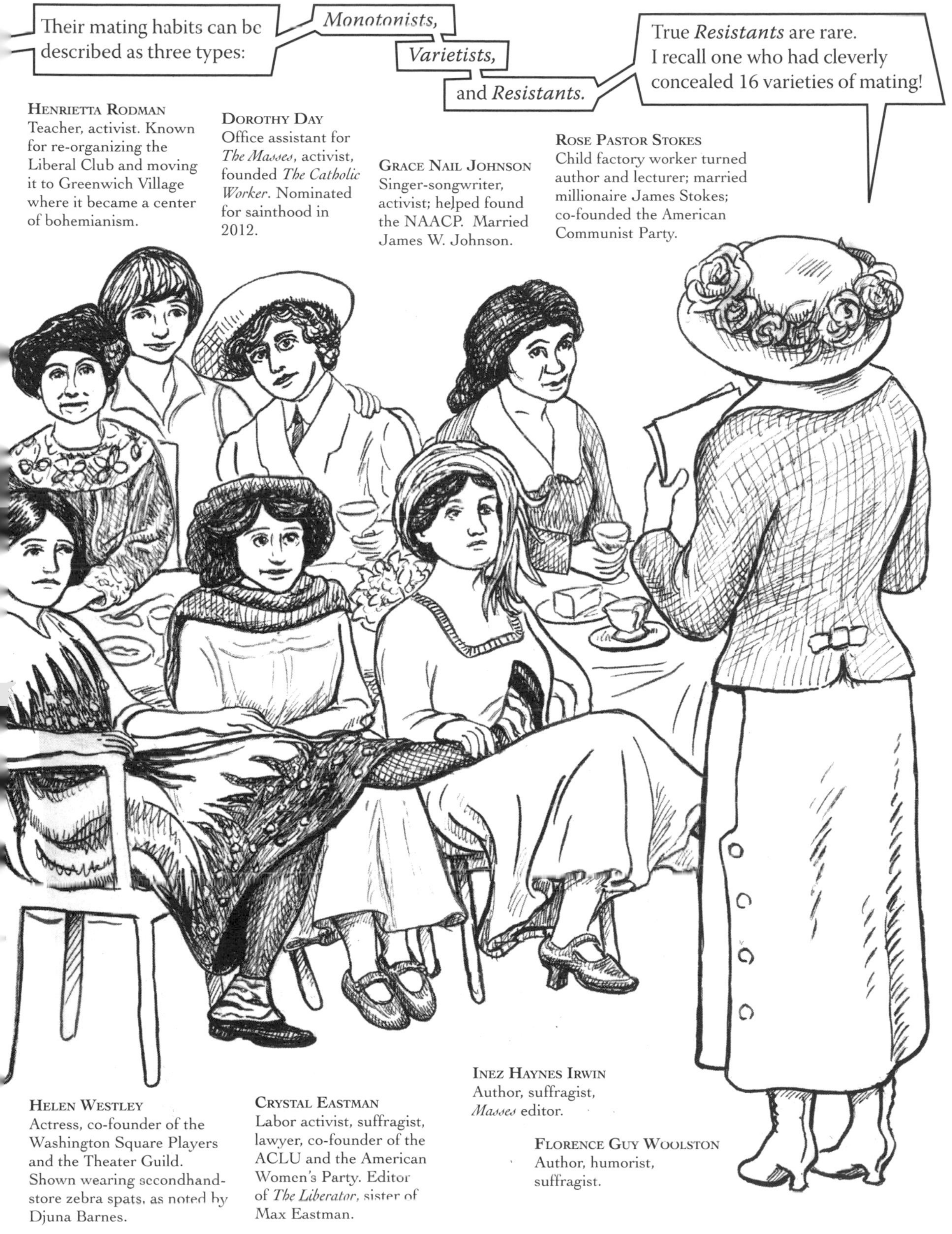
Their mating habits can be described as three types:
Monotonists,
Varietists,
and Resistants.
True Resistants are rare. I recall one who had cleverly concealed 16 varieties of mating!
HENRIETTA RODMAN Teacher, activist. Known for re-organizing the Liberal Club and moving it to Greenwich Village where it became a center of bohemianism.
DOROTHY DAY Office assistant for The Masses, activist, founded The Catholic Worker. Nominated for sainthood in 2012.
GRACE NAIL JOHNSON Singer-songwriter, activist; helped found the NAACP. Married James W. Johnson.
ROSE PASTOR STOKES Child factory worker turned author and lecturer; married millionaire James Stokes; co-founded the American Communist Party.
HELEN WESTLEY Actress, co-founder of the Washington Square Players and the Theater Guild. Shown wearing secondhand-store zebra spats, as noted by Djuna Barnes.
CRYSTAL EASTMAN Labor activist, suffragist, lawyer, co-founder of the ACLU and the American Women's Party. Editor of The Liberator, sister of Max Eastman.
INEZ HAYNES IRWIN Author, suffragist, Masses editor.
FLORENCE GUY WOOLSTON Author, humorist, suffragist.

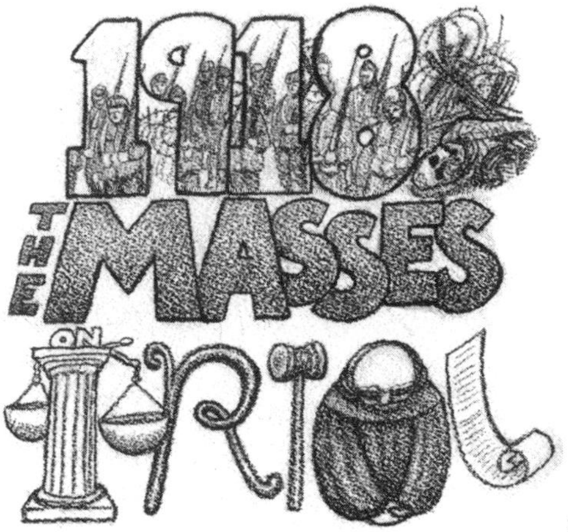
1918
THE MASSES
ON
TRIAL

Always in the trenches fighting for free speech, *The Masses* has a long history in court. In August 1917 the magazine is dealt a fatal blow.

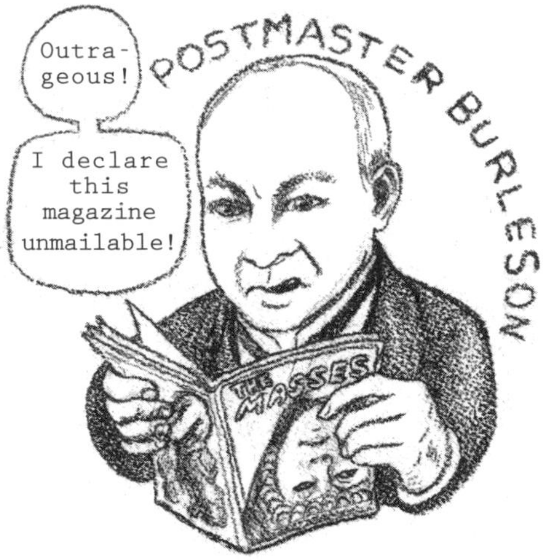
Outra-
geous!
I declare this magazine unmailable!
POSTMASTER BURLESON
THE MASSES

After losing a legal battle over the censorship of the August issue, *The Masses* closes its offices in December 1917.

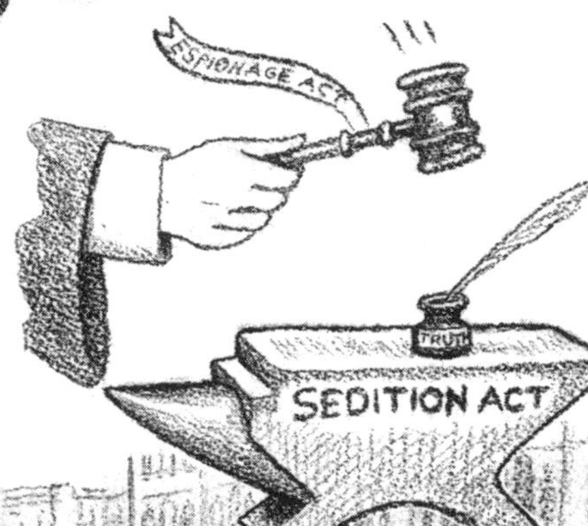
ESPIONAGE ACT
TRUTH
SEDITION ACT

In 1918 Max Eastman, Art Young, Floyd Dell, John Reed, Henry Glintenkamp and *Masses* business manager Merrill Rogers are indicted under the Espionage Act.

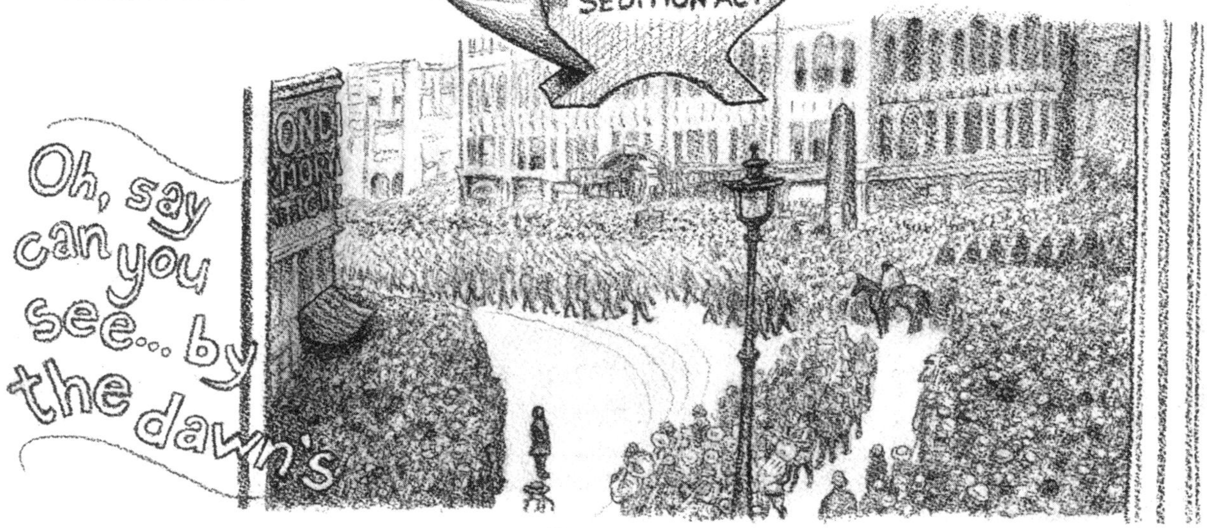
Oh, say can you see... by the dawn's

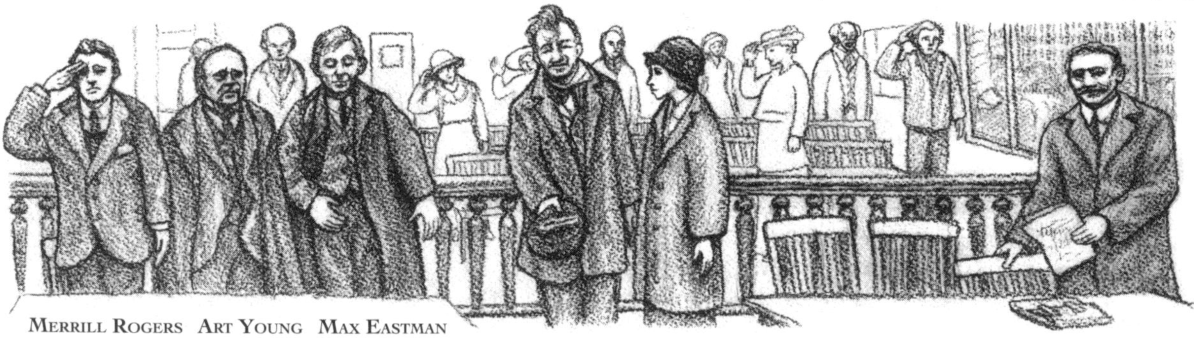

Merrill Rogers Art Young Max Eastman

Floyd Dell Edna St. Vincent Millay Morris Hillquit, Lawyer

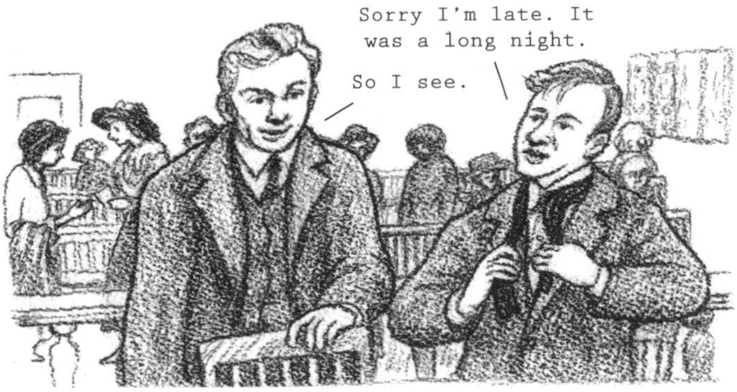
Sorry I'm late. It was a long night.
So I see.

The spectators are a host of Greenwich Village characters. The trial takes place across from a war-bond office, where a brass band trumpets patriotic airs.

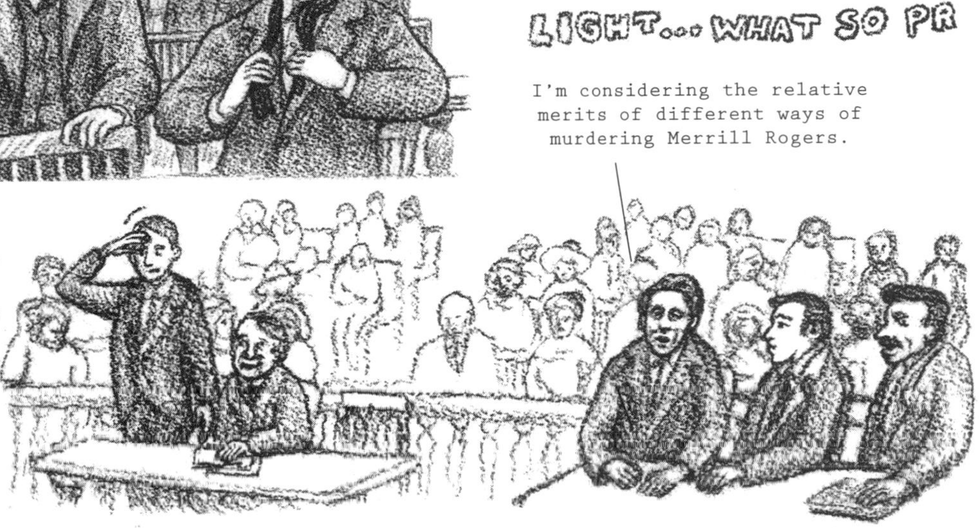
LIGHT... WHAT SO PR
I'm considering the relative merits of different ways of murdering Merrill Rogers.

Every time the band plays "The Star Spangled Banner," Rogers leaps to his feet and stands at attention, and everyone else follows suit.

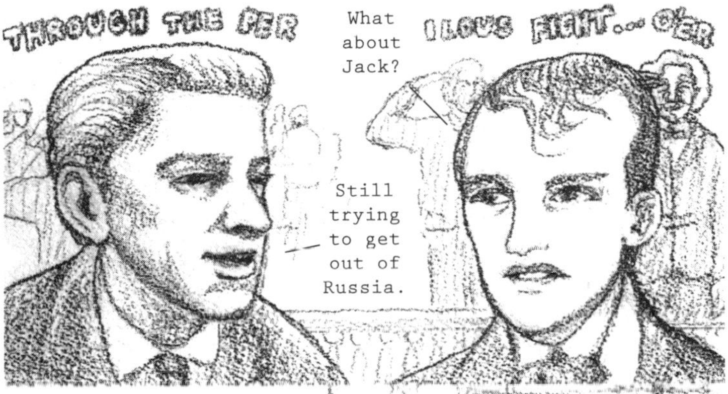
THROUGH THE PER
ILOUS FIGHT... O'ER
What about Jack?
Still trying to get out of Russia.

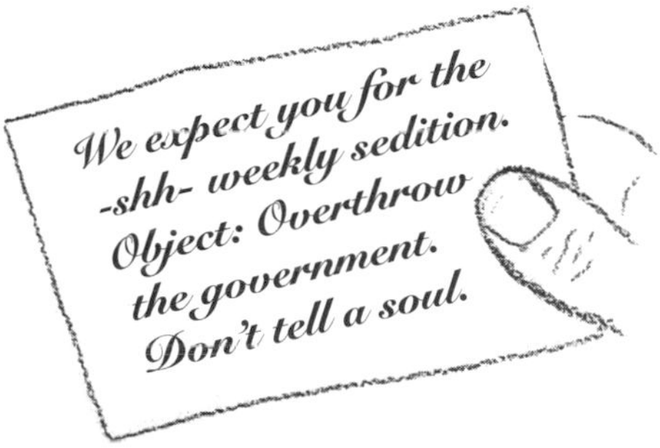
We expect you for the -shh- weekly sedition. Object: Overthrow the government. Don't tell a soul.

Max and Crystal Eastman have already founded a successor to *The Masses*. Accounts of the trial are published in *The Liberator*.

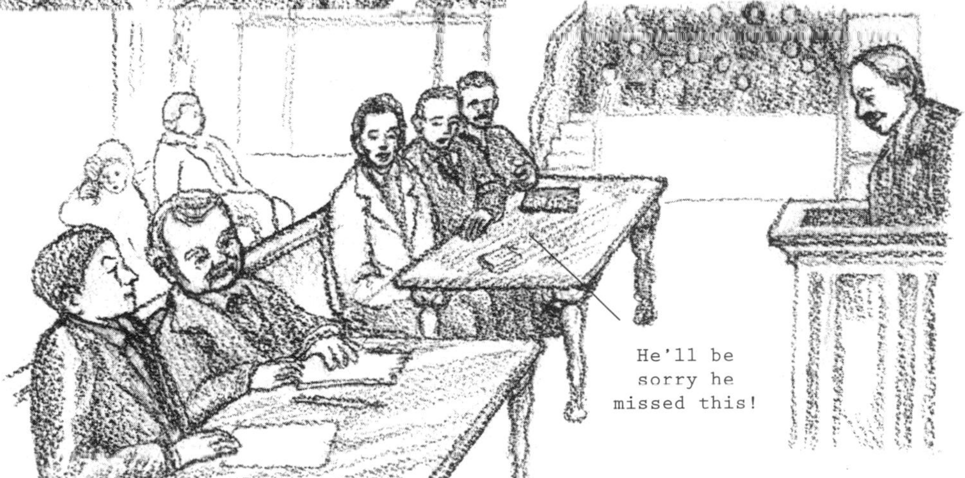
He'll be sorry he missed this!

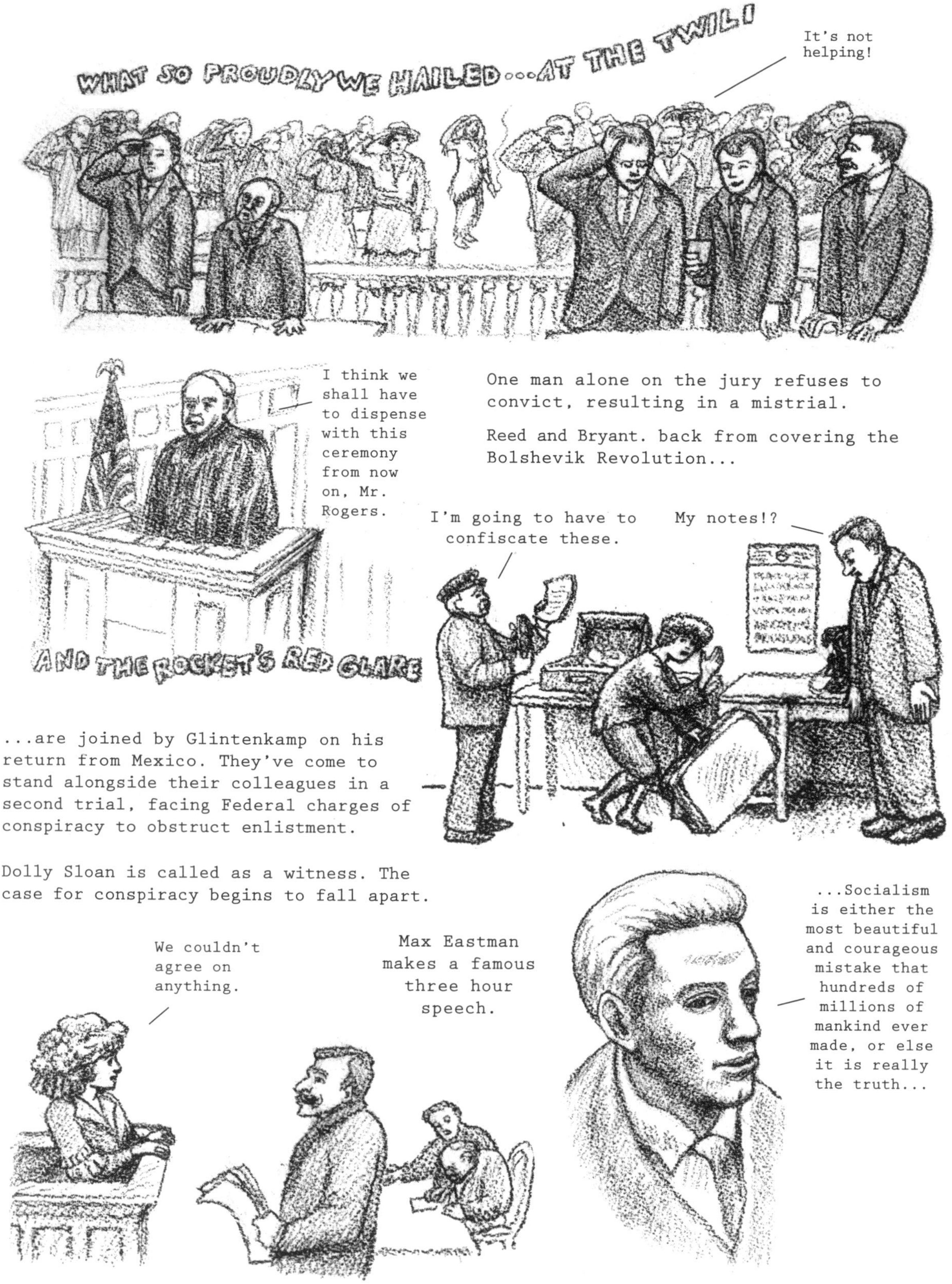
WHAT SO PROUDLY WE HAILED...AT THE TWILI
It's not helping!
I think we shall have to dispense with this ceremony from now on, Mr. Rogers.
AND THE ROCKET'S RED GLARE
One man alone on the jury refuses to convict, resulting in a mistrial.
Reed and Bryant. back from covering the Bolshevik Revolution...
I'm going to have to confiscate these.
My notes!?
...are joined by Glintenkamp on his return from Mexico. They've come to stand alongside their colleagues in a second trial, facing Federal charges of conspiracy to obstruct enlistment.
Dolly Sloan is called as a witness. The case for conspiracy begins to fall apart.
We couldn't agree on anything.
Max Eastman makes a famous three hour speech.
...Socialism is either the most beautiful and courageous mistake that hundreds of millions of mankind ever made, or else it is really the truth...

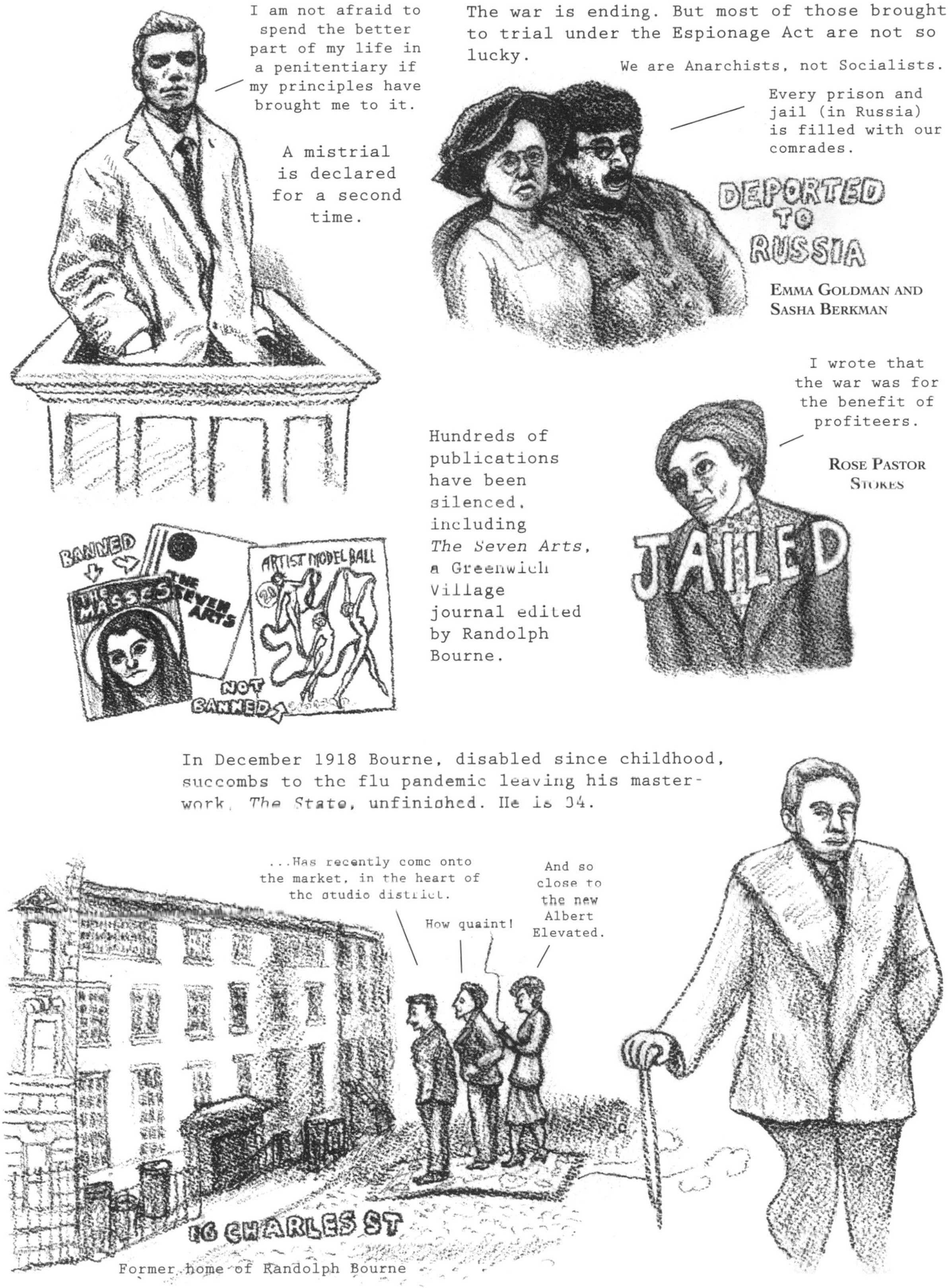
I am not afraid to spend the better part of my life in a penitentiary if my principles have brought me to it.
A mistrial is declared for a second time.
The war is ending. But most of those brought to trial under the Espionage Act are not so lucky.
We are Anarchists, not Socialists.
Every prison and jail (in Russia) is filled with our comrades.
DEPORTED TO RUSSIA
EMMA GOLDMAN AND SASHA BERKMAN
BANNED
THE MASSES
THE SEVEN ARTS
ARTIST MODEL BALL
NOT BANNED
Hundreds of publications have been silenced, including *The Seven Arts*, a Greenwich Village journal edited by Randolph Bourne.
I wrote that the war was for the benefit of profiteers.
ROSE PASTOR STOKES
JAILED
In December 1918 Bourne, disabled since childhood, succombs to the flu pandemic leaving his master-work, *The State*, unfinished. He is 34.
...Has recently come onto the market, in the heart of the studio district.
How quaint!
And so close to the new Albert Elevated.
16 CHARLES ST
Former home of Randolph Bourne

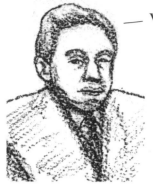

— **War is the health of the State.**

It automatically sets in motion throughout society those irresistible forces for uniformity, for passionate cooperation with the Government in coercing into obedience the minority groups and individuals which lack the larger herd sense.

Randolph Bourne

John Dos Passos will later write:

If any man has a ghost, Bourne has a ghost, a tiny, twisted, unscared ghost in a long black cloak, hopping along the grimy old brick brownstone streets still left in downtown New York, crying out in a shrill soundless giggle:

War is the Health of the State!

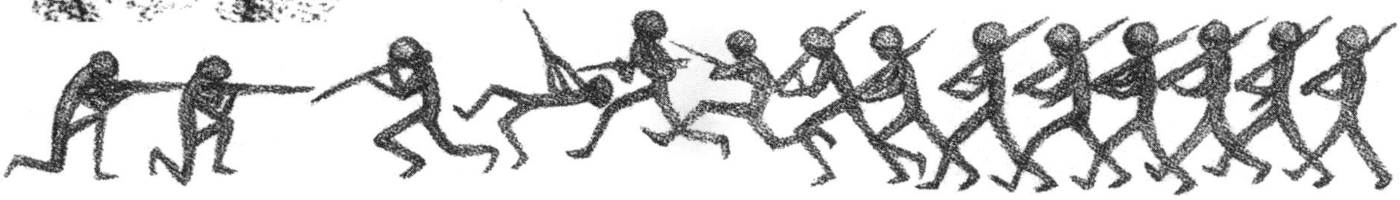

Louise Bryant and Jack Reed write their famous eyewitness reports on the Russian Revolution.

Jack Reed returns to Russia in 1919. His letters home abruptly cease.

TEN DAYS THAT SHOOK THE WORLD
SIX RED MONTHS IN RUSSIA

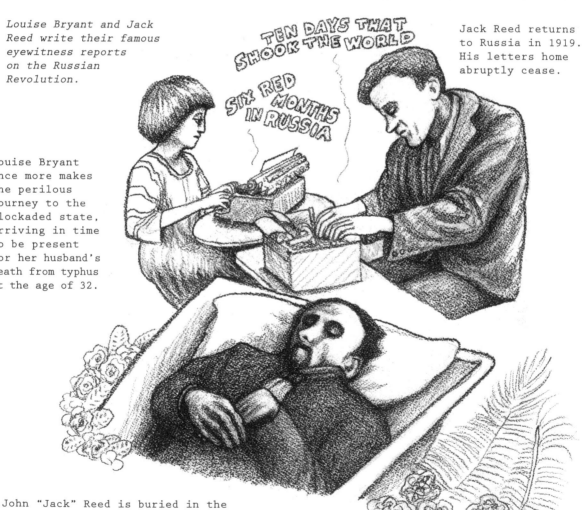

Louise Bryant once more makes the perilous journey to the blockaded state, arriving in time to be present for her husband's death from typhus at the age of 32.

John "Jack" Reed is buried in the Kremlin in 1920, with full honors.

MABEL DODGE

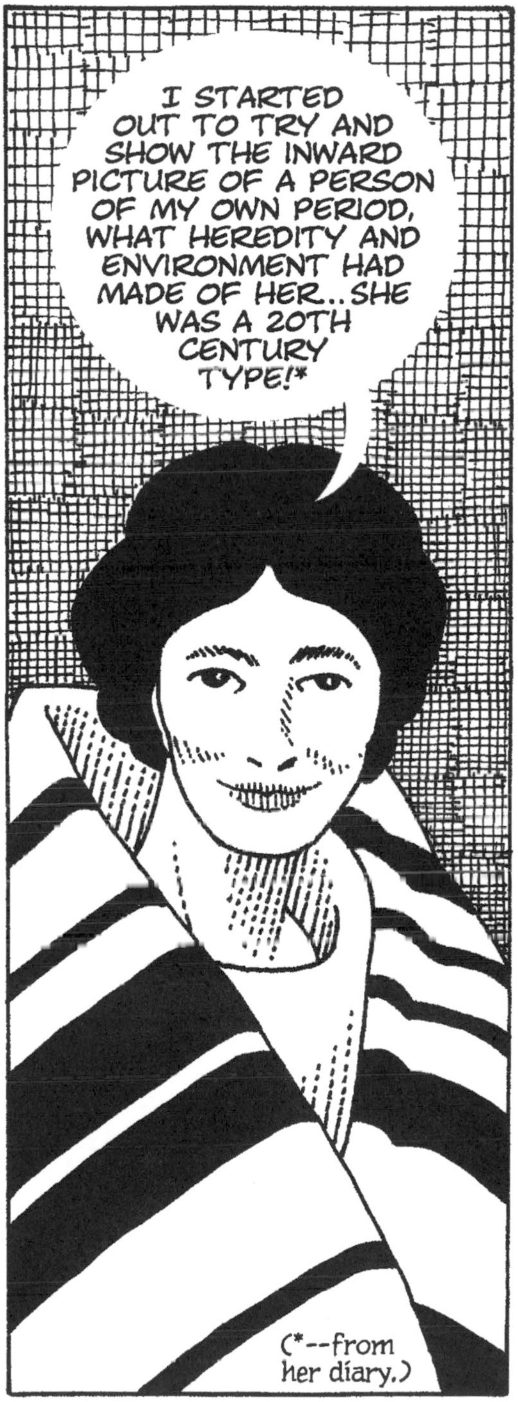
I STARTED OUT TO TRY AND SHOW THE INWARD PICTURE OF A PERSON OF MY OWN PERIOD, WHAT HEREDITY AND ENVIRONMENT HAD MADE OF HER...SHE WAS A 20TH CENTURY TYPE!*
(*--from her diary.)

Script: PAUL BUHLE
Art: MATT HOWARTH

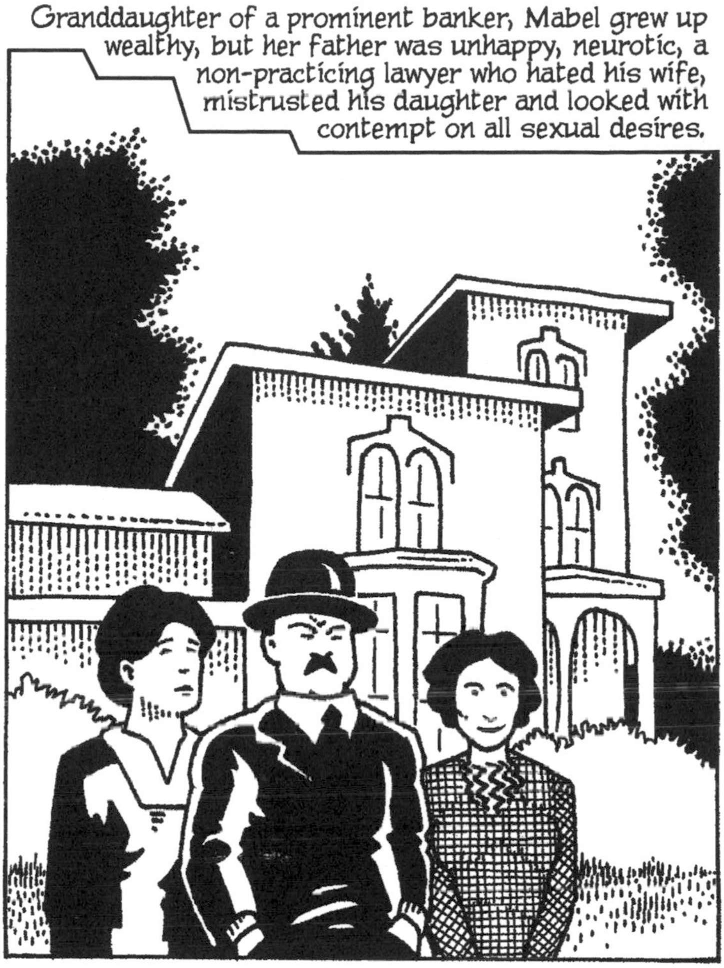
Granddaughter of a prominent banker, Mabel grew up wealthy, but her father was unhappy, neurotic, a non-practicing lawyer who hated his wife, mistrusted his daughter and looked with contempt on all sexual desires.

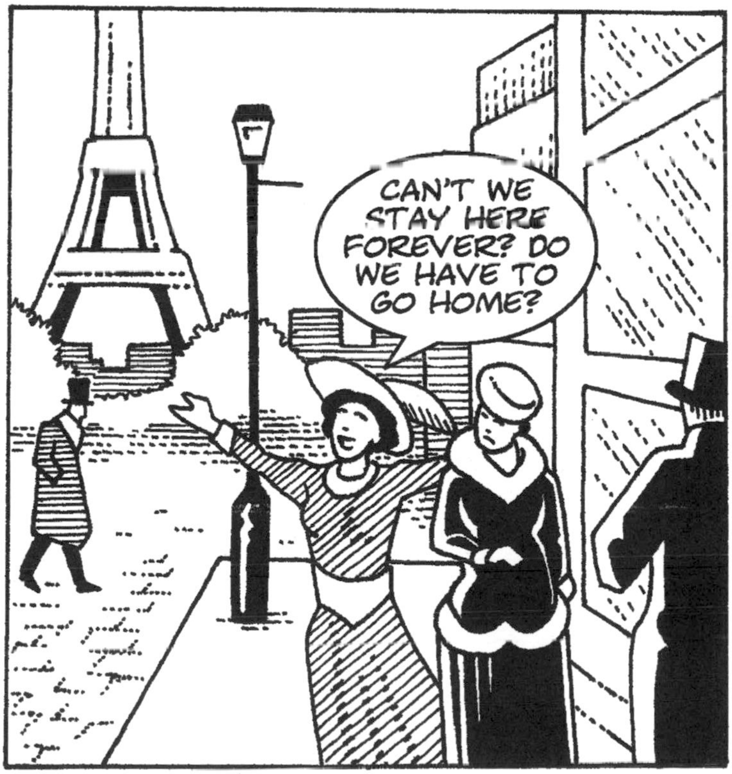
CAN'T WE STAY HERE FOREVER? DO WE HAVE TO GO HOME?

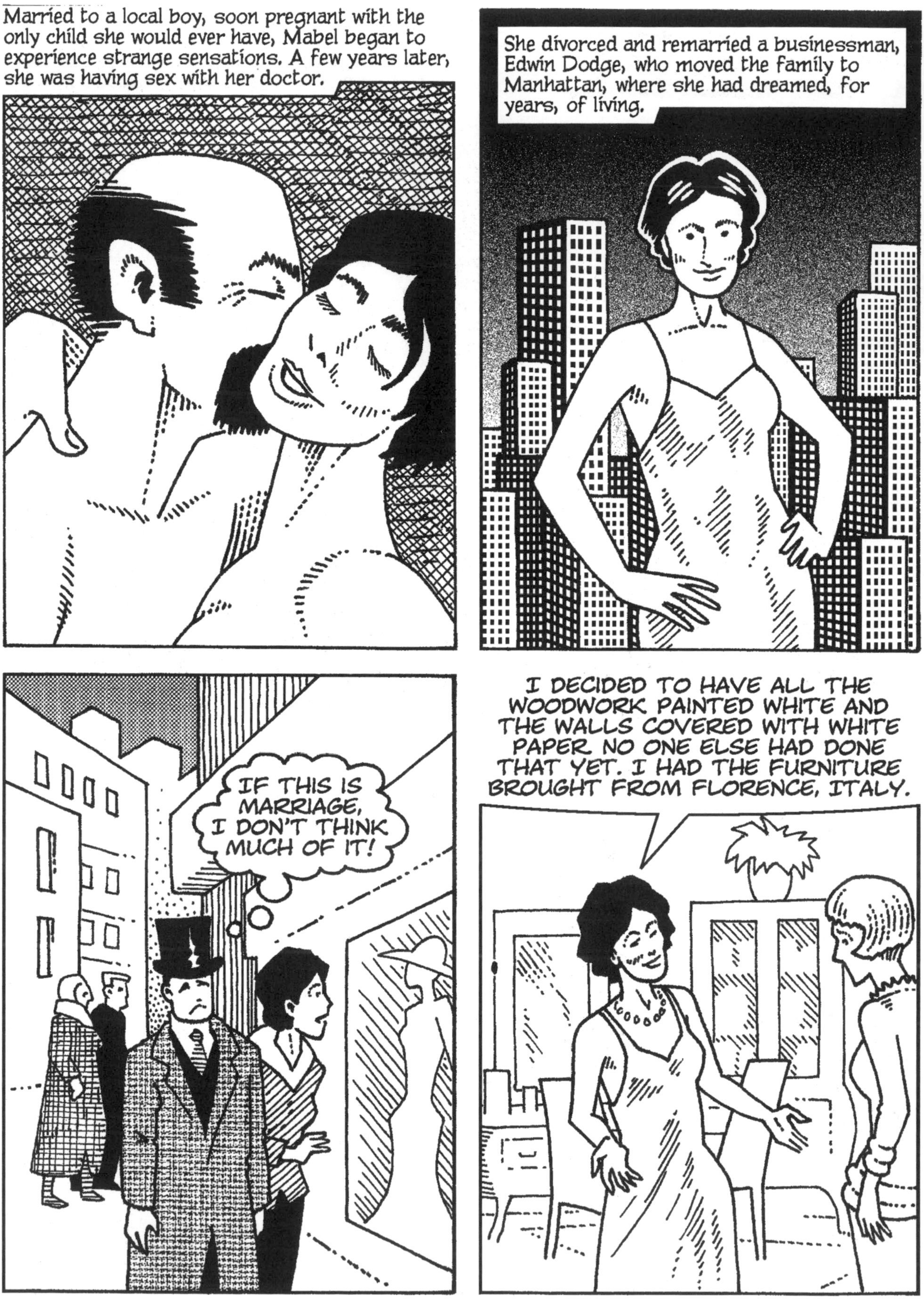
Married to a local boy, soon pregnant with the only child she would ever have, Mabel began to experience strange sensations. A few years later, she was having sex with her doctor.
She divorced and remarried a businessman, Edwin Dodge, who moved the family to Manhattan, where she had dreamed, for years, of living.
IF THIS IS MARRIAGE, I DON'T THINK MUCH OF IT!
I DECIDED TO HAVE ALL THE WOODWORK PAINTED WHITE AND THE WALLS COVERED WITH WHITE PAPER. NO ONE ELSE HAD DONE THAT YET. I HAD THE FURNITURE BROUGHT FROM FLORENCE, ITALY.

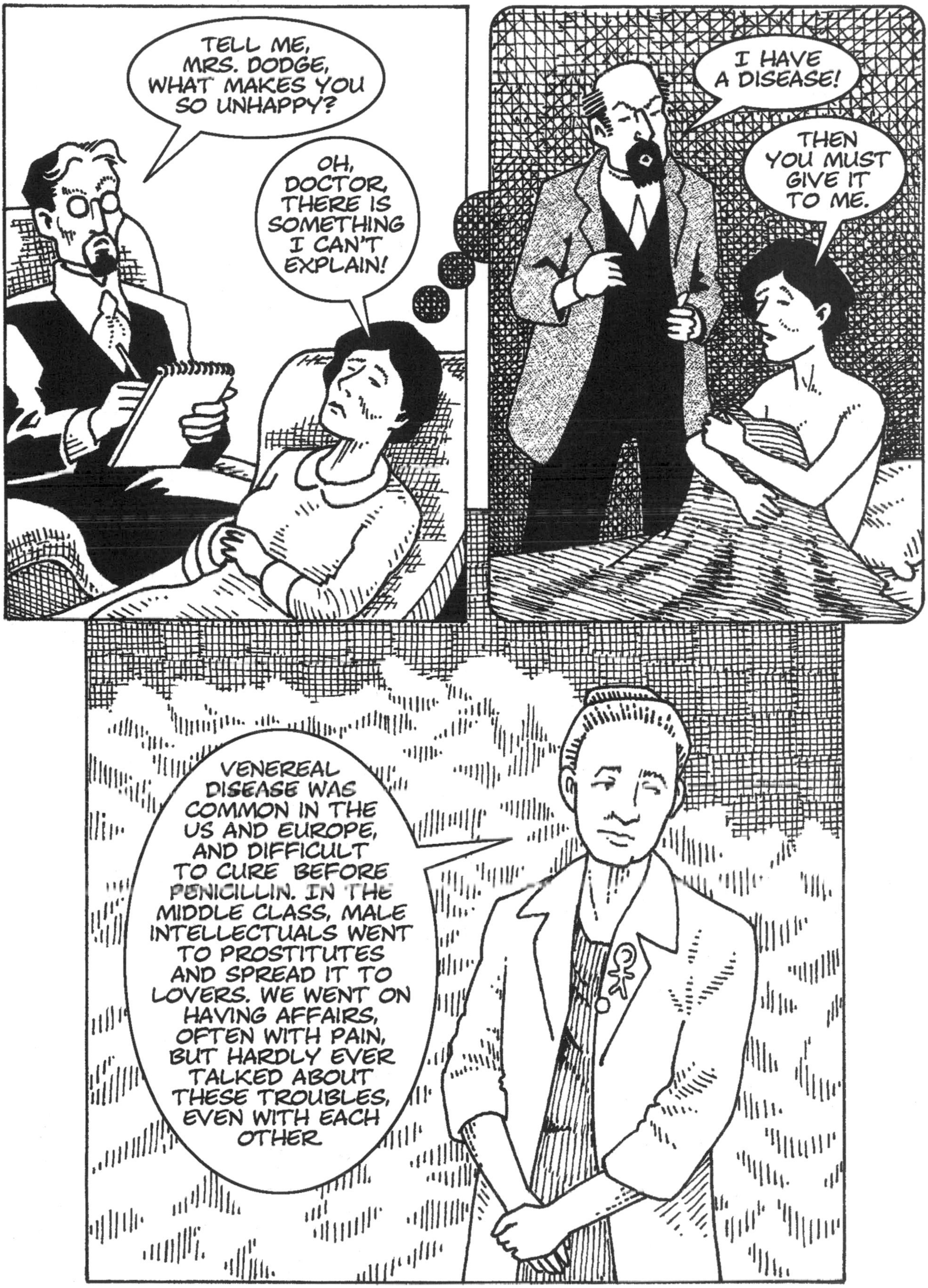
TELL ME, MRS. DODGE, WHAT MAKES YOU SO UNHAPPY?
OH, DOCTOR, THERE IS SOMETHING I CAN'T EXPLAIN!
I HAVE A DISEASE!
THEN YOU MUST GIVE IT TO ME.
VENEREAL DISEASE WAS COMMON IN THE US AND EUROPE, AND DIFFICULT TO CURE BEFORE PENICILLIN. IN THE MIDDLE CLASS, MALE INTELLECTUALS WENT TO PROSTITUTES AND SPREAD IT TO LOVERS. WE WENT ON HAVING AFFAIRS, OFTEN WITH PAIN, BUT HARDLY EVER TALKED ABOUT THESE TROUBLES, EVEN WITH EACH OTHER

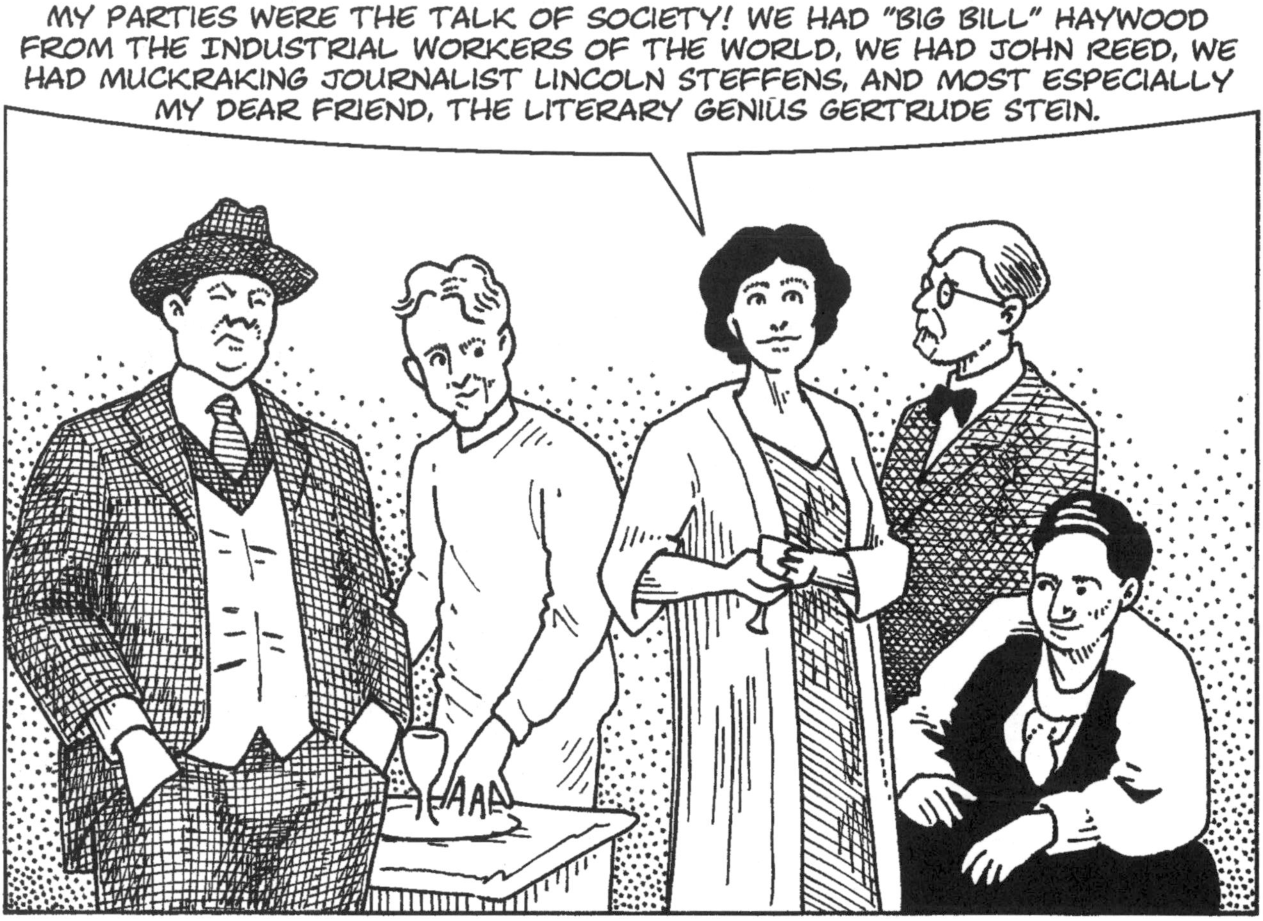
MY PARTIES WERE THE TALK OF SOCIETY! WE HAD "BIG BILL" HAYWOOD FROM THE INDUSTRIAL WORKERS OF THE WORLD, WE HAD JOHN REED, WE HAD MUCKRAKING JOURNALIST LINCOLN STEFFENS, AND MOST ESPECIALLY MY DEAR FRIEND, THE LITERARY GENIUS GERTRUDE STEIN.

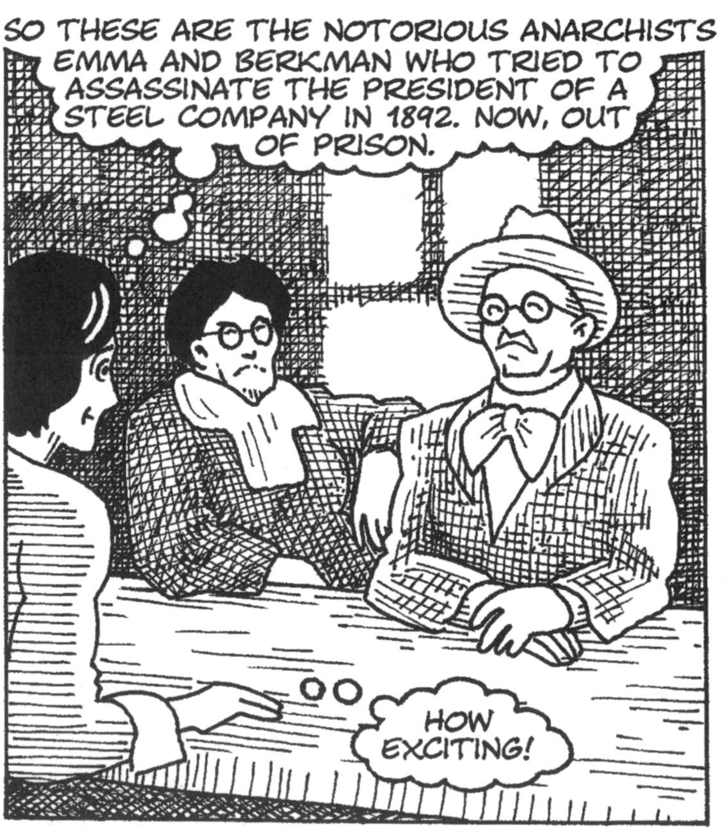
SO THESE ARE THE NOTORIOUS ANARCHISTS EMMA AND BERKMAN WHO TRIED TO ASSASSINATE THE PRESIDENT OF A STEEL COMPANY IN 1892. NOW, OUT OF PRISON.
HOW EXCITING!

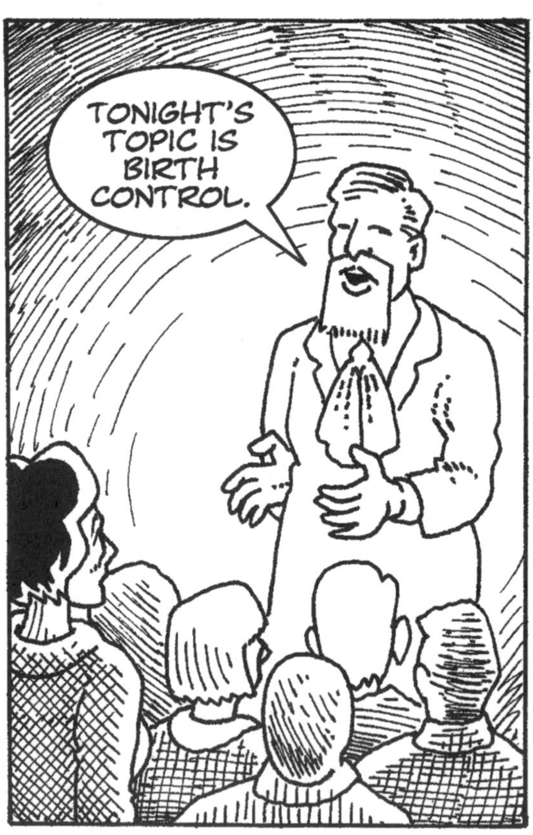
TONIGHT'S TOPIC IS BIRTH CONTROL.

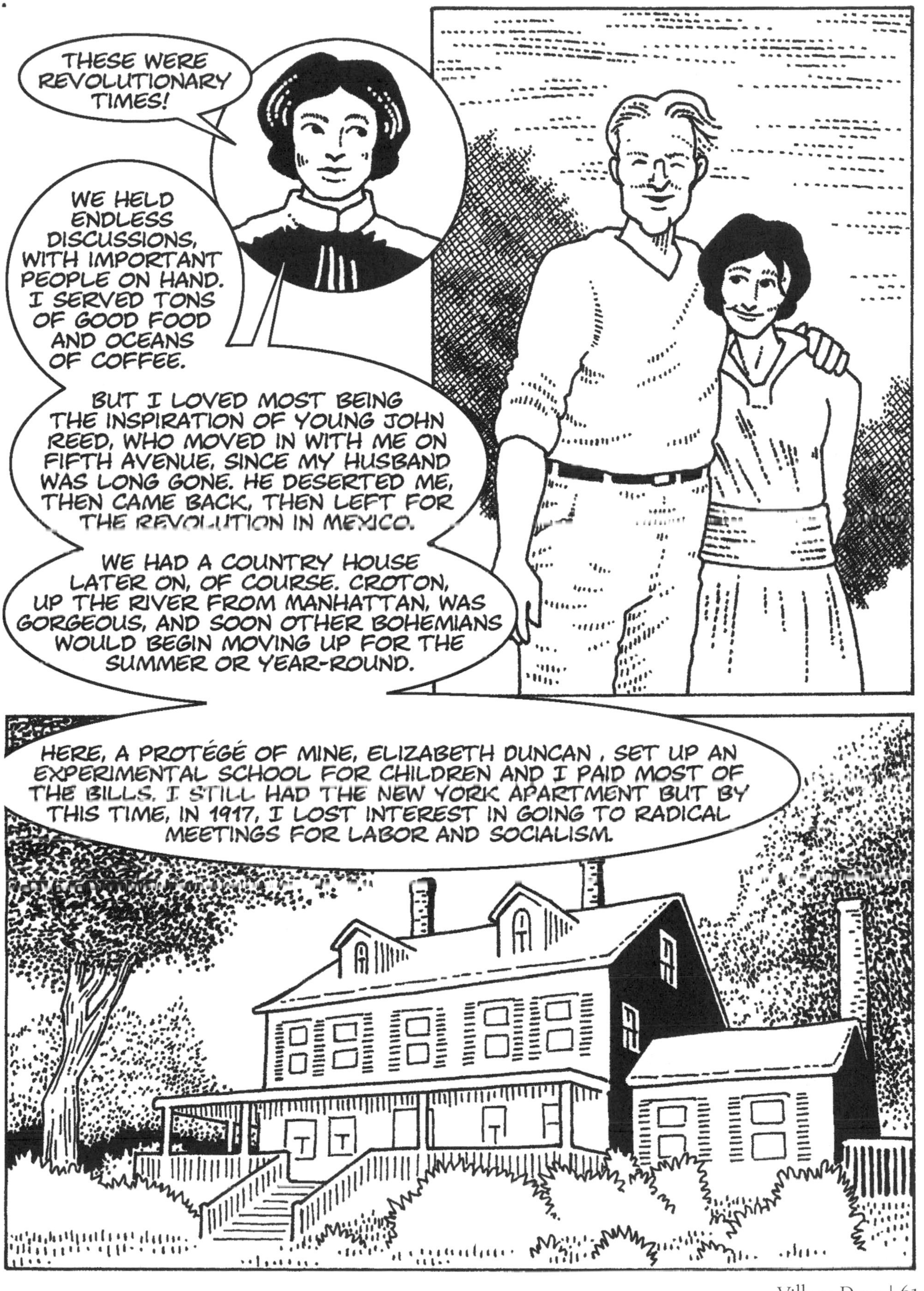
THESE WERE REVOLUTIONARY TIMES!
WE HELD ENDLESS DISCUSSIONS, WITH IMPORTANT PEOPLE ON HAND. I SERVED TONS OF GOOD FOOD AND OCEANS OF COFFEE.
BUT I LOVED MOST BEING THE INSPIRATION OF YOUNG JOHN REED, WHO MOVED IN WITH ME ON FIFTH AVENUE, SINCE MY HUSBAND WAS LONG GONE. HE DESERTED ME, THEN CAME BACK, THEN LEFT FOR THE REVOLUTION IN MEXICO.
WE HAD A COUNTRY HOUSE LATER ON, OF COURSE. CROTON, UP THE RIVER FROM MANHATTAN, WAS GORGEOUS, AND SOON OTHER BOHEMIANS WOULD BEGIN MOVING UP FOR THE SUMMER OR YEAR-ROUND.
HERE, A PROTÉGÉ OF MINE, ELIZABETH DUNCAN , SET UP AN EXPERIMENTAL SCHOOL FOR CHILDREN AND I PAID MOST OF THE BILLS. I STILL HAD THE NEW YORK APARTMENT BUT BY THIS TIME, IN 1917, I LOST INTEREST IN GOING TO RADICAL MEETINGS FOR LABOR AND SOCIALISM.

ARTURO GIOVANNITTI

Bohemian rebel, labor champion, and poet

TEXT: LUISA CETTI

ART: STEVE STILES

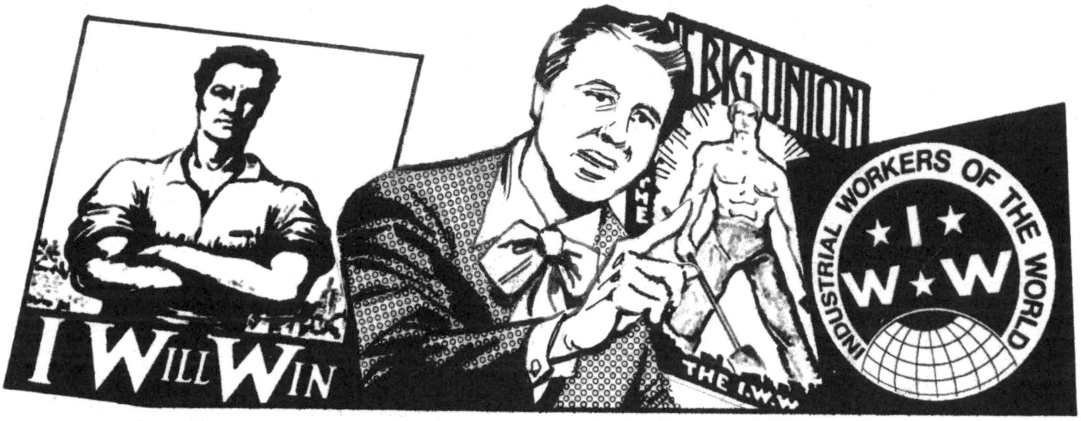
I WILL WIN
BIG UNION
INDUSTRIAL WORKERS OF THE WORLD
I W W
THE I.W.W

IN 1901, AT SEVENTEEN, ARTURO GIOVANNITTI, LEFT HIS LITTLE TOWN IN SOUTHERN ITALY FOR AMERICA, IN SEARCH OF THE FREEDOM HE COULD NOT FIND IN HIS COUNTRY. LIKE SO MANY IMMIGRANTS, HE WAS LOOKING FOR NEW OPPORTUNITIES, BUT LOVE FOR DEMOCRACY INSPIRED HIS CHOICE TOO.

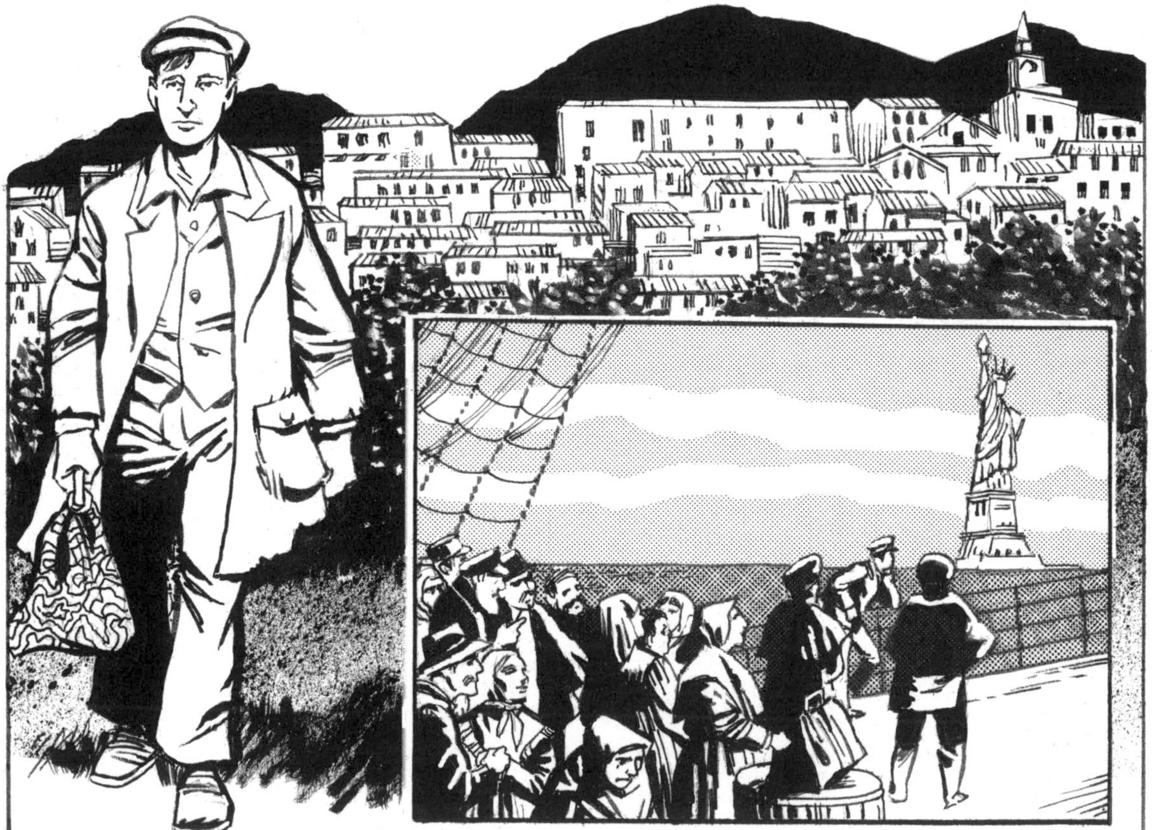

FROM PROTESTANT MINISTER TO RADICAL ACTIVIST

FOLLOWING HIS MYSTICAL AND RELIGIOUS FEELINGS, ARTURO STUDIED AT A PROTESTANT SEMINARY IN CANADA AND WAS ORDAINED AS A MINISTER. AT 20, HE IMMIGRATED TO THE UNITED STATES TO PREACH AMONG THE COAL MINERS OF PENNSYLVANIA. THE MISERY, DISILLUSION, AND DEGRADATION OF THE FOREIGN WORKERS STRIVING FOR A BETTER LIFE EASED A QUICK AND NATURAL TRANSITION FROM AN EVANGELICAL MISSION TO A RADICAL GOSPEL OF SOCIAL JUSTICE AND INTENSE POLITICAL ACTIVITY. HE BECAME A LABOR ORGANISER, ACTIVE IN THE SOCIALIST MOVEMENT; HE LED STRIKES, WAS A POWERFUL ORATOR, AND WROTE LYRICAL VERSES.

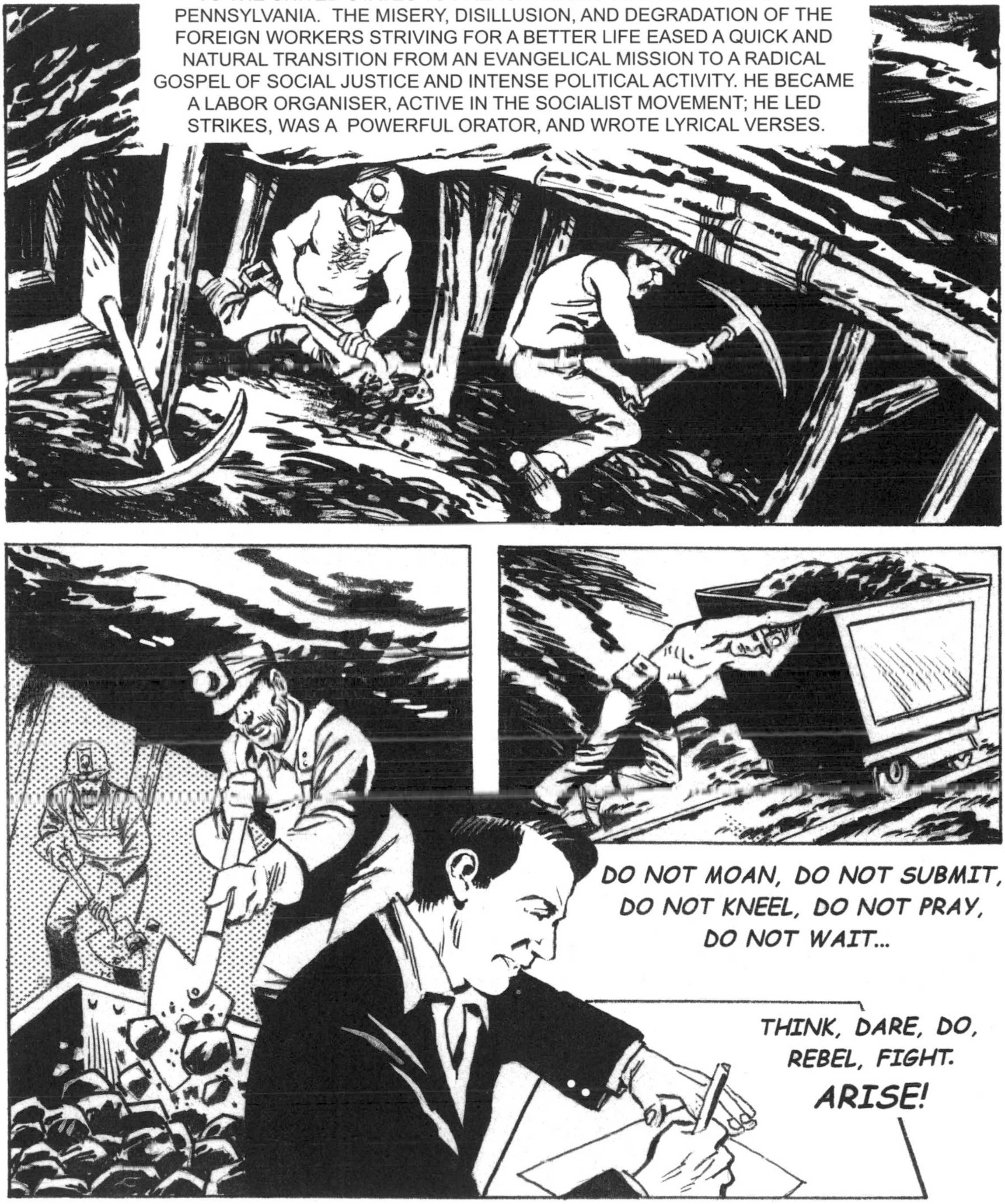
DO NOT MOAN, DO NOT SUBMIT, DO NOT KNEEL, DO NOT PRAY, DO NOT WAIT...
THINK, DARE, DO, REBEL, FIGHT. ARISE!

THE LAWRENCE STRIKE

IN 1912, DURING THE LAWRENCE STRIKE, WHEN WOOLEN MILL WORKERS LEFT THEIR JOB IN PROTEST AGAINST A REDUCTION OF WAGES, A STRIKER, ANNA LO PIZZO, WAS KILLED BY THE POLICE AND IWW ORGANIZERS GIOVANNITTI AND JOSEPH ETTOR WERE ACCUSED OF INSPIRING THE LAWRENCE STRIKERS TO VIOLENCE AND CHARGED WITH RESPONSIBLITY FOR HER DEATH. THE CASE GAINED NATIONAL PROMINENCE AND GIOVANNITTI WAS ALLOWED TO SPEAK TO THE JURY, GIVING HIS FIRST SPEECH IN ENGLISH.

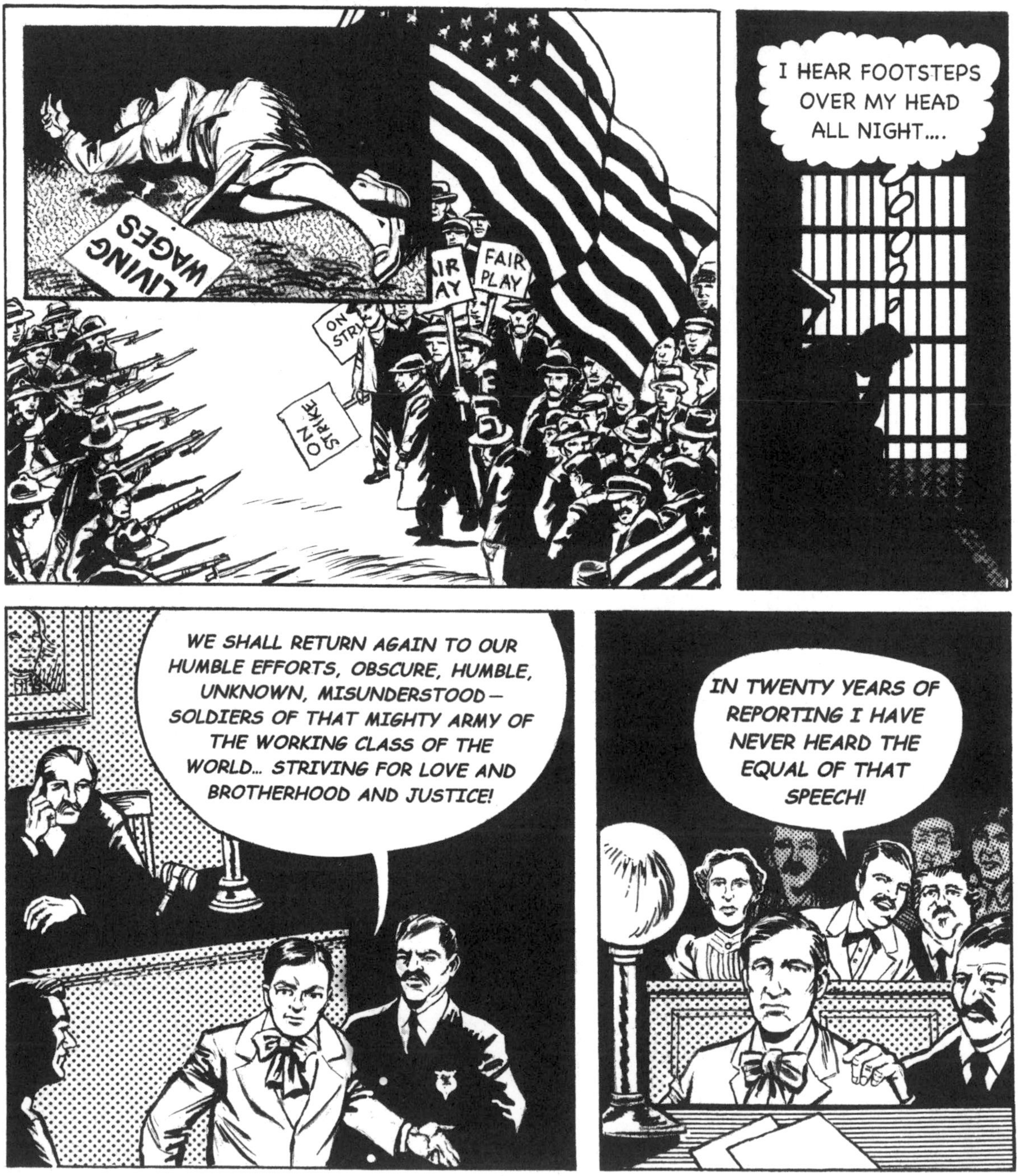
LIVING WAGES
FAIR PLAY
ON STRIKE
I HEAR FOOTSTEPS OVER MY HEAD ALL NIGHT....
WE SHALL RETURN AGAIN TO OUR HUMBLE EFFORTS, OBSCURE, HUMBLE, UNKNOWN, MISUNDERSTOOD— SOLDIERS OF THAT MIGHTY ARMY OF THE WORKING CLASS OF THE WORLD... STRIVING FOR LOVE AND BROTHERHOOD AND JUSTICE!
IN TWENTY YEARS OF REPORTING I HAVE NEVER HEARD THE EQUAL OF THAT SPEECH!

INTERNATIONAL SOLIDARITY FOR ETTOR AND GIOVANNITTI

ECHOES ABROAD OF THE LAWRENCE STRIKE AND THE ARREST OF ETTOR AND GIOVANNITTI WERE STRONG. IN ITALY THERE WAS A LARGE SOLIDARITY MOVEMENT: COMMITTEES FOR E & G SPRANG UP IN EVERY TOWN, AND THERE WERE PROTESTS AND DEMONSTRATIONS AGAINST THEIR ARREST.

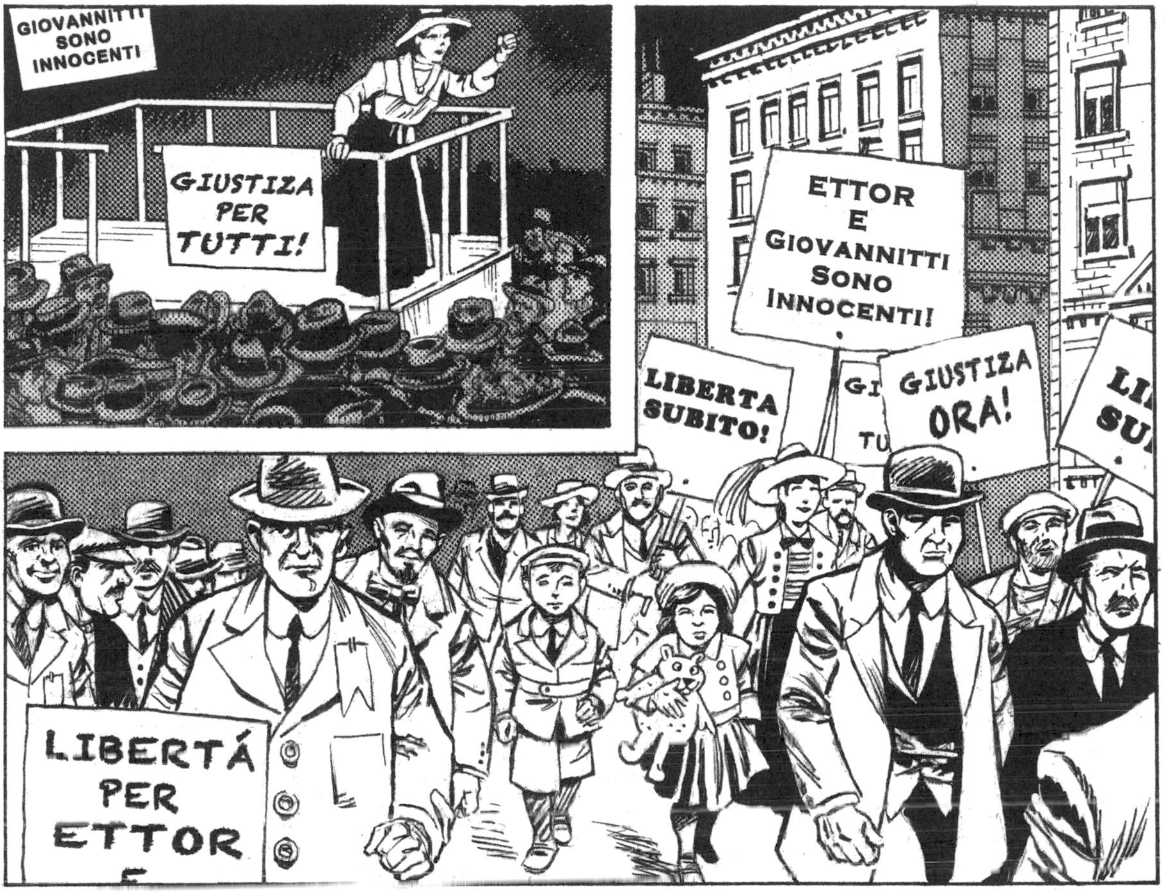
GIOVANNITTI SONO INNOCENTI
GIUSTIZA PER TUTTI!
ETTOR E GIOVANNITTI SONO INNOCENTI!
LIBERTA SUBITO!
GIUSTIZA ORA!
LIBERTÁ PER ETTOR

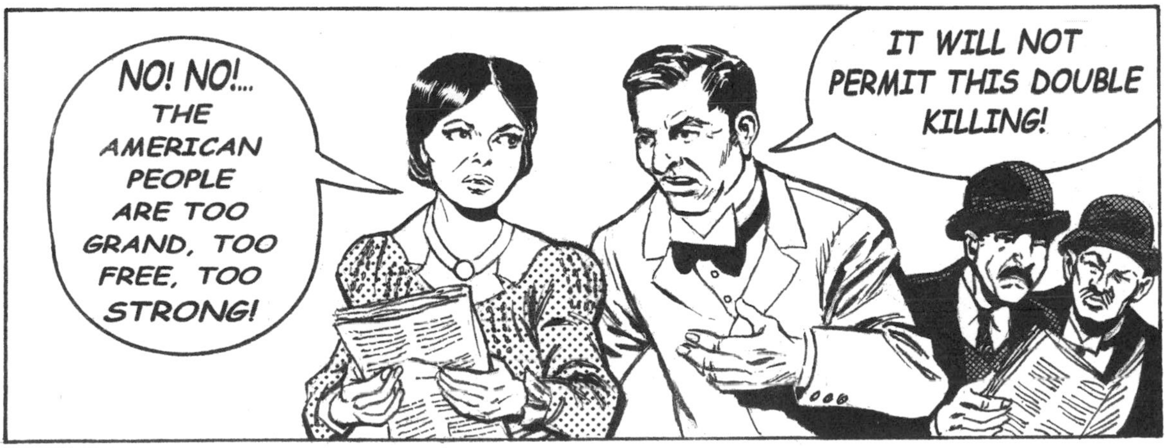
NO! NO!... THE AMERICAN PEOPLE ARE TOO GRAND, TOO FREE, TOO STRONG!
IT WILL NOT PERMIT THIS DOUBLE KILLING!

ETTOR AND GIOVANNETTI RECEIVED MORE THAN ***15,000*** LETTERS AND TELEGRAMS OF SUPPORT FROM ITALY. THE CASE RAISED THE ATTENTION OF THE INTERNATIONAL PRESS: THE PRISON AUTHORITES WERE OBLIGED TO FIX A LIMIT TO THE E & G INTERVIEWS TO NOT MORE THAN THREE A DAY.

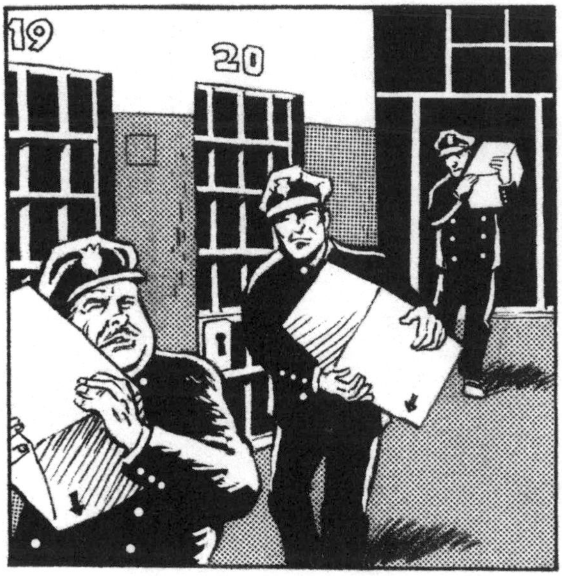
19
20

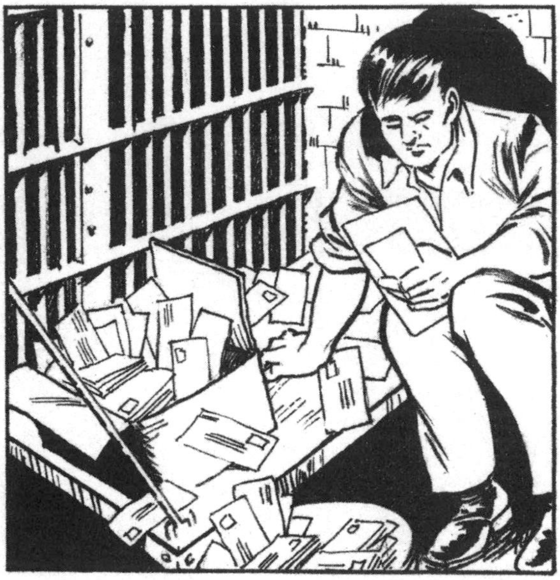

IN LONDON AND BRUSSELS, IN PARIS AND IN BERLIN, IN BRAZIL AND IN AUSTRALIA, EVERYWHERE IN THE WORLD ITALIAN IMMIGRANT WORKERS AND LOCAL RADICALS RALLIED FOR ETTOR AND GIOVANNITTI. SWEDISH AND FRENCH WORKERS PROPOSED A BOYCOTT OF WOOLEN GOODS FROM THE UNITED STATES AND A REFUSAL TO LOAD SHIPS GOING TO THE U. S. IN RIPABOTTONI, ARTURO'S HOME VILLAGE, WHERE THE SOLIDARITY MOVEMENT STARTED. ARTURO'S LIBERATION IN DECEMBER 1912 WAS GREETED BY A MASS CELEBRATION.

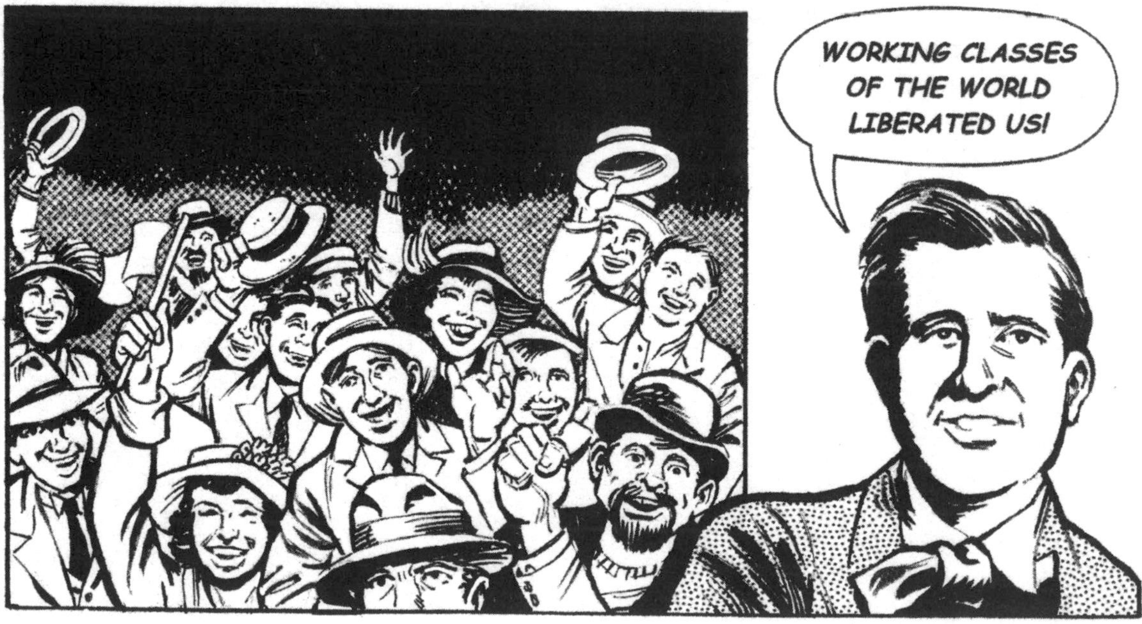
WORKING CLASSES OF THE WORLD LIBERATED US!

HAPPY COMRADES

IN THE FIRST DECADES OF THE 20TH CENTURY, THE CAFES AND LITTLE RESTAURANTS OF GREENWICH VILLAGE WERE THE PERFECT MEETING PLACES FOR REBELS OF ALL KINDS. AT THE HEART OF THE VILLAGE, A HANDFUL OF ITALIAN ARTISTS AND RADICALS CROSSED THE ETHNIC BOUNDARIES AND BECAME PART OF THE BOHEMIAN FERMENT OF THOSE DAYS.

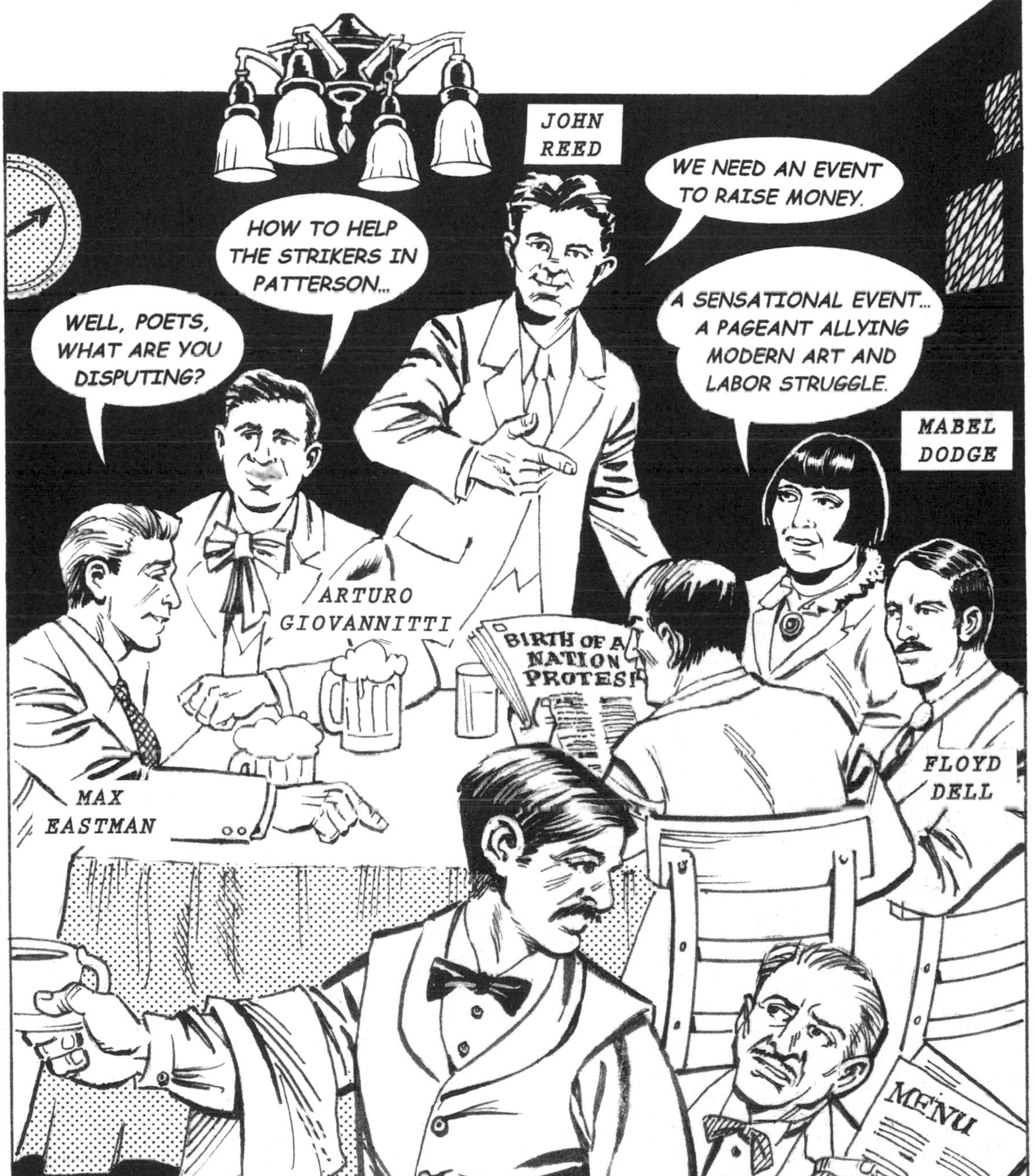
JOHN REED
WELL, POETS, WHAT ARE YOU DISPUTING?
HOW TO HELP THE STRIKERS IN PATTERSON...
WE NEED AN EVENT TO RAISE MONEY.
A SENSATIONAL EVENT... A PAGEANT ALLYING MODERN ART AND LABOR STRUGGLE.
MABEL DODGE
ARTURO GIOVANNITTI
BIRTH OF A NATION PROTEST
MAX EASTMAN
FLOYD DELL
MENU

ART AND STRUGGLE

A GIFTED ORATATOR, AS WELL AS A RENOWNED WORKING CLASS POET, GIOVANNITTI WAS GREETED WITH ENTHUSIASM TO UNION PICNICS AND EVENTS. HIS ROOM ON WEST 28TH STREET WAS THE USUAL MEETING PLACE FOR A BUNCH OF ARTISTS OF ALL NATIONALITIES DISCUSSING ART, LITERATURE, AND POLITICS. IN 1914, TOGETHER WITH THE SCULPTOR ONORIO RUOTOLO, HE STARTED A SHORT LIVED “MAGAZINE OF ART AND STRUGGLE,” ***IL FUOCO.*** WHEN ITALY ENTERED WWI, GIOVANNITTI OPPOSED ITALY’S PARTICIPATION. GIOVANNITTI RESUMED HIS ROLE AS A MILITANT IN THE STRUGGLE FOR SOCIAL CHANGE.

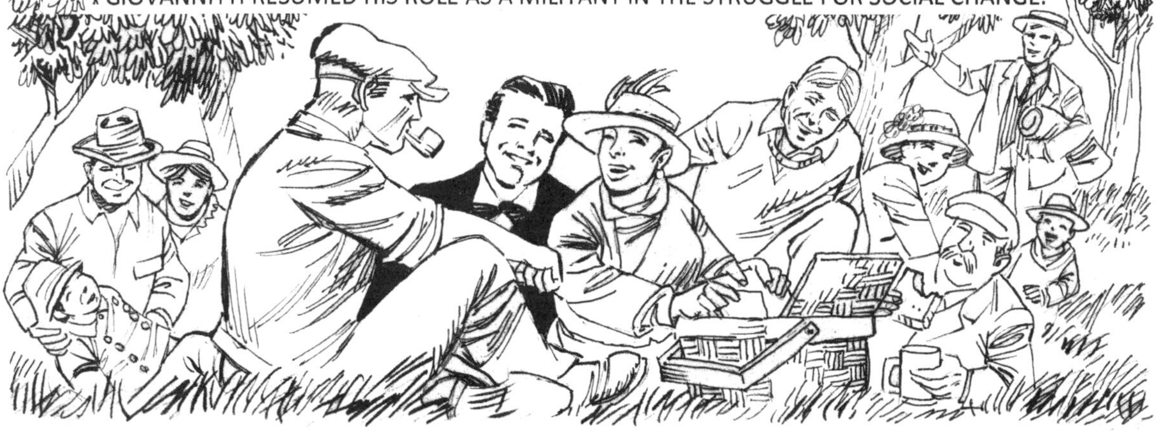

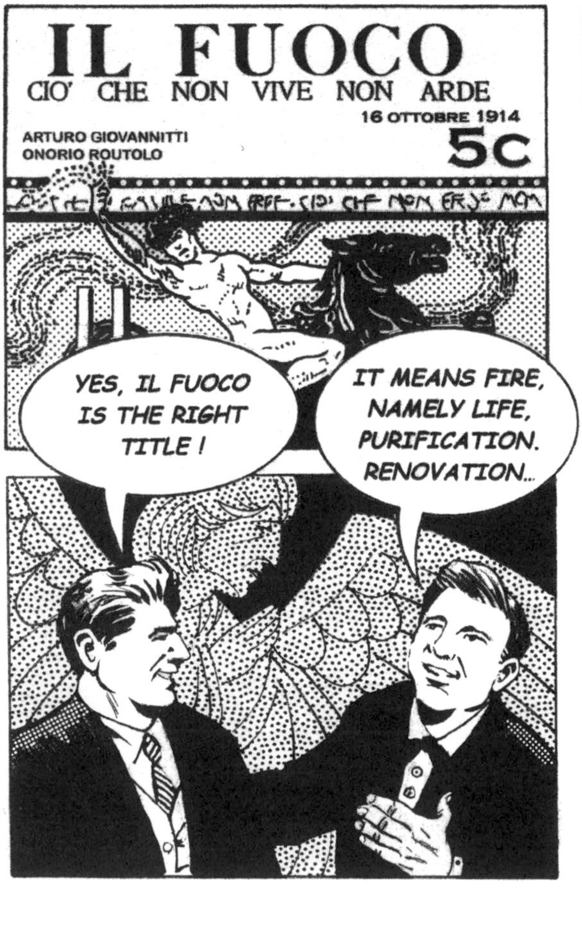
IL FUOCO
CIO' CHE NON VIVE NON ARDE
16 OTTOBRE 1914
ARTURO GIOVANNITTI
ONORIO ROUTOLO
5C
YES, IL FUOCO IS THE RIGHT TITLE !
IT MEANS FIRE, NAMELY LIFE, PURIFICATION. RENOVATION...

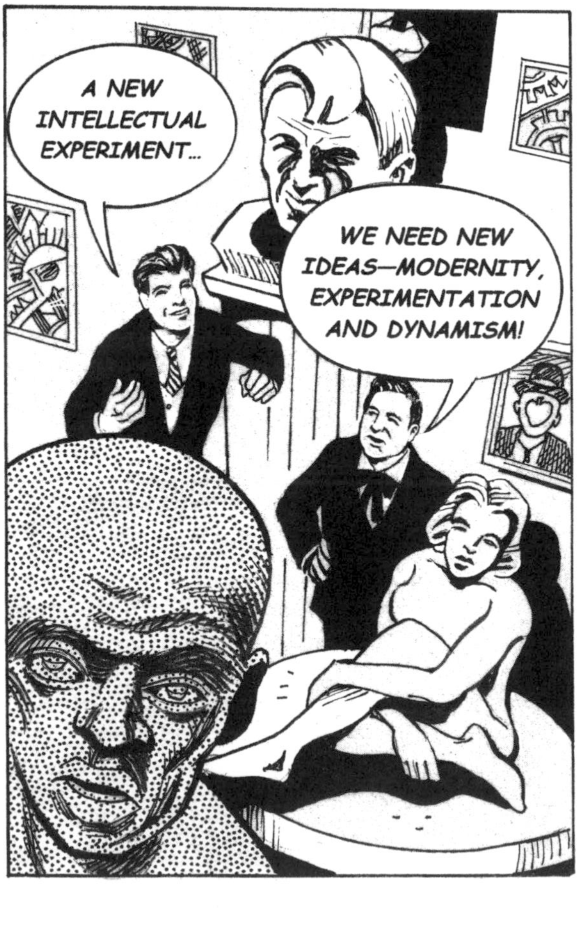
A NEW INTELLECTUAL EXPERIMENT...
WE NEED NEW IDEAS—MODERNITY, EXPERIMENTATION AND DYNAMISM!

REBEL DREAMS FACING HARSH REALITY

BY 1917, THE POLITICAL CLIMATE WAS MORE AND MORE TENSE AND BITTER FOR RADICAL ITALIAN-AMERICANS, CULMINATING IN THE EXECUTION OF SACCO AND VANZETTI IN 1927. YET GIOVANNITTI REMAINED ACTIVE IN THE ITALIAN-AMERICAN LABOR MOVEMENT AND IN ARTISTIC AND LITERARY CIRCLES OF NEW YORK. HE HAD A LEADING ROLE IN THE ANTIFASCIST MOVEMENT IN THE U.S. IN THE 1930S AND '40S, DESPITE HIS FAILING HEALTH AND INCREASING ALCOHOLISM. ECHOING THESE DIFFICULT TIMES, HIS POETRY LOST THE VIBRANT FLAME OF 1910'S HEROIC REVOLUTIONARY AND GAINED A SORT OF DOLEFUL GRACE.

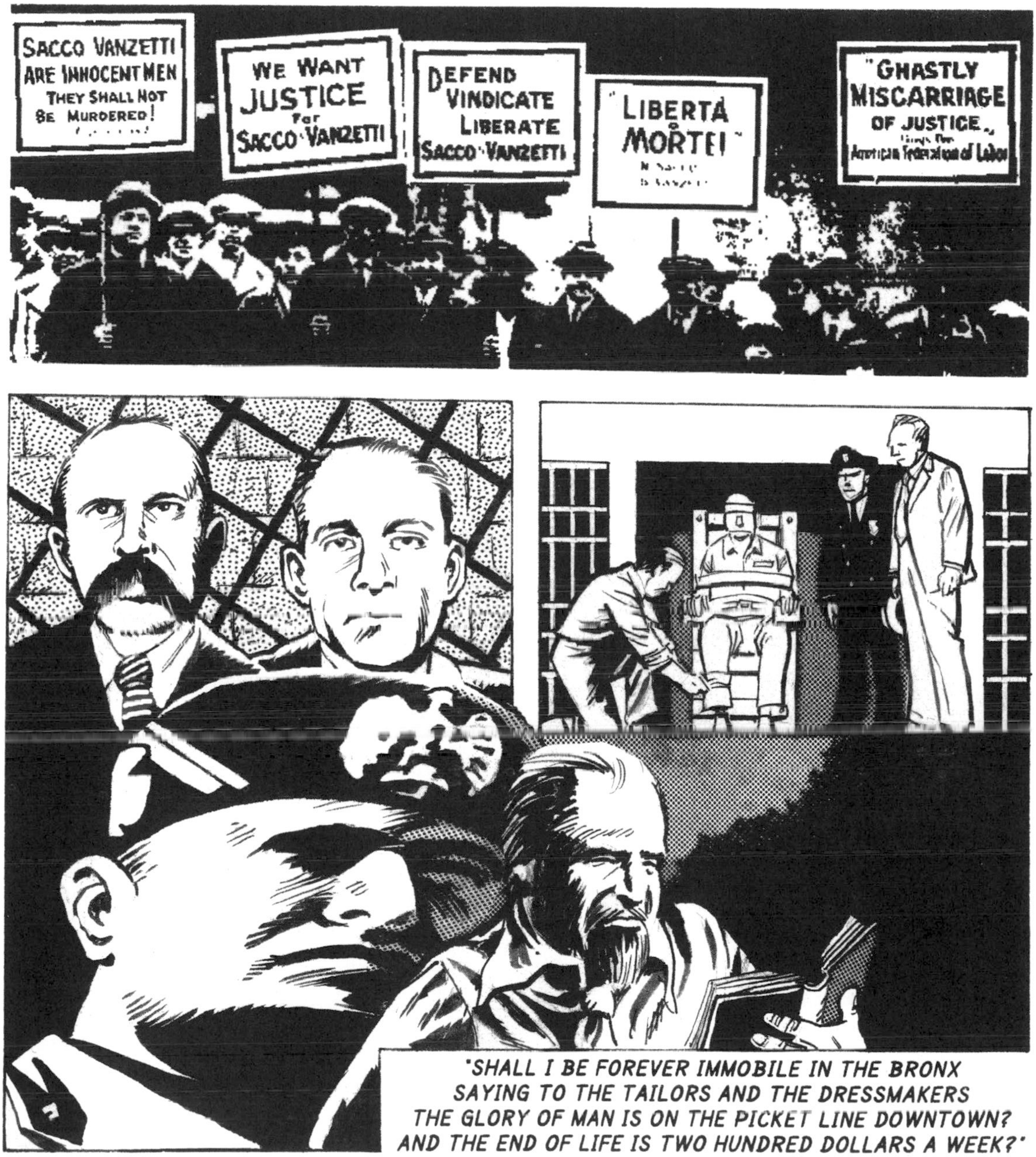
SACCO VANZETTI ARE INNOCENT MEN THEY SHALL NOT BE MURDERED!
WE WANT JUSTICE for SACCO-VANZETTI
DEFEND VINDICATE LIBERATE SACCO-VANZETTI
"LIBERTÀ O MORTE!"
"GHASTLY MISCARRIAGE OF JUSTICE"
'SHALL I BE FOREVER IMMOBILE IN THE BRONX
SAYING TO THE TAILORS AND THE DRESSMAKERS
THE GLORY OF MAN IS ON THE PICKET LINE DOWNTOWN?
AND THE END OF LIFE IS TWO HUNDRED DOLLARS A WEEK?'

Chapter Five

Art and the Artist

By wartime, it was an advanced section of the global avant-garde that took shape in and around New York, thanks both to temporary visitors and a handful of American experimenters.

This development had been almost two decades in the making. The semi-documentary styles of Alfred Steiglitz's artistic photography, for instance, actually lent themselves to ostensibly European innovations like Dada, the reformulation of daily life detritus to a new purpose. Here, a urinal signed by "R. Mutt," aka Marcel Duchamp, was offered up as an artful entry into a major show, a few years after Duchamp's "Nude Descending a Staircase" made artistic history with its combination of painting and simulated mechanical or bodily motion.

The art of Steiglitz, Man Ray and others remarkably reconceived the world, as did Harlem, the center of modern African-American culture, with artists like Claude McKay, who transcended all boundaries.

American artists and intellectuals were in touch with those in Europe as never before, ironically at the tragic moment when world war wiped out a long phase of optimism about society's future. The consequences would be profound.

The FROWNING PROPHET and The SMILING REVOLUTIONARY

MODERN ART ARRIVES IN NEW YORK

WORDS and ART BY DAN STEFFAN

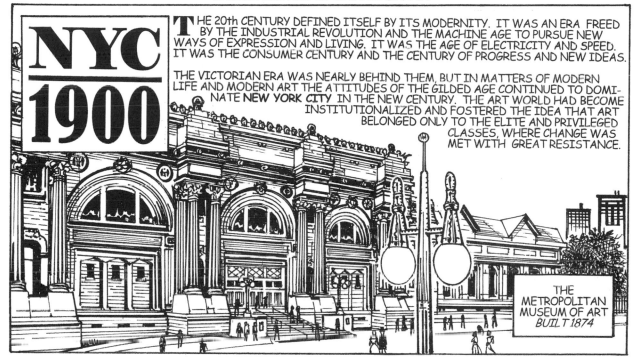

NYC 1900

THE 20th CENTURY DEFINED ITSELF BY ITS MODERNITY. IT WAS AN ERA FREED BY THE INDUSTRIAL REVOLUTION AND THE MACHINE AGE TO PURSUE NEW WAYS OF EXPRESSION AND LIVING. IT WAS THE AGE OF ELECTRICITY AND SPEED. IT WAS THE CONSUMER CENTURY AND THE CENTURY OF PROGRESS AND NEW IDEAS.

THE VICTORIAN ERA WAS NEARLY BEHIND THEM, BUT IN MATTERS OF MODERN LIFE AND MODERN ART THE ATTITUDES OF THE GILDED AGE CONTINUED TO DOMINATE **NEW YORK CITY** IN THE NEW CENTURY. THE ART WORLD HAD BECOME INSTITUTIONALIZED AND FOSTERED THE IDEA THAT ART BELONGED ONLY TO THE ELITE AND PRIVILEGED CLASSES, WHERE CHANGE WAS MET WITH GREAT RESISTANCE.

THE METROPOLITAN MUSEUM OF ART BUILT 1874

FORTUNATELY, NOT EVERYONE FELT THAT WAY. **ALFRED STIEGLITZ** (1864-1946), FOR INSTANCE, WAS A RENOWNED PHOTOGRAPHER WHO BELIEVED THAT TRADITIONAL ART HAD BECOME "FANCIFUL SYMBOLISM," AND THAT THERE SHOULD BE NO BARRIER BETWEEN ART AND LIFE. PHOTOGRAPHY HAD TAUGHT HIM THAT ANYONE COULD MAKE ART.

THE GOAL OF ART IS THE VITAL EXPRESSION OF SELF. IN PHOTOGRAPHY THERE IS A REALITY SO SUBTLE THAT IT BECOMES MORE REAL THAN REALITY.

STIEGLITZ WANTED TO BREAK DOWN THE BARRIERS BETWEEN ART AND TECHNOLOGY. HE WANTED HIS CAMERA TO "SERVE THE HUMAN SPIRIT" AND PROVE THAT PHOTOGRAPHY WAS A LEGITIMATE FORM OF PICTORIAL EXPRESSION. A CONTRARIAN BY NATURE, HE RELISHED THE CHALLENGE OF OPENING CLOSED MINDS AND NEW DOORS OF PERCEPTION.

TOWARDS THIS END, STIEGLITZ AND A COMPATRIOT NAMED **EDWARD STEICHEN** (1879-1973) HELPED ORGANIZE AN EXHIBITION OF AMERICAN PICTORIAL PHOTOGRAPHY IN 1902, AT THE NATIONAL ARTS CLUB OF MANHATTAN. "GIVE EVERY MAN WHO HAS A MESSAGE A CHANCE TO BE HEARD," WAS THEIR MOTTO.

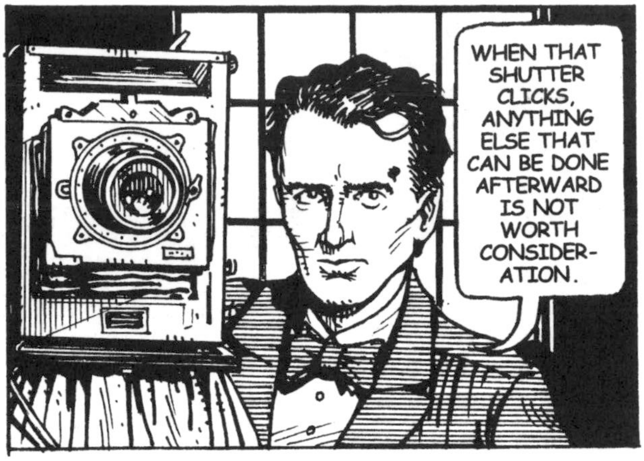
WHEN THAT SHUTTER CLICKS, ANYTHING ELSE THAT CAN BE DONE AFTERWARD IS NOT WORTH CONSIDERATION.

THEY CALLED THEMSELVES **PHOTO-SECESSIONISTS** TO SET THEIR WORK APART FROM THEIR CONSERVATIVE CONTEMPORARIES AND TO CHALLENGE THE ACCEPTED IDEA OF WHAT CONSTITUTED AN ARTISTIC PHOTOGRAPH. IT WAS THE 1st TIME MODERN PHOTOGRAPHERS WERE JUDGED BY A JURY OF THEIR PEERS.

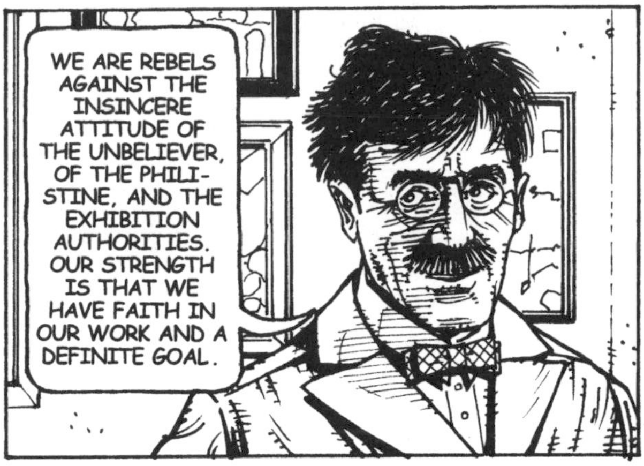
WE ARE REBELS AGAINST THE INSINCERE ATTITUDE OF THE UNBELIEVER, OF THE PHILISTINE, AND THE EXHIBITION AUTHORITIES. OUR STRENGTH IS THAT WE HAVE FAITH IN OUR WORK AND A DEFINITE GOAL.

ENCOURAGED BY THE EXHIBIT'S SUCCESS, STIEGLITZ BEGAN PLANNING A MAGAZINE TO PROMOTE HIS RADICAL IDEAS ABOUT PHOTOGRAPHY AS FINE ART. HIS OBJECTIVE WAS TO EXPOSE THE READERS TO THE PREMISE THAT PICTORIAL PHOTOGRAPHS SHOULD BE JUDGED SOLELY AS WORKS OF ART, WITHOUT CONSIDERING THAT THEY'D BEEN PRODUCED USING A CAMERA.

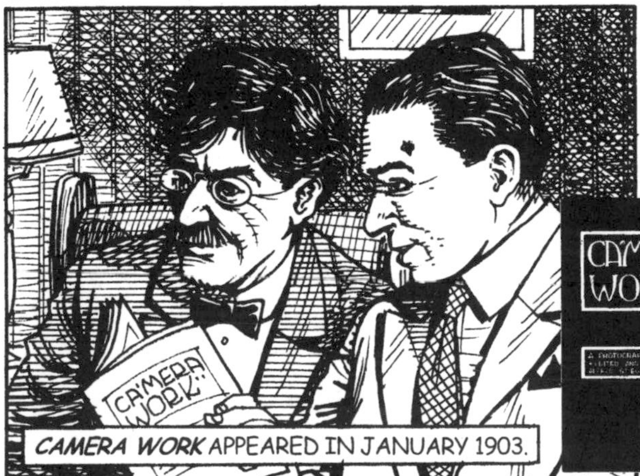
CAMERA WORK
CAMERA WORK
CAMERA WORK APPEARED IN JANUARY 1903.

THE PHOTO-SECESSION EXHIBIT AND STIEGLITZ'S *CAMERA WORK* ATTRACTED PHOTOGRAPHERS AND CRITICS ALIKE AND PROVIDED THEM WITH A FORUM FOR DEBATE THAT HAD BEEN MISSING. CURTIS BELL, THE PRESIDENT OF THE AMERICAN FEDERATION OF PHOTOGRAPHY, CONDEMNED THEIR EFFORTS AND WENT SO FAR AS TO STAGE A COMPETING EXHIBIT.

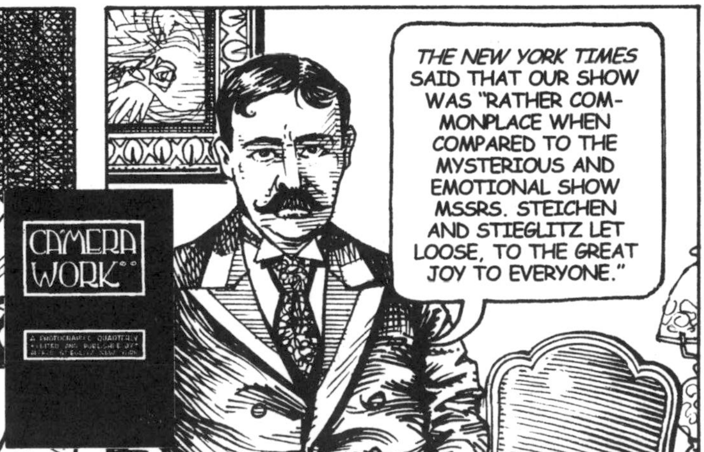
THE NEW YORK TIMES SAID THAT OUR SHOW WAS "RATHER COMMONPLACE WHEN COMPARED TO THE MYSTERIOUS AND EMOTIONAL SHOW MSSRS. STEICHEN AND STIEGLITZ LET LOOSE, TO THE GREAT JOY TO EVERYONE."

STIEGLITZ AND STEICHEN WERE NOT ALONE IN THEIR DISSATISFACTION WITH THE ART ESTABLISHMENT. THE FOUNDING MEMBERS OF THE **ASHCAN SCHOOL** OF PAINTERS, **ROBERT HENRI** (1865-1929) AND **JOHN SLOAN** (1871-1951) CAME TO NEW YORK FROM PHILADELPHIA ON A QUEST FOR "BEAUTY IN TRUTH," BUT HAD MET ONLY RESISTANCE TO THEIR ART.

HENRI FOUGHT THE PROBLEM FROM THE INSIDE BY TEACHING PAINTING AT THE NEW YORK SCHOOL OF ART, WHERE STUDENTS LIKE JOSEPH STELLA, EDWARD HOPPER, GEORGE BELLOWS AND ROCKWELL KENT EMBRACED HIS NEW AESTHETIC, AND CHANGED THEIR ART TO REFLECT THE WORLD AROUND THEM. SLOAN WORKED AS AN ILLUSTRATOR AND USED JOURNALISTIC REALISM IN HIS PUBLISHED WORKS.

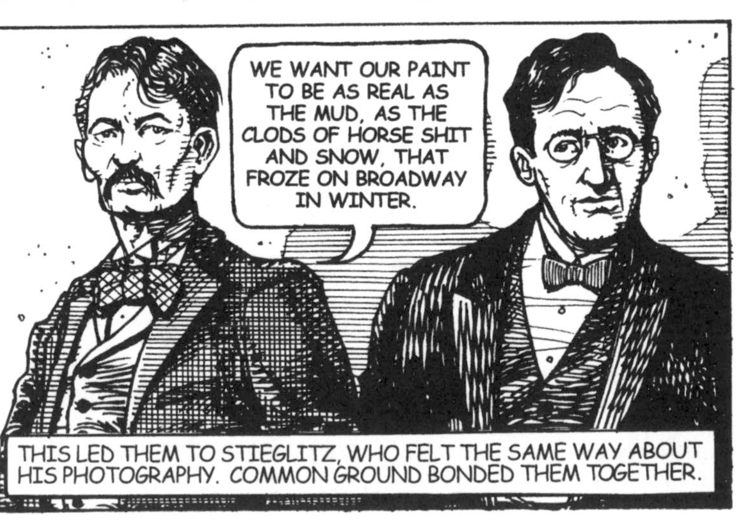
WE WANT OUR PAINT TO BE AS REAL AS THE MUD, AS THE CLODS OF HORSE SHIT AND SNOW, THAT FROZE ON BROADWAY IN WINTER.
THIS LED THEM TO STIEGLITZ, WHO FELT THE SAME WAY ABOUT HIS PHOTOGRAPHY. COMMON GROUND BONDED THEM TOGETHER.

IN 1905 STEICHEN CONVINCED A SKEPTICAL STIEGLITZ TO RENT THE SPACE ACROSS FROM HIS STUDIO AT 291 FIFTH AVENUE AND TURN IT INTO A GALLERY SPECIALIZING IN NEW PHOTOGRAPHY. THEY CALLED IT **THE LITTLE GALLERIES OF PHOTO-SECESSION**.

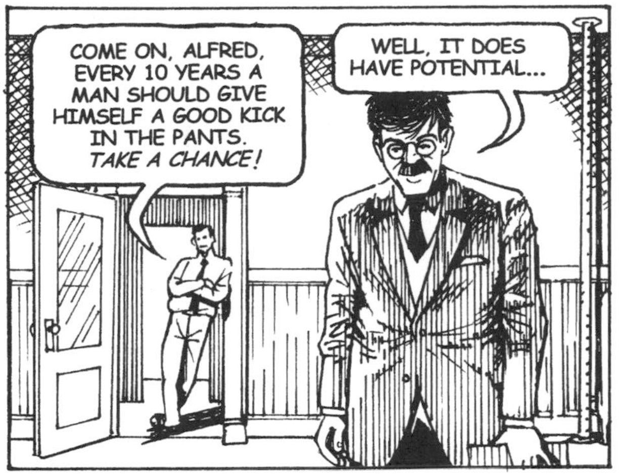
COME ON, ALFRED, EVERY 10 YEARS A MAN SHOULD GIVE HIMSELF A GOOD KICK IN THE PANTS. TAKE A CHANCE!
WELL, IT DOES HAVE POTENTIAL...

THE LITTLE GALLERIES BECAME NOT ONLY EXHIBITION SPACE, BUT AN EDUCATIONAL FACILITY FOR ARTISTS AND PHOTOGRAPHERS AND A MEETING PLACE FOR ART LOVERS. DESPITE ITS MODEST SUCCESS, STIEGLITZ WAS WORRIED THAT IT WOULD NOT LAST.

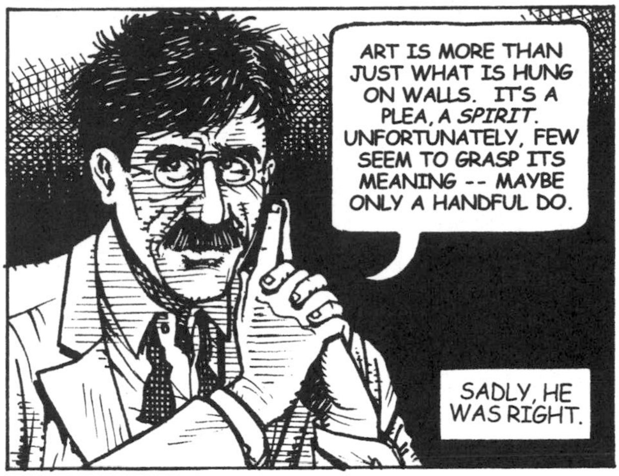
ART IS MORE THAN JUST WHAT IS HUNG ON WALLS. IT'S A PLEA, A SPIRIT. UNFORTUNATELY, FEW SEEM TO GRASP ITS MEANING -- MAYBE ONLY A HANDFUL DO.
SADLY, HE WAS RIGHT.

IN ITS EARLY DAYS, THE LITTLE GALLERIES' REPUTATION BROUGHT STIEGLITZ UNEXPECTED FAME AND INFLUENCE, WHICH HE WISELY USED TO SPONSOR EXHIBITS BY NEW PHOTOGRAPHERS FROM FRANCE, ENGLAND, GERMANY AND AUSTRIA, IN ADDITION TO MANY SHOWS BY THE PHOTO-SECESSIONISTS THEMSELVES.

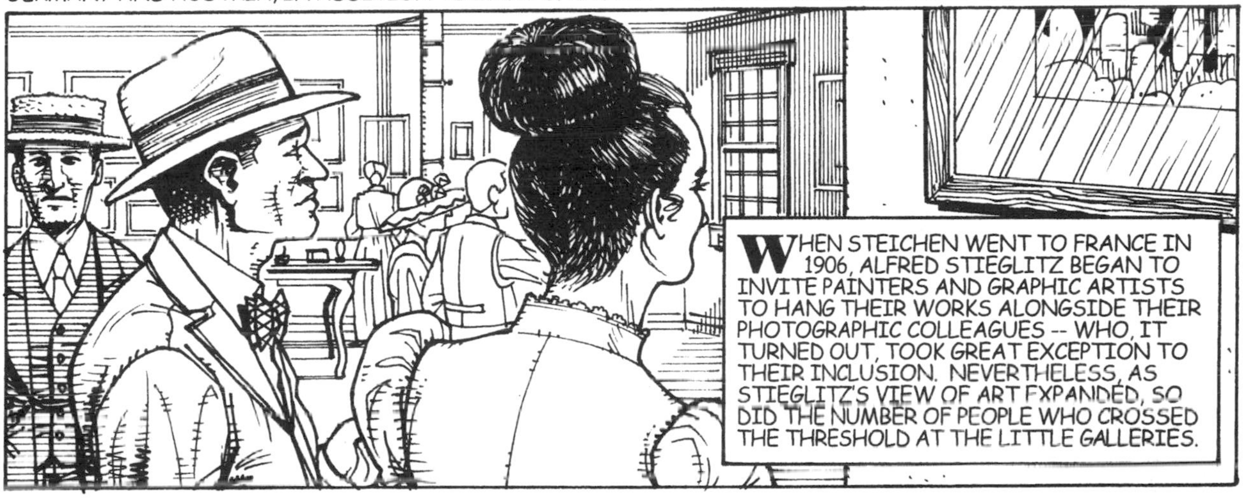
WHEN STEICHEN WENT TO FRANCE IN 1906, ALFRED STIEGLITZ BEGAN TO INVITE PAINTERS AND GRAPHIC ARTISTS TO HANG THEIR WORKS ALONGSIDE THEIR PHOTOGRAPHIC COLLEAGUES -- WHO, IT TURNED OUT, TOOK GREAT EXCEPTION TO THEIR INCLUSION. NEVERTHELESS, AS STIEGLITZ'S VIEW OF ART EXPANDED, SO DID THE NUMBER OF PEOPLE WHO CROSSED THE THRESHOLD AT THE LITTLE GALLERIES.

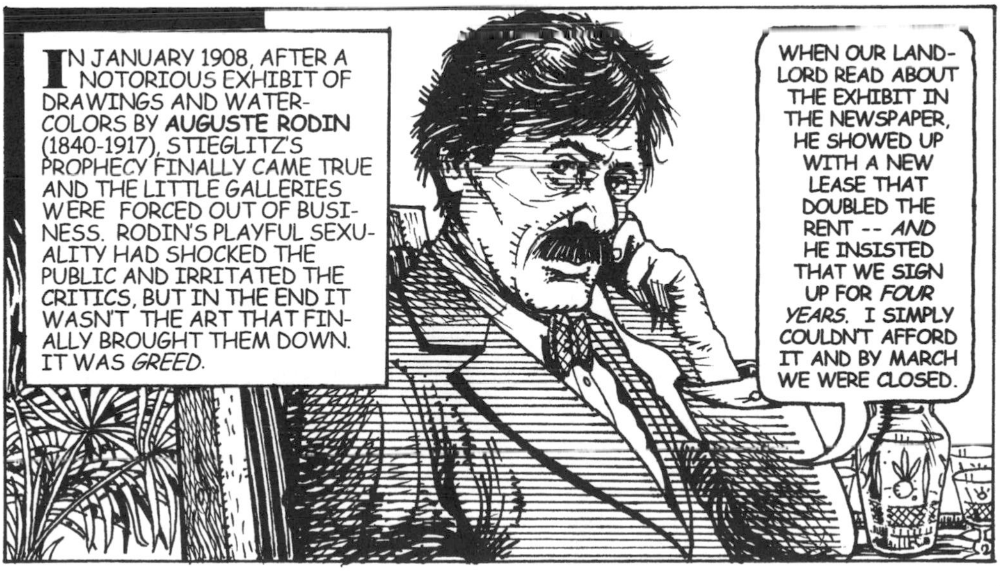
IN JANUARY 1908, AFTER A NOTORIOUS EXHIBIT OF DRAWINGS AND WATERCOLORS BY AUGUSTE RODIN (1840-1917), STIEGLITZ'S PROPHECY FINALLY CAME TRUE AND THE LITTLE GALLERIES WERE FORCED OUT OF BUSINESS. RODIN'S PLAYFUL SEXUALITY HAD SHOCKED THE PUBLIC AND IRRITATED THE CRITICS, BUT IN THE END IT WASN'T THE ART THAT FINALLY BROUGHT THEM DOWN. IT WAS GREED.
WHEN OUR LANDLORD READ ABOUT THE EXHIBIT IN THE NEWSPAPER, HE SHOWED UP WITH A NEW LEASE THAT DOUBLED THE RENT -- AND HE INSISTED THAT WE SIGN UP FOR FOUR YEARS. I SIMPLY COULDN'T AFFORD IT AND BY MARCH WE WERE CLOSED.

YEARS LATER, **GEORGIA O'KEEFFE** (1887-1986) RECALLED GOING TO THE RODIN SHOW WHILE A STUDENT.

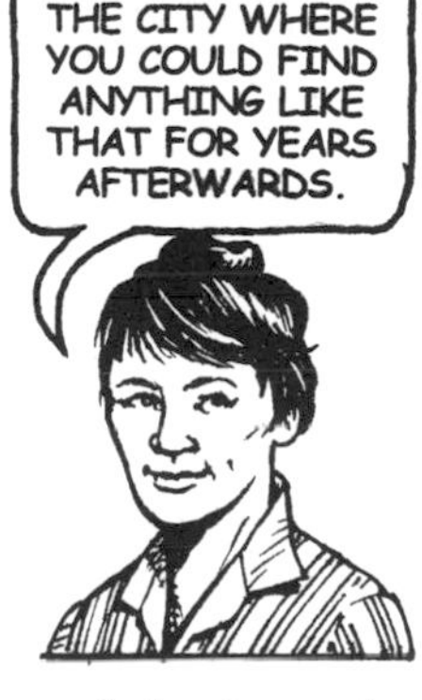
THERE WERE NO OTHER PLACES IN THE CITY WHERE YOU COULD FIND ANYTHING LIKE THAT FOR YEARS AFTERWARDS.

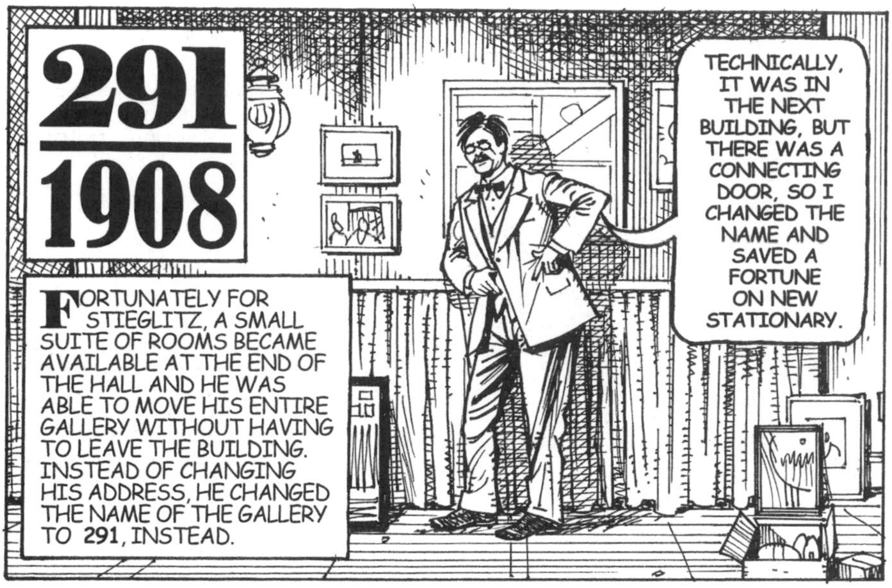
291
1908
FORTUNATELY FOR STIEGLITZ, A SMALL SUITE OF ROOMS BECAME AVAILABLE AT THE END OF THE HALL AND HE WAS ABLE TO MOVE HIS ENTIRE GALLERY WITHOUT HAVING TO LEAVE THE BUILDING. INSTEAD OF CHANGING HIS ADDRESS, HE CHANGED THE NAME OF THE GALLERY TO 291, INSTEAD.
TECHNICALLY, IT WAS IN THE NEXT BUILDING, BUT THERE WAS A CONNECTING DOOR, SO I CHANGED THE NAME AND SAVED A FORTUNE ON NEW STATIONARY.

THE OTHER PHOTO-SECESSIONISTS HADN'T LIKED ALFRED'S IDEA OF SHARING THE GALLERY WITH PAINTERS AND CHOSE NOT TO FOLLOW HIM DOWN THE HALL TO HIS NEW LOCATION. "THEIR RAMPANT JEALOUSY WAS IN DANGER OF HARMING EVERYTHING I WAS ATTEMPTING TO BUILD," HE SAID. "IT WAS TIME TO EVOLVE."

THE NEW ATTITUDE AT 291 ATTRACTED A SMALL CROWD OF INTELLECTUALS AND ARTISTS WHO SYMPATHIZED WITH STIEGLITZ'S IDEALS. SOON HE FOUND HIMSELF SURROUNDED BY ARTISTS, JOURNALISTS AUTHORS, CRITICS AND THEIR EDITORS -- AS WELL AS THE OCCASIONAL PAYING CUSTOMER.

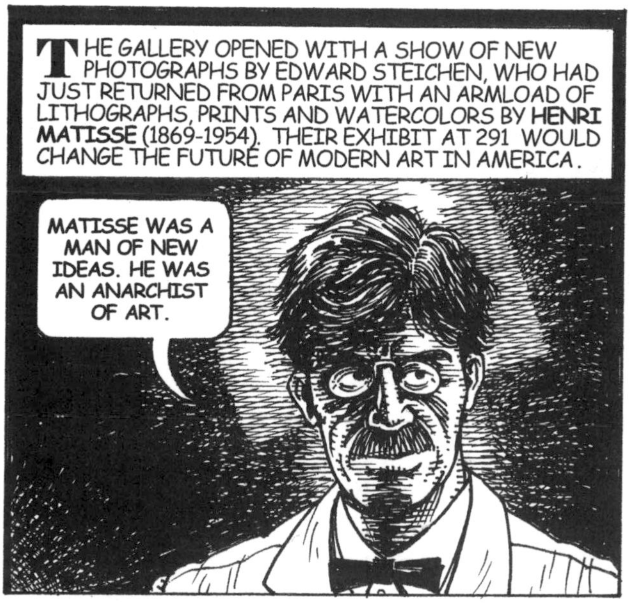
THE GALLERY OPENED WITH A SHOW OF NEW PHOTOGRAPHS BY EDWARD STEICHEN, WHO HAD JUST RETURNED FROM PARIS WITH AN ARMLOAD OF LITHOGRAPHS, PRINTS AND WATERCOLORS BY HENRI MATISSE (1869-1954). THEIR EXHIBIT AT 291 WOULD CHANGE THE FUTURE OF MODERN ART IN AMERICA.
MATISSE WAS A MAN OF NEW IDEAS. HE WAS AN ANARCHIST OF ART.

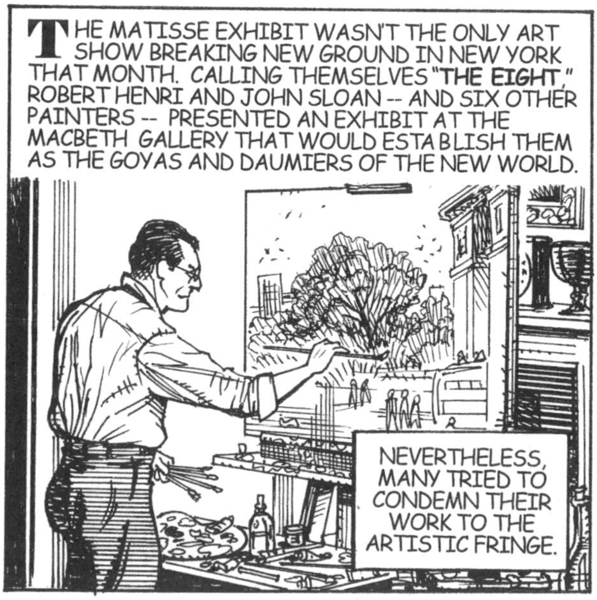
THE MATISSE EXHIBIT WASN'T THE ONLY ART SHOW BREAKING NEW GROUND IN NEW YORK THAT MONTH. CALLING THEMSELVES "THE EIGHT," ROBERT HENRI AND JOHN SLOAN -- AND SIX OTHER PAINTERS -- PRESENTED AN EXHIBIT AT THE MACBETH GALLERY THAT WOULD ESTABLISH THEM AS THE GOYAS AND DAUMIERS OF THE NEW WORLD.
NEVERTHELESS, MANY TRIED TO CONDEMN THEIR WORK TO THE ARTISTIC FRINGE.

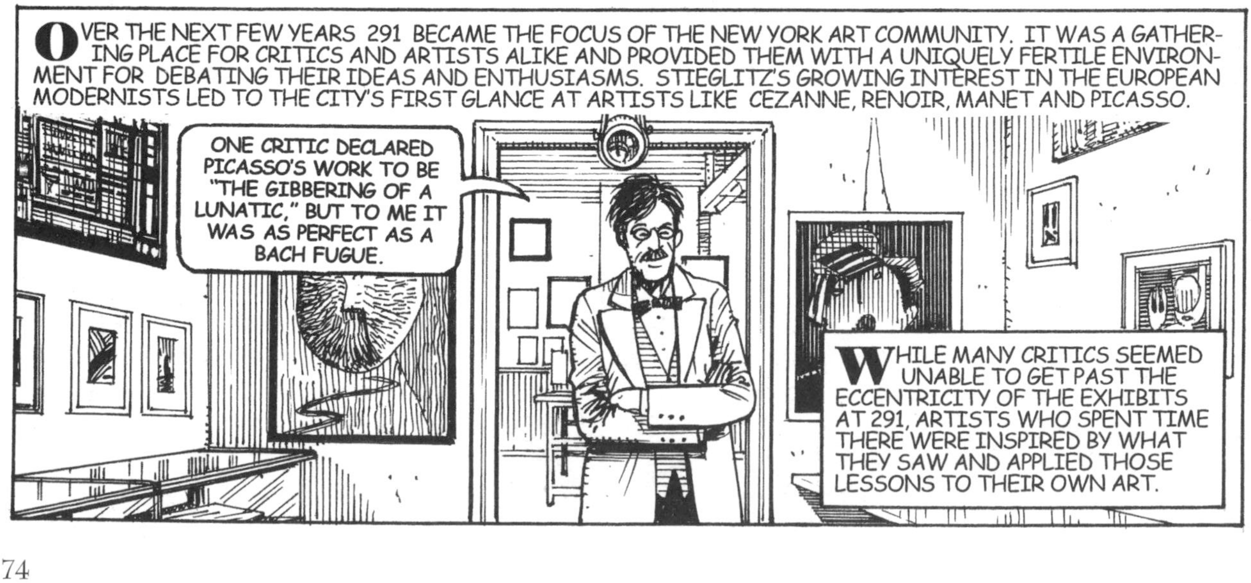
OVER THE NEXT FEW YEARS 291 BECAME THE FOCUS OF THE NEW YORK ART COMMUNITY. IT WAS A GATHERING PLACE FOR CRITICS AND ARTISTS ALIKE AND PROVIDED THEM WITH A UNIQUELY FERTILE ENVIRONMENT FOR DEBATING THEIR IDEAS AND ENTHUSIASMS. STIEGLITZ'S GROWING INTEREST IN THE EUROPEAN MODERNISTS LED TO THE CITY'S FIRST GLANCE AT ARTISTS LIKE CEZANNE, RENOIR, MANET AND PICASSO.
ONE CRITIC DECLARED PICASSO'S WORK TO BE "THE GIBBERING OF A LUNATIC," BUT TO ME IT WAS AS PERFECT AS A BACH FUGUE.
WHILE MANY CRITICS SEEMED UNABLE TO GET PAST THE ECCENTRICITY OF THE EXHIBITS AT 291, ARTISTS WHO SPENT TIME THERE WERE INSPIRED BY WHAT THEY SAW AND APPLIED THOSE LESSONS TO THEIR OWN ART.

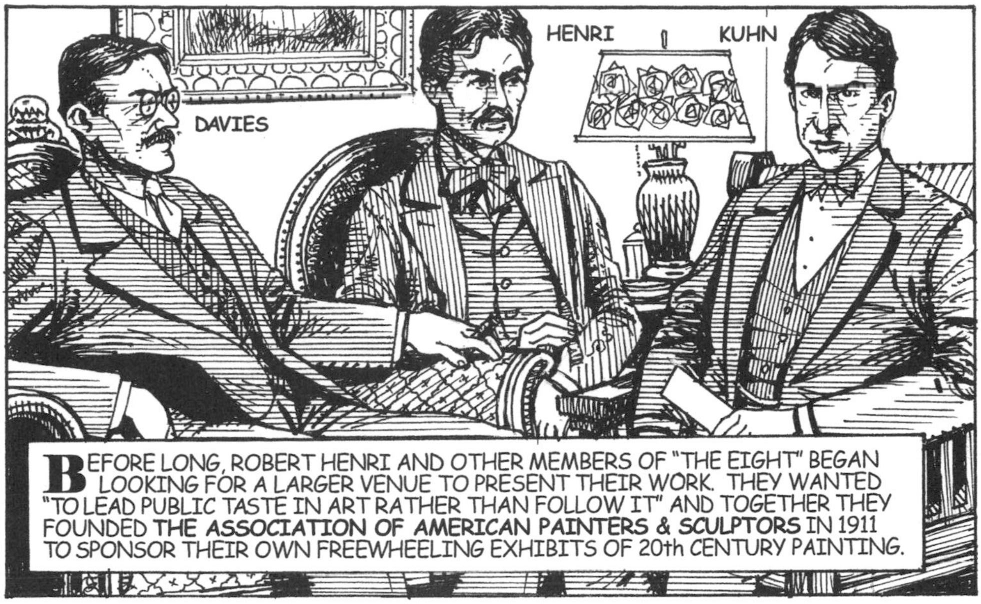
HENRI
KUHN
DAVIES
BEFORE LONG, ROBERT HENRI AND OTHER MEMBERS OF "THE EIGHT" BEGAN LOOKING FOR A LARGER VENUE TO PRESENT THEIR WORK. THEY WANTED "TO LEAD PUBLIC TASTE IN ART RATHER THAN FOLLOW IT" AND TOGETHER THEY FOUNDED **THE ASSOCIATION OF AMERICAN PAINTERS & SCULPTORS** IN 1911 TO SPONSOR THEIR OWN FREEWHEELING EXHIBITS OF 20th CENTURY PAINTING.

HENRI PASSED ON THE HONOR OF BEING THEIR FIRST PRESIDENT, NOMINATING **ARTHUR B. DAVIES** (1862-1928) FOR THE JOB. DAVIES -- YET ANOTHER ONE OF "THE EIGHT" -- THEN APPOINTED HIS DISCIPLE, **WALT KUHN** (1877-1928) AS THE GROUP'S EXECUTIVE SECRETARY BECAUSE OF HIS CONSIDERABLE ORGANIZATIONAL SKILLS AND HIS MANY ART WORLD CONTACTS.

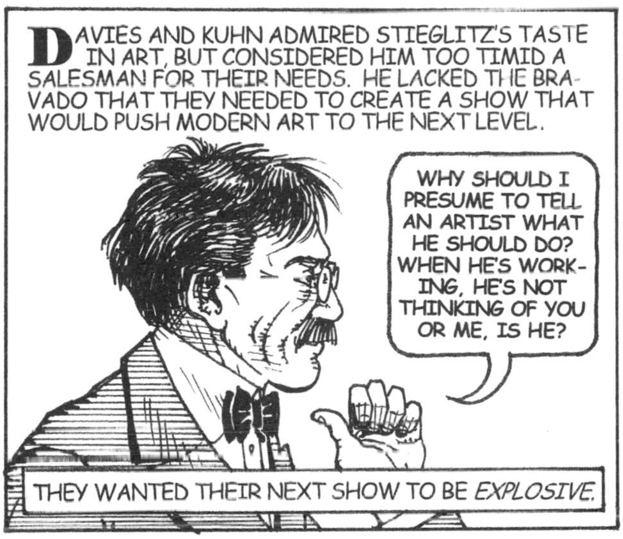
DAVIES AND KUHN ADMIRED STIEGLITZ'S TASTE IN ART, BUT CONSIDERED HIM TOO TIMID A SALESMAN FOR THEIR NEEDS. HE LACKED THE BRAVADO THAT THEY NEEDED TO CREATE A SHOW THAT WOULD PUSH MODERN ART TO THE NEXT LEVEL.
WHY SHOULD I PRESUME TO TELL AN ARTIST WHAT HE SHOULD DO? WHEN HE'S WORKING, HE'S NOT THINKING OF YOU OR ME, IS HE?
THEY WANTED THEIR NEXT SHOW TO BE *EXPLOSIVE.*

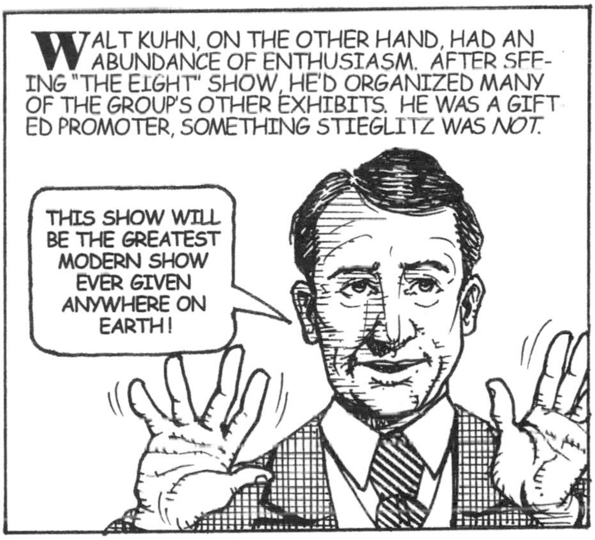
WALT KUHN, ON THE OTHER HAND, HAD AN ABUNDANCE OF ENTHUSIASM. AFTER SEEING "THE EIGHT" SHOW, HE'D ORGANIZED MANY OF THE GROUP'S OTHER EXHIBITS. HE WAS A GIFTED PROMOTER, SOMETHING STIEGLITZ WAS *NOT.*
THIS SHOW WILL BE THE GREATEST MODERN SHOW EVER GIVEN ANYWHERE ON EARTH!

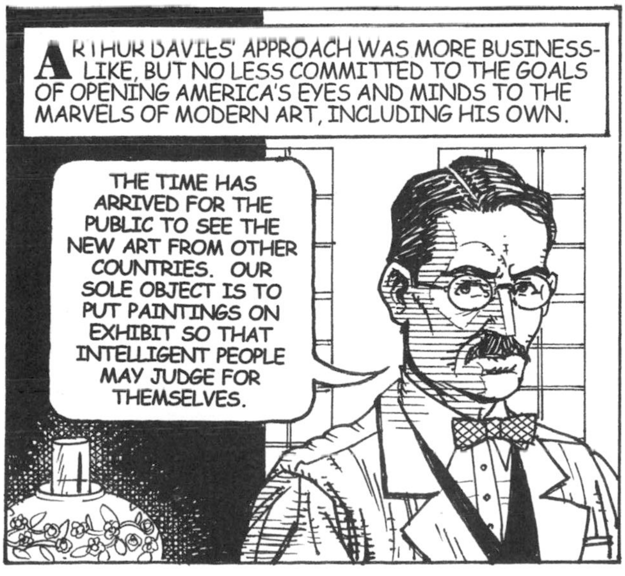
ARTHUR DAVIES' APPROACH WAS MORE BUSINESSLIKE, BUT NO LESS COMMITTED TO THE GOALS OF OPENING AMERICA'S EYES AND MINDS TO THE MARVELS OF MODERN ART, INCLUDING HIS OWN.
THE TIME HAS ARRIVED FOR THE PUBLIC TO SEE THE NEW ART FROM OTHER COUNTRIES. OUR SOLE OBJECT IS TO PUT PAINTINGS ON EXHIBIT SO THAT INTELLIGENT PEOPLE MAY JUDGE FOR THEMSELVES.

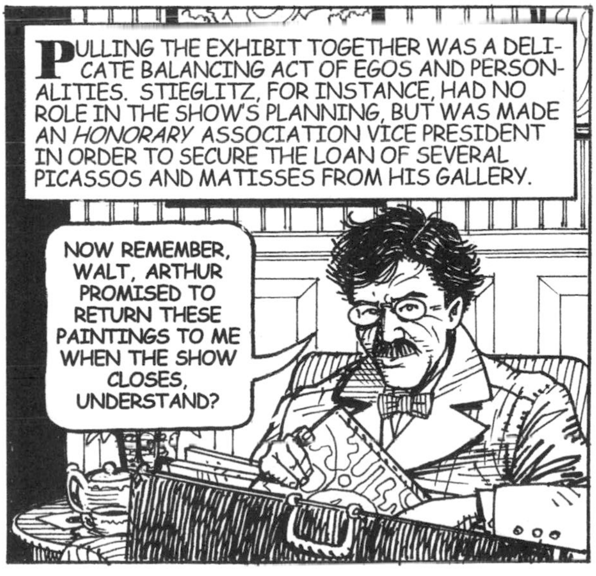
PULLING THE EXHIBIT TOGETHER WAS A DELICATE BALANCING ACT OF EGOS AND PERSONALITIES. STIEGLITZ, FOR INSTANCE, HAD NO ROLE IN THE SHOW'S PLANNING, BUT WAS MADE AN *HONORARY* ASSOCIATION VICE PRESIDENT IN ORDER TO SECURE THE LOAN OF SEVERAL PICASSOS AND MATISSES FROM HIS GALLERY.
NOW REMEMBER, WALT, ARTHUR PROMISED TO RETURN THESE PAINTINGS TO ME WHEN THE SHOW CLOSES, UNDERSTAND?

BY THE END OF 1912 KUHN'S PROMOTIONAL CAMPAIGN WAS IN HIGH GEAR AND THE ASSOCIATION'S AMBITION WAS MATCHED ONLY BY THEIR EARNEST OPTIMISM. THOUSANDS OF POSTERS, POSTCARDS, AND LAPEL PINS FLOODED NEW YORK CITY'S NEIGHBORHOODS -- THEY EVEN ADVERTISED ON THE STREET CARS.

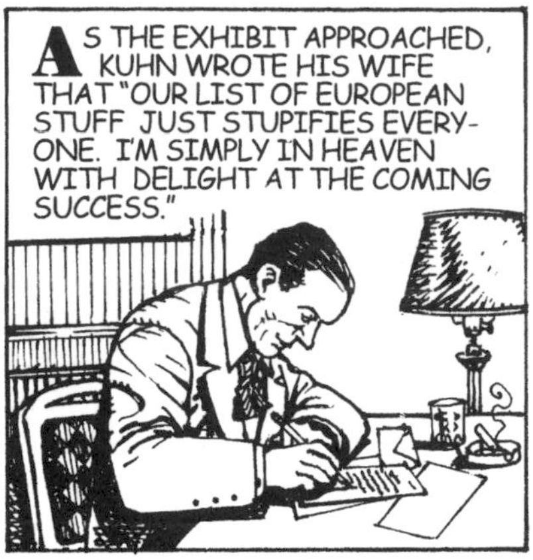
AS THE EXHIBIT APPROACHED, KUHN WROTE HIS WIFE THAT "OUR LIST OF EUROPEAN STUFF JUST STUPIFIES EVERYONE. I'M SIMPLY IN HEAVEN WITH DELIGHT AT THE COMING SUCCESS."

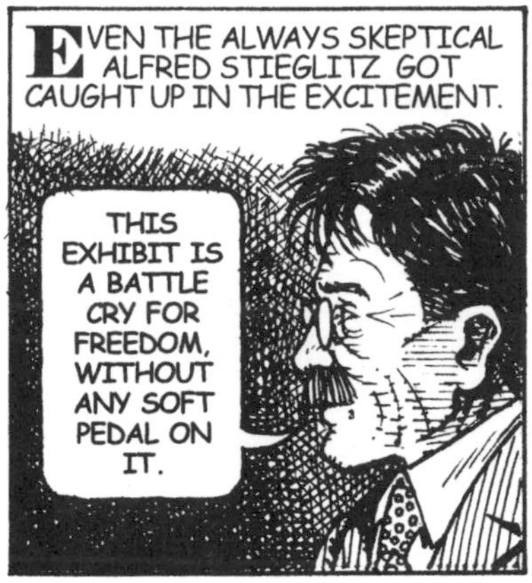
EVEN THE ALWAYS SKEPTICAL ALFRED STIEGLITZ GOT CAUGHT UP IN THE EXCITEMENT.
THIS EXHIBIT IS A BATTLE CRY FOR FREEDOM, WITHOUT ANY SOFT PEDAL ON IT.

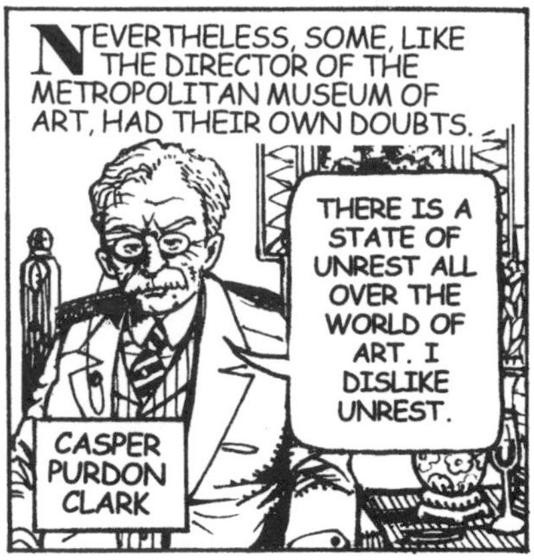
NEVERTHELESS, SOME, LIKE THE DIRECTOR OF THE METROPOLITAN MUSEUM OF ART, HAD THEIR OWN DOUBTS.
THERE IS A STATE OF UNREST ALL OVER THE WORLD OF ART. I DISLIKE UNREST.
CASPER PURDON CLARK

THE NEW YORK TIMES PREDICTED THAT THE UPCOMING **INTERNATIONAL EXHIBITION OF MODERN ART** WOULD "THROW A BOMB INTO OUR ART WORLD AND MANY GOOD LEADERS WILL GET HIT." THEY WERE RIGHT.

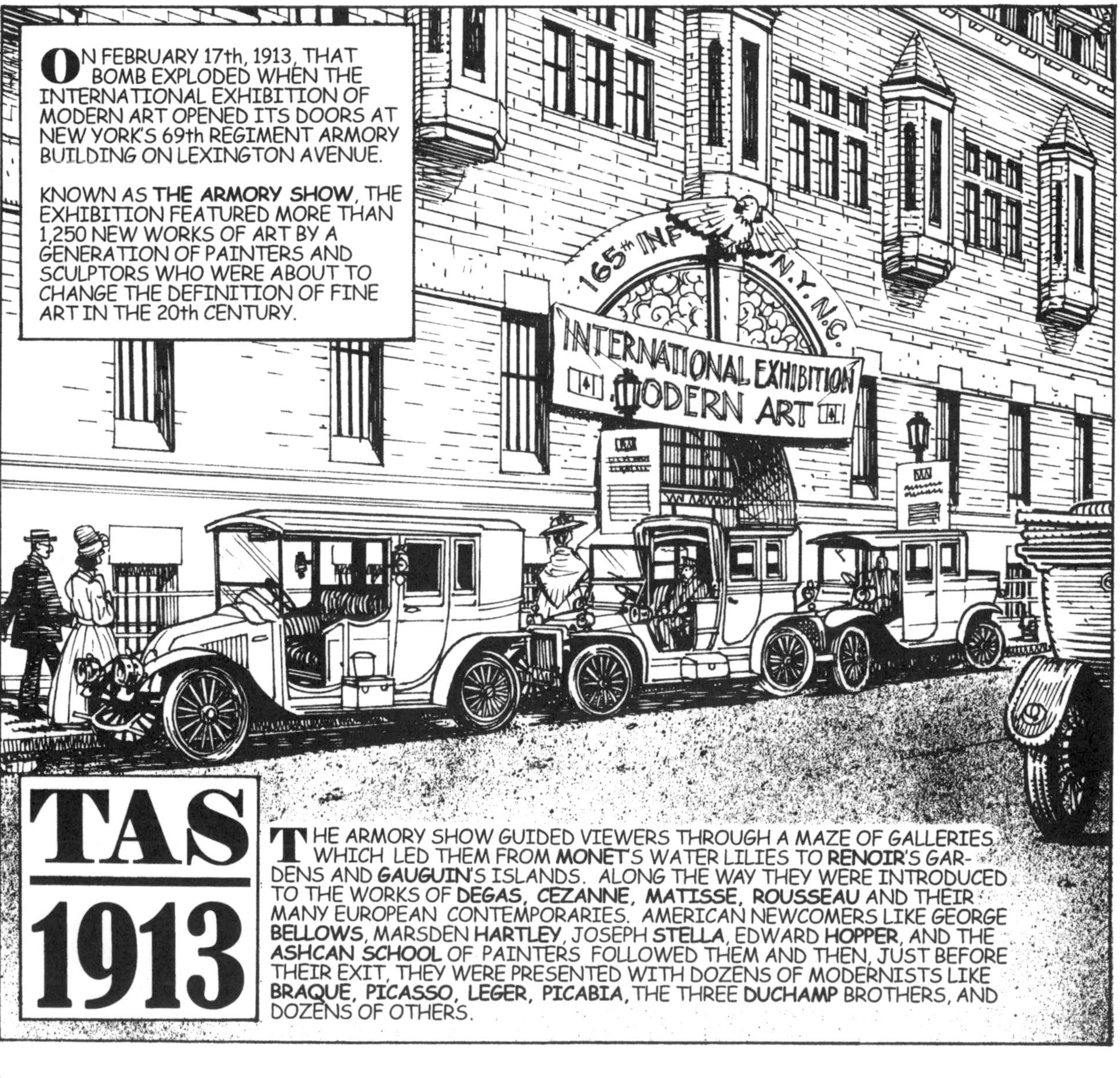
ON FEBRUARY 17th, 1913, THAT BOMB EXPLODED WHEN THE INTERNATIONAL EXHIBITION OF MODERN ART OPENED ITS DOORS AT NEW YORK'S 69th REGIMENT ARMORY BUILDING ON LEXINGTON AVENUE.
KNOWN AS THE ARMORY SHOW, THE EXHIBITION FEATURED MORE THAN 1,250 NEW WORKS OF ART BY A GENERATION OF PAINTERS AND SCULPTORS WHO WERE ABOUT TO CHANGE THE DEFINITION OF FINE ART IN THE 20th CENTURY.
165th INF
N.Y.N.G.
INTERNATIONAL EXHIBITION
MODERN ART
TAS
1913
THE ARMORY SHOW GUIDED VIEWERS THROUGH A MAZE OF GALLERIES WHICH LED THEM FROM MONET'S WATER LILIES TO RENOIR'S GARDENS AND GAUGUIN'S ISLANDS. ALONG THE WAY THEY WERE INTRODUCED TO THE WORKS OF DEGAS, CEZANNE, MATISSE, ROUSSEAU AND THEIR MANY EUROPEAN CONTEMPORARIES. AMERICAN NEWCOMERS LIKE GEORGE BELLOWS, MARSDEN HARTLEY, JOSEPH STELLA, EDWARD HOPPER, AND THE ASHCAN SCHOOL OF PAINTERS FOLLOWED THEM AND THEN, JUST BEFORE THEIR EXIT, THEY WERE PRESENTED WITH DOZENS OF MODERNISTS LIKE BRAQUE, PICASSO, LEGER, PICABIA, THE THREE DUCHAMP BROTHERS, AND DOZENS OF OTHERS.

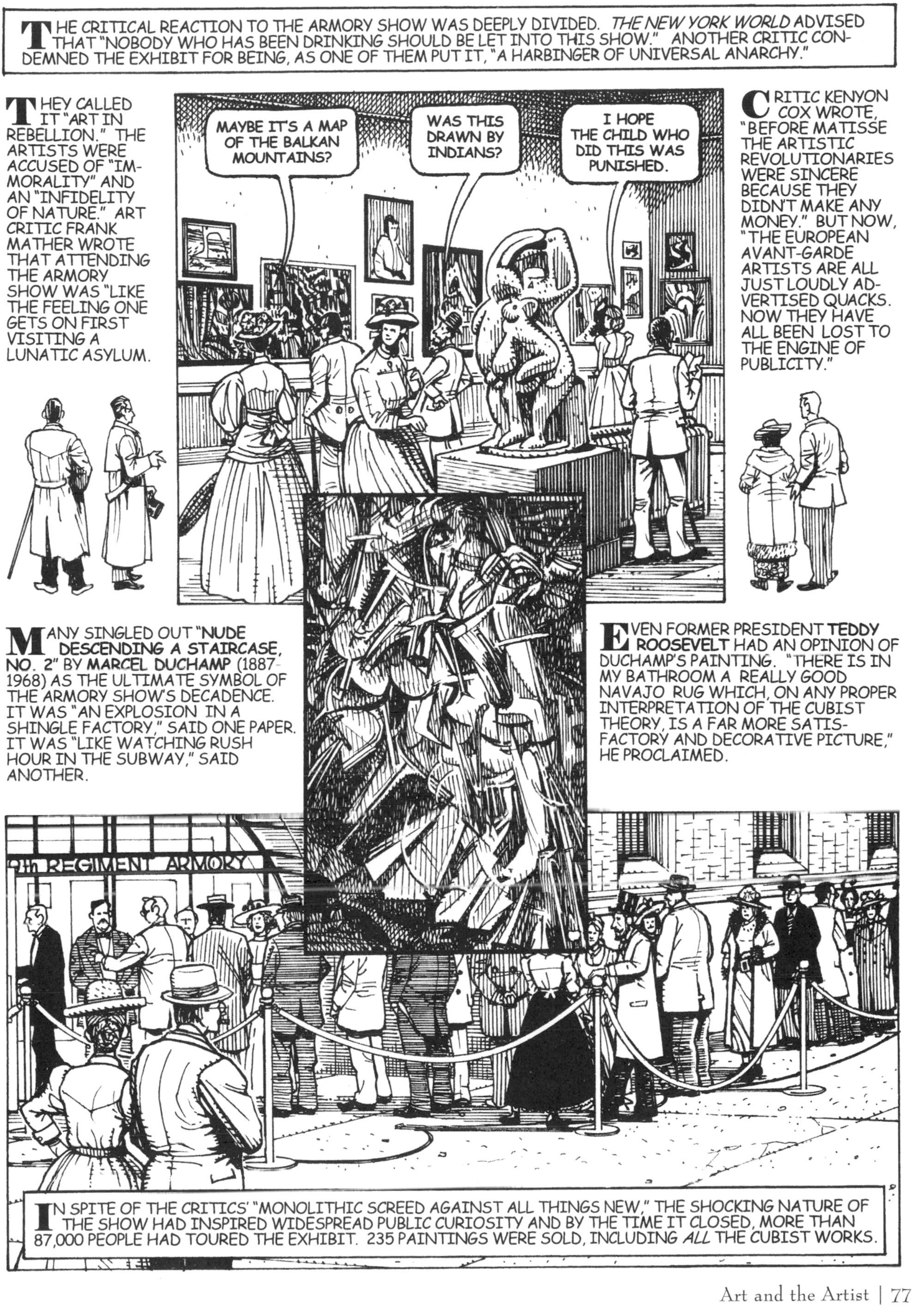
THE CRITICAL REACTION TO THE ARMORY SHOW WAS DEEPLY DIVIDED. *THE NEW YORK WORLD* ADVISED THAT "NOBODY WHO HAS BEEN DRINKING SHOULD BE LET INTO THIS SHOW." ANOTHER CRITIC CONDEMNED THE EXHIBIT FOR BEING, AS ONE OF THEM PUT IT, "A HARBINGER OF UNIVERSAL ANARCHY."
THEY CALLED IT "ART IN REBELLION." THE ARTISTS WERE ACCUSED OF "IMMORALITY" AND AN "INFIDELITY OF NATURE." ART CRITIC FRANK MATHER WROTE THAT ATTENDING THE ARMORY SHOW WAS "LIKE THE FEELING ONE GETS ON FIRST VISITING A LUNATIC ASYLUM.
MAYBE IT'S A MAP OF THE BALKAN MOUNTAINS?
WAS THIS DRAWN BY INDIANS?
I HOPE THE CHILD WHO DID THIS WAS PUNISHED.
CRITIC KENYON COX WROTE, "BEFORE MATISSE THE ARTISTIC REVOLUTIONARIES WERE SINCERE BECAUSE THEY DIDN'T MAKE ANY MONEY." BUT NOW, "THE EUROPEAN AVANT-GARDE ARTISTS ARE ALL JUST LOUDLY ADVERTISED QUACKS. NOW THEY HAVE ALL BEEN LOST TO THE ENGINE OF PUBLICITY."
MANY SINGLED OUT "**NUDE DESCENDING A STAIRCASE, NO. 2**" BY **MARCEL DUCHAMP** (1887-1968) AS THE ULTIMATE SYMBOL OF THE ARMORY SHOW'S DECADENCE. IT WAS "AN EXPLOSION IN A SHINGLE FACTORY," SAID ONE PAPER. IT WAS "LIKE WATCHING RUSH HOUR IN THE SUBWAY," SAID ANOTHER.
EVEN FORMER PRESIDENT **TEDDY ROOSEVELT** HAD AN OPINION OF DUCHAMP'S PAINTING. "THERE IS IN MY BATHROOM A REALLY GOOD NAVAJO RUG WHICH, ON ANY PROPER INTERPRETATION OF THE CUBIST THEORY, IS A FAR MORE SATISFACTORY AND DECORATIVE PICTURE," HE PROCLAIMED.
REGIMENT ARMORY
IN SPITE OF THE CRITICS' "MONOLITHIC SCREED AGAINST ALL THINGS NEW," THE SHOCKING NATURE OF THE SHOW HAD INSPIRED WIDESPREAD PUBLIC CURIOSITY AND BY THE TIME IT CLOSED, MORE THAN 87,000 PEOPLE HAD TOURED THE EXHIBIT. 235 PAINTINGS WERE SOLD, INCLUDING *ALL* THE CUBIST WORKS.

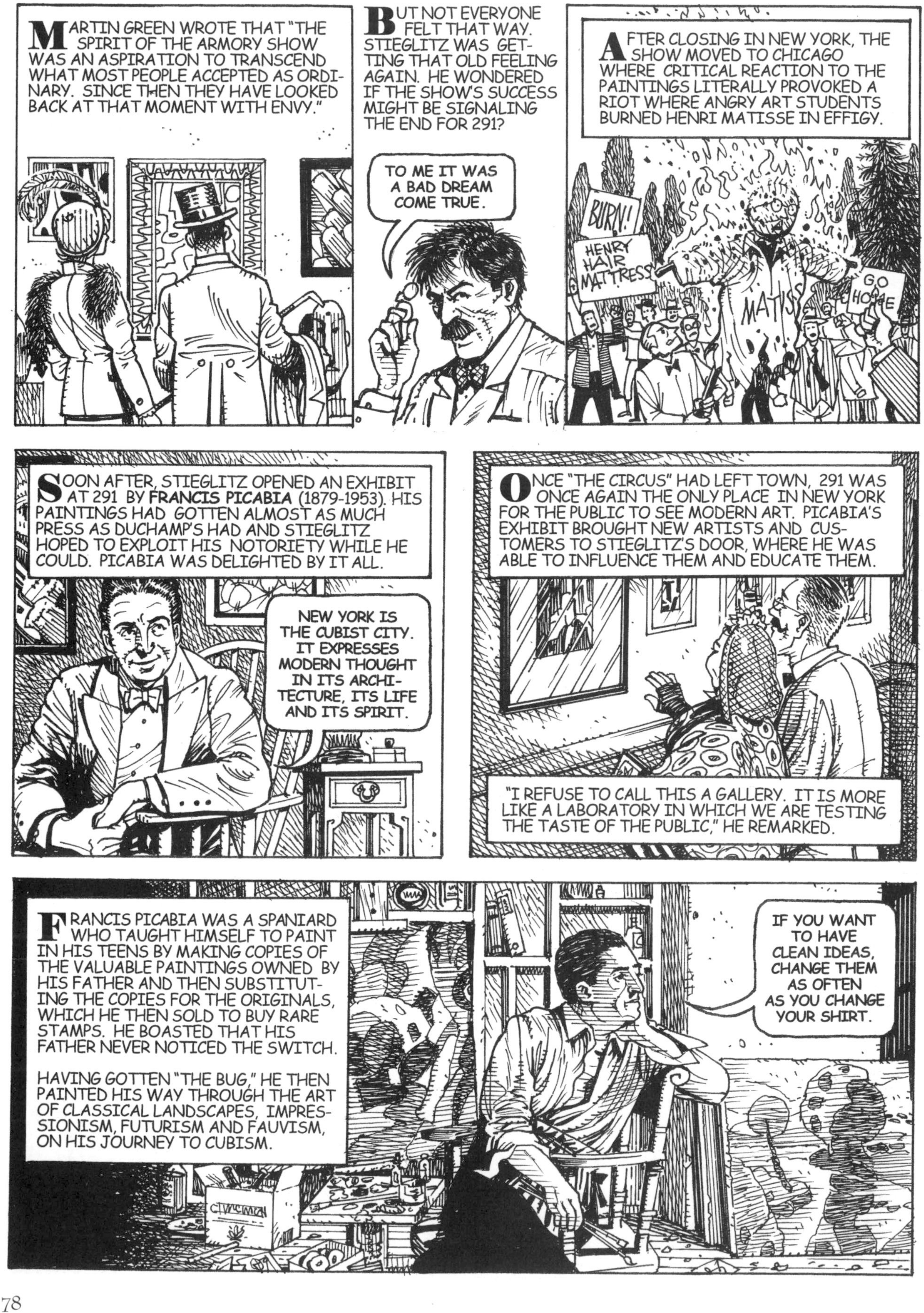
MARTIN GREEN WROTE THAT "THE SPIRIT OF THE ARMORY SHOW WAS AN ASPIRATION TO TRANSCEND WHAT MOST PEOPLE ACCEPTED AS ORDINARY. SINCE THEN THEY HAVE LOOKED BACK AT THAT MOMENT WITH ENVY."
BUT NOT EVERYONE FELT THAT WAY. STIEGLITZ WAS GETTING THAT OLD FEELING AGAIN. HE WONDERED IF THE SHOW'S SUCCESS MIGHT BE SIGNALING THE END FOR 291?
TO ME IT WAS A BAD DREAM COME TRUE.
AFTER CLOSING IN NEW YORK, THE SHOW MOVED TO CHICAGO WHERE CRITICAL REACTION TO THE PAINTINGS LITERALLY PROVOKED A RIOT WHERE ANGRY ART STUDENTS BURNED HENRI MATISSE IN EFFIGY.
BURN!
HENRY HAIR MATTRESS
GO HOME
MATISS
SOON AFTER, STIEGLITZ OPENED AN EXHIBIT AT 291 BY FRANCIS PICABIA (1879-1953). HIS PAINTINGS HAD GOTTEN ALMOST AS MUCH PRESS AS DUCHAMP'S HAD AND STIEGLITZ HOPED TO EXPLOIT HIS NOTORIETY WHILE HE COULD. PICABIA WAS DELIGHTED BY IT ALL.
NEW YORK IS THE CUBIST CITY. IT EXPRESSES MODERN THOUGHT IN ITS ARCHITECTURE, ITS LIFE AND ITS SPIRIT.
ONCE "THE CIRCUS" HAD LEFT TOWN, 291 WAS ONCE AGAIN THE ONLY PLACE IN NEW YORK FOR THE PUBLIC TO SEE MODERN ART. PICABIA'S EXHIBIT BROUGHT NEW ARTISTS AND CUSTOMERS TO STIEGLITZ'S DOOR, WHERE HE WAS ABLE TO INFLUENCE THEM AND EDUCATE THEM.
"I REFUSE TO CALL THIS A GALLERY. IT IS MORE LIKE A LABORATORY IN WHICH WE ARE TESTING THE TASTE OF THE PUBLIC," HE REMARKED.
FRANCIS PICABIA WAS A SPANIARD WHO TAUGHT HIMSELF TO PAINT IN HIS TEENS BY MAKING COPIES OF THE VALUABLE PAINTINGS OWNED BY HIS FATHER AND THEN SUBSTITUTING THE COPIES FOR THE ORIGINALS, WHICH HE THEN SOLD TO BUY RARE STAMPS. HE BOASTED THAT HIS FATHER NEVER NOTICED THE SWITCH.
HAVING GOTTEN "THE BUG," HE THEN PAINTED HIS WAY THROUGH THE ART OF CLASSICAL LANDSCAPES, IMPRESSIONISM, FUTURISM AND FAUVISM, ON HIS JOURNEY TO CUBISM.
IF YOU WANT TO HAVE CLEAN IDEAS, CHANGE THEM AS OFTEN AS YOU CHANGE YOUR SHIRT.

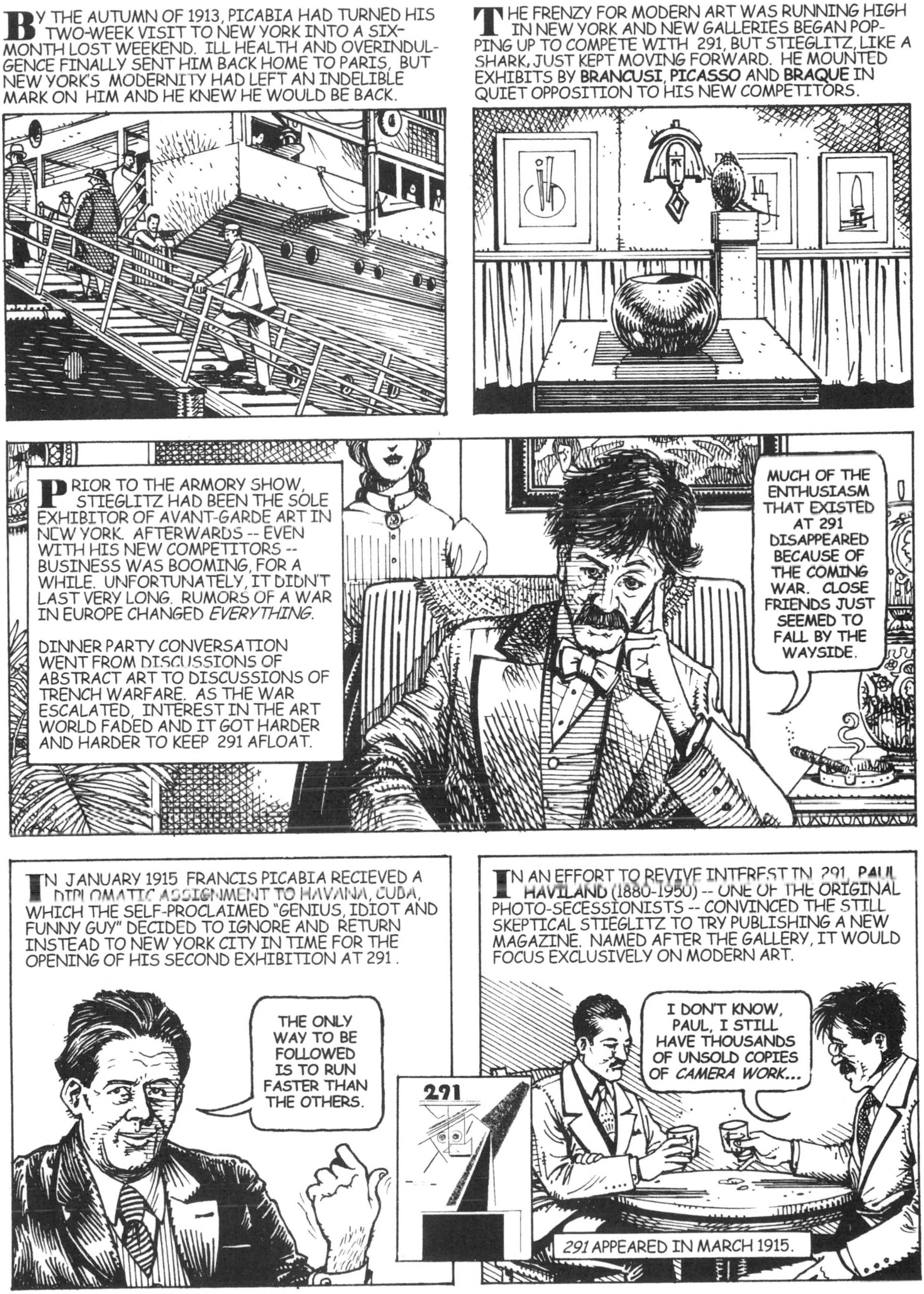
BY THE AUTUMN OF 1913, PICABIA HAD TURNED HIS TWO-WEEK VISIT TO NEW YORK INTO A SIX-MONTH LOST WEEKEND. ILL HEALTH AND OVERINDULGENCE FINALLY SENT HIM BACK HOME TO PARIS, BUT NEW YORK'S MODERNITY HAD LEFT AN INDELIBLE MARK ON HIM AND HE KNEW HE WOULD BE BACK.
THE FRENZY FOR MODERN ART WAS RUNNING HIGH IN NEW YORK AND NEW GALLERIES BEGAN POPPING UP TO COMPETE WITH 291, BUT STIEGLITZ, LIKE A SHARK, JUST KEPT MOVING FORWARD. HE MOUNTED EXHIBITS BY **BRANCUSI**, **PICASSO** AND **BRAQUE** IN QUIET OPPOSITION TO HIS NEW COMPETITORS.
PRIOR TO THE ARMORY SHOW, STIEGLITZ HAD BEEN THE SOLE EXHIBITOR OF AVANT-GARDE ART IN NEW YORK. AFTERWARDS -- EVEN WITH HIS NEW COMPETITORS -- BUSINESS WAS BOOMING, FOR A WHILE. UNFORTUNATELY, IT DIDN'T LAST VERY LONG. RUMORS OF A WAR IN EUROPE CHANGED *EVERYTHING*.
DINNER PARTY CONVERSATION WENT FROM DISCUSSIONS OF ABSTRACT ART TO DISCUSSIONS OF TRENCH WARFARE. AS THE WAR ESCALATED, INTEREST IN THE ART WORLD FADED AND IT GOT HARDER AND HARDER TO KEEP 291 AFLOAT.
MUCH OF THE ENTHUSIASM THAT EXISTED AT 291 DISAPPEARED BECAUSE OF THE COMING WAR. CLOSE FRIENDS JUST SEEMED TO FALL BY THE WAYSIDE.
IN JANUARY 1915 FRANCIS PICABIA RECIEVED A DIPLOMATIC ASSIGNMENT TO HAVANA, CUBA, WHICH THE SELF-PROCLAIMED "GENIUS, IDIOT AND FUNNY GUY" DECIDED TO IGNORE AND RETURN INSTEAD TO NEW YORK CITY IN TIME FOR THE OPENING OF HIS SECOND EXHIBITION AT 291.
THE ONLY WAY TO BE FOLLOWED IS TO RUN FASTER THAN THE OTHERS.
291
IN AN EFFORT TO REVIVE INTEREST IN 291, **PAUL HAVILAND** (1880-1950) -- ONE OF THE ORIGINAL PHOTO-SECESSIONISTS -- CONVINCED THE STILL SKEPTICAL STIEGLITZ TO TRY PUBLISHING A NEW MAGAZINE. NAMED AFTER THE GALLERY, IT WOULD FOCUS EXCLUSIVELY ON MODERN ART.
I DON'T KNOW, PAUL, I STILL HAVE THOUSANDS OF UNSOLD COPIES OF *CAMERA WORK*...
291 APPEARED IN MARCH 1915.

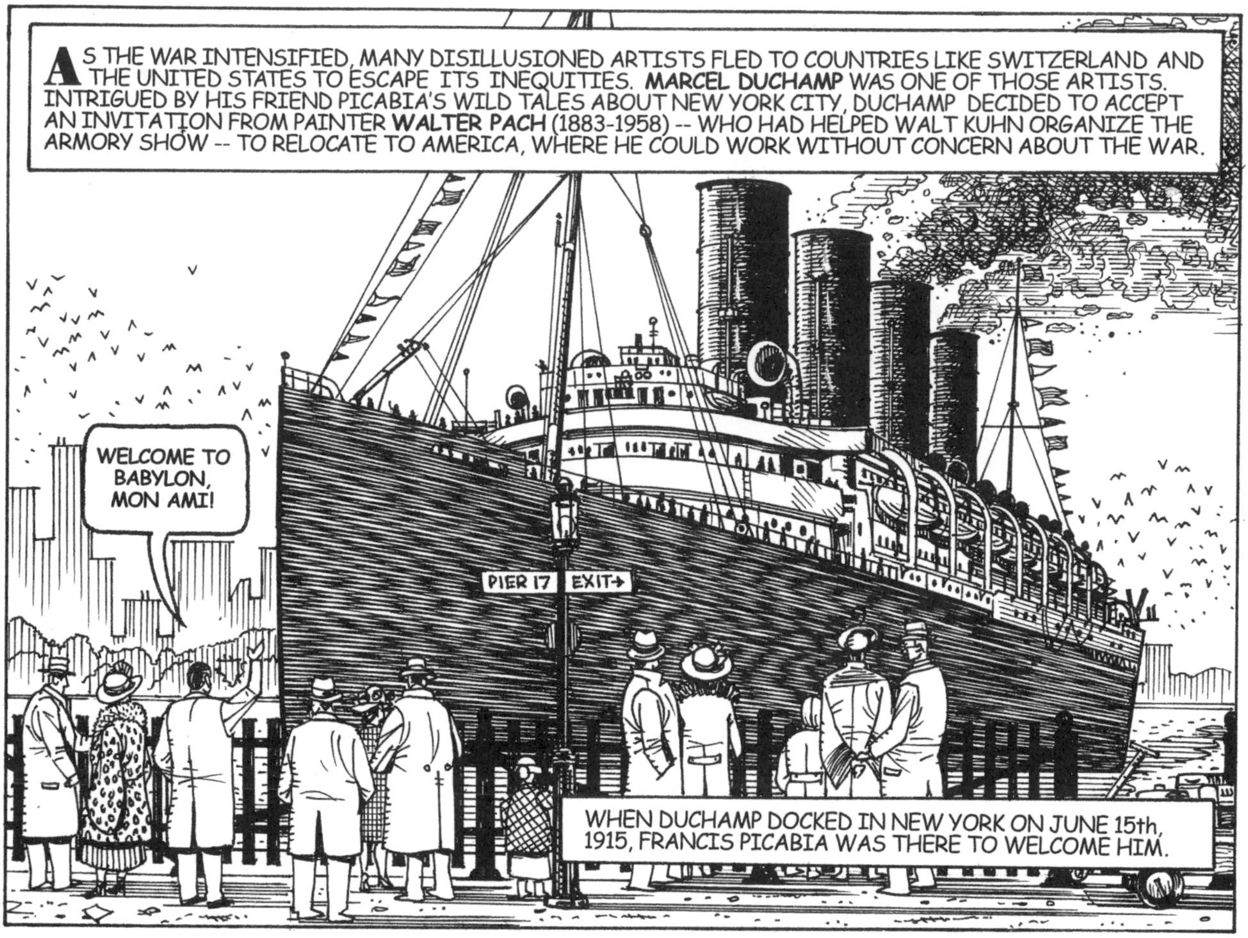
AS THE WAR INTENSIFIED, MANY DISILLUSIONED ARTISTS FLED TO COUNTRIES LIKE SWITZERLAND AND THE UNITED STATES TO ESCAPE ITS INEQUITIES. MARCEL DUCHAMP WAS ONE OF THOSE ARTISTS. INTRIGUED BY HIS FRIEND PICABIA'S WILD TALES ABOUT NEW YORK CITY, DUCHAMP DECIDED TO ACCEPT AN INVITATION FROM PAINTER WALTER PACH (1883-1958) -- WHO HAD HELPED WALT KUHN ORGANIZE THE ARMORY SHOW -- TO RELOCATE TO AMERICA, WHERE HE COULD WORK WITHOUT CONCERN ABOUT THE WAR.
WELCOME TO BABYLON, MON AMI!
PIER 17
EXIT→
WHEN DUCHAMP DOCKED IN NEW YORK ON JUNE 15th, 1915, FRANCIS PICABIA WAS THERE TO WELCOME HIM.

PICABIA HAD KNOWN MARCEL DUCHAMP FOR FIVE YEARS. THEY'D MET AT THE 1910 AUTUMN SALON IN PARIS, WHERE PICABIA HAD BEEN CHRISTENED THE *ENFANT TERRIBLE* OF THE FAUVIST PAINTERS. THEY WERE KINDRED SPIRITS WHO ENJOYED TALKING ABOUT ART AS MUCH, IF NOT MORE, THAN THEY LIKED MAKING IT.

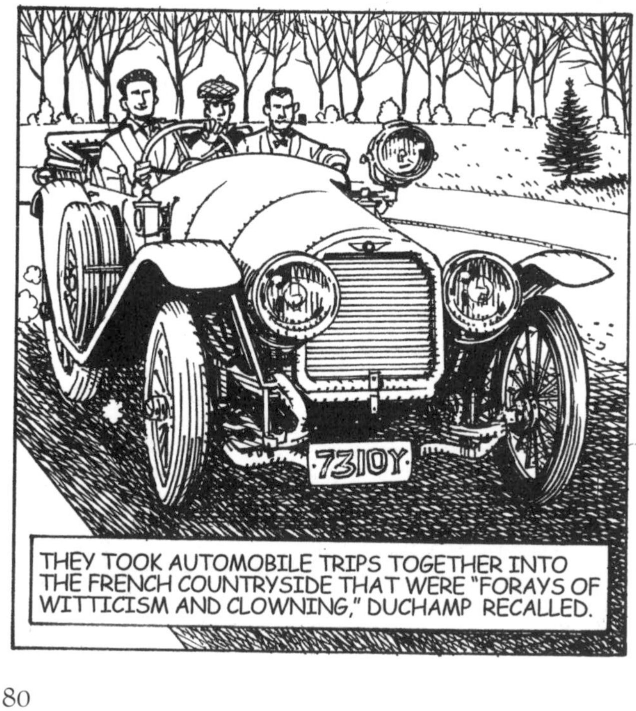
7310Y
THEY TOOK AUTOMOBILE TRIPS TOGETHER INTO THE FRENCH COUNTRYSIDE THAT WERE "FORAYS OF WITTICISM AND CLOWNING," DUCHAMP RECALLED.

THE FIRST PLACE PICABIA TOOK DUCHAMP AFTER HE'D LANDED WAS THE APARTMENT OF **LOUISE & WALTER ARENSBERG** (1878-1954) -- WEALTHY ART COLLECTORS HE'D MET THROUGH ALFRED STIEGLITZ. THEY WERE ECSTATIC TO MEET HIM AND IMMEDIATELY OFFERED THE PROMISE OF THEIR PATRONAGE.

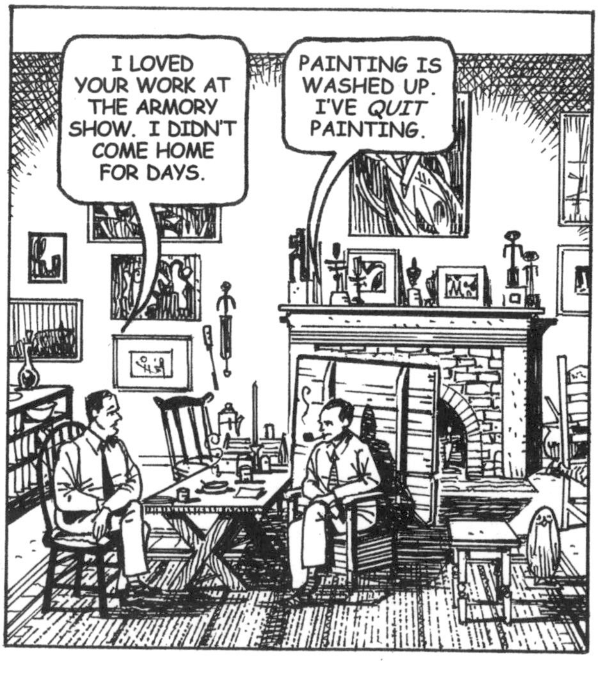
I LOVED YOUR WORK AT THE ARMORY SHOW. I DIDN'T COME HOME FOR DAYS.
PAINTING IS WASHED UP. I'VE QUIT PAINTING.

TO MOST NEW YORKERS MARCEL DUCHAMP WAS INFAMOUS FOR CREATING "NUDE DESCENDING A STAIRCASE. NO. 2," -- MODERN ART'S MOST NOTORIOUS PAINTING -- BUT THERE WAS MUCH MORE TO HIM THAN THAT. HE WAS FROM A FAMILY OF ARTISTS, INCLUDING HIS BROTHERS **JACQUES VILLON** AND **RAYMOND DUCHAMP-VILLON**, AND HAD EXPLORED IMPRESSIONISM, FAUVISM, INTIMISM AND FUTURISM, BEFORE TRYING HIS HAND AT CUBISM.

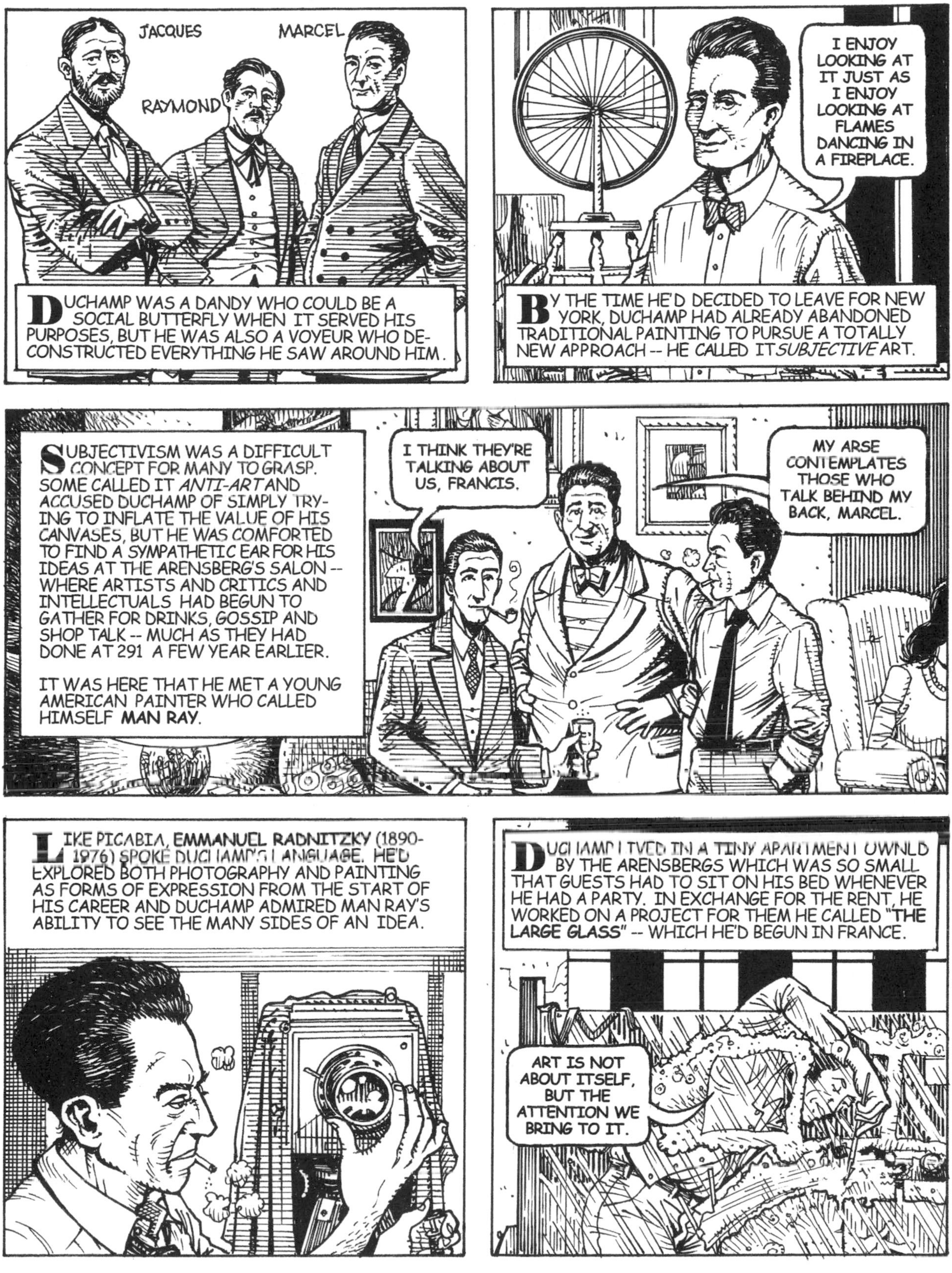
JACQUES
MARCEL
RAYMOND
DUCHAMP WAS A DANDY WHO COULD BE A SOCIAL BUTTERFLY WHEN IT SERVED HIS PURPOSES, BUT HE WAS ALSO A VOYEUR WHO DE-CONSTRUCTED EVERYTHING HE SAW AROUND HIM.
I ENJOY LOOKING AT IT JUST AS I ENJOY LOOKING AT FLAMES DANCING IN A FIREPLACE.
BY THE TIME HE'D DECIDED TO LEAVE FOR NEW YORK, DUCHAMP HAD ALREADY ABANDONED TRADITIONAL PAINTING TO PURSUE A TOTALLY NEW APPROACH -- HE CALLED IT *SUBJECTIVE* ART.
SUBJECTIVISM WAS A DIFFICULT CONCEPT FOR MANY TO GRASP. SOME CALLED IT *ANTI-ART* AND ACCUSED DUCHAMP OF SIMPLY TRYING TO INFLATE THE VALUE OF HIS CANVASES, BUT HE WAS COMFORTED TO FIND A *SYMPATHETIC EAR* FOR HIS IDEAS AT THE ARENSBERG'S SALON -- WHERE ARTISTS AND CRITICS AND INTELLECTUALS HAD BEGUN TO GATHER FOR DRINKS, GOSSIP AND SHOP TALK -- MUCH AS THEY HAD DONE AT 291 A FEW YEAR EARLIER.
IT WAS HERE THAT HE MET A YOUNG AMERICAN PAINTER WHO CALLED HIMSELF **MAN RAY**.
I THINK THEY'RE TALKING ABOUT US, FRANCIS.
MY ARSE CONTEMPLATES THOSE WHO TALK BEHIND MY BACK, MARCEL.
LIKE PICABIA, **EMMANUEL RADNITZKY** (1890-1976) SPOKE DUCHAMP'S LANGUAGE. HE'D EXPLORED BOTH PHOTOGRAPHY AND PAINTING AS FORMS OF EXPRESSION FROM THE START OF HIS CAREER AND DUCHAMP ADMIRED MAN RAY'S ABILITY TO SEE THE MANY SIDES OF AN IDEA.
DUCHAMP LIVED IN A TINY APARTMENT OWNED BY THE ARENSBERGS WHICH WAS SO SMALL THAT GUESTS HAD TO SIT ON HIS BED WHENEVER HE HAD A PARTY. IN EXCHANGE FOR THE RENT, HE WORKED ON A PROJECT FOR THEM HE CALLED "**THE LARGE GLASS**" -- WHICH HE'D BEGUN IN FRANCE.
ART IS NOT ABOUT ITSELF, BUT THE ATTENTION WE BRING TO IT.

WHILE DUCHAMP AND MAN RAY WERE PURSUING THEIR NEW KIND OF ART, PICABIA WAS MAKING WHAT HE CALLED **MECHANOMORPHS**. THEY WERE PORTRAITS THAT USED MACHINE PARTS TO REFLECT THEIR SUBJECT'S FEATURES AND PERSONALITIES.

THE YEAR ENDED WITH AN EXHIBIT OF MAN RAY'S CUBIST PAINTINGS. HE'D BEGUN TAKING ART CLASSES IN 1909 FROM ROBERT HENRI AND CONTINUED TO PAINT FOR THE REST OF HIS LIFE, EVEN AFTER HIS LATER ACCLAIM AS A PHOTOGRAPHER.

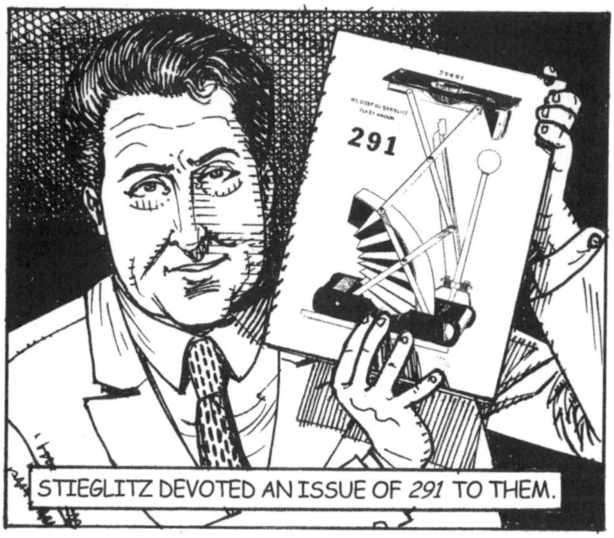
291
STIEGLITZ DEVOTED AN ISSUE OF *291* TO THEM.

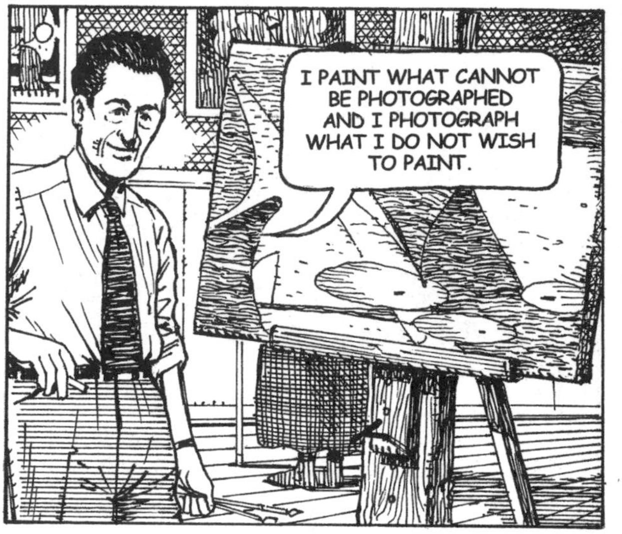
I PAINT WHAT CANNOT BE PHOTOGRAPHED AND I PHOTOGRAPH WHAT I DO NOT WISH TO PAINT.

THE ARENSBERG'S SALON BECAME THE NEW SOCIAL CENTER OF NEW YORK'S ART SCENE. THEIR PARTIES ATTRACTED A YOUNGER GROUP OF ARTISTS AND WRITERS THAN THE OLD GUARD WHO MET AT 291. AS THEIR RESIDENT *GENIUS*, DUCHAMP MET MANY OF THE MEMORABLE ARTISTS AND ECCENTRICS OF THE DAY. WOMEN, IN PARTICULAR, WERE TITILLATED BY HIS INTELLIGENCE, HIS TALENT, HIS HUMOR AND, OF COURSE, HIS ACCENT.

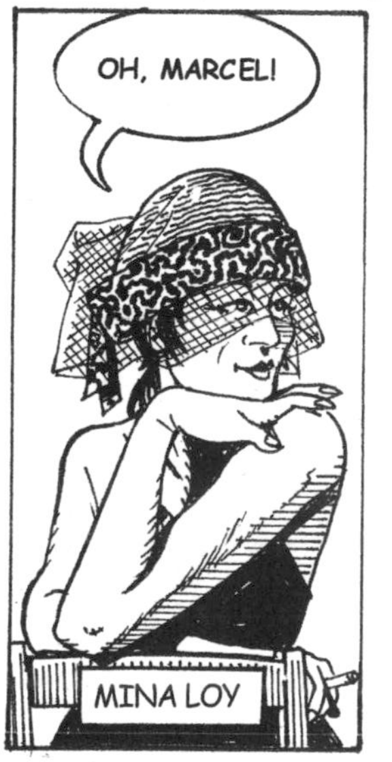
OH, MARCEL!
MINA LOY

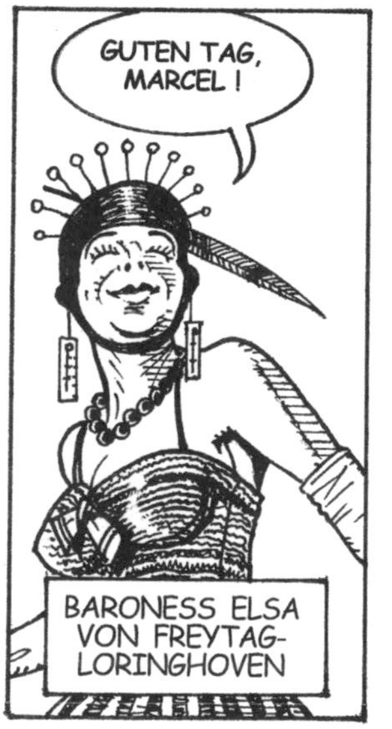
GUTEN TAG, MARCEL!
BARONESS ELSA VON FREYTAG-LORINGHOVEN

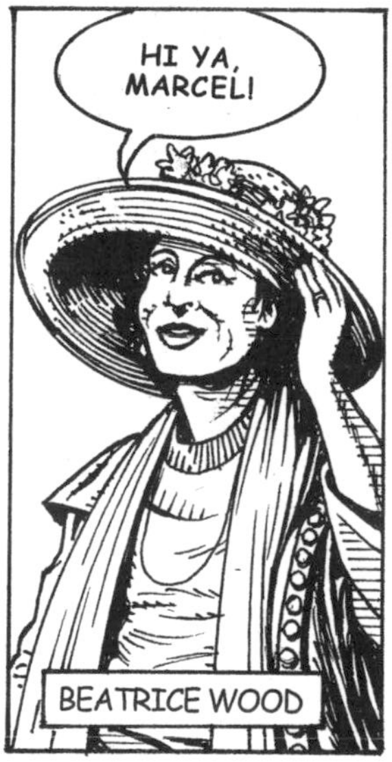
HI YA, MARCEL!
BEATRICE WOOD

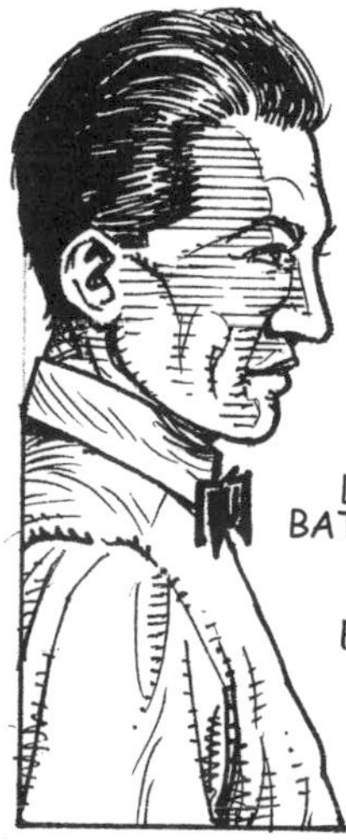

"I TOLD THEM ALL THAT I HAD CHOSEN TO LIVE A CELIBATE LIFE, BUT IT JUST SEEMED TO ENCOURAGE THEM."

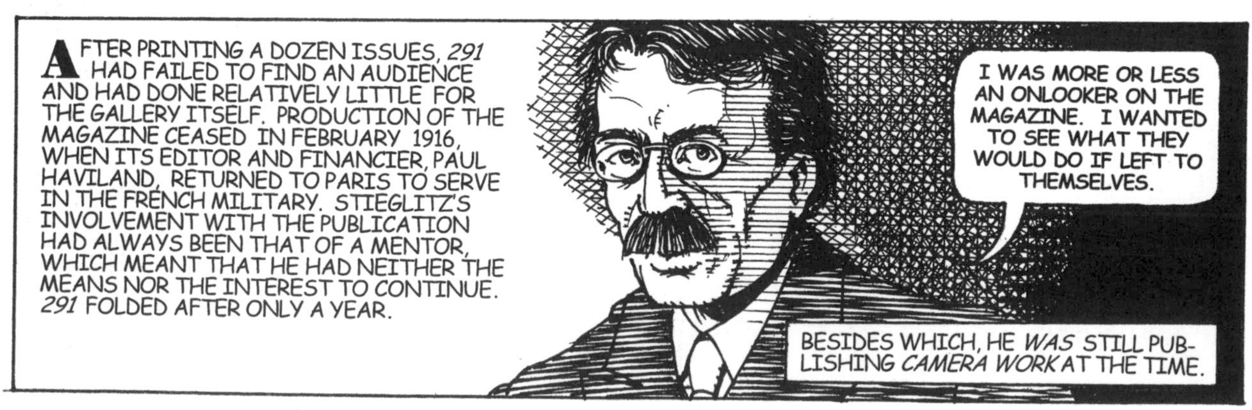
AFTER PRINTING A DOZEN ISSUES, *291* HAD FAILED TO FIND AN AUDIENCE AND HAD DONE RELATIVELY LITTLE FOR THE GALLERY ITSELF. PRODUCTION OF THE MAGAZINE CEASED IN FEBRUARY 1916, WHEN ITS EDITOR AND FINANCIER, PAUL HAVILAND, RETURNED TO PARIS TO SERVE IN THE FRENCH MILITARY. STIEGLITZ'S INVOLVEMENT WITH THE PUBLICATION HAD ALWAYS BEEN THAT OF A MENTOR, WHICH MEANT THAT HE HAD NEITHER THE MEANS NOR THE INTEREST TO CONTINUE. *291* FOLDED AFTER ONLY A YEAR.
I WAS MORE OR LESS AN ONLOOKER ON THE MAGAZINE. I WANTED TO SEE WHAT THEY WOULD DO IF LEFT TO THEMSELVES.
BESIDES WHICH, HE *WAS* STILL PUBLISHING *CAMERA WORK* AT THE TIME.

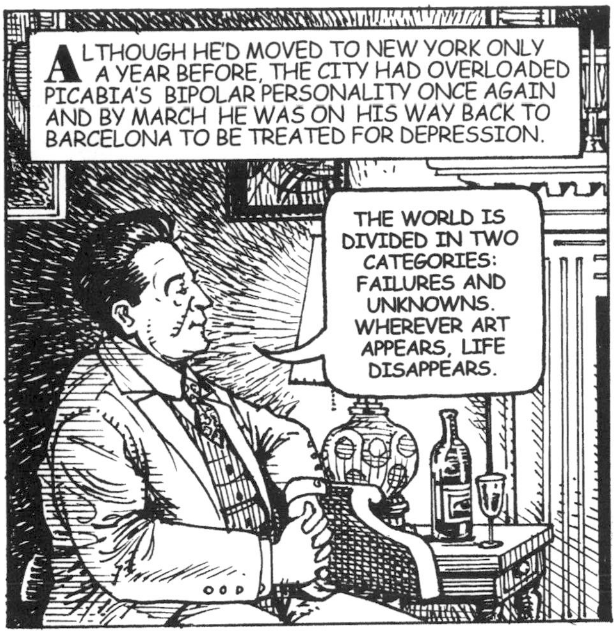
ALTHOUGH HE'D MOVED TO NEW YORK ONLY A YEAR BEFORE, THE CITY HAD OVERLOADED PICABIA'S BIPOLAR PERSONALITY ONCE AGAIN AND BY MARCH HE WAS ON HIS WAY BACK TO BARCELONA TO BE TREATED FOR DEPRESSION.
THE WORLD IS DIVIDED IN TWO CATEGORIES: FAILURES AND UNKNOWNS. WHEREVER ART APPEARS, LIFE DISAPPEARS.

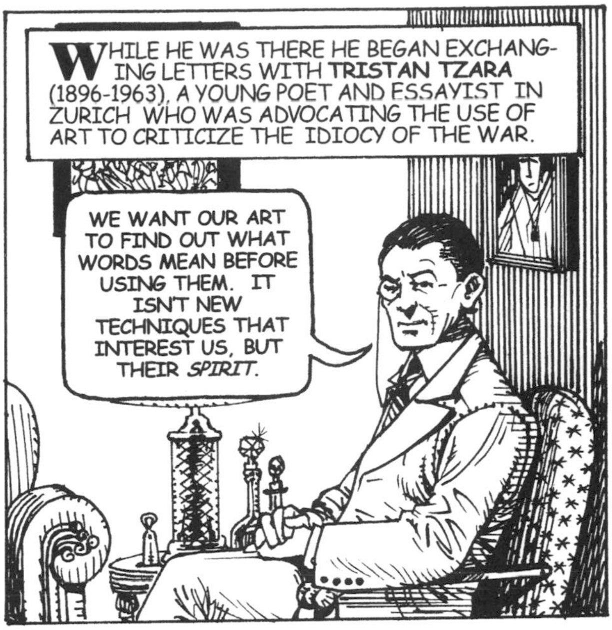
WHILE HE WAS THERE HE BEGAN EXCHANGING LETTERS WITH **TRISTAN TZARA** (1896-1963), A YOUNG POET AND ESSAYIST IN ZURICH WHO WAS ADVOCATING THE USE OF ART TO CRITICIZE THE IDIOCY OF THE WAR.
WE WANT OUR ART TO FIND OUT WHAT WORDS MEAN BEFORE USING THEM. IT ISN'T NEW TECHNIQUES THAT INTEREST US, BUT THEIR *SPIRIT*.

DURING VISITS TO ZURICH, PICABIA SPENT HOURS WITH TZARA AND **HUGO BALL** (1886-1927) AT THEIR LOCAL ARTIST'S SALOON, **CABARET VOLTAIRE**, DISCUSSING THE HORRIBLE TOLL THE WAR WAS TAKING ON THEIR LIVES AND WHAT THEY, AS ARTISTS, COULD DO ABOUT IT. HE TOLD THEM ABOUT DUCHAMP AND HIS RADICAL NEW CREATIVE THEORIES -- INCLUDING SUBJECTIVE ART AND THE USE OF HUMOR AS A WEAPON AGAINST OPPRESSION. THEY, IN TURN, TOLD HIM ABOUT THEIR NEW SATIRICAL PROTEST MOVEMENT CALLED **DADA**.

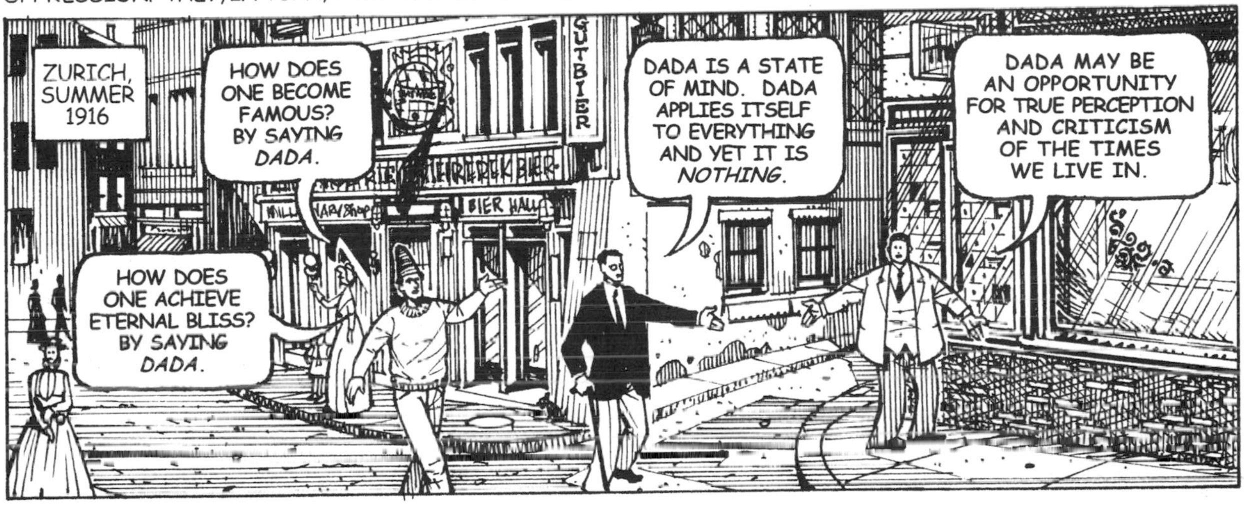
ZURICH, SUMMER 1916
HOW DOES ONE BECOME FAMOUS? BY SAYING *DADA*.
HOW DOES ONE ACHIEVE ETERNAL BLISS? BY SAYING *DADA*.
DADA IS A STATE OF MIND. DADA APPLIES ITSELF TO EVERYTHING AND YET IT IS *NOTHING*.
DADA MAY BE AN OPPORTUNITY FOR TRUE PERCEPTION AND CRITICISM OF THE TIMES WE LIVE IN.
GUTBIER
BIER HALL

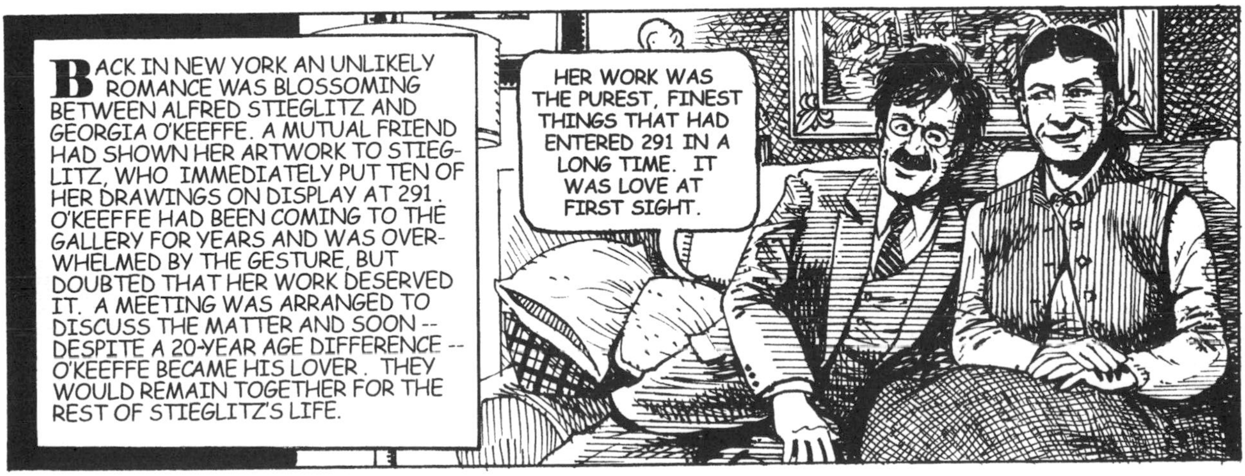
BACK IN NEW YORK AN UNLIKELY ROMANCE WAS BLOSSOMING BETWEEN ALFRED STIEGLITZ AND GEORGIA O'KEEFFE. A MUTUAL FRIEND HAD SHOWN HER ARTWORK TO STIEGLITZ, WHO IMMEDIATELY PUT TEN OF HER DRAWINGS ON DISPLAY AT 291. O'KEEFFE HAD BEEN COMING TO THE GALLERY FOR YEARS AND WAS OVERWHELMED BY THE GESTURE, BUT DOUBTED THAT HER WORK DESERVED IT. A MEETING WAS ARRANGED TO DISCUSS THE MATTER AND SOON -- DESPITE A 20-YEAR AGE DIFFERENCE -- O'KEEFFE BECAME HIS LOVER. THEY WOULD REMAIN TOGETHER FOR THE REST OF STIEGLITZ'S LIFE.
HER WORK WAS THE PUREST, FINEST THINGS THAT HAD ENTERED 291 IN A LONG TIME. IT WAS LOVE AT FIRST SIGHT.

AS MODERN ART'S MOST FAMOUS REBEL, MARCEL DUCHAMP WAS EXPECTED TO DO SOMETHING REVOLUTIONARY TO FOLLOW HIS TRIUMPH AT THE ARMORY SHOW AND HE DID *NOT* DISAPPOINT. HE WANTED TO PUT HIS THEORIES ABOUT SUBJECTIVISM TO THEIR TEST, SO HE DECIDED TO REVISIT AN IDEA HE HAD BEGUN EXPLORING WHILE HE WAS STILL LIVING IN FRANCE. HE CALLED THEM **READYMADES**.

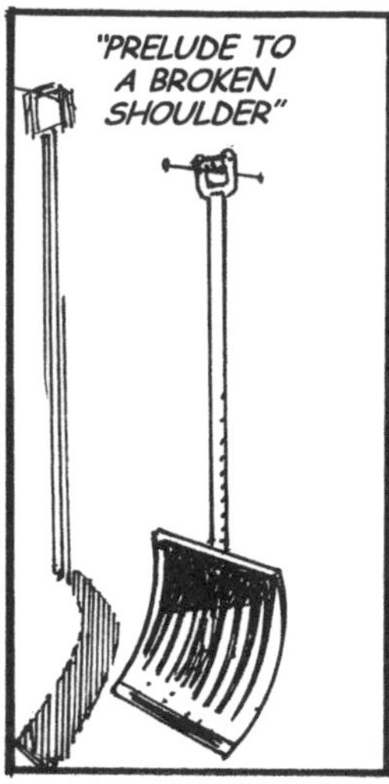
"PRELUDE TO A BROKEN SHOULDER"

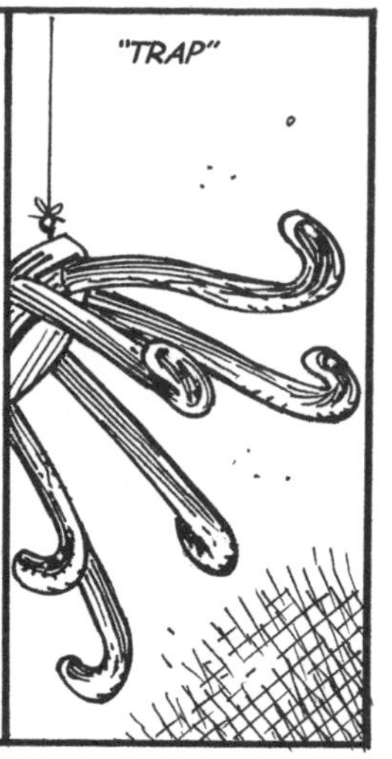
"TRAP"

READYMADES WERE A TYPE OF **FOUND ART** BASED ON THE CONCEPT THAT MANUFACTURED OBJECTS COULD BE TURNED *INTO* ART BY SIMPLY DECLARING THEM TO *BE* ART. THEY WERE ABOUT FINDING BEAUTY AND HUMOR IN THE MUNDANE WORLD.

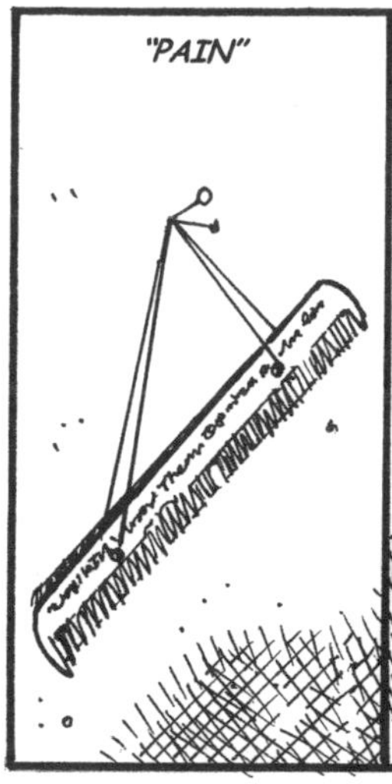
"PAIN"

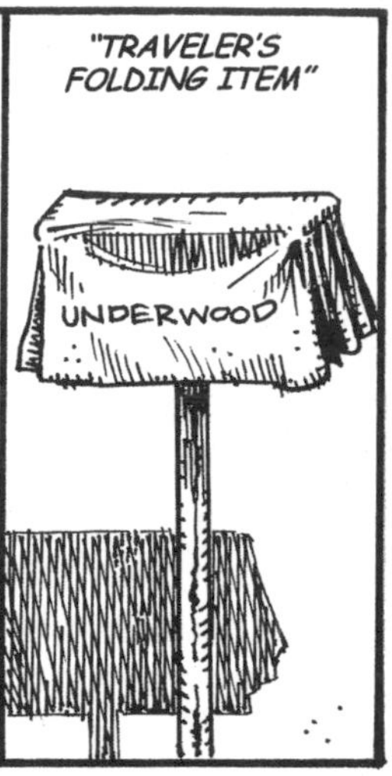
"TRAVELER'S FOLDING ITEM"
UNDERWOOD

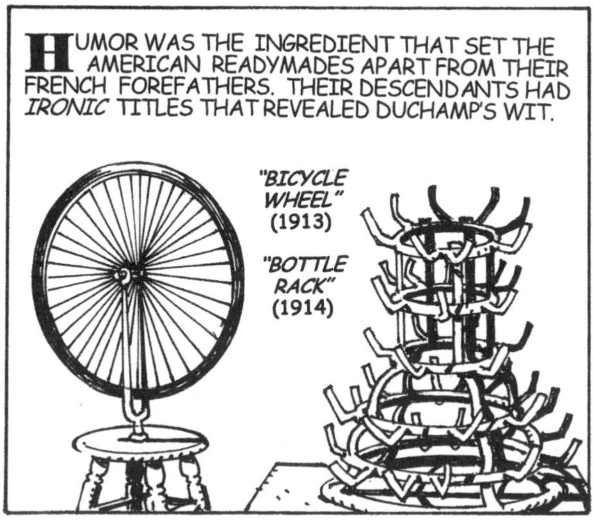
HUMOR WAS THE INGREDIENT THAT SET THE AMERICAN READYMADES APART FROM THEIR FRENCH FOREFATHERS. THEIR DESCENDANTS HAD *IRONIC* TITLES THAT REVEALED DUCHAMP'S WIT.
"BICYCLE WHEEL" (1913)
"BOTTLE RACK" (1914)

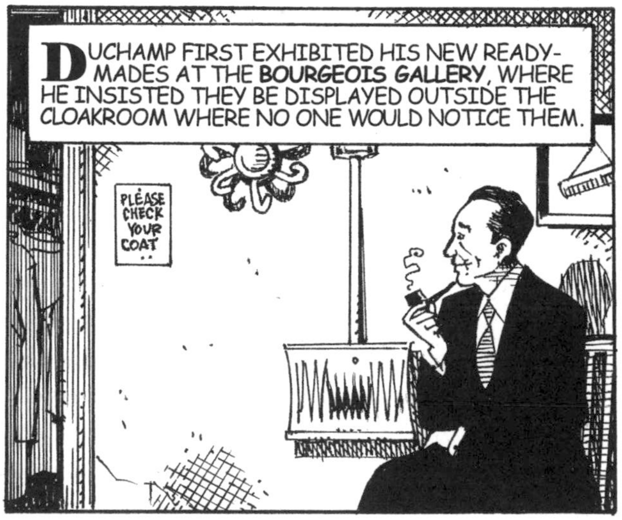
DUCHAMP FIRST EXHIBITED HIS NEW READYMADES AT THE **BOURGEOIS GALLERY**, WHERE HE INSISTED THEY BE DISPLAYED OUTSIDE THE CLOAKROOM WHERE NO ONE WOULD NOTICE THEM.
PLEASE CHECK YOUR COAT

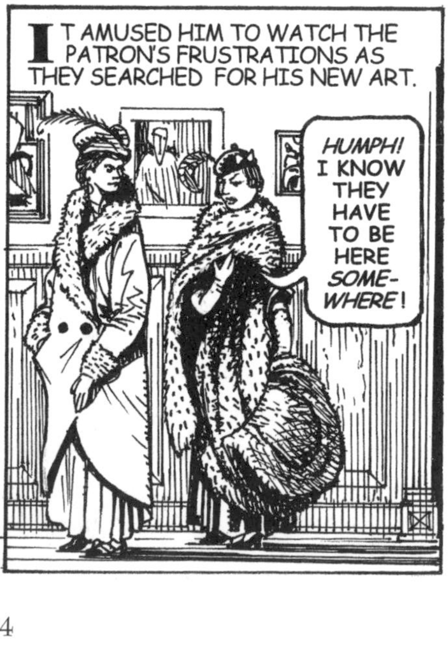
IT AMUSED HIM TO WATCH THE PATRON'S FRUSTRATIONS AS THEY SEARCHED FOR HIS NEW ART.
HUMPH! I KNOW THEY HAVE TO BE HERE SOMEWHERE!

THAT AUTUMN DUCHAMP BECAME ONE OF THE FOUNDERS OF **THE SOCIETY OF INDEPENDENT ARTISTS**. THEIR MISSION WAS TO HOST EXHIBITS THAT WOULD HAVE NO RESTRICTIONS ON CONTENT, NO JURY, AND NO AWARDS. THE ONLY QUALIFICATION WAS AN ENTRANT'S ABILITY TO PAY THE SMALL REGISTRATION FEE OF *SIX DOLLARS*. NO ARTIST COULD BE EXCLUDED FROM THEIR SHOWS FOR ANY REASON.

LITTLE DID HE REALIZE THAT A PRESENT FROM BARONESS ELSA VON FREYTAG-LORINGHOVEN WOULD SOON BRING THEIR SO-CALLED *MISSION* TO ITS KNEES.

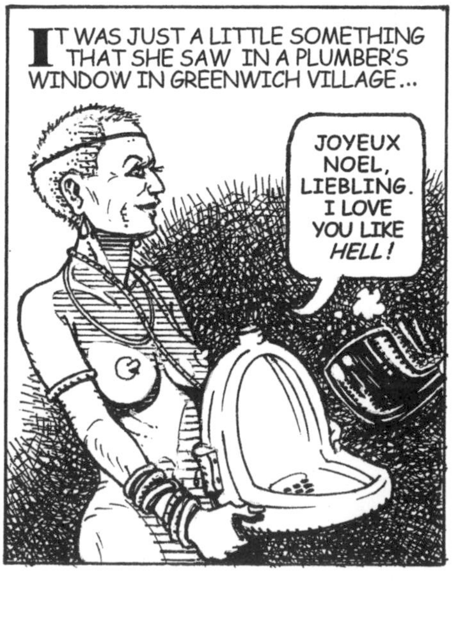
IT WAS JUST A LITTLE SOMETHING THAT SHE SAW IN A PLUMBER'S WINDOW IN GREENWICH VILLAGE...
JOYEUX NOEL, LIEBLING. I LOVE YOU LIKE HELL!

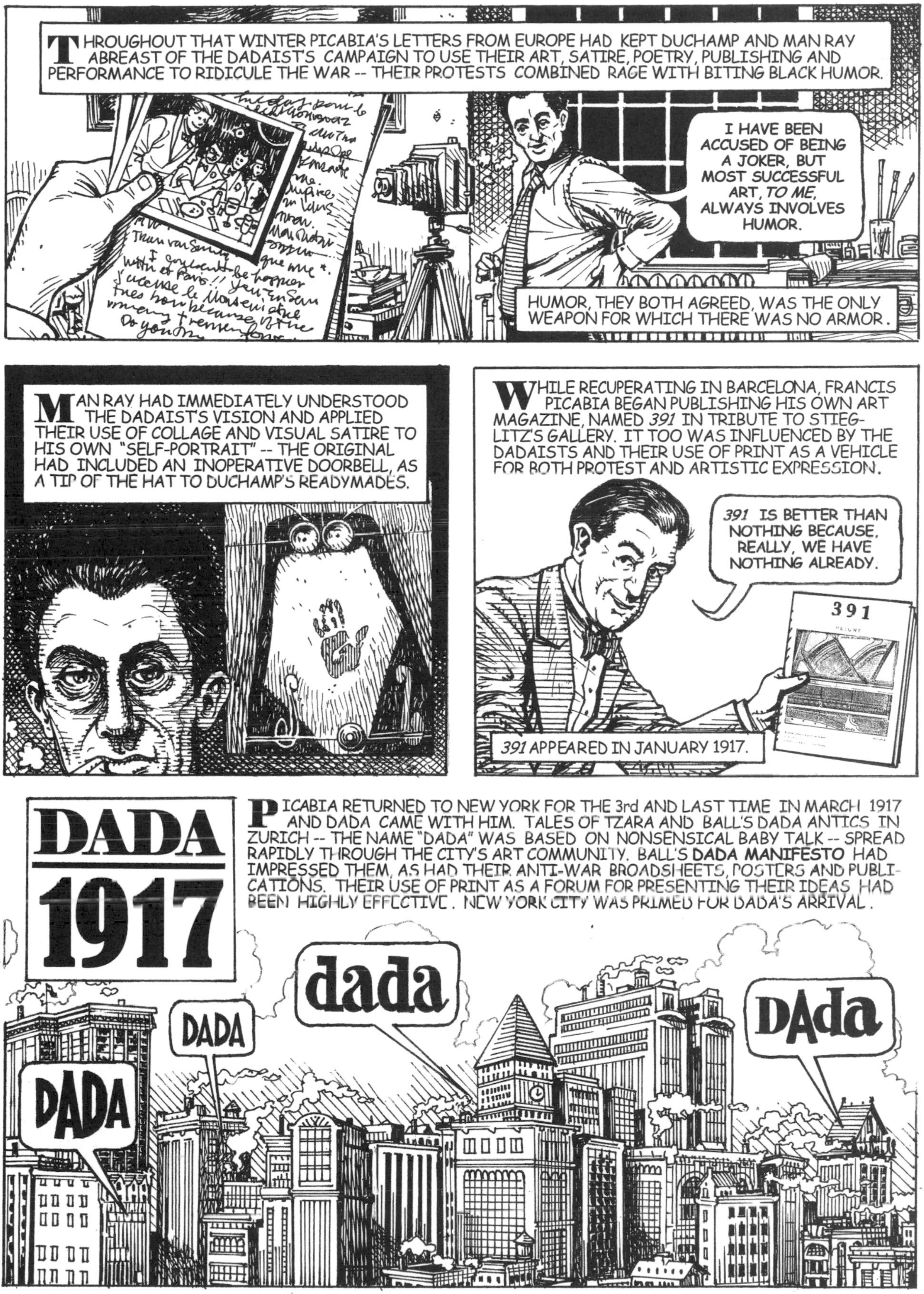
THROUGHOUT THAT WINTER PICABIA'S LETTERS FROM EUROPE HAD KEPT DUCHAMP AND MAN RAY ABREAST OF THE DADAIST'S CAMPAIGN TO USE THEIR ART, SATIRE, POETRY, PUBLISHING AND PERFORMANCE TO RIDICULE THE WAR -- THEIR PROTESTS COMBINED RAGE WITH BITING BLACK HUMOR.
I HAVE BEEN ACCUSED OF BEING A JOKER, BUT MOST SUCCESSFUL ART, *TO ME*, ALWAYS INVOLVES HUMOR.
HUMOR, THEY BOTH AGREED, WAS THE ONLY WEAPON FOR WHICH THERE WAS NO ARMOR.
MAN RAY HAD IMMEDIATELY UNDERSTOOD THE DADAIST'S VISION AND APPLIED THEIR USE OF COLLAGE AND VISUAL SATIRE TO HIS OWN "SELF-PORTRAIT" -- THE ORIGINAL HAD INCLUDED AN INOPERATIVE DOORBELL, AS A TIP OF THE HAT TO DUCHAMP'S READYMADES.
WHILE RECUPERATING IN BARCELONA, FRANCIS PICABIA BEGAN PUBLISHING HIS OWN ART MAGAZINE, NAMED *391* IN TRIBUTE TO STIEGLITZ'S GALLERY. IT TOO WAS INFLUENCED BY THE DADAISTS AND THEIR USE OF PRINT AS A VEHICLE FOR BOTH PROTEST AND ARTISTIC EXPRESSION.
391 IS BETTER THAN NOTHING BECAUSE, REALLY, WE HAVE NOTHING ALREADY.
391
391 APPEARED IN JANUARY 1917.
DADA 1917
PICABIA RETURNED TO NEW YORK FOR THE 3rd AND LAST TIME IN MARCH 1917 AND DADA CAME WITH HIM. TALES OF TZARA AND BALL'S DADA ANTICS IN ZURICH -- THE NAME "DADA" WAS BASED ON NONSENSICAL BABY TALK -- SPREAD RAPIDLY THROUGH THE CITY'S ART COMMUNITY. BALL'S **DADA MANIFESTO** HAD IMPRESSED THEM, AS HAD THEIR ANTI-WAR BROADSHEETS, POSTERS AND PUBLICATIONS. THEIR USE OF PRINT AS A FORUM FOR PRESENTING THEIR IDEAS HAD BEEN HIGHLY EFFECTIVE. NEW YORK CITY WAS PRIMED FOR DADA'S ARRIVAL.
DADA
DADA
dada
DAda

THAT SPRING, WITH PICABIA'S INJECTION OF DADA IN THEIR BLOODSTREAMS, THE DENIZENS OF 291 AND THE ARENSBERG'S SALON WENT INTO A FRENZY OF CREATIVE ENERGY, ESPECIALLY DUCHAMP.

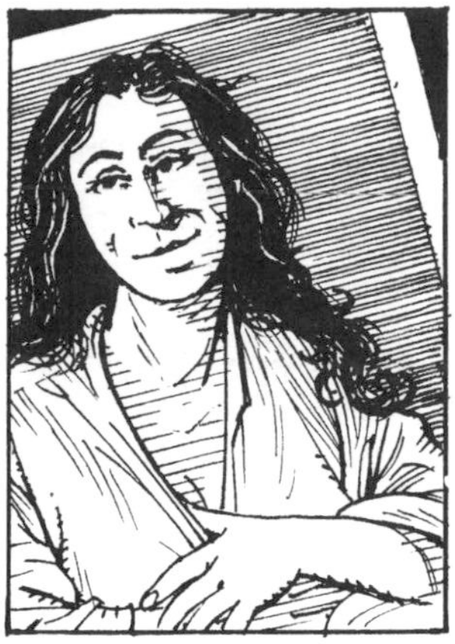

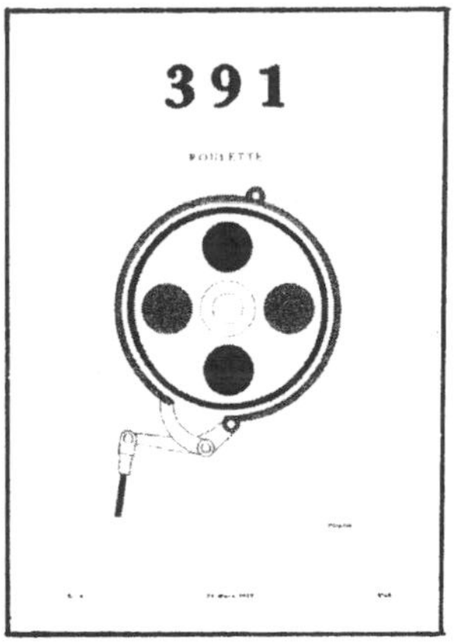
391

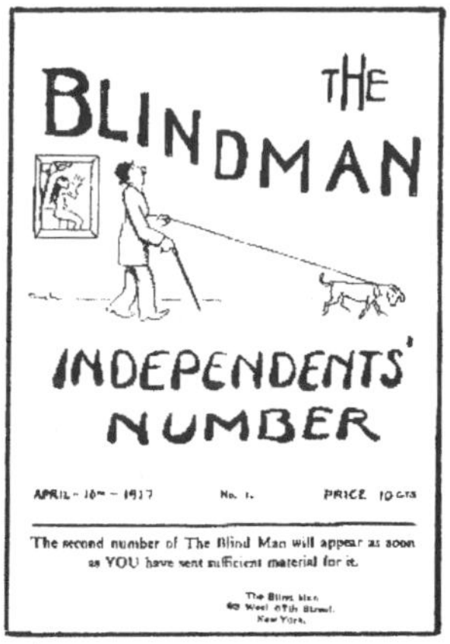
THE BLINDMAN
INDEPENDENTS' NUMBER
APRIL - 10th - 1917 No. 1. PRICE 10 CTS
The second number of The Blind Man will appear as soon as YOU have sent sufficient material for it.

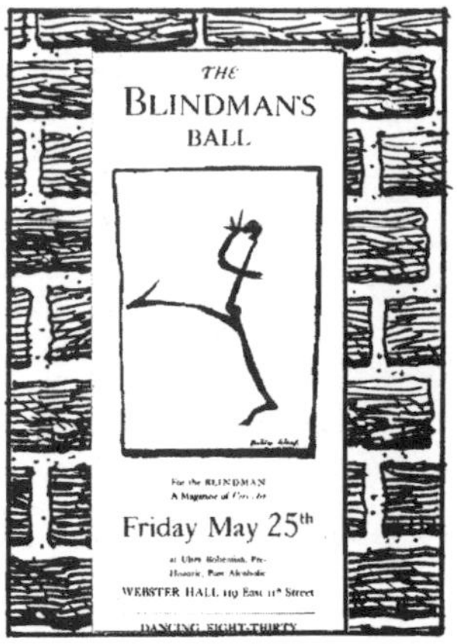
THE BLINDMAN'S BALL
Friday May 25th
WEBSTER HALL 119 East 11th Street

INSPIRED BY COMMERCIAL ART TECHNIQUES, MAN RAY BEGAN PAINTING WITH STENCILS AND AN AIRBRUSH. STIEGLITZ BEGAN OBSESSIVELY FOCUSING HIS LENS ON O'KEEFFE'S RUGGED BEAUTY -- *OFTEN IN THE NUDE*. WITH DUCHAMP'S HELP, PICABIA PUBLISHED A FEW NEW ISSUES OF *391*, WHILE **BEATRICE WOOD** (1893-1998) AND **HENRI-PIERRE ROCHE** (1879-1959) -- THE AUTHOR OF *JULES AND JIM* -- PRESENTED THE PREMIER OF NEW YORK'S FIRST DADA-STYLE MAGAZINE, ***THE BLINDMAN***, PUBLISHED TO PROMOTE A DADA-INSPIRED GALA CALLED **THE BLINDMAN'S BALL**, WHICH THEY HOPED WOULD FURTHER SOCIALIZE THE CITY'S ARTS COMMUNITY.

DUCHAMP ENCOURAGED THEM ALL AND THEY, IN TURN, INSPIRED HIM TO FINISH HIS ENTRY FOR THE SOCIETY OF INDEPENDENT ARTISTS EXHIBITION. HE CALLED IT "**FOUNTAIN**" AND CONSIDERED IT HIS FINEST READYMADE TO DATE. UNFORTUNATELY THE EXHIBIT'S ADMINISTRATORS DISAGREED, BANNING IT FROM THE SHOW. DUCHAMP WAS *STUNNED*. HOW COULD A SOCIETY THAT HE HAD CO-FOUNDED REJECT HIS LATEST WORK?

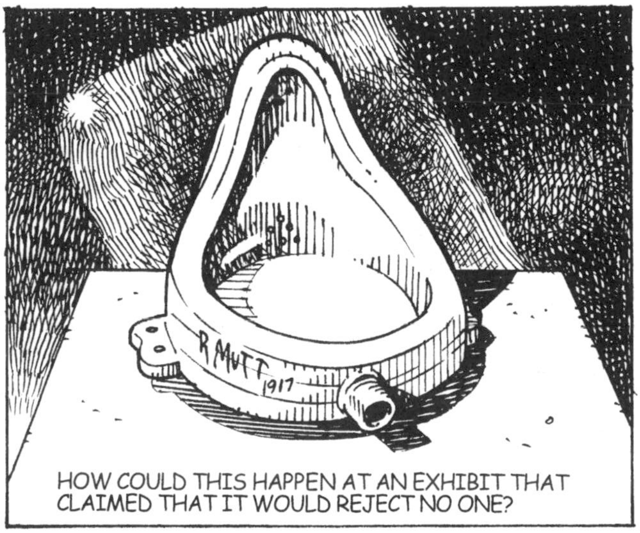
R MUTT 1917
HOW COULD THIS HAPPEN AT AN EXHIBIT THAT CLAIMED THAT IT WOULD REJECT NO ONE?

THE SOCIETY CITED THEIR CONCERNS ABOUT THE PUBLIC'S REACTION AS THE GROUNDS FOR THE REJECTION, BUT DUCHAMP WOULD HEAR NONE OF IT. ARTISTIC FREEDOM WAS THE *WHOLE POINT* OF THE SHOW AND FOR THEM TO REJECT "FOUNTAIN" WAS THE SAME AS REJECTING THE SOCIETY'S OWN CHARTER. HE RESIGNED HIS DIRECTORSHIP IN DISGUST AND THEN QUIT THE SOCIETY OUTRIGHT. OTHERS, LIKE MAN RAY, SOON FOLLOWED HIM.

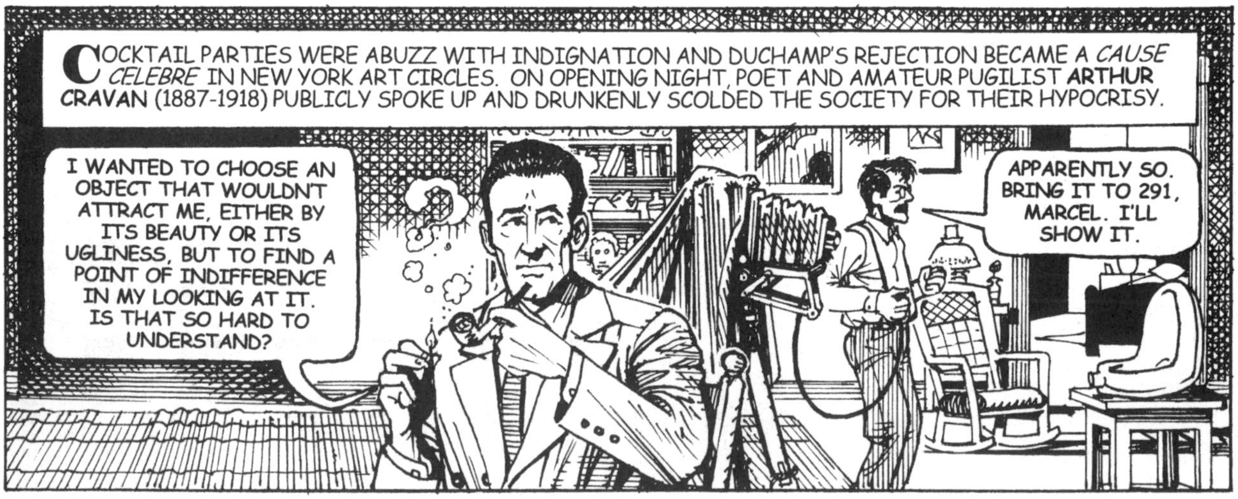
COCKTAIL PARTIES WERE ABUZZ WITH INDIGNATION AND DUCHAMP'S REJECTION BECAME A *CAUSE CELEBRE* IN NEW YORK ART CIRCLES. ON OPENING NIGHT, POET AND AMATEUR PUGILIST **ARTHUR CRAVAN** (1887-1918) PUBLICLY SPOKE UP AND DRUNKENLY SCOLDED THE SOCIETY FOR THEIR HYPOCRISY.
I WANTED TO CHOOSE AN OBJECT THAT WOULDN'T ATTRACT ME, EITHER BY ITS BEAUTY OR ITS UGLINESS, BUT TO FIND A POINT OF INDIFFERENCE IN MY LOOKING AT IT. IS THAT SO HARD TO UNDERSTAND?
APPARENTLY SO. BRING IT TO 291, MARCEL. I'LL SHOW IT.

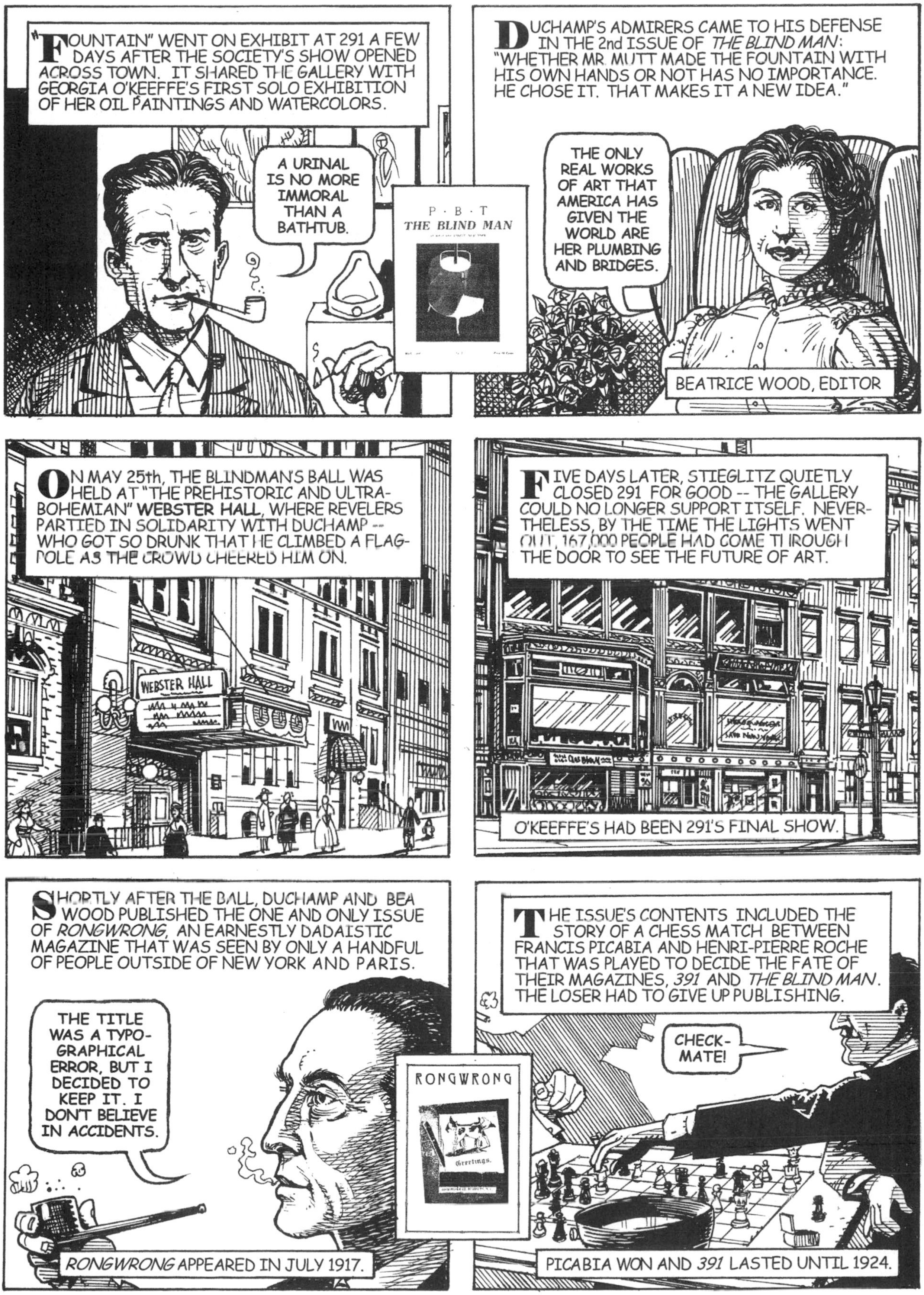
"FOUNTAIN" WENT ON EXHIBIT AT 291 A FEW DAYS AFTER THE SOCIETY'S SHOW OPENED ACROSS TOWN. IT SHARED THE GALLERY WITH GEORGIA O'KEEFFE'S FIRST SOLO EXHIBITION OF HER OIL PAINTINGS AND WATERCOLORS.
A URINAL IS NO MORE IMMORAL THAN A BATHTUB.
P · B · T
THE BLIND MAN
DUCHAMP'S ADMIRERS CAME TO HIS DEFENSE IN THE 2nd ISSUE OF *THE BLIND MAN*: "WHETHER MR. MUTT MADE THE FOUNTAIN WITH HIS OWN HANDS OR NOT HAS NO IMPORTANCE. HE CHOSE IT. THAT MAKES IT A NEW IDEA."
THE ONLY REAL WORKS OF ART THAT AMERICA HAS GIVEN THE WORLD ARE HER PLUMBING AND BRIDGES.
BEATRICE WOOD, EDITOR
ON MAY 25th, THE BLINDMAN'S BALL WAS HELD AT "THE PREHISTORIC AND ULTRA-BOHEMIAN" **WEBSTER HALL**, WHERE REVELERS PARTIED IN SOLIDARITY WITH DUCHAMP -- WHO GOT SO DRUNK THAT HE CLIMBED A FLAG-POLE AS THE CROWD CHEERED HIM ON.
WEBSTER HALL
FIVE DAYS LATER, STIEGLITZ QUIETLY CLOSED 291 FOR GOOD -- THE GALLERY COULD NO LONGER SUPPORT ITSELF. NEVER-THELESS, BY THE TIME THE LIGHTS WENT OUT, 167,000 PEOPLE HAD COME THROUGH THE DOOR TO SEE THE FUTURE OF ART.
O'KEEFFE'S HAD BEEN 291'S FINAL SHOW.
SHORTLY AFTER THE BALL, DUCHAMP AND BEA WOOD PUBLISHED THE ONE AND ONLY ISSUE OF *RONGWRONG*, AN EARNESTLY DADAISTIC MAGAZINE THAT WAS SEEN BY ONLY A HANDFUL OF PEOPLE OUTSIDE OF NEW YORK AND PARIS.
THE TITLE WAS A TYPO-GRAPHICAL ERROR, BUT I DECIDED TO KEEP IT. I DON'T BELIEVE IN ACCIDENTS.
RONGWRONG
Greetings.
RONGWRONG APPEARED IN JULY 1917.
THE ISSUE'S CONTENTS INCLUDED THE STORY OF A CHESS MATCH BETWEEN FRANCIS PICABIA AND HENRI-PIERRE ROCHE THAT WAS PLAYED TO DECIDE THE FATE OF THEIR MAGAZINES, *391* AND *THE BLIND MAN*. THE LOSER HAD TO GIVE UP PUBLISHING.
CHECK-MATE!
PICABIA WON AND *391* LASTED UNTIL 1924.

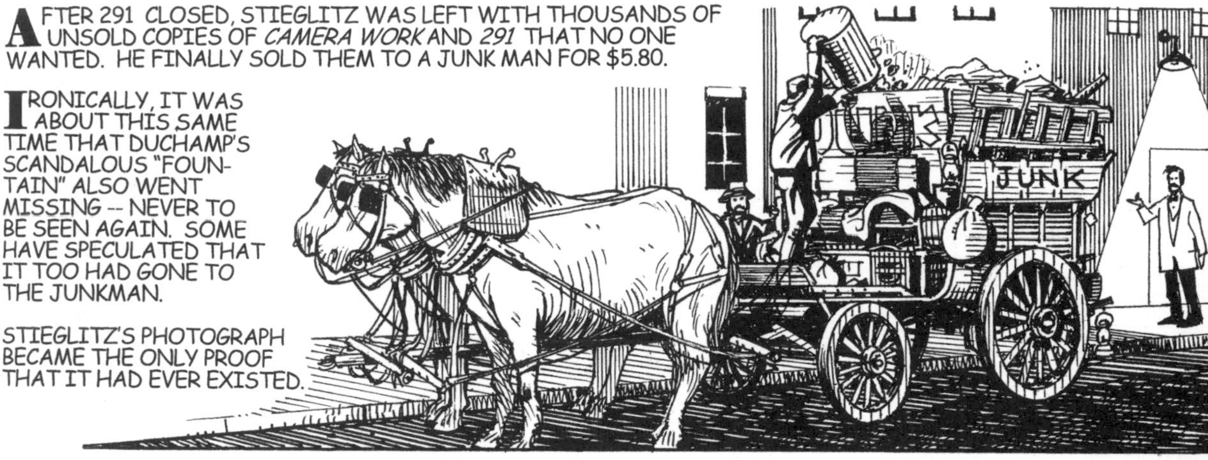
AFTER 291 CLOSED, STIEGLITZ WAS LEFT WITH THOUSANDS OF UNSOLD COPIES OF *CAMERA WORK* AND *291* THAT NO ONE WANTED. HE FINALLY SOLD THEM TO A JUNK MAN FOR $5.80.
IRONICALLY, IT WAS ABOUT THIS *SAME* TIME THAT DUCHAMP'S SCANDALOUS "FOUNTAIN" ALSO WENT MISSING -- NEVER TO BE SEEN AGAIN. SOME HAVE SPECULATED THAT IT TOO HAD GONE TO THE JUNKMAN.
STIEGLITZ'S PHOTOGRAPH BECAME THE ONLY PROOF THAT IT HAD EVER EXISTED.
JUNK

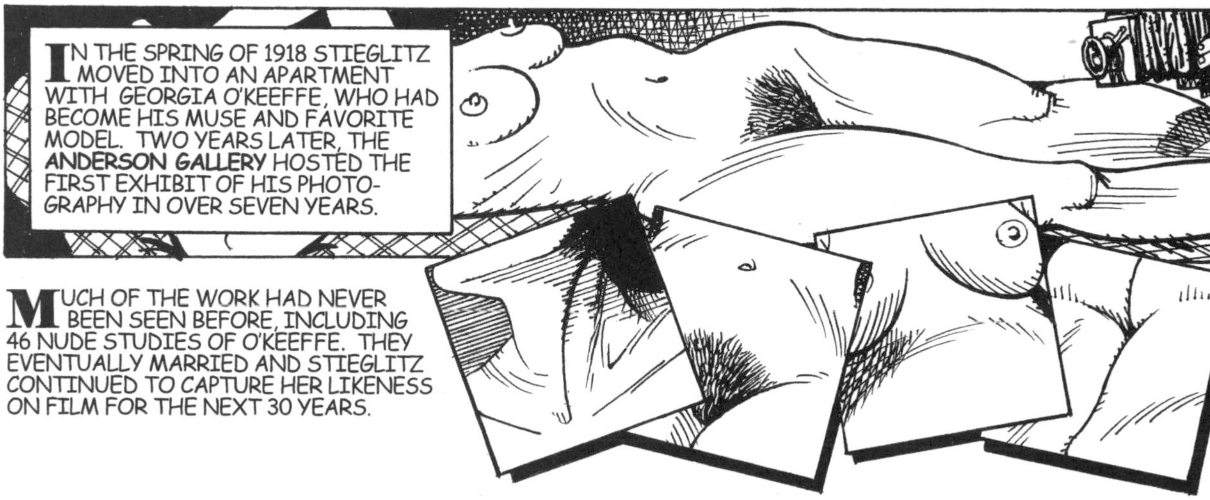
IN THE SPRING OF 1918 STIEGLITZ MOVED INTO AN APARTMENT WITH GEORGIA O'KEEFFE, WHO HAD BECOME HIS MUSE AND FAVORITE MODEL. TWO YEARS LATER, THE **ANDERSON GALLERY** HOSTED THE FIRST EXHIBIT OF HIS PHOTOGRAPHY IN OVER SEVEN YEARS.
MUCH OF THE WORK HAD NEVER BEEN SEEN BEFORE, INCLUDING 46 NUDE STUDIES OF O'KEEFFE. THEY EVENTUALLY MARRIED AND STIEGLITZ CONTINUED TO CAPTURE HER LIKENESS ON FILM FOR THE NEXT 30 YEARS.

DUCHAMP SPENT SEVERAL MONTHS TRYING TO MAKE ENOUGH MONEY TO TRAVEL. HE TAUGHT FRENCH LESSONS TO EARN EXTRA CASH AND LIVED FRUGALLY. HE WORKED EXACTLY TWO HOURS A DAY ON "THE LARGE GLASS" -- USING THE ROUTINE TO KEEP HIM FOCUSED ON HIS WORK. THE REST OF HIS TIME WAS SPENT PLAYING CHESS. "I AM A VICTIM OF CHESS," HE SAID. "IT HAS ALL THE BEAUTY OF ART AND MORE."

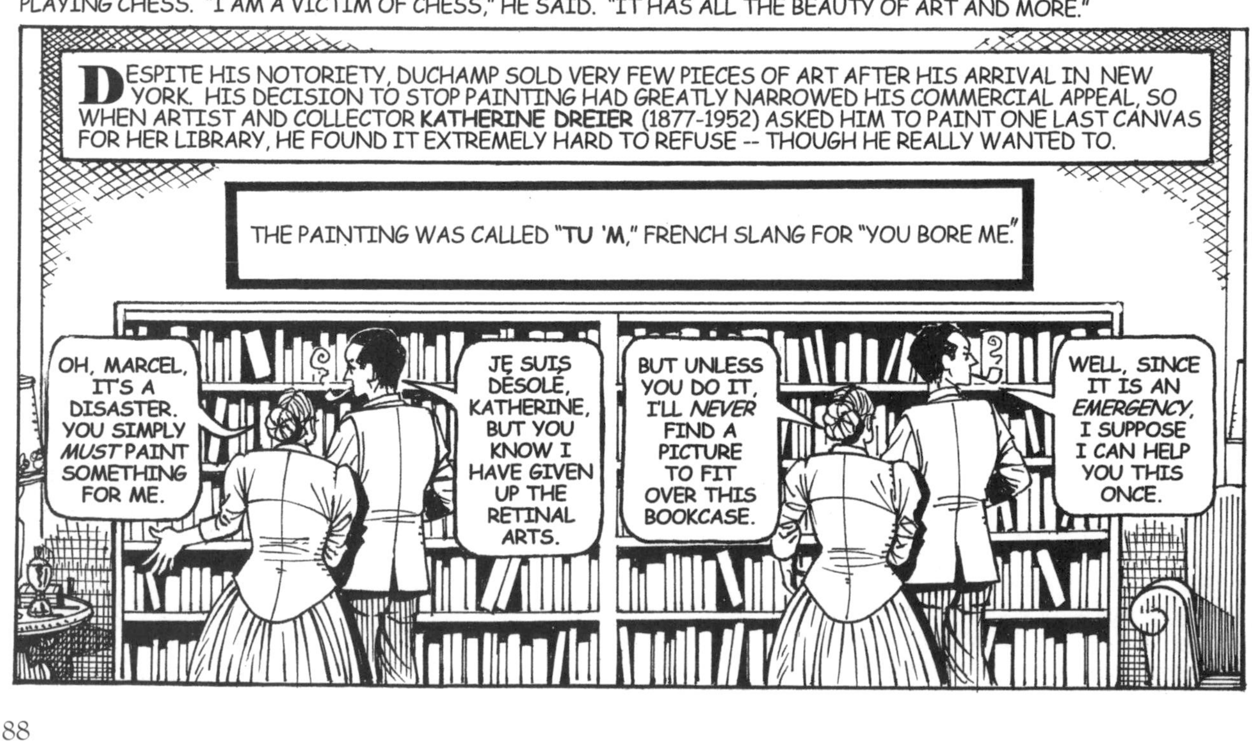
DESPITE HIS NOTORIETY, DUCHAMP SOLD VERY FEW PIECES OF ART AFTER HIS ARRIVAL IN NEW YORK. HIS DECISION TO STOP PAINTING HAD GREATLY NARROWED HIS COMMERCIAL APPEAL, SO WHEN ARTIST AND COLLECTOR **KATHERINE DREIER** (1877-1952) ASKED HIM TO PAINT ONE LAST CANVAS FOR HER LIBRARY, HE FOUND IT EXTREMELY HARD TO REFUSE -- THOUGH HE REALLY WANTED TO.
THE PAINTING WAS CALLED "**TU 'M**," FRENCH SLANG FOR "YOU BORE ME."
OH, MARCEL, IT'S A DISASTER. YOU SIMPLY *MUST* PAINT SOMETHING FOR ME.
JE SUIS DÉSOLÉ, KATHERINE, BUT YOU KNOW I HAVE GIVEN UP THE RETINAL ARTS.
BUT UNLESS YOU DO IT, I'LL *NEVER* FIND A PICTURE TO FIT OVER THIS BOOKCASE.
WELL, SINCE IT IS AN *EMERGENCY*, I SUPPOSE I CAN HELP YOU THIS ONCE.

AFTER FINISHING DREIER'S BOOKCASE PAINTING, DUCHAMP SPENT NINE MONTHS PLAYING CHESS IN BUENOS AIRES. WHEN HE RETURNED IN MAY 1919 HE WAS INVIGORATED AND RENEWED, BUT FOUND NEW YORK'S ART COMMUNITY -- ESPECIALLY HIS DADAIST COMRADES -- IN DISARRAY. MANY OF THEM HAD SIMPLY LEFT TOWN.

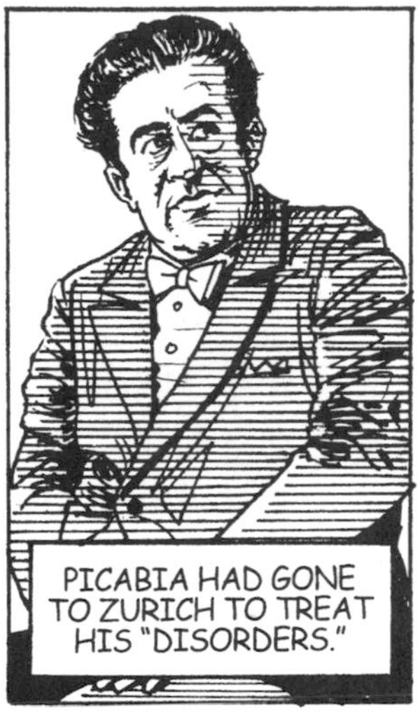
PICABIA HAD GONE TO ZURICH TO TREAT HIS "DISORDERS."

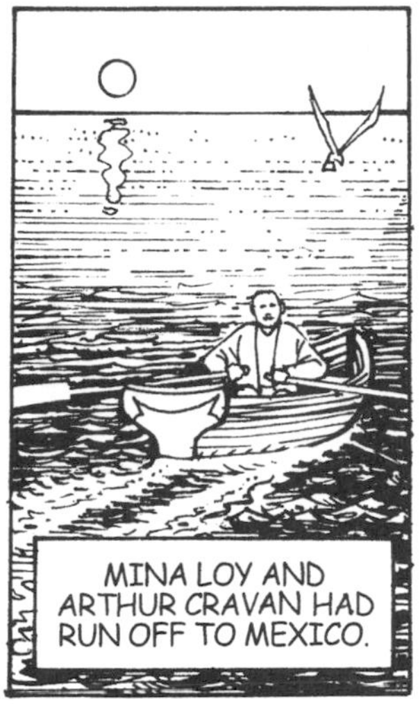
MINA LOY AND ARTHUR CRAVAN HAD RUN OFF TO MEXICO.

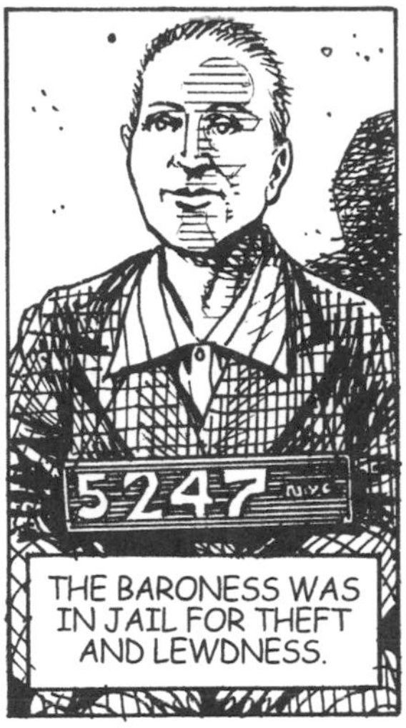
5247
THE BARONESS WAS IN JAIL FOR THEFT AND LEWDNESS.

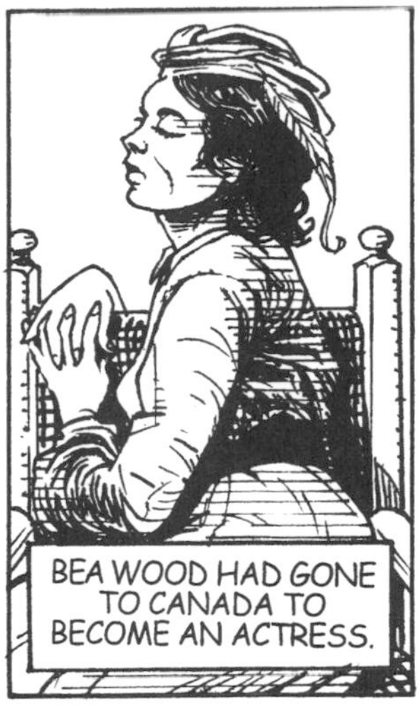
BEA WOOD HAD GONE TO CANADA TO BECOME AN ACTRESS.

AFTER THE WAR, MANY REFUGEE ARTISTS HAD RETURNED TO EUROPE. THE ARENSBERGS BEGAN SPENDING MORE TIME IN CALIFORNIA, LEAVING NEW YORK'S ARTISTS WITHOUT A PLACE TO GO FOR FREE DRINKS AND CHIT-CHAT, SO DUCHAMP DECIDED TO RETURN TO FRANCE FOR THE FIRST TIME IN MORE THAN FOUR YEARS.

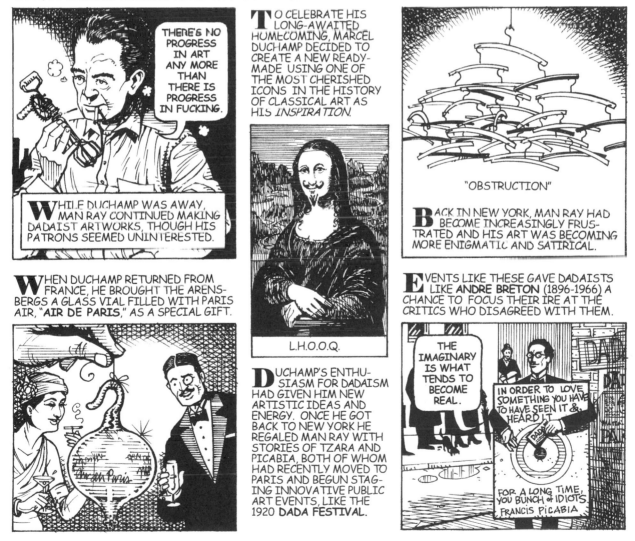

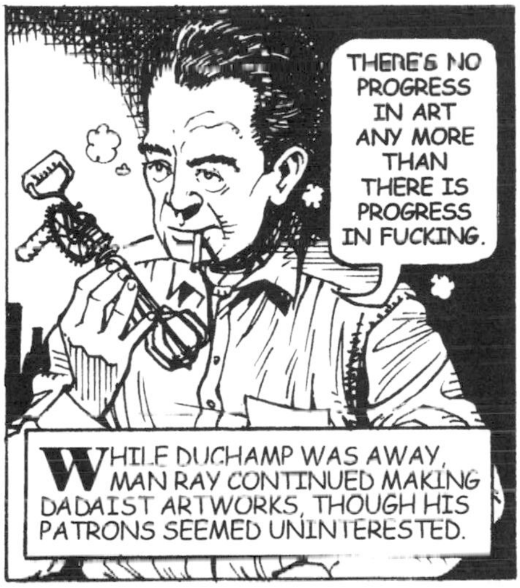
THERE'S NO PROGRESS IN ART ANY MORE THAN THERE IS PROGRESS IN FUCKING.
WHILE DUCHAMP WAS AWAY, MAN RAY CONTINUED MAKING DADAIST ARTWORKS, THOUGH HIS PATRONS SEEMED UNINTERESTED.

TO CELEBRATE HIS LONG-AWAITED HOMECOMING, MARCEL DUCHAMP DECIDED TO CREATE A NEW READY-MADE USING ONE OF THE MOST CHERISHED ICONS IN THE HISTORY OF CLASSICAL ART AS HIS *INSPIRATION*.

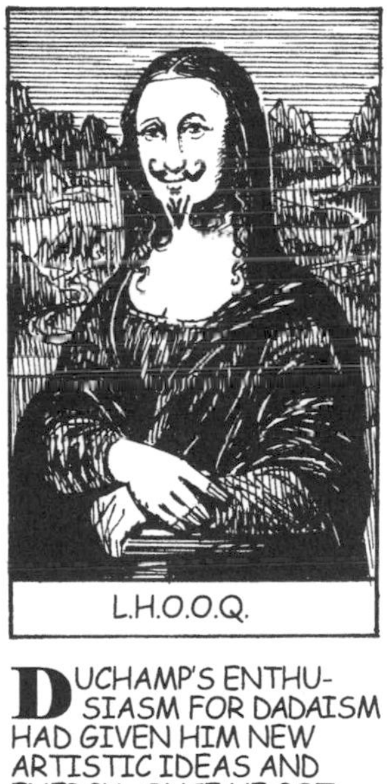
L.H.O.O.Q.

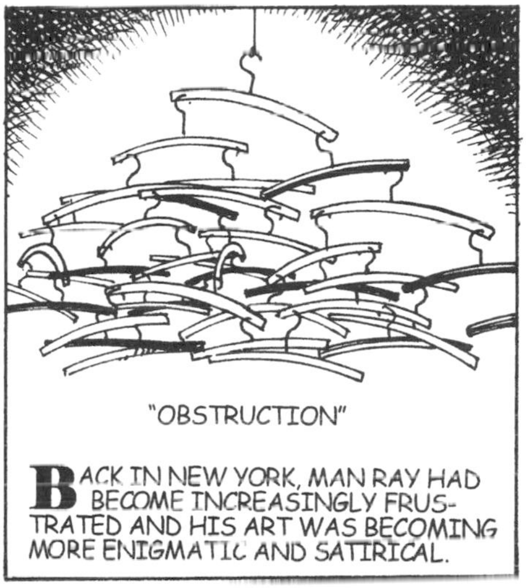
"OBSTRUCTION"
BACK IN NEW YORK, MAN RAY HAD BECOME INCREASINGLY FRUSTRATED AND HIS ART WAS BECOMING MORE ENIGMATIC AND SATIRICAL.

WHEN DUCHAMP RETURNED FROM FRANCE, HE BROUGHT THE ARENSBERGS A GLASS VIAL FILLED WITH PARIS AIR, "**AIR DE PARIS**," AS A SPECIAL GIFT.

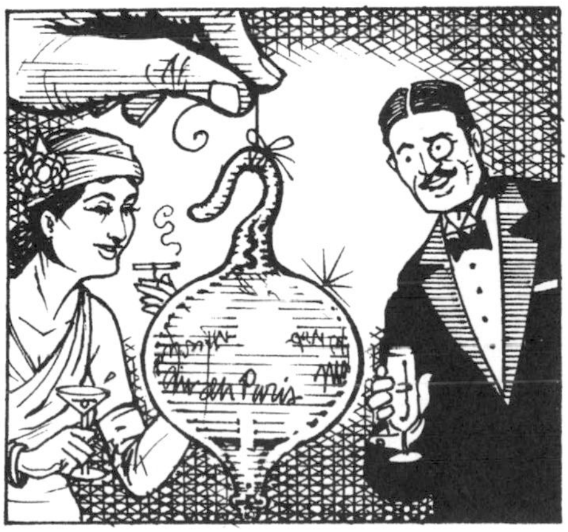

DUCHAMP'S ENTHUSIASM FOR DADAISM HAD GIVEN HIM NEW ARTISTIC IDEAS AND ENERGY. ONCE HE GOT BACK TO NEW YORK HE REGALED MAN RAY WITH STORIES OF TZARA AND PICABIA, BOTH OF WHOM HAD RECENTLY MOVED TO PARIS AND BEGUN STAGING INNOVATIVE PUBLIC ART EVENTS, LIKE THE 1920 **DADA FESTIVAL**.

EVENTS LIKE THESE GAVE DADAISTS LIKE **ANDRE BRETON** (1896-1966) A CHANCE TO FOCUS THEIR IRE AT THE CRITICS WHO DISAGREED WITH THEM.

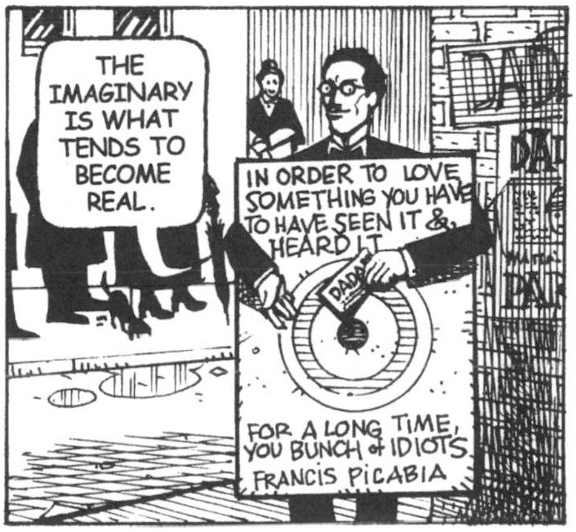
THE IMAGINARY IS WHAT TENDS TO BECOME REAL.
IN ORDER TO LOVE SOMETHING YOU HAVE TO HAVE SEEN IT & HEARD IT FOR A LONG TIME, YOU BUNCH of IDIOTS. FRANCIS PICABIA

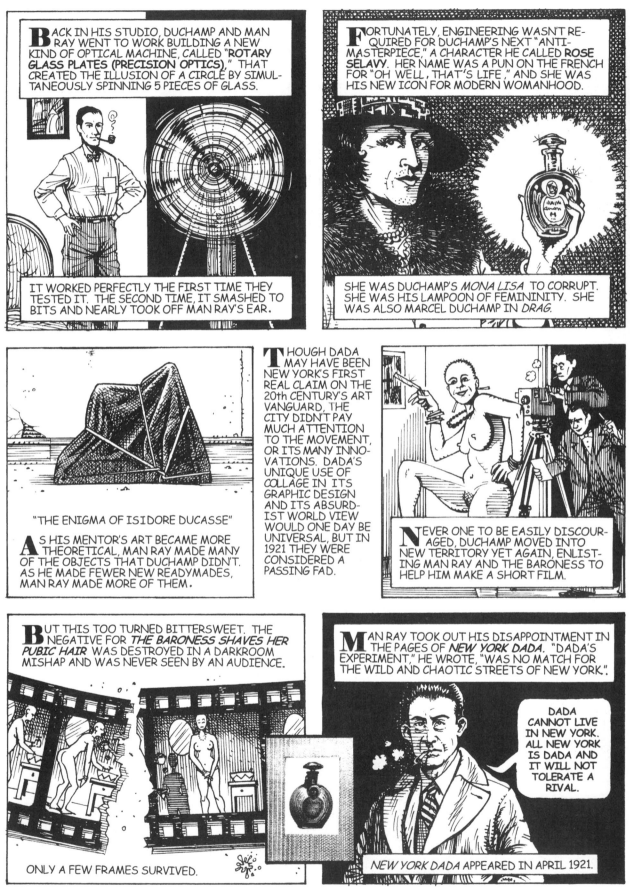

BACK IN HIS STUDIO, DUCHAMP AND MAN RAY WENT TO WORK BUILDING A NEW KIND OF OPTICAL MACHINE, CALLED "**ROTARY GLASS PLATES (PRECISION OPTICS),**" THAT CREATED THE ILLUSION OF A CIRCLE BY SIMULTANEOUSLY SPINNING 5 PIECES OF GLASS.

IT WORKED PERFECTLY THE FIRST TIME THEY TESTED IT. THE SECOND TIME, IT SMASHED TO BITS AND NEARLY TOOK OFF MAN RAY'S EAR.

FORTUNATELY, ENGINEERING WASN'T REQUIRED FOR DUCHAMP'S NEXT "ANTIMASTERPIECE," A CHARACTER HE CALLED **ROSE SELAVY.** HER NAME WAS A PUN ON THE FRENCH FOR "OH WELL, THAT'S LIFE," AND SHE WAS HIS NEW ICON FOR MODERN WOMANHOOD.

SHE WAS DUCHAMP'S *MONA LISA* TO CORRUPT. SHE WAS HIS LAMPOON OF FEMININITY. SHE WAS ALSO MARCEL DUCHAMP IN *DRAG.*

"THE ENIGMA OF ISIDORE DUCASSE"

AS HIS MENTOR'S ART BECAME MORE THEORETICAL, MAN RAY MADE MANY OF THE OBJECTS THAT DUCHAMP DIDN'T. AS HE MADE FEWER NEW READYMADES, MAN RAY MADE MORE OF THEM.

THOUGH DADA MAY HAVE BEEN NEW YORK'S FIRST REAL CLAIM ON THE 20th CENTURY'S ART VANGUARD, THE CITY DIDN'T PAY MUCH ATTENTION TO THE MOVEMENT, OR ITS MANY INNOVATIONS. DADA'S UNIQUE USE OF COLLAGE IN ITS GRAPHIC DESIGN AND ITS ABSURDIST WORLD VIEW WOULD ONE DAY BE UNIVERSAL, BUT IN 1921 THEY WERE CONSIDERED A PASSING FAD.

NEVER ONE TO BE EASILY DISCOURAGED, DUCHAMP MOVED INTO NEW TERRITORY YET AGAIN, ENLISTING MAN RAY AND THE BARONESS TO HELP HIM MAKE A SHORT FILM.

BUT THIS TOO TURNED BITTERSWEET. THE NEGATIVE FOR *THE BARONESS SHAVES HER PUBIC HAIR* WAS DESTROYED IN A DARKROOM MISHAP AND WAS NEVER SEEN BY AN AUDIENCE.

ONLY A FEW FRAMES SURVIVED.

MAN RAY TOOK OUT HIS DISAPPOINTMENT IN THE PAGES OF *NEW YORK DADA.* "DADA'S EXPERIMENT," HE WROTE, "WAS NO MATCH FOR THE WILD AND *CHAOTIC* STREETS OF NEW YORK."

DADA CANNOT LIVE IN NEW YORK. ALL NEW YORK IS DADA AND IT WILL NOT TOLERATE A RIVAL.

NEW YORK DADA APPEARED IN APRIL 1921.

THE DESTRUCTION OF *THE BARONESS SHAVES HER PUBIC HAIR* WAS THE FINAL STRAW FOR MAN RAY. FOLLOWING SO CLOSELY AFTER THE FAILURE OF "ROTARY GLASS PLATES," HE FELT AS IF HIS LUCK HAD CHANGED. EVERYTHING SEEMED TO HAVE SPOILED. "DADA CANNOT LIVE IN NEW YORK," HE WROTE TZARA.

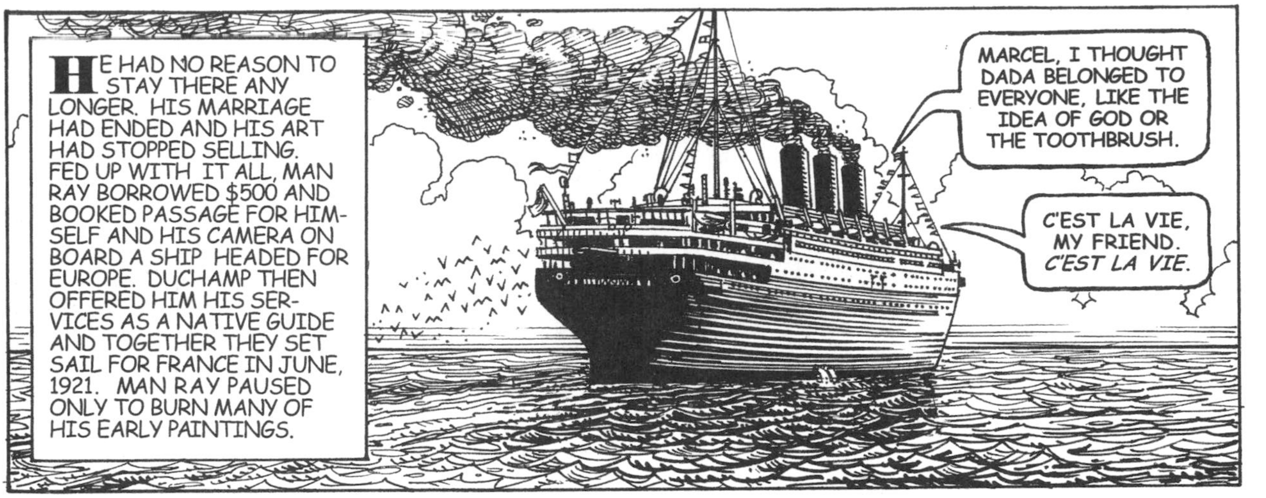
HE HAD NO REASON TO STAY THERE ANY LONGER. HIS MARRIAGE HAD ENDED AND HIS ART HAD STOPPED SELLING. FED UP WITH IT ALL, MAN RAY BORROWED $500 AND BOOKED PASSAGE FOR HIMSELF AND HIS CAMERA ON BOARD A SHIP HEADED FOR EUROPE. DUCHAMP THEN OFFERED HIM HIS SERVICES AS A NATIVE GUIDE AND TOGETHER THEY SET SAIL FOR FRANCE IN JUNE, 1921. MAN RAY PAUSED ONLY TO BURN MANY OF HIS EARLY PAINTINGS.
MARCEL, I THOUGHT DADA BELONGED TO EVERYONE, LIKE THE IDEA OF GOD OR THE TOOTHBRUSH.
C'EST LA VIE, MY FRIEND. *C'EST LA VIE*.

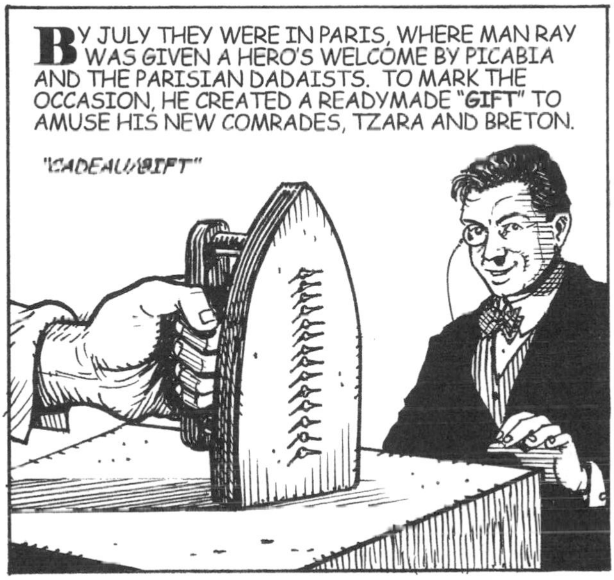
BY JULY THEY WERE IN PARIS, WHERE MAN RAY WAS GIVEN A HERO'S WELCOME BY PICABIA AND THE PARISIAN DADAISTS. TO MARK THE OCCASION, HE CREATED A READYMADE "**GIFT**" TO AMUSE HIS NEW COMRADES, TZARA AND BRETON.
"CADEAU/GIFT"

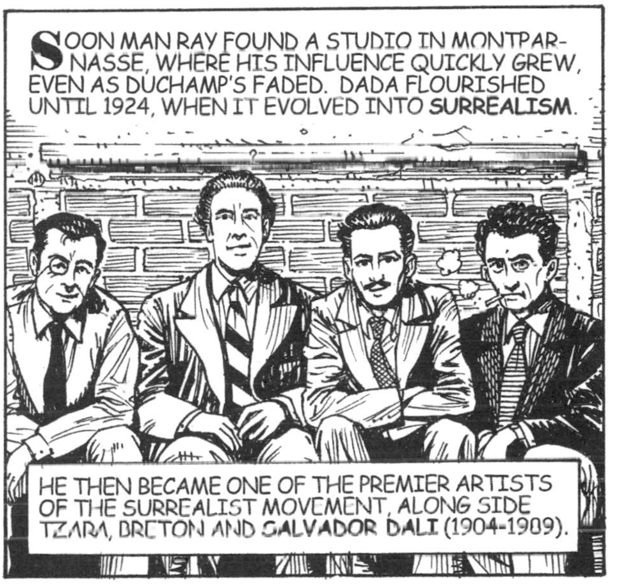
SOON MAN RAY FOUND A STUDIO IN MONTPARNASSE, WHERE HIS INFLUENCE QUICKLY GREW, EVEN AS DUCHAMP'S FADED. DADA FLOURISHED UNTIL 1924, WHEN IT EVOLVED INTO **SURREALISM**.
HE THEN BECAME ONE OF THE PREMIER ARTISTS OF THE SURREALIST MOVEMENT, ALONG SIDE TZARA, BRETON AND **SALVADOR DALI** (1904-1989).

DUCHAMP PERIODICALLY RETURNED TO NEW YORK TO CONTINUE WORKING ON "THE LARGE GLASS" -- ALSO KNOWN AS "**THE BRIDE STRIPPED BARE BY HER BACHELORS**" -- UNTIL IT WAS "FINISHED" IN 1923. FROM THEN ON HE SEEMED TO HAVE LITTLE TIME FOR SUCH THINGS. HE SPENT MOST OF THE NEXT 45 YEARS PLAYING CHESS AND PROVING THAT THE ONLY *TRUE* ART IS THE ART OF LIVING, ALTHOUGH THE OCCASIONAL CAREER RETROSPECTIVE DOESN'T HURT, EITHER.

FOR LYNN

DAN STEFFAN 2012

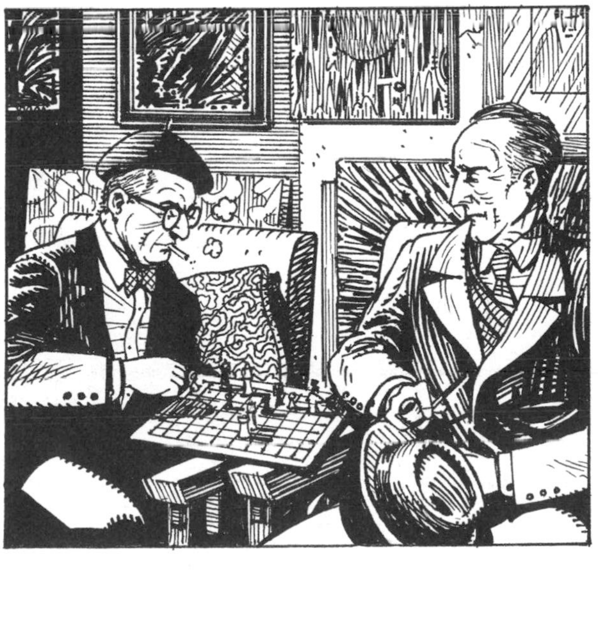

MAN RAY AND DUCHAMP WERE FRIENDS FOR MORE THAN 50 YEARS AND CONTINUED TO BE CLOSE UNTIL, LITERALLY, THE VERY END. ON OCTOBER 2nd, 1968, MAN RAY AND HIS WIFE WERE DINNER GUESTS AT DUCHAMP'S HOME IN NEUILLY, FRANCE, WHERE THEY ATE WELL AND TOASTED EACH OTHER'S HEALTH. CONVERSATION AND A GAME OF CHESS FOLLOWED THE MEAL -- AS WAS THEIR HABIT. AFTER SAYING *ADIEU*, DUCHAMP WENT TO BED AND NEVER WOKE UP.

FIN

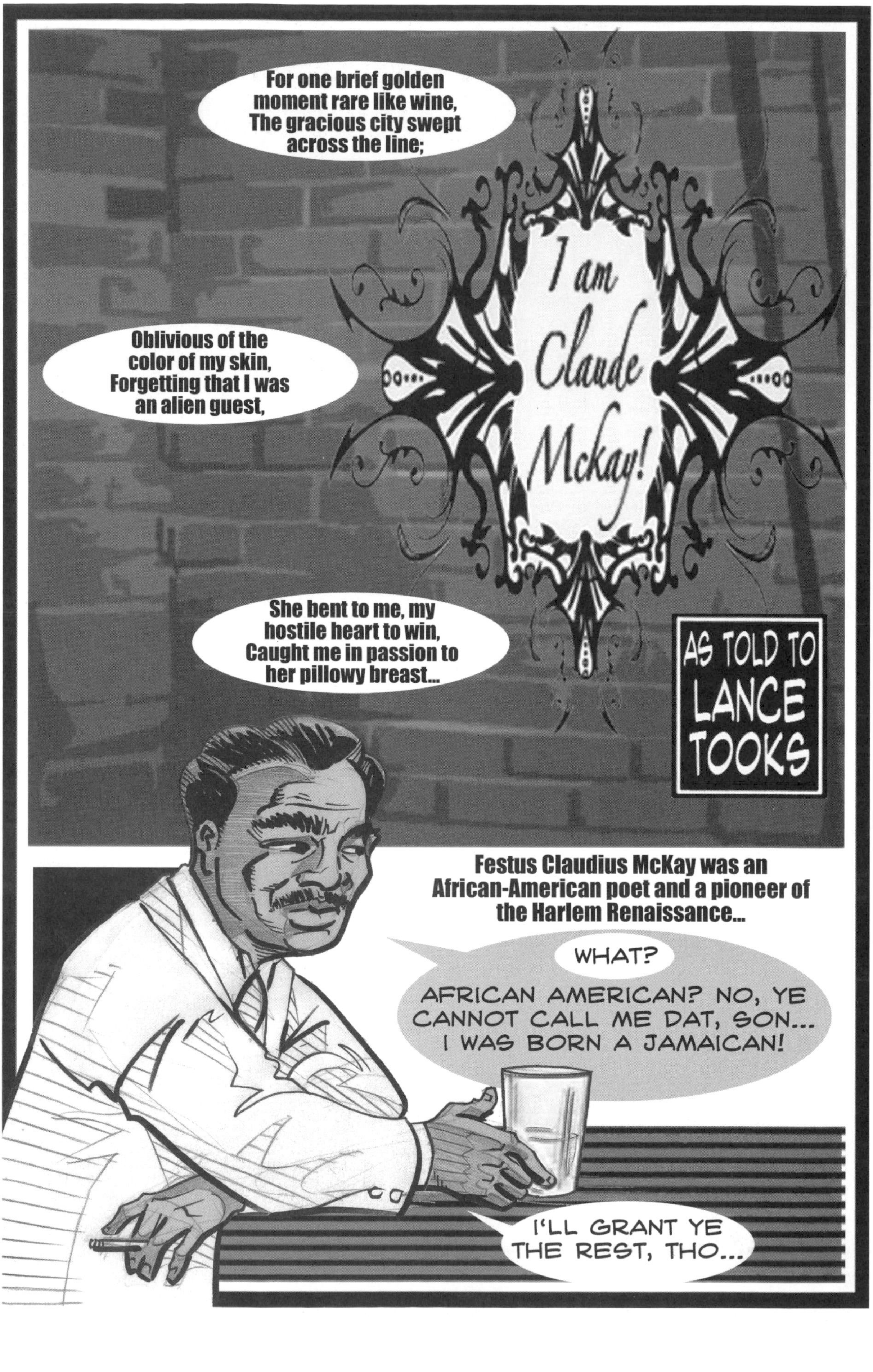
For one brief golden moment rare like wine, The gracious city swept across the line;
I am Claude Mckay!
Oblivious of the color of my skin, Forgetting that I was an alien guest,
She bent to me, my hostile heart to win, Caught me in passion to her pillowy breast...
AS TOLD TO LANCE TOOKS
Festus Claudius McKay was an African-American poet and a pioneer of the Harlem Renaissance...
WHAT?
AFRICAN AMERICAN? NO, YE CANNOT CALL ME DAT, SON... I WAS BORN A JAMAICAN!
I'LL GRANT YE THE REST, THO...

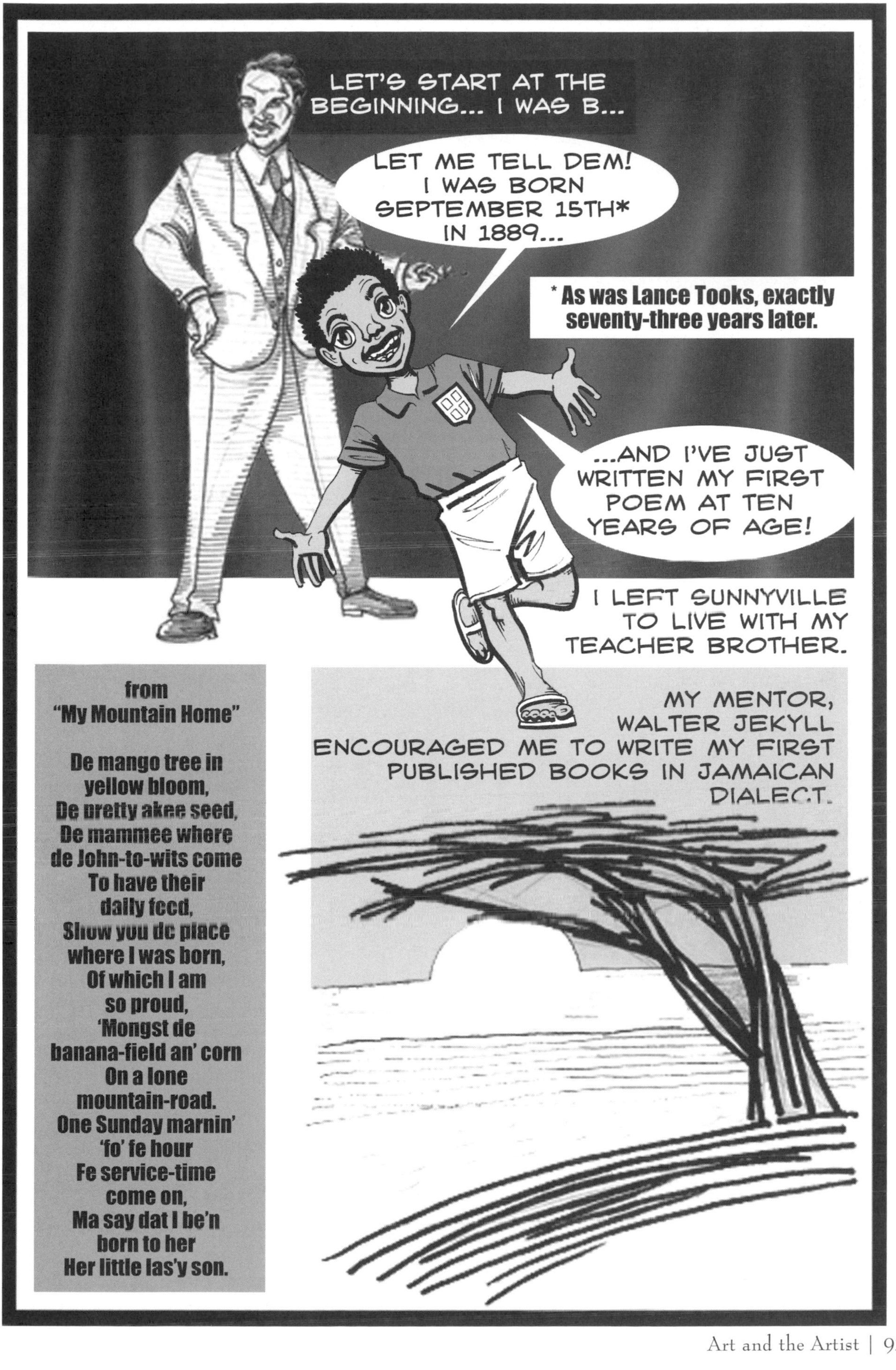
LET'S START AT THE BEGINNING... I WAS B...
LET ME TELL DEM! I WAS BORN SEPTEMBER 15TH* IN 1889...
* As was Lance Tooks, exactly seventy-three years later.
...AND I'VE JUST WRITTEN MY FIRST POEM AT TEN YEARS OF AGE!
I LEFT SUNNYVILLE TO LIVE WITH MY TEACHER BROTHER.
from
"My Mountain Home"
De mango tree in
yellow bloom,
De pretty akee seed,
De mammee where
de John-to-wits come
To have their
daily feed,
Show you de place
where I was born,
Of which I am
so proud,
'Mongst de
banana-field an' corn
On a lone
mountain-road.
One Sunday marnin'
'fo' fe hour
Fe service-time
come on,
Ma say dat I be'n
born to her
Her little las'y son.
MY MENTOR, WALTER JEKYLL ENCOURAGED ME TO WRITE MY FIRST PUBLISHED BOOKS IN JAMAICAN DIALECT.

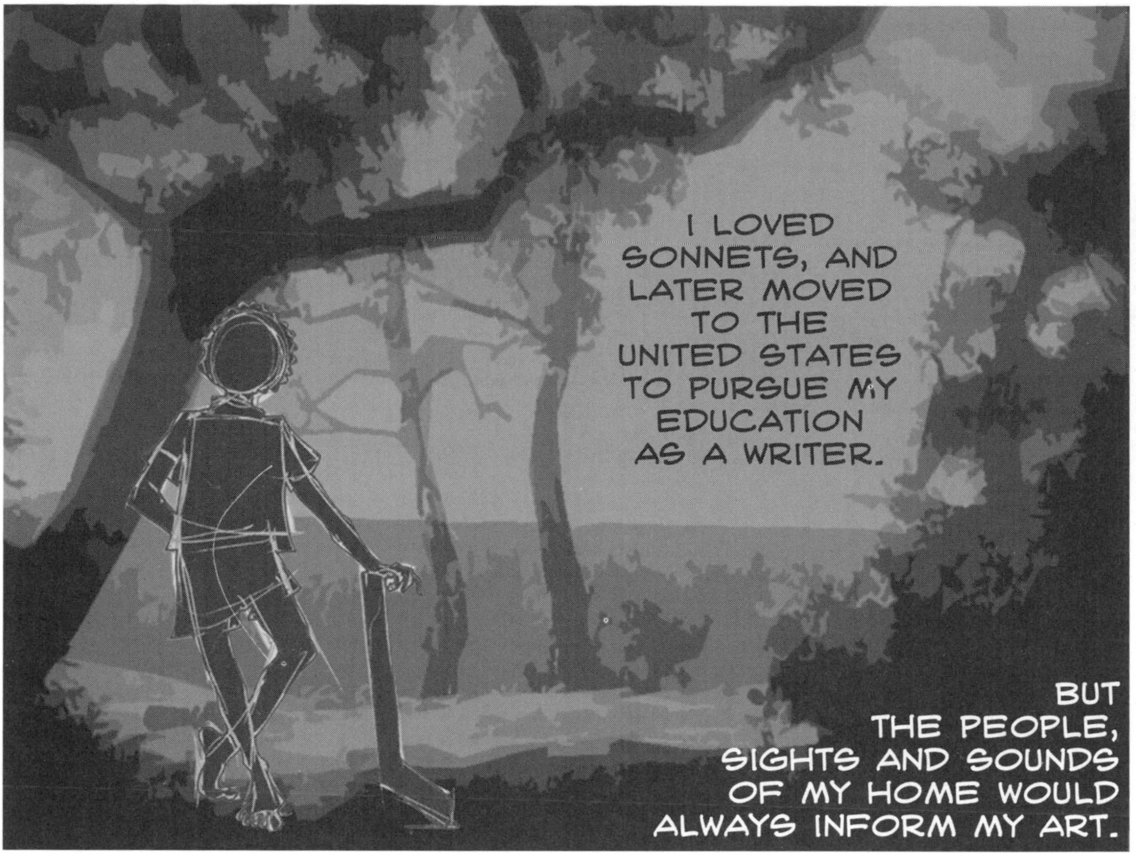
I LOVED SONNETS, AND LATER MOVED TO THE UNITED STATES TO PURSUE MY EDUCATION AS A WRITER.
BUT THE PEOPLE, SIGHTS AND SOUNDS OF MY HOME WOULD ALWAYS INFORM MY ART.

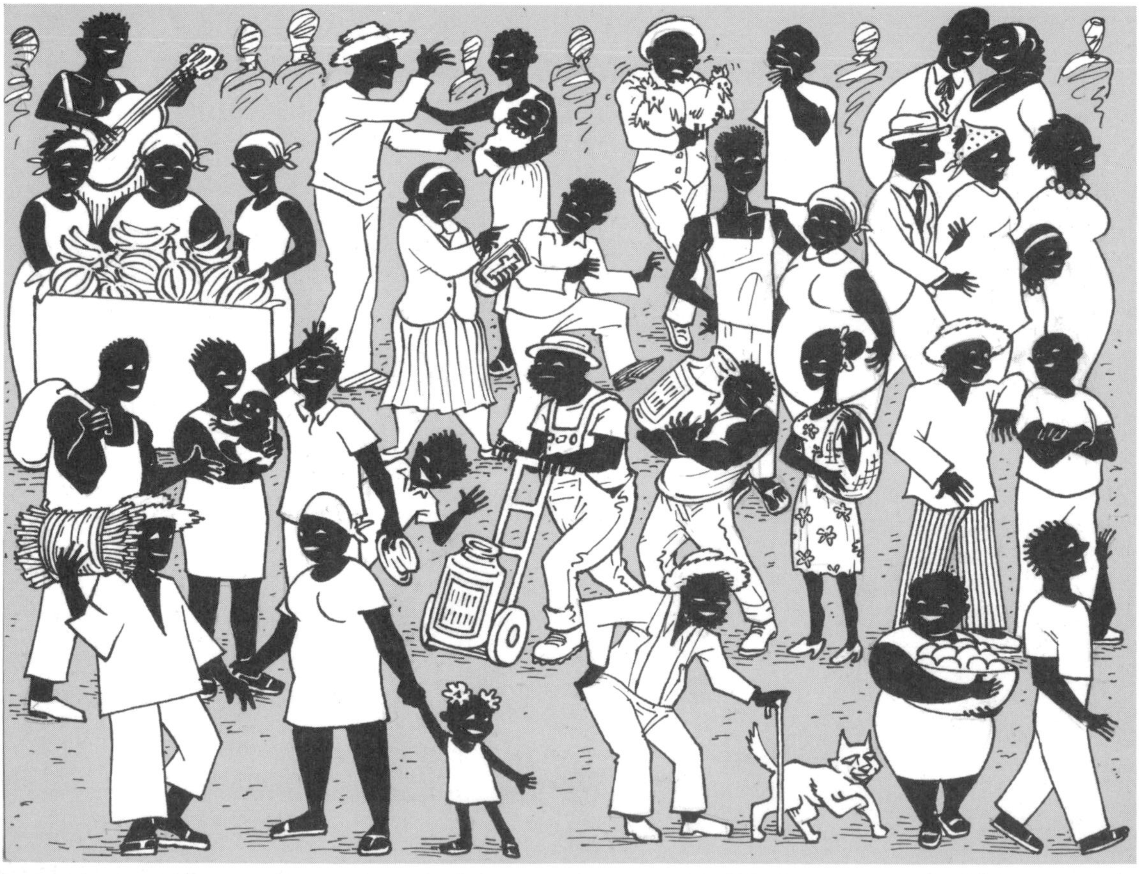

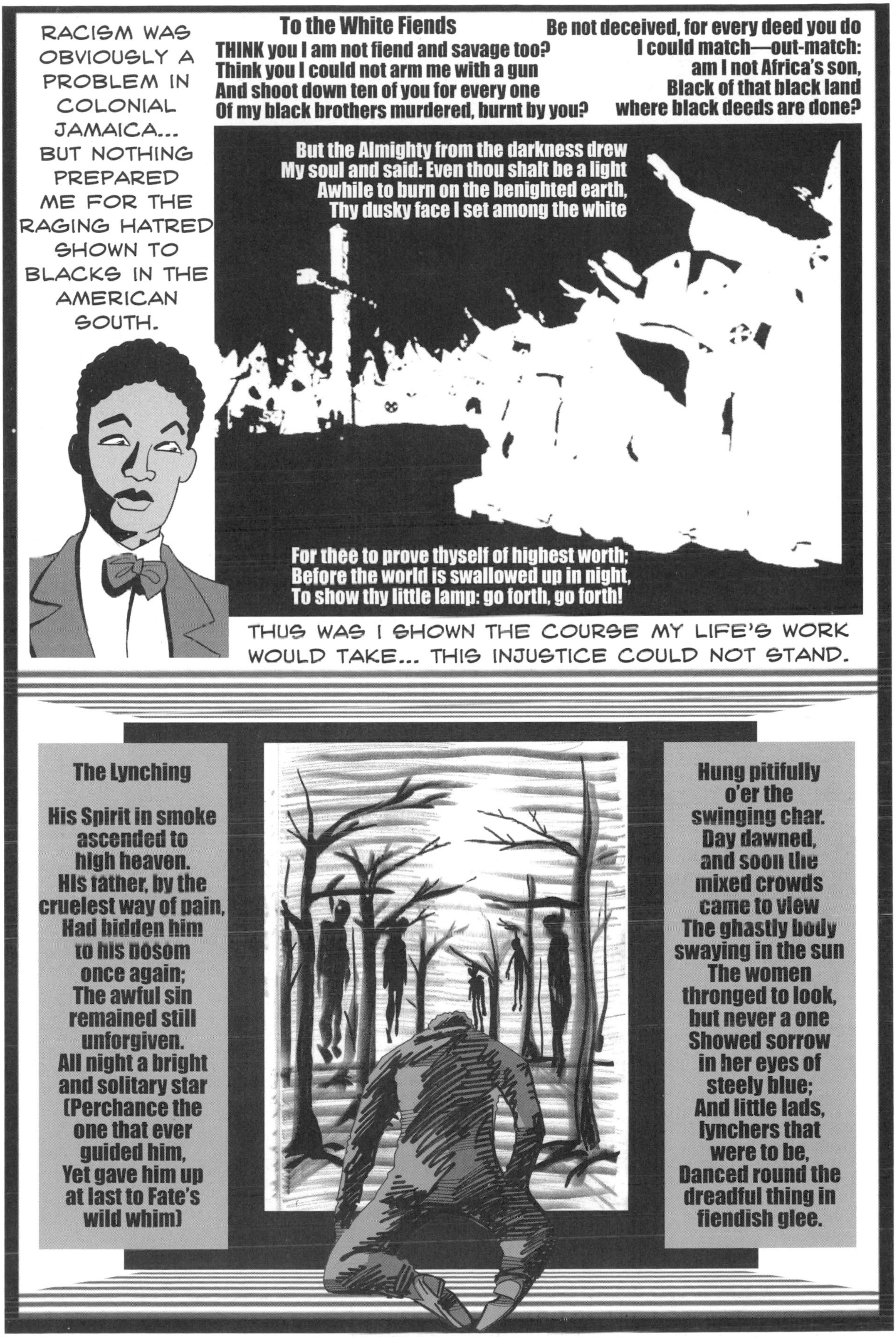

RACISM WAS OBVIOUSLY A PROBLEM IN COLONIAL JAMAICA... BUT NOTHING PREPARED ME FOR THE RAGING HATRED SHOWN TO BLACKS IN THE AMERICAN SOUTH.
To the White Fiends
THINK you I am not fiend and savage too?
Think you I could not arm me with a gun
And shoot down ten of you for every one
Of my black brothers murdered, burnt by you?
Be not deceived, for every deed you do
I could match—out-match:
am I not Africa's son,
Black of that black land
where black deeds are done?
But the Almighty from the darkness drew
My soul and said: Even thou shalt be a light
Awhile to burn on the benighted earth,
Thy dusky face I set among the white
For thee to prove thyself of highest worth;
Before the world is swallowed up in night,
To show thy little lamp: go forth, go forth!
THUS WAS I SHOWN THE COURSE MY LIFE'S WORK WOULD TAKE... THIS INJUSTICE COULD NOT STAND.
The Lynching
His Spirit in smoke
ascended to
high heaven.
His father, by the
cruelest way of pain,
Had bidden him
to his bosom
once again;
The awful sin
remained still
unforgiven.
All night a bright
and solitary star
(Perchance the
one that ever
guided him,
Yet gave him up
at last to Fate's
wild whim)
Hung pitifully
o'er the
swinging char.
Day dawned,
and soon the
mixed crowds
came to view
The ghastly body
swaying in the sun
The women
thronged to look,
but never a one
Showed sorrow
in her eyes of
steely blue;
And little lads,
lynchers that
were to be,
Danced round the
dreadful thing in
fiendish glee.

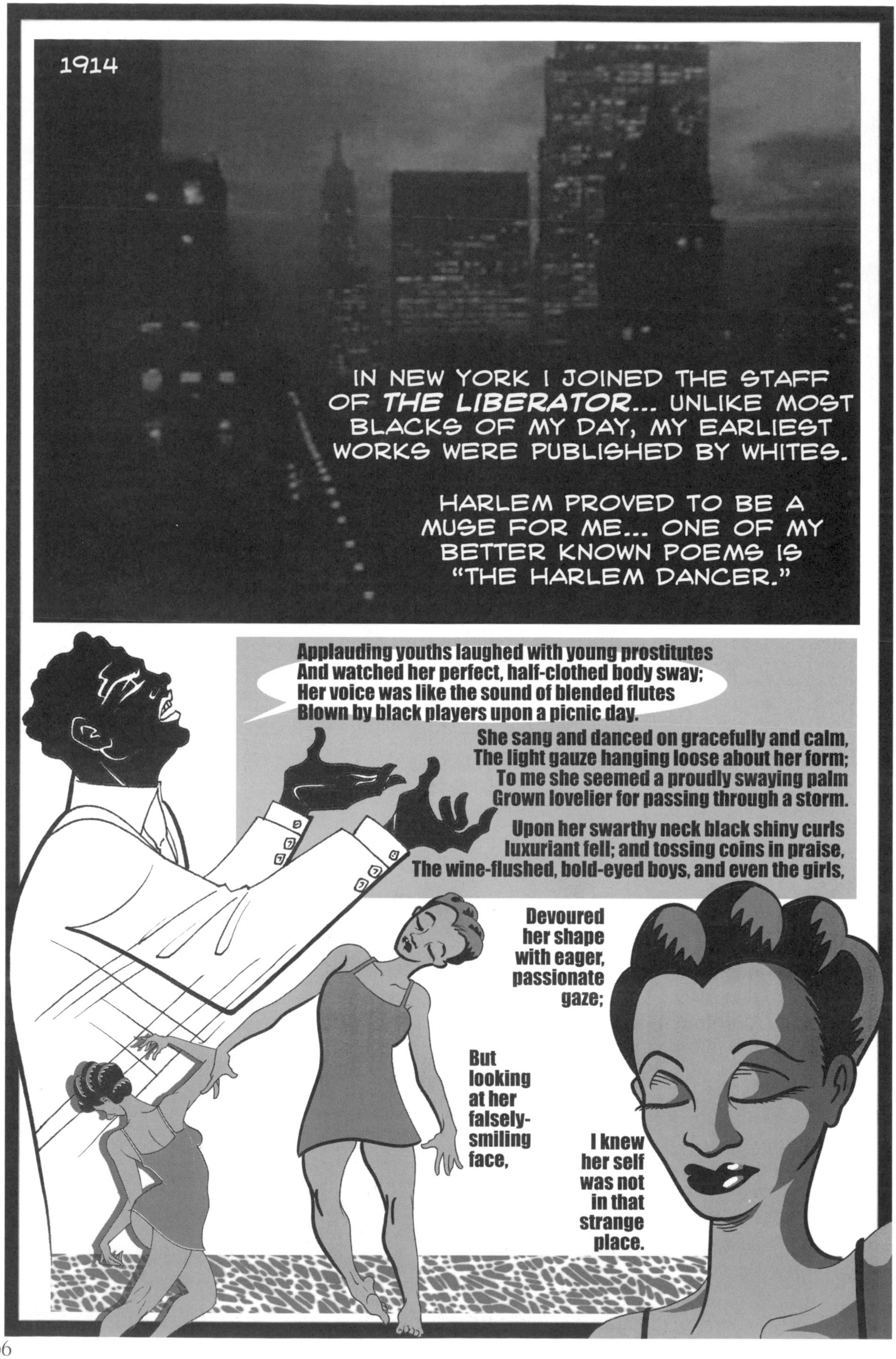
1914
IN NEW YORK I JOINED THE STAFF OF *THE LIBERATOR*... UNLIKE MOST BLACKS OF MY DAY, MY EARLIEST WORKS WERE PUBLISHED BY WHITES.
HARLEM PROVED TO BE A MUSE FOR ME... ONE OF MY BETTER KNOWN POEMS IS "THE HARLEM DANCER."
Applauding youths laughed with young prostitutes
And watched her perfect, half-clothed body sway;
Her voice was like the sound of blended flutes
Blown by black players upon a picnic day.
She sang and danced on gracefully and calm,
The light gauze hanging loose about her form;
To me she seemed a proudly swaying palm
Grown lovelier for passing through a storm.
Upon her swarthy neck black shiny curls
luxuriant fell; and tossing coins in praise,
The wine-flushed, bold-eyed boys, and even the girls,
Devoured her shape with eager, passionate gaze;
But looking at her falsely-smiling face,
I knew her self was not in that strange place.

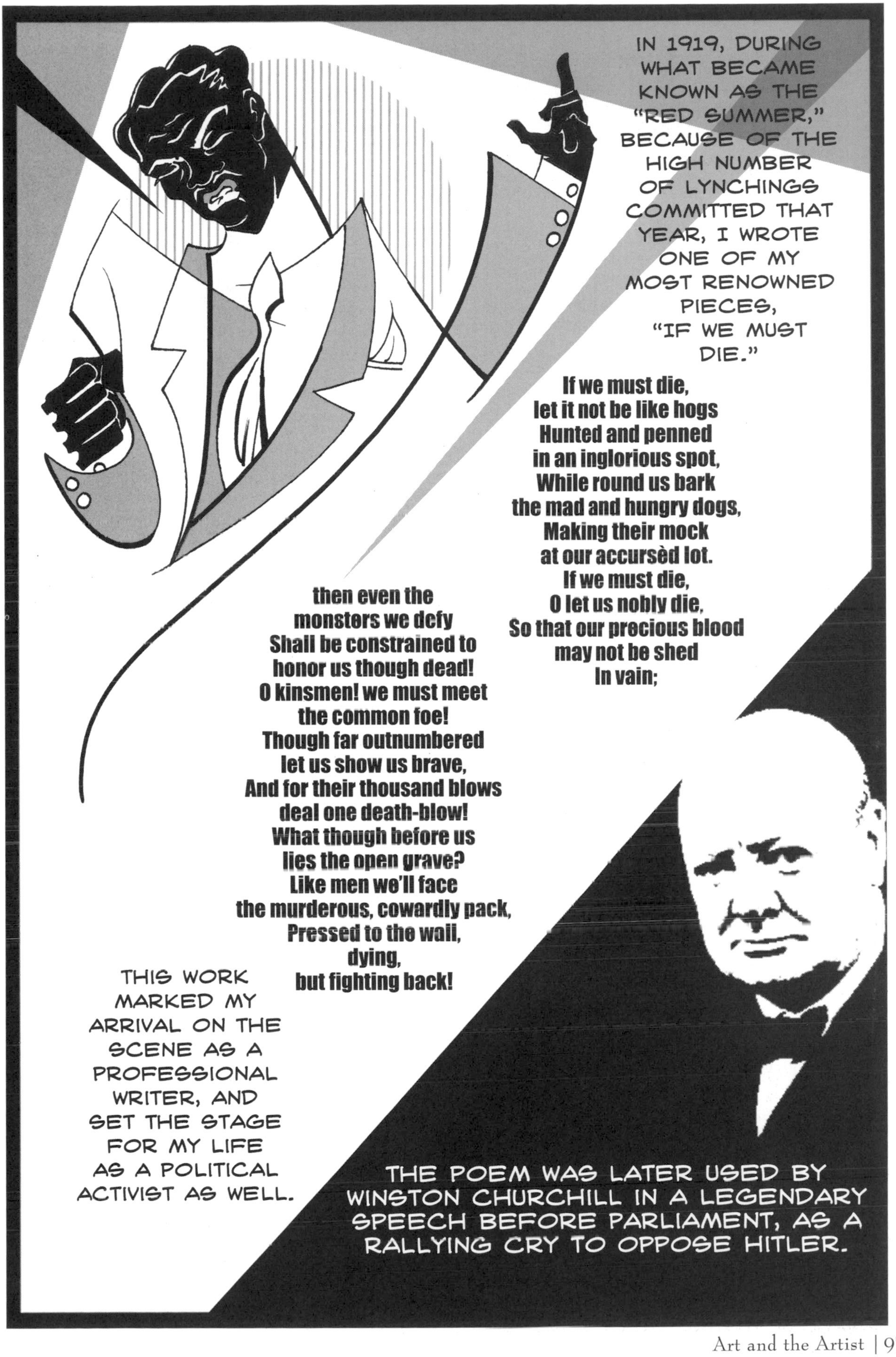
IN 1919, DURING WHAT BECAME KNOWN AS THE "RED SUMMER," BECAUSE OF THE HIGH NUMBER OF LYNCHINGS COMMITTED THAT YEAR, I WROTE ONE OF MY MOST RENOWNED PIECES, "IF WE MUST DIE."
If we must die,
let it not be like hogs
Hunted and penned
in an inglorious spot,
While round us bark
the mad and hungry dogs,
Making their mock
at our accursèd lot.
If we must die,
O let us nobly die,
So that our precious blood
may not be shed
In vain;
then even the
monsters we defy
Shall be constrained to
honor us though dead!
O kinsmen! we must meet
the common foe!
Though far outnumbered
let us show us brave,
And for their thousand blows
deal one death-blow!
What though before us
lies the open grave?
Like men we'll face
the murderous, cowardly pack,
Pressed to the wall,
dying,
but fighting back!
THIS WORK MARKED MY ARRIVAL ON THE SCENE AS A PROFESSIONAL WRITER, AND SET THE STAGE FOR MY LIFE AS A POLITICAL ACTIVIST AS WELL.
THE POEM WAS LATER USED BY WINSTON CHURCHILL IN A LEGENDARY SPEECH BEFORE PARLIAMENT, AS A RALLYING CRY TO OPPOSE HITLER.

December, 1919

Last night I heard
your voice, mother,
The words you sang to me
When I, a little barefoot boy,
Knelt down against
your knee.

And tears gushed from
my heart, mother,
And passed beyond its wall,
But though the fountain
reached my throat
The drops refused to fall.

'Tis ten years since
you died, mother,
Just ten dark years of pain,
And oh, I only wish that I
Could weep just once again.

I MOVED TO LONDON IN 1919. I JOINED ATHEIST AND SOCIALIST GROUPS AND GOT INVOLVED. I BECAME AN AVID MARXIST AND WROTE FOR *THE WORKER'S DREADNOUGHT* AND *THE CAMBRIDGE MAGAZINE.*

I WAS THE FIRST WORKING BLACK JOURNALIST IN BRITAIN.

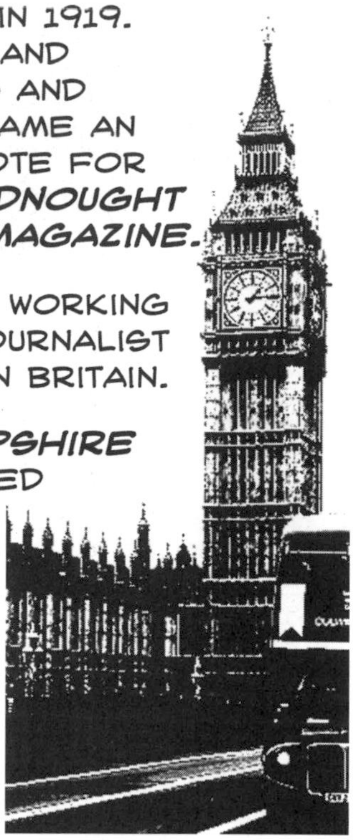

SPRING IN NEW HAMPSHIRE WAS MY THIRD PUBLISHED VERSE COLLECTION, WHICH CONTAINED "HARLEM SHADOWS," ABOUT AMERICA'S DEGREDATION OF MY PEOPLE. IT BECAME THE TITLE OF A LATER COLLECTION AS WELL.

Harlem Shadows

I hear the halting footsteps of a lass
In Negro Harlem when the night
lets fall its veil.
I see the shapes of girls who pass
To bend and barter at desire's call.
Ah, little dark girls who in slippered feet
Go prowling through the night
from street to street!

Through the long night until the silver break
Of day the little gray feet know no rest;
Through the lone night
until the last snow-flake
Has dropped from heaven upon
the earth's white breast,
The dusky, half-clad girls of tired feet
Are trudging, thinly shod,
from street to street.

Ah, stern harsh world,
that in the wretched way
Of poverty, dishonor and disgrace,
Has pushed the timid little feet of clay,
The sacred brown feet of my fallen race!
Ah, heart of me, the weary, weary feet
In Harlem wandering
from street to street.

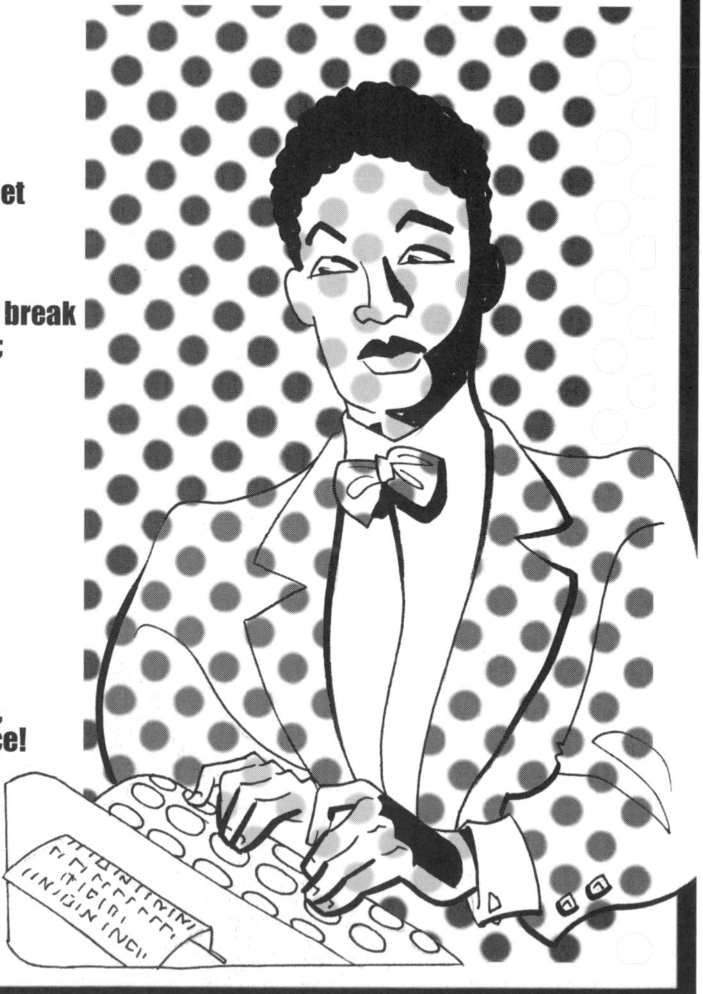

I TRAVELLED THE WORLD, WRITING... TO HOLLAND, BELGIUM, MOROCCO, PARIS, BERLIN...

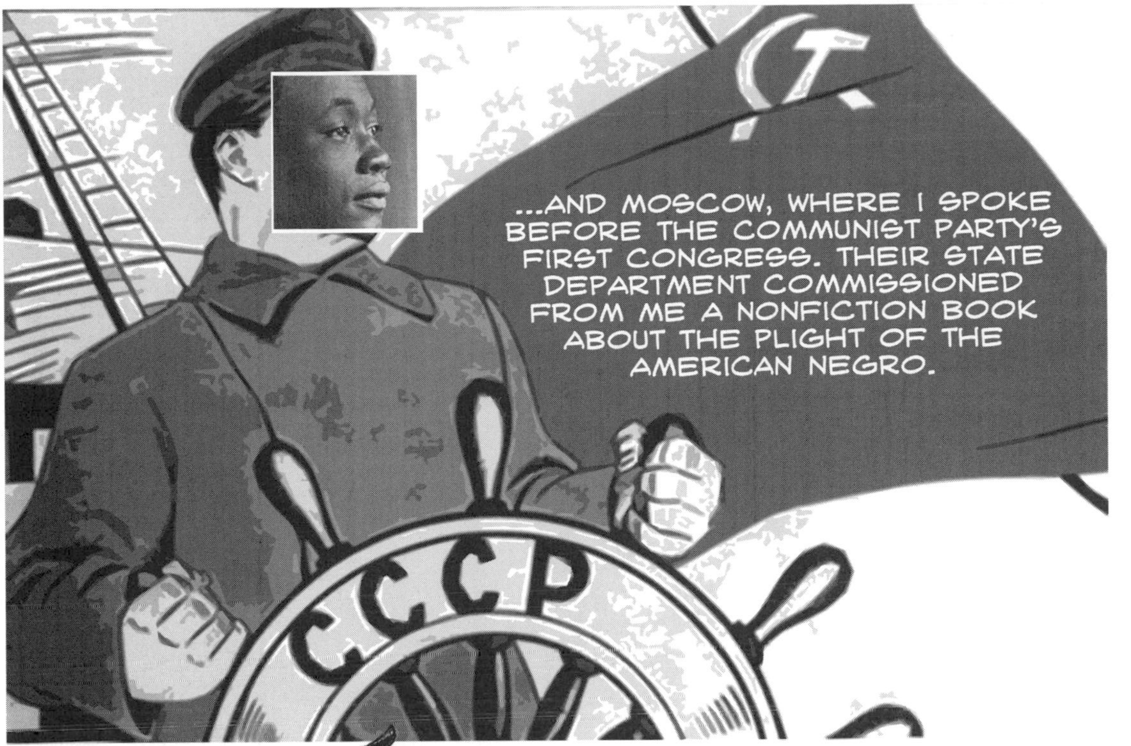
...AND MOSCOW, WHERE I SPOKE BEFORE THE COMMUNIST PARTY'S FIRST CONGRESS. THEIR STATE DEPARTMENT COMMISSIONED FROM ME A NONFICTION BOOK ABOUT THE PLIGHT OF THE AMERICAN NEGRO.
CCCP

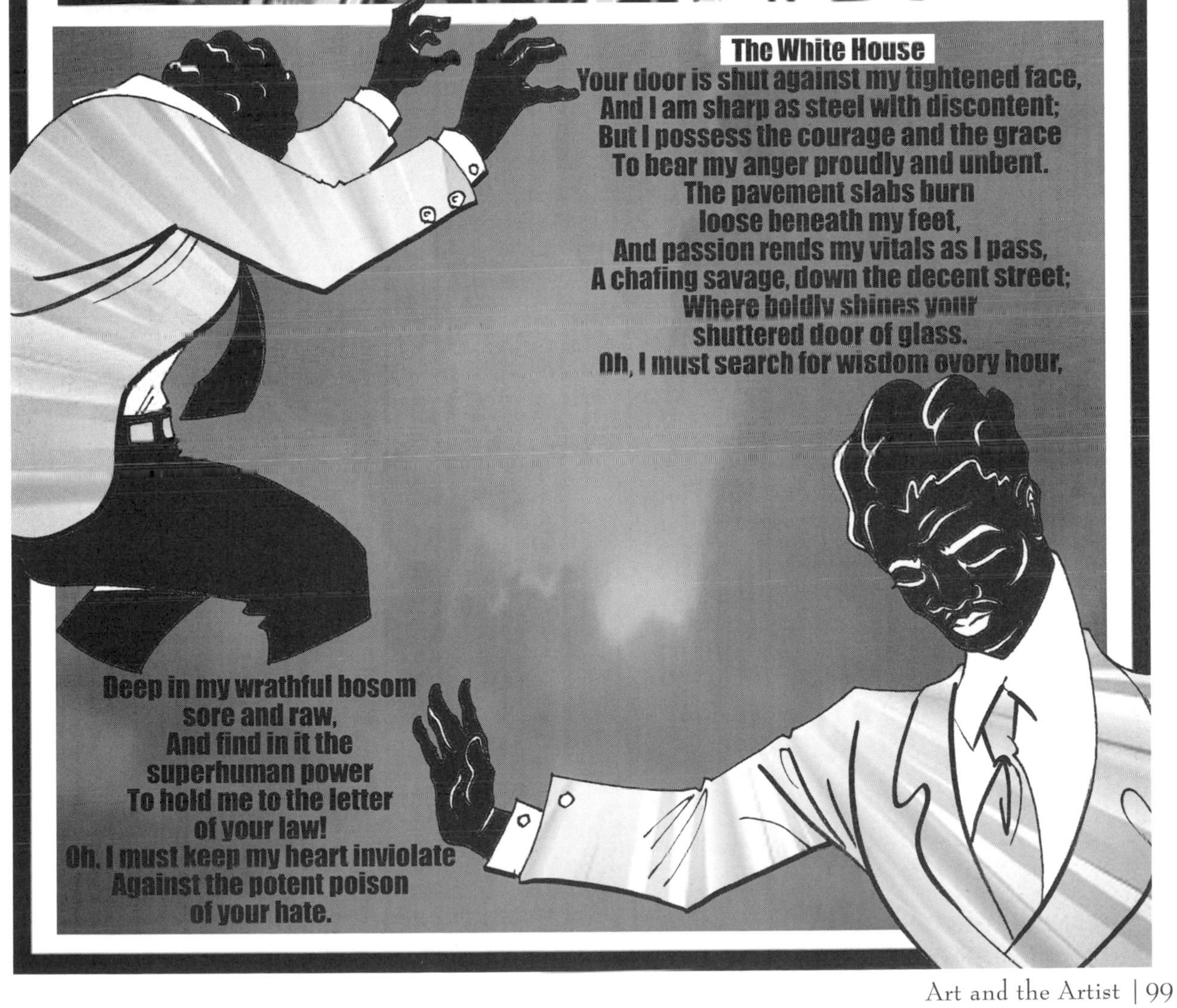
The White House
Your door is shut against my tightened face,
And I am sharp as steel with discontent;
But I possess the courage and the grace
To bear my anger proudly and unbent.
The pavement slabs burn
loose beneath my feet,
And passion rends my vitals as I pass,
A chafing savage, down the decent street;
Where boldly shines your
shuttered door of glass.
Oh, I must search for wisdom every hour,
Deep in my wrathful bosom
sore and raw,
And find in it the
superhuman power
To hold me to the letter
of your law!
Oh, I must keep my heart inviolate
Against the potent poison
of your hate.

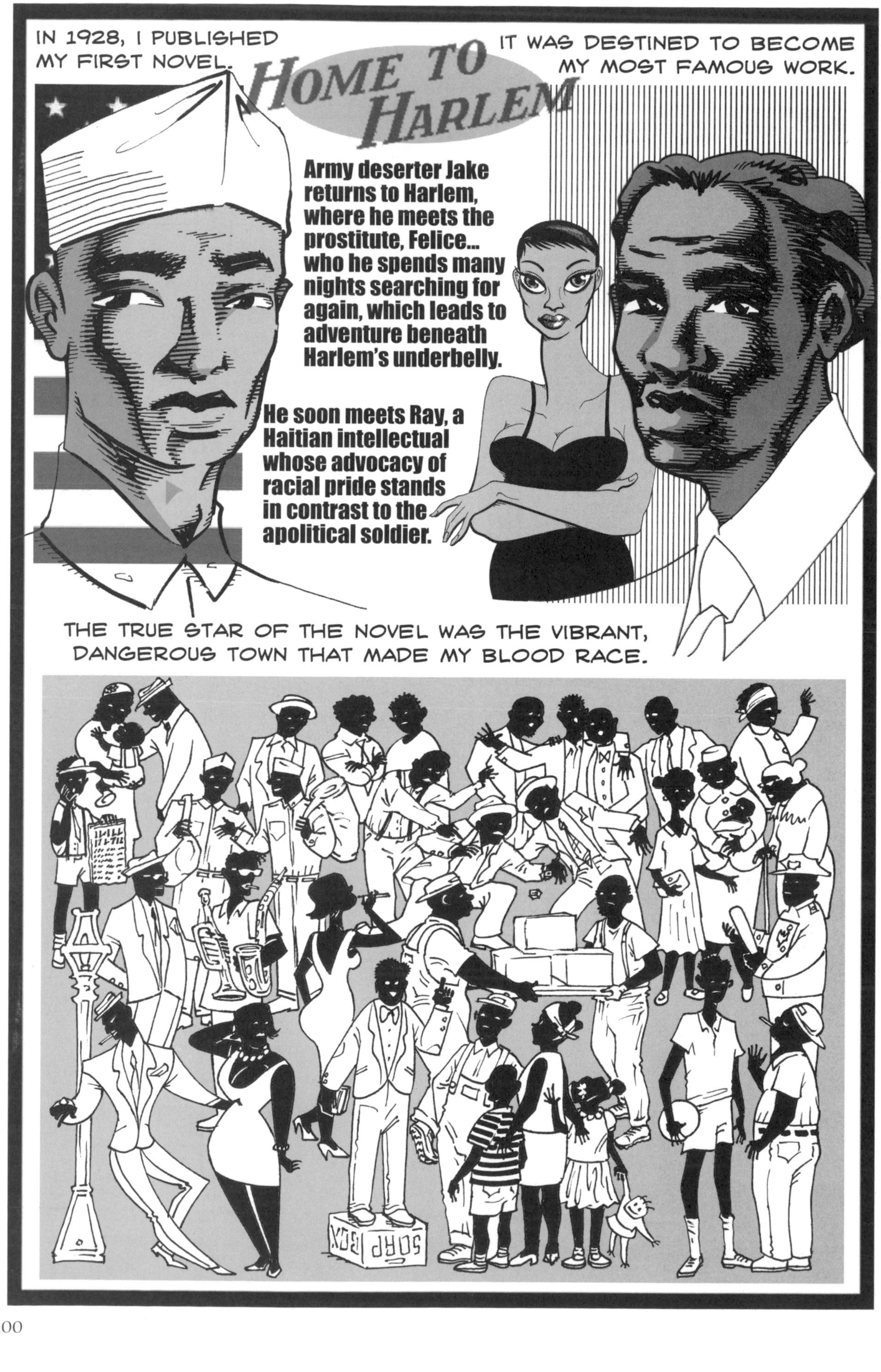

IN 1928, I PUBLISHED MY FIRST NOVEL.
HOME TO HARLEM
IT WAS DESTINED TO BECOME MY MOST FAMOUS WORK.
Army deserter Jake returns to Harlem, where he meets the prostitute, Felice... who he spends many nights searching for again, which leads to adventure beneath Harlem's underbelly.
He soon meets Ray, a Haitian intellectual whose advocacy of racial pride stands in contrast to the apolitical soldier.
THE TRUE STAR OF THE NOVEL WAS THE VIBRANT, DANGEROUS TOWN THAT MADE MY BLOOD RACE.
SOAP BOX

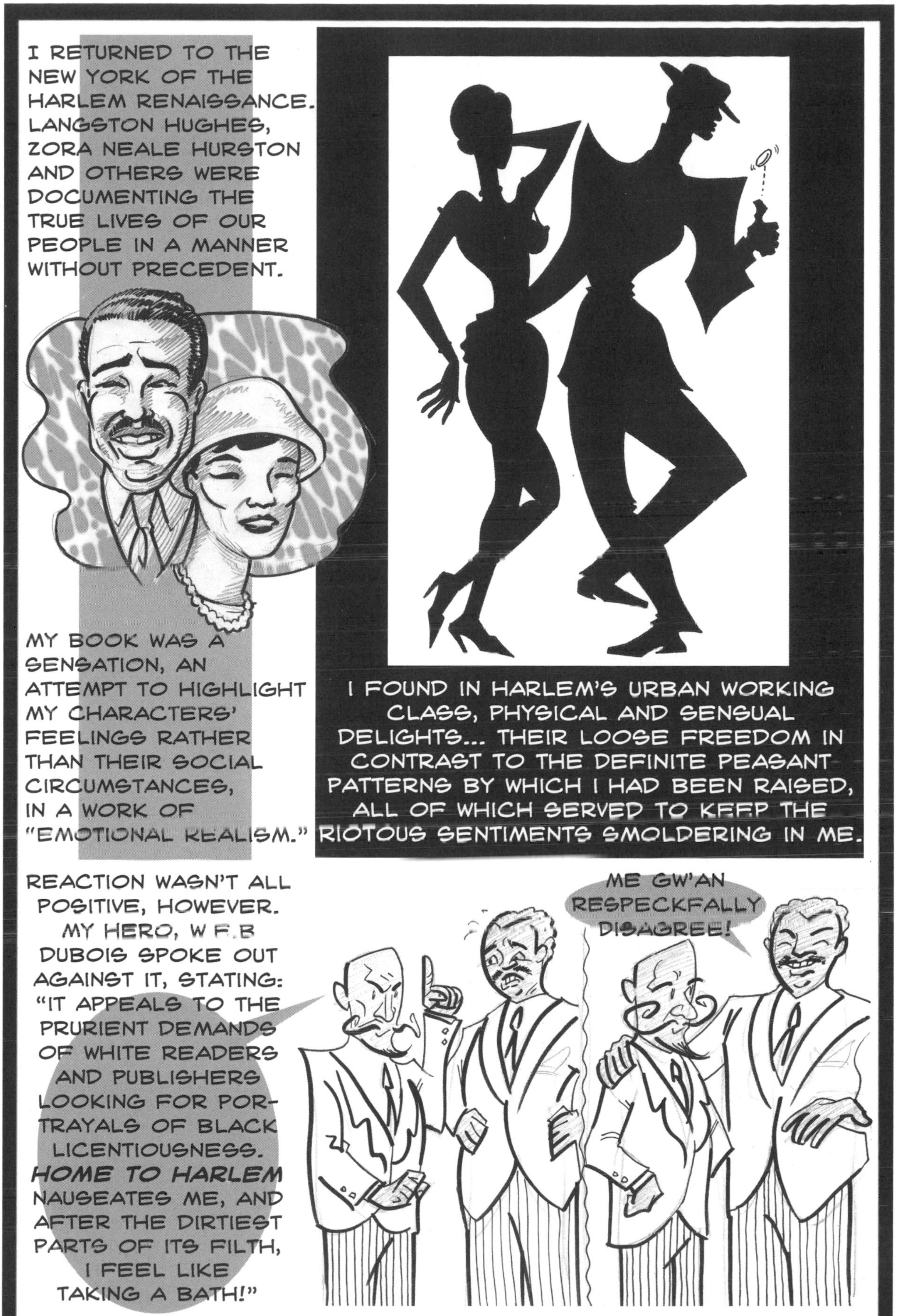

I RETURNED TO THE NEW YORK OF THE HARLEM RENAISSANCE. LANGSTON HUGHES, ZORA NEALE HURSTON AND OTHERS WERE DOCUMENTING THE TRUE LIVES OF OUR PEOPLE IN A MANNER WITHOUT PRECEDENT.
MY BOOK WAS A SENSATION, AN ATTEMPT TO HIGHLIGHT MY CHARACTERS' FEELINGS RATHER THAN THEIR SOCIAL CIRCUMSTANCES, IN A WORK OF "EMOTIONAL REALISM."
I FOUND IN HARLEM'S URBAN WORKING CLASS, PHYSICAL AND SENSUAL DELIGHTS... THEIR LOOSE FREEDOM IN CONTRAST TO THE DEFINITE PEASANT PATTERNS BY WHICH I HAD BEEN RAISED, ALL OF WHICH SERVED TO KEEP THE RIOTOUS SENTIMENTS SMOLDERING IN ME.
REACTION WASN'T ALL POSITIVE, HOWEVER. MY HERO, W.E.B DUBOIS SPOKE OUT AGAINST IT, STATING:
"IT APPEALS TO THE PRURIENT DEMANDS OF WHITE READERS AND PUBLISHERS LOOKING FOR PORTRAYALS OF BLACK LICENTIOUSNESS. HOME TO HARLEM NAUSEATES ME, AND AFTER THE DIRTIEST PARTS OF ITS FILTH, I FEEL LIKE TAKING A BATH!"
ME GW'AN RESPECKFALLY DISAGREE!

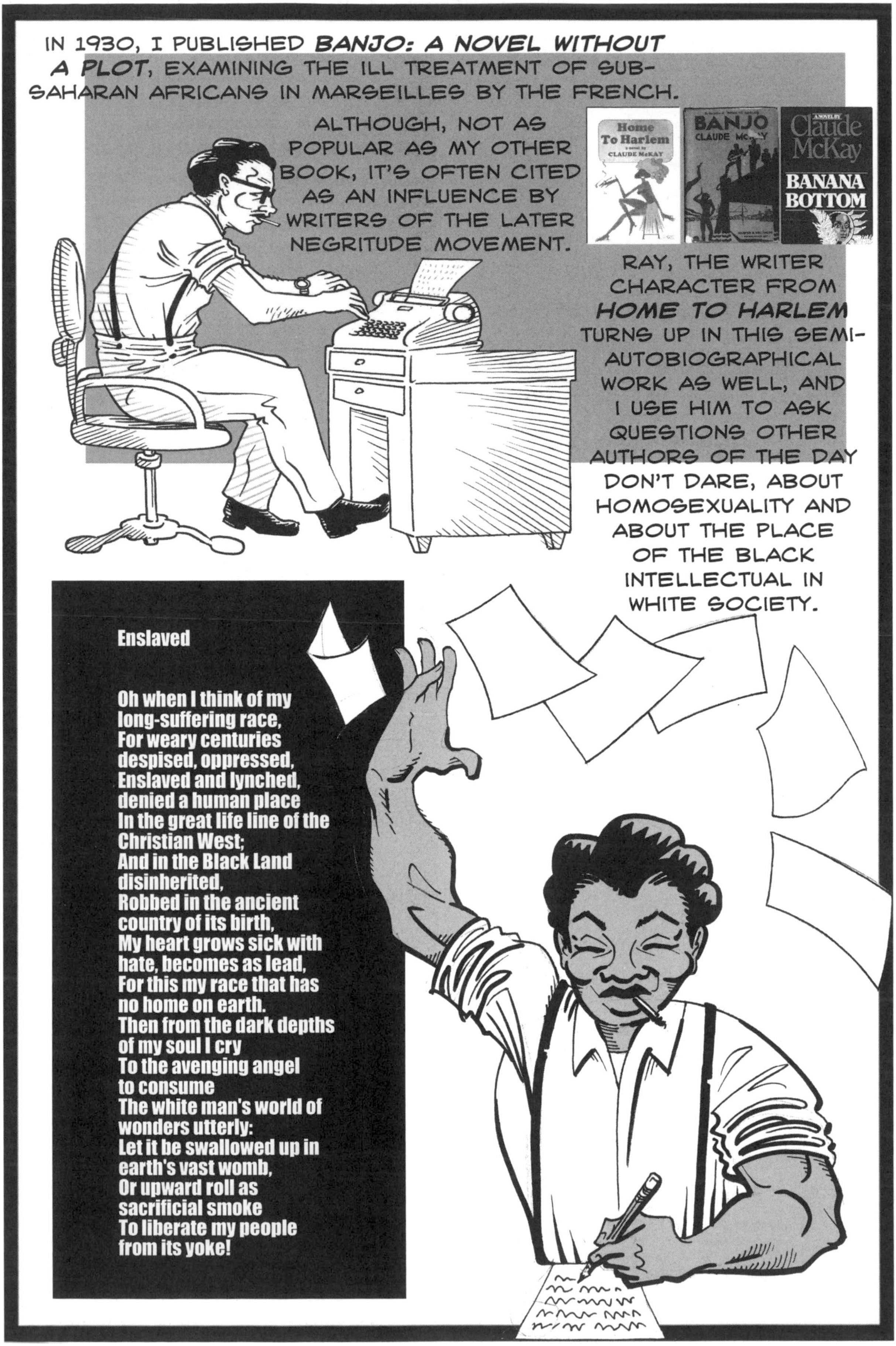
IN 1930, I PUBLISHED ***BANJO: A NOVEL WITHOUT A PLOT***, EXAMINING THE ILL TREATMENT OF SUB-SAHARAN AFRICANS IN MARSEILLES BY THE FRENCH.
ALTHOUGH, NOT AS POPULAR AS MY OTHER BOOK, IT'S OFTEN CITED AS AN INFLUENCE BY WRITERS OF THE LATER NEGRITUDE MOVEMENT.
Home To Harlem
CLAUDE McKAY
BANJO
CLAUDE McKAY
Claude McKay
BANANA BOTTOM
RAY, THE WRITER CHARACTER FROM ***HOME TO HARLEM*** TURNS UP IN THIS SEMI-AUTOBIOGRAPHICAL WORK AS WELL, AND I USE HIM TO ASK QUESTIONS OTHER AUTHORS OF THE DAY DON'T DARE, ABOUT HOMOSEXUALITY AND ABOUT THE PLACE OF THE BLACK INTELLECTUAL IN WHITE SOCIETY.
Enslaved
Oh when I think of my
long-suffering race,
For weary centuries
despised, oppressed,
Enslaved and lynched,
denied a human place
In the great life line of the
Christian West;
And in the Black Land
disinherited,
Robbed in the ancient
country of its birth,
My heart grows sick with
hate, becomes as lead,
For this my race that has
no home on earth.
Then from the dark depths
of my soul I cry
To the avenging angel
to consume
The white man's world of
wonders utterly:
Let it be swallowed up in
earth's vast womb,
Or upward roll as
sacrificial smoke
To liberate my people
from its yoke!

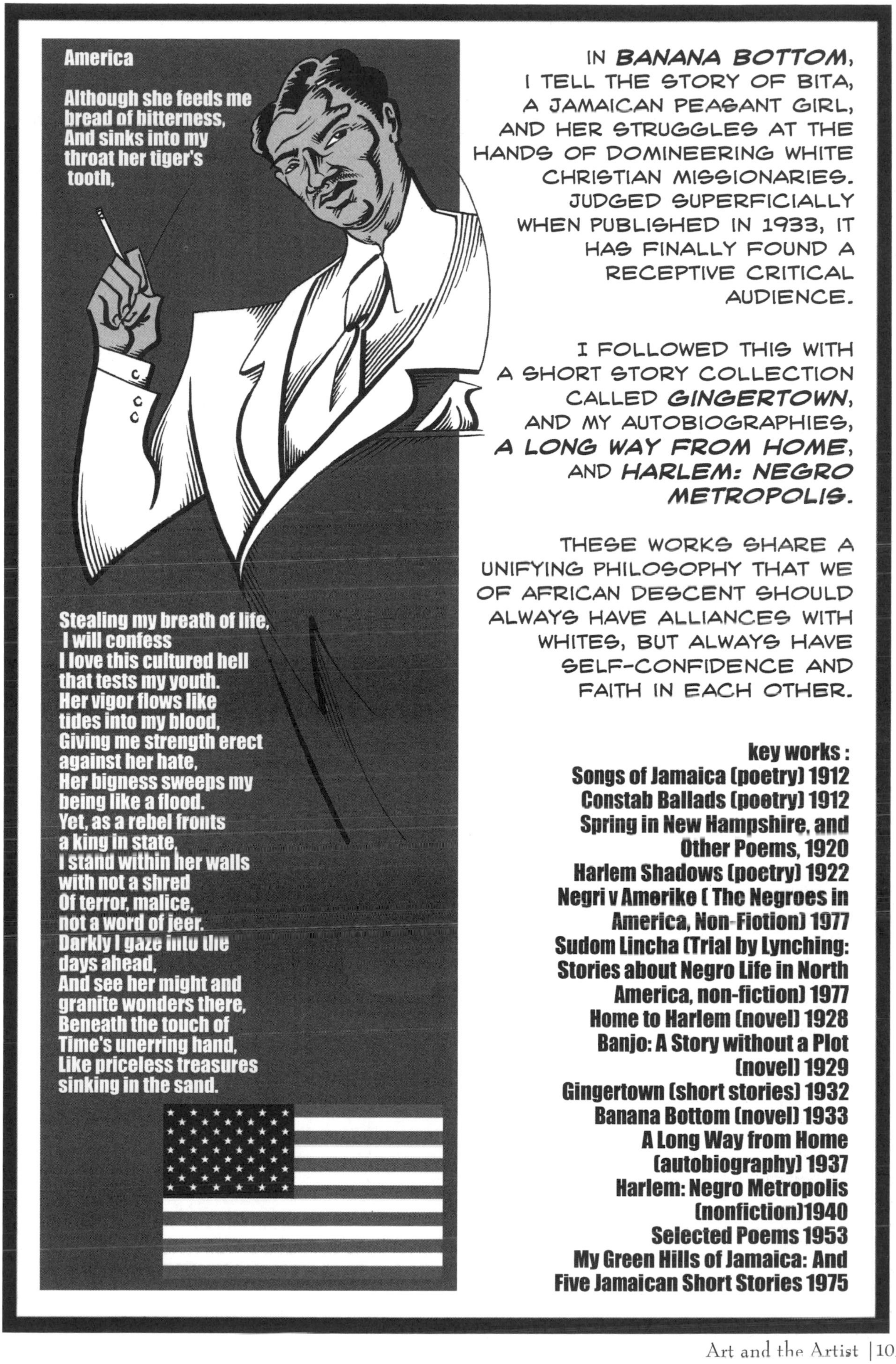
IN *BANANA BOTTOM*, I TELL THE STORY OF BITA, A JAMAICAN PEASANT GIRL, AND HER STRUGGLES AT THE HANDS OF DOMINEERING WHITE CHRISTIAN MISSIONARIES. JUDGED SUPERFICIALLY WHEN PUBLISHED IN 1933, IT HAS FINALLY FOUND A RECEPTIVE CRITICAL AUDIENCE.
I FOLLOWED THIS WITH A SHORT STORY COLLECTION CALLED *GINGERTOWN*, AND MY AUTOBIOGRAPHIES, *A LONG WAY FROM HOME*, AND *HARLEM: NEGRO METROPOLIS*.
THESE WORKS SHARE A UNIFYING PHILOSOPHY THAT WE OF AFRICAN DESCENT SHOULD ALWAYS HAVE ALLIANCES WITH WHITES, BUT ALWAYS HAVE SELF-CONFIDENCE AND FAITH IN EACH OTHER.
America
Although she feeds me bread of bitterness, And sinks into my throat her tiger's tooth,
Stealing my breath of life, I will confess I love this cultured hell that tests my youth. Her vigor flows like tides into my blood, Giving me strength erect against her hate, Her bigness sweeps my being like a flood. Yet, as a rebel fronts a king in state, I stand within her walls with not a shred Of terror, malice, not a word of jeer. Darkly I gaze into the days ahead, And see her might and granite wonders there, Beneath the touch of Time's unerring hand, Like priceless treasures sinking in the sand.
key works :
Songs of Jamaica (poetry) 1912
Constab Ballads (poetry) 1912
Spring in New Hampshire, and Other Poems, 1920
Harlem Shadows (poetry) 1922
Negri v Amerike (The Negroes in America, Non-Fiotion) 1977
Sudom Lincha (Trial by Lynching: Stories about Negro Life in North America, non-fiction) 1977
Home to Harlem (novel) 1928
Banjo: A Story without a Plot (novel) 1929
Gingertown (short stories) 1932
Banana Bottom (novel) 1933
A Long Way from Home (autobiography) 1937
Harlem: Negro Metropolis (nonfiction)1940
Selected Poems 1953
My Green Hills of Jamaica: And Five Jamaican Short Stories 1975

To Winter

Stay, season of calm love
and soulful snows!
There is a subtle sweetness
in the sun,
The ripples on the stream's
breast gaily run,
The wind more boisterously
by me blows,
And each succeeding day
now longer grows.
The birds a gladder music
have begun,
The squirrel, full of mischief
and of fun,
From maples' topmost branch
the brown twig throws.
I read these pregnant signs,
know what they mean:
I know that thou art making
ready to go.
Oh stay! I fled a land where
fields are green
Always, and palms wave
gently to and fro,
And winds are balmy, blue
brooks ever sheen,
To ease my heart of its
impassioned woe.

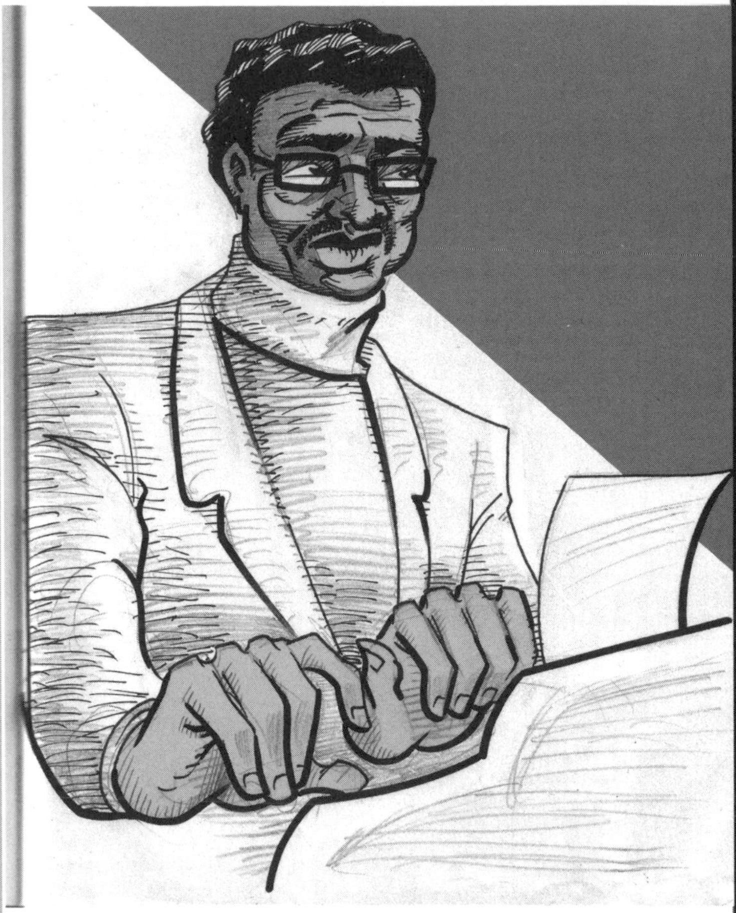

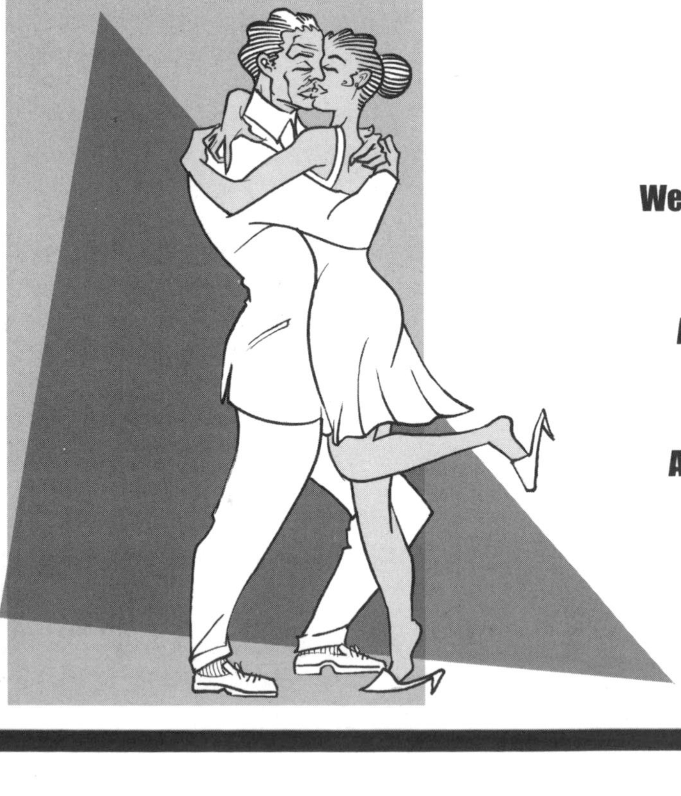

After the Winter

Some day, when trees
have shed their leaves
And against the morning's white
The shivering birds
beneath the eaves
Have sheltered for the night,
We'll turn our faces southward, love,
Toward the summer isle
Where bamboos spire
the shafted grove
And wide-mouthed orchids smile.

And we will seek the quiet hill
Where towers the cotton tree,
And leaps the laughing crystal rill,
And works the droning bee.
And we will build a cottage there
Beside an open glade,
With black-ribbed blue-bells
blowing near,
And ferns that never fade.

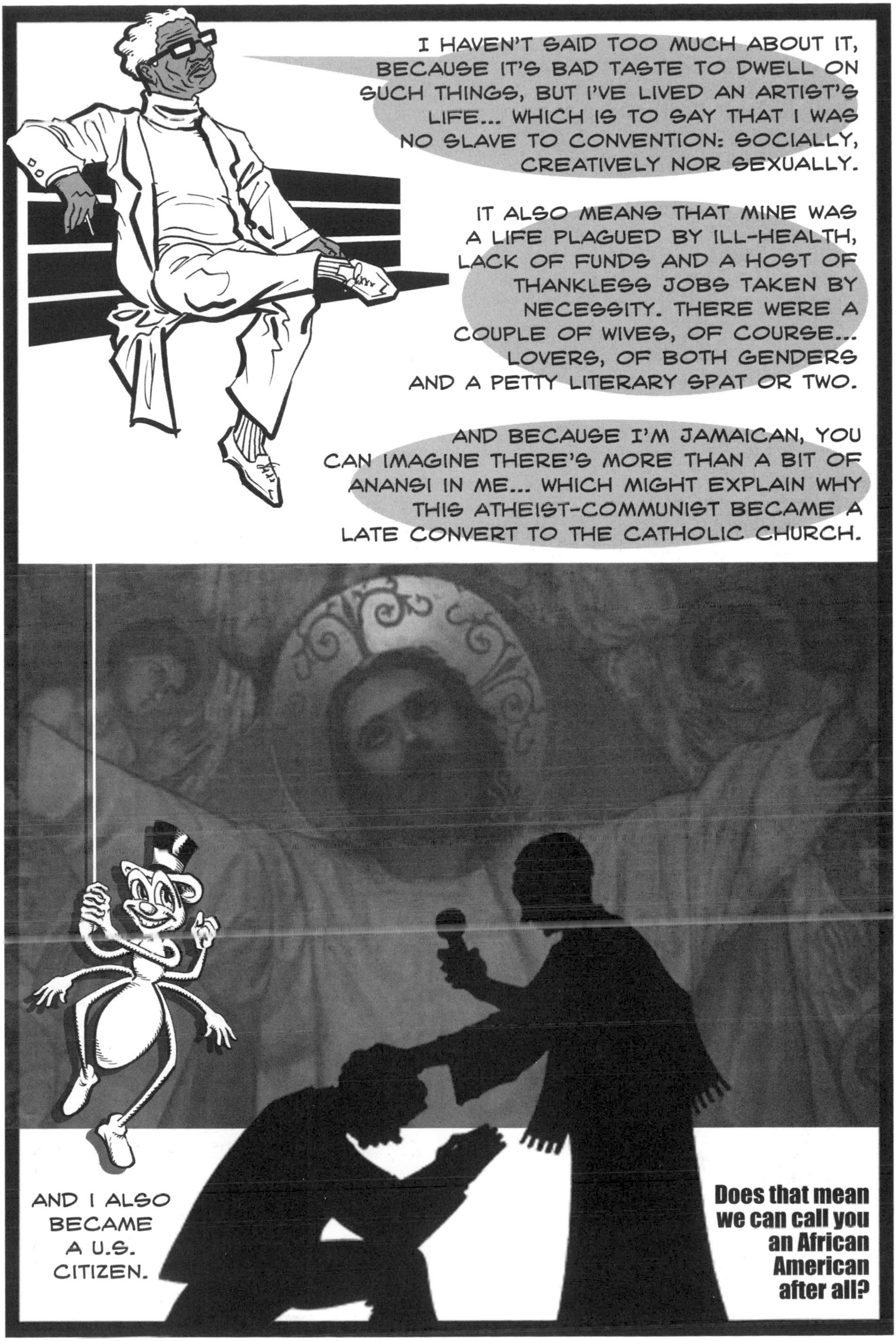
I HAVEN'T SAID TOO MUCH ABOUT IT, BECAUSE IT'S BAD TASTE TO DWELL ON SUCH THINGS, BUT I'VE LIVED AN ARTIST'S LIFE... WHICH IS TO SAY THAT I WAS NO SLAVE TO CONVENTION: SOCIALLY, CREATIVELY NOR SEXUALLY.
IT ALSO MEANS THAT MINE WAS A LIFE PLAGUED BY ILL-HEALTH, LACK OF FUNDS AND A HOST OF THANKLESS JOBS TAKEN BY NECESSITY. THERE WERE A COUPLE OF WIVES, OF COURSE... LOVERS, OF BOTH GENDERS AND A PETTY LITERARY SPAT OR TWO.
AND BECAUSE I'M JAMAICAN, YOU CAN IMAGINE THERE'S MORE THAN A BIT OF ANANSI IN ME... WHICH MIGHT EXPLAIN WHY THIS ATHEIST-COMMUNIST BECAME A LATE CONVERT TO THE CATHOLIC CHURCH.
AND I ALSO BECAME A U.S. CITIZEN.
Does that mean we can call you an African American after all?

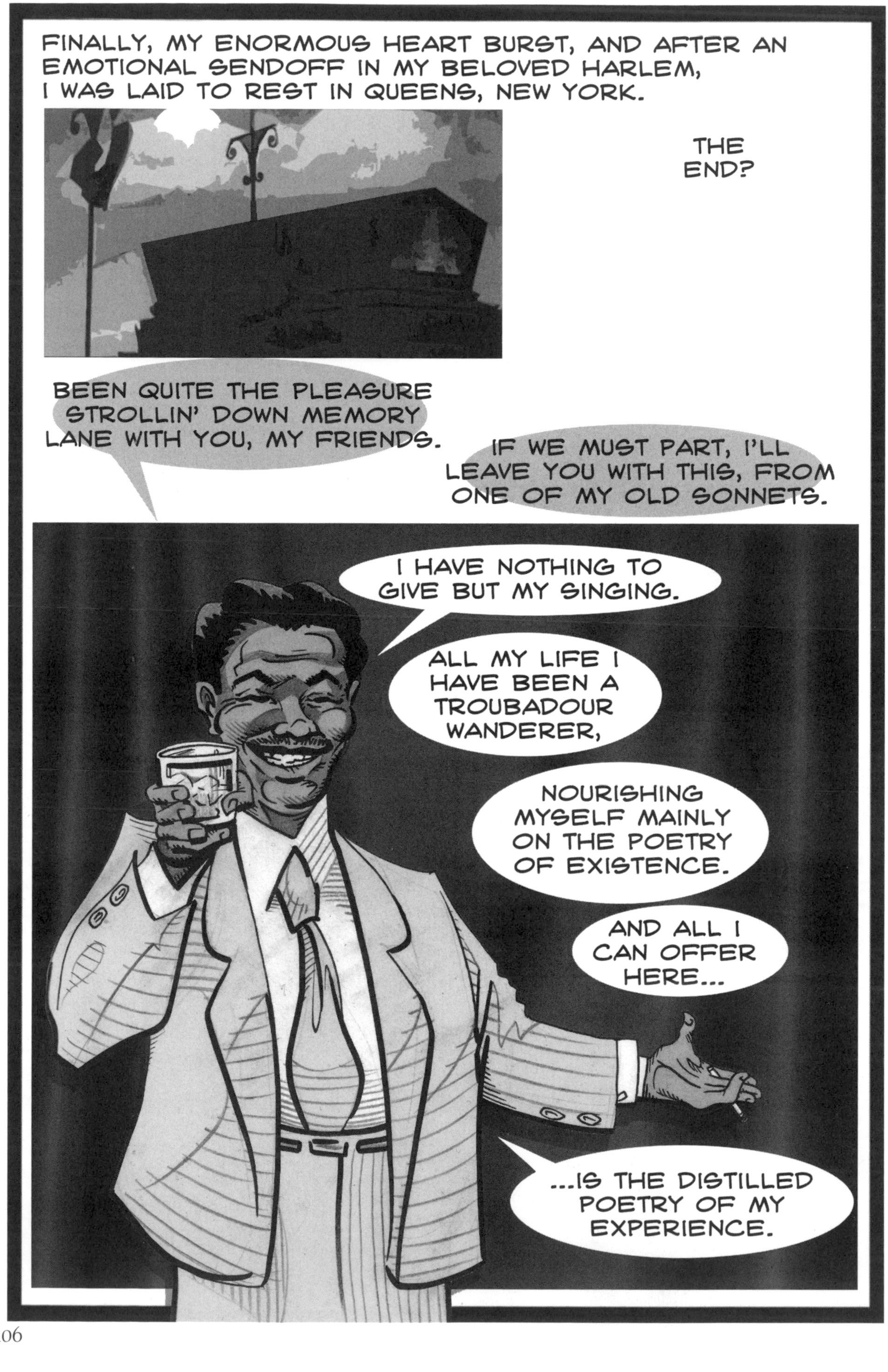
FINALLY, MY ENORMOUS HEART BURST, AND AFTER AN EMOTIONAL SENDOFF IN MY BELOVED HARLEM, I WAS LAID TO REST IN QUEENS, NEW YORK.
THE END?
BEEN QUITE THE PLEASURE STROLLIN' DOWN MEMORY LANE WITH YOU, MY FRIENDS.
IF WE MUST PART, I'LL LEAVE YOU WITH THIS, FROM ONE OF MY OLD SONNETS.
I HAVE NOTHING TO GIVE BUT MY SINGING.
ALL MY LIFE I HAVE BEEN A TROUBADOUR WANDERER,
NOURISHING MYSELF MAINLY ON THE POETRY OF EXISTENCE.
AND ALL I CAN OFFER HERE...
...IS THE DISTILLED POETRY OF MY EXPERIENCE.

Chapter Six

Outward Bound

The 1920s, famously remembered as a moment of cultural exile—with future luminaries, from Ernest Hemingway to Gertrude Stein and Ezra Pound, traveling and writing in Europe—has a more complex history than its reputation for Modernism has widely earned.

In the 1920s, Greenwich Village seemed a colony of escapees from a generally conservative nation run, at least in several states, by the Ku Klux Klan. Labor unions were beaten down, business success and the astronomical stock market rise proclaimed the "Americanism" that would defeat Russian Bolshevism.

From this arose a Yiddish bohemia, largely working class in character, part of a golden age of Yiddish culture in theater and music occurring in Greater New York, as well as places as far afield as Eastern Europe and Buenos Aires. A lively cerebral bohemia emerged, too, epitomized by the confident projection of advancing sexuality as a prime means to overcome American conservatism. And not least among these developments, the cultural declaration that Harlem was more than an exotic extra, but a space for the most extraordinary possibilities in the artistic life of the New World.

Paris still beckoned of course, in greater ways than it ever had before or could again. More Americans had the money to travel and others like Henry Miller could live on the cheap. Black artists like Josephine Baker had an urgent need for audiences more cosmopolitan, more sophisticated than the U.S. had to offer. The exiled literati, as with Carl Van Vechten back at home (if "home" is New York), added a homoeroticism that had been closeted within bohemia before, but now became a permanent part of the scene.

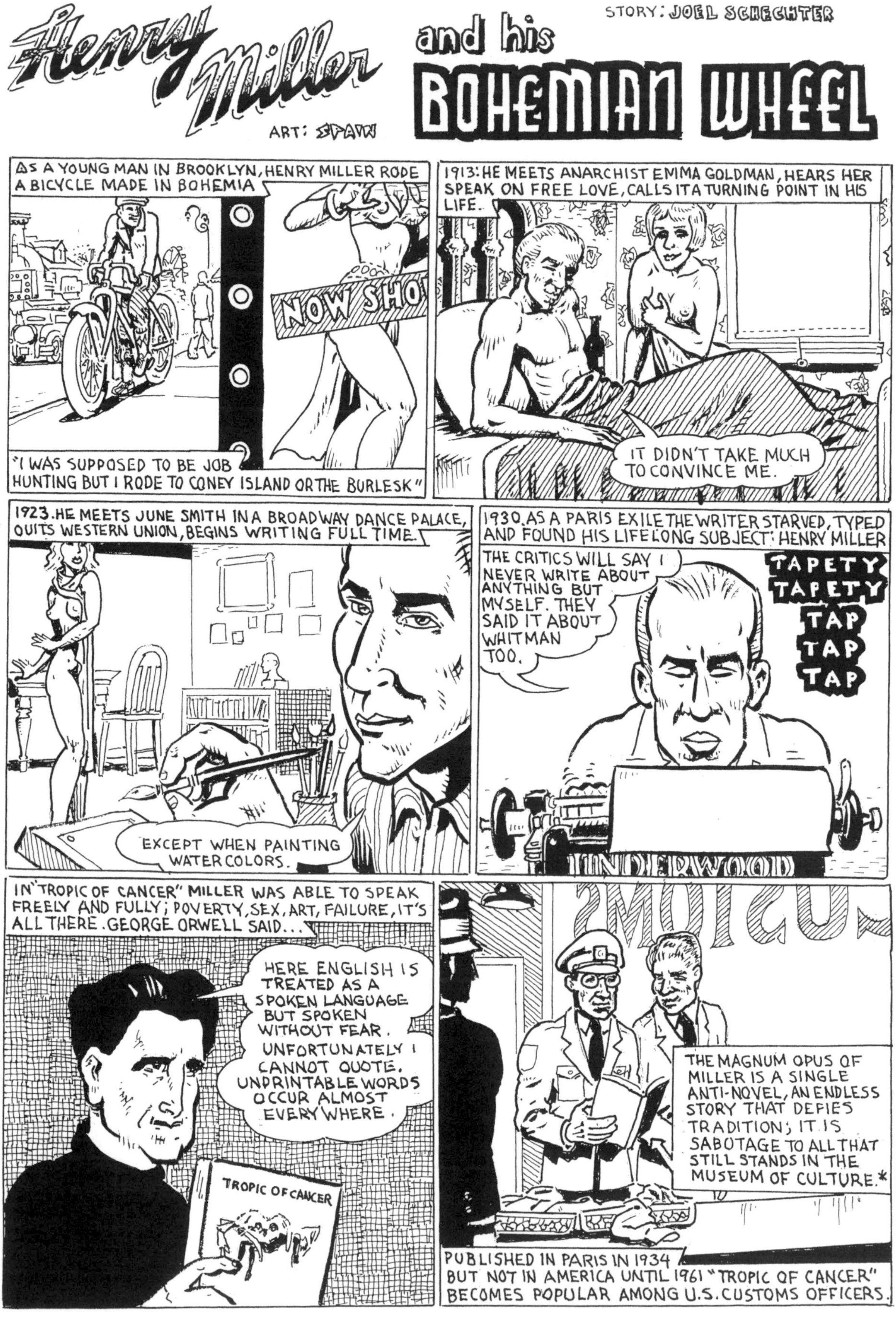
STORY: JOEL SCHECHTER
Henry Miller and his BOHEMIAN WHEEL
ART: SPAIN
AS A YOUNG MAN IN BROOKLYN, HENRY MILLER RODE A BICYCLE MADE IN BOHEMIA
NOW SHO
"I WAS SUPPOSED TO BE JOB HUNTING BUT I RODE TO CONEY ISLAND OR THE BURLESK"
1913: HE MEETS ANARCHIST EMMA GOLDMAN, HEARS HER SPEAK ON FREE LOVE, CALLS IT A TURNING POINT IN HIS LIFE.
IT DIDN'T TAKE MUCH TO CONVINCE ME.
1923. HE MEETS JUNE SMITH IN A BROADWAY DANCE PALACE, QUITS WESTERN UNION, BEGINS WRITING FULL TIME.
EXCEPT WHEN PAINTING WATER COLORS.
1930. AS A PARIS EXILE THE WRITER STARVED, TYPED AND FOUND HIS LIFELONG SUBJECT: HENRY MILLER
THE CRITICS WILL SAY I NEVER WRITE ABOUT ANYTHING BUT MYSELF. THEY SAID IT ABOUT WHITMAN TOO.
TAPETY TAPETY TAP TAP TAP
UNDERWOOD
IN "TROPIC OF CANCER" MILLER WAS ABLE TO SPEAK FREELY AND FULLY; POVERTY, SEX, ART, FAILURE, IT'S ALL THERE. GEORGE ORWELL SAID...
HERE ENGLISH IS TREATED AS A SPOKEN LANGUAGE BUT SPOKEN WITHOUT FEAR. UNFORTUNATELY I CANNOT QUOTE. UNPRINTABLE WORDS OCCUR ALMOST EVERYWHERE.
TROPIC OF CANCER
CUSTOMS
THE MAGNUM OPUS OF MILLER IS A SINGLE ANTI-NOVEL, AN ENDLESS STORY THAT DEFIES TRADITION; IT IS SABOTAGE TO ALL THAT STILL STANDS IN THE MUSEUM OF CULTURE.*
* KARL SHAPIRO
PUBLISHED IN PARIS IN 1934 BUT NOT IN AMERICA UNTIL 1961 "TROPIC OF CANCER" BECOMES POPULAR AMONG U.S. CUSTOMS OFFICERS.

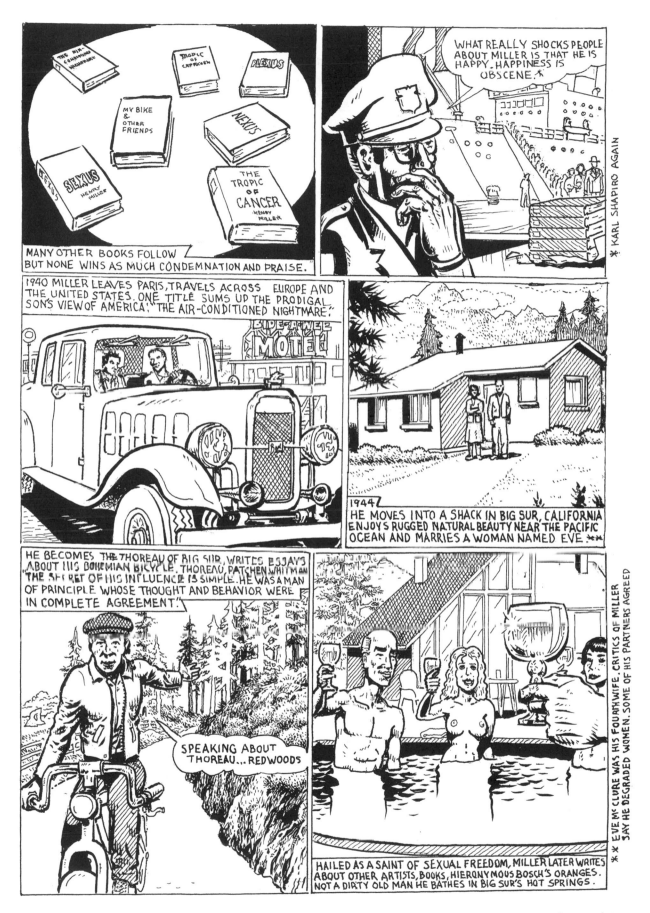

MY BIKE & OTHER FRIENDS
SEXUS HENRY MILLER
PLEXUS
NEXUS
THE TROPIC OF CANCER HENRY MILLER
MANY OTHER BOOKS FOLLOW BUT NONE WINS AS MUCH CONDEMNATION AND PRAISE.
WHAT REALLY SHOCKS PEOPLE ABOUT MILLER IS THAT HE IS HAPPY. HAPPINESS IS OBSCENE.*
* KARL SHAPIRO AGAIN
1940 MILLER LEAVES PARIS, TRAVELS ACROSS EUROPE AND THE UNITED STATES. ONE TITLE SUMS UP THE PRODIGAL SON'S VIEW OF AMERICA, "THE AIR-CONDITIONED NIGHTMARE."
MOTEL
1944
HE MOVES INTO A SHACK IN BIG SUR, CALIFORNIA ENJOYS RUGGED NATURAL BEAUTY NEAR THE PACIFIC OCEAN AND MARRIES A WOMAN NAMED EVE.**
HE BECOMES THE THOREAU OF BIG SUR, WRITES ESSAYS ABOUT HIS BOHEMIAN BICYCLE, THOREAU, PATCHEN, WHITMAN "THE SECRET OF HIS INFLUENCE IS SIMPLE. HE WAS A MAN OF PRINCIPLE WHOSE THOUGHT AND BEHAVIOR WERE IN COMPLETE AGREEMENT."
SPEAKING ABOUT THOREAU... REDWOODS
HAILED AS A SAINT OF SEXUAL FREEDOM, MILLER LATER WRITES ABOUT OTHER ARTISTS, BOOKS, HIERONYMOUS BOSCH'S ORANGES. NOT A DIRTY OLD MAN HE BATHES IN BIG SUR'S HOT SPRINGS.
** EVE MCCLURE WAS HIS FOURTH WIFE. CRITICS OF MILLER SAY HE DEGRADED WOMEN. SOME OF HIS PARTNERS AGREED

"The Sex Boys" and the Libidinal Left

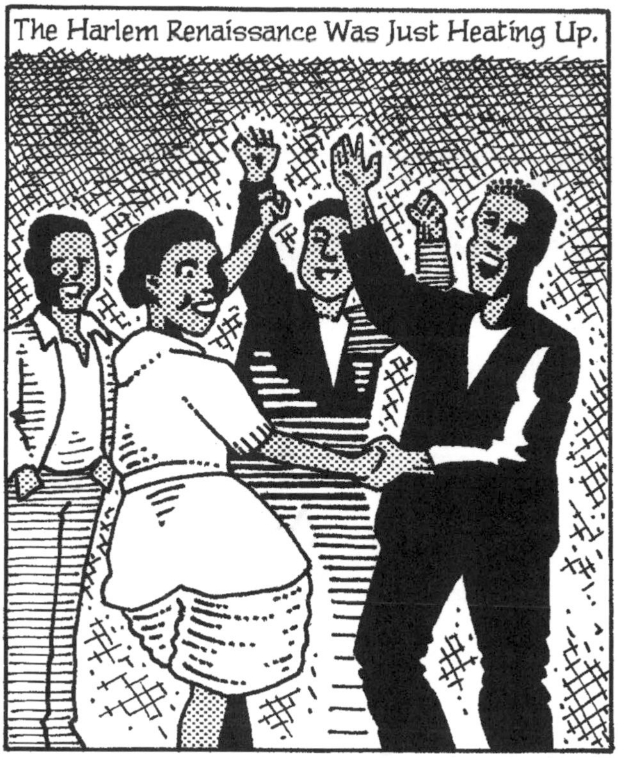
The Harlem Renaissance Was Just Heating Up.

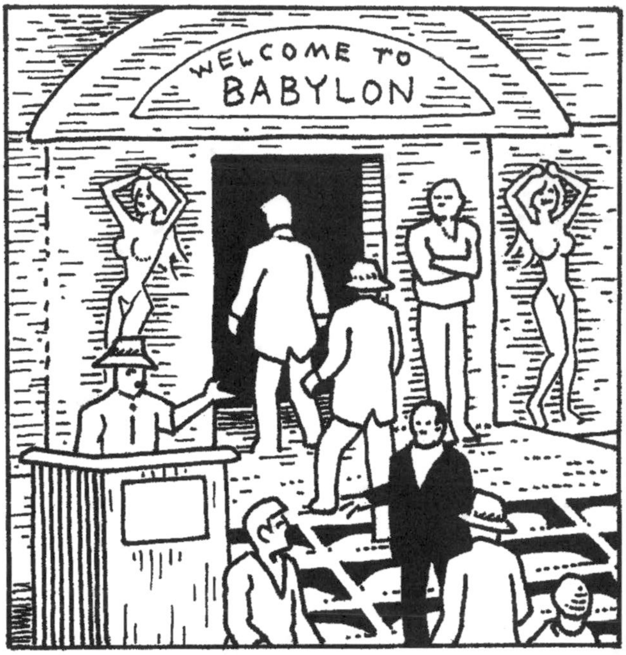
WELCOME TO
BABYLON

What were called "Cooch Shows" featuring scantily-clad women had become a big business in almost every part of the country.

But the Greenwich Village revolution in morals had run aground. Young people across the country had largely caught up with free love in their own ways.

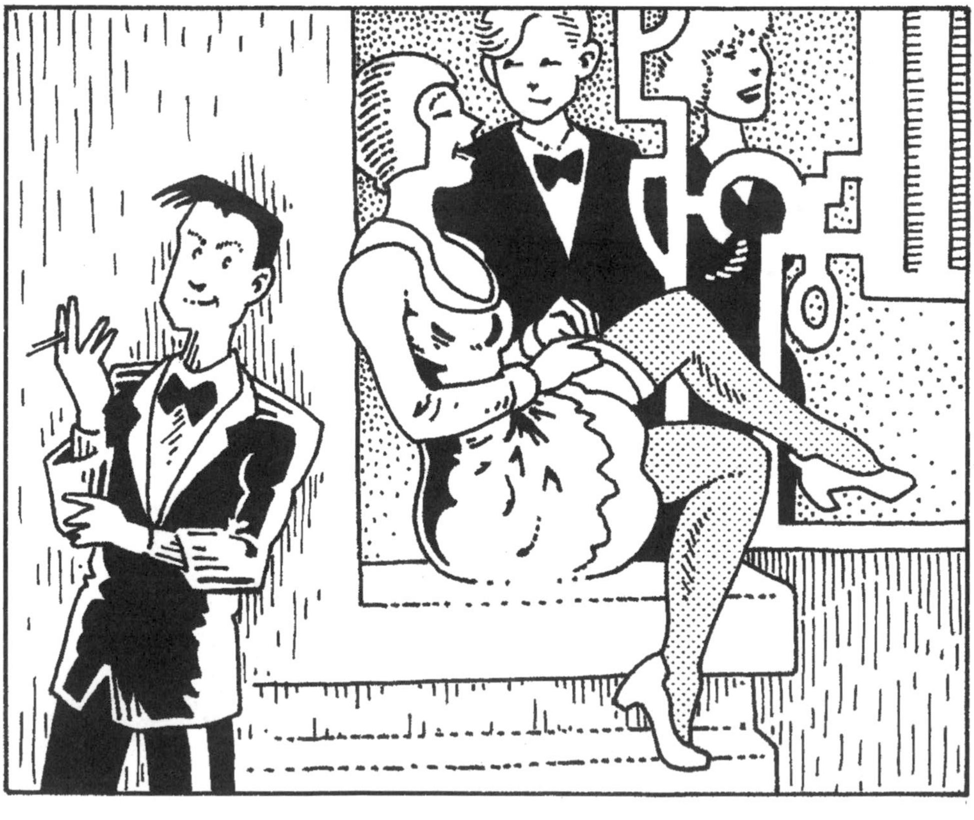

SCRIPT:
Paul Buhle

ART:
Matt Howarth

In the living room of VF Calverton...

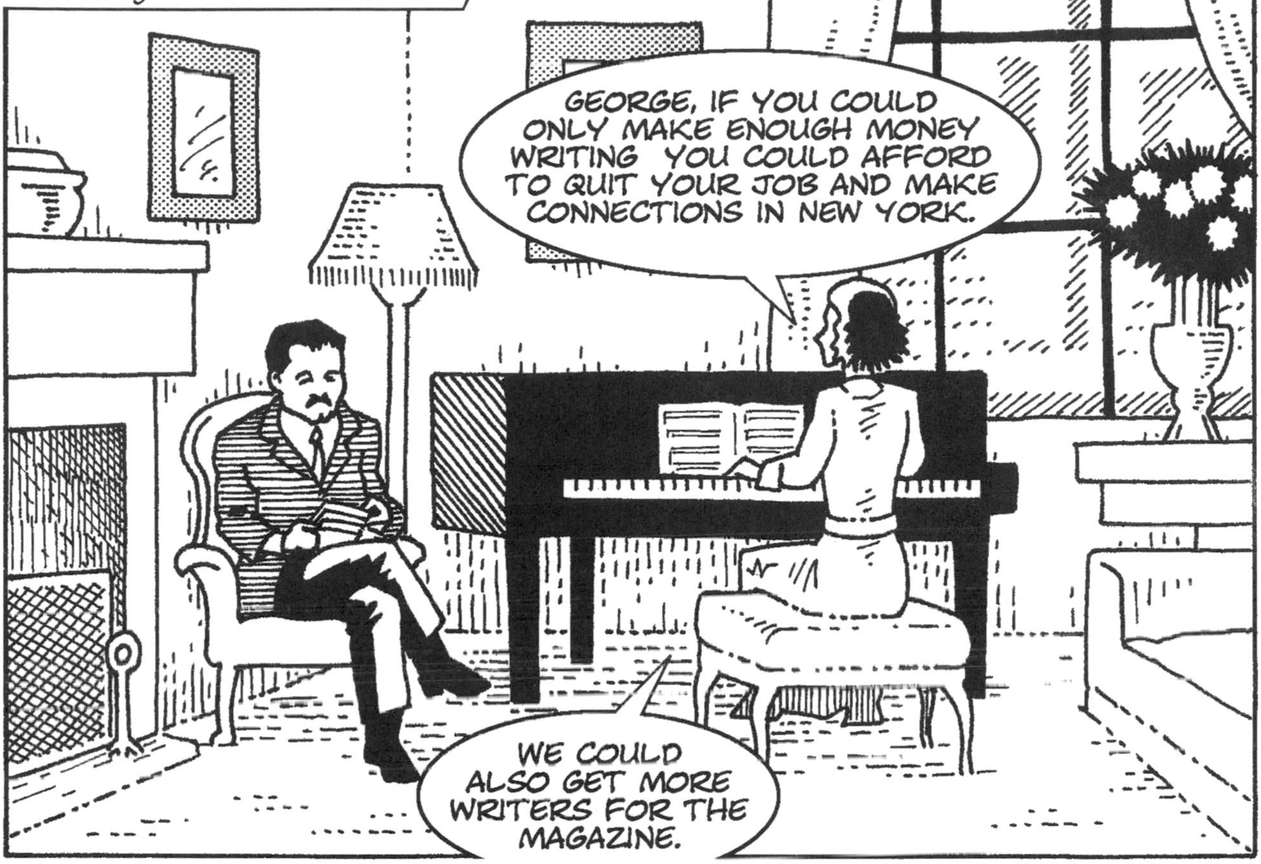
GEORGE, IF YOU COULD ONLY MAKE ENOUGH MONEY WRITING YOU COULD AFFORD TO QUIT YOUR JOB AND MAKE CONNECTIONS IN NEW YORK.
WE COULD ALSO GET MORE WRITERS FOR THE MAGAZINE.

In VF Calverton's editorial office...

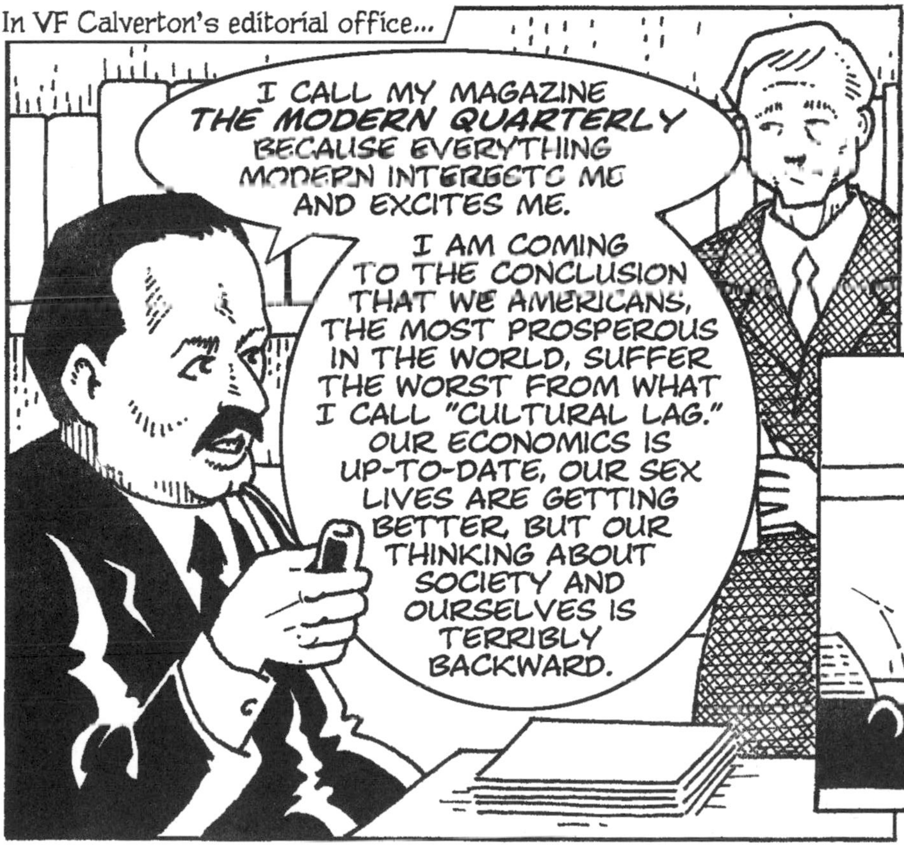
I CALL MY MAGAZINE *THE MODERN QUARTERLY* BECAUSE EVERYTHING MODERN INTERESTS ME AND EXCITES ME.
I AM COMING TO THE CONCLUSION THAT WE AMERICANS, THE MOST PROSPEROUS IN THE WORLD, SUFFER THE WORST FROM WHAT I CALL "CULTURAL LAG." OUR ECONOMICS IS UP-TO-DATE, OUR SEX LIVES ARE GETTING BETTER, BUT OUR THINKING ABOUT SOCIETY AND OURSELVES IS TERRIBLY BACKWARD.

Calverton sought out black writers and white authors who could write sympathetically on subjects like American Black culture, anti-colonial struggles in Africa and Asia, and the cultural implications.

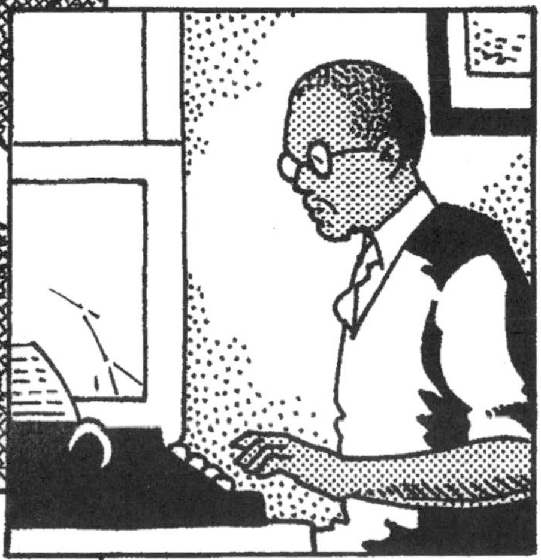

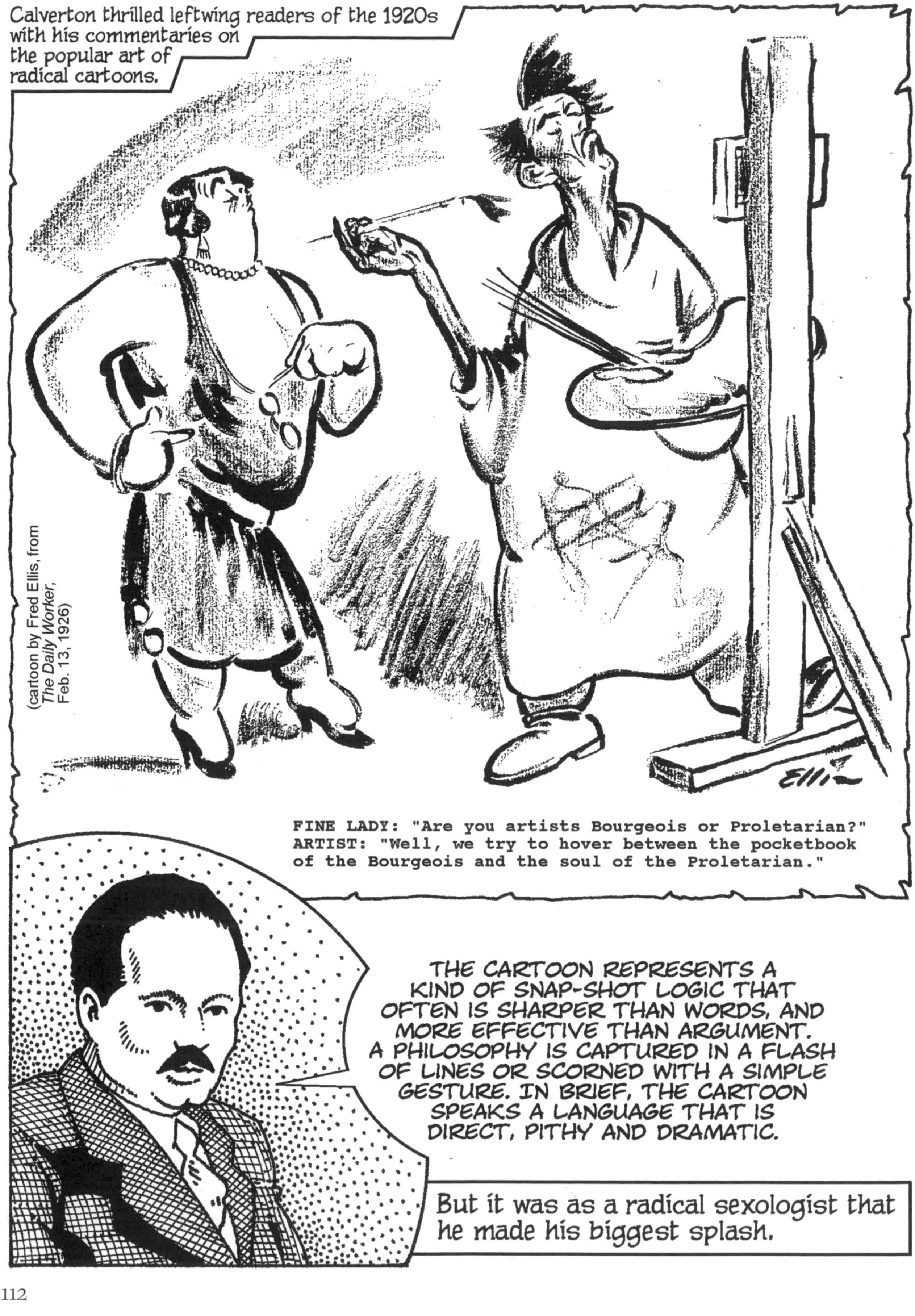

Calverton thrilled leftwing readers of the 1920s with his commentaries on the popular art of radical cartoons.
(cartoon by Fred Ellis, from The Daily Worker, Feb. 13, 1926)
Ellis
FINE LADY: "Are you artists Bourgeois or Proletarian?"
ARTIST: "Well, we try to hover between the pocketbook of the Bourgeois and the soul of the Proletarian."
THE CARTOON REPRESENTS A KIND OF SNAP-SHOT LOGIC THAT OFTEN IS SHARPER THAN WORDS, AND MORE EFFECTIVE THAN ARGUMENT. A PHILOSOPHY IS CAPTURED IN A FLASH OF LINES OR SCORNED WITH A SIMPLE GESTURE. IN BRIEF, THE CARTOON SPEAKS A LANGUAGE THAT IS DIRECT, PITHY AND DRAMATIC.
But it was as a radical sexologist that he made his biggest splash.

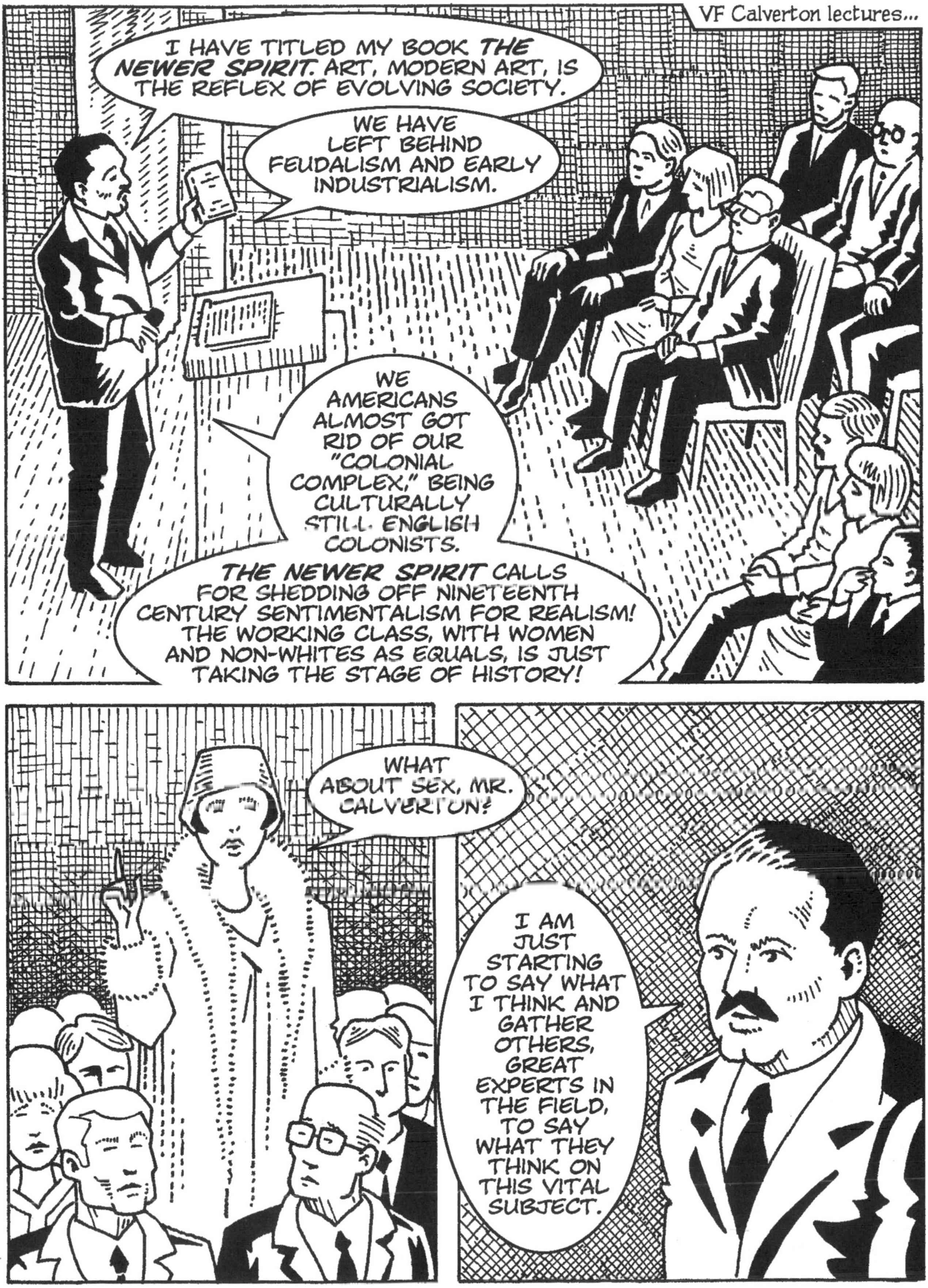
VF Calverton lectures...
I HAVE TITLED MY BOOK *THE NEWER SPIRIT.* ART, MODERN ART, IS THE REFLEX OF EVOLVING SOCIETY.
WE HAVE LEFT BEHIND FEUDALISM AND EARLY INDUSTRIALISM.
WE AMERICANS ALMOST GOT RID OF OUR "COLONIAL COMPLEX," BEING CULTURALLY STILL ENGLISH COLONISTS.
THE NEWER SPIRIT CALLS FOR SHEDDING OFF NINETEENTH CENTURY SENTIMENTALISM FOR REALISM! THE WORKING CLASS, WITH WOMEN AND NON-WHITES AS EQUALS, IS JUST TAKING THE STAGE OF HISTORY!
WHAT ABOUT SEX, MR. CALVERTON?
I AM JUST STARTING TO SAY WHAT I THINK AND GATHER OTHERS, GREAT EXPERTS IN THE FIELD, TO SAY WHAT THEY THINK ON THIS VITAL SUBJECT.

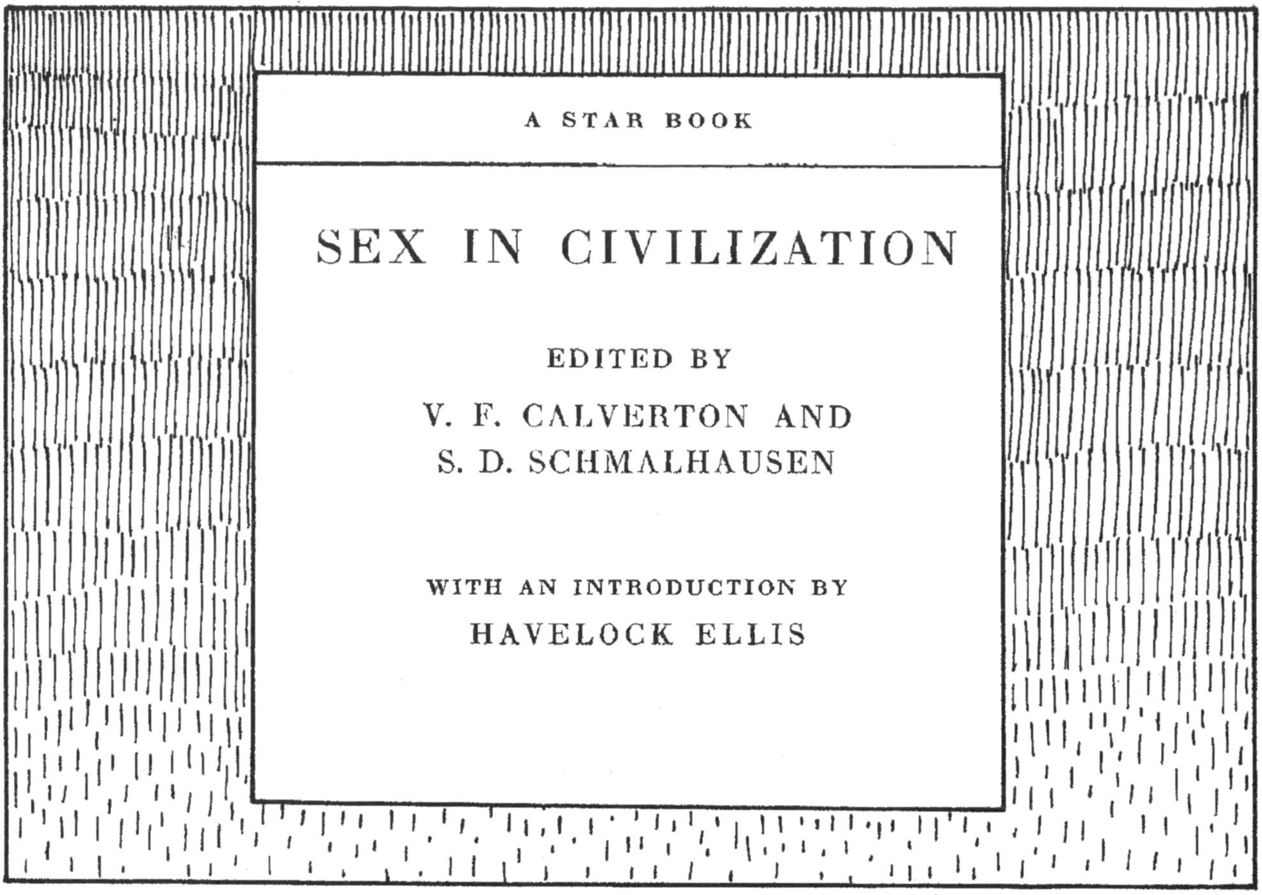
A STAR BOOK
SEX IN CIVILIZATION
EDITED BY
V. F. CALVERTON AND
S. D. SCHMALHAUSEN
WITH AN INTRODUCTION BY
HAVELOCK ELLIS

By 1929, Calverton and his fellow editor Samuel D. Schmalhausen were known popularly, in the press and at Manhttan cocktail parties, as the "Sex Boys." Their volume SEX IN CIVILIZATION gathered the foremost experts in the world, led by the greatest and most popular writer on sexual subjects, Havelock Ellis.

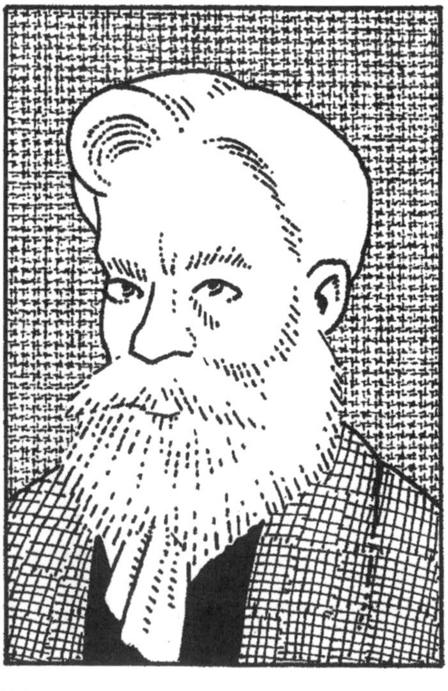

Havelock Ellis.

With the Depression, hemlines went down, free love faded and so did Calverton. He and his magazine died in 1940.

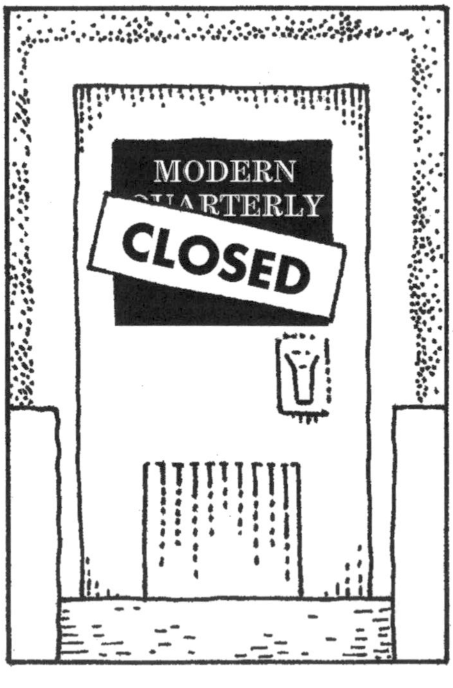
MODERN
CLOSED

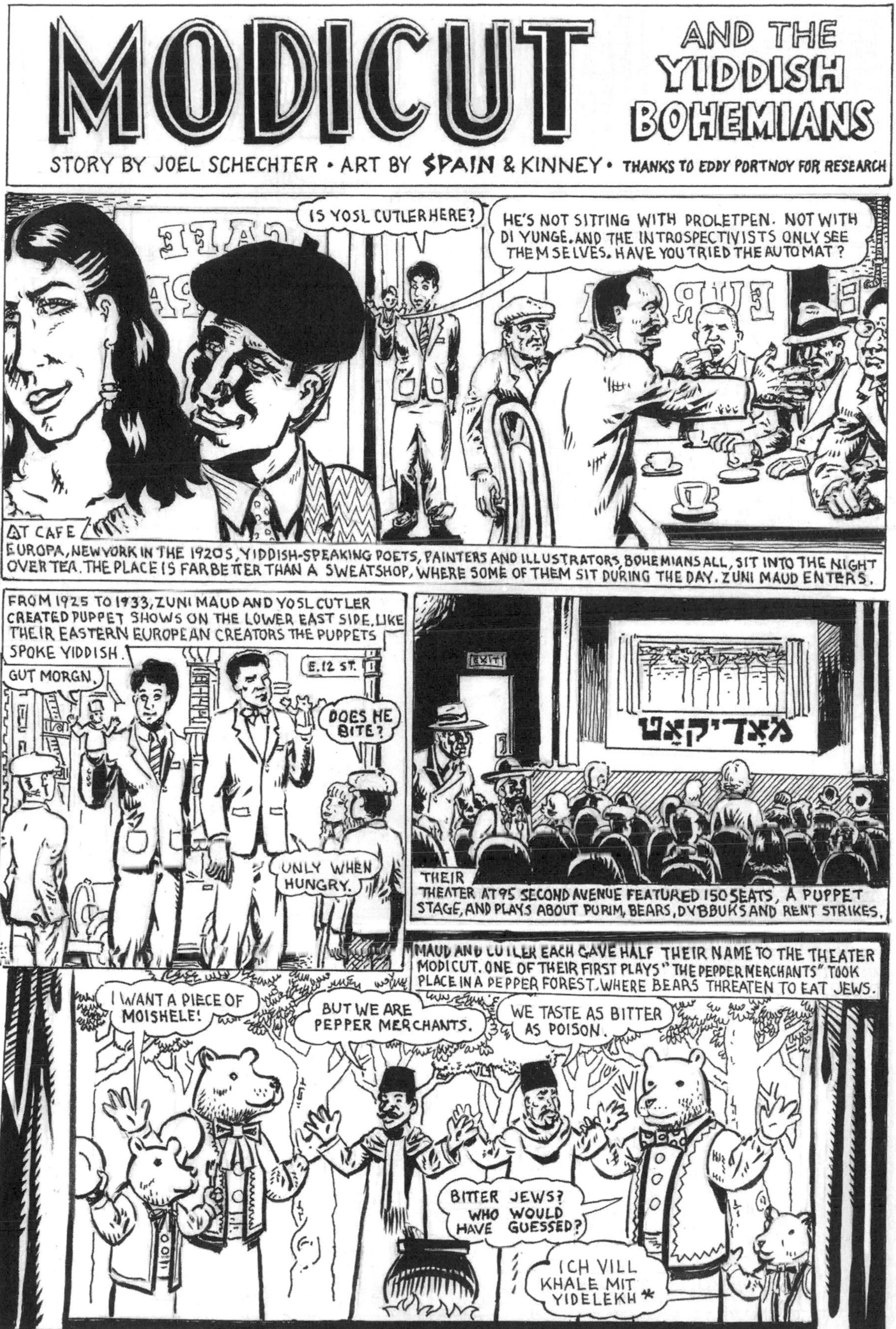

MODICUT AND THE YIDDISH BOHEMIANS
STORY BY JOEL SCHECHTER • ART BY SPAIN & KINNEY • THANKS TO EDDY PORTNOY FOR RESEARCH
CAFE EUROPA
IS YOSL CUTLER HERE?
HE'S NOT SITTING WITH PROLETPEN. NOT WITH DI YUNGE. AND THE INTROSPECTIVISTS ONLY SEE THEMSELVES. HAVE YOU TRIED THE AUTOMAT?
AT CAFE EUROPA, NEW YORK IN THE 1920S, YIDDISH-SPEAKING POETS, PAINTERS AND ILLUSTRATORS, BOHEMIANS ALL, SIT INTO THE NIGHT OVER TEA. THE PLACE IS FAR BETTER THAN A SWEATSHOP, WHERE SOME OF THEM SIT DURING THE DAY. ZUNI MAUD ENTERS.
FROM 1925 TO 1933, ZUNI MAUD AND YOSL CUTLER CREATED PUPPET SHOWS ON THE LOWER EAST SIDE. LIKE THEIR EASTERN EUROPEAN CREATORS THE PUPPETS SPOKE YIDDISH.
E. 12 ST.
GUT MORGN.
DOES HE BITE?
ONLY WHEN HUNGRY.
EXIT
THEIR THEATER AT 95 SECOND AVENUE FEATURED 150 SEATS, A PUPPET STAGE, AND PLAYS ABOUT PURIM, BEARS, DYBBUKS AND RENT STRIKES.
MAUD AND CUTLER EACH GAVE HALF THEIR NAME TO THE THEATER MODICUT. ONE OF THEIR FIRST PLAYS "THE PEPPER MERCHANTS" TOOK PLACE IN A PEPPER FOREST, WHERE BEARS THREATEN TO EAT JEWS.
I WANT A PIECE OF MOISHELE!
BUT WE ARE PEPPER MERCHANTS.
WE TASTE AS BITTER AS POISON.
BITTER JEWS? WHO WOULD HAVE GUESSED?
ICH VILL KHALE MIT YIDELEKH*
*I WANT CHALLAH WITH MY JEWS.

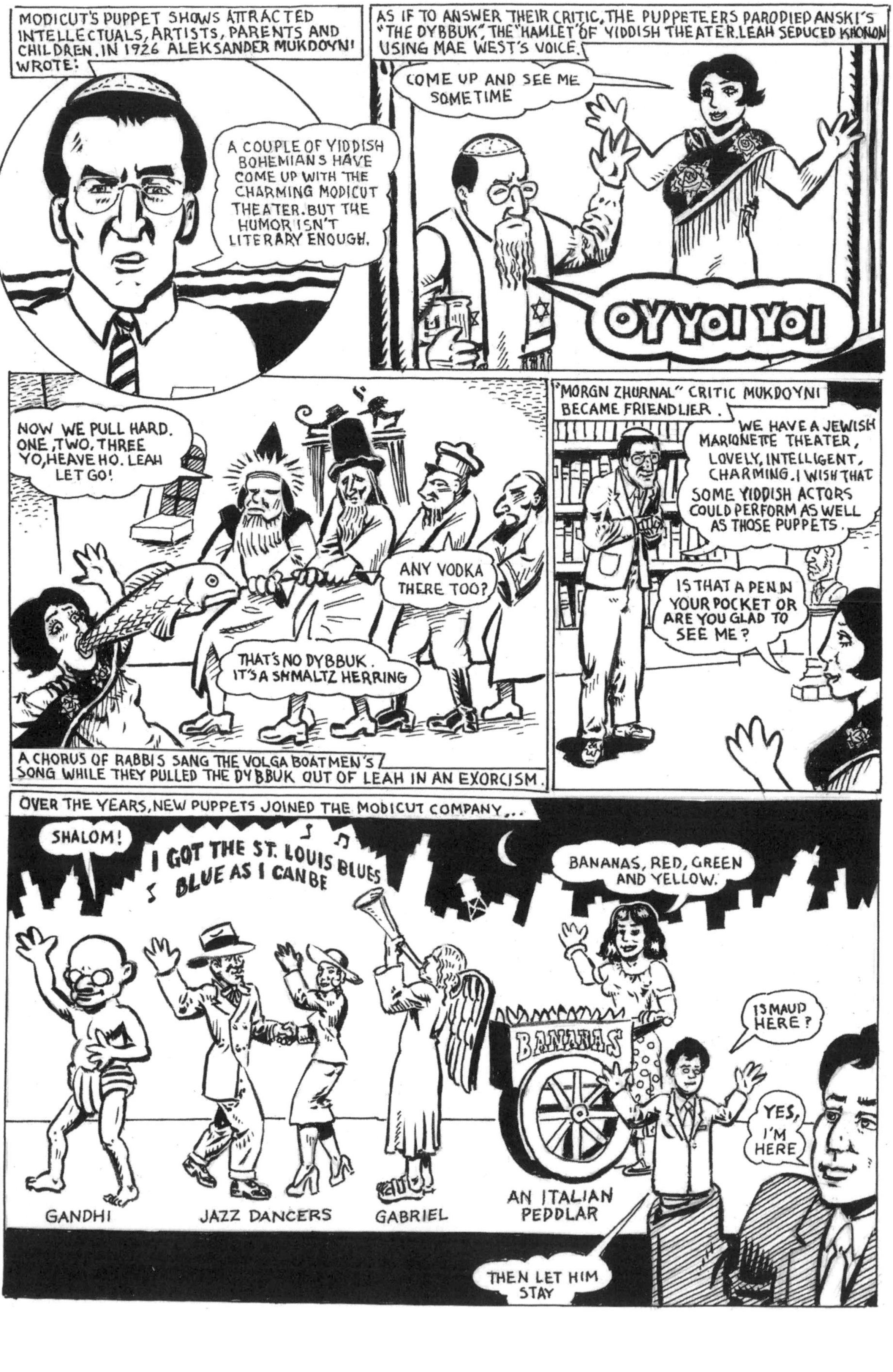

MODICUT'S PUPPET SHOWS ATTRACTED INTELLECTUALS, ARTISTS, PARENTS AND CHILDREN. IN 1926 ALEKSANDER MUKDOYNI WROTE:
A COUPLE OF YIDDISH BOHEMIANS HAVE COME UP WITH THE CHARMING MODICUT THEATER. BUT THE HUMOR ISN'T LITERARY ENOUGH.
AS IF TO ANSWER THEIR CRITIC, THE PUPPETEERS PARODIED ANSKI'S "THE DYBBUK", THE "HAMLET" OF YIDDISH THEATER. LEAH SEDUCED KHONON USING MAE WEST'S VOICE.
COME UP AND SEE ME SOMETIME
OY YOI YOI
NOW WE PULL HARD. ONE, TWO, THREE YO, HEAVE HO. LEAH LET GO!
ANY VODKA THERE TOO?
THAT'S NO DYBBUK. IT'S A SHMALTZ HERRING
A CHORUS OF RABBIS SANG THE VOLGA BOATMEN'S SONG WHILE THEY PULLED THE DYBBUK OUT OF LEAH IN AN EXORCISM.
"MORGN ZHURNAL" CRITIC MUKDOYNI BECAME FRIENDLIER.
WE HAVE A JEWISH MARIONETTE THEATER, LOVELY, INTELLIGENT, CHARMING. I WISH THAT SOME YIDDISH ACTORS COULD PERFORM AS WELL AS THOSE PUPPETS.
IS THAT A PEN IN YOUR POCKET OR ARE YOU GLAD TO SEE ME?
OVER THE YEARS, NEW PUPPETS JOINED THE MODICUT COMPANY...
SHALOM!
I GOT THE ST. LOUIS BLUES BLUE AS I CAN BE
BANANAS, RED, GREEN AND YELLOW.
BANANAS
IS MAUD HERE?
YES, I'M HERE
GANDHI
JAZZ DANCERS
GABRIEL
AN ITALIAN PEDDLAR
THEN LET HIM STAY

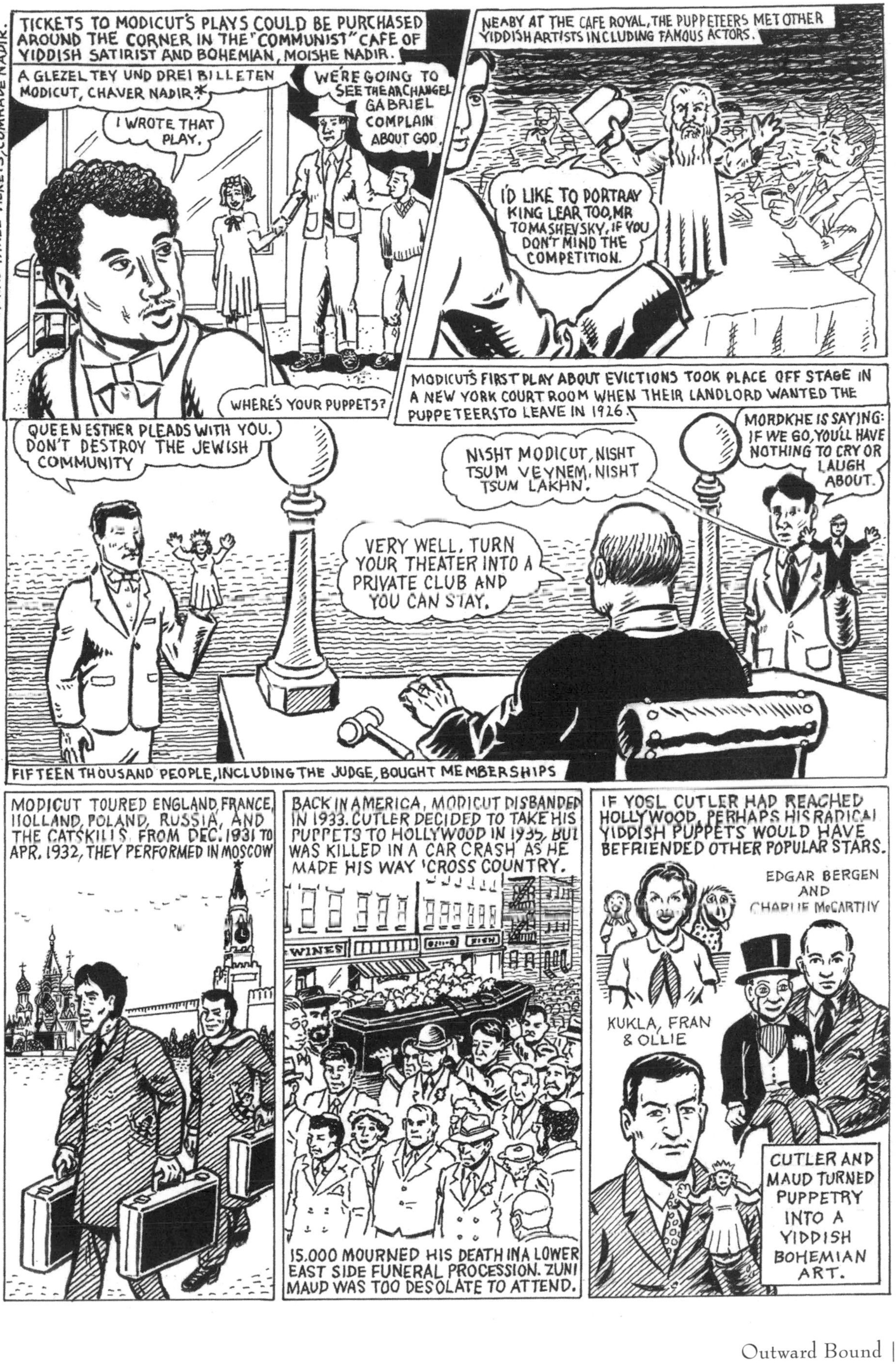
TICKETS TO MODICUT'S PLAYS COULD BE PURCHASED AROUND THE CORNER IN THE "COMMUNIST" CAFE OF YIDDISH SATIRIST AND BOHEMIAN, MOISHE NADIR.
A GLEZEL TEY UND DREI BILLETEN MODICUT, CHAVER NADIR.*
I WROTE THAT PLAY.
WE'RE GOING TO SEE THE ARCHANGEL GABRIEL COMPLAIN ABOUT GOD.
WHERE'S YOUR PUPPETS?
*A GLASS OF TEA AND THREE TICKETS, COMRADE NADIR.
NEABY AT THE CAFE ROYAL, THE PUPPETEERS MET OTHER YIDDISH ARTISTS INCLUDING FAMOUS ACTORS.
I'D LIKE TO PORTRAY KING LEAR TOO, MR TOMASHEVSKY, IF YOU DON'T MIND THE COMPETITION.
MODICUT'S FIRST PLAY ABOUT EVICTIONS TOOK PLACE OFF STAGE IN A NEW YORK COURT ROOM WHEN THEIR LANDLORD WANTED THE PUPPETEERS TO LEAVE IN 1926.
QUEEN ESTHER PLEADS WITH YOU. DON'T DESTROY THE JEWISH COMMUNITY
NISHT MODICUT, NISHT TSUM VEYNEM, NISHT TSUM LAKHN.
MORDKHE IS SAYING: IF WE GO, YOU'LL HAVE NOTHING TO CRY OR LAUGH ABOUT.
VERY WELL. TURN YOUR THEATER INTO A PRIVATE CLUB AND YOU CAN STAY.
FIFTEEN THOUSAND PEOPLE, INCLUDING THE JUDGE, BOUGHT MEMBERSHIPS
MODICUT TOURED ENGLAND, FRANCE, HOLLAND, POLAND, RUSSIA, AND THE CATSKILLS. FROM DEC. 1931 TO APR. 1932, THEY PERFORMED IN MOSCOW
BACK IN AMERICA, MODICUT DISBANDED IN 1933. CUTLER DECIDED TO TAKE HIS PUPPETS TO HOLLYWOOD IN 1935, BUT WAS KILLED IN A CAR CRASH AS HE MADE HIS WAY 'CROSS COUNTRY.
WINES
FISH
15,000 MOURNED HIS DEATH IN A LOWER EAST SIDE FUNERAL PROCESSION. ZUNI MAUD WAS TOO DESOLATE TO ATTEND.
IF YOSL CUTLER HAD REACHED HOLLYWOOD, PERHAPS HIS RADICAL YIDDISH PUPPETS WOULD HAVE BEFRIENDED OTHER POPULAR STARS.
EDGAR BERGEN AND CHARLIE McCARTHY
KUKLA, FRAN & OLLIE
CUTLER AND MAUD TURNED PUPPETRY INTO A YIDDISH BOHEMIAN ART.

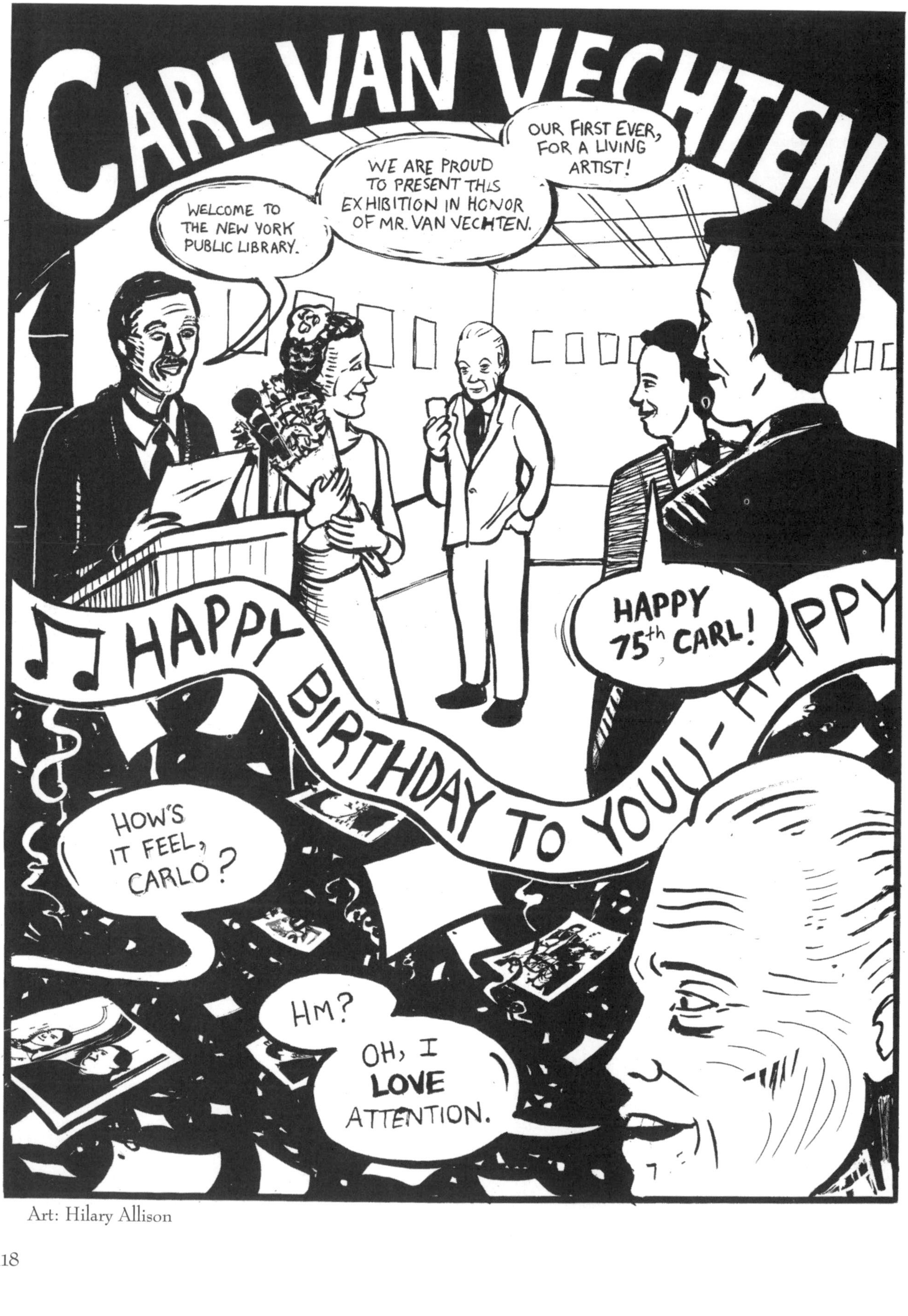
CARL VAN VECHTEN
WELCOME TO THE NEW YORK PUBLIC LIBRARY.
WE ARE PROUD TO PRESENT THIS EXHIBITION IN HONOR OF MR. VAN VECHTEN.
OUR FIRST EVER, FOR A LIVING ARTIST!
HAPPY BIRTHDAY TO YOUU- HAPPY
HAPPY 75th, CARL!
HOW'S IT FEEL, CARLO?
HM?
OH, I LOVE ATTENTION.
Art: Hilary Allison

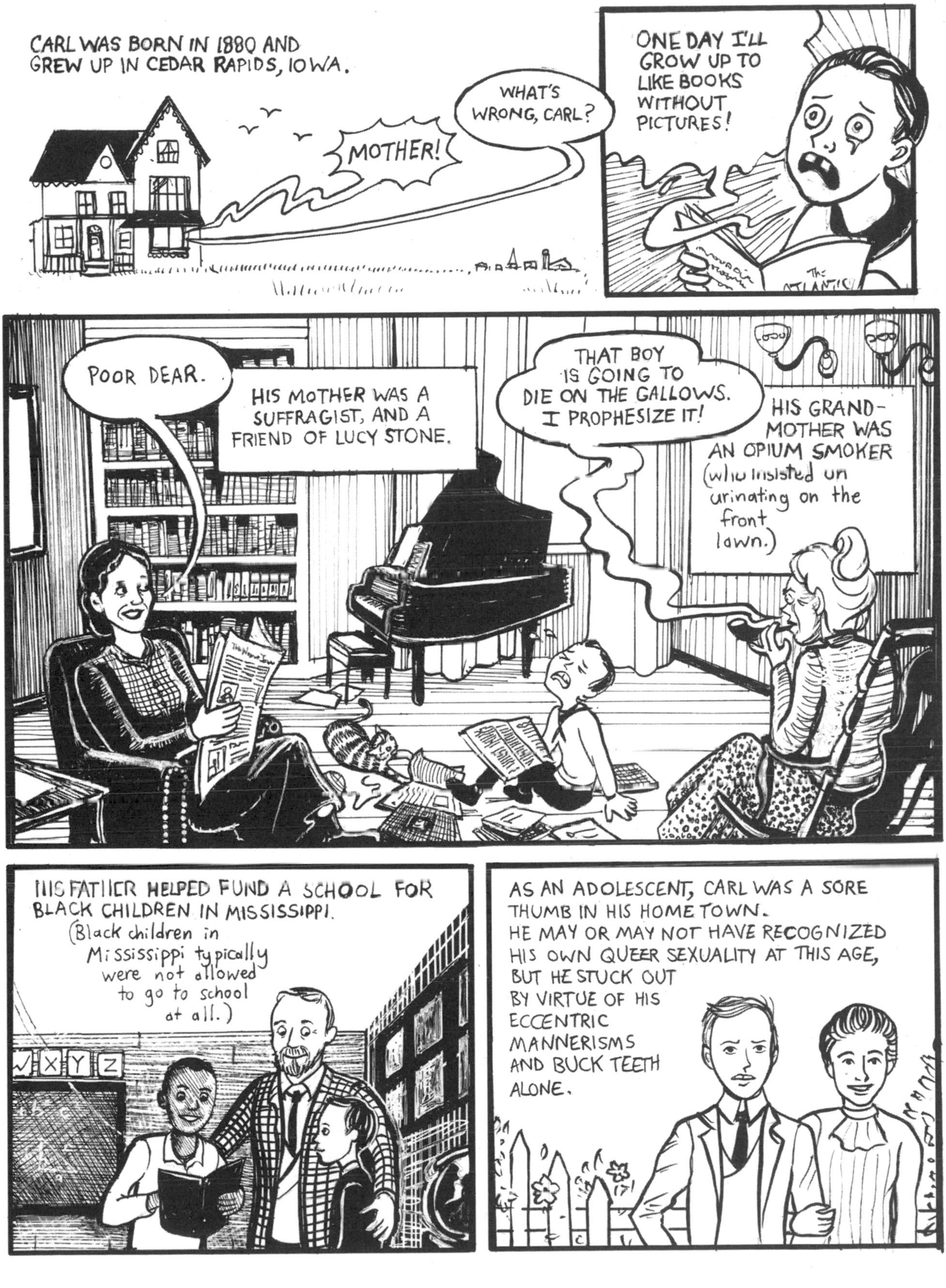

CARL WAS BORN IN 1880 AND GREW UP IN CEDAR RAPIDS, IOWA.
MOTHER!
WHAT'S WRONG, CARL?
ONE DAY I'LL GROW UP TO LIKE BOOKS WITHOUT PICTURES!
POOR DEAR.
HIS MOTHER WAS A SUFFRAGIST, AND A FRIEND OF LUCY STONE.
THAT BOY IS GOING TO DIE ON THE GALLOWS. I PROPHESIZE IT!
HIS GRAND-MOTHER WAS AN OPIUM SMOKER (who insisted on urinating on the front lawn.)
HIS FATHER HELPED FUND A SCHOOL FOR BLACK CHILDREN IN MISSISSIPPI.
(Black children in Mississippi typically were not allowed to go to school at all.)
W X Y Z
AS AN ADOLESCENT, CARL WAS A SORE THUMB IN HIS HOMETOWN.
HE MAY OR MAY NOT HAVE RECOGNIZED HIS OWN QUEER SEXUALITY AT THIS AGE, BUT HE STUCK OUT BY VIRTUE OF HIS ECCENTRIC MANNERISMS AND BUCK TEETH ALONE.

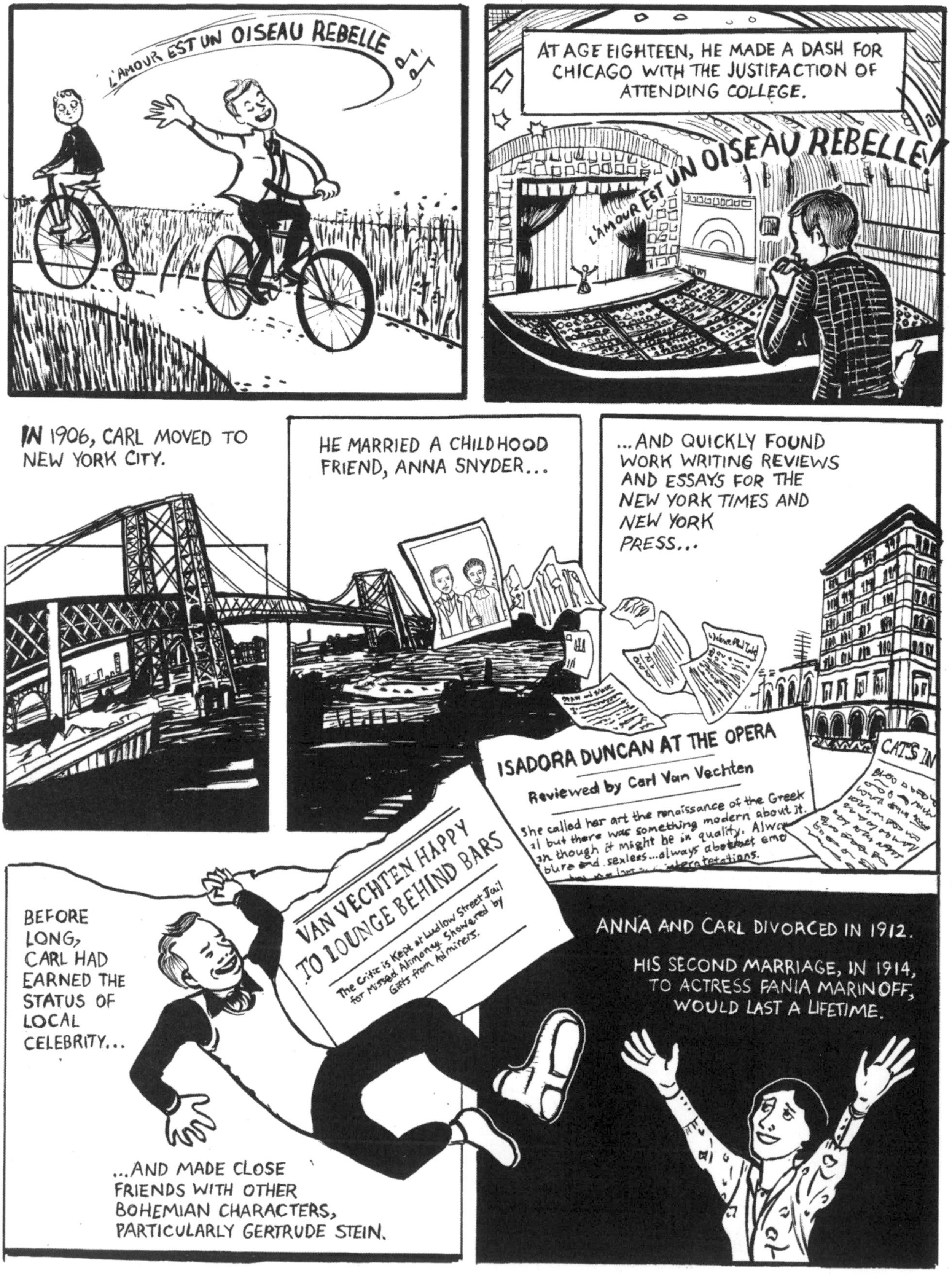

L'AMOUR EST UN OISEAU REBELLE
AT AGE EIGHTEEN, HE MADE A DASH FOR CHICAGO WITH THE JUSTIFACTION OF ATTENDING COLLEGE.
L'AMOUR EST UN OISEAU REBELLE!
IN 1906, CARL MOVED TO NEW YORK CITY.
HE MARRIED A CHILDHOOD FRIEND, ANNA SNYDER...
...AND QUICKLY FOUND WORK WRITING REVIEWS AND ESSAYS FOR THE NEW YORK TIMES AND NEW YORK PRESS...
ISADORA DUNCAN AT THE OPERA
Reviewed by Carl Van Vechten
CAT'S IN
VAN VECHTEN HAPPY TO LOUNGE BEHIND BARS
The Critic is Kept at Ludlow Street Jail for Missed Alimony. Showered by Gifts from Admirers.
BEFORE LONG, CARL HAD EARNED THE STATUS OF LOCAL CELEBRITY...
...AND MADE CLOSE FRIENDS WITH OTHER BOHEMIAN CHARACTERS, PARTICULARLY GERTRUDE STEIN.
ANNA AND CARL DIVORCED IN 1912.
HIS SECOND MARRIAGE, IN 1914, TO ACTRESS FANIA MARINOFF, WOULD LAST A LIFETIME.

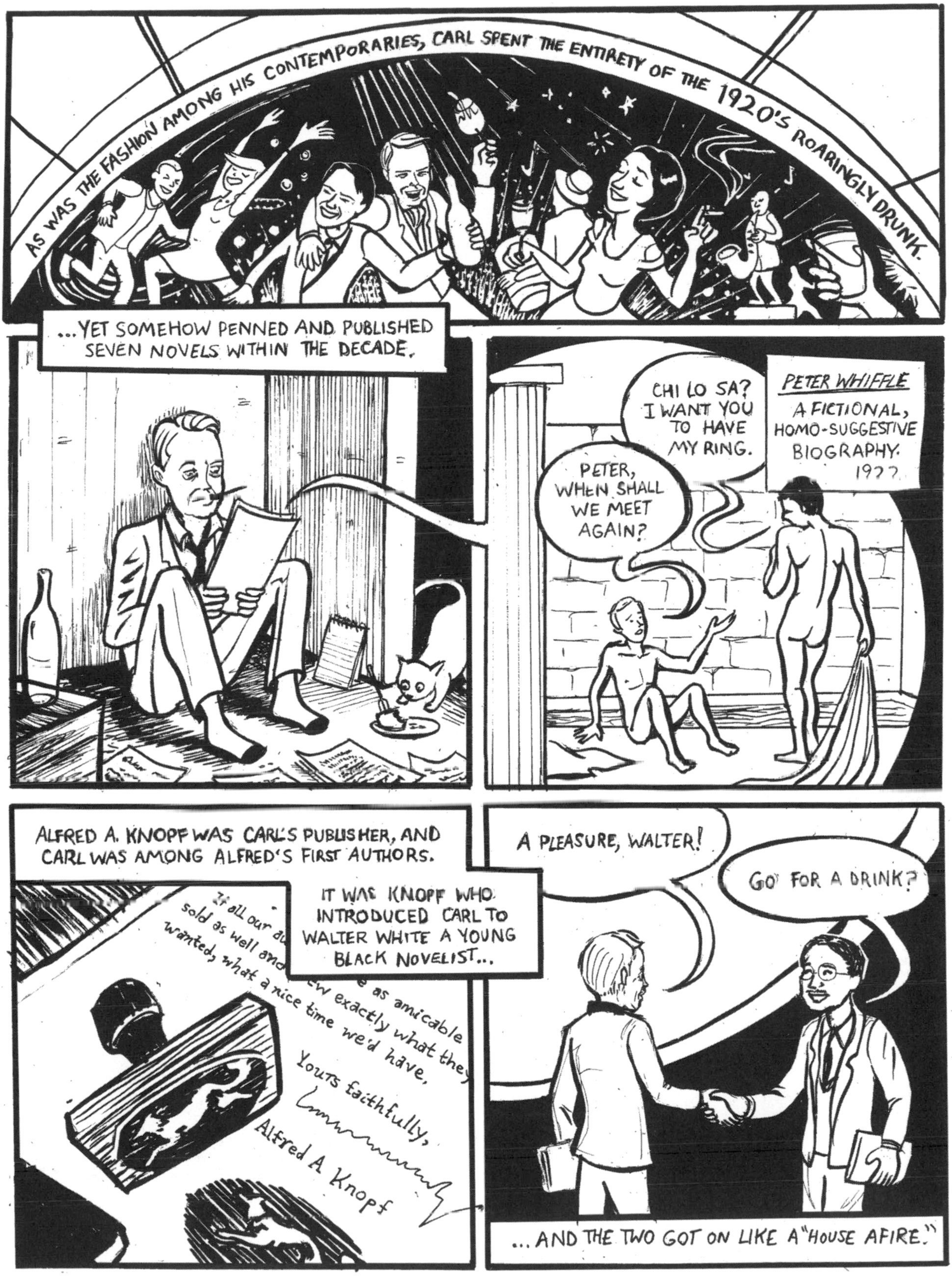
AS WAS THE FASHION AMONG HIS CONTEMPORARIES, CARL SPENT THE ENTIRETY OF THE 1920'S ROARINGLY DRUNK.
...YET SOMEHOW PENNED AND PUBLISHED SEVEN NOVELS WITHIN THE DECADE.
PETER WHIFFLE
A FICTIONAL, HOMO-SUGGESTIVE BIOGRAPHY. 1922
CHI LO SA? I WANT YOU TO HAVE MY RING.
PETER, WHEN SHALL WE MEET AGAIN?
ALFRED A. KNOPF WAS CARL'S PUBLISHER, AND CARL WAS AMONG ALFRED'S FIRST AUTHORS.
IT WAS KNOPF WHO INTRODUCED CARL TO WALTER WHITE A YOUNG BLACK NOVELIST...
If all our au
sold as well and
as amicable
w exactly what they
wanted, what a nice time we'd have.
Yours faithfully,
Alfred A Knopf
A PLEASURE, WALTER!
GO FOR A DRINK?
...AND THE TWO GOT ON LIKE A "HOUSE AFIRE."

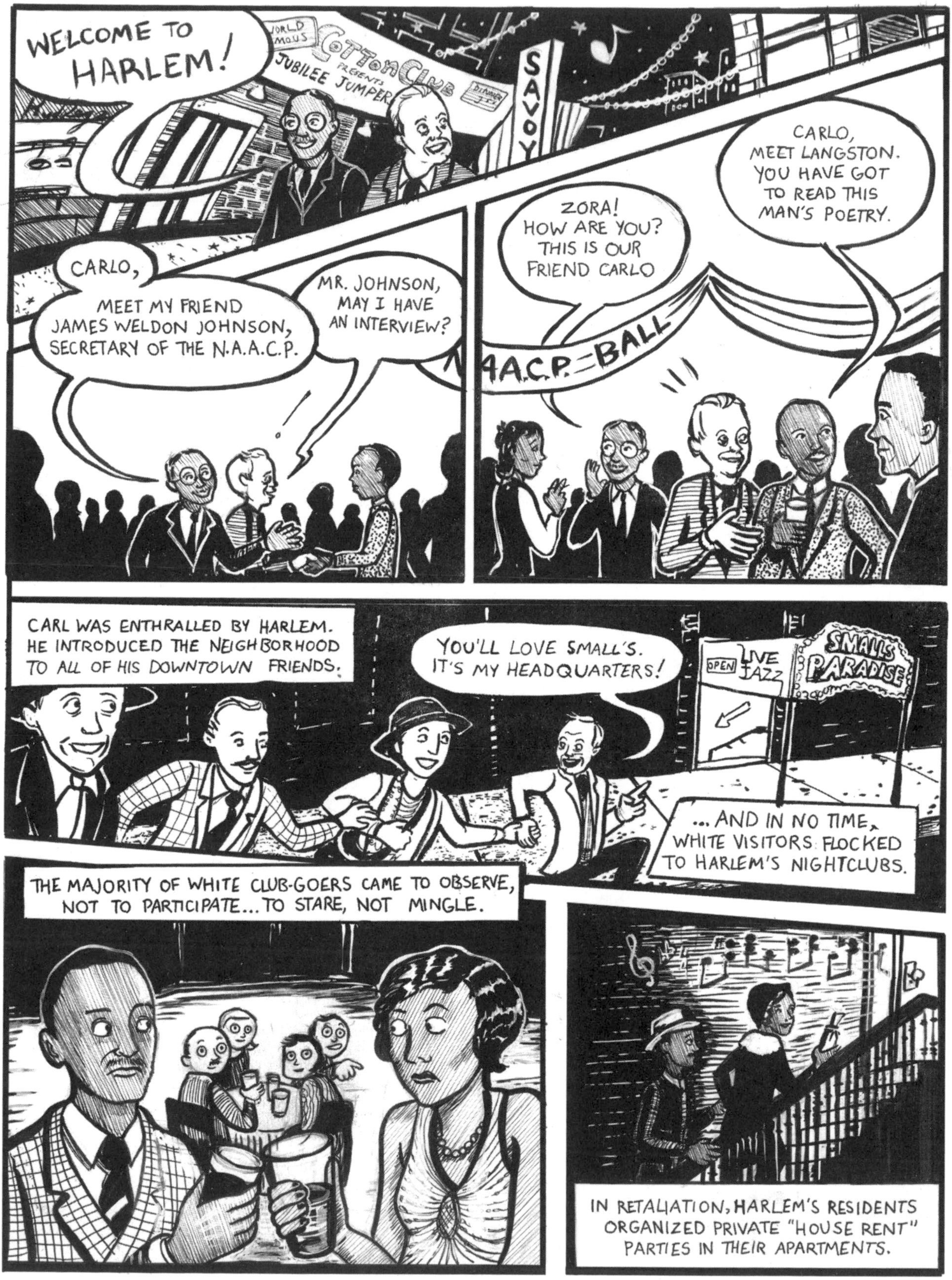
WELCOME TO HARLEM!
WORLD FAMOUS COTTON CLUB PRESENTS JUBILEE JUMPERS
SAVOY
CARLO,
MEET MY FRIEND JAMES WELDON JOHNSON, SECRETARY OF THE N.A.A.C.P.
MR. JOHNSON, MAY I HAVE AN INTERVIEW?
N.A.A.C.P. BALL
ZORA! HOW ARE YOU? THIS IS OUR FRIEND CARLO
CARLO, MEET LANGSTON. YOU HAVE GOT TO READ THIS MAN'S POETRY.
CARL WAS ENTHRALLED BY HARLEM. HE INTRODUCED THE NEIGHBORHOOD TO ALL OF HIS DOWNTOWN FRIENDS.
YOU'LL LOVE SMALL'S. IT'S MY HEADQUARTERS!
OPEN
LIVE JAZZ
SMALLS PARADISE
...AND IN NO TIME, WHITE VISITORS FLOCKED TO HARLEM'S NIGHTCLUBS.
THE MAJORITY OF WHITE CLUB-GOERS CAME TO OBSERVE, NOT TO PARTICIPATE... TO STARE, NOT MINGLE.
IN RETALIATION, HARLEM'S RESIDENTS ORGANIZED PRIVATE "HOUSE RENT" PARTIES IN THEIR APARTMENTS.

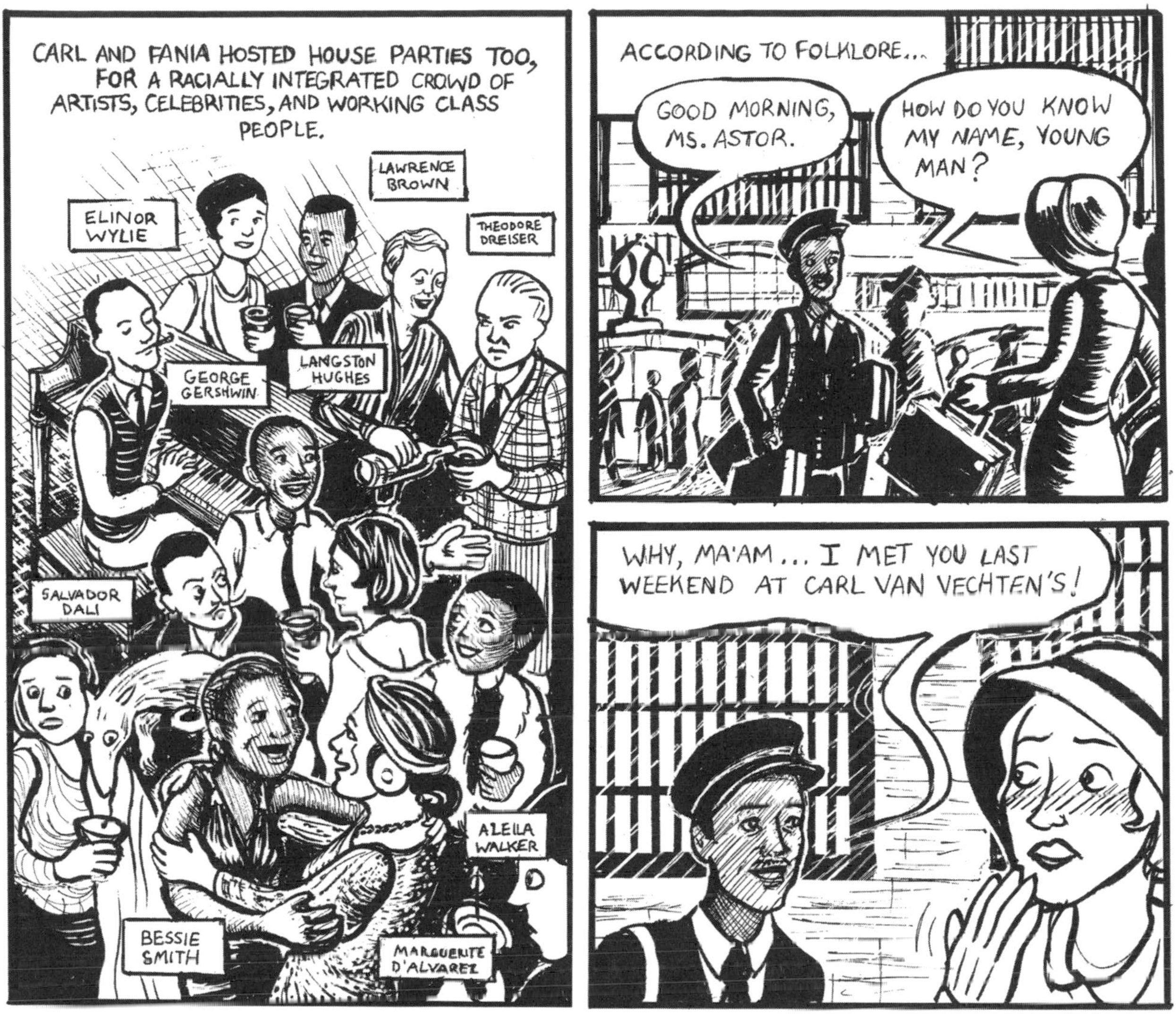
CARL AND FANIA HOSTED HOUSE PARTIES TOO, FOR A RACIALLY INTEGRATED CROWD OF ARTISTS, CELEBRITIES, AND WORKING CLASS PEOPLE.
LAWRENCE BROWN
ELINOR WYLIE
THEODORE DREISER
GEORGE GERSHWIN
LANGSTON HUGHES
SALVADOR DALI
AZELIA WALKER
BESSIE SMITH
MARGUERITE D'ALVAREZ
ACCORDING TO FOLKLORE...
GOOD MORNING, MS. ASTOR.
HOW DO YOU KNOW MY NAME, YOUNG MAN?
WHY, MA'AM... I MET YOU LAST WEEKEND AT CARL VAN VECHTEN'S!

HARLEM'S DRAG BALLS WERE ALSO INTEGRATED. CARL OFTEN SERVED AS JUDGE...

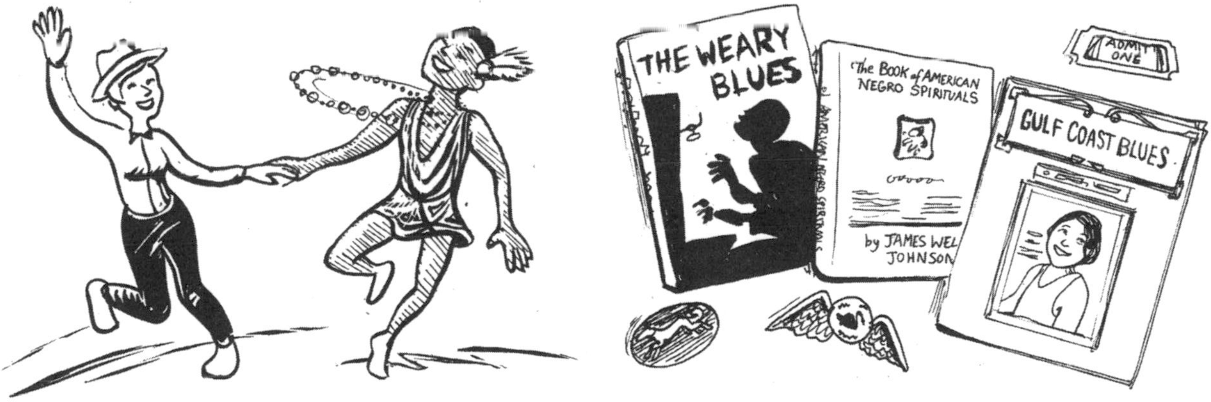
THE WEARY BLUES
The Book of AMERICAN NEGRO SPIRITUALS
by JAMES WEL JOHNSON
ADMIT ONE
GULF COAST BLUES

...ALL THE WHILE WRITING REVIEWS AND ADVOCATING PUBLICATION OF BLACK ARTISTS, INTRODUCING THEIR WORK TO A RAVENOUS WHITE AUDIENCE. BLACK NEWSPAPERS HAILED CARL AS A WHITE ALLY... UNTIL, THAT IS, HE ATTEMPTED TO DOCUMENT HARLEM IN A NOVEL... *NIGGER HEAVEN.*

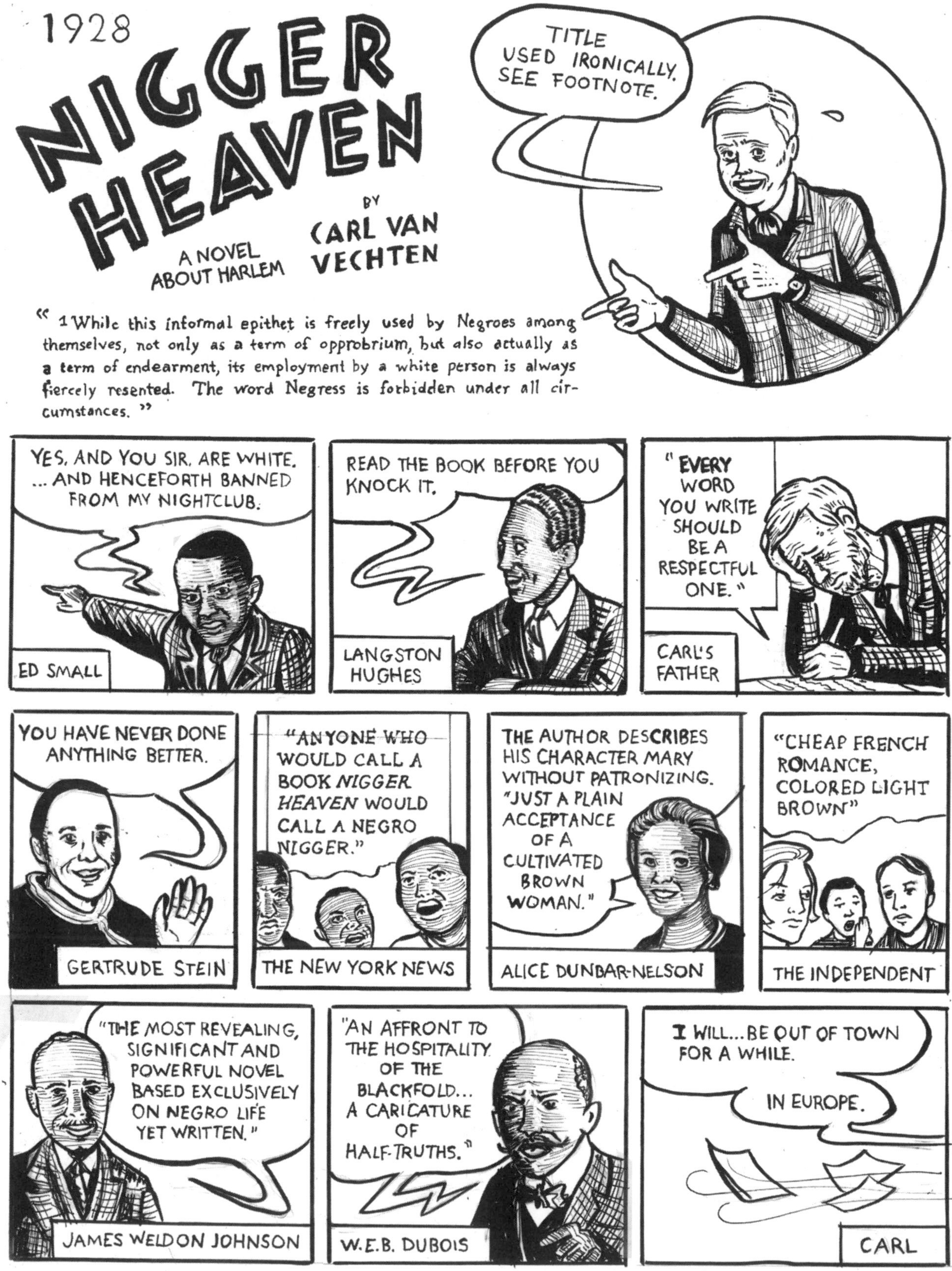
1928
NIGGER HEAVEN
BY CARL VAN VECHTEN
A NOVEL ABOUT HARLEM
TITLE USED IRONICALLY. SEE FOOTNOTE.
" 1 While this informal epithet is freely used by Negroes among themselves, not only as a term of opprobrium, but also actually as a term of endearment, its employment by a white person is always fiercely resented. The word Negress is forbidden under all circumstances. "
YES, AND YOU SIR, ARE WHITE. ... AND HENCEFORTH BANNED FROM MY NIGHTCLUB.
ED SMALL
READ THE BOOK BEFORE YOU KNOCK IT.
LANGSTON HUGHES
" EVERY WORD YOU WRITE SHOULD BE A RESPECTFUL ONE. "
CARL'S FATHER
YOU HAVE NEVER DONE ANYTHING BETTER.
GERTRUDE STEIN
"ANYONE WHO WOULD CALL A BOOK NIGGER HEAVEN WOULD CALL A NEGRO NIGGER."
THE NEW YORK NEWS
THE AUTHOR DESCRIBES HIS CHARACTER MARY WITHOUT PATRONIZING. "JUST A PLAIN ACCEPTANCE OF A CULTIVATED BROWN WOMAN."
ALICE DUNBAR-NELSON
"CHEAP FRENCH ROMANCE, COLORED LIGHT BROWN"
THE INDEPENDENT
"THE MOST REVEALING, SIGNIFICANT AND POWERFUL NOVEL BASED EXCLUSIVELY ON NEGRO LIFE YET WRITTEN."
JAMES WELDON JOHNSON
"AN AFFRONT TO THE HOSPITALITY OF THE BLACKFOLD... A CARICATURE OF HALF-TRUTHS."
W.E.B. DUBOIS
I WILL... BE OUT OF TOWN FOR A WHILE.
IN EUROPE.
CARL

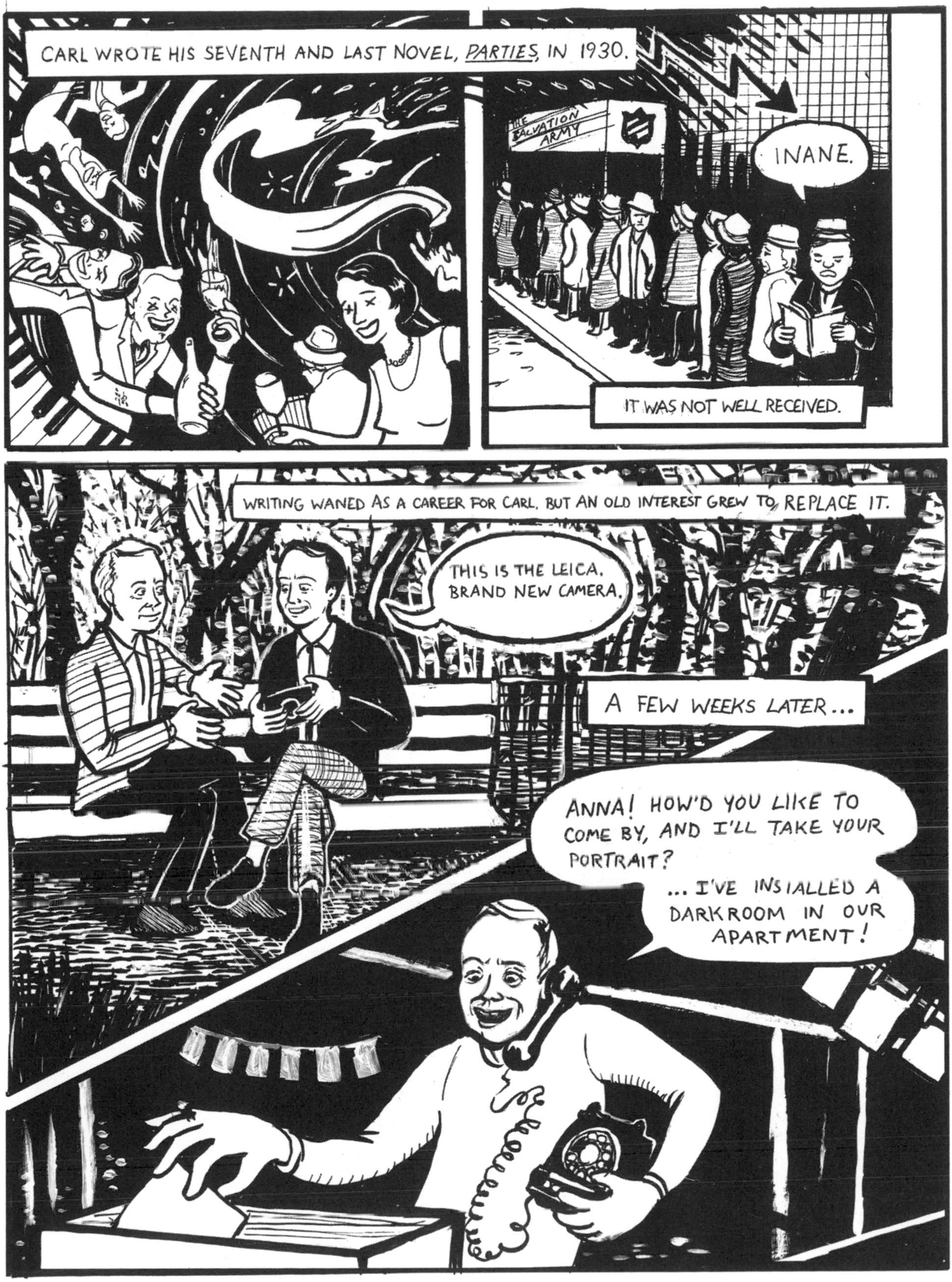
CARL WROTE HIS SEVENTH AND LAST NOVEL, PARTIES, IN 1930.
THE SALVATION ARMY
INANE.
IT WAS NOT WELL RECEIVED.
WRITING WANED AS A CAREER FOR CARL, BUT AN OLD INTEREST GREW TO REPLACE IT.
THIS IS THE LEICA. BRAND NEW CAMERA.
A FEW WEEKS LATER...
ANNA! HOW'D YOU LIKE TO COME BY, AND I'LL TAKE YOUR PORTRAIT?
... I'VE INSTALLED A DARKROOM IN OUR APARTMENT!

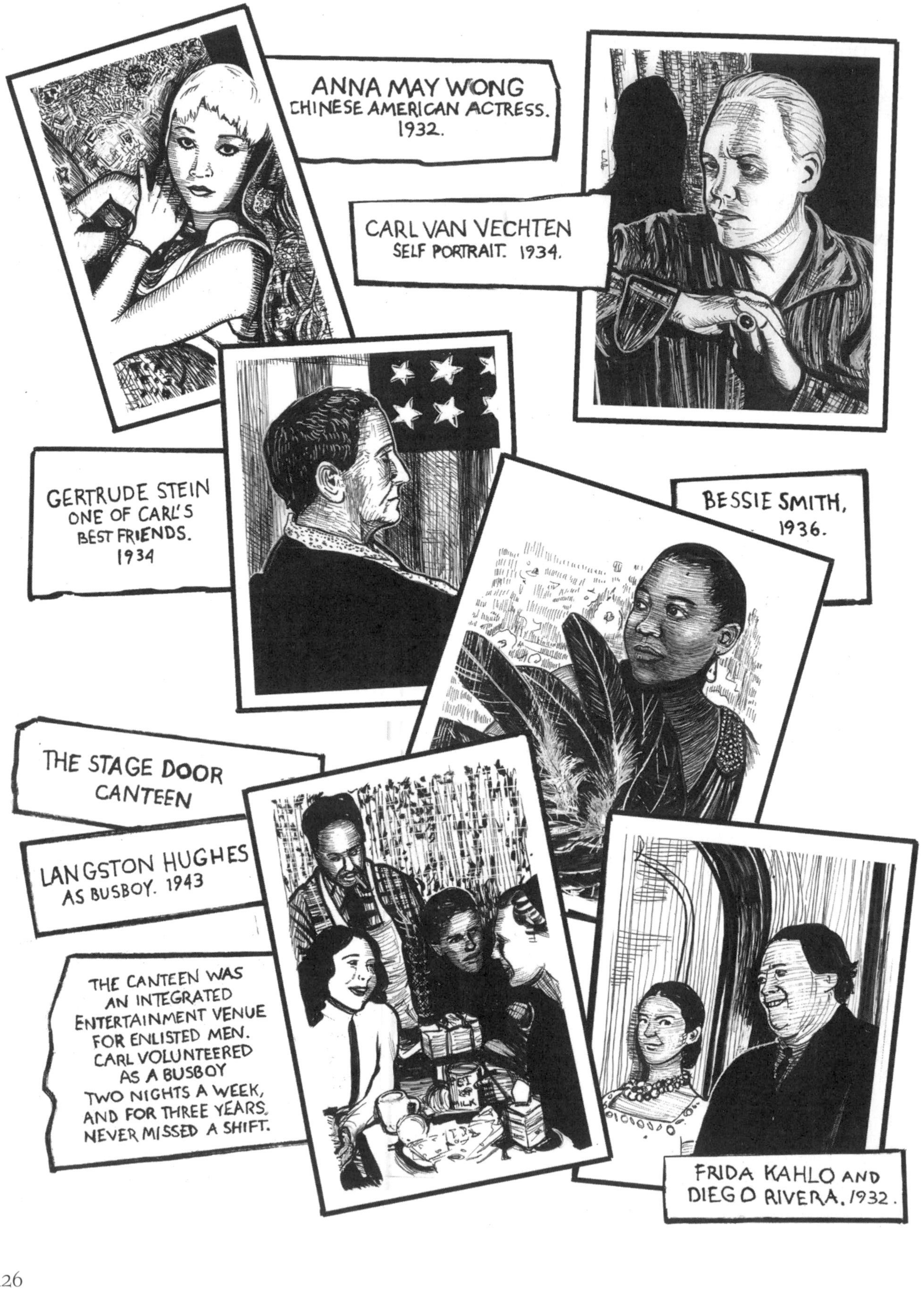
ANNA MAY WONG
CHINESE AMERICAN ACTRESS.
1932.
CARL VAN VECHTEN
SELF PORTRAIT. 1934.
GERTRUDE STEIN
ONE OF CARL'S
BEST FRIENDS.
1934
BESSIE SMITH,
1936.
THE STAGE DOOR
CANTEEN
LANGSTON HUGHES
AS BUSBOY. 1943
THE CANTEEN WAS
AN INTEGRATED
ENTERTAINMENT VENUE
FOR ENLISTED MEN.
CARL VOLUNTEERED
AS A BUSBOY
TWO NIGHTS A WEEK,
AND FOR THREE YEARS,
NEVER MISSED A SHIFT.
FRIDA KAHLO AND
DIEGO RIVERA. 1932.

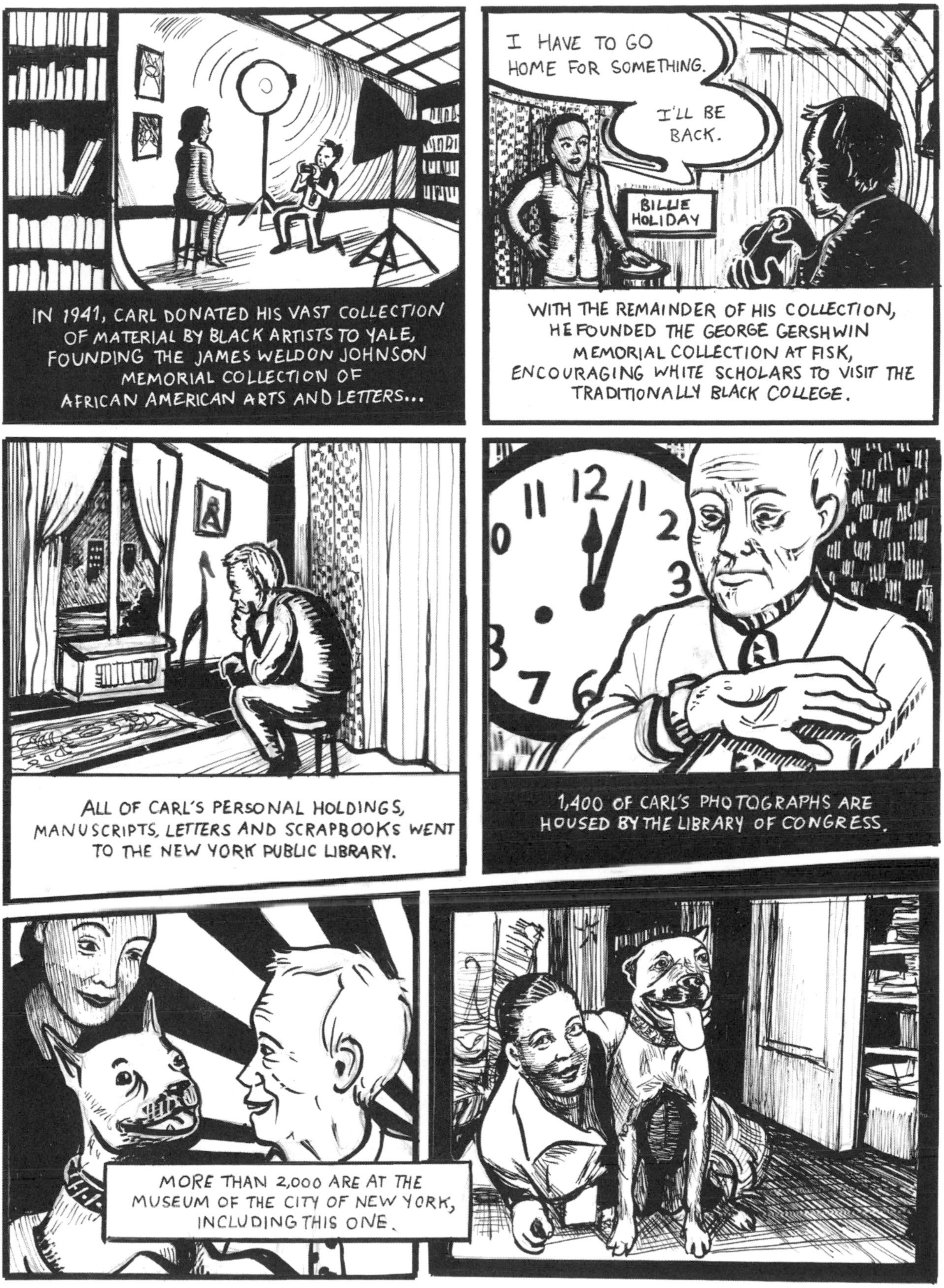
IN 1941, CARL DONATED HIS VAST COLLECTION OF MATERIAL BY BLACK ARTISTS TO YALE, FOUNDING THE JAMES WELDON JOHNSON MEMORIAL COLLECTION OF AFRICAN AMERICAN ARTS AND LETTERS...
I HAVE TO GO HOME FOR SOMETHING.
I'LL BE BACK.
BILLIE HOLIDAY
WITH THE REMAINDER OF HIS COLLECTION, HE FOUNDED THE GEORGE GERSHWIN MEMORIAL COLLECTION AT FISK, ENCOURAGING WHITE SCHOLARS TO VISIT THE TRADITIONALLY BLACK COLLEGE.
ALL OF CARL'S PERSONAL HOLDINGS, MANUSCRIPTS, LETTERS AND SCRAPBOOKS WENT TO THE NEW YORK PUBLIC LIBRARY.
1,400 OF CARL'S PHOTOGRAPHS ARE HOUSED BY THE LIBRARY OF CONGRESS.
MORE THAN 2,000 ARE AT THE MUSEUM OF THE CITY OF NEW YORK, INCLUDING THIS ONE.

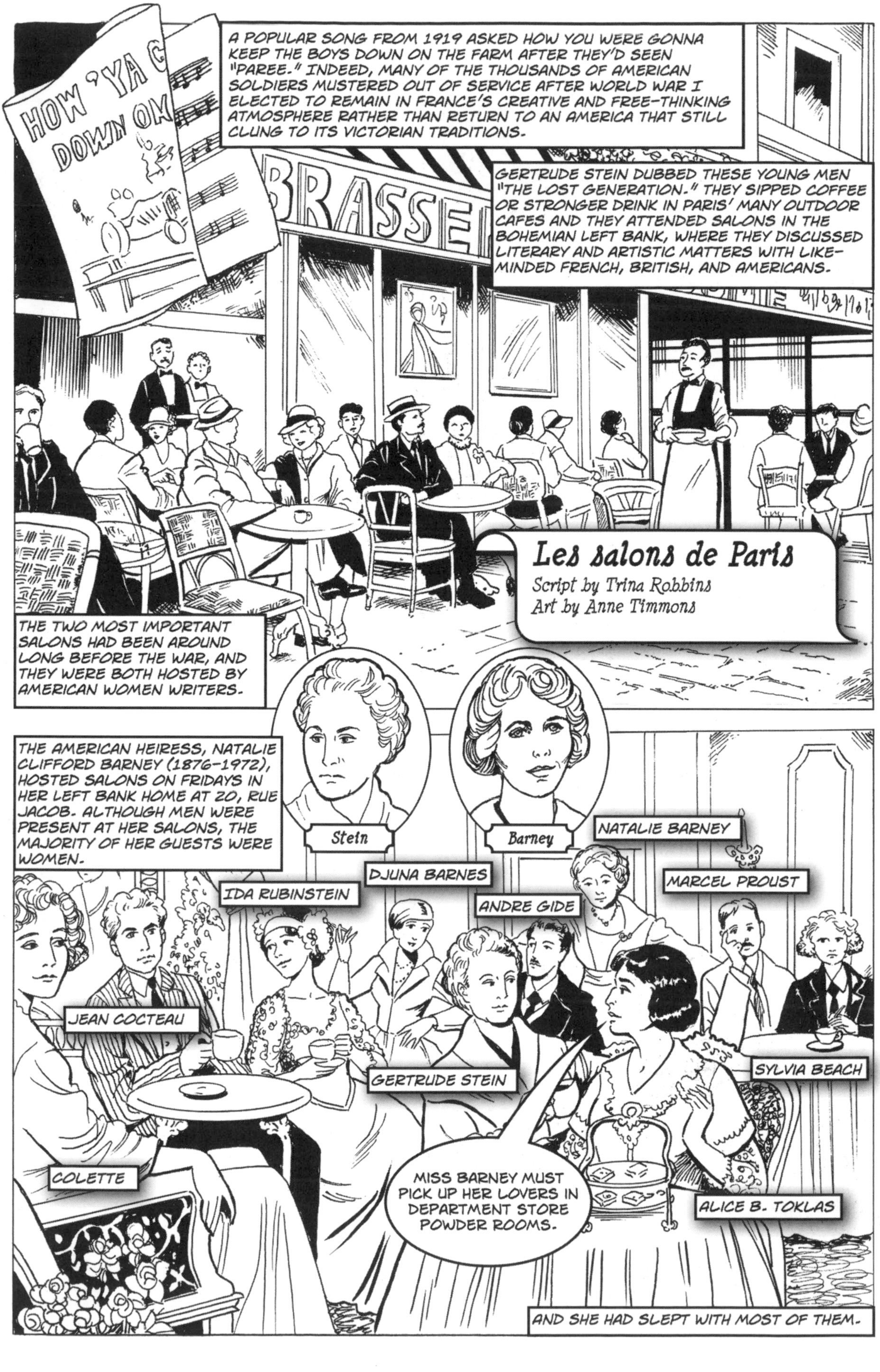
HOW 'YA G
DOWN ON
A POPULAR SONG FROM 1919 ASKED HOW YOU WERE GONNA KEEP THE BOYS DOWN ON THE FARM AFTER THEY'D SEEN "PAREE." INDEED, MANY OF THE THOUSANDS OF AMERICAN SOLDIERS MUSTERED OUT OF SERVICE AFTER WORLD WAR I ELECTED TO REMAIN IN FRANCE'S CREATIVE AND FREE-THINKING ATMOSPHERE RATHER THAN RETURN TO AN AMERICA THAT STILL CLUNG TO ITS VICTORIAN TRADITIONS.
BRASSE
GERTRUDE STEIN DUBBED THESE YOUNG MEN "THE LOST GENERATION." THEY SIPPED COFFEE OR STRONGER DRINK IN PARIS' MANY OUTDOOR CAFES AND THEY ATTENDED SALONS IN THE BOHEMIAN LEFT BANK, WHERE THEY DISCUSSED LITERARY AND ARTISTIC MATTERS WITH LIKE-MINDED FRENCH, BRITISH, AND AMERICANS.
Les salons de Paris
Script by Trina Robbins
Art by Anne Timmons
THE TWO MOST IMPORTANT SALONS HAD BEEN AROUND LONG BEFORE THE WAR, AND THEY WERE BOTH HOSTED BY AMERICAN WOMEN WRITERS.
Stein
Barney
THE AMERICAN HEIRESS, NATALIE CLIFFORD BARNEY (1876–1972), HOSTED SALONS ON FRIDAYS IN HER LEFT BANK HOME AT 20, RUE JACOB. ALTHOUGH MEN WERE PRESENT AT HER SALONS, THE MAJORITY OF HER GUESTS WERE WOMEN.
NATALIE BARNEY
DJUNA BARNES
IDA RUBINSTEIN
MARCEL PROUST
ANDRE GIDE
JEAN COCTEAU
GERTRUDE STEIN
SYLVIA BEACH
COLETTE
MISS BARNEY MUST PICK UP HER LOVERS IN DEPARTMENT STORE POWDER ROOMS.
ALICE B. TOKLAS
AND SHE HAD SLEPT WITH MOST OF THEM.

SYLVIA BEACH HAD SOME SNIDE THINGS TO SAY ABOUT THE WOMEN WHO FREQUENTED BARNEY'S SALONS.

HMPH! LADIES WITH HIGH COLLARS AND MONOCLES.

SYLVIA BEACH'S ENGLISH-LANGUAGE BOOKSTORE, SHAKESPEARE AND COMPANY, WAS SITUATED ACROSS THE STREET FROM LA MAISON DES AMIS DES LIVRES, A FRENCH-LANGUAGE BOOKSTORE OWNED BY HER LOVER, ADRIENNE MONNIER.

LA MAISON DES AMIS DES LIVRE

THE TWO WOMEN LIVED TOGETHER IN AN APARTMENT OVER MONNIER'S BOOKSTORE.

NATALIE BARNEY'S EXTREME WEALTH ALLOWED HER TO BE AN OUT LESBIAN AT A TIME WHEN NO ONE SPOKE THE WORD ALOUD IN DECENT SOCIETY. BECAUSE OF HER OUTSPOKEN LESBIANISM AND BECAUSE SHE RODE HORSES ASTRIDE RATHER THAN SIDESADDLE, SHE EARNED THE NICKNAME "THE AMAZON."

ALBINOS AREN'T REPROACHED FOR HAVING PINK EYES AND WHITISH HAIR, WHY SHOULD THEY HOLD IT AGAINST ME FOR BEING A LESBIAN?

...AN INTERESTING REMARK, CONSIDERING THAT BEACH, PUBLISHER OF JAMES JOYCE'S ULYSSES, FAVORED MANNISH ATTIRE HERSELF.

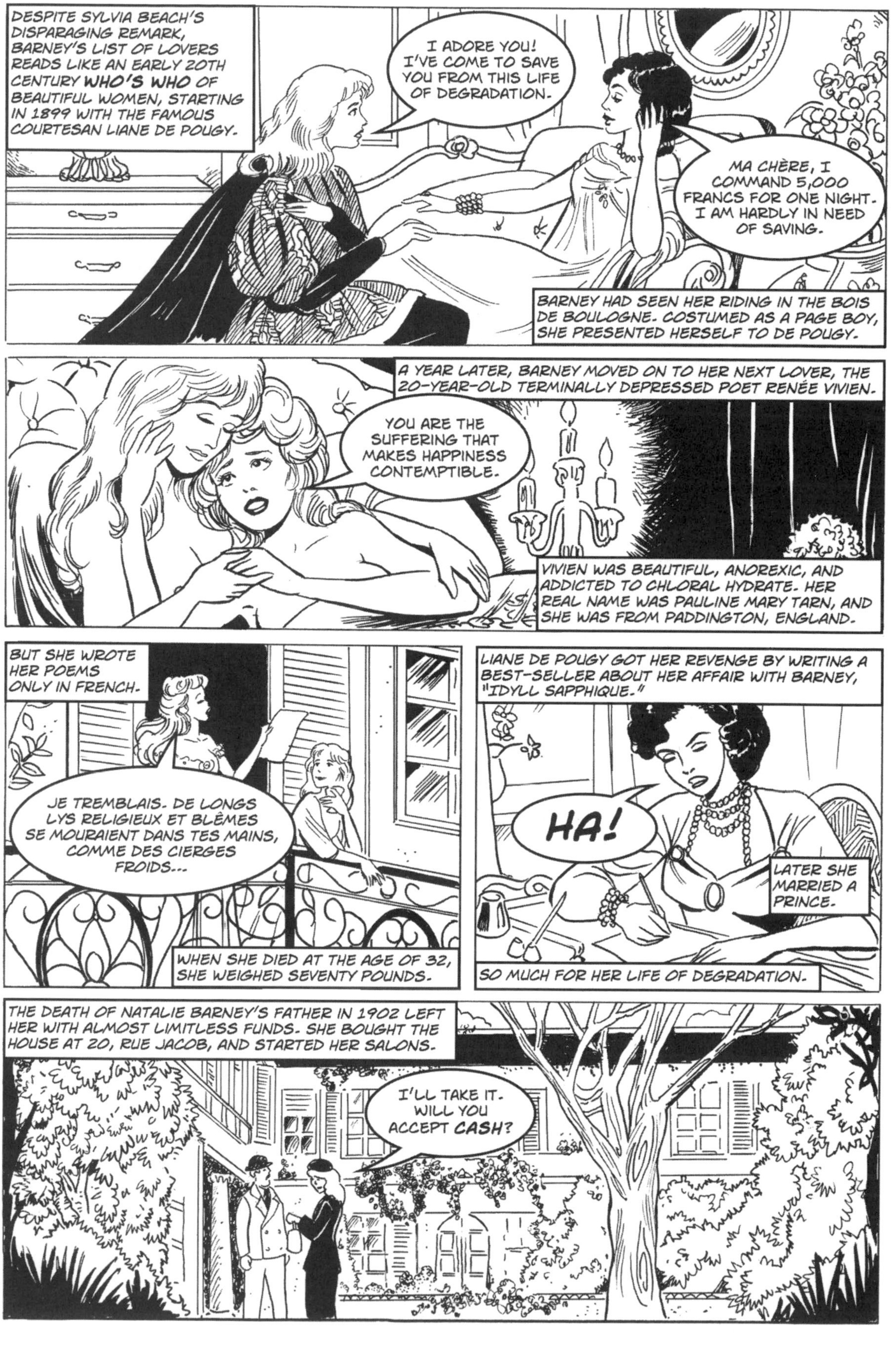
DESPITE SYLVIA BEACH'S DISPARAGING REMARK, BARNEY'S LIST OF LOVERS READS LIKE AN EARLY 20TH CENTURY **WHO'S WHO** OF BEAUTIFUL WOMEN, STARTING IN 1899 WITH THE FAMOUS COURTESAN LIANE DE POUGY.
I ADORE YOU! I'VE COME TO SAVE YOU FROM THIS LIFE OF DEGRADATION.
MA CHÈRE, I COMMAND 5,000 FRANCS FOR ONE NIGHT. I AM HARDLY IN NEED OF SAVING.
BARNEY HAD SEEN HER RIDING IN THE BOIS DE BOULOGNE. COSTUMED AS A PAGE BOY, SHE PRESENTED HERSELF TO DE POUGY.
A YEAR LATER, BARNEY MOVED ON TO HER NEXT LOVER, THE 20-YEAR-OLD TERMINALLY DEPRESSED POET RENÉE VIVIEN.
YOU ARE THE SUFFERING THAT MAKES HAPPINESS CONTEMPTIBLE.
VIVIEN WAS BEAUTIFUL, ANOREXIC, AND ADDICTED TO CHLORAL HYDRATE. HER REAL NAME WAS PAULINE MARY TARN, AND SHE WAS FROM PADDINGTON, ENGLAND.
BUT SHE WROTE HER POEMS ONLY IN FRENCH.
JE TREMBLAIS. DE LONGS LYS RELIGIEUX ET BLÊMES SE MOURAIENT DANS TES MAINS, COMME DES CIERGES FROIDS...
WHEN SHE DIED AT THE AGE OF 32, SHE WEIGHED SEVENTY POUNDS.
LIANE DE POUGY GOT HER REVENGE BY WRITING A BEST-SELLER ABOUT HER AFFAIR WITH BARNEY, "IDYLL SAPPHIQUE."
HA!
LATER SHE MARRIED A PRINCE.
SO MUCH FOR HER LIFE OF DEGRADATION.
THE DEATH OF NATALIE BARNEY'S FATHER IN 1902 LEFT HER WITH ALMOST LIMITLESS FUNDS. SHE BOUGHT THE HOUSE AT 20, RUE JACOB, AND STARTED HER SALONS.
I'LL TAKE IT. WILL YOU ACCEPT **CASH**?

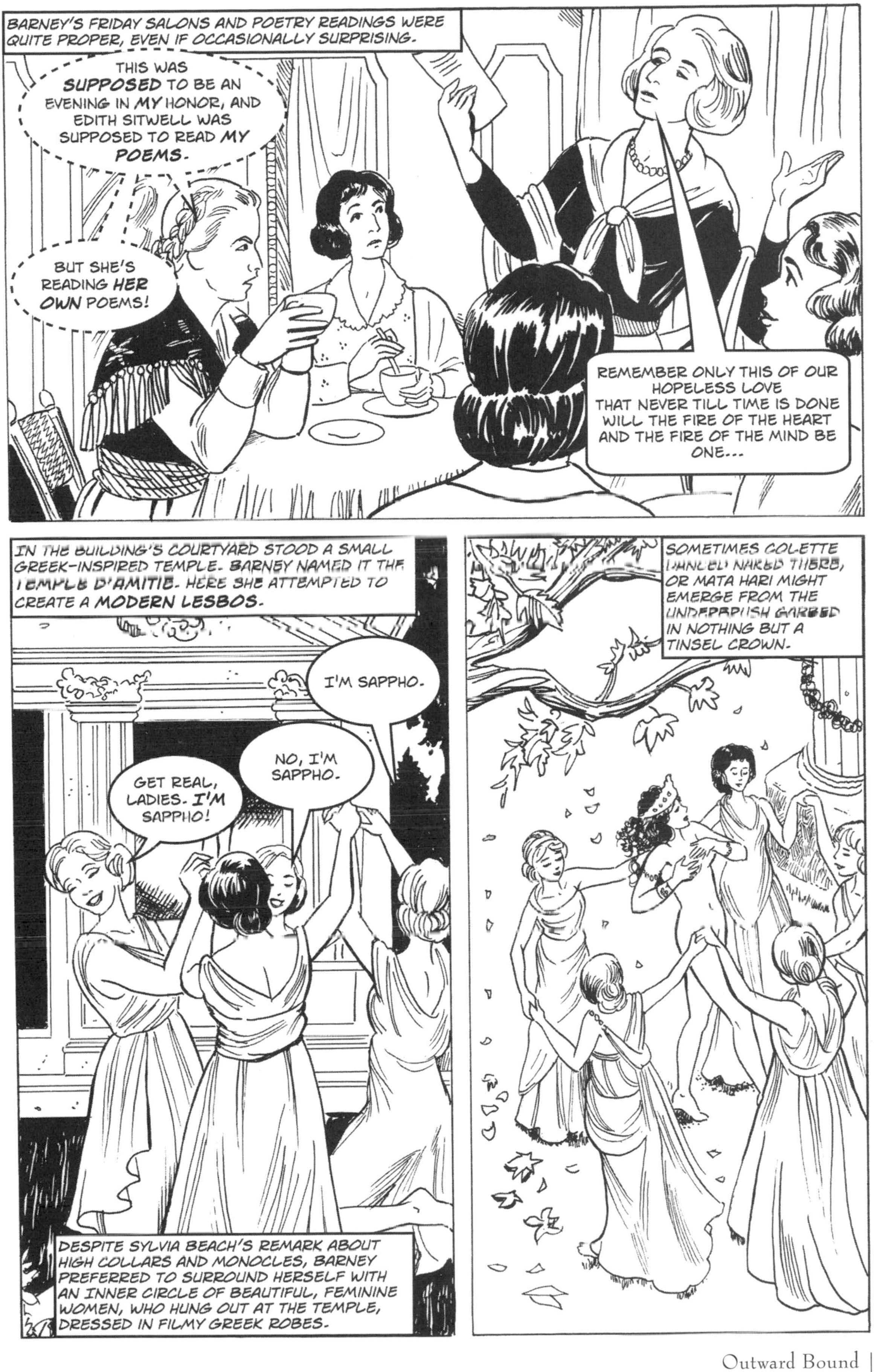

BARNEY'S FRIDAY SALONS AND POETRY READINGS WERE QUITE PROPER, EVEN IF OCCASIONALLY SURPRISING.
THIS WAS SUPPOSED TO BE AN EVENING IN MY HONOR, AND EDITH SITWELL WAS SUPPOSED TO READ MY POEMS.
BUT SHE'S READING HER OWN POEMS!
REMEMBER ONLY THIS OF OUR HOPELESS LOVE THAT NEVER TILL TIME IS DONE WILL THE FIRE OF THE HEART AND THE FIRE OF THE MIND BE ONE...
IN THE BUILDING'S COURTYARD STOOD A SMALL GREEK-INSPIRED TEMPLE. BARNEY NAMED IT THE TEMPLE D'AMITIE. HERE SHE ATTEMPTED TO CREATE A MODERN LESBOS.
I'M SAPPHO.
NO, I'M SAPPHO.
GET REAL, LADIES. I'M SAPPHO!
DESPITE SYLVIA BEACH'S REMARK ABOUT HIGH COLLARS AND MONOCLES, BARNEY PREFERRED TO SURROUND HERSELF WITH AN INNER CIRCLE OF BEAUTIFUL, FEMININE WOMEN, WHO HUNG OUT AT THE TEMPLE, DRESSED IN FILMY GREEK ROBES.
SOMETIMES COLETTE DANCED NAKED THERE, OR MATA HARI MIGHT EMERGE FROM THE UNDERBRUSH GARBED IN NOTHING BUT A TINSEL CROWN.

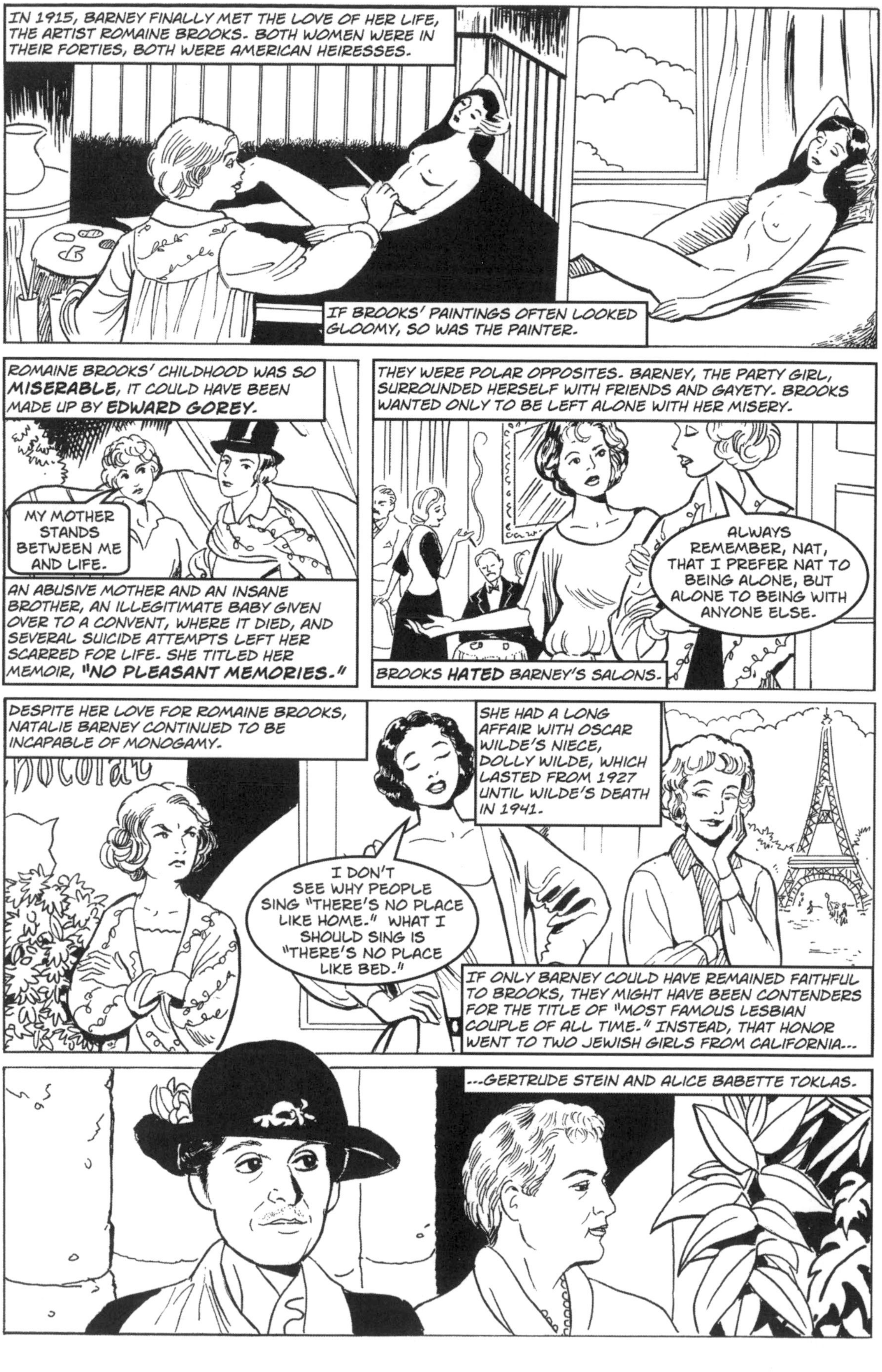
IN 1915, BARNEY FINALLY MET THE LOVE OF HER LIFE, THE ARTIST ROMAINE BROOKS. BOTH WOMEN WERE IN THEIR FORTIES, BOTH WERE AMERICAN HEIRESSES.
IF BROOKS' PAINTINGS OFTEN LOOKED GLOOMY, SO WAS THE PAINTER.
ROMAINE BROOKS' CHILDHOOD WAS SO MISERABLE, IT COULD HAVE BEEN MADE UP BY EDWARD GOREY.
MY MOTHER STANDS BETWEEN ME AND LIFE.
AN ABUSIVE MOTHER AND AN INSANE BROTHER, AN ILLEGITIMATE BABY GIVEN OVER TO A CONVENT, WHERE IT DIED, AND SEVERAL SUICIDE ATTEMPTS LEFT HER SCARRED FOR LIFE. SHE TITLED HER MEMOIR, "NO PLEASANT MEMORIES."
THEY WERE POLAR OPPOSITES. BARNEY, THE PARTY GIRL, SURROUNDED HERSELF WITH FRIENDS AND GAYETY. BROOKS WANTED ONLY TO BE LEFT ALONE WITH HER MISERY.
ALWAYS REMEMBER, NAT, THAT I PREFER NAT TO BEING ALONE, BUT ALONE TO BEING WITH ANYONE ELSE.
BROOKS HATED BARNEY'S SALONS.
DESPITE HER LOVE FOR ROMAINE BROOKS, NATALIE BARNEY CONTINUED TO BE INCAPABLE OF MONOGAMY.
SHE HAD A LONG AFFAIR WITH OSCAR WILDE'S NIECE, DOLLY WILDE, WHICH LASTED FROM 1927 UNTIL WILDE'S DEATH IN 1941.
I DON'T SEE WHY PEOPLE SING "THERE'S NO PLACE LIKE HOME." WHAT I SHOULD SING IS "THERE'S NO PLACE LIKE BED."
IF ONLY BARNEY COULD HAVE REMAINED FAITHFUL TO BROOKS, THEY MIGHT HAVE BEEN CONTENDERS FOR THE TITLE OF "MOST FAMOUS LESBIAN COUPLE OF ALL TIME." INSTEAD, THAT HONOR WENT TO TWO JEWISH GIRLS FROM CALIFORNIA...
...GERTRUDE STEIN AND ALICE BABETTE TOKLAS.

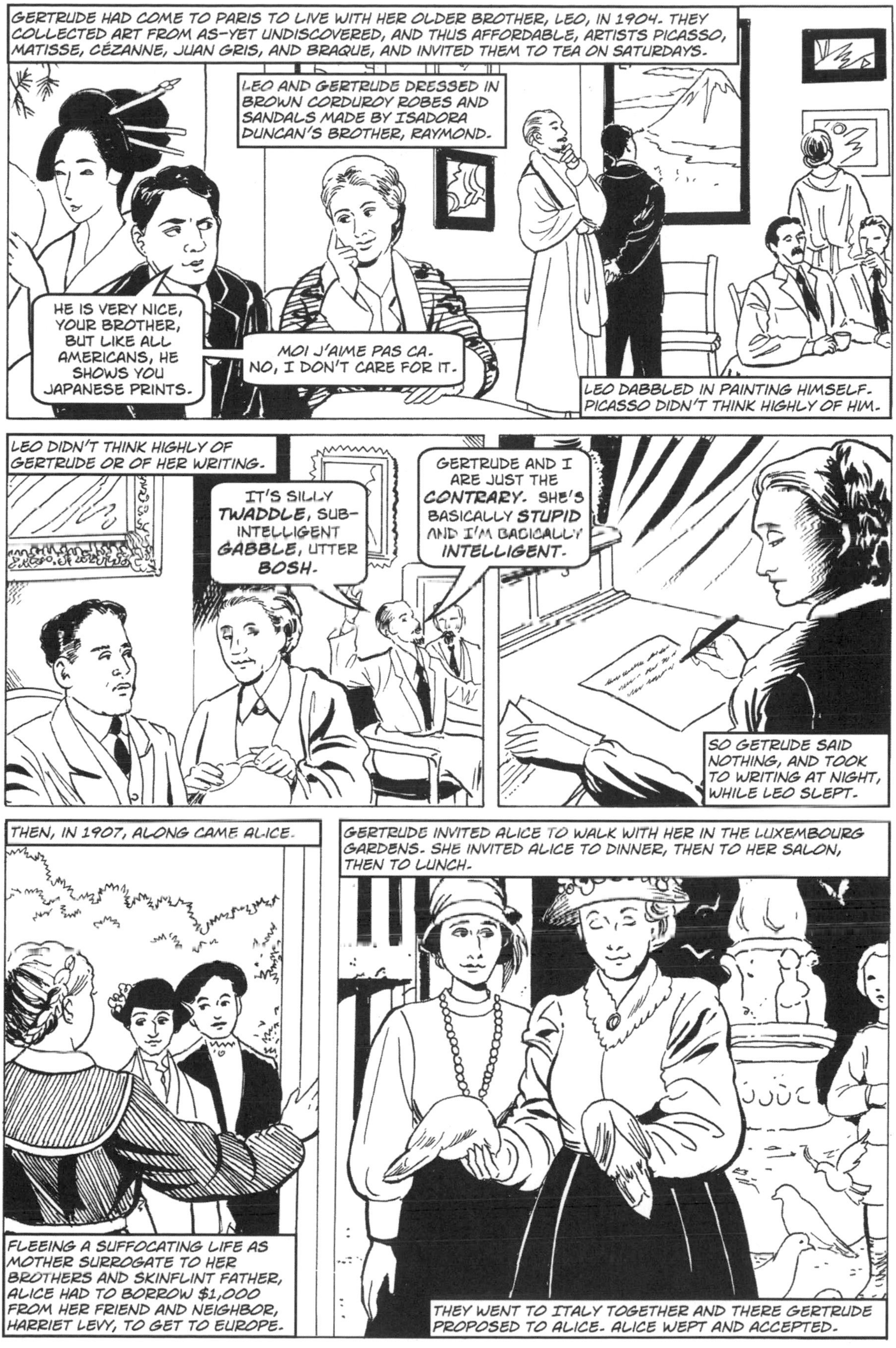
GERTRUDE HAD COME TO PARIS TO LIVE WITH HER OLDER BROTHER, LEO, IN 1904. THEY COLLECTED ART FROM AS-YET UNDISCOVERED, AND THUS AFFORDABLE, ARTISTS PICASSO, MATISSE, CÉZANNE, JUAN GRIS, AND BRAQUE, AND INVITED THEM TO TEA ON SATURDAYS.
LEO AND GERTRUDE DRESSED IN BROWN CORDUROY ROBES AND SANDALS MADE BY ISADORA DUNCAN'S BROTHER, RAYMOND.
HE IS VERY NICE, YOUR BROTHER, BUT LIKE ALL AMERICANS, HE SHOWS YOU JAPANESE PRINTS.
MOI J'AIME PAS CA. NO, I DON'T CARE FOR IT.
LEO DABBLED IN PAINTING HIMSELF. PICASSO DIDN'T THINK HIGHLY OF HIM.
LEO DIDN'T THINK HIGHLY OF GERTRUDE OR OF HER WRITING.
IT'S SILLY TWADDLE, SUB-INTELLIGENT GABBLE, UTTER BOSH.
GERTRUDE AND I ARE JUST THE CONTRARY. SHE'S BASICALLY STUPID AND I'M BASICALLY INTELLIGENT.
SO GETRUDE SAID NOTHING, AND TOOK TO WRITING AT NIGHT, WHILE LEO SLEPT.
THEN, IN 1907, ALONG CAME ALICE.
FLEEING A SUFFOCATING LIFE AS MOTHER SURROGATE TO HER BROTHERS AND SKINFLINT FATHER, ALICE HAD TO BORROW $1,000 FROM HER FRIEND AND NEIGHBOR, HARRIET LEVY, TO GET TO EUROPE.
GERTRUDE INVITED ALICE TO WALK WITH HER IN THE LUXEMBOURG GARDENS. SHE INVITED ALICE TO DINNER, THEN TO HER SALON, THEN TO LUNCH.
THEY WENT TO ITALY TOGETHER AND THERE GERTRUDE PROPOSED TO ALICE. ALICE WEPT AND ACCEPTED.

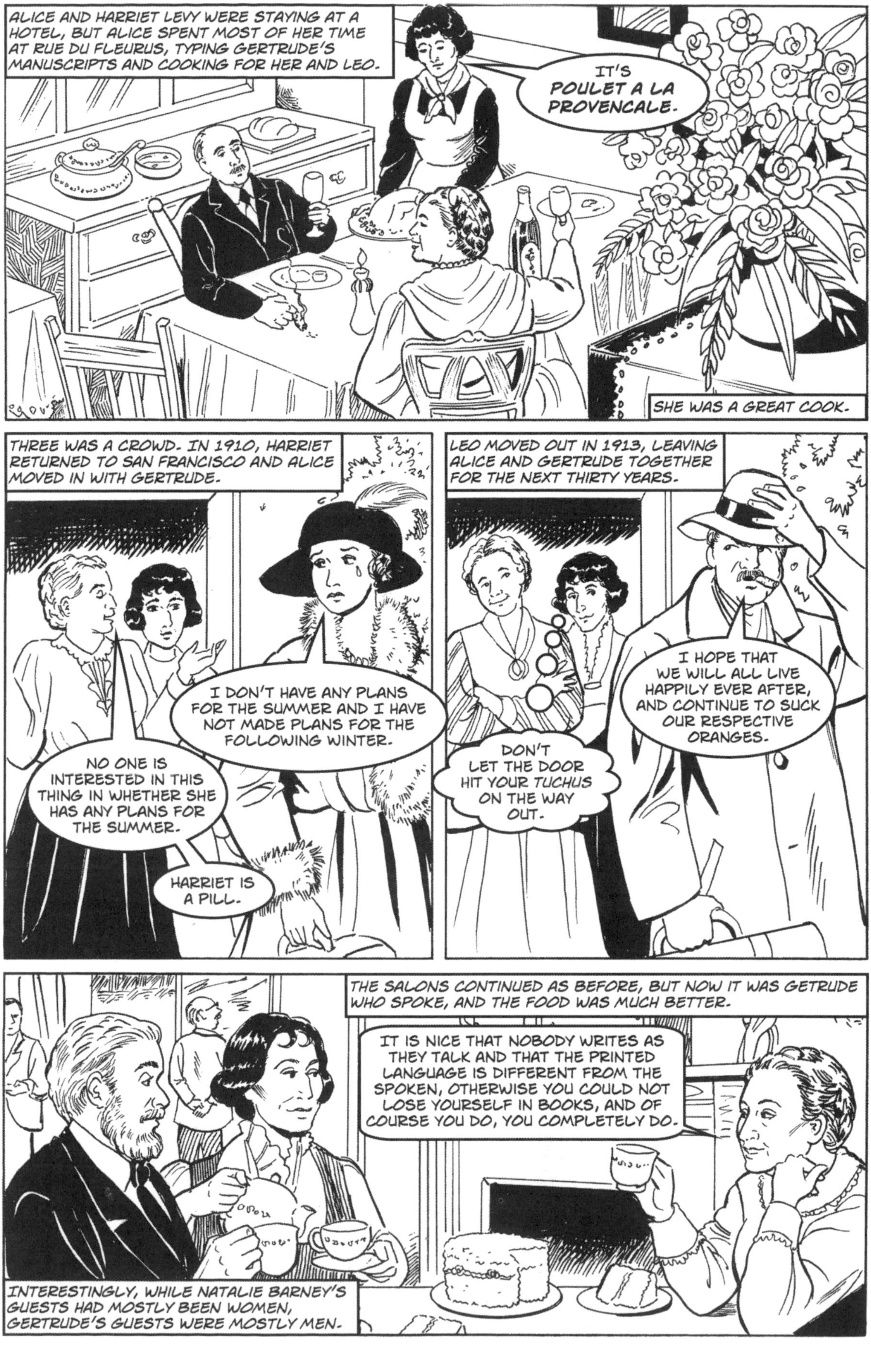

ALICE AND HARRIET LEVY WERE STAYING AT A HOTEL, BUT ALICE SPENT MOST OF HER TIME AT RUE DU FLEURUS, TYPING GERTRUDE'S MANUSCRIPTS AND COOKING FOR HER AND LEO.
IT'S POULET A LA PROVENCALE.
SHE WAS A GREAT COOK.
THREE WAS A CROWD. IN 1910, HARRIET RETURNED TO SAN FRANCISCO AND ALICE MOVED IN WITH GERTRUDE.
I DON'T HAVE ANY PLANS FOR THE SUMMER AND I HAVE NOT MADE PLANS FOR THE FOLLOWING WINTER.
NO ONE IS INTERESTED IN THIS THING IN WHETHER SHE HAS ANY PLANS FOR THE SUMMER.
HARRIET IS A PILL.
LEO MOVED OUT IN 1913, LEAVING ALICE AND GERTRUDE TOGETHER FOR THE NEXT THIRTY YEARS.
I HOPE THAT WE WILL ALL LIVE HAPPILY EVER AFTER, AND CONTINUE TO SUCK OUR RESPECTIVE ORANGES.
DON'T LET THE DOOR HIT YOUR TUCHUS ON THE WAY OUT.
THE SALONS CONTINUED AS BEFORE, BUT NOW IT WAS GETRUDE WHO SPOKE, AND THE FOOD WAS MUCH BETTER.
IT IS NICE THAT NOBODY WRITES AS THEY TALK AND THAT THE PRINTED LANGUAGE IS DIFFERENT FROM THE SPOKEN, OTHERWISE YOU COULD NOT LOSE YOURSELF IN BOOKS, AND OF COURSE YOU DO, YOU COMPLETELY DO.
INTERESTINGLY, WHILE NATALIE BARNEY'S GUESTS HAD MOSTLY BEEN WOMEN, GERTRUDE'S GUESTS WERE MOSTLY MEN.

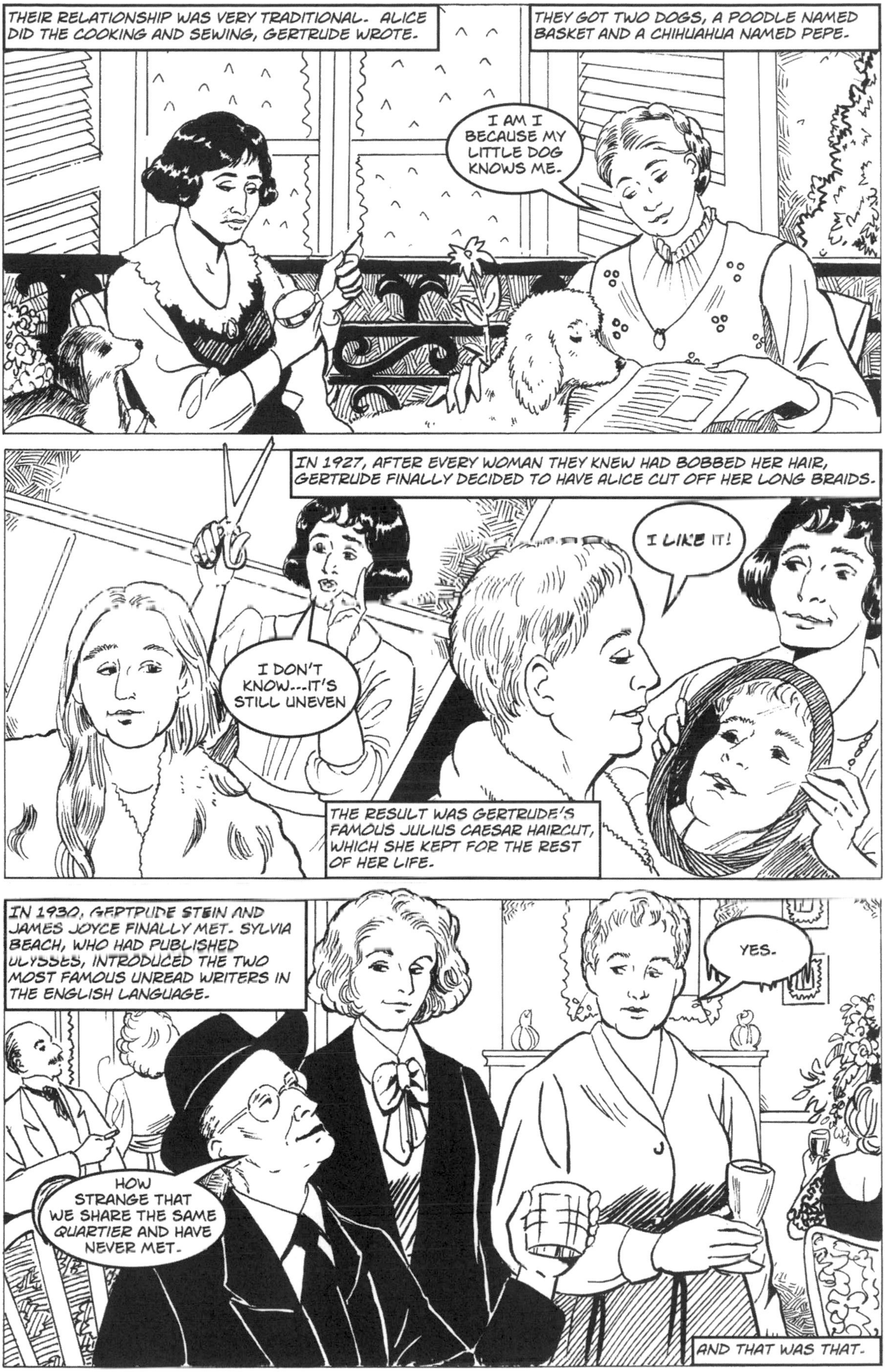
THEIR RELATIONSHIP WAS VERY TRADITIONAL. ALICE DID THE COOKING AND SEWING, GERTRUDE WROTE.
THEY GOT TWO DOGS, A POODLE NAMED BASKET AND A CHIHUAHUA NAMED PEPE.
I AM I BECAUSE MY LITTLE DOG KNOWS ME.
IN 1927, AFTER EVERY WOMAN THEY KNEW HAD BOBBED HER HAIR, GERTRUDE FINALLY DECIDED TO HAVE ALICE CUT OFF HER LONG BRAIDS.
I DON'T KNOW...IT'S STILL UNEVEN
I LIKE IT!
THE RESULT WAS GERTRUDE'S FAMOUS JULIUS CAESAR HAIRCUT, WHICH SHE KEPT FOR THE REST OF HER LIFE.
IN 1930, GERTRUDE STEIN AND JAMES JOYCE FINALLY MET. SYLVIA BEACH, WHO HAD PUBLISHED ULYSSES, INTRODUCED THE TWO MOST FAMOUS UNREAD WRITERS IN THE ENGLISH LANGUAGE.
YES.
HOW STRANGE THAT WE SHARE THE SAME QUARTIER AND HAVE NEVER MET.
AND THAT WAS THAT.

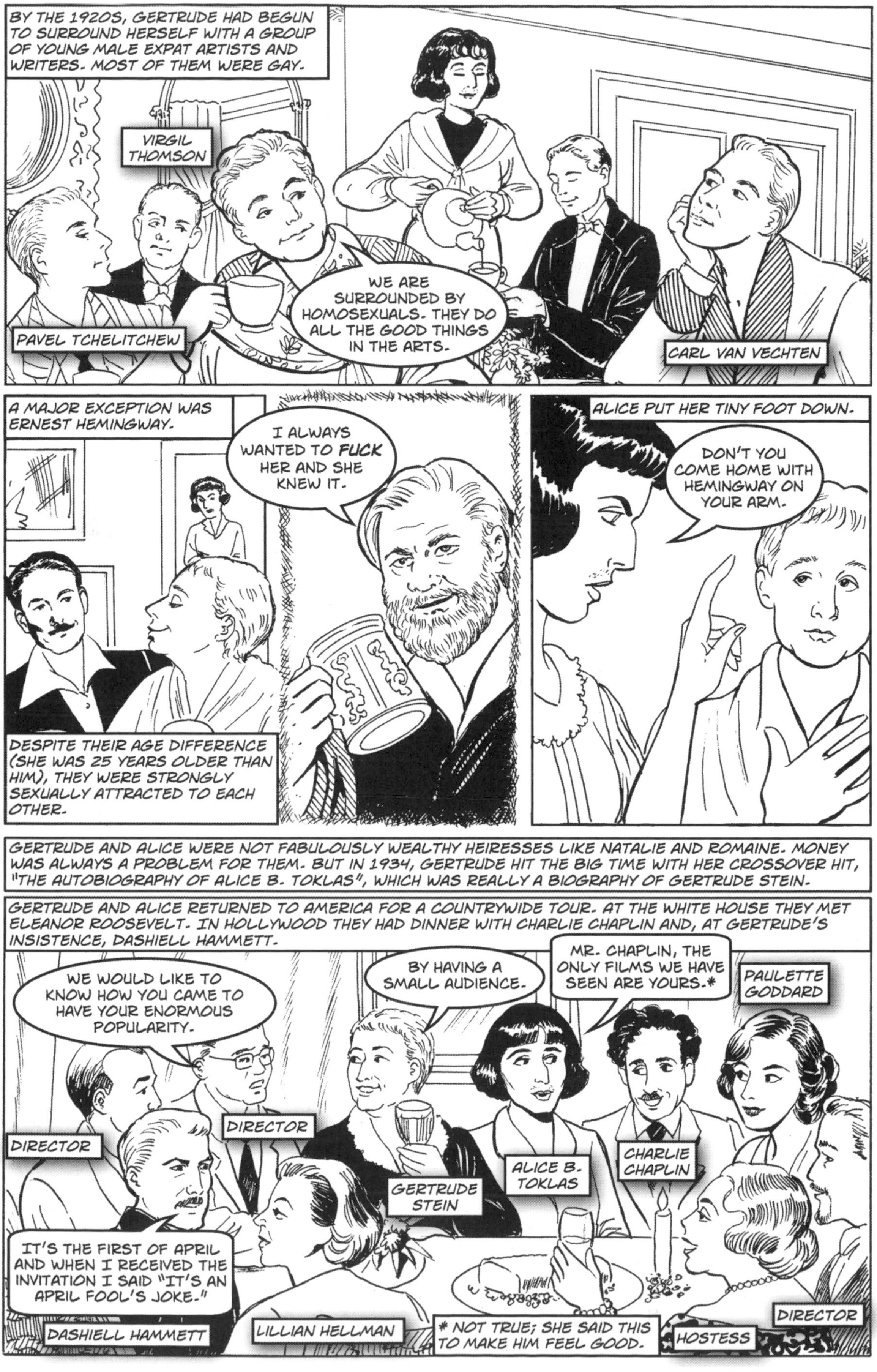

BY THE 1920S, GERTRUDE HAD BEGUN TO SURROUND HERSELF WITH A GROUP OF YOUNG MALE EXPAT ARTISTS AND WRITERS. MOST OF THEM WERE GAY.
VIRGIL THOMSON
WE ARE SURROUNDED BY HOMOSEXUALS. THEY DO ALL THE GOOD THINGS IN THE ARTS.
PAVEL TCHELITCHEW
CARL VAN VECHTEN
A MAJOR EXCEPTION WAS ERNEST HEMINGWAY.
DESPITE THEIR AGE DIFFERENCE (SHE WAS 25 YEARS OLDER THAN HIM), THEY WERE STRONGLY SEXUALLY ATTRACTED TO EACH OTHER.
I ALWAYS WANTED TO **FUCK** HER AND SHE KNEW IT.
ALICE PUT HER TINY FOOT DOWN.
DON'T YOU COME HOME WITH HEMINGWAY ON YOUR ARM.
GERTRUDE AND ALICE WERE NOT FABULOUSLY WEALTHY HEIRESSES LIKE NATALIE AND ROMAINE. MONEY WAS ALWAYS A PROBLEM FOR THEM. BUT IN 1934, GERTRUDE HIT THE BIG TIME WITH HER CROSSOVER HIT, "THE AUTOBIOGRAPHY OF ALICE B. TOKLAS", WHICH WAS REALLY A BIOGRAPHY OF GERTRUDE STEIN.
GERTRUDE AND ALICE RETURNED TO AMERICA FOR A COUNTRYWIDE TOUR. AT THE WHITE HOUSE THEY MET ELEANOR ROOSEVELT. IN HOLLYWOOD THEY HAD DINNER WITH CHARLIE CHAPLIN AND, AT GERTRUDE'S INSISTENCE, DASHIELL HAMMETT.
WE WOULD LIKE TO KNOW HOW YOU CAME TO HAVE YOUR ENORMOUS POPULARITY.
BY HAVING A SMALL AUDIENCE.
MR. CHAPLIN, THE ONLY FILMS WE HAVE SEEN ARE YOURS.*
PAULETTE GODDARD
DIRECTOR
DIRECTOR
GERTRUDE STEIN
ALICE B. TOKLAS
CHARLIE CHAPLIN
IT'S THE FIRST OF APRIL AND WHEN I RECEIVED THE INVITATION I SAID "IT'S AN APRIL FOOL'S JOKE."
DASHIELL HAMMETT
LILLIAN HELLMAN
* NOT TRUE; SHE SAID THIS TO MAKE HIM FEEL GOOD.
HOSTESS
DIRECTOR

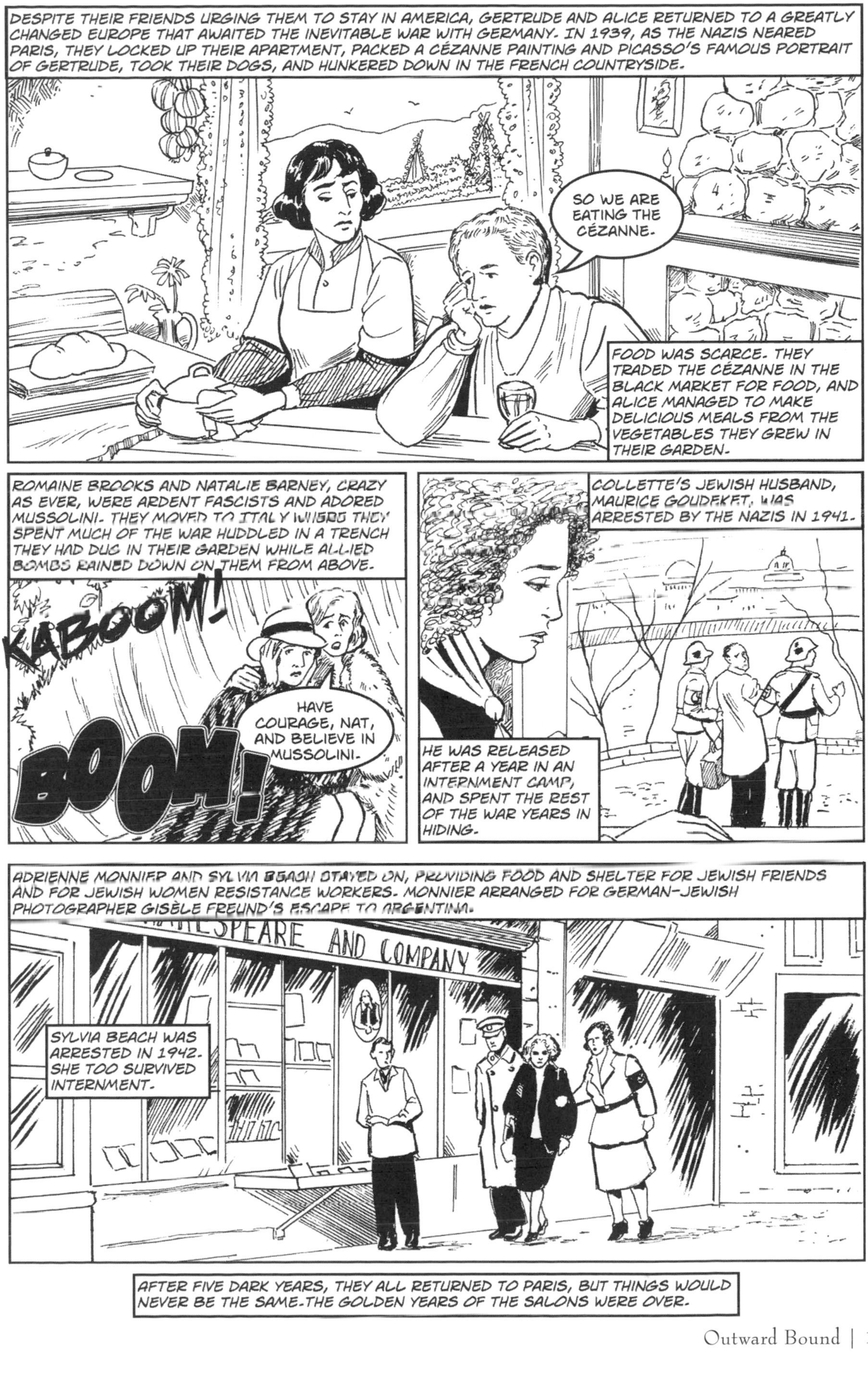
DESPITE THEIR FRIENDS URGING THEM TO STAY IN AMERICA, GERTRUDE AND ALICE RETURNED TO A GREATLY CHANGED EUROPE THAT AWAITED THE INEVITABLE WAR WITH GERMANY. IN 1939, AS THE NAZIS NEARED PARIS, THEY LOCKED UP THEIR APARTMENT, PACKED A CÉZANNE PAINTING AND PICASSO'S FAMOUS PORTRAIT OF GERTRUDE, TOOK THEIR DOGS, AND HUNKERED DOWN IN THE FRENCH COUNTRYSIDE.
SO WE ARE EATING THE CÉZANNE.
FOOD WAS SCARCE. THEY TRADED THE CÉZANNE IN THE BLACK MARKET FOR FOOD, AND ALICE MANAGED TO MAKE DELICIOUS MEALS FROM THE VEGETABLES THEY GREW IN THEIR GARDEN.
ROMAINE BROOKS AND NATALIE BARNEY, CRAZY AS EVER, WERE ARDENT FASCISTS AND ADORED MUSSOLINI. THEY MOVED TO ITALY WHERE THEY SPENT MUCH OF THE WAR HUDDLED IN A TRENCH THEY HAD DUG IN THEIR GARDEN WHILE ALLIED BOMBS RAINED DOWN ON THEM FROM ABOVE.
KABOOOM!
HAVE COURAGE, NAT, AND BELIEVE IN MUSSOLINI.
BOOM!
COLLETTE'S JEWISH HUSBAND, MAURICE GOUDEKET, WAS ARRESTED BY THE NAZIS IN 1941.
HE WAS RELEASED AFTER A YEAR IN AN INTERNMENT CAMP, AND SPENT THE REST OF THE WAR YEARS IN HIDING.
ADRIENNE MONNIER AND SYLVIA BEACH STAYED ON, PROVIDING FOOD AND SHELTER FOR JEWISH FRIENDS AND FOR JEWISH WOMEN RESISTANCE WORKERS. MONNIER ARRANGED FOR GERMAN-JEWISH PHOTOGRAPHER GISÈLE FREUND'S ESCAPE TO ARGENTINA.
AND COMPANY
SYLVIA BEACH WAS ARRESTED IN 1942. SHE TOO SURVIVED INTERNMENT.
AFTER FIVE DARK YEARS, THEY ALL RETURNED TO PARIS, BUT THINGS WOULD NEVER BE THE SAME. THE GOLDEN YEARS OF THE SALONS WERE OVER.

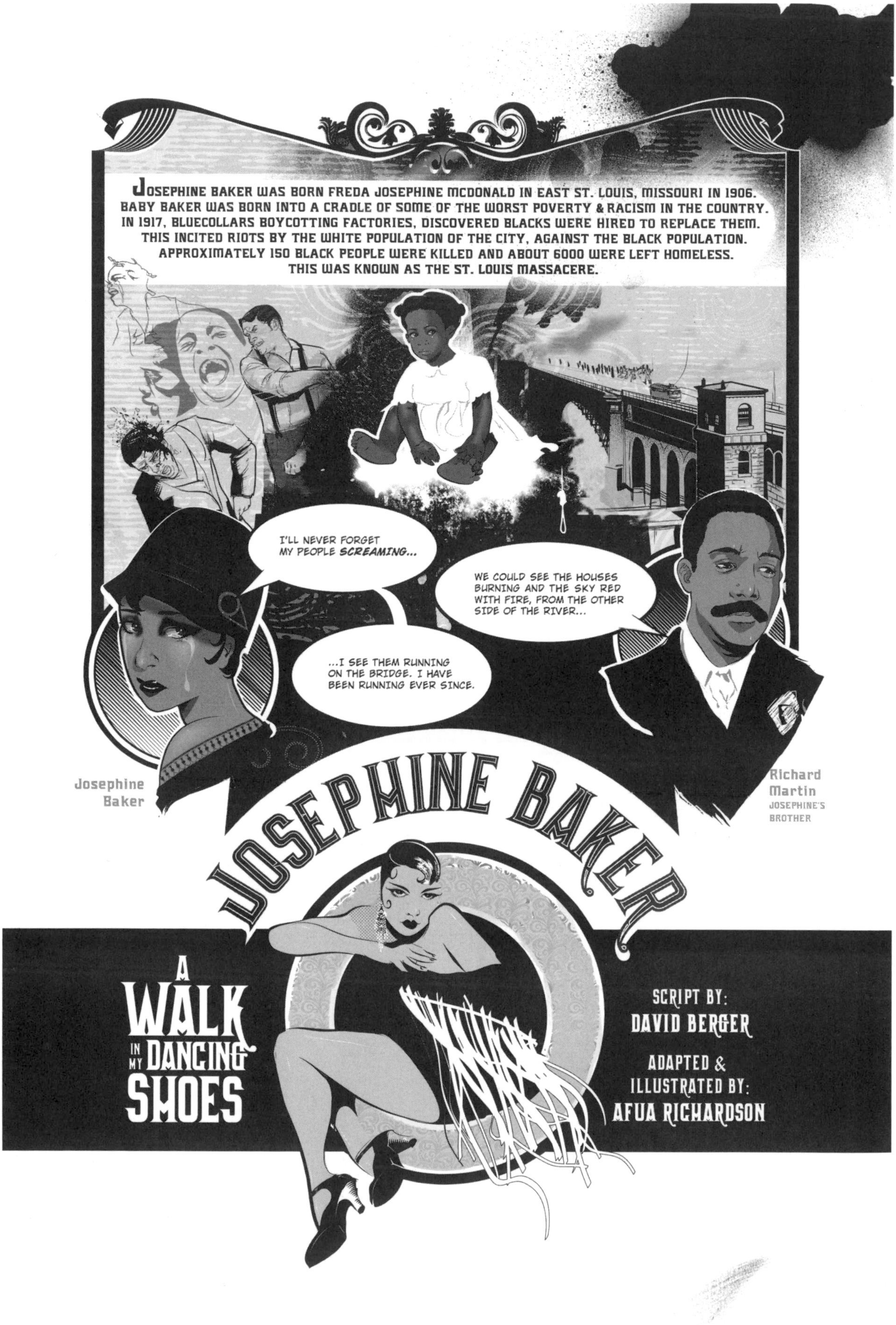

JOSEPHINE BAKER WAS BORN FREDA JOSEPHINE MCDONALD IN EAST ST. LOUIS, MISSOURI IN 1906. BABY BAKER WAS BORN INTO A CRADLE OF SOME OF THE WORST POVERTY & RACISM IN THE COUNTRY. IN 1917, BLUECOLLARS BOYCOTTING FACTORIES, DISCOVERED BLACKS WERE HIRED TO REPLACE THEM. THIS INCITED RIOTS BY THE WHITE POPULATION OF THE CITY, AGAINST THE BLACK POPULATION. APPROXIMATELY 150 BLACK PEOPLE WERE KILLED AND ABOUT 6000 WERE LEFT HOMELESS. THIS WAS KNOWN AS THE ST. LOUIS MASSACERE.
I'LL NEVER FORGET MY PEOPLE SCREAMING...
...I SEE THEM RUNNING ON THE BRIDGE. I HAVE BEEN RUNNING EVER SINCE.
WE COULD SEE THE HOUSES BURNING AND THE SKY RED WITH FIRE, FROM THE OTHER SIDE OF THE RIVER...
Josephine Baker
Richard Martin JOSEPHINE'S BROTHER
JOSEPHINE BAKER
A WALK IN MY DANCING SHOES
SCRIPT BY: DAVID BERGER
ADAPTED & ILLUSTRATED BY: AFUA RICHARDSON

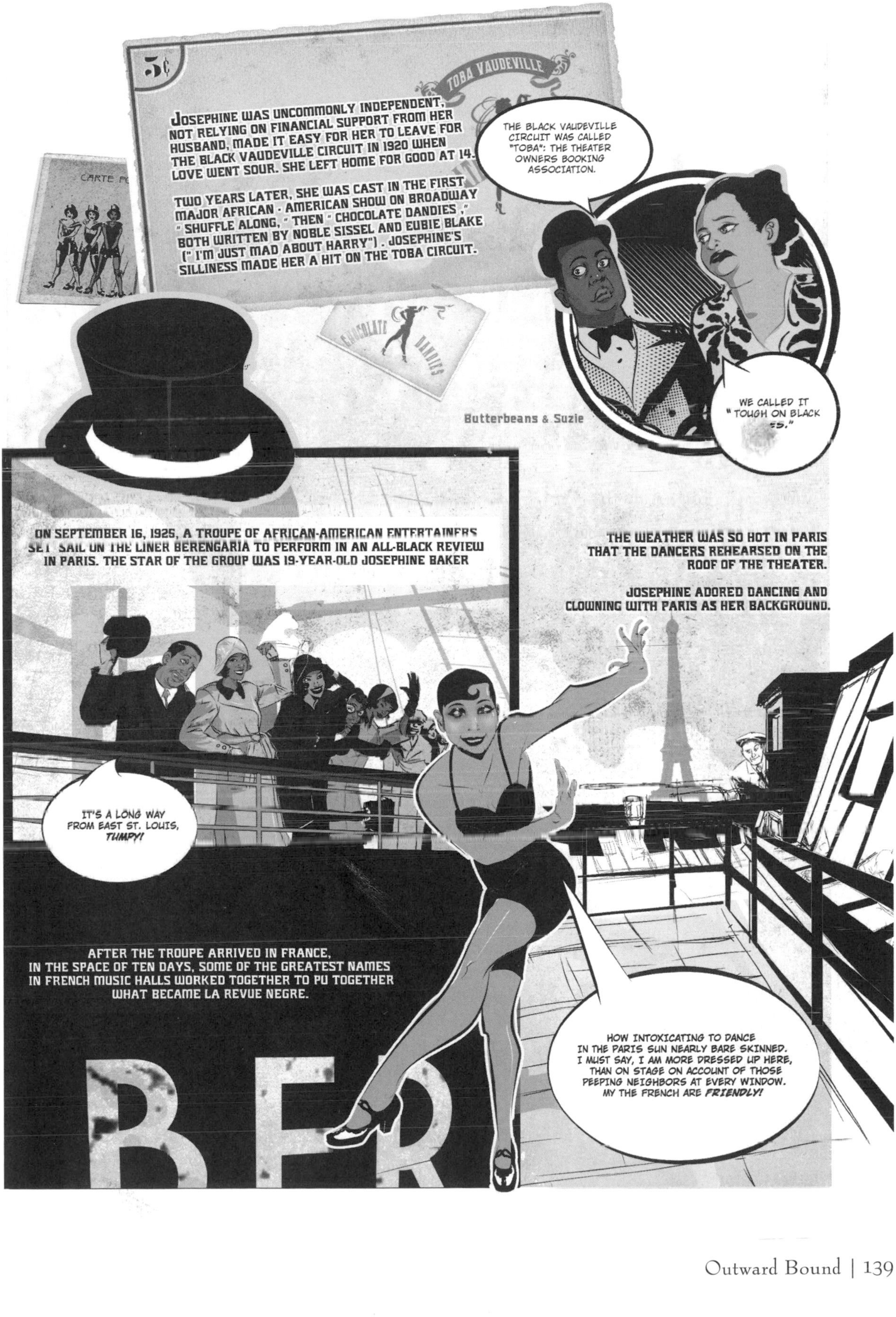
5¢
TOBA VAUDEVILLE
JOSEPHINE WAS UNCOMMONLY INDEPENDENT, NOT RELYING ON FINANCIAL SUPPORT FROM HER HUSBAND, MADE IT EASY FOR HER TO LEAVE FOR THE BLACK VAUDEVILLE CIRCUIT IN 1920 WHEN LOVE WENT SOUR. SHE LEFT HOME FOR GOOD AT 14.
TWO YEARS LATER, SHE WAS CAST IN THE FIRST MAJOR AFRICAN - AMERICAN SHOW ON BROADWAY " SHUFFLE ALONG, " THEN " CHOCOLATE DANDIES ," BOTH WRITTEN BY NOBLE SISSEL AND EUBIE BLAKE (" I'M JUST MAD ABOUT HARRY") . JOSEPHINE'S SILLINESS MADE HER A HIT ON THE TOBA CIRCUIT.
CARTE PO
CHOCOLATE DANDIES
THE BLACK VAUDEVILLE CIRCUIT WAS CALLED "TOBA": THE THEATER OWNERS BOOKING ASSOCIATION.
WE CALLED IT " TOUGH ON BLACK
Butterbeans & Suzie
ON SEPTEMBER 16, 1925, A TROUPE OF AFRICAN-AMERICAN ENTERTAINERS SET SAIL ON THE LINER BERENGARIA TO PERFORM IN AN ALL-BLACK REVIEW IN PARIS. THE STAR OF THE GROUP WAS 19-YEAR-OLD JOSEPHINE BAKER
IT'S A LONG WAY FROM EAST ST. LOUIS, TUMPY!
AFTER THE TROUPE ARRIVED IN FRANCE, IN THE SPACE OF TEN DAYS, SOME OF THE GREATEST NAMES IN FRENCH MUSIC HALLS WORKED TOGETHER TO PU TOGETHER WHAT BECAME LA REVUE NEGRE.
BER
THE WEATHER WAS SO HOT IN PARIS THAT THE DANCERS REHEARSED ON THE ROOF OF THE THEATER.
JOSEPHINE ADORED DANCING AND CLOWNING WITH PARIS AS HER BACKGROUND.
HOW INTOXICATING TO DANCE IN THE PARIS SUN NEARLY BARE SKINNED. I MUST SAY, I AM MORE DRESSED UP HERE, THAN ON STAGE ON ACCOUNT OF THOSE PEEPING NEIGHBORS AT EVERY WINDOW. MY THE FRENCH ARE FRIENDLY!

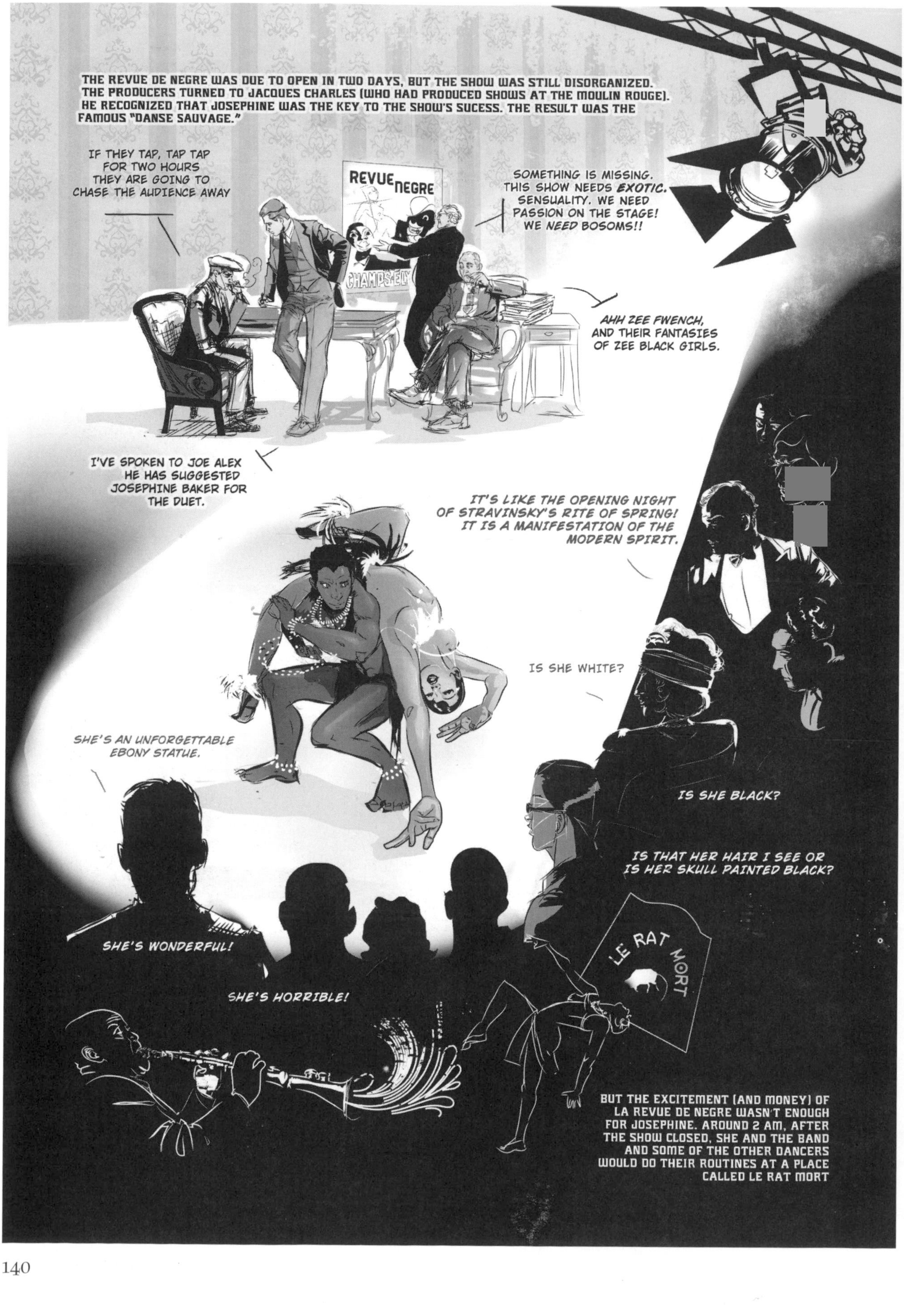
THE REVUE DE NEGRE WAS DUE TO OPEN IN TWO DAYS, BUT THE SHOW WAS STILL DISORGANIZED. THE PRODUCERS TURNED TO JACQUES CHARLES (WHO HAD PRODUCED SHOWS AT THE MOULIN ROUGE). HE RECOGNIZED THAT JOSEPHINE WAS THE KEY TO THE SHOW'S SUCESS. THE RESULT WAS THE FAMOUS "DANSE SAUVAGE."
IF THEY TAP, TAP TAP FOR TWO HOURS THEY ARE GOING TO CHASE THE AUDIENCE AWAY
REVUE NEGRE
CHAMPS-ELY
SOMETHING IS MISSING. THIS SHOW NEEDS EXOTIC. SENSUALITY. WE NEED PASSION ON THE STAGE! WE NEED BOSOMS!!
AHH ZEE FWENCH, AND THEIR FANTASIES OF ZEE BLACK GIRLS.
I'VE SPOKEN TO JOE ALEX HE HAS SUGGESTED JOSEPHINE BAKER FOR THE DUET.
IT'S LIKE THE OPENING NIGHT OF STRAVINSKY'S RITE OF SPRING! IT IS A MANIFESTATION OF THE MODERN SPIRIT.
IS SHE WHITE?
SHE'S AN UNFORGETTABLE EBONY STATUE.
IS SHE BLACK?
IS THAT HER HAIR I SEE OR IS HER SKULL PAINTED BLACK?
SHE'S WONDERFUL!
SHE'S HORRIBLE!
LE RAT MORT
BUT THE EXCITEMENT (AND MONEY) OF LA REVUE DE NEGRE WASN'T ENOUGH FOR JOSEPHINE. AROUND 2 AM, AFTER THE SHOW CLOSED, SHE AND THE BAND AND SOME OF THE OTHER DANCERS WOULD DO THEIR ROUTINES AT A PLACE CALLED LE RAT MORT

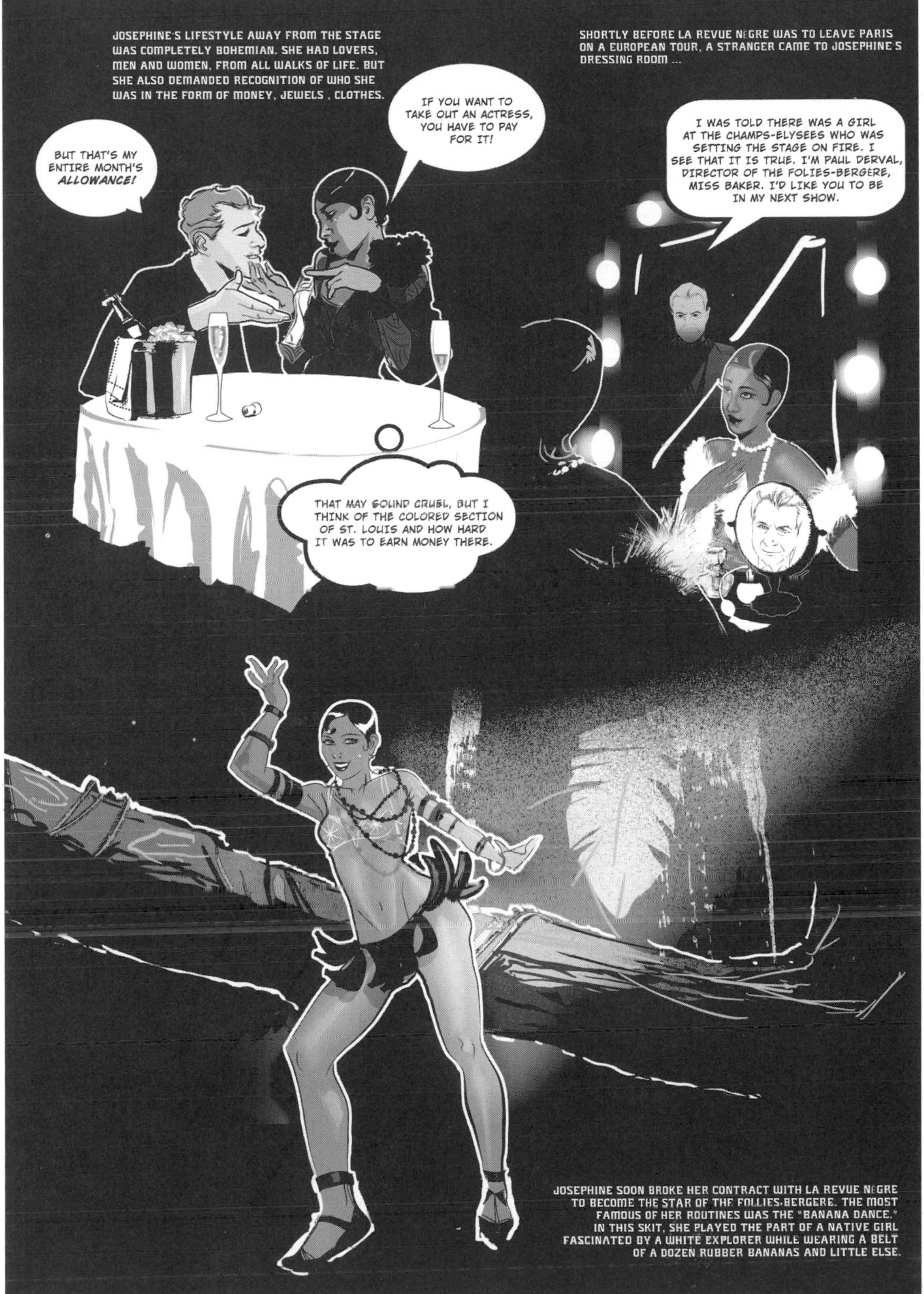
JOSEPHINE'S LIFESTYLE AWAY FROM THE STAGE WAS COMPLETELY BOHEMIAN. SHE HAD LOVERS, MEN AND WOMEN, FROM ALL WALKS OF LIFE. BUT SHE ALSO DEMANDED RECOGNITION OF WHO SHE WAS IN THE FORM OF MONEY, JEWELS , CLOTHES.
IF YOU WANT TO TAKE OUT AN ACTRESS, YOU HAVE TO PAY FOR IT!
BUT THAT'S MY ENTIRE MONTH'S ALLOWANCE!
THAT MAY SOUND CRUEL, BUT I THINK OF THE COLORED SECTION OF ST. LOUIS AND HOW HARD IT WAS TO EARN MONEY THERE.
SHORTLY BEFORE LA REVUE NEGRE WAS TO LEAVE PARIS ON A EUROPEAN TOUR, A STRANGER CAME TO JOSEPHINE'S DRESSING ROOM ...
I WAS TOLD THERE WAS A GIRL AT THE CHAMPS-ELYSEES WHO WAS SETTING THE STAGE ON FIRE. I SEE THAT IT IS TRUE. I'M PAUL DERVAL, DIRECTOR OF THE FOLIES-BERGERE, MISS BAKER. I'D LIKE YOU TO BE IN MY NEXT SHOW.
JOSEPHINE SOON BROKE HER CONTRACT WITH LA REVUE NEGRE TO BECOME THE STAR OF THE FOLLIES-BERGERE. THE MOST FAMOUS OF HER ROUTINES WAS THE "BANANA DANCE." IN THIS SKIT, SHE PLAYED THE PART OF A NATIVE GIRL FASCINATED BY A WHITE EXPLORER WHILE WEARING A BELT OF A DOZEN RUBBER BANANAS AND LITTLE ELSE.

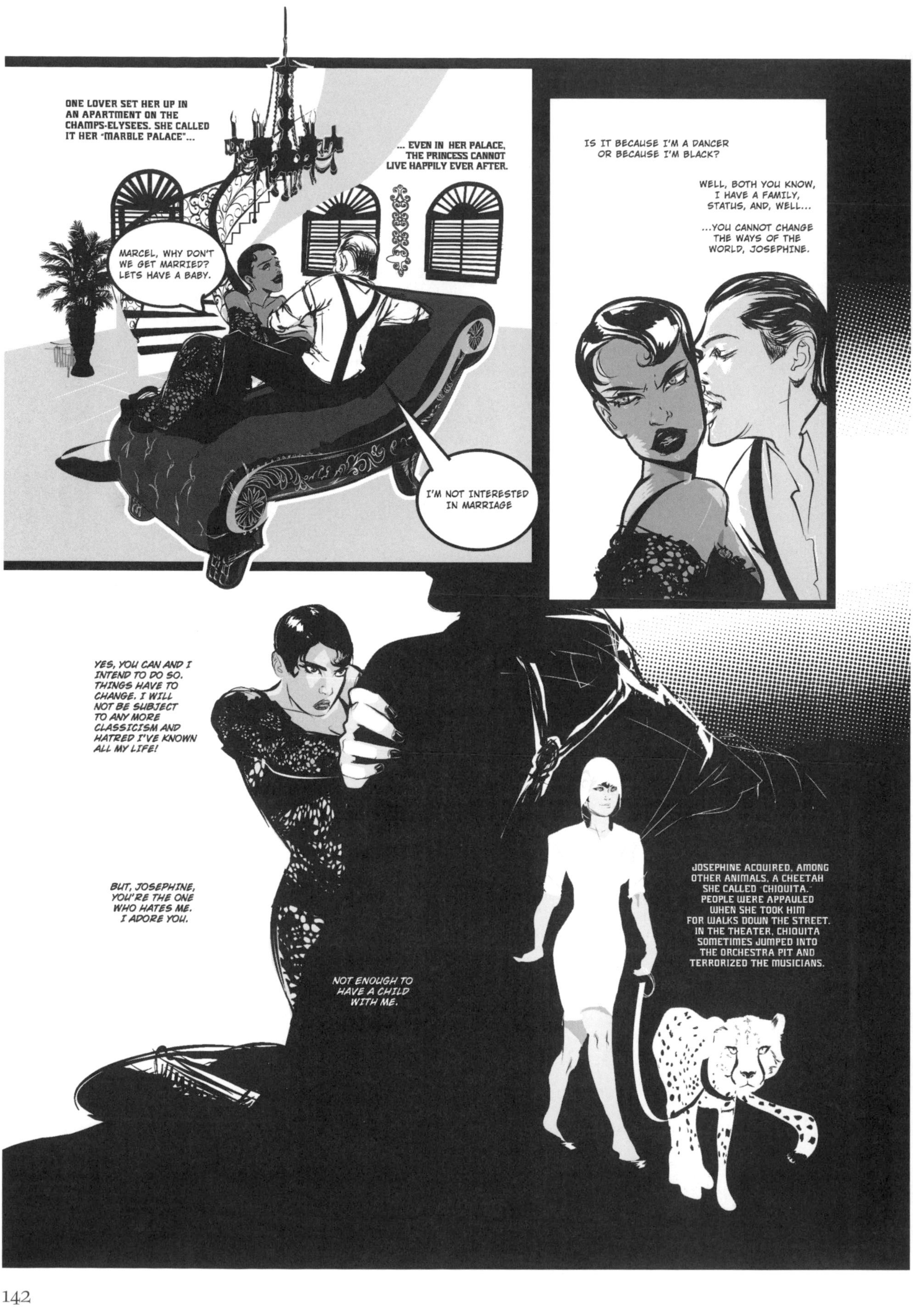
ONE LOVER SET HER UP IN AN APARTMENT ON THE CHAMPS-ELYSEES. SHE CALLED IT HER "MARBLE PALACE"...
... EVEN IN HER PALACE, THE PRINCESS CANNOT LIVE HAPPILY EVER AFTER.
MARCEL, WHY DON'T WE GET MARRIED? LETS HAVE A BABY.
I'M NOT INTERESTED IN MARRIAGE
IS IT BECAUSE I'M A DANCER OR BECAUSE I'M BLACK?
WELL, BOTH YOU KNOW, I HAVE A FAMILY, STATUS, AND, WELL...
...YOU CANNOT CHANGE THE WAYS OF THE WORLD, JOSEPHINE.
YES, YOU CAN AND I INTEND TO DO SO. THINGS HAVE TO CHANGE. I WILL NOT BE SUBJECT TO ANY MORE CLASSICISM AND HATRED I'VE KNOWN ALL MY LIFE!
BUT, JOSEPHINE, YOU'RE THE ONE WHO HATES ME. I ADORE YOU.
NOT ENOUGH TO HAVE A CHILD WITH ME.
JOSEPHINE ACQUIRED, AMONG OTHER ANIMALS, A CHEETAH SHE CALLED "CHIQUITA." PEOPLE WERE APPAULED WHEN SHE TOOK HIM FOR WALKS DOWN THE STREET. IN THE THEATER, CHIQUITA SOMETIMES JUMPED INTO THE ORCHESTRA PIT AND TERRORIZED THE MUSICIANS.

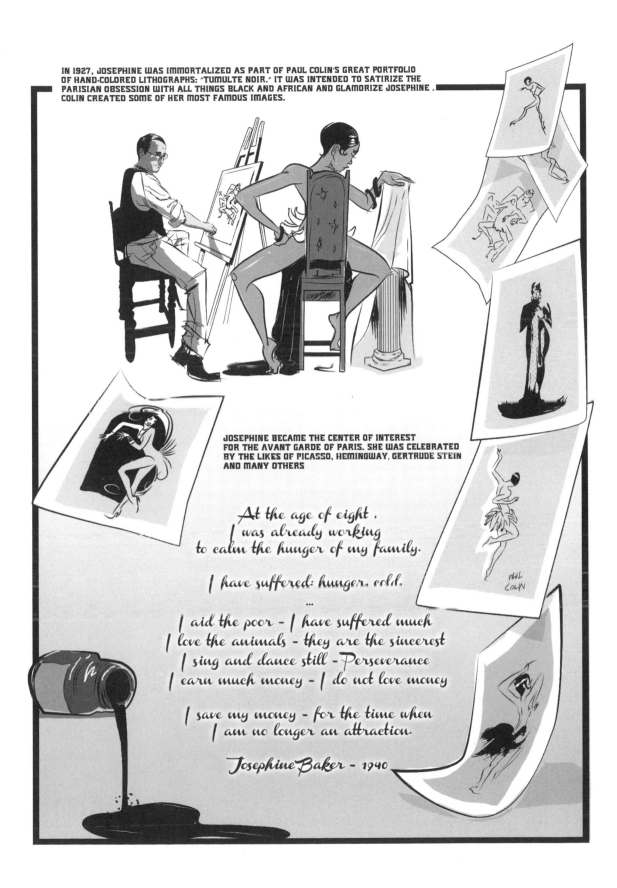

IN 1927, JOSEPHINE WAS IMMORTALIZED AS PART OF PAUL COLIN'S GREAT PORTFOLIO OF HAND-COLORED LITHOGRAPHS: "TUMULTE NOIR." IT WAS INTENDED TO SATIRIZE THE PARISIAN OBSESSION WITH ALL THINGS BLACK AND AFRICAN AND GLAMORIZE JOSEPHINE. COLIN CREATED SOME OF HER MOST FAMOUS IMAGES.

JOSEPHINE BECAME THE CENTER OF INTEREST FOR THE AVANT GARDE OF PARIS. SHE WAS CELEBRATED BY THE LIKES OF PICASSO, HEMINGWAY, GERTRUDE STEIN AND MANY OTHERS

At the age of eight,
I was already working
to calm the hunger of my family.

I have suffered: hunger, cold.
...

I aid the poor - I have suffered much
I love the animals - they are the sincerest
I sing and dance still - Perseverance
I earn much money - I do not love money

I save my money - for the time when
I am no longer an attraction.

Josephine Baker - 1940

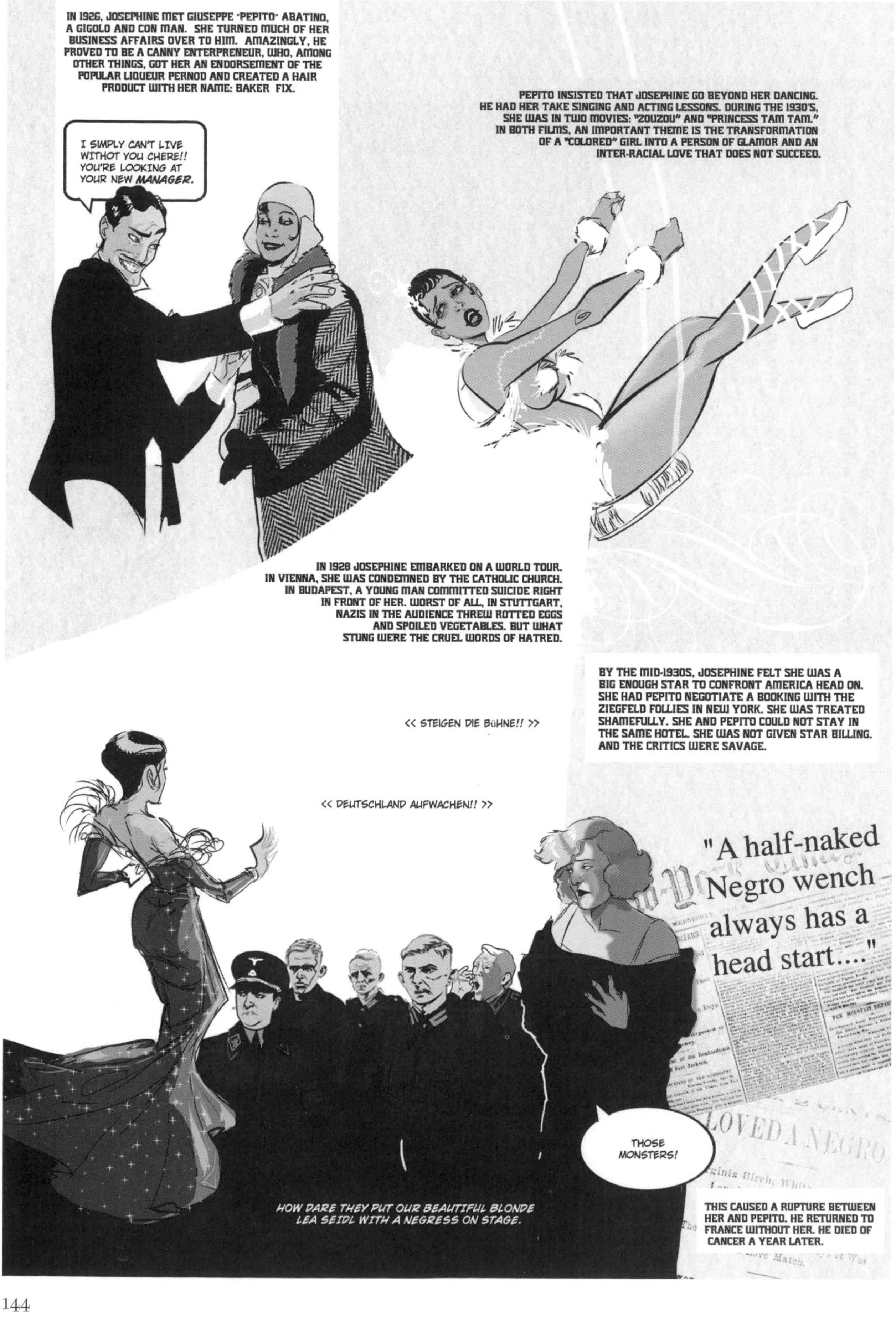
IN 1926, JOSEPHINE MET GIUSEPPE "PEPITO" ABATINO, A GIGOLO AND CON MAN. SHE TURNED MUCH OF HER BUSINESS AFFAIRS OVER TO HIM. AMAZINGLY, HE PROVED TO BE A CANNY ENTERPRENEUR, WHO, AMONG OTHER THINGS, GOT HER AN ENDORSEMENT OF THE POPULAR LIQUEUR PERNOD AND CREATED A HAIR PRODUCT WITH HER NAME: BAKER FIX.
I SIMPLY CAN'T LIVE WITHOT YOU CHERE!! YOU'RE LOOKING AT YOUR NEW MANAGER.
PEPITO INSISTED THAT JOSEPHINE GO BEYOND HER DANCING. HE HAD HER TAKE SINGING AND ACTING LESSONS. DURING THE 1930'S, SHE WAS IN TWO MOVIES: "ZOUZOU" AND "PRINCESS TAM TAM." IN BOTH FILMS, AN IMPORTANT THEME IS THE TRANSFORMATION OF A "COLORED" GIRL INTO A PERSON OF GLAMOR AND AN INTER-RACIAL LOVE THAT DOES NOT SUCCEED.
IN 1928 JOSEPHINE EMBARKED ON A WORLD TOUR. IN VIENNA, SHE WAS CONDEMNED BY THE CATHOLIC CHURCH. IN BUDAPEST, A YOUNG MAN COMMITTED SUICIDE RIGHT IN FRONT OF HER. WORST OF ALL, IN STUTTGART, NAZIS IN THE AUDIENCE THREW ROTTED EGGS AND SPOILED VEGETABLES. BUT WHAT STUNG WERE THE CRUEL WORDS OF HATRED.
<< STEIGEN DIE BüHNE!! >>
<< DEUTSCHLAND AUFWACHEN!! >>
HOW DARE THEY PUT OUR BEAUTIFUL BLONDE LEA SEIDL WITH A NEGRESS ON STAGE.
BY THE MID-1930S, JOSEPHINE FELT SHE WAS A BIG ENOUGH STAR TO CONFRONT AMERICA HEAD ON. SHE HAD PEPITO NEGOTIATE A BOOKING WITH THE ZIEGFELD FOLLIES IN NEW YORK. SHE WAS TREATED SHAMEFULLY. SHE AND PEPITO COULD NOT STAY IN THE SAME HOTEL. SHE WAS NOT GIVEN STAR BILLING. AND THE CRITICS WERE SAVAGE.
"A half-naked Negro wench always has a head start...."
LOVED A NEGRO
THOSE MONSTERS!
THIS CAUSED A RUPTURE BETWEEN HER AND PEPITO. HE RETURNED TO FRANCE WITHOUT HER. HE DIED OF CANCER A YEAR LATER.

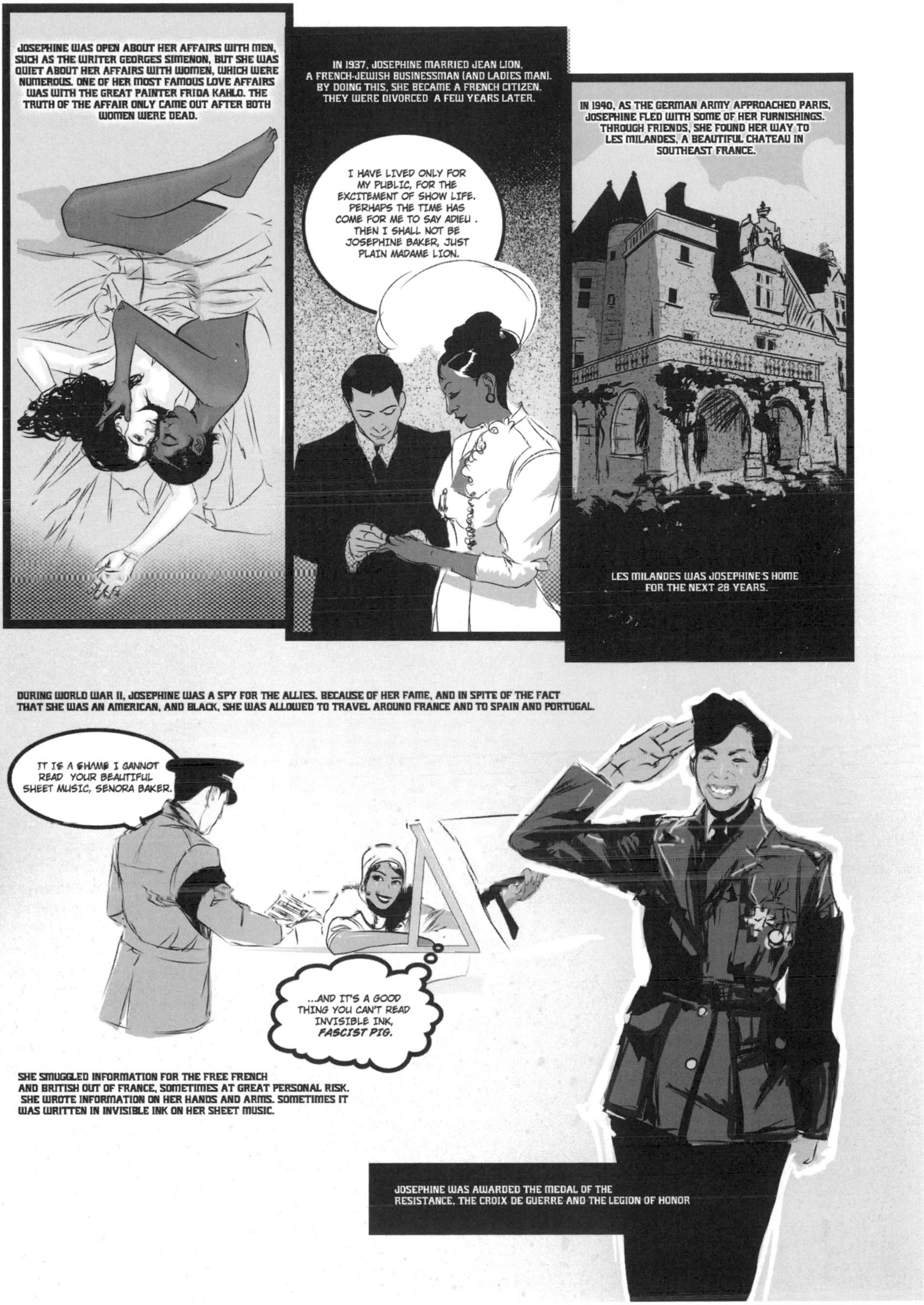
JOSEPHINE WAS OPEN ABOUT HER AFFAIRS WITH MEN, SUCH AS THE WRITER GEORGES SIMENON, BUT SHE WAS QUIET ABOUT HER AFFAIRS WITH WOMEN, WHICH WERE NUMEROUS. ONE OF HER MOST FAMOUS LOVE AFFAIRS WAS WITH THE GREAT PAINTER FRIDA KAHLO. THE TRUTH OF THE AFFAIR ONLY CAME OUT AFTER BOTH WOMEN WERE DEAD.
IN 1937, JOSEPHINE MARRIED JEAN LION, A FRENCH-JEWISH BUSINESSMAN (AND LADIES MAN). BY DOING THIS, SHE BECAME A FRENCH CITIZEN. THEY WERE DIVORCED A FEW YEARS LATER.
I HAVE LIVED ONLY FOR MY PUBLIC, FOR THE EXCITEMENT OF SHOW LIFE. PERHAPS THE TIME HAS COME FOR ME TO SAY ADIEU . THEN I SHALL NOT BE JOSEPHINE BAKER, JUST PLAIN MADAME LION.
IN 1940, AS THE GERMAN ARMY APPROACHED PARIS, JOSEPHINE FLED WITH SOME OF HER FURNISHINGS. THROUGH FRIENDS, SHE FOUND HER WAY TO LES MILANDES, A BEAUTIFUL CHATEAU IN SOUTHEAST FRANCE.
LES MILANDES WAS JOSEPHINE'S HOME FOR THE NEXT 28 YEARS.
DURING WORLD WAR II, JOSEPHINE WAS A SPY FOR THE ALLIES. BECAUSE OF HER FAME, AND IN SPITE OF THE FACT THAT SHE WAS AN AMERICAN, AND BLACK, SHE WAS ALLOWED TO TRAVEL AROUND FRANCE AND TO SPAIN AND PORTUGAL.
IT IS A SHAME I CANNOT READ YOUR BEAUTIFUL SHEET MUSIC, SENORA BAKER.
...AND IT'S A GOOD THING YOU CAN'T READ INVISIBLE INK, FASCIST PIG.
SHE SMUGGLED INFORMATION FOR THE FREE FRENCH AND BRITISH OUT OF FRANCE, SOMETIMES AT GREAT PERSONAL RISK. SHE WROTE INFORMATION ON HER HANDS AND ARMS. SOMETIMES IT WAS WRITTEN IN INVISIBLE INK ON HER SHEET MUSIC.
JOSEPHINE WAS AWARDED THE MEDAL OF THE RESISTANCE, THE CROIX DE GUERRE AND THE LEGION OF HONOR

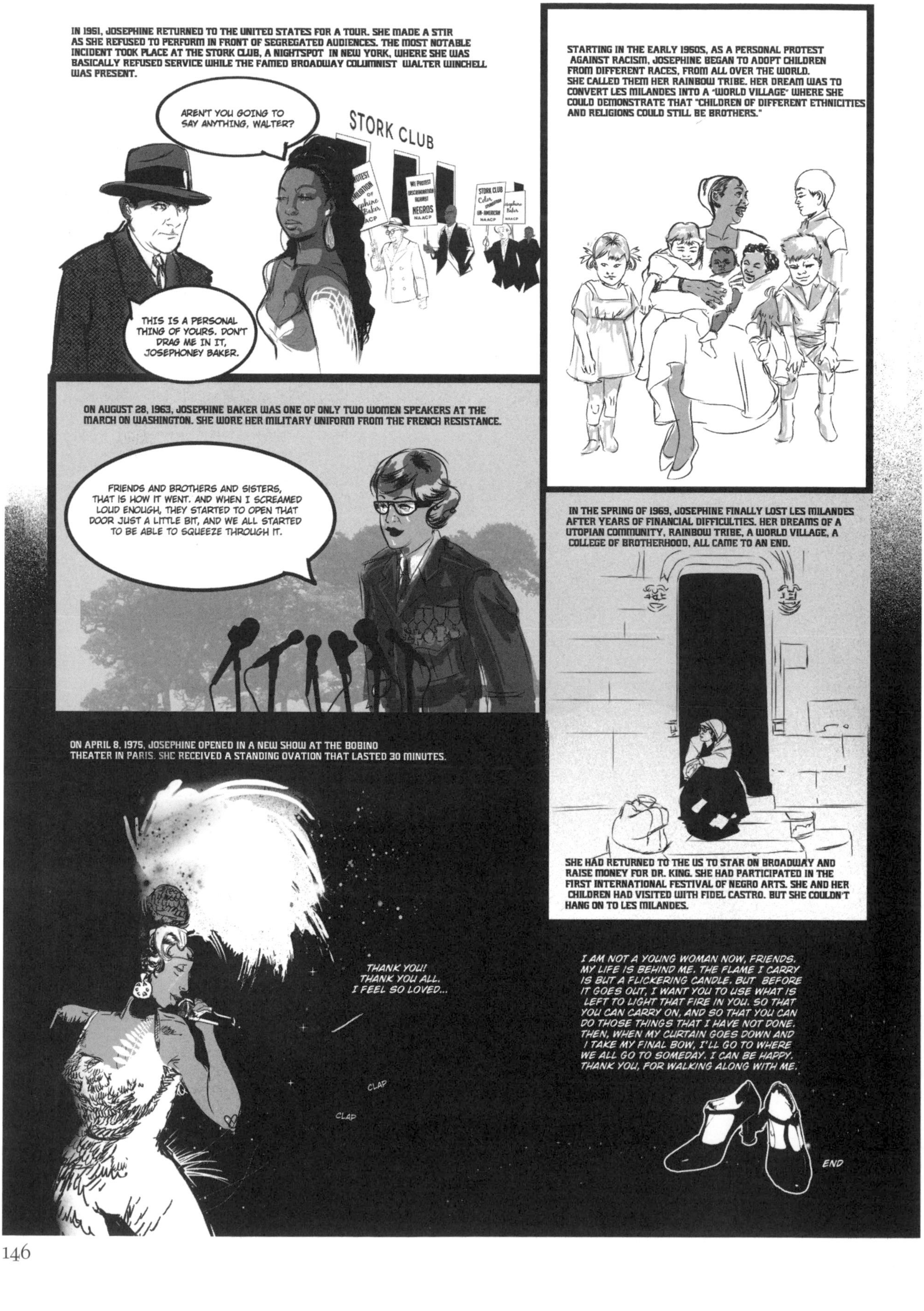
IN 1951, JOSEPHINE RETURNED TO THE UNITED STATES FOR A TOUR. SHE MADE A STIR AS SHE REFUSED TO PERFORM IN FRONT OF SEGREGATED AUDIENCES. THE MOST NOTABLE INCIDENT TOOK PLACE AT THE STORK CLUB, A NIGHTSPOT IN NEW YORK, WHERE SHE WAS BASICALLY REFUSED SERVICE WHILE THE FAMED BROADWAY COLUMNIST WALTER WINCHELL WAS PRESENT.
AREN'T YOU GOING TO SAY ANYTHING, WALTER?
STORK CLUB
THIS IS A PERSONAL THING OF YOURS. DON'T DRAG ME IN IT, JOSEPHONEY BAKER.
STARTING IN THE EARLY 1960S, AS A PERSONAL PROTEST AGAINST RACISM, JOSEPHINE BEGAN TO ADOPT CHILDREN FROM DIFFERENT RACES, FROM ALL OVER THE WORLD. SHE CALLED THEM HER RAINBOW TRIBE. HER DREAM WAS TO CONVERT LES MILANDES INTO A "WORLD VILLAGE" WHERE SHE COULD DEMONSTRATE THAT "CHILDREN OF DIFFERENT ETHNICITIES AND RELIGIONS COULD STILL BE BROTHERS."
ON AUGUST 28, 1963, JOSEPHINE BAKER WAS ONE OF ONLY TWO WOMEN SPEAKERS AT THE MARCH ON WASHINGTON. SHE WORE HER MILITARY UNIFORM FROM THE FRENCH RESISTANCE.
FRIENDS AND BROTHERS AND SISTERS, THAT IS HOW IT WENT. AND WHEN I SCREAMED LOUD ENOUGH, THEY STARTED TO OPEN THAT DOOR JUST A LITTLE BIT, AND WE ALL STARTED TO BE ABLE TO SQUEEZE THROUGH IT.
IN THE SPRING OF 1969, JOSEPHINE FINALLY LOST LES MILANDES AFTER YEARS OF FINANCIAL DIFFICULTIES. HER DREAMS OF A UTOPIAN COMMUNITY, RAINBOW TRIBE, A WORLD VILLAGE, A COLLEGE OF BROTHERHOOD, ALL CAME TO AN END.
SHE HAD RETURNED TO THE US TO STAR ON BROADWAY AND RAISE MONEY FOR DR. KING. SHE HAD PARTICIPATED IN THE FIRST INTERNATIONAL FESTIVAL OF NEGRO ARTS. SHE AND HER CHILDREN HAD VISITED WITH FIDEL CASTRO. BUT SHE COULDN'T HANG ON TO LES MILANDES.
ON APRIL 8, 1975, JOSEPHINE OPENED IN A NEW SHOW AT THE BOBINO THEATER IN PARIS. SHE RECEIVED A STANDING OVATION THAT LASTED 30 MINUTES.
THANK YOU! THANK YOU ALL. I FEEL SO LOVED...
CLAP
CLAP
I AM NOT A YOUNG WOMAN NOW, FRIENDS. MY LIFE IS BEHIND ME. THE FLAME I CARRY IS BUT A FLICKERING CANDLE. BUT BEFORE IT GOES OUT, I WANT YOU TO USE WHAT IS LEFT TO LIGHT THAT FIRE IN YOU. SO THAT YOU CAN CARRY ON, AND SO THAT YOU CAN DO THOSE THINGS THAT I HAVE NOT DONE. THEN, WHEN MY CURTAIN GOES DOWN AND I TAKE MY FINAL BOW, I'LL GO TO WHERE WE ALL GO TO SOMEDAY. I CAN BE HAPPY. THANK YOU, FOR WALKING ALONG WITH ME.
END

Chapter Seven

Bringing Bohemia Home

The 1930s era of Franklin Roosevelt and the New Deal was also a moment of homecoming for wide radical impulses held in abeyance during the politically conservative, Aspirin Age 1920s. The rise of industrial unionism after a series of near-general strikes in several cities, the emergence of radical theater (and even a handful of left-written films on social themes), and a spirit of populist culture in dance, photography and mural painting, meant that serious artists had found audiences on their own turf, had learned to speak their language.

African-American culture was moving out of the shadows and out of Harlem into the public eye and the public dance floor, though black artists still faced daunting racist discrimination. This simple fact brought the shared culture forward by centuries in only a few years. Woody Guthrie, ostensibly outside this shift, found himself on platforms with Leadbelly and others, just as the 1930s faded into the war years. Meanwhile, the public, very much including the working-class public, was educating itself through its own exuberant expression, seeking to create, as a forgotten 1910s socialist and editor of *Modern Dance* magazine put it, an art in their own lives, on the dance floor.

The tragic side to this could not be much hidden. W.E.B. DuBois explained decades earlier that Black cultural expression had come out of pain more than pleasure, and the popular sensation that was Billie Holiday singing "Strange Fruit" epitomized the ongoing agonies. Katherine Dunham and Pearl Primus fought their way through the muck, and triumphed but ... at a cost.

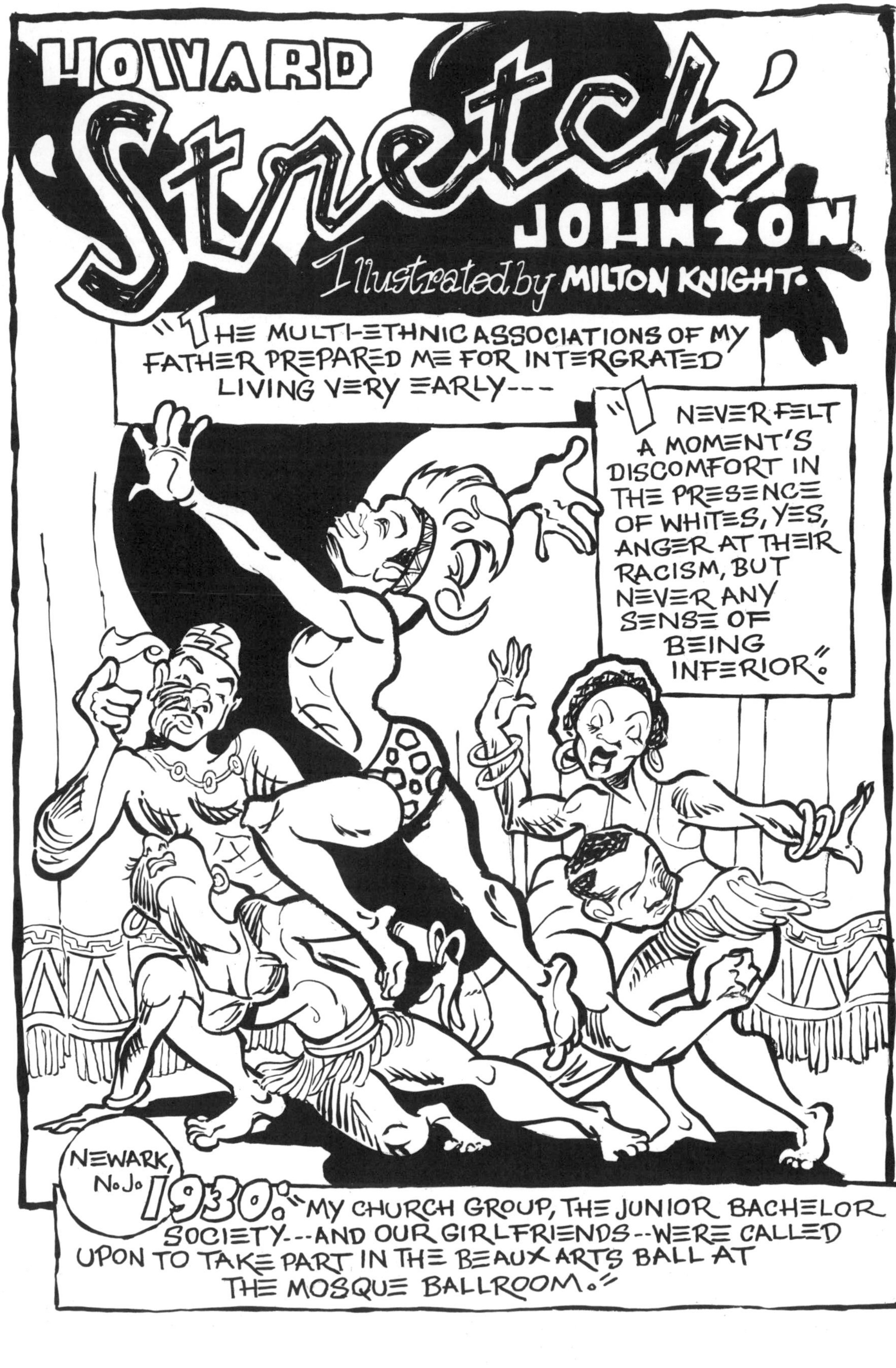
HOWARD 'Stretch' JOHNSON
Illustrated by MILTON KNIGHT.
"THE MULTI-ETHNIC ASSOCIATIONS OF MY FATHER PREPARED ME FOR INTERGRATED LIVING VERY EARLY---
"I NEVER FELT A MOMENT'S DISCOMFORT IN THE PRESENCE OF WHITES, YES, ANGER AT THEIR RACISM, BUT NEVER ANY SENSE OF BEING INFERIOR."
NEWARK, N.J. 1930. "MY CHURCH GROUP, THE JUNIOR BACHELOR SOCIETY---AND OUR GIRLFRIENDS--WERE CALLED UPON TO TAKE PART IN THE BEAUX ARTS BALL AT THE MOSQUE BALLROOM."

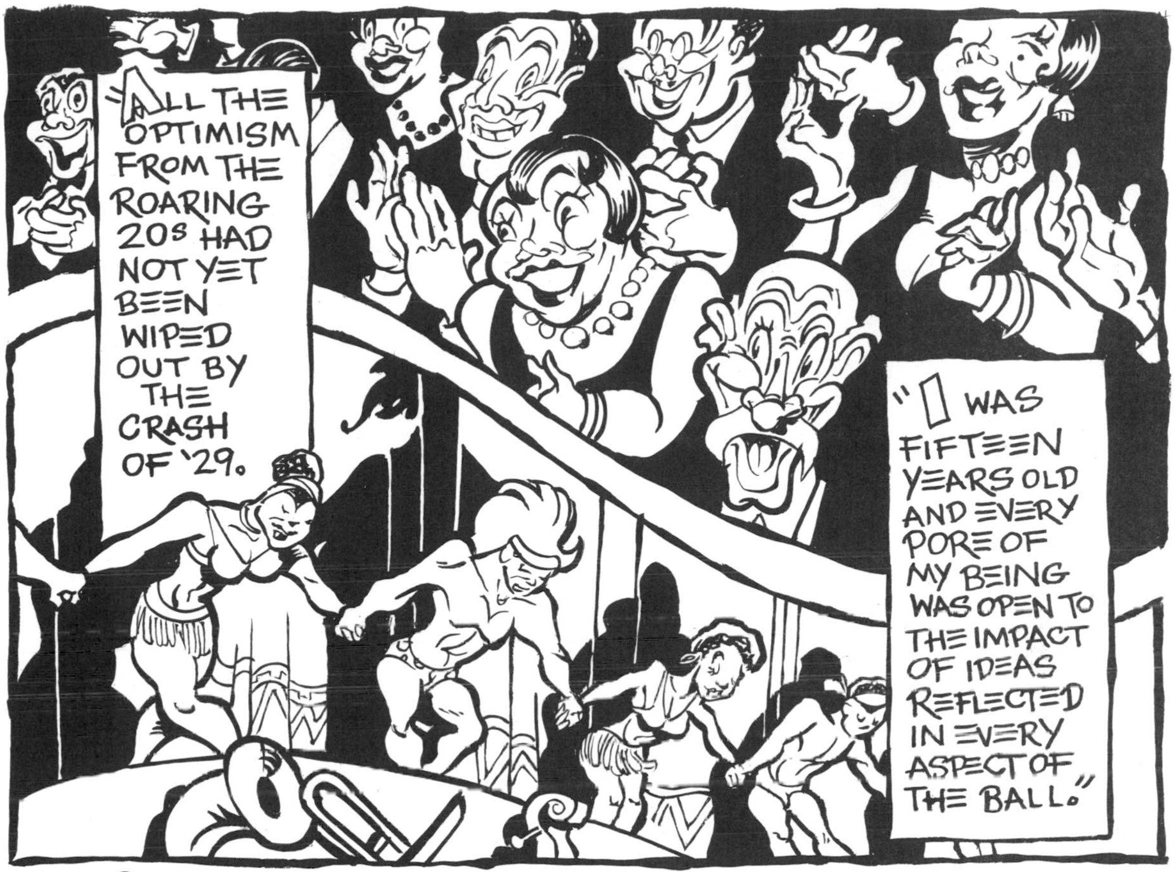
"ALL THE OPTIMISM FROM THE ROARING 20s HAD NOT YET BEEN WIPED OUT BY THE CRASH OF '29.
"I WAS FIFTEEN YEARS OLD AND EVERY PORE OF MY BEING WAS OPEN TO THE IMPACT OF IDEAS REFLECTED IN EVERY ASPECT OF THE BALL."

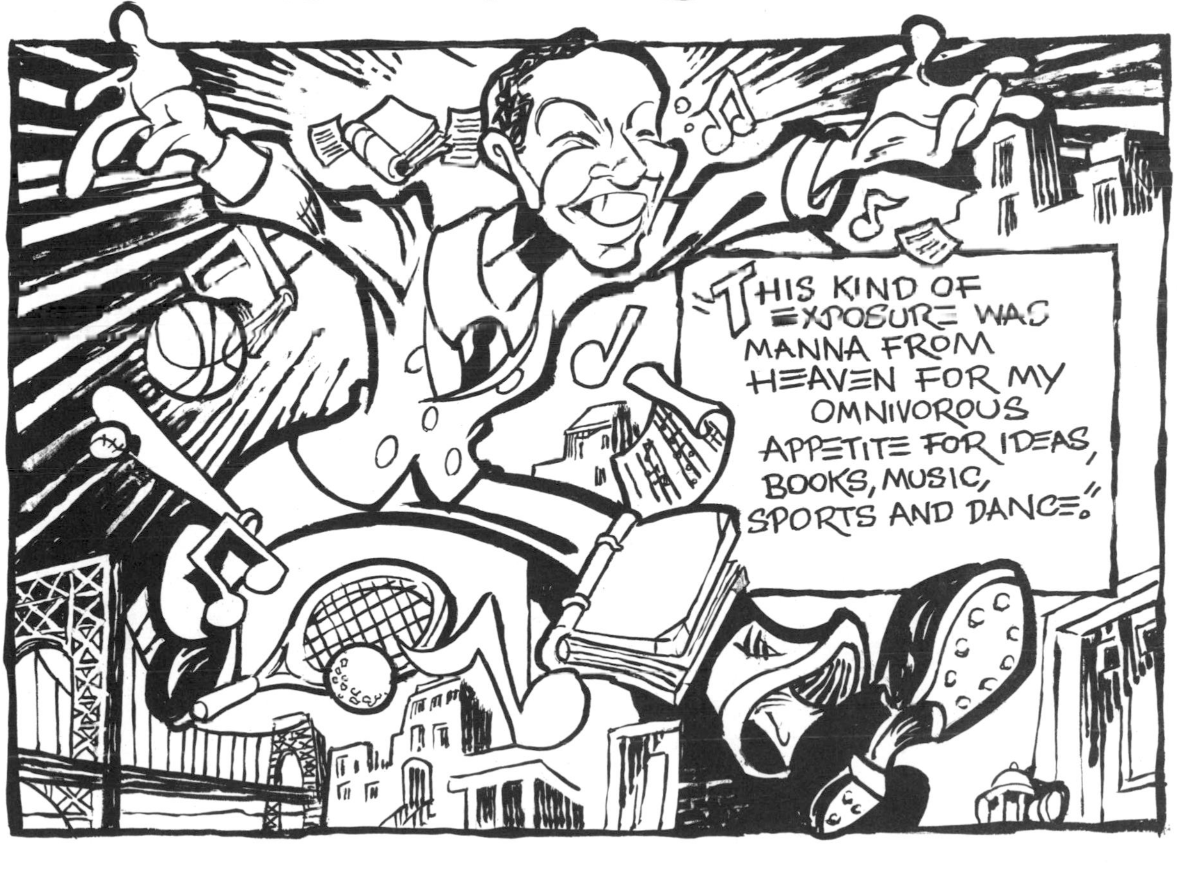
"THIS KIND OF EXPOSURE WAS MANNA FROM HEAVEN FOR MY OMNIVOROUS APPETITE FOR IDEAS, BOOKS, MUSIC, SPORTS AND DANCE."

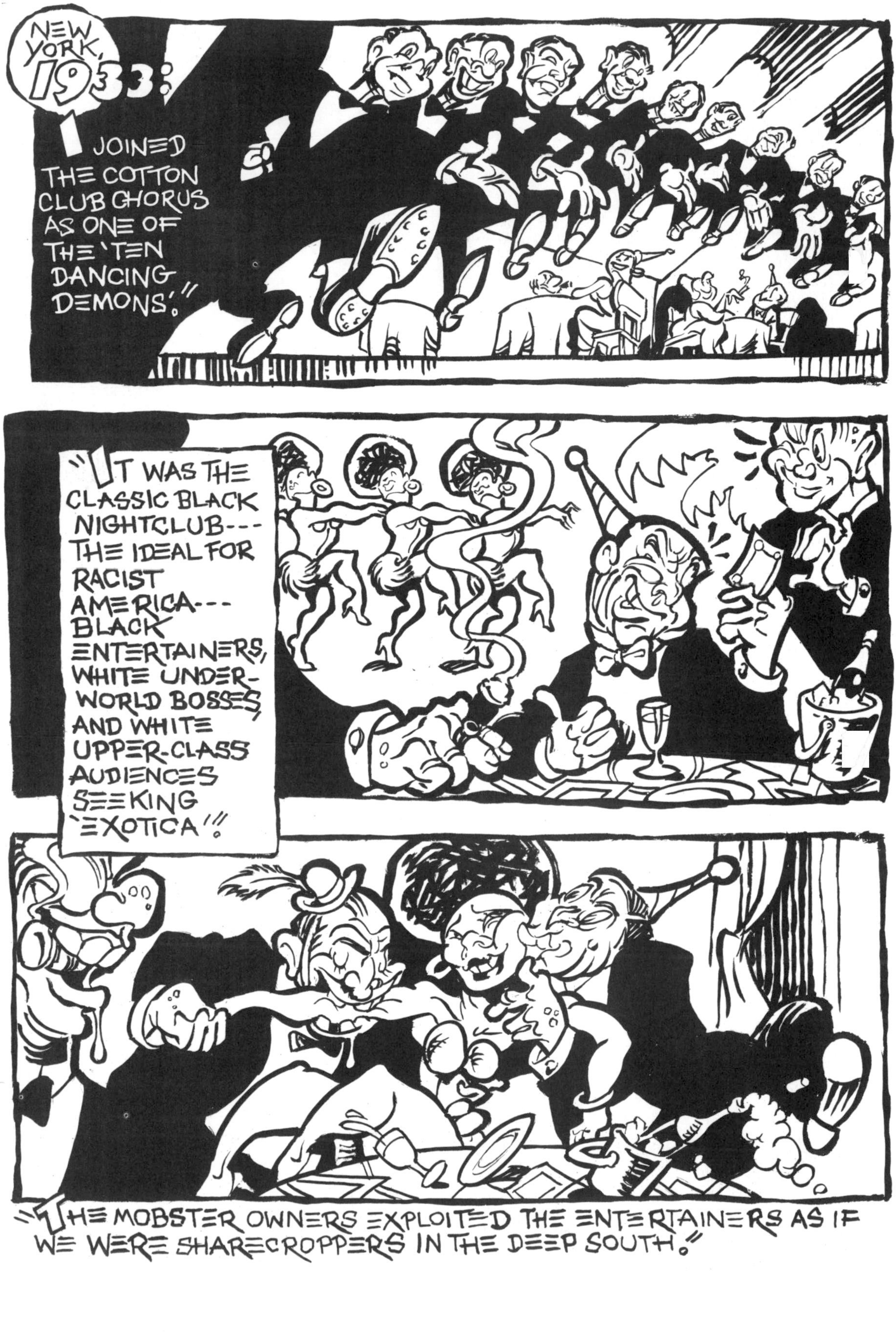
NEW YORK, 1933:
I JOINED THE COTTON CLUB CHORUS AS ONE OF THE 'TEN DANCING DEMONS'."
"IT WAS THE CLASSIC BLACK NIGHTCLUB--- THE IDEAL FOR RACIST AMERICA--- BLACK ENTERTAINERS, WHITE UNDER-WORLD BOSSES, AND WHITE UPPER-CLASS AUDIENCES SEEKING 'EXOTICA'!"
"THE MOBSTER OWNERS EXPLOITED THE ENTERTAINERS AS IF WE WERE SHARECROPPERS IN THE DEEP SOUTH."

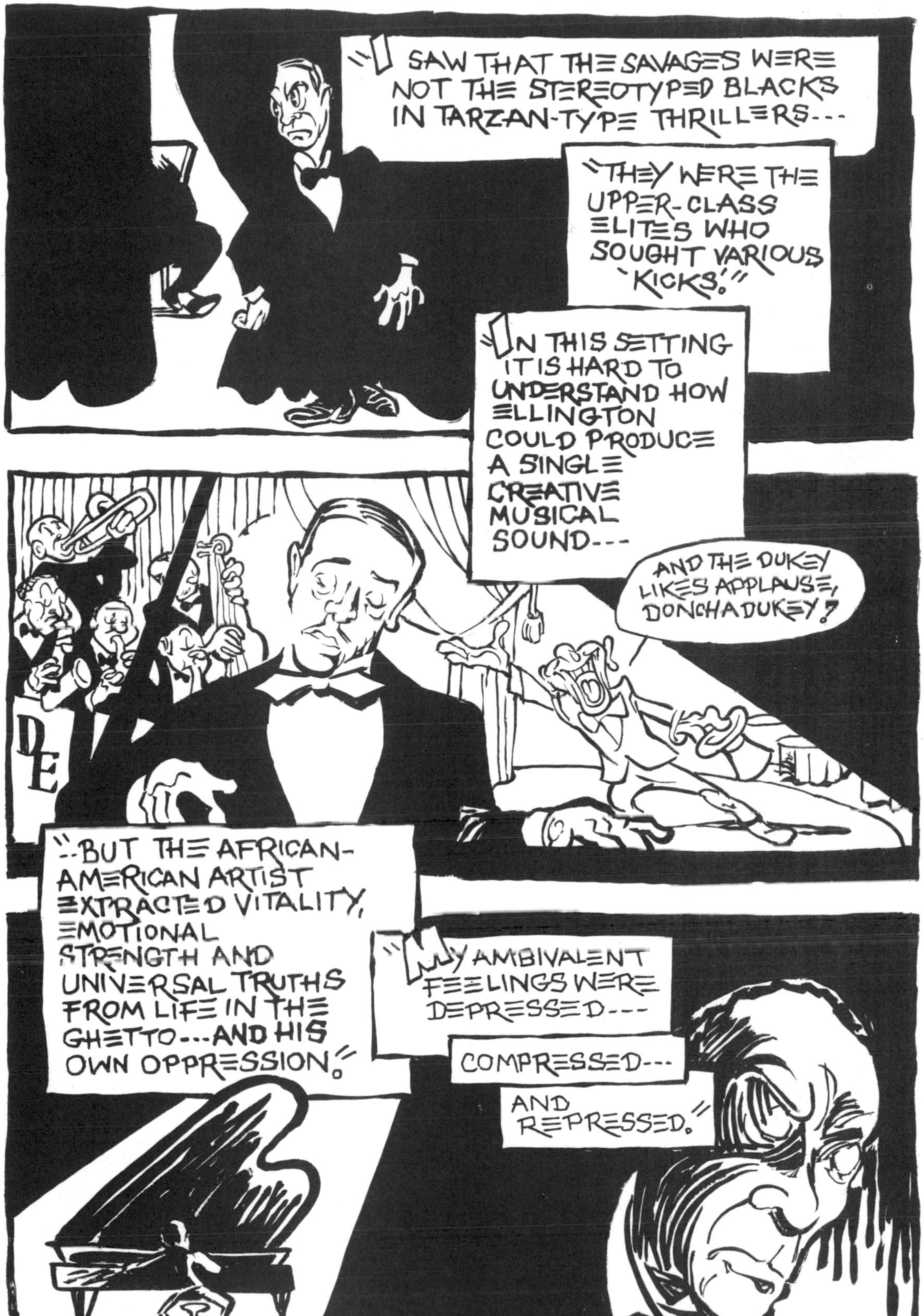
"I SAW THAT THE SAVAGES WERE NOT THE STEREOTYPED BLACKS IN TARZAN-TYPE THRILLERS---
"THEY WERE THE UPPER-CLASS ELITES WHO SOUGHT VARIOUS 'KICKS.'"
"IN THIS SETTING IT IS HARD TO UNDERSTAND HOW ELLINGTON COULD PRODUCE A SINGLE CREATIVE MUSICAL SOUND---
AND THE DUKEY LIKES APPLAUSE, DONCHADUKEY?
DE
"--BUT THE AFRICAN-AMERICAN ARTIST EXTRACTED VITALITY, EMOTIONAL STRENGTH AND UNIVERSAL TRUTHS FROM LIFE IN THE GHETTO---AND HIS OWN OPPRESSION."
"MY AMBIVALENT FEELINGS WERE DEPRESSED---
COMPRESSED---
AND REPRESSED."

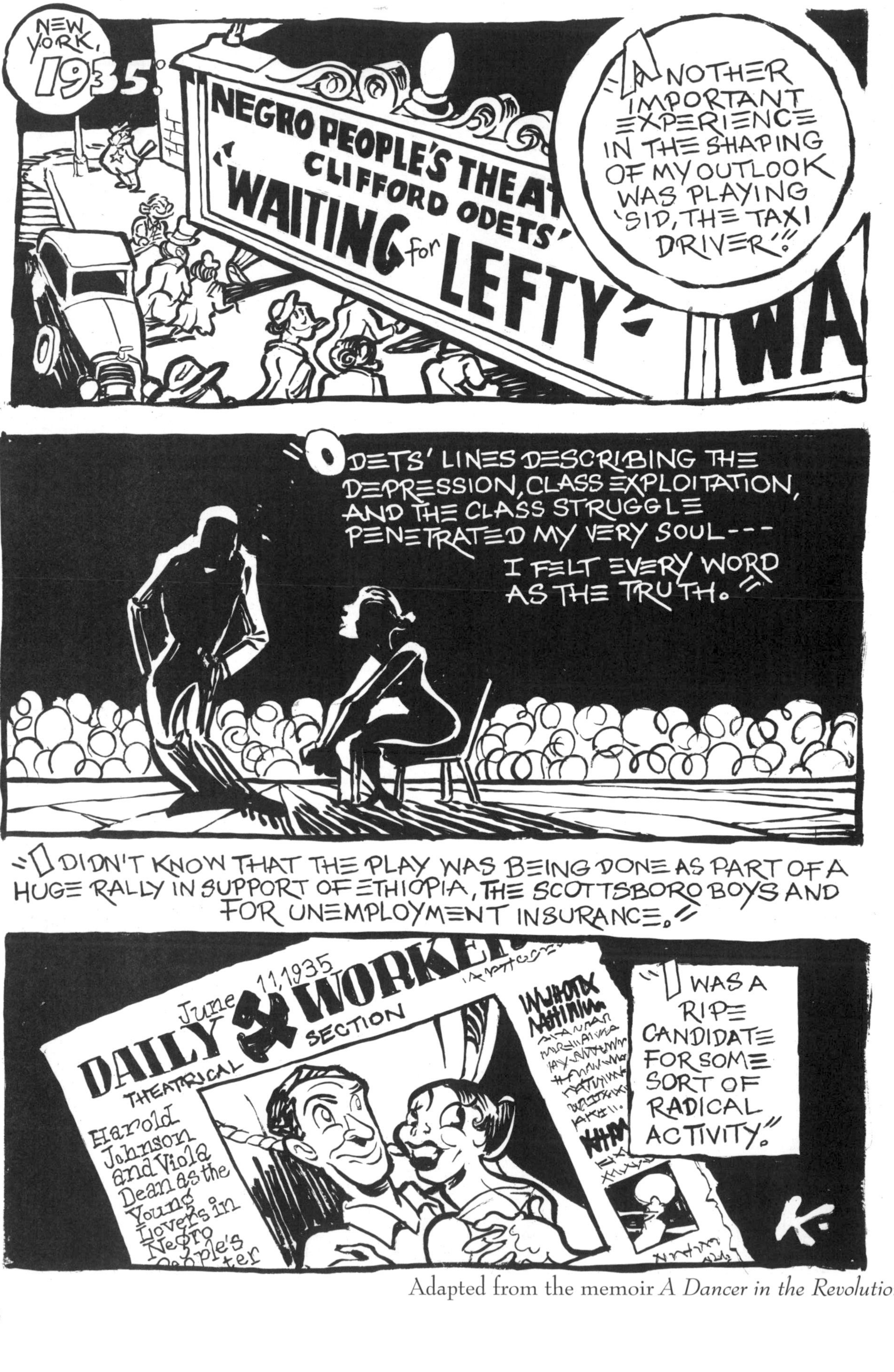
NEW YORK, 1935.
NEGRO PEOPLE'S THEAT
CLIFFORD ODETS'
"WAITING for LEFTY"
WA
"ANOTHER IMPORTANT EXPERIENCE IN THE SHAPING OF MY OUTLOOK WAS PLAYING 'SID, THE TAXI DRIVER'."
"ODETS' LINES DESCRIBING THE DEPRESSION, CLASS EXPLOITATION, AND THE CLASS STRUGGLE PENETRATED MY VERY SOUL--- I FELT EVERY WORD AS THE TRUTH."
"I DIDN'T KNOW THAT THE PLAY WAS BEING DONE AS PART OF A HUGE RALLY IN SUPPORT OF ETHIOPIA, THE SCOTTSBORO BOYS AND FOR UNEMPLOYMENT INSURANCE."
June 11, 1935
DAILY WORKER
THEATRICAL SECTION
Harold Johnson and Viola Dean as the Young Lovers in Negro People's
"I WAS A RIPE CANDIDATE FOR SOME SORT OF RADICAL ACTIVITY."
K.

Adapted from the memoir *A Dancer in the Revolution*

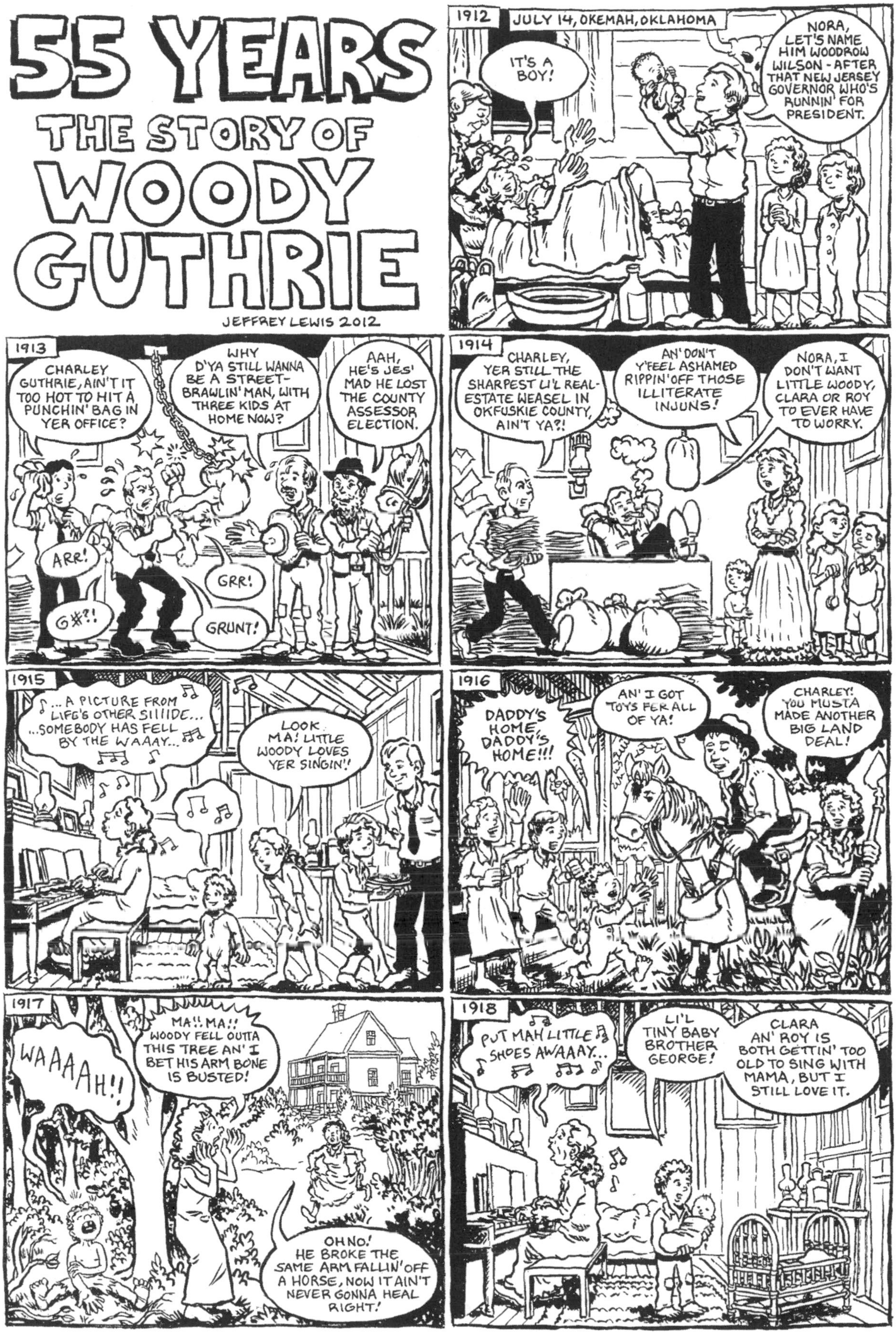
55 YEARS
THE STORY OF
WOODY GUTHRIE
JEFFREY LEWIS 2012
1912
JULY 14, OKEMAH, OKLAHOMA
IT'S A BOY!
NORA, LET'S NAME HIM WOODROW WILSON - AFTER THAT NEW JERSEY GOVERNOR WHO'S RUNNIN' FOR PRESIDENT.
1913
CHARLEY GUTHRIE, AIN'T IT TOO HOT TO HIT A PUNCHIN' BAG IN YER OFFICE?
WHY D'YA STILL WANNA BE A STREET-BRAWLIN' MAN, WITH THREE KIDS AT HOME NOW?
AAH, HE'S JES' MAD HE LOST THE COUNTY ASSESSOR ELECTION.
ARR!
G#?!
GRR!
GRUNT!
1914
CHARLEY, YER STILL THE SHARPEST LI'L REAL-ESTATE WEASEL IN OKFUSKIE COUNTY, AIN'T YA?!
AN' DON'T Y'FEEL ASHAMED RIPPIN' OFF THOSE ILLITERATE INJUNS!
NORA, I DON'T WANT LITTLE WOODY, CLARA OR ROY TO EVER HAVE TO WORRY.
1915
...A PICTURE FROM LIFE'S OTHER SIIIIDE... ...SOMEBODY HAS FELL BY THE WAAAY...
LOOK MA! LITTLE WOODY LOVES YER SINGIN'!
1916
DADDY'S HOME, DADDY'S HOME!!!
AN' I GOT TOYS FER ALL OF YA!
CHARLEY! YOU MUSTA MADE ANOTHER BIG LAND DEAL!
1917
WAAAAAH!!
MA!! MA!! WOODY FELL OUTTA THIS TREE AN' I BET HIS ARM BONE IS BUSTED!
OH NO! HE BROKE THE SAME ARM FALLIN' OFF A HORSE, NOW IT AIN'T NEVER GONNA HEAL RIGHT!
1918
PUT MAH LITTLE SHOES AWAAAY...
LI'L TINY BABY BROTHER GEORGE!
CLARA AN' ROY IS BOTH GETTIN' TOO OLD TO SING WITH MAMA, BUT I STILL LOVE IT.

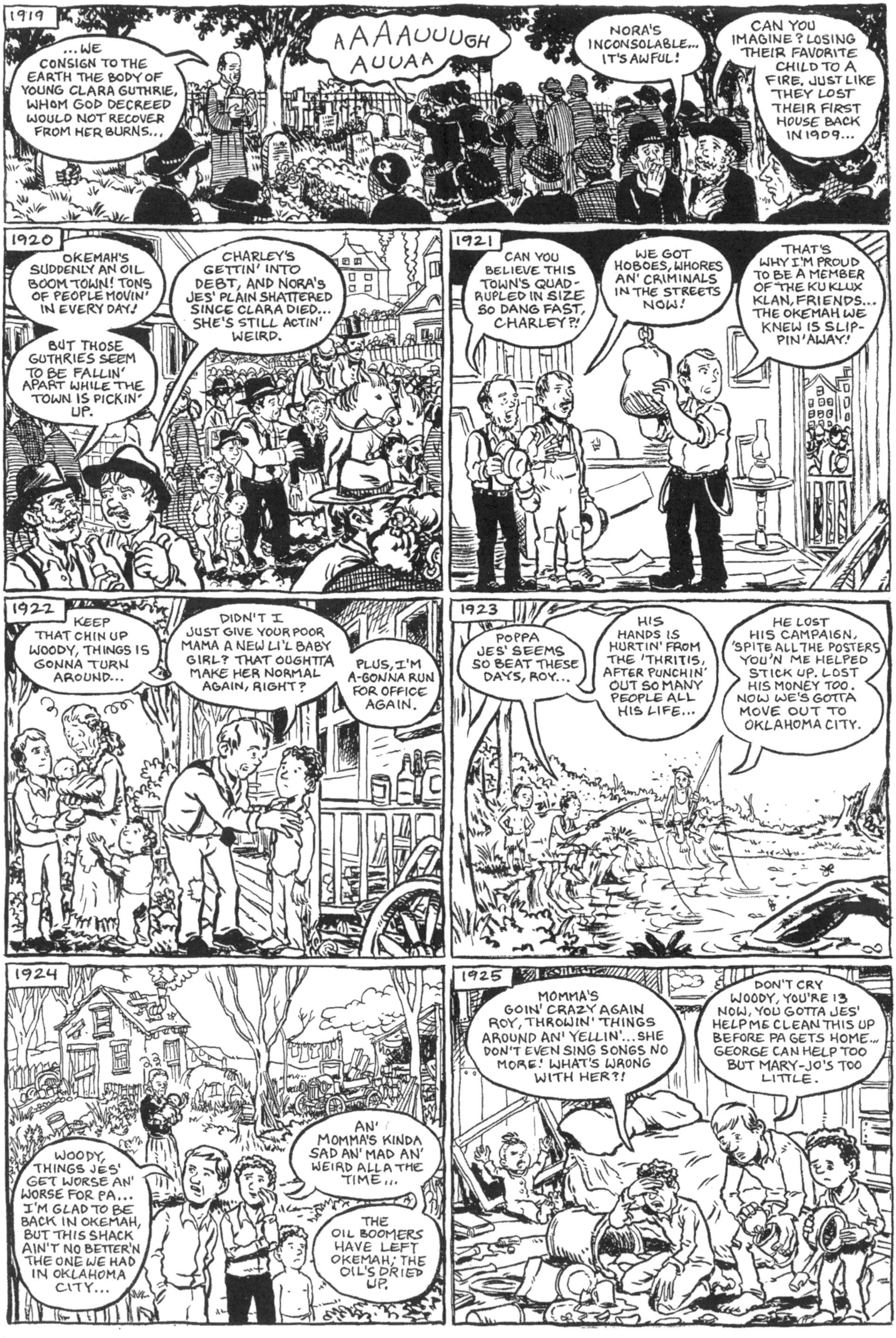
1919
...WE CONSIGN TO THE EARTH THE BODY OF YOUNG CLARA GUTHRIE, WHOM GOD DECREED WOULD NOT RECOVER FROM HER BURNS...
AAAAUUUGH AUUAA
NORA'S INCONSOLABLE... IT'S AWFUL!
CAN YOU IMAGINE? LOSING THEIR FAVORITE CHILD TO A FIRE, JUST LIKE THEY LOST THEIR FIRST HOUSE BACK IN 1909...
1920
OKEMAH'S SUDDENLY AN OIL BOOM TOWN! TONS OF PEOPLE MOVIN' IN EVERY DAY!
BUT THOSE GUTHRIES SEEM TO BE FALLIN' APART WHILE THE TOWN IS PICKIN' UP.
CHARLEY'S GETTIN' INTO DEBT, AND NORA'S JES' PLAIN SHATTERED SINCE CLARA DIED... SHE'S STILL ACTIN' WEIRD.
1921
CAN YOU BELIEVE THIS TOWN'S QUADRUPLED IN SIZE SO DANG FAST, CHARLEY?!
WE GOT HOBOES, WHORES AN' CRIMINALS IN THE STREETS NOW!
THAT'S WHY I'M PROUD TO BE A MEMBER OF THE KU KLUX KLAN, FRIENDS... THE OKEMAH WE KNEW IS SLIPPIN' AWAY!
1922
KEEP THAT CHIN UP WOODY, THINGS IS GONNA TURN AROUND...
DIDN'T I JUST GIVE YOUR POOR MAMA A NEW LI'L BABY GIRL? THAT OUGHTTA MAKE HER NORMAL AGAIN, RIGHT?
PLUS, I'M A-GONNA RUN FOR OFFICE AGAIN.
1923
POPPA JES' SEEMS SO BEAT THESE DAYS, ROY...
HIS HANDS IS HURTIN' FROM THE 'THRITIS, AFTER PUNCHIN' OUT SO MANY PEOPLE ALL HIS LIFE...
HE LOST HIS CAMPAIGN, 'SPITE ALL THE POSTERS YOU'N ME HELPED STICK UP. LOST HIS MONEY TOO. NOW WE'S GOTTA MOVE OUT TO OKLAHOMA CITY.
1924
WOODY, THINGS JES' GET WORSE AN' WORSE FOR PA... I'M GLAD TO BE BACK IN OKEMAH, BUT THIS SHACK AIN'T NO BETTER'N THE ONE WE HAD IN OKLAHOMA CITY...
AN' MOMMA'S KINDA SAD AN' MAD AN' WEIRD ALLA THE TIME...
THE OIL BOOMERS HAVE LEFT OKEMAH; THE OIL'S DRIED UP.
1925
MOMMA'S GOIN' CRAZY AGAIN ROY, THROWIN' THINGS AROUND AN' YELLIN'... SHE DON'T EVEN SING SONGS NO MORE! WHAT'S WRONG WITH HER?!
DON'T CRY WOODY, YOU'RE 13 NOW, YOU GOTTA JES' HELP ME CLEAN THIS UP BEFORE PA GETS HOME... GEORGE CAN HELP TOO BUT MARY-JO'S TOO LITTLE.

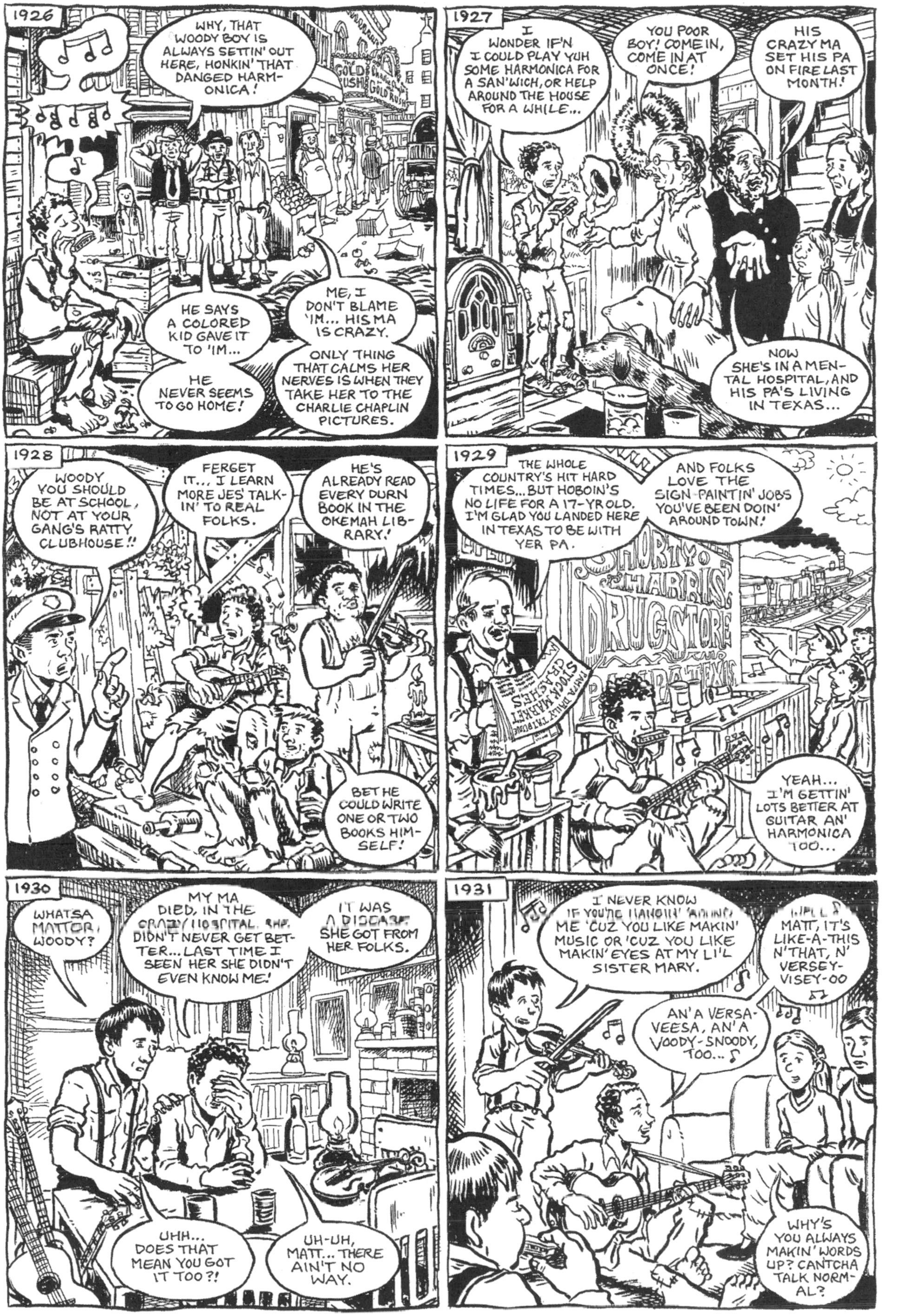
1926
WHY, THAT WOODY BOY IS ALWAYS SETTIN' OUT HERE, HONKIN' THAT DANGED HARMONICA!
GOLD RUSH
HE SAYS A COLORED KID GAVE IT TO 'IM...
HE NEVER SEEMS TO GO HOME!
ME, I DON'T BLAME 'IM... HIS MA IS CRAZY.
ONLY THING THAT CALMS HER NERVES IS WHEN THEY TAKE HER TO THE CHARLIE CHAPLIN PICTURES.
1927
I WONDER IF'N I COULD PLAY YUH SOME HARMONICA FOR A SAN'WICH, OR HELP AROUND THE HOUSE FOR A WHILE...
YOU POOR BOY! COME IN, COME IN AT ONCE!
HIS CRAZY MA SET HIS PA ON FIRE LAST MONTH!
NOW SHE'S IN A MENTAL HOSPITAL, AND HIS PA'S LIVING IN TEXAS...
1928
WOODY YOU SHOULD BE AT SCHOOL, NOT AT YOUR GANG'S RATTY CLUBHOUSE!!
FERGET IT... I LEARN MORE JES' TALKIN' TO REAL FOLKS.
HE'S ALREADY READ EVERY DURN BOOK IN THE OKEMAH LIBRARY!
BET HE COULD WRITE ONE OR TWO BOOKS HIMSELF!
1929
THE WHOLE COUNTRY'S HIT HARD TIMES... BUT HOBOIN'S NO LIFE FOR A 17-YR OLD. I'M GLAD YOU LANDED HERE IN TEXAS TO BE WITH YER PA.
AND FOLKS LOVE THE SIGN-PAINTIN' JOBS YOU'VE BEEN DOIN' AROUND TOWN!
SHORTY HARRIS' DRUGSTORE
STOCK MARKET CRASHES
YEAH... I'M GETTIN' LOTS BETTER AT GUITAR AN' HARMONICA TOO...
1930
WHATSA MATTER, WOODY?
MY MA DIED, IN THE CRAZY HOSPITAL. SHE DIDN'T NEVER GET BETTER... LAST TIME I SEEN HER SHE DIDN'T EVEN KNOW ME!
IT WAS A DISEASE SHE GOT FROM HER FOLKS.
UHH... DOES THAT MEAN YOU GOT IT TOO?!
UH-UH, MATT... THERE AIN'T NO WAY.
1931
I NEVER KNOW IF YOU'RE HANGIN' 'ROUND ME 'CUZ YOU LIKE MAKIN' MUSIC OR 'CUZ YOU LIKE MAKIN' EYES AT MY LI'L SISTER MARY.
WELL MATT, IT'S LIKE-A-THIS N'THAT, N' VERSEY-VISEY-OO
AN'A VERSA-VEESA, AN'A VOODY-SNOODY, TOO...
WHY'S YOU ALWAYS MAKIN' WORDS UP? CANTCHA TALK NORMAL?

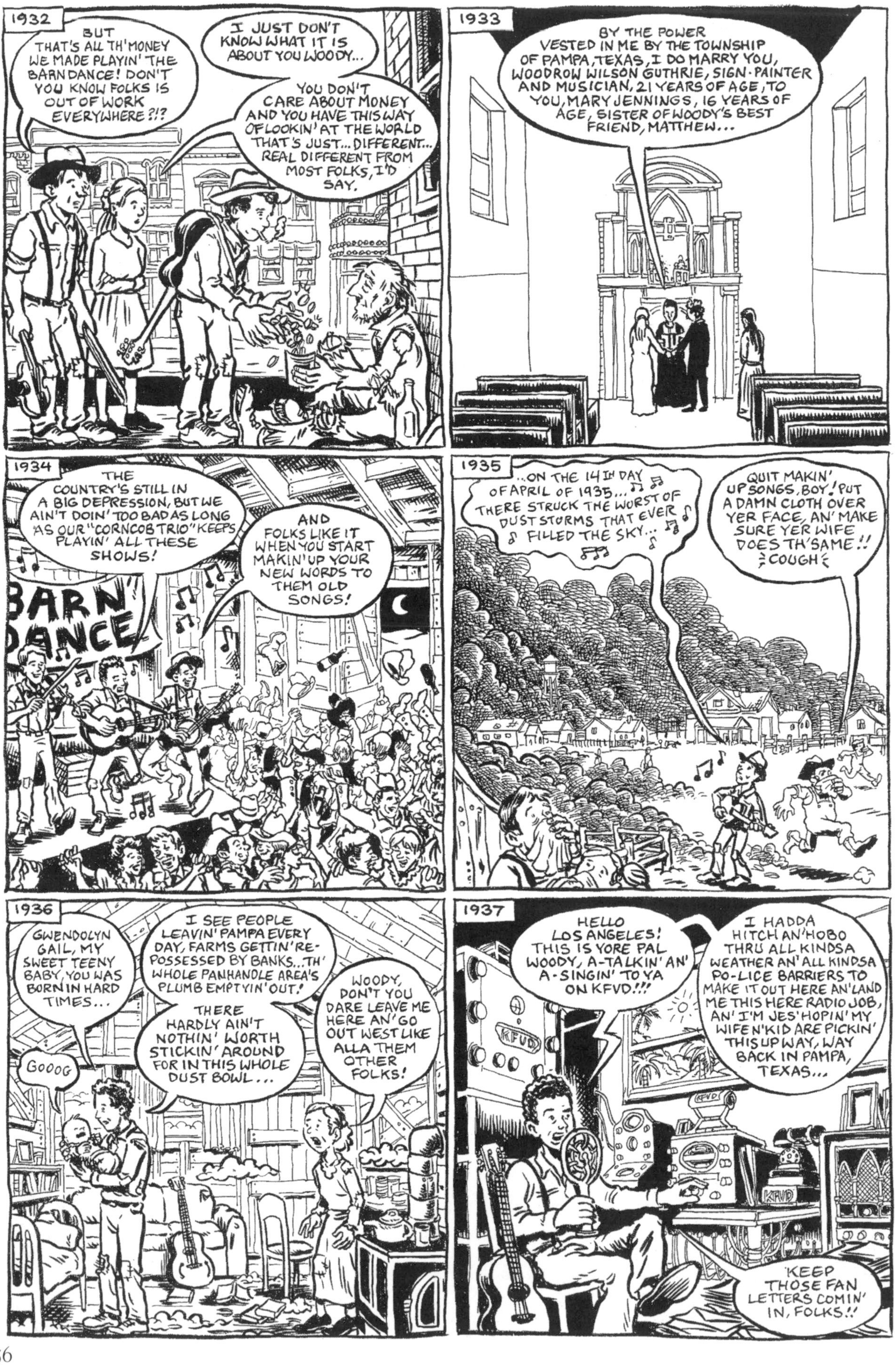
1932
BUT THAT'S ALL TH' MONEY WE MADE PLAYIN' THE BARN DANCE! DON'T YOU KNOW FOLKS IS OUT OF WORK EVERYWHERE?!?
I JUST DON'T KNOW WHAT IT IS ABOUT YOU WOODY...
YOU DON'T CARE ABOUT MONEY AND YOU HAVE THIS WAY OF LOOKIN' AT THE WORLD THAT'S JUST... DIFFERENT... REAL DIFFERENT FROM MOST FOLKS, I'D SAY.
1933
BY THE POWER VESTED IN ME BY THE TOWNSHIP OF PAMPA, TEXAS, I DO MARRY YOU, WOODROW WILSON GUTHRIE, SIGN-PAINTER AND MUSICIAN, 21 YEARS OF AGE, TO YOU, MARY JENNINGS, 16 YEARS OF AGE, SISTER OF WOODY'S BEST FRIEND, MATTHEW...
1934
THE COUNTRY'S STILL IN A BIG DEPRESSION, BUT WE AIN'T DOIN' TOO BAD AS LONG AS OUR "CORNCOB TRIO" KEEPS PLAYIN' ALL THESE SHOWS!
AND FOLKS LIKE IT WHEN YOU START MAKIN' UP YOUR NEW WORDS TO THEM OLD SONGS!
BARN DANCE
1935
...ON THE 14TH DAY OF APRIL OF 1935... THERE STRUCK THE WORST OF DUST STORMS THAT EVER FILLED THE SKY...
QUIT MAKIN' UP SONGS, BOY! PUT A DAMN CLOTH OVER YER FACE, AN' MAKE SURE YER WIFE DOES TH' SAME!! COUGH
1936
GWENDOLYN GAIL, MY SWEET TEENY BABY, YOU WAS BORN IN HARD TIMES...
GOOOG
I SEE PEOPLE LEAVIN' PAMPA EVERY DAY, FARMS GETTIN' RE-POSSESSED BY BANKS... TH' WHOLE PANHANDLE AREA'S PLUMB EMPTYIN' OUT!
THERE HARDLY AIN'T NOTHIN' WORTH STICKIN' AROUND FOR IN THIS WHOLE DUST BOWL...
WOODY, DON'T YOU DARE LEAVE ME HERE AN' GO OUT WEST LIKE ALLA THEM OTHER FOLKS!
1937
HELLO LOS ANGELES! THIS IS YORE PAL WOODY, A-TALKIN' AN' A-SINGIN' TO YA ON KFVD!!!
I HADDA HITCH AN' HOBO THRU ALL KINDSA WEATHER AN' ALL KINDSA PO-LICE BARRIERS TO MAKE IT OUT HERE AN' LAND ME THIS HERE RADIO JOB, AN' I'M JES' HOPIN' MY WIFE N' KID ARE PICKIN' THIS UP WAY, WAY BACK IN PAMPA, TEXAS...
KFVD
KEEP THOSE FAN LETTERS COMIN' IN, FOLKS!!

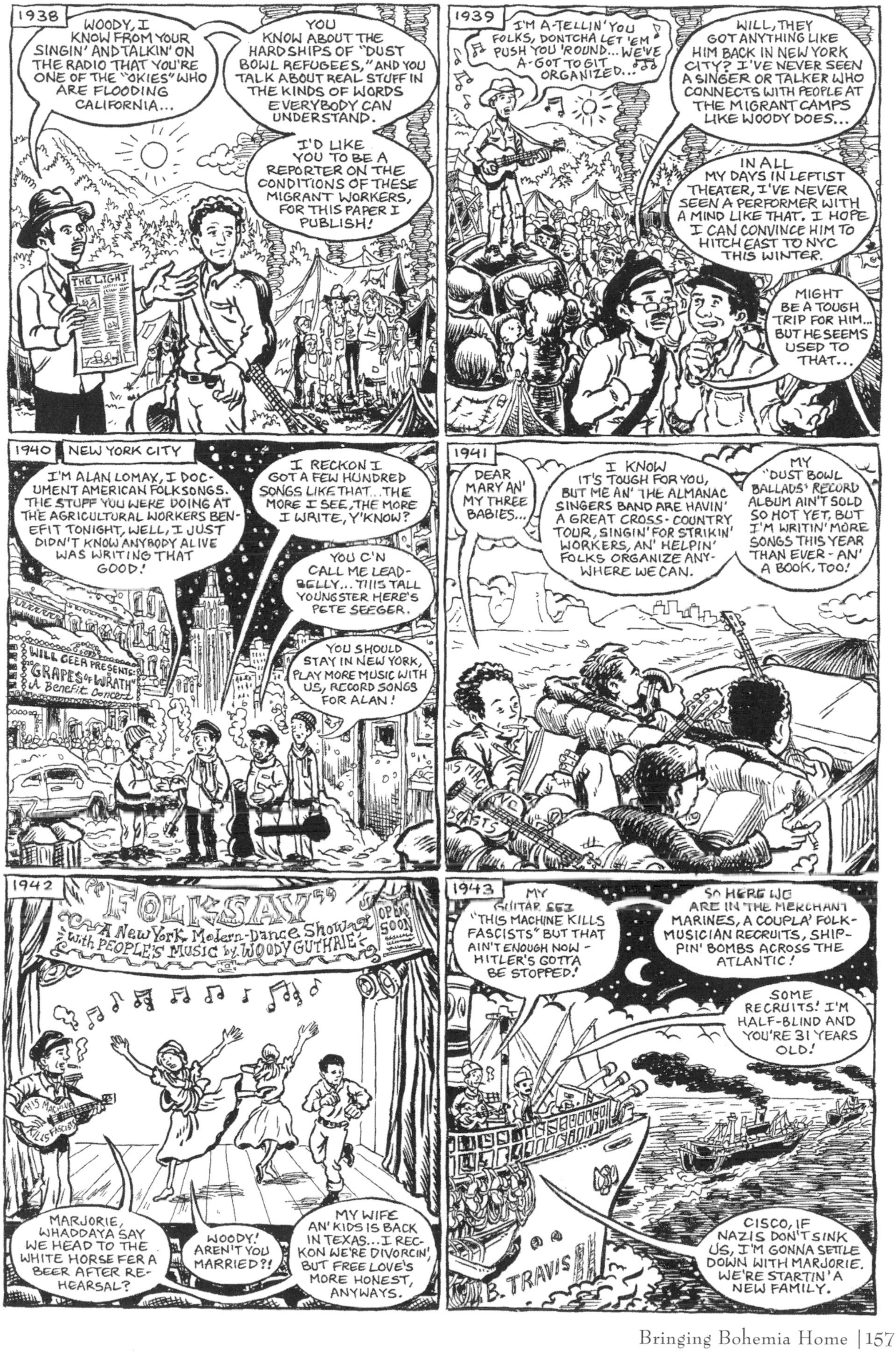
1938
WOODY, I KNOW FROM YOUR SINGIN' AND TALKIN' ON THE RADIO THAT YOU'RE ONE OF THE "OKIES" WHO ARE FLOODING CALIFORNIA...
YOU KNOW ABOUT THE HARDSHIPS OF "DUST BOWL REFUGEES," AND YOU TALK ABOUT REAL STUFF IN THE KINDS OF WORDS EVERYBODY CAN UNDERSTAND.
I'D LIKE YOU TO BE A REPORTER ON THE CONDITIONS OF THESE MIGRANT WORKERS, FOR THIS PAPER I PUBLISH!
THE LIGHT
1939
I'M A-TELLIN' YOU FOLKS, DONTCHA LET 'EM PUSH YOU 'ROUND... WE'VE A-GOT TO GIT ORGANIZED...
WILL, THEY GOT ANYTHING LIKE HIM BACK IN NEW YORK CITY? I'VE NEVER SEEN A SINGER OR TALKER WHO CONNECTS WITH PEOPLE AT THE MIGRANT CAMPS LIKE WOODY DOES...
IN ALL MY DAYS IN LEFTIST THEATER, I'VE NEVER SEEN A PERFORMER WITH A MIND LIKE THAT. I HOPE I CAN CONVINCE HIM TO HITCH EAST TO NYC THIS WINTER.
MIGHT BE A TOUGH TRIP FOR HIM... BUT HE SEEMS USED TO THAT...
1940
NEW YORK CITY
I'M ALAN LOMAX, I DOCUMENT AMERICAN FOLKSONGS. THE STUFF YOU WERE DOING AT THE AGRICULTURAL WORKERS BENEFIT TONIGHT, WELL, I JUST DIDN'T KNOW ANYBODY ALIVE WAS WRITING THAT GOOD!
I RECKON I GOT A FEW HUNDRED SONGS LIKE THAT... THE MORE I SEE, THE MORE I WRITE, Y'KNOW?
YOU C'N CALL ME LEADBELLY... THIS TALL YOUNGSTER HERE'S PETE SEEGER.
YOU SHOULD STAY IN NEW YORK, PLAY MORE MUSIC WITH US, RECORD SONGS FOR ALAN!
WILL GEER PRESENTS: "GRAPES of WRATH" A Benefit Concert
1941
DEAR MARY AN' MY THREE BABIES...
I KNOW IT'S TOUGH FOR YOU, BUT ME AN' THE ALMANAC SINGERS BAND ARE HAVIN' A GREAT CROSS-COUNTRY TOUR, SINGIN' FOR STRIKIN' WORKERS, AN' HELPIN' FOLKS ORGANIZE ANYWHERE WE CAN.
MY "DUST BOWL BALLADS" RECORD ALBUM AIN'T SOLD SO HOT YET, BUT I'M WRITIN' MORE SONGS THIS YEAR THAN EVER - AN' A BOOK, TOO!
1942
"FOLKSAY"
A New York Modern-Dance Show with PEOPLE'S MUSIC by WOODY GUTHRIE!
OPENS SOON
THIS MACHINE KILLS FASCISTS
MARJORIE, WHADDAYA SAY WE HEAD TO THE WHITE HORSE FER A BEER AFTER REHEARSAL?
WOODY! AREN'T YOU MARRIED?!
MY WIFE AN' KIDS IS BACK IN TEXAS... I RECKON WE'RE DIVORCIN', BUT FREE LOVE'S MORE HONEST, ANYWAYS.
1943
MY GUITAR SEZ "THIS MACHINE KILLS FASCISTS" BUT THAT AIN'T ENOUGH NOW - HITLER'S GOTTA BE STOPPED!
SO HERE WE ARE IN THE MERCHANT MARINES, A COUPLA' FOLK-MUSICIAN RECRUITS, SHIPPIN' BOMBS ACROSS THE ATLANTIC!
SOME RECRUITS! I'M HALF-BLIND AND YOU'RE 31 YEARS OLD!
CISCO, IF NAZIS DON'T SINK US, I'M GONNA SETTLE DOWN WITH MARJORIE. WE'RE STARTIN' A NEW FAMILY.
B. TRAVIS

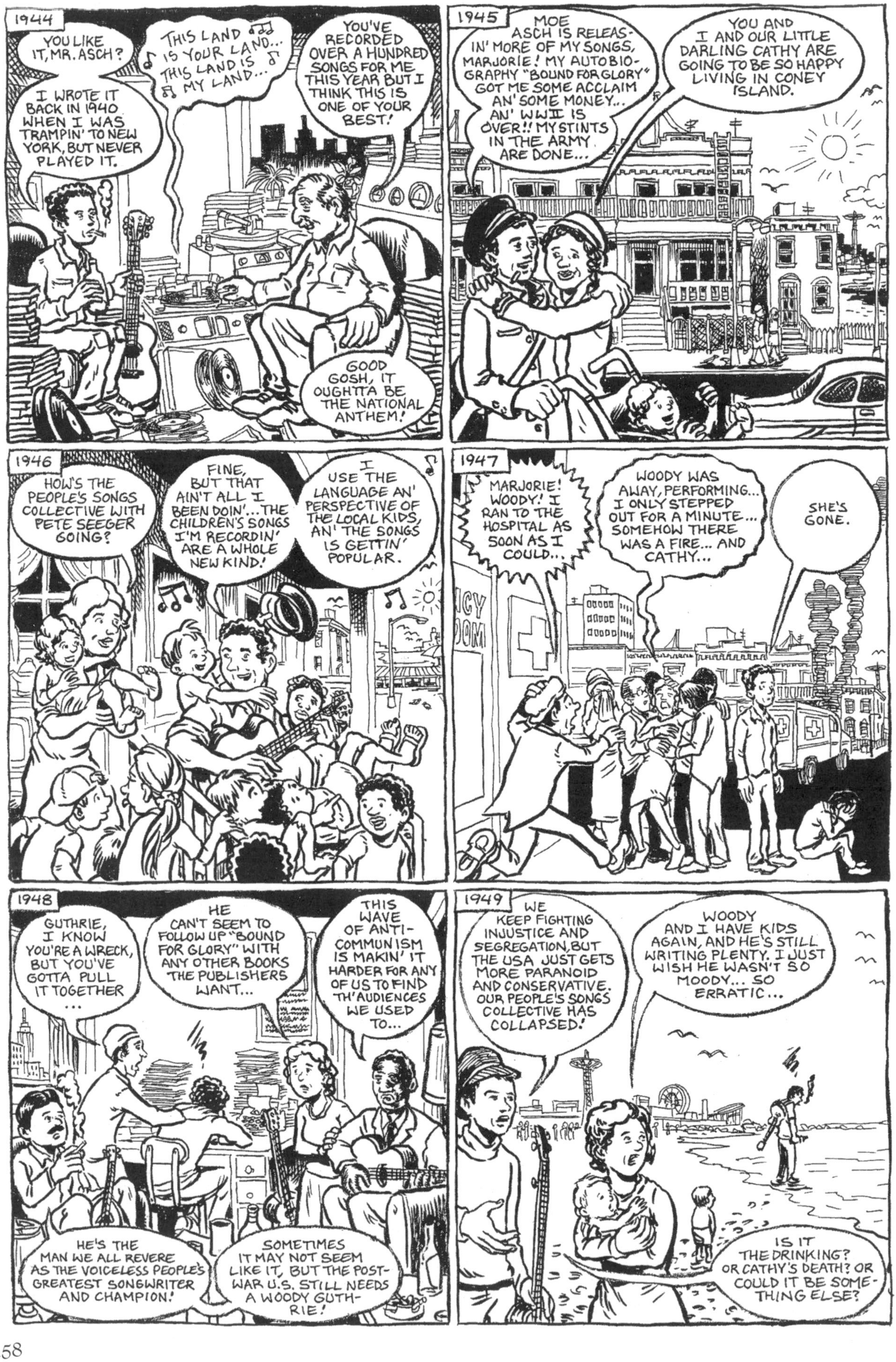
1944
YOU LIKE IT, MR. ASCH?
I WROTE IT BACK IN 1940 WHEN I WAS TRAMPIN' TO NEW YORK, BUT NEVER PLAYED IT.
THIS LAND IS YOUR LAND... THIS LAND IS MY LAND...
YOU'VE RECORDED OVER A HUNDRED SONGS FOR ME THIS YEAR BUT I THINK THIS IS ONE OF YOUR BEST!
GOOD GOSH, IT OUGHTTA BE THE NATIONAL ANTHEM!
1945
MOE ASCH IS RELEASIN' MORE OF MY SONGS, MARJORIE! MY AUTOBIOGRAPHY "BOUND FOR GLORY" GOT ME SOME ACCLAIM AN' SOME MONEY... AN' WWII IS OVER!! MY STINTS IN THE ARMY ARE DONE...
YOU AND I AND OUR LITTLE DARLING CATHY ARE GOING TO BE SO HAPPY LIVING IN CONEY ISLAND.
1946
HOW'S THE PEOPLE'S SONGS COLLECTIVE WITH PETE SEEGER GOING?
FINE, BUT THAT AIN'T ALL I BEEN DOIN'... THE CHILDREN'S SONGS I'M RECORDIN' ARE A WHOLE NEW KIND!
I USE THE LANGUAGE AN' PERSPECTIVE OF THE LOCAL KIDS, AN' THE SONGS IS GETTIN' POPULAR.
1947
MARJORIE! WOODY! I RAN TO THE HOSPITAL AS SOON AS I COULD...
WOODY WAS AWAY, PERFORMING... I ONLY STEPPED OUT FOR A MINUTE... SOMEHOW THERE WAS A FIRE... AND CATHY...
SHE'S GONE.
1948
GUTHRIE, I KNOW YOU'RE A WRECK, BUT YOU'VE GOTTA PULL IT TOGETHER ...
HE CAN'T SEEM TO FOLLOW UP "BOUND FOR GLORY" WITH ANY OTHER BOOKS THE PUBLISHERS WANT...
THIS WAVE OF ANTI-COMMUNISM IS MAKIN' IT HARDER FOR ANY OF US TO FIND TH' AUDIENCES WE USED TO...
HE'S THE MAN WE ALL REVERE AS THE VOICELESS PEOPLE'S GREATEST SONGWRITER AND CHAMPION!
SOMETIMES IT MAY NOT SEEM LIKE IT, BUT THE POST-WAR U.S. STILL NEEDS A WOODY GUTHRIE!
1949
WE KEEP FIGHTING INJUSTICE AND SEGREGATION, BUT THE USA JUST GETS MORE PARANOID AND CONSERVATIVE. OUR PEOPLE'S SONGS COLLECTIVE HAS COLLAPSED!
WOODY AND I HAVE KIDS AGAIN, AND HE'S STILL WRITING PLENTY. I JUST WISH HE WASN'T SO MOODY... SO ERRATIC...
IS IT THE DRINKING? OR CATHY'S DEATH? OR COULD IT BE SOMETHING ELSE?

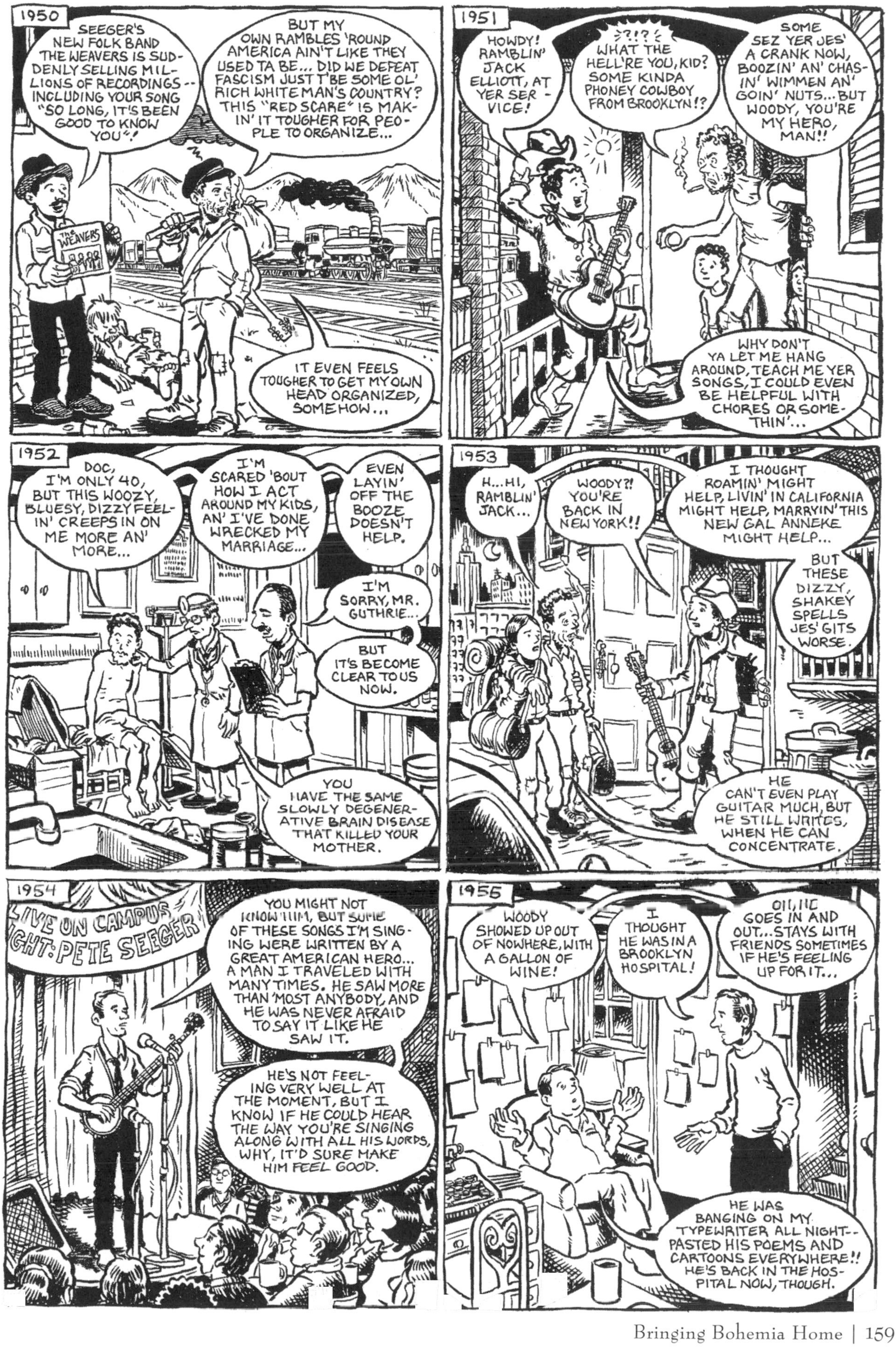
1950
SEEGER'S NEW FOLK BAND THE WEAVERS IS SUDDENLY SELLING MILLIONS OF RECORDINGS -- INCLUDING YOUR SONG "SO LONG, IT'S BEEN GOOD TO KNOW YOU"!
BUT MY OWN RAMBLES 'ROUND AMERICA AIN'T LIKE THEY USED TA BE... DID WE DEFEAT FASCISM JUST T'BE SOME OL' RICH WHITE MAN'S COUNTRY? THIS "RED SCARE" IS MAKIN' IT TOUGHER FOR PEOPLE TO ORGANIZE...
THE WEAVERS
IT EVEN FEELS TOUGHER TO GET MY OWN HEAD ORGANIZED, SOMEHOW...
1951
HOWDY! RAMBLIN' JACK ELLIOTT, AT YER SERVICE!
?!?! WHAT THE HELL'RE YOU, KID? SOME KINDA PHONEY COWBOY FROM BROOKLYN!?
SOME SEZ YER JES' A CRANK NOW, BOOZIN' AN' CHASIN' WIMMEN AN' GOIN' NUTS... BUT WOODY, YOU'RE MY HERO, MAN!!
WHY DON'T YA LET ME HANG AROUND, TEACH ME YER SONGS, I COULD EVEN BE HELPFUL WITH CHORES OR SOMETHIN'...
1952
DOC, I'M ONLY 40, BUT THIS WOOZY, BLUESY, DIZZY FEELIN' CREEPS IN ON ME MORE AN' MORE...
I'M SCARED 'BOUT HOW I ACT AROUND MY KIDS, AN' I'VE DONE WRECKED MY MARRIAGE...
EVEN LAYIN' OFF THE BOOZE DOESN'T HELP.
I'M SORRY, MR. GUTHRIE...
BUT IT'S BECOME CLEAR TO US NOW.
YOU HAVE THE SAME SLOWLY DEGENERATIVE BRAIN DISEASE THAT KILLED YOUR MOTHER.
1953
H...HI, RAMBLIN' JACK...
WOODY?! YOU'RE BACK IN NEW YORK!!
I THOUGHT ROAMIN' MIGHT HELP, LIVIN' IN CALIFORNIA MIGHT HELP, MARRYIN' THIS NEW GAL ANNEKE MIGHT HELP...
BUT THESE DIZZY, SHAKEY SPELLS JES' GITS WORSE.
HE CAN'T EVEN PLAY GUITAR MUCH, BUT HE STILL WRITES, WHEN HE CAN CONCENTRATE.
1954
LIVE ON CAMPUS
IGHT: PETE SEEGER
YOU MIGHT NOT KNOW HIM, BUT SOME OF THESE SONGS I'M SINGING WERE WRITTEN BY A GREAT AMERICAN HERO... A MAN I TRAVELED WITH MANY TIMES. HE SAW MORE THAN 'MOST ANYBODY, AND HE WAS NEVER AFRAID TO SAY IT LIKE HE SAW IT.
HE'S NOT FEELING VERY WELL AT THE MOMENT, BUT I KNOW IF HE COULD HEAR THE WAY YOU'RE SINGING ALONG WITH ALL HIS WORDS, WHY, IT'D SURE MAKE HIM FEEL GOOD.
1956
WOODY SHOWED UP OUT OF NOWHERE, WITH A GALLON OF WINE!
I THOUGHT HE WAS IN A BROOKLYN HOSPITAL!
OH, HE GOES IN AND OUT... STAYS WITH FRIENDS SOMETIMES IF HE'S FEELING UP FOR IT...
HE WAS BANGING ON MY TYPEWRITER ALL NIGHT -- PASTED HIS POEMS AND CARTOONS EVERYWHERE!! HE'S BACK IN THE HOSPITAL NOW, THOUGH.

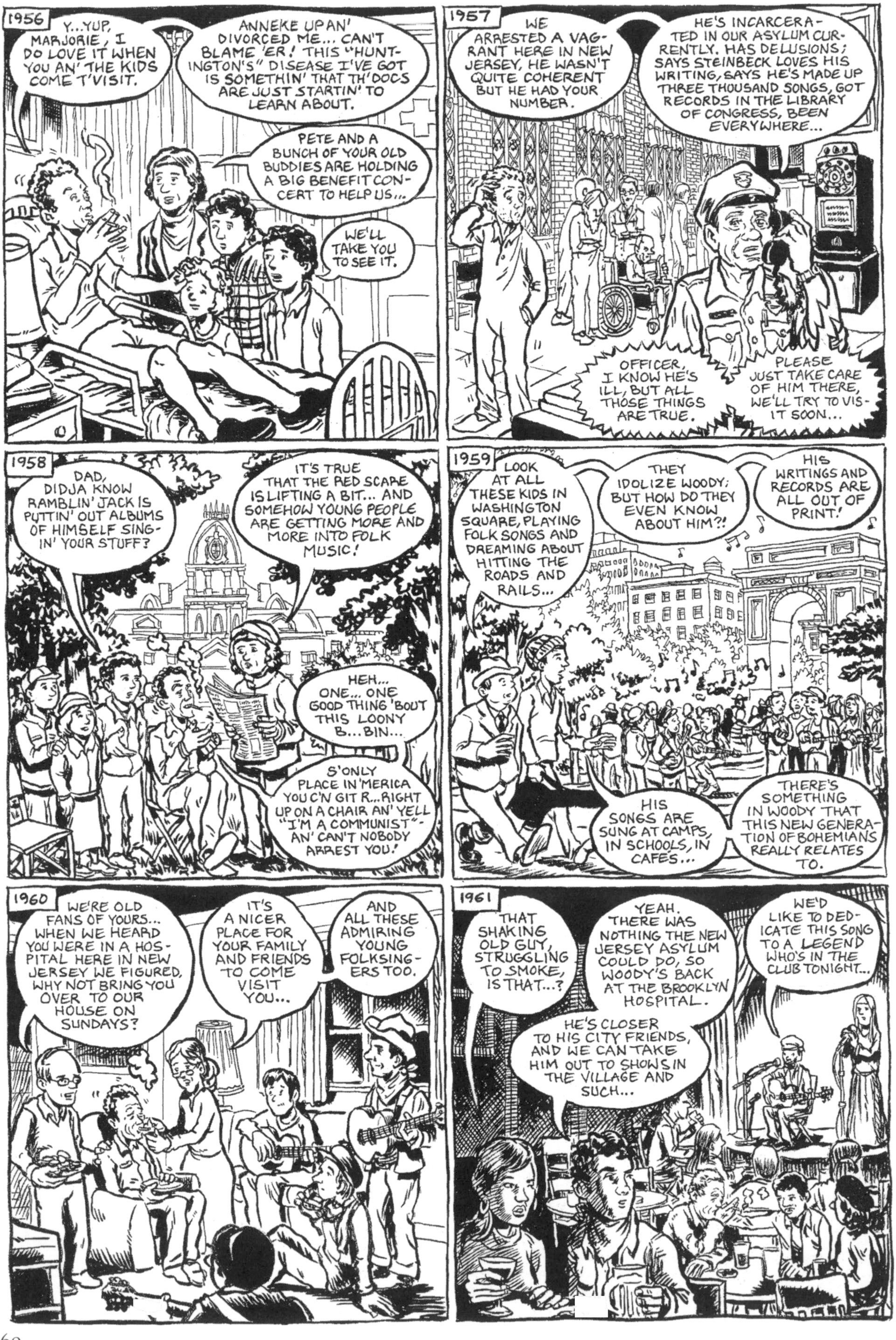
1956
Y...YUP, MARJORIE, I DO LOVE IT WHEN YOU AN' THE KIDS COME T'VISIT.
ANNEKE UP AN' DIVORCED ME... CAN'T BLAME 'ER! THIS "HUNTINGTON'S" DISEASE I'VE GOT IS SOMETHIN' THAT TH'DOCS ARE JUST STARTIN' TO LEARN ABOUT.
PETE AND A BUNCH OF YOUR OLD BUDDIES ARE HOLDING A BIG BENEFIT CONCERT TO HELP US...
WE'LL TAKE YOU TO SEE IT.
1957
WE ARRESTED A VAGRANT HERE IN NEW JERSEY, HE WASN'T QUITE COHERENT BUT HE HAD YOUR NUMBER.
HE'S INCARCERATED IN OUR ASYLUM CURRENTLY. HAS DELUSIONS; SAYS STEINBECK LOVES HIS WRITING, SAYS HE'S MADE UP THREE THOUSAND SONGS, GOT RECORDS IN THE LIBRARY OF CONGRESS, BEEN EVERYWHERE...
OFFICER, I KNOW HE'S ILL, BUT ALL THOSE THINGS ARE TRUE.
PLEASE JUST TAKE CARE OF HIM THERE, WE'LL TRY TO VISIT SOON...
1958
DAD, DIDJA KNOW RAMBLIN' JACK IS PUTTIN' OUT ALBUMS OF HIMSELF SINGIN' YOUR STUFF?
IT'S TRUE THAT THE RED SCARE IS LIFTING A BIT... AND SOMEHOW YOUNG PEOPLE ARE GETTING MORE AND MORE INTO FOLK MUSIC!
HEH... ONE... ONE GOOD THING 'BOUT THIS LOONY B...BIN...
S'ONLY PLACE IN 'MERICA YOU C'N GIT R...RIGHT UP ON A CHAIR AN' YELL "I'M A COMMUNIST"—AN' CAN'T NOBODY ARREST YOU!
1959
LOOK AT ALL THESE KIDS IN WASHINGTON SQUARE, PLAYING FOLK SONGS AND DREAMING ABOUT HITTING THE ROADS AND RAILS...
THEY IDOLIZE WOODY; BUT HOW DO THEY EVEN KNOW ABOUT HIM?!
HIS WRITINGS AND RECORDS ARE ALL OUT OF PRINT!
HIS SONGS ARE SUNG AT CAMPS, IN SCHOOLS, IN CAFES...
THERE'S SOMETHING IN WOODY THAT THIS NEW GENERATION OF BOHEMIANS REALLY RELATES TO.
1960
WE'RE OLD FANS OF YOURS... WHEN WE HEARD YOU WERE IN A HOSPITAL HERE IN NEW JERSEY WE FIGURED, WHY NOT BRING YOU OVER TO OUR HOUSE ON SUNDAYS?
IT'S A NICER PLACE FOR YOUR FAMILY AND FRIENDS TO COME VISIT YOU...
AND ALL THESE ADMIRING YOUNG FOLKSINGERS TOO.
1961
THAT SHAKING OLD GUY, STRUGGLING TO SMOKE, IS THAT...?
YEAH. THERE WAS NOTHING THE NEW JERSEY ASYLUM COULD DO, SO WOODY'S BACK AT THE BROOKLYN HOSPITAL.
HE'S CLOSER TO HIS CITY FRIENDS, AND WE CAN TAKE HIM OUT TO SHOWS IN THE VILLAGE AND SUCH...
WE'D LIKE TO DEDICATE THIS SONG TO A LEGEND WHO'S IN THE CLUB TONIGHT...

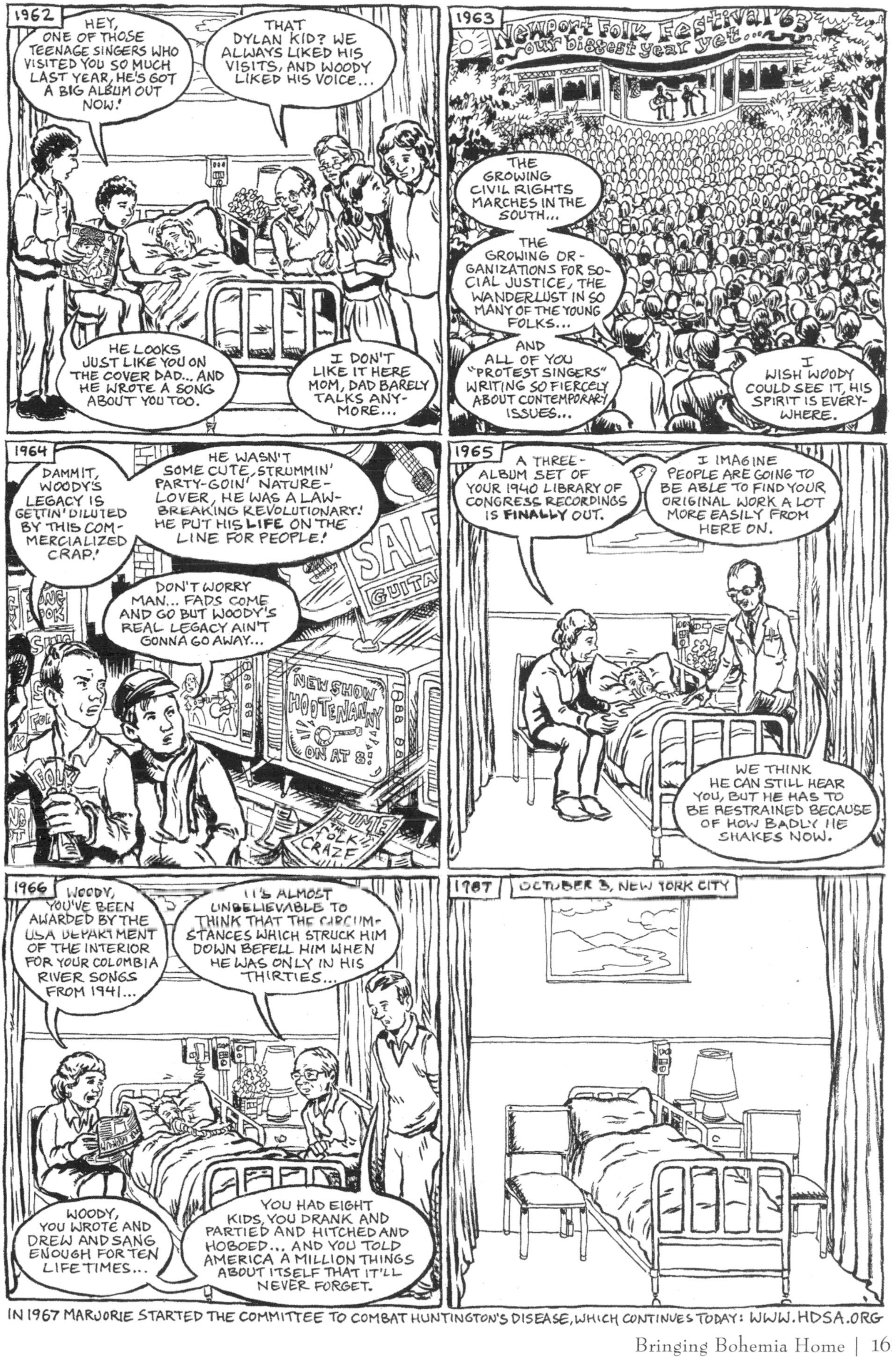
1962
HEY, ONE OF THOSE TEENAGE SINGERS WHO VISITED YOU SO MUCH LAST YEAR, HE'S GOT A BIG ALBUM OUT NOW!
THAT DYLAN KID? WE ALWAYS LIKED HIS VISITS, AND WOODY LIKED HIS VOICE...
HE LOOKS JUST LIKE YOU ON THE COVER DAD... AND HE WROTE A SONG ABOUT YOU TOO.
I DON'T LIKE IT HERE MOM, DAD BARELY TALKS ANY-MORE...
1963
Newport Folk Festival '63 our biggest year yet...
THE GROWING CIVIL RIGHTS MARCHES IN THE SOUTH...
THE GROWING OR-GANIZATIONS FOR SO-CIAL JUSTICE, THE WANDERLUST IN SO MANY OF THE YOUNG FOLKS...
AND ALL OF YOU "PROTEST SINGERS" WRITING SO FIERCELY ABOUT CONTEMPORARY ISSUES...
I WISH WOODY COULD SEE IT, HIS SPIRIT IS EVERY-WHERE.
1964
DAMMIT, WOODY'S LEGACY IS GETTIN' DILUTED BY THIS COM-MERCIALIZED CRAP!
HE WASN'T SOME CUTE, STRUMMIN' PARTY-GOIN' NATURE-LOVER, HE WAS A LAW-BREAKING REVOLUTIONARY! HE PUT HIS LIFE ON THE LINE FOR PEOPLE!
DON'T WORRY MAN... FADS COME AND GO BUT WOODY'S REAL LEGACY AIN'T GONNA GO AWAY...
NEW SHOW HOOTENANNY ON AT 8!
TIME THE FOLK CRAZE
1965
A THREE-ALBUM SET OF YOUR 1940 LIBRARY OF CONGRESS RECORDINGS IS FINALLY OUT.
I IMAGINE PEOPLE ARE GOING TO BE ABLE TO FIND YOUR ORIGINAL WORK A LOT MORE EASILY FROM HERE ON.
WE THINK HE CAN STILL HEAR YOU, BUT HE HAS TO BE RESTRAINED BECAUSE OF HOW BADLY HE SHAKES NOW.
1966
WOODY, YOU'VE BEEN AWARDED BY THE USA DEPARTMENT OF THE INTERIOR FOR YOUR COLOMBIA RIVER SONGS FROM 1941...
IT'S ALMOST UNBELIEVABLE TO THINK THAT THE CIRCUM-STANCES WHICH STRUCK HIM DOWN BEFELL HIM WHEN HE WAS ONLY IN HIS THIRTIES...
WOODY, YOU WROTE AND DREW AND SANG ENOUGH FOR TEN LIFE TIMES...
YOU HAD EIGHT KIDS, YOU DRANK AND PARTIED AND HITCHED AND HOBOED... AND YOU TOLD AMERICA A MILLION THINGS ABOUT ITSELF THAT IT'LL NEVER FORGET.
1967
OCTOBER 3, NEW YORK CITY

IN 1967 MARJORIE STARTED THE COMMITTEE TO COMBAT HUNTINGTON'S DISEASE, WHICH CONTINUES TODAY: WWW.HDSA.ORG

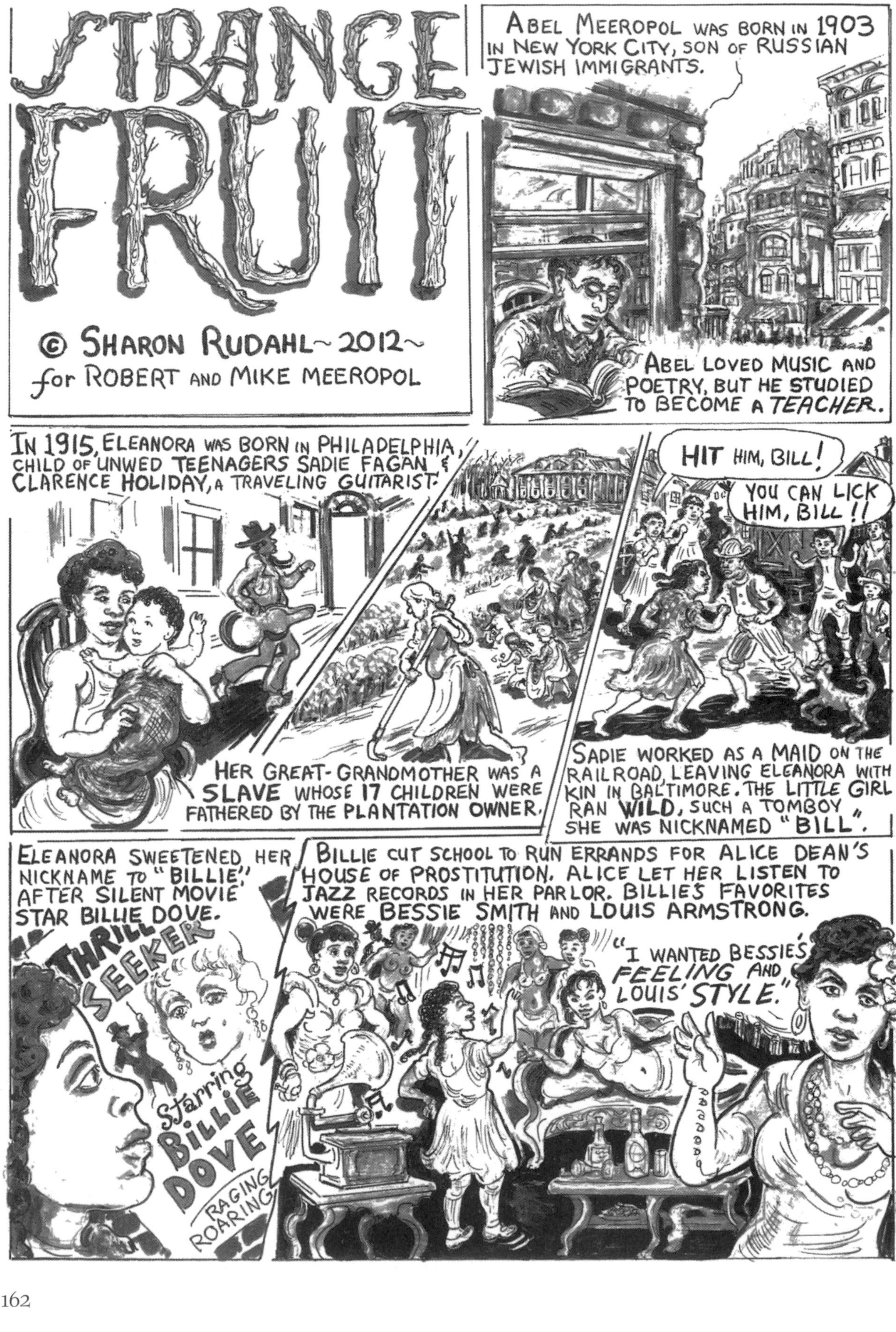
STRANGE FRUIT
© SHARON RUDAHL ~ 2012 ~
for ROBERT AND MIKE MEEROPOL
ABEL MEEROPOL WAS BORN IN 1903 IN NEW YORK CITY, SON OF RUSSIAN JEWISH IMMIGRANTS.
ABEL LOVED MUSIC AND POETRY, BUT HE STUDIED TO BECOME A TEACHER.
IN 1915, ELEANORA WAS BORN IN PHILADELPHIA, CHILD OF UNWED TEENAGERS SADIE FAGAN & CLARENCE HOLIDAY, A TRAVELING GUITARIST.
HER GREAT-GRANDMOTHER WAS A SLAVE WHOSE 17 CHILDREN WERE FATHERED BY THE PLANTATION OWNER.
HIT HIM, BILL!
YOU CAN LICK HIM, BILL!!
SADIE WORKED AS A MAID ON THE RAILROAD, LEAVING ELEANORA WITH KIN IN BALTIMORE. THE LITTLE GIRL RAN WILD, SUCH A TOMBOY SHE WAS NICKNAMED "BILL".
ELEANORA SWEETENED HER NICKNAME TO "BILLIE," AFTER SILENT MOVIE STAR BILLIE DOVE.
THRILL SEEKER
Starring BILLIE DOVE
RAGING ROARING
BILLIE CUT SCHOOL TO RUN ERRANDS FOR ALICE DEAN'S HOUSE OF PROSTITUTION. ALICE LET HER LISTEN TO JAZZ RECORDS IN HER PARLOR. BILLIE'S FAVORITES WERE BESSIE SMITH AND LOUIS ARMSTRONG.
"I WANTED BESSIE'S FEELING AND LOUIS' STYLE."

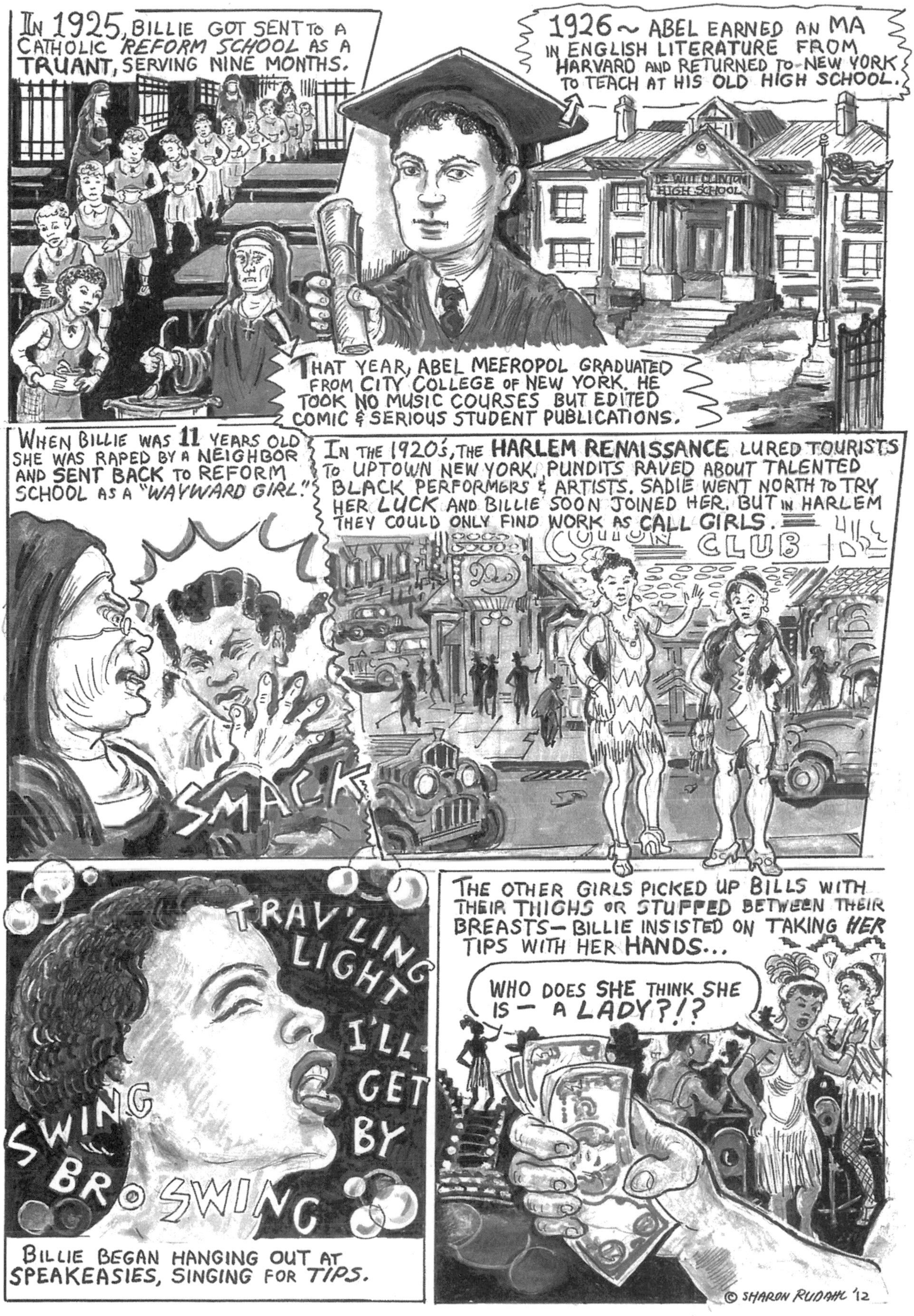
IN 1925, BILLIE GOT SENT TO A CATHOLIC REFORM SCHOOL AS A TRUANT, SERVING NINE MONTHS.
1926 ~ ABEL EARNED AN MA IN ENGLISH LITERATURE FROM HARVARD AND RETURNED TO NEW YORK TO TEACH AT HIS OLD HIGH SCHOOL.
DE WITT CLINTON HIGH SCHOOL
THAT YEAR, ABEL MEEROPOL GRADUATED FROM CITY COLLEGE OF NEW YORK. HE TOOK NO MUSIC COURSES BUT EDITED COMIC & SERIOUS STUDENT PUBLICATIONS.
WHEN BILLIE WAS 11 YEARS OLD SHE WAS RAPED BY A NEIGHBOR AND SENT BACK TO REFORM SCHOOL AS A "WAYWARD GIRL."
SMACK
IN THE 1920'S, THE HARLEM RENAISSANCE LURED TOURISTS TO UPTOWN NEW YORK. PUNDITS RAVED ABOUT TALENTED BLACK PERFORMERS & ARTISTS. SADIE WENT NORTH TO TRY HER LUCK AND BILLIE SOON JOINED HER. BUT IN HARLEM THEY COULD ONLY FIND WORK AS CALL GIRLS.
CLUB
TRAV'LING LIGHT I'LL GET BY
SWING BRO SWING
BILLIE BEGAN HANGING OUT AT SPEAKEASIES, SINGING FOR TIPS.
THE OTHER GIRLS PICKED UP BILLS WITH THEIR THIGHS OR STUFFED BETWEEN THEIR BREASTS— BILLIE INSISTED ON TAKING HER TIPS WITH HER HANDS...
WHO DOES SHE THINK SHE IS — A LADY?!?
© SHARON RUDAHL '12

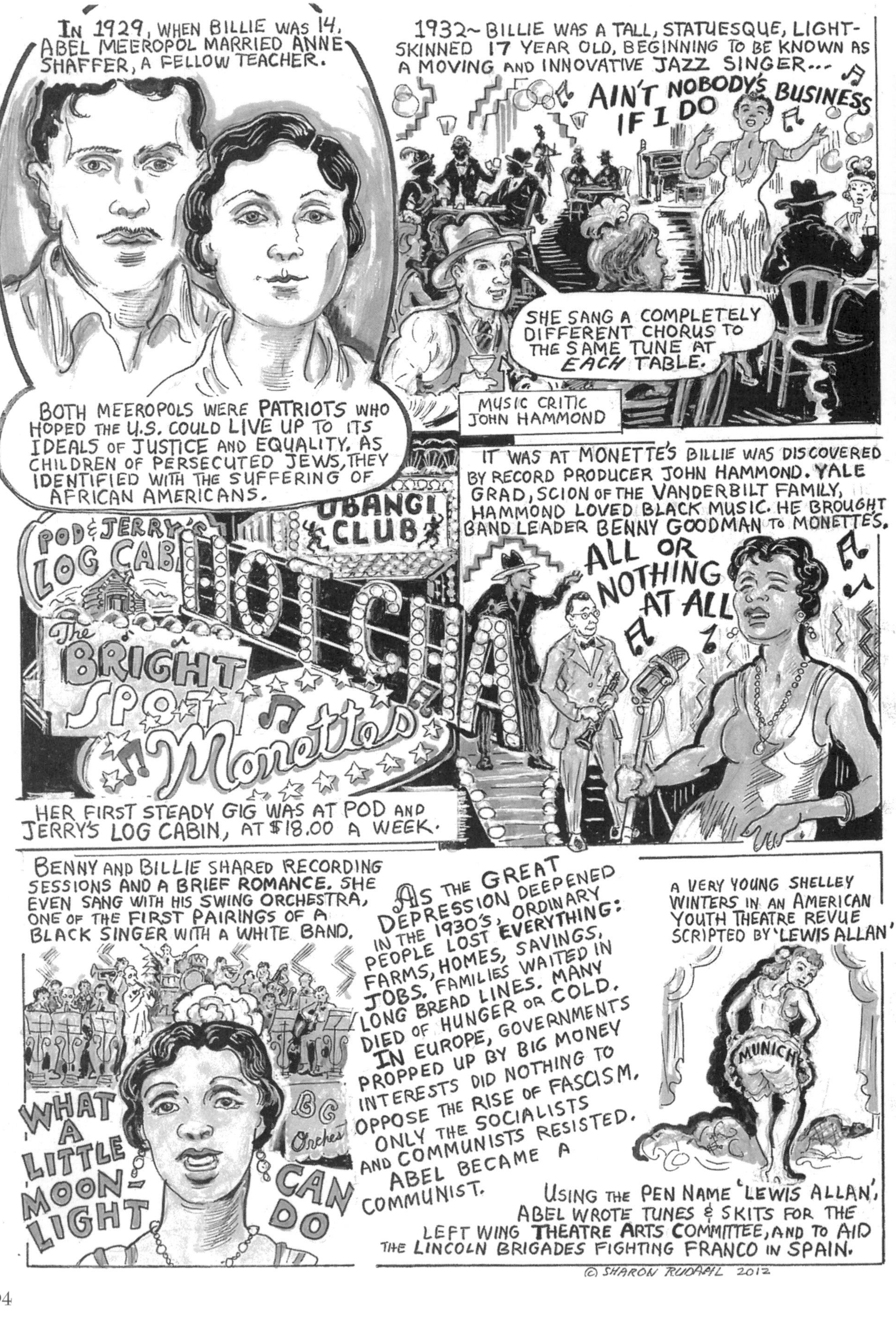
IN 1929, WHEN BILLIE WAS 14, ABEL MEEROPOL MARRIED ANNE SHAFFER, A FELLOW TEACHER.
BOTH MEEROPOLS WERE PATRIOTS WHO HOPED THE U.S. COULD LIVE UP TO ITS IDEALS OF JUSTICE AND EQUALITY. AS CHILDREN OF PERSECUTED JEWS, THEY IDENTIFIED WITH THE SUFFERING OF AFRICAN AMERICANS.
1932~ BILLIE WAS A TALL, STATUESQUE, LIGHT-SKINNED 17 YEAR OLD, BEGINNING TO BE KNOWN AS A MOVING AND INNOVATIVE JAZZ SINGER...
AIN'T NOBODY'S BUSINESS IF I DO
SHE SANG A COMPLETELY DIFFERENT CHORUS TO THE SAME TUNE AT EACH TABLE.
MUSIC CRITIC JOHN HAMMOND
POD & JERRY'S LOG CAB
UBANGI CLUB
HOT CHA
The BRIGHT SPOT
Monette's
HER FIRST STEADY GIG WAS AT POD AND JERRY'S LOG CABIN, AT $18.00 A WEEK.
IT WAS AT MONETTE'S BILLIE WAS DISCOVERED BY RECORD PRODUCER JOHN HAMMOND. YALE GRAD, SCION OF THE VANDERBILT FAMILY, HAMMOND LOVED BLACK MUSIC. HE BROUGHT BAND LEADER BENNY GOODMAN TO MONETTE'S.
ALL OR NOTHING AT ALL
BENNY AND BILLIE SHARED RECORDING SESSIONS AND A BRIEF ROMANCE. SHE EVEN SANG WITH HIS SWING ORCHESTRA, ONE OF THE FIRST PAIRINGS OF A BLACK SINGER WITH A WHITE BAND.
BG Orches
WHAT A LITTLE MOON-LIGHT CAN DO
AS THE GREAT DEPRESSION DEEPENED IN THE 1930'S, ORDINARY PEOPLE LOST EVERYTHING: FARMS, HOMES, SAVINGS, JOBS. FAMILIES WAITED IN LONG BREAD LINES. MANY DIED OF HUNGER OR COLD. IN EUROPE, GOVERNMENTS PROPPED UP BY BIG MONEY INTERESTS DID NOTHING TO OPPOSE THE RISE OF FASCISM. ONLY THE SOCIALISTS AND COMMUNISTS RESISTED. ABEL BECAME A COMMUNIST.
A VERY YOUNG SHELLEY WINTERS IN AN AMERICAN YOUTH THEATRE REVUE SCRIPTED BY 'LEWIS ALLAN'
MUNICH
USING THE PEN NAME 'LEWIS ALLAN', ABEL WROTE TUNES & SKITS FOR THE LEFT WING THEATRE ARTS COMMITTEE, AND TO AID THE LINCOLN BRIGADES FIGHTING FRANCO IN SPAIN.
© SHARON RUDAHL 2012

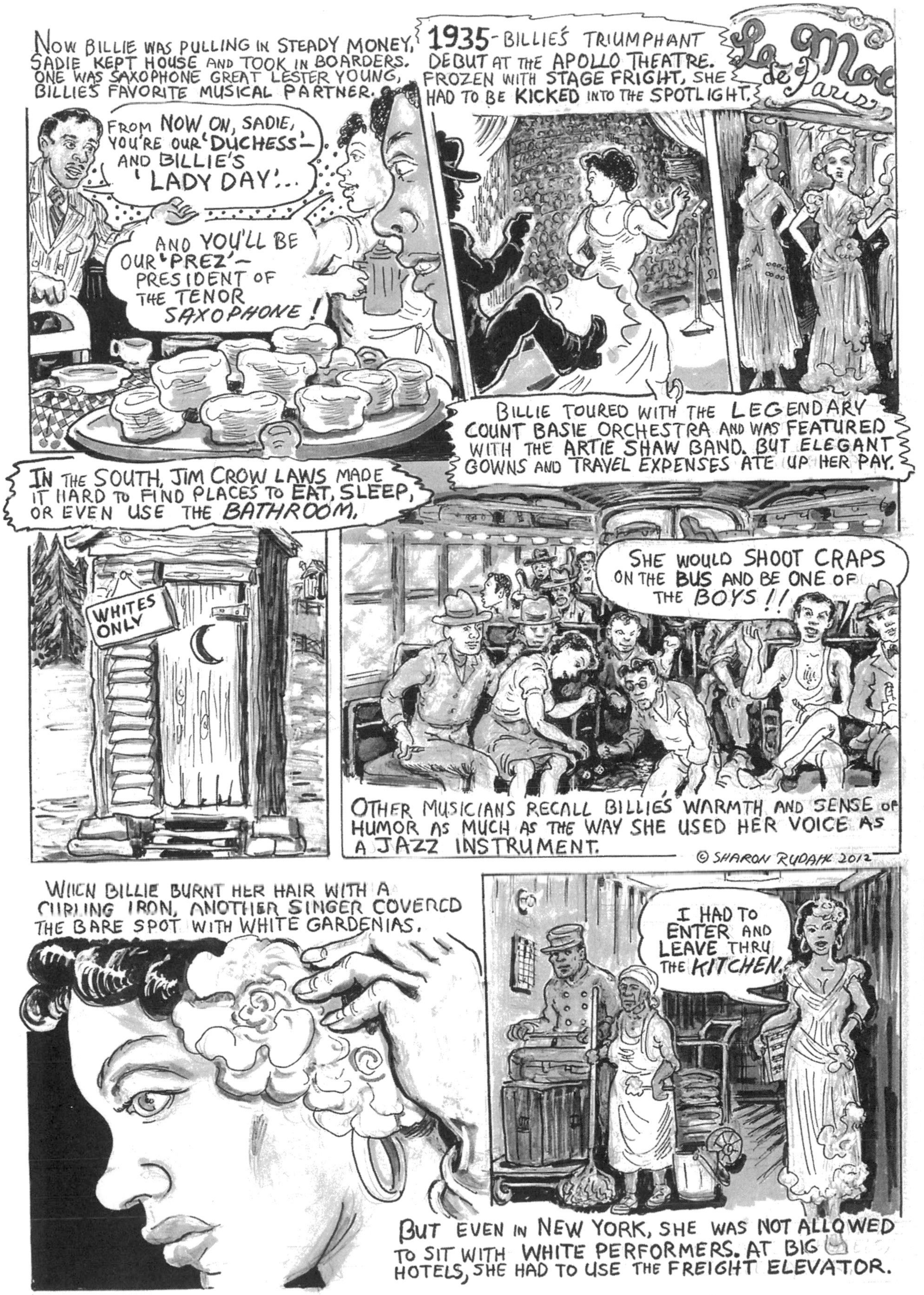

NOW BILLIE WAS PULLING IN STEADY MONEY, SADIE KEPT HOUSE AND TOOK IN BOARDERS. ONE WAS SAXOPHONE GREAT LESTER YOUNG, BILLIE'S FAVORITE MUSICAL PARTNER.
FROM NOW ON, SADIE, YOU'RE OUR 'DUCHESS'— AND BILLIE'S 'LADY DAY'...
AND YOU'LL BE OUR 'PREZ'— PRESIDENT OF THE TENOR SAXOPHONE!
1935- BILLIE'S TRIUMPHANT DEBUT AT THE APOLLO THEATRE. FROZEN WITH STAGE FRIGHT, SHE HAD TO BE KICKED INTO THE SPOTLIGHT.
La Mode de Paris
BILLIE TOURED WITH THE LEGENDARY COUNT BASIE ORCHESTRA AND WAS FEATURED WITH THE ARTIE SHAW BAND. BUT ELEGANT GOWNS AND TRAVEL EXPENSES ATE UP HER PAY.
IN THE SOUTH, JIM CROW LAWS MADE IT HARD TO FIND PLACES TO EAT, SLEEP, OR EVEN USE THE BATHROOM.
WHITES ONLY
SHE WOULD SHOOT CRAPS ON THE BUS AND BE ONE OF THE BOYS!!
OTHER MUSICIANS RECALL BILLIE'S WARMTH AND SENSE OF HUMOR AS MUCH AS THE WAY SHE USED HER VOICE AS A JAZZ INSTRUMENT.
© SHARON RUDAHL 2012
WHEN BILLIE BURNT HER HAIR WITH A CURLING IRON, ANOTHER SINGER COVERED THE BARE SPOT WITH WHITE GARDENIAS.
I HAD TO ENTER AND LEAVE THRU THE KITCHEN.
BUT EVEN IN NEW YORK, SHE WAS NOT ALLOWED TO SIT WITH WHITE PERFORMERS. AT BIG HOTELS, SHE HAD TO USE THE FREIGHT ELEVATOR.

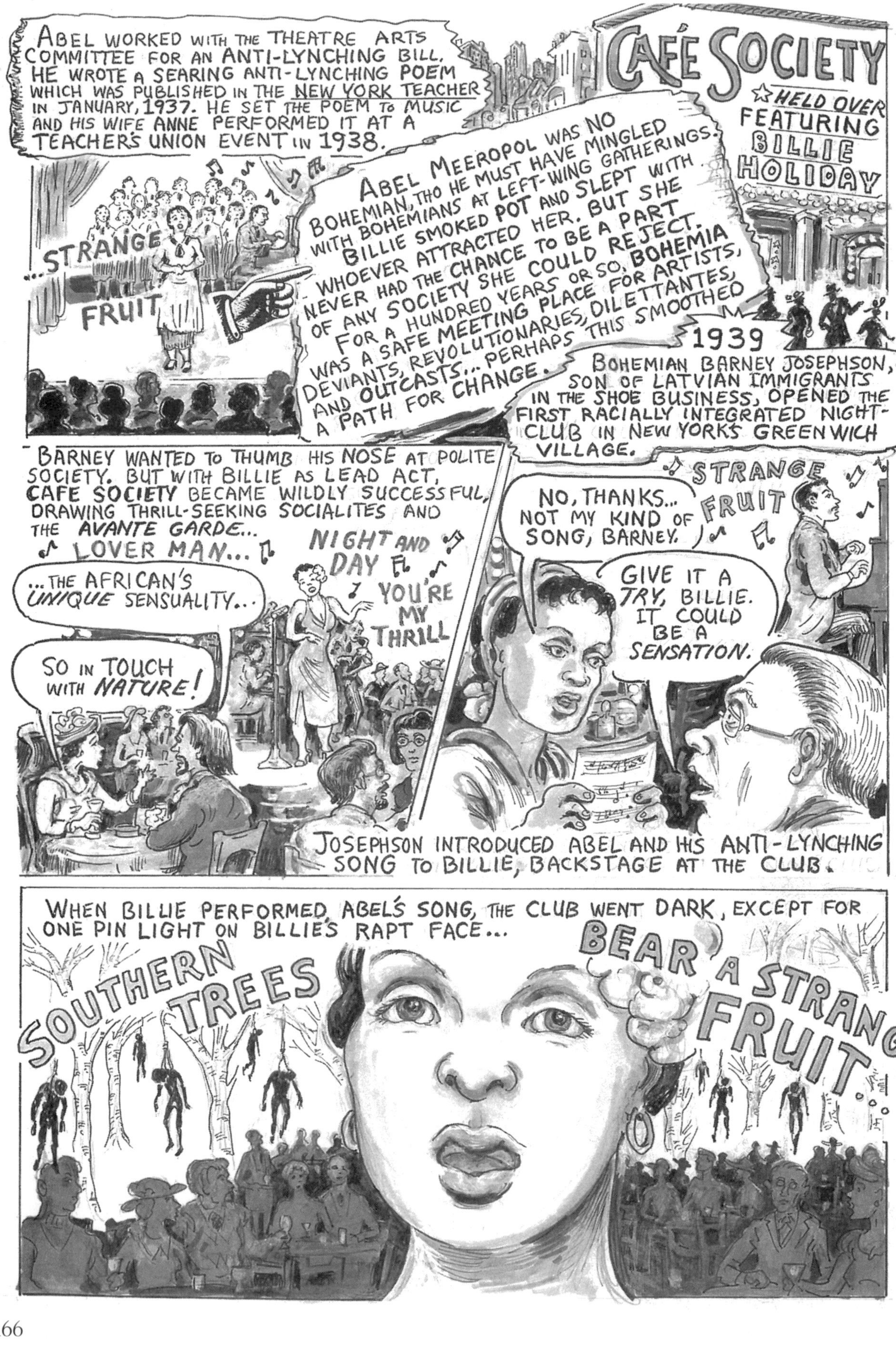
ABEL WORKED WITH THE THEATRE ARTS COMMITTEE FOR AN ANTI-LYNCHING BILL. HE WROTE A SEARING ANTI-LYNCHING POEM WHICH WAS PUBLISHED IN THE NEW YORK TEACHER IN JANUARY, 1937. HE SET THE POEM TO MUSIC AND HIS WIFE ANNE PERFORMED IT AT A TEACHER'S UNION EVENT IN 1938.
...STRANGE FRUIT
ABEL MEEROPOL WAS NO BOHEMIAN, THO HE MUST HAVE MINGLED WITH BOHEMIANS AT LEFT-WING GATHERINGS. BILLIE SMOKED POT AND SLEPT WITH WHOEVER ATTRACTED HER. BUT SHE NEVER HAD THE CHANCE TO BE A PART OF ANY SOCIETY SHE COULD REJECT. FOR A HUNDRED YEARS OR SO, BOHEMIA WAS A SAFE MEETING PLACE FOR ARTISTS, DEVIANTS, REVOLUTIONARIES, DILETTANTES, AND OUTCASTS... PERHAPS THIS SMOOTHED A PATH FOR CHANGE.
CAFÉ SOCIETY
HELD OVER
FEATURING
BILLIE HOLIDAY
1939
BOHEMIAN BARNEY JOSEPHSON, SON OF LATVIAN IMMIGRANTS IN THE SHOE BUSINESS, OPENED THE FIRST RACIALLY INTEGRATED NIGHT-CLUB IN NEW YORK'S GREENWICH VILLAGE.
BARNEY WANTED TO THUMB HIS NOSE AT POLITE SOCIETY. BUT WITH BILLIE AS LEAD ACT, CAFE SOCIETY BECAME WILDLY SUCCESSFUL, DRAWING THRILL-SEEKING SOCIALITES AND THE AVANTE GARDE...
LOVER MAN...
NIGHT AND DAY
YOU'RE MY THRILL
...THE AFRICAN'S UNIQUE SENSUALITY...
SO IN TOUCH WITH NATURE!
STRANGE FRUIT
NO, THANKS... NOT MY KIND OF SONG, BARNEY.
GIVE IT A TRY, BILLIE. IT COULD BE A SENSATION.
JOSEPHSON INTRODUCED ABEL AND HIS ANTI-LYNCHING SONG TO BILLIE, BACKSTAGE AT THE CLUB.
WHEN BILLIE PERFORMED ABEL'S SONG, THE CLUB WENT DARK, EXCEPT FOR ONE PIN LIGHT ON BILLIE'S RAPT FACE...
SOUTHERN TREES
BEAR A STRANGE FRUIT...

AS BILLIE BEGAN TO SING, THE AUDIENCE SAW STATELY SOUTHERN MANSIONS SURROUNDED BY TALL TREES...

BUT THESE TREE TRUNKS WERE SLICK WITH BLOOD, BLOOD TRICKLING DOWN INTO THE EARTH...

FROM THE BRANCHES HUNG HIDEOUS SHAPES - THE TWISTED BODIES OF LYNCHED BLACK MEN...

EYES BULGING, MOUTHS DISTORTED IN THE AGONY OF DEATH...

CAW CAW CAW CAW CAW

PECKED BY THE CROWS, PARCHED BY THE SUN, ROTTED BY THE RAINS...

CAW CAW CAW CAW CAW CAW CAW CAW CAW CAW

"HERE IS A STRANGE...AND BITTER...CROP!!"

WHEN BILLIE FINISHED THE CLUB WAS SILENT. IT SEEMED THE SONG HAD FAILED. THEN SHE HEARD GASPS, SOBS, AND WILD APPLAUSE.

CLAP CLAP CLAP CLAP CLAP CLAP CLAP CLAP CLAP CLAP CLAP CLAP CLAP

© SHARON RUDAHL 2017

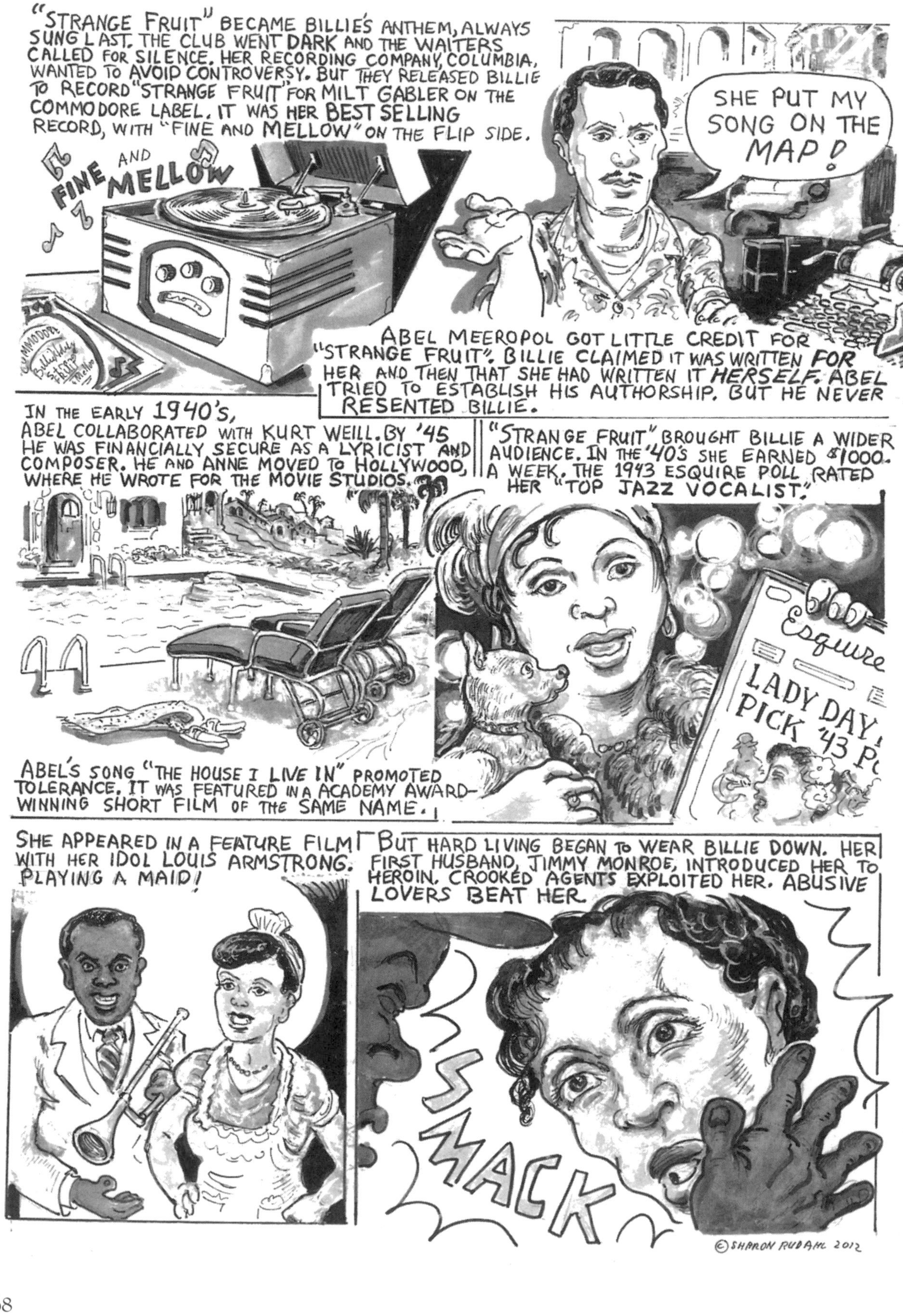
"STRANGE FRUIT" BECAME BILLIE'S ANTHEM, ALWAYS SUNG LAST. THE CLUB WENT DARK AND THE WAITERS CALLED FOR SILENCE. HER RECORDING COMPANY, COLUMBIA, WANTED TO AVOID CONTROVERSY. BUT THEY RELEASED BILLIE TO RECORD "STRANGE FRUIT" FOR MILT GABLER ON THE COMMODORE LABEL. IT WAS HER BEST SELLING RECORD, WITH "FINE AND MELLOW" ON THE FLIP SIDE.
FINE AND MELLOW
SHE PUT MY SONG ON THE MAP!
ABEL MEEROPOL GOT LITTLE CREDIT FOR "STRANGE FRUIT". BILLIE CLAIMED IT WAS WRITTEN FOR HER AND THEN THAT SHE HAD WRITTEN IT HERSELF. ABEL TRIED TO ESTABLISH HIS AUTHORSHIP. BUT HE NEVER RESENTED BILLIE.
IN THE EARLY 1940's, ABEL COLLABORATED WITH KURT WEILL. BY '45 HE WAS FINANCIALLY SECURE AS A LYRICIST AND COMPOSER. HE AND ANNE MOVED TO HOLLYWOOD, WHERE HE WROTE FOR THE MOVIE STUDIOS.
ABEL'S SONG "THE HOUSE I LIVE IN" PROMOTED TOLERANCE. IT WAS FEATURED IN A ACADEMY AWARD-WINNING SHORT FILM OF THE SAME NAME.
"STRANGE FRUIT" BROUGHT BILLIE A WIDER AUDIENCE. IN THE '40's SHE EARNED $1000. A WEEK. THE 1943 ESQUIRE POLL RATED HER "TOP JAZZ VOCALIST."
Esquire
LADY DAY PICK '43
SHE APPEARED IN A FEATURE FILM WITH HER IDOL LOUIS ARMSTRONG. PLAYING A MAID!
BUT HARD LIVING BEGAN TO WEAR BILLIE DOWN. HER FIRST HUSBAND, JIMMY MONROE, INTRODUCED HER TO HEROIN. CROOKED AGENTS EXPLOITED HER. ABUSIVE LOVERS BEAT HER.
SMACK
©SHARON RUDAHL 2012

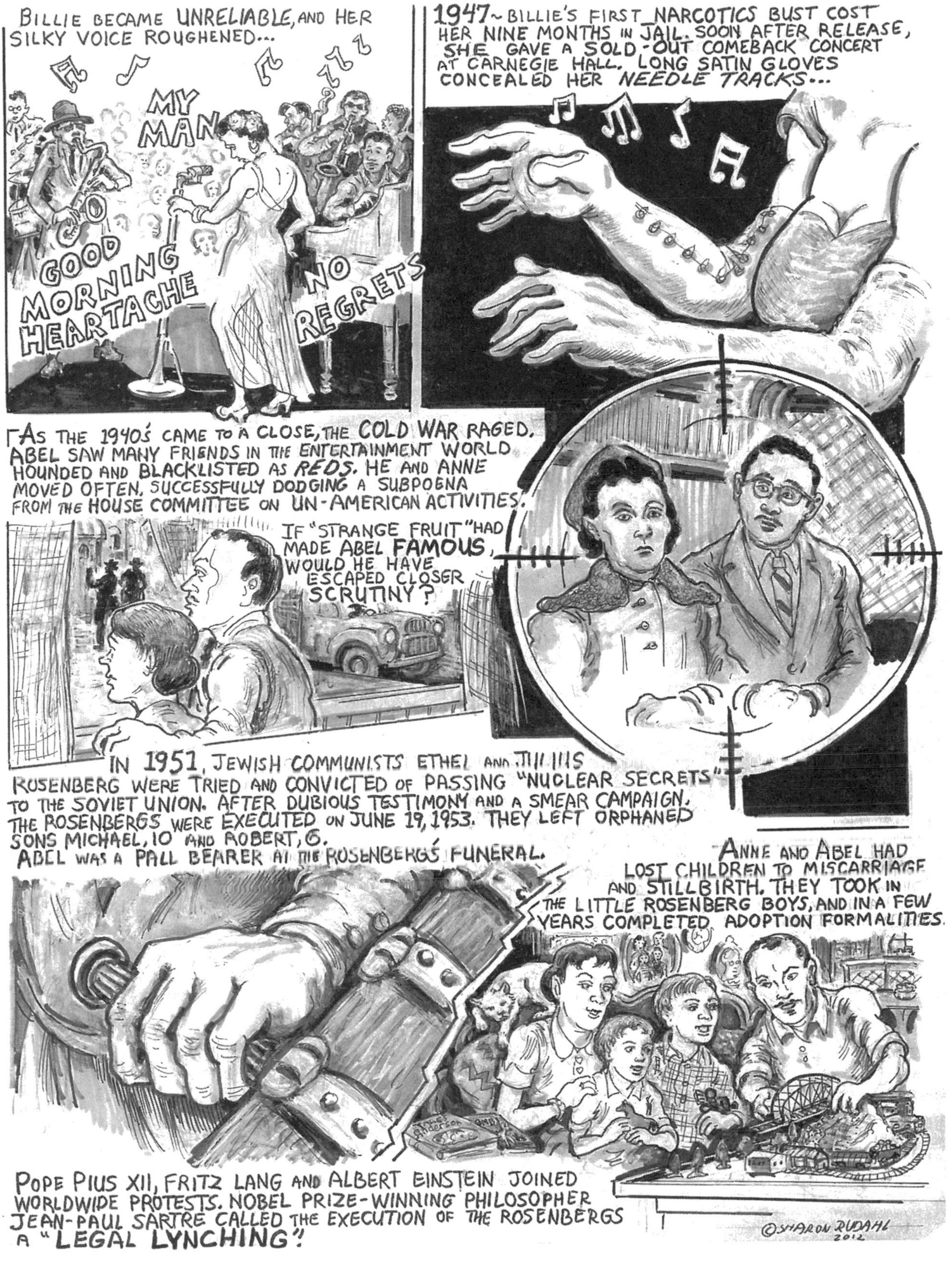
BILLIE BECAME UNRELIABLE, AND HER SILKY VOICE ROUGHENED...
MY MAN
GOOD MORNING HEARTACHE
NO REGRETS
1947 ~ BILLIE'S FIRST NARCOTICS BUST COST HER NINE MONTHS IN JAIL. SOON AFTER RELEASE, SHE GAVE A SOLD-OUT COMEBACK CONCERT AT CARNEGIE HALL. LONG SATIN GLOVES CONCEALED HER NEEDLE TRACKS...
AS THE 1940'S CAME TO A CLOSE, THE COLD WAR RAGED. ABEL SAW MANY FRIENDS IN THE ENTERTAINMENT WORLD HOUNDED AND BLACKLISTED AS REDS. HE AND ANNE MOVED OFTEN, SUCCESSFULLY DODGING A SUBPOENA FROM THE HOUSE COMMITTEE ON UN-AMERICAN ACTIVITIES.
IF "STRANGE FRUIT" HAD MADE ABEL FAMOUS, WOULD HE HAVE ESCAPED CLOSER SCRUTINY?
IN 1951, JEWISH COMMUNISTS ETHEL AND JULIUS ROSENBERG WERE TRIED AND CONVICTED OF PASSING "NUCLEAR SECRETS" TO THE SOVIET UNION. AFTER DUBIOUS TESTIMONY AND A SMEAR CAMPAIGN, THE ROSENBERGS WERE EXECUTED ON JUNE 19, 1953. THEY LEFT ORPHANED SONS MICHAEL, 10 AND ROBERT, 6.
ABEL WAS A PALL BEARER AT THE ROSENBERGS' FUNERAL.
ANNE AND ABEL HAD LOST CHILDREN TO MISCARRIAGE AND STILLBIRTH. THEY TOOK IN THE LITTLE ROSENBERG BOYS, AND IN A FEW YEARS COMPLETED ADOPTION FORMALITIES.
POPE PIUS XII, FRITZ LANG AND ALBERT EINSTEIN JOINED WORLDWIDE PROTESTS. NOBEL PRIZE-WINNING PHILOSOPHER JEAN-PAUL SARTRE CALLED THE EXECUTION OF THE ROSENBERGS A "LEGAL LYNCHING"!
©SHARON RUDAHL 2012

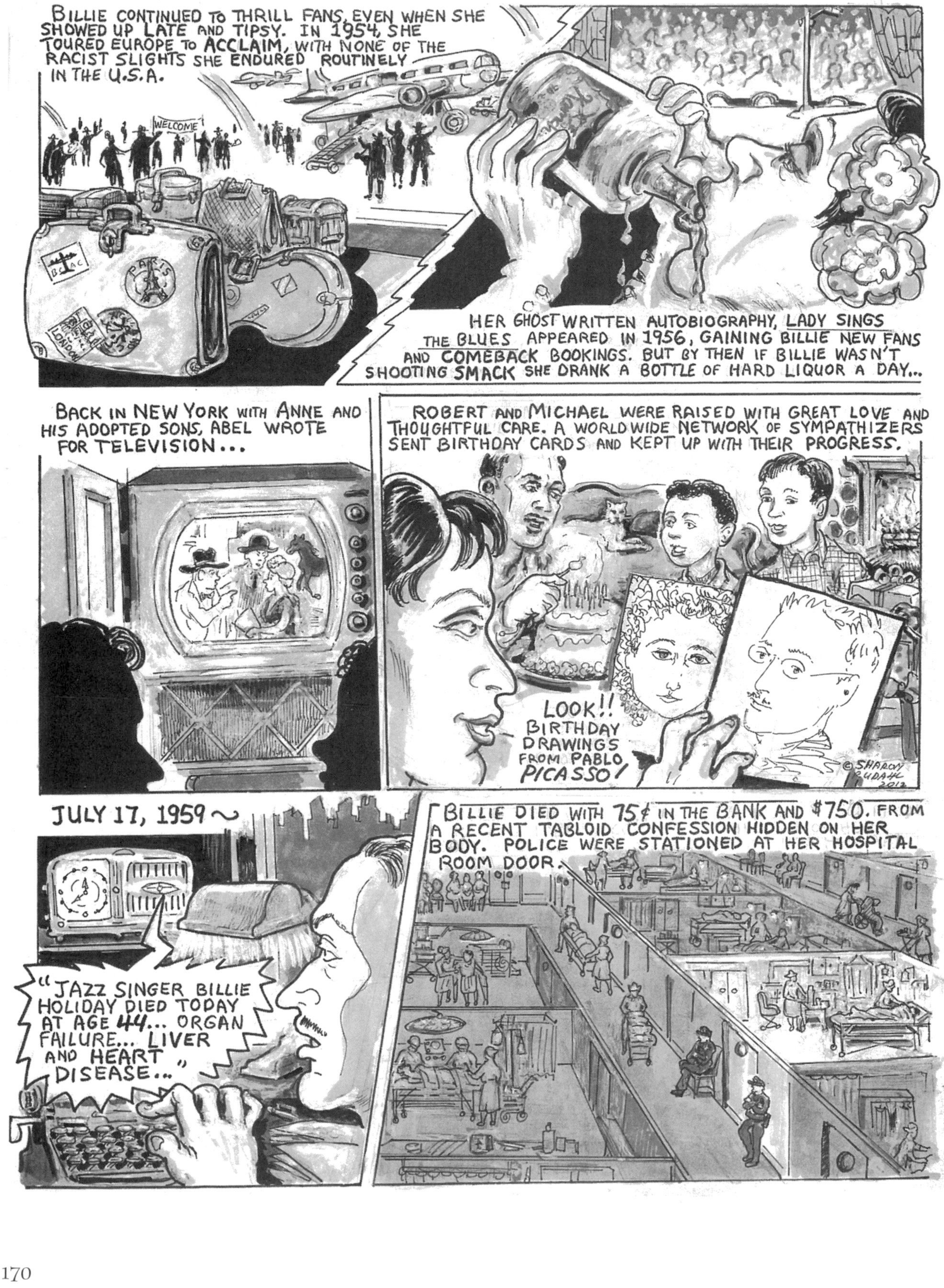
BILLIE CONTINUED TO THRILL FANS, EVEN WHEN SHE SHOWED UP LATE AND TIPSY. IN 1954, SHE TOURED EUROPE TO ACCLAIM, WITH NONE OF THE RACIST SLIGHTS SHE ENDURED ROUTINELY IN THE U.S.A.
WELCOME
PARIS
LONDON
HER GHOSTWRITTEN AUTOBIOGRAPHY, LADY SINGS THE BLUES APPEARED IN 1956, GAINING BILLIE NEW FANS AND COMEBACK BOOKINGS. BUT BY THEN IF BILLIE WASN'T SHOOTING SMACK SHE DRANK A BOTTLE OF HARD LIQUOR A DAY...
BACK IN NEW YORK WITH ANNE AND HIS ADOPTED SONS, ABEL WROTE FOR TELEVISION...
ROBERT AND MICHAEL WERE RAISED WITH GREAT LOVE AND THOUGHTFUL CARE. A WORLDWIDE NETWORK OF SYMPATHIZERS SENT BIRTHDAY CARDS AND KEPT UP WITH THEIR PROGRESS.
LOOK!! BIRTHDAY DRAWINGS FROM PABLO PICASSO!
© SHARON RUDAHL 2012
JULY 17, 1959 ~
"JAZZ SINGER BILLIE HOLIDAY DIED TODAY AT AGE 44... ORGAN FAILURE... LIVER AND HEART DISEASE..."
BILLIE DIED WITH 75¢ IN THE BANK AND $750. FROM A RECENT TABLOID CONFESSION HIDDEN ON HER BODY. POLICE WERE STATIONED AT HER HOSPITAL ROOM DOOR.

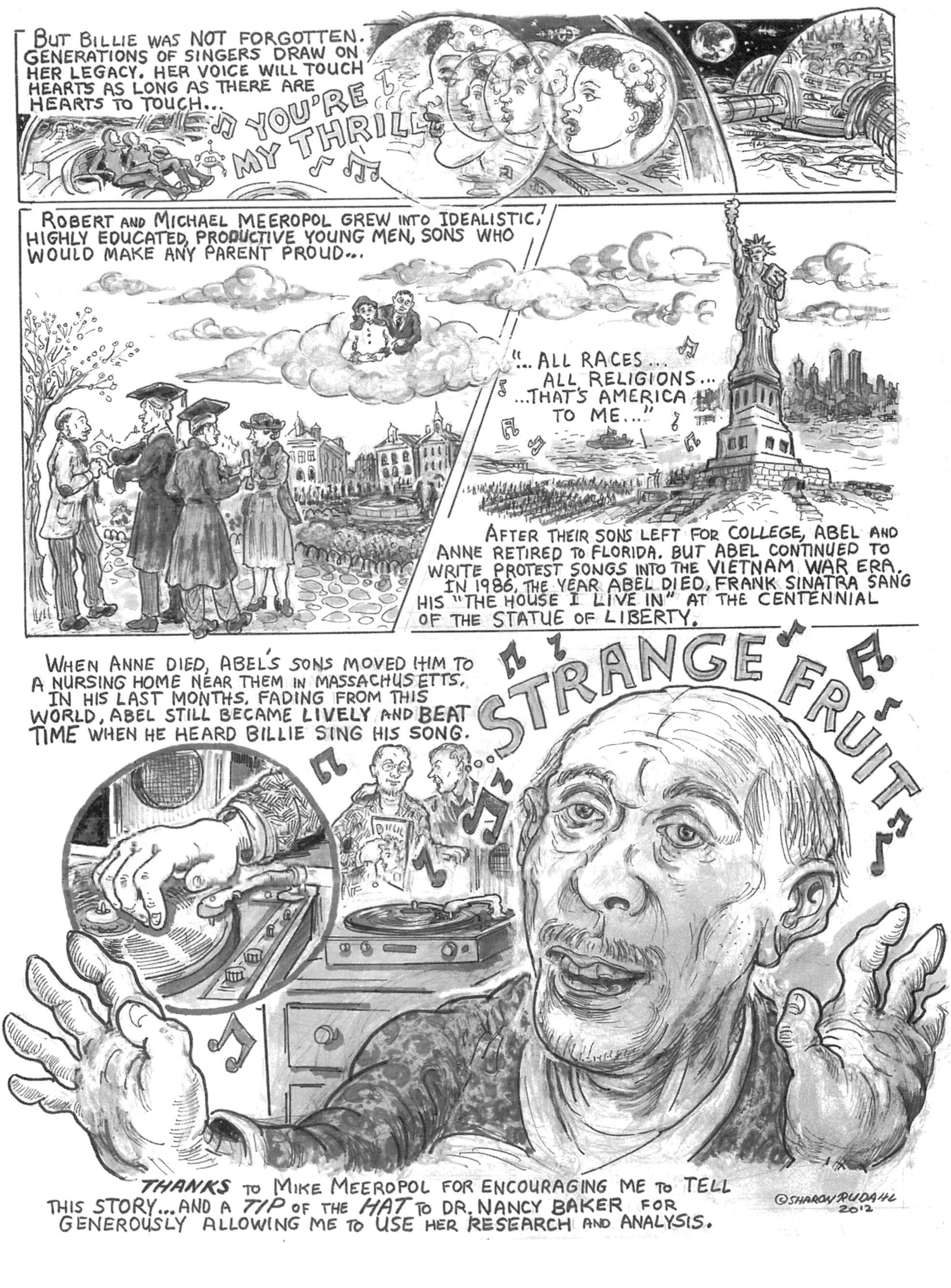
BUT BILLIE WAS NOT FORGOTTEN. GENERATIONS OF SINGERS DRAW ON HER LEGACY. HER VOICE WILL TOUCH HEARTS AS LONG AS THERE ARE HEARTS TO TOUCH...
YOU'RE MY THRILL
ROBERT AND MICHAEL MEEROPOL GREW INTO IDEALISTIC, HIGHLY EDUCATED, PRODUCTIVE YOUNG MEN, SONS WHO WOULD MAKE ANY PARENT PROUD...
"...ALL RACES... ALL RELIGIONS... ...THAT'S AMERICA TO ME..."
AFTER THEIR SONS LEFT FOR COLLEGE, ABEL AND ANNE RETIRED TO FLORIDA. BUT ABEL CONTINUED TO WRITE PROTEST SONGS INTO THE VIETNAM WAR ERA. IN 1986, THE YEAR ABEL DIED, FRANK SINATRA SANG HIS "THE HOUSE I LIVE IN" AT THE CENTENNIAL OF THE STATUE OF LIBERTY.
WHEN ANNE DIED, ABEL'S SONS MOVED HIM TO A NURSING HOME NEAR THEM IN MASSACHUSETTS. IN HIS LAST MONTHS, FADING FROM THIS WORLD, ABEL STILL BECAME LIVELY AND BEAT TIME WHEN HE HEARD BILLIE SING HIS SONG.
...STRANGE FRUIT...
THANKS TO MIKE MEEROPOL FOR ENCOURAGING ME TO TELL THIS STORY... AND A TIP OF THE HAT TO DR. NANCY BAKER FOR GENEROUSLY ALLOWING ME TO USE HER RESEARCH AND ANALYSIS.
©SHARON RUDAHL 2012

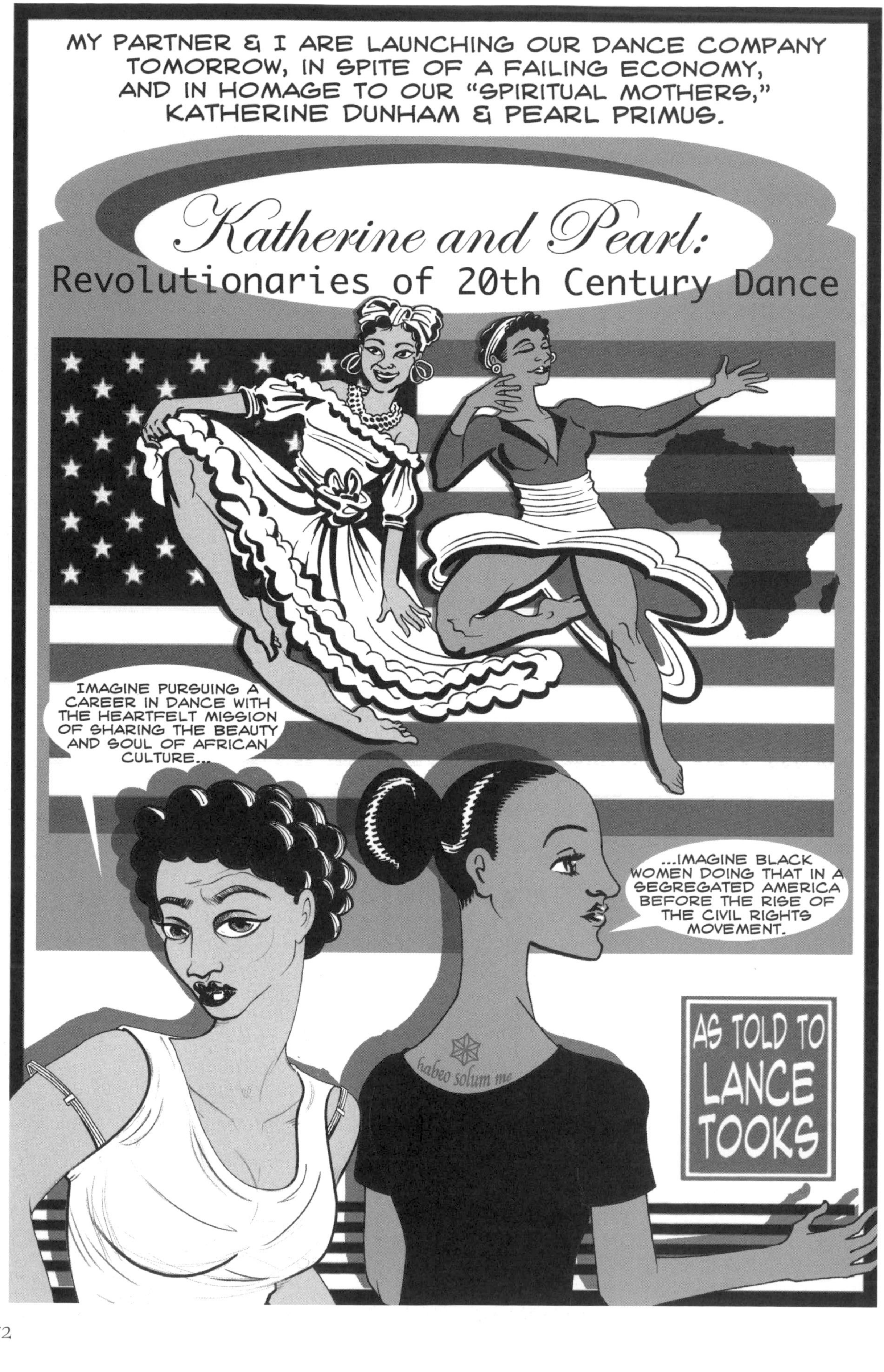
MY PARTNER & I ARE LAUNCHING OUR DANCE COMPANY TOMORROW, IN SPITE OF A FAILING ECONOMY, AND IN HOMAGE TO OUR "SPIRITUAL MOTHERS," KATHERINE DUNHAM & PEARL PRIMUS.
Katherine and Pearl:
Revolutionaries of 20th Century Dance
IMAGINE PURSUING A CAREER IN DANCE WITH THE HEARTFELT MISSION OF SHARING THE BEAUTY AND SOUL OF AFRICAN CULTURE...
...IMAGINE BLACK WOMEN DOING THAT IN A SEGREGATED AMERICA BEFORE THE RISE OF THE CIVIL RIGHTS MOVEMENT.
habeo solum me
AS TOLD TO LANCE TOOKS

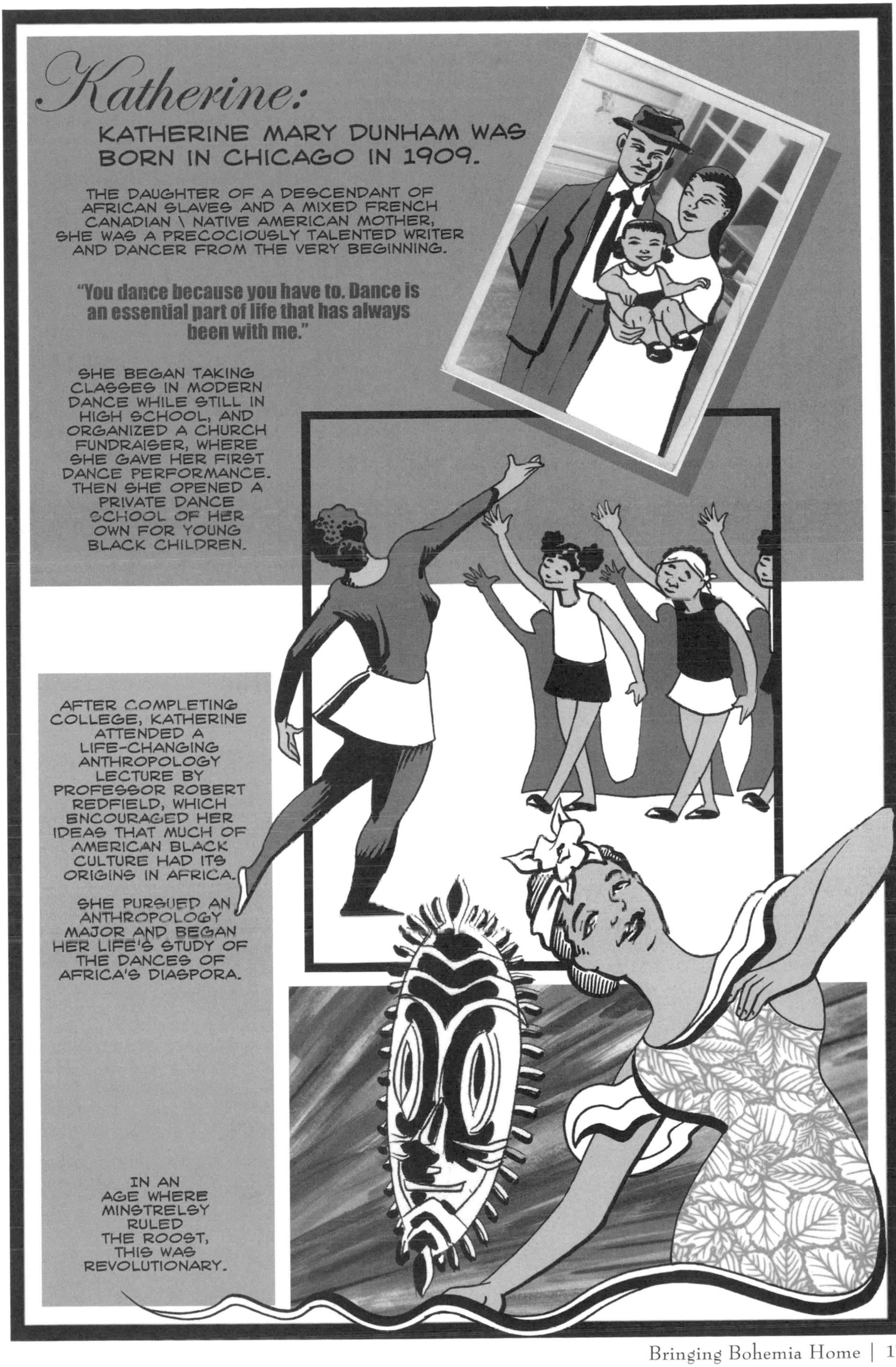
Katherine:
KATHERINE MARY DUNHAM WAS BORN IN CHICAGO IN 1909.
THE DAUGHTER OF A DESCENDANT OF AFRICAN SLAVES AND A MIXED FRENCH CANADIAN \ NATIVE AMERICAN MOTHER, SHE WAS A PRECOCIOUSLY TALENTED WRITER AND DANCER FROM THE VERY BEGINNING.
"You dance because you have to. Dance is an essential part of life that has always been with me."
SHE BEGAN TAKING CLASSES IN MODERN DANCE WHILE STILL IN HIGH SCHOOL, AND ORGANIZED A CHURCH FUNDRAISER, WHERE SHE GAVE HER FIRST DANCE PERFORMANCE. THEN SHE OPENED A PRIVATE DANCE SCHOOL OF HER OWN FOR YOUNG BLACK CHILDREN.
AFTER COMPLETING COLLEGE, KATHERINE ATTENDED A LIFE-CHANGING ANTHROPOLOGY LECTURE BY PROFESSOR ROBERT REDFIELD, WHICH ENCOURAGED HER IDEAS THAT MUCH OF AMERICAN BLACK CULTURE HAD ITS ORIGINS IN AFRICA.
SHE PURSUED AN ANTHROPOLOGY MAJOR AND BEGAN HER LIFE'S STUDY OF THE DANCES OF AFRICA'S DIASPORA.
IN AN AGE WHERE MINSTRELSY RULED THE ROOST, THIS WAS REVOLUTIONARY.

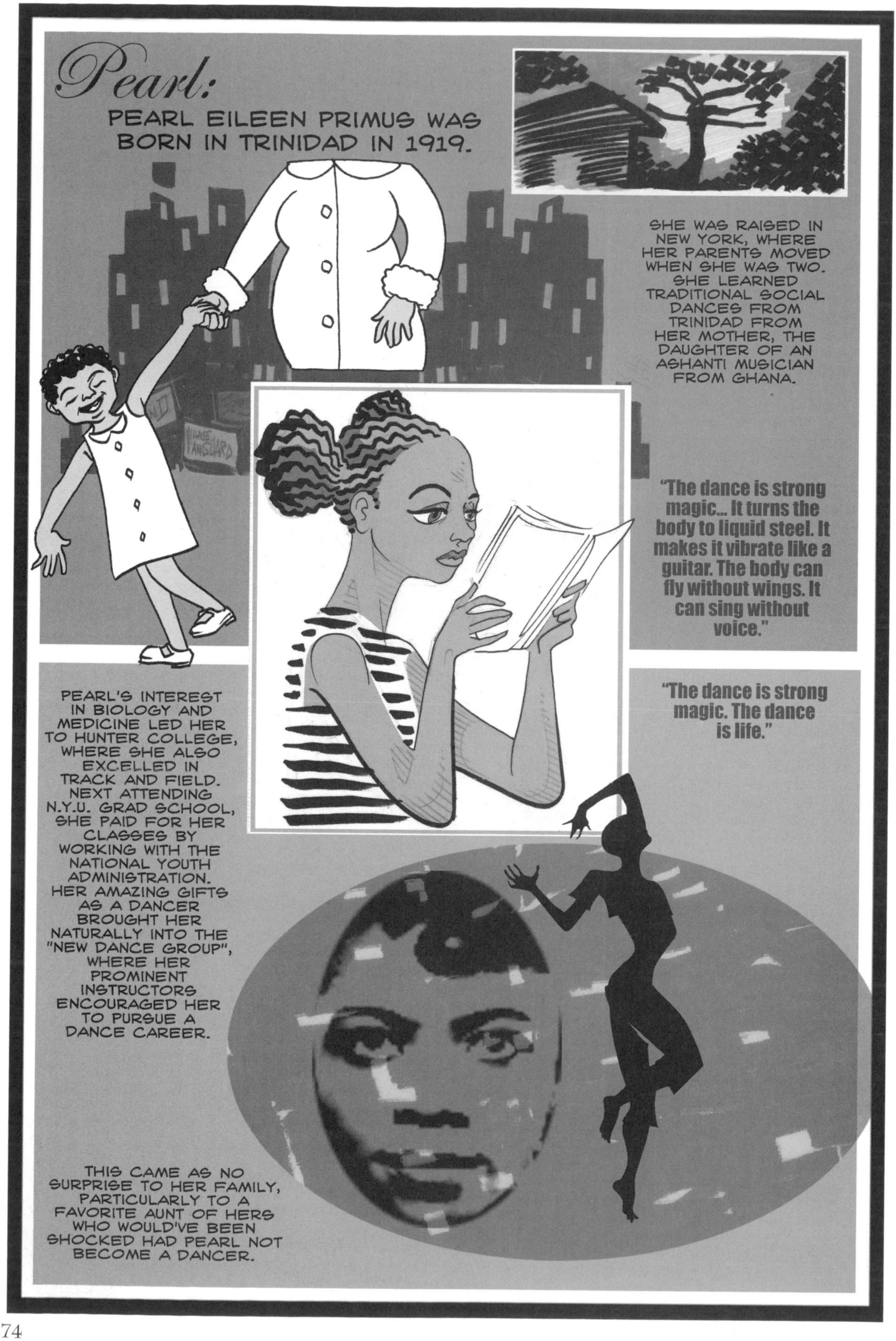
Pearl:
PEARL EILEEN PRIMUS WAS BORN IN TRINIDAD IN 1919.
SHE WAS RAISED IN NEW YORK, WHERE HER PARENTS MOVED WHEN SHE WAS TWO. SHE LEARNED TRADITIONAL SOCIAL DANCES FROM TRINIDAD FROM HER MOTHER, THE DAUGHTER OF AN ASHANTI MUSICIAN FROM GHANA.
"The dance is strong magic... It turns the body to liquid steel. It makes it vibrate like a guitar. The body can fly without wings. It can sing without voice."
PEARL'S INTEREST IN BIOLOGY AND MEDICINE LED HER TO HUNTER COLLEGE, WHERE SHE ALSO EXCELLED IN TRACK AND FIELD. NEXT ATTENDING N.Y.U. GRAD SCHOOL, SHE PAID FOR HER CLASSES BY WORKING WITH THE NATIONAL YOUTH ADMINISTRATION. HER AMAZING GIFTS AS A DANCER BROUGHT HER NATURALLY INTO THE "NEW DANCE GROUP", WHERE HER PROMINENT INSTRUCTORS ENCOURAGED HER TO PURSUE A DANCE CAREER.
"The dance is strong magic. The dance is life."
THIS CAME AS NO SURPRISE TO HER FAMILY, PARTICULARLY TO A FAVORITE AUNT OF HERS WHO WOULD'VE BEEN SHOCKED HAD PEARL NOT BECOME A DANCER.

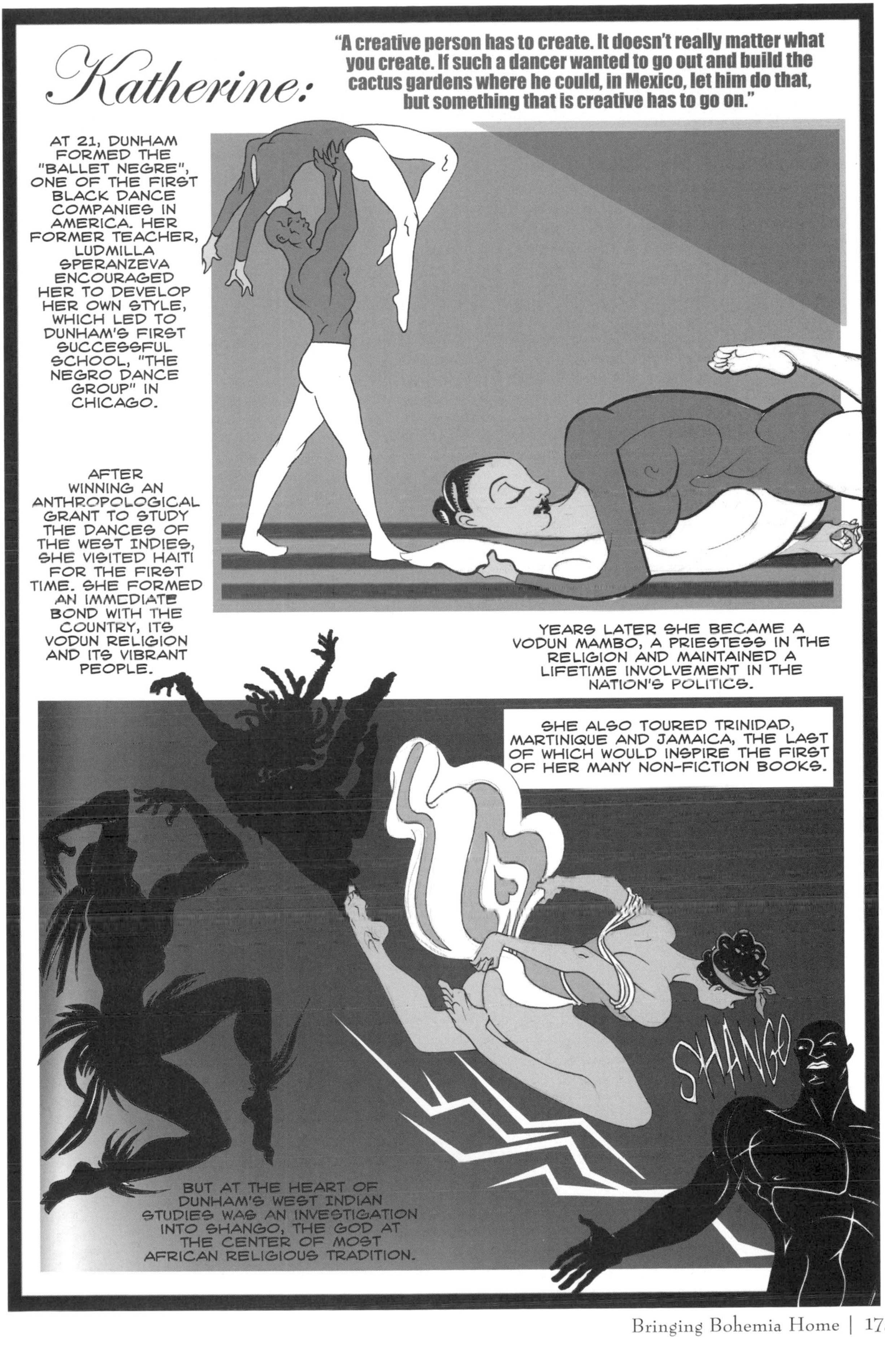
Katherine:
"A creative person has to create. It doesn't really matter what you create. If such a dancer wanted to go out and build the cactus gardens where he could, in Mexico, let him do that, but something that is creative has to go on."
AT 21, DUNHAM FORMED THE "BALLET NEGRE", ONE OF THE FIRST BLACK DANCE COMPANIES IN AMERICA. HER FORMER TEACHER, LUDMILLA SPERANZEVA ENCOURAGED HER TO DEVELOP HER OWN STYLE, WHICH LED TO DUNHAM'S FIRST SUCCESSFUL SCHOOL, "THE NEGRO DANCE GROUP" IN CHICAGO.
AFTER WINNING AN ANTHROPOLOGICAL GRANT TO STUDY THE DANCES OF THE WEST INDIES, SHE VISITED HAITI FOR THE FIRST TIME. SHE FORMED AN IMMEDIATE BOND WITH THE COUNTRY, ITS VODUN RELIGION AND ITS VIBRANT PEOPLE.
YEARS LATER SHE BECAME A VODUN MAMBO, A PRIESTESS IN THE RELIGION AND MAINTAINED A LIFETIME INVOLVEMENT IN THE NATION'S POLITICS.
SHE ALSO TOURED TRINIDAD, MARTINIQUE AND JAMAICA, THE LAST OF WHICH WOULD INSPIRE THE FIRST OF HER MANY NON-FICTION BOOKS.
SHANGO
BUT AT THE HEART OF DUNHAM'S WEST INDIAN STUDIES WAS AN INVESTIGATION INTO SHANGO, THE GOD AT THE CENTER OF MOST AFRICAN RELIGIOUS TRADITION.

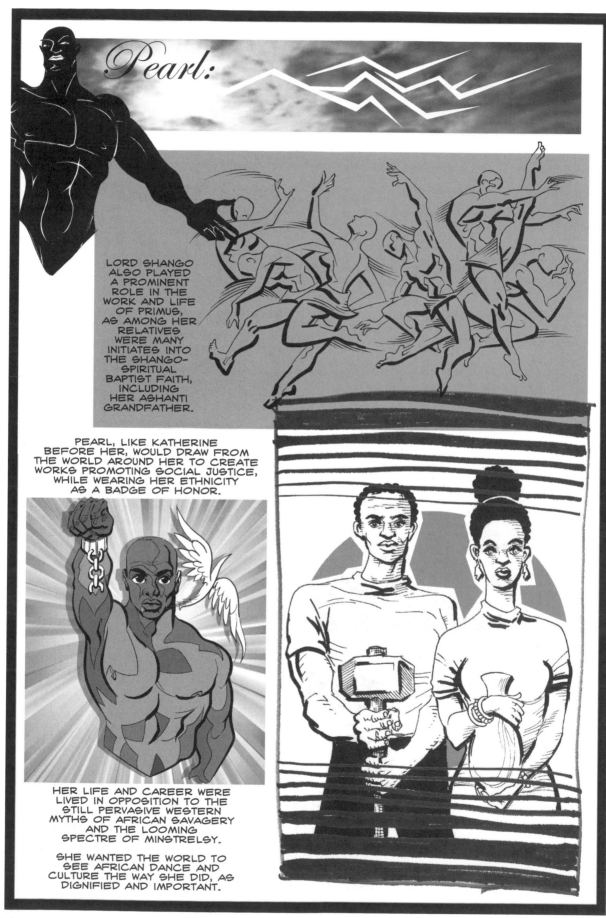

Pearl:

LORD SHANGO ALSO PLAYED A PROMINENT ROLE IN THE WORK AND LIFE OF PRIMUS, AS AMONG HER RELATIVES WERE MANY INITIATES INTO THE SHANGO-SPIRITUAL BAPTIST FAITH, INCLUDING HER ASHANTI GRANDFATHER.

PEARL, LIKE KATHERINE BEFORE HER, WOULD DRAW FROM THE WORLD AROUND HER TO CREATE WORKS PROMOTING SOCIAL JUSTICE, WHILE WEARING HER ETHNICITY AS A BADGE OF HONOR.

HER LIFE AND CAREER WERE LIVED IN OPPOSITION TO THE STILL PERVASIVE WESTERN MYTHS OF AFRICAN SAVAGERY AND THE LOOMING SPECTRE OF MINSTRELSY.

SHE WANTED THE WORLD TO SEE AFRICAN DANCE AND CULTURE THE WAY SHE DID, AS DIGNIFIED AND IMPORTANT.

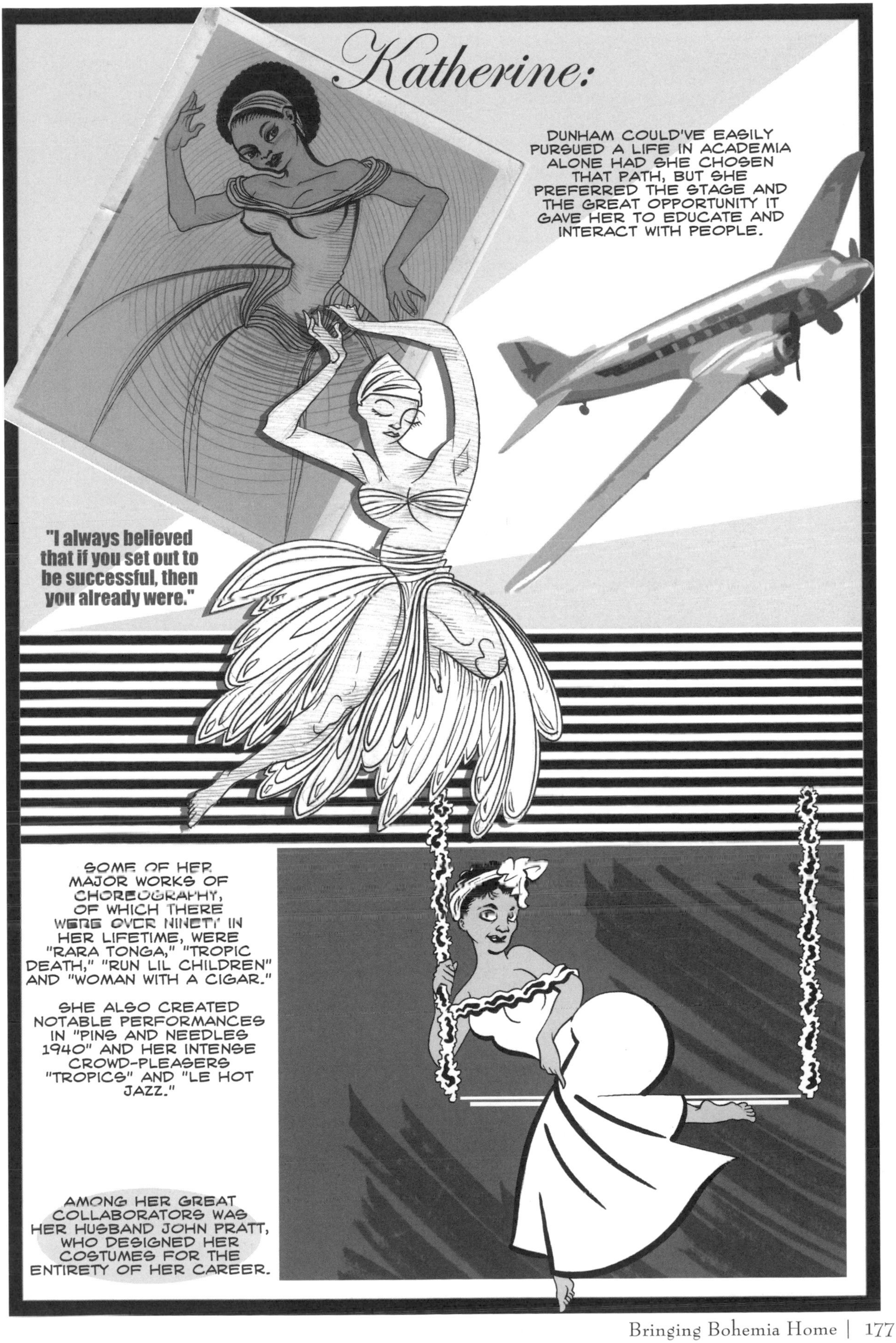
Katherine:
DUNHAM COULD'VE EASILY PURSUED A LIFE IN ACADEMIA ALONE HAD SHE CHOSEN THAT PATH, BUT SHE PREFERRED THE STAGE AND THE GREAT OPPORTUNITY IT GAVE HER TO EDUCATE AND INTERACT WITH PEOPLE.
"I always believed that if you set out to be successful, then you already were."
SOME OF HER MAJOR WORKS OF CHOREOGRAPHY, OF WHICH THERE WERE OVER NINETY IN HER LIFETIME, WERE "RARA TONGA," "TROPIC DEATH," "RUN LIL CHILDREN" AND "WOMAN WITH A CIGAR."
SHE ALSO CREATED NOTABLE PERFORMANCES IN "PINS AND NEEDLES 1940" AND HER INTENSE CROWD-PLEASERS "TROPICS" AND "LE HOT JAZZ."
AMONG HER GREAT COLLABORATORS WAS HER HUSBAND JOHN PRATT, WHO DESIGNED HER COSTUMES FOR THE ENTIRETY OF HER CAREER.

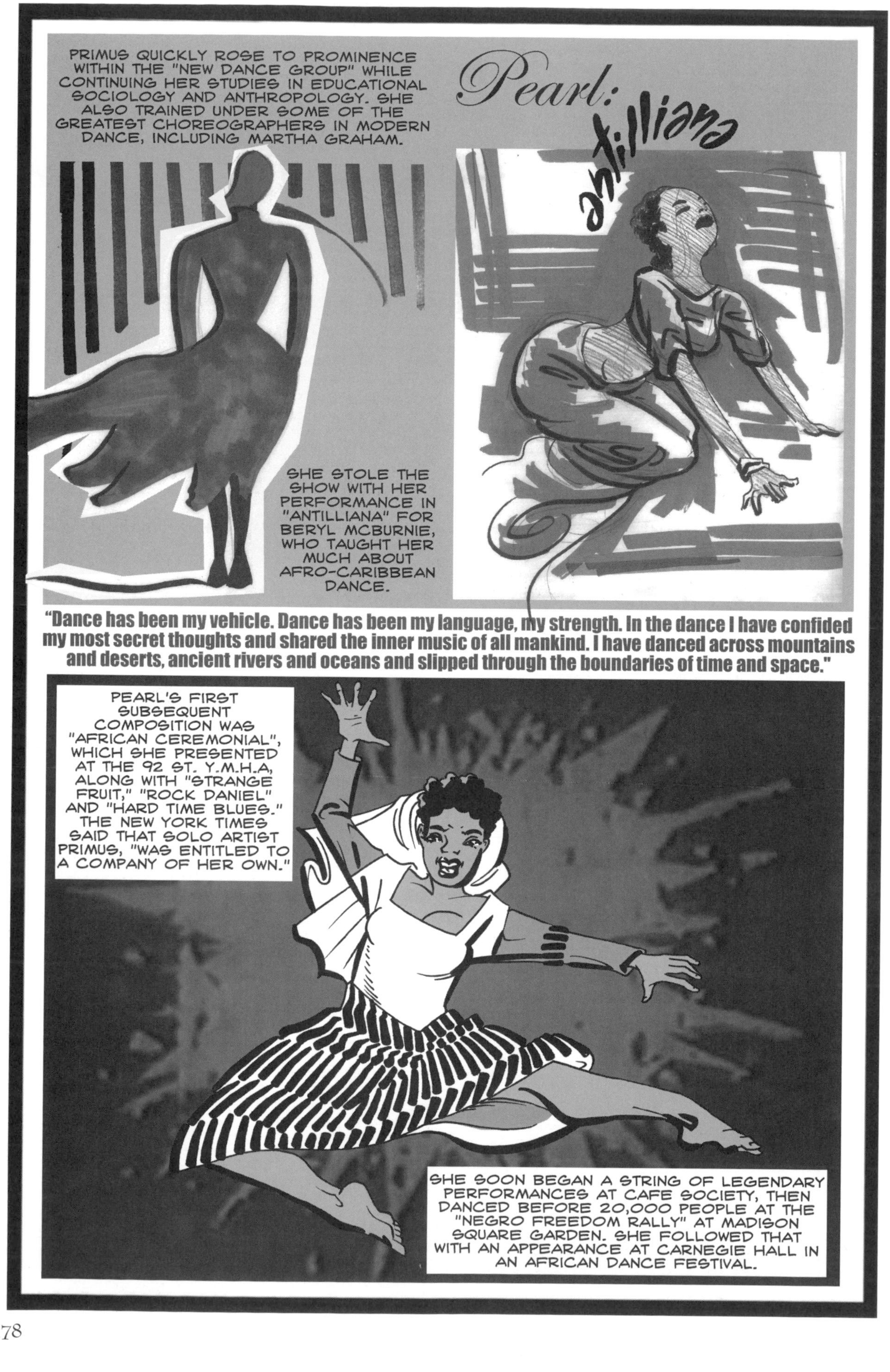
PRIMUS QUICKLY ROSE TO PROMINENCE WITHIN THE "NEW DANCE GROUP" WHILE CONTINUING HER STUDIES IN EDUCATIONAL SOCIOLOGY AND ANTHROPOLOGY. SHE ALSO TRAINED UNDER SOME OF THE GREATEST CHOREOGRAPHERS IN MODERN DANCE, INCLUDING MARTHA GRAHAM.
Pearl:
antilliana
SHE STOLE THE SHOW WITH HER PERFORMANCE IN "ANTILLIANA" FOR BERYL MCBURNIE, WHO TAUGHT HER MUCH ABOUT AFRO-CARIBBEAN DANCE.
"Dance has been my vehicle. Dance has been my language, my strength. In the dance I have confided my most secret thoughts and shared the inner music of all mankind. I have danced across mountains and deserts, ancient rivers and oceans and slipped through the boundaries of time and space."
PEARL'S FIRST SUBSEQUENT COMPOSITION WAS "AFRICAN CEREMONIAL", WHICH SHE PRESENTED AT THE 92 ST. Y.M.H.A, ALONG WITH "STRANGE FRUIT," "ROCK DANIEL" AND "HARD TIME BLUES." THE NEW YORK TIMES SAID THAT SOLO ARTIST PRIMUS, "WAS ENTITLED TO A COMPANY OF HER OWN."
SHE SOON BEGAN A STRING OF LEGENDARY PERFORMANCES AT CAFE SOCIETY, THEN DANCED BEFORE 20,000 PEOPLE AT THE "NEGRO FREEDOM RALLY" AT MADISON SQUARE GARDEN. SHE FOLLOWED THAT WITH AN APPEARANCE AT CARNEGIE HALL IN AN AFRICAN DANCE FESTIVAL.

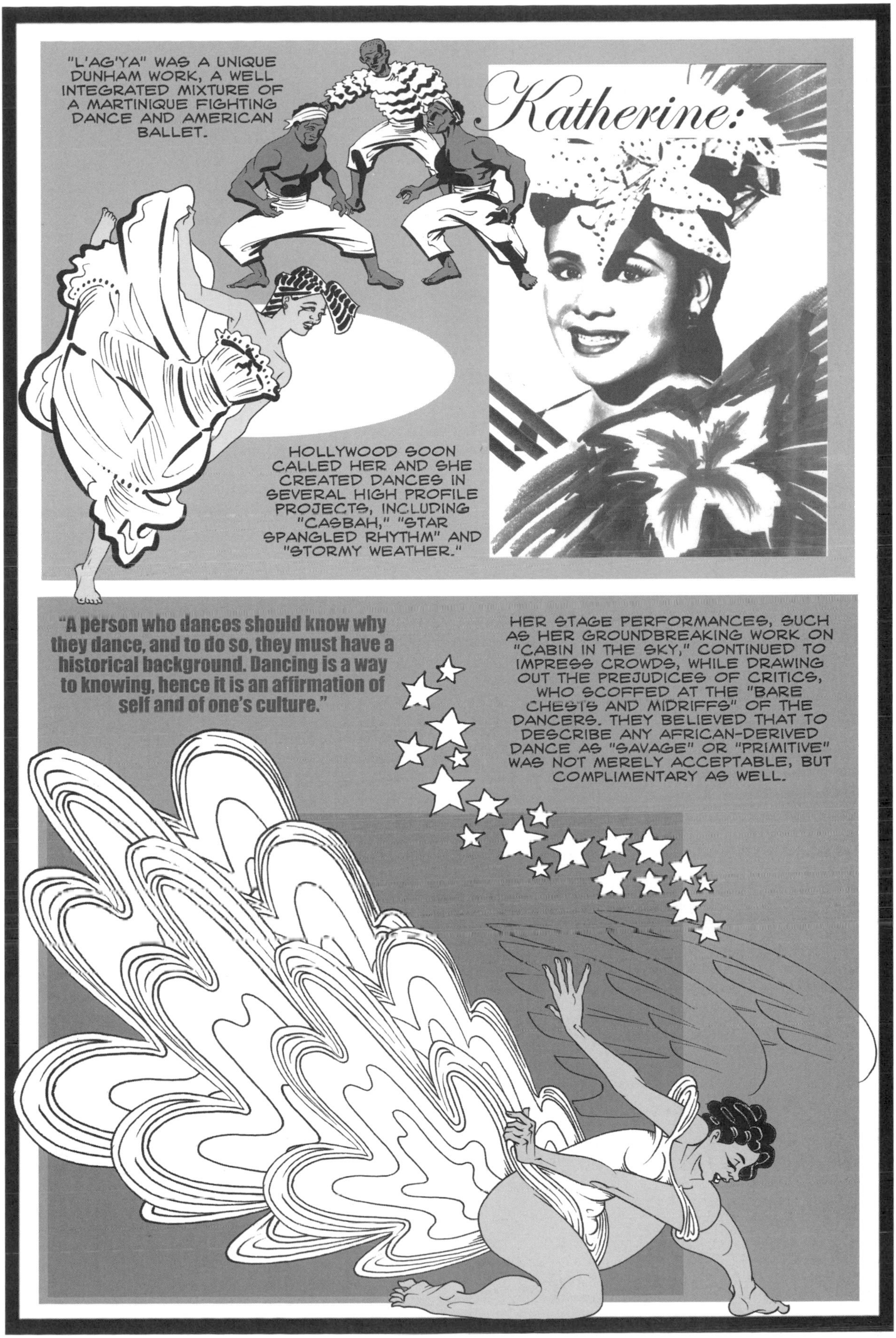
"L'AG'YA" WAS A UNIQUE DUNHAM WORK, A WELL INTEGRATED MIXTURE OF A MARTINIQUE FIGHTING DANCE AND AMERICAN BALLET.
Katherine:
HOLLYWOOD SOON CALLED HER AND SHE CREATED DANCES IN SEVERAL HIGH PROFILE PROJECTS, INCLUDING "CASBAH," "STAR SPANGLED RHYTHM" AND "STORMY WEATHER."
"A person who dances should know why they dance, and to do so, they must have a historical background. Dancing is a way to knowing, hence it is an affirmation of self and of one's culture."
HER STAGE PERFORMANCES, SUCH AS HER GROUNDBREAKING WORK ON "CABIN IN THE SKY," CONTINUED TO IMPRESS CROWDS, WHILE DRAWING OUT THE PREJUDICES OF CRITICS, WHO SCOFFED AT THE "BARE CHESTS AND MIDRIFFS" OF THE DANCERS. THEY BELIEVED THAT TO DESCRIBE ANY AFRICAN-DERIVED DANCE AS "SAVAGE" OR "PRIMITIVE" WAS NOT MERELY ACCEPTABLE, BUT COMPLIMENTARY AS WELL.

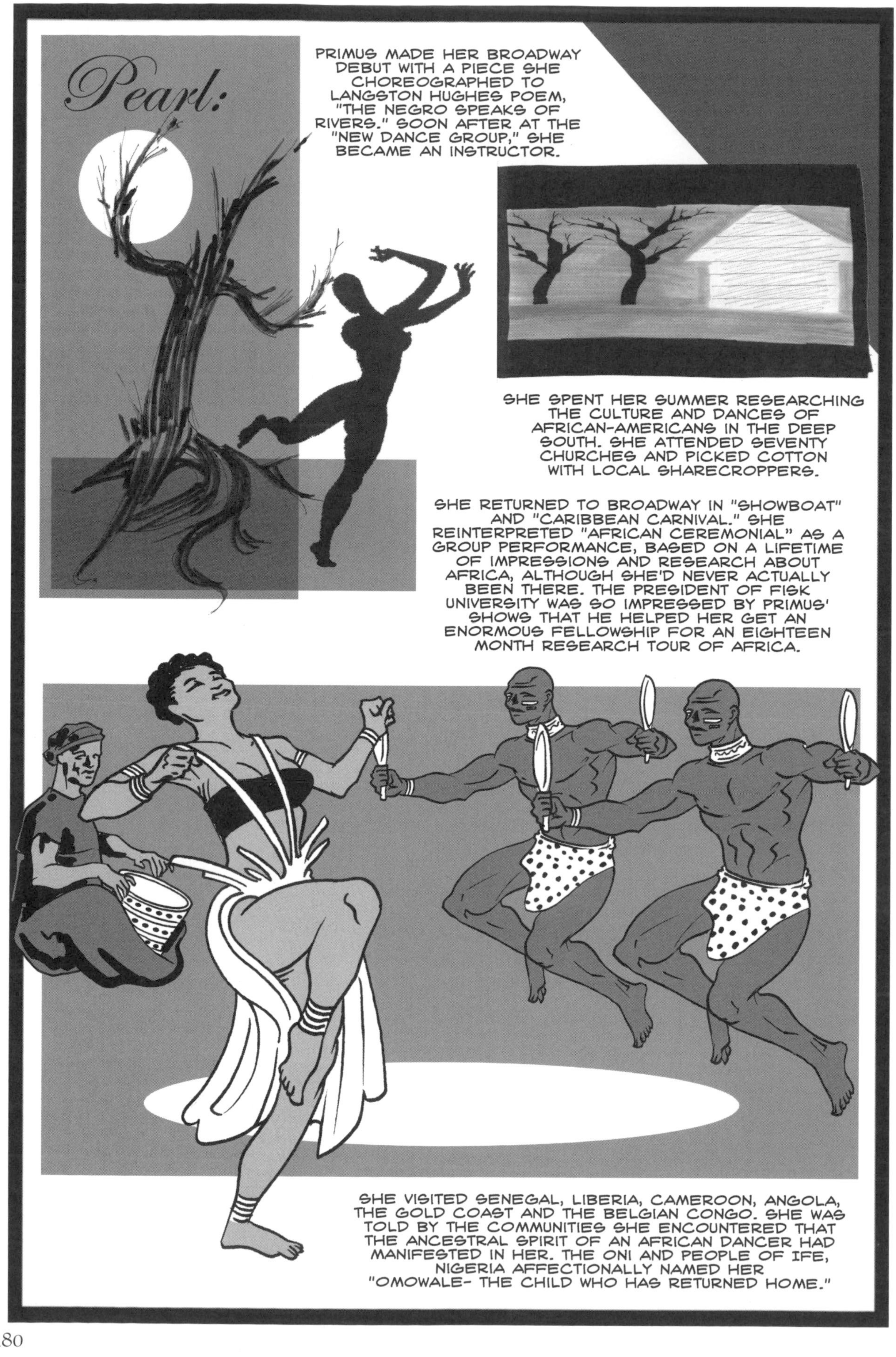
Pearl:
PRIMUS MADE HER BROADWAY DEBUT WITH A PIECE SHE CHOREOGRAPHED TO LANGSTON HUGHES POEM, "THE NEGRO SPEAKS OF RIVERS." SOON AFTER AT THE "NEW DANCE GROUP," SHE BECAME AN INSTRUCTOR.
SHE SPENT HER SUMMER RESEARCHING THE CULTURE AND DANCES OF AFRICAN-AMERICANS IN THE DEEP SOUTH. SHE ATTENDED SEVENTY CHURCHES AND PICKED COTTON WITH LOCAL SHARECROPPERS.
SHE RETURNED TO BROADWAY IN "SHOWBOAT" AND "CARIBBEAN CARNIVAL." SHE REINTERPRETED "AFRICAN CEREMONIAL" AS A GROUP PERFORMANCE, BASED ON A LIFETIME OF IMPRESSIONS AND RESEARCH ABOUT AFRICA, ALTHOUGH SHE'D NEVER ACTUALLY BEEN THERE. THE PRESIDENT OF FISK UNIVERSITY WAS SO IMPRESSED BY PRIMUS' SHOWS THAT HE HELPED HER GET AN ENORMOUS FELLOWSHIP FOR AN EIGHTEEN MONTH RESEARCH TOUR OF AFRICA.
SHE VISITED SENEGAL, LIBERIA, CAMEROON, ANGOLA, THE GOLD COAST AND THE BELGIAN CONGO. SHE WAS TOLD BY THE COMMUNITIES SHE ENCOUNTERED THAT THE ANCESTRAL SPIRIT OF AN AFRICAN DANCER HAD MANIFESTED IN HER. THE ONI AND PEOPLE OF IFE, NIGERIA AFFECTIONATELY NAMED HER "OMOWALE- THE CHILD WHO HAS RETURNED HOME."

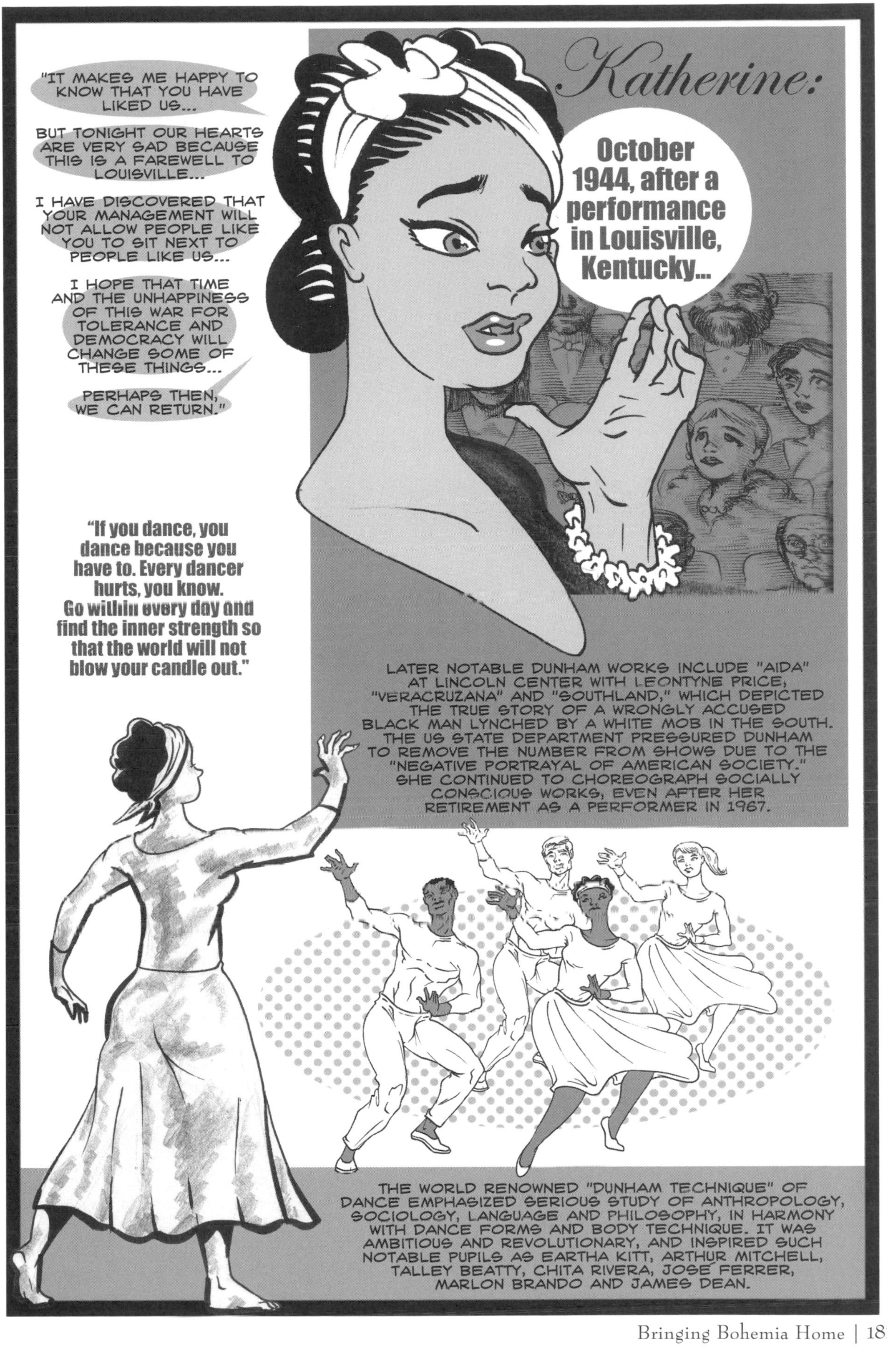
Katherine:
"IT MAKES ME HAPPY TO KNOW THAT YOU HAVE LIKED US...
BUT TONIGHT OUR HEARTS ARE VERY SAD BECAUSE THIS IS A FAREWELL TO LOUISVILLE...
I HAVE DISCOVERED THAT YOUR MANAGEMENT WILL NOT ALLOW PEOPLE LIKE YOU TO SIT NEXT TO PEOPLE LIKE US...
I HOPE THAT TIME AND THE UNHAPPINESS OF THIS WAR FOR TOLERANCE AND DEMOCRACY WILL CHANGE SOME OF THESE THINGS...
PERHAPS THEN, WE CAN RETURN."
October 1944, after a performance in Louisville, Kentucky...
"If you dance, you dance because you have to. Every dancer hurts, you know. Go within every day and find the inner strength so that the world will not blow your candle out."
LATER NOTABLE DUNHAM WORKS INCLUDE "AIDA" AT LINCOLN CENTER WITH LEONTYNE PRICE, "VERACRUZANA" AND "SOUTHLAND," WHICH DEPICTED THE TRUE STORY OF A WRONGLY ACCUSED BLACK MAN LYNCHED BY A WHITE MOB IN THE SOUTH. THE US STATE DEPARTMENT PRESSURED DUNHAM TO REMOVE THE NUMBER FROM SHOWS DUE TO THE "NEGATIVE PORTRAYAL OF AMERICAN SOCIETY." SHE CONTINUED TO CHOREOGRAPH SOCIALLY CONSCIOUS WORKS, EVEN AFTER HER RETIREMENT AS A PERFORMER IN 1967.
THE WORLD RENOWNED "DUNHAM TECHNIQUE" OF DANCE EMPHASIZED SERIOUS STUDY OF ANTHROPOLOGY, SOCIOLOGY, LANGUAGE AND PHILOSOPHY, IN HARMONY WITH DANCE FORMS AND BODY TECHNIQUE. IT WAS AMBITIOUS AND REVOLUTIONARY, AND INSPIRED SUCH NOTABLE PUPILS AS EARTHA KITT, ARTHUR MITCHELL, TALLEY BEATTY, CHITA RIVERA, JOSÉ FERRER, MARLON BRANDO AND JAMES DEAN.

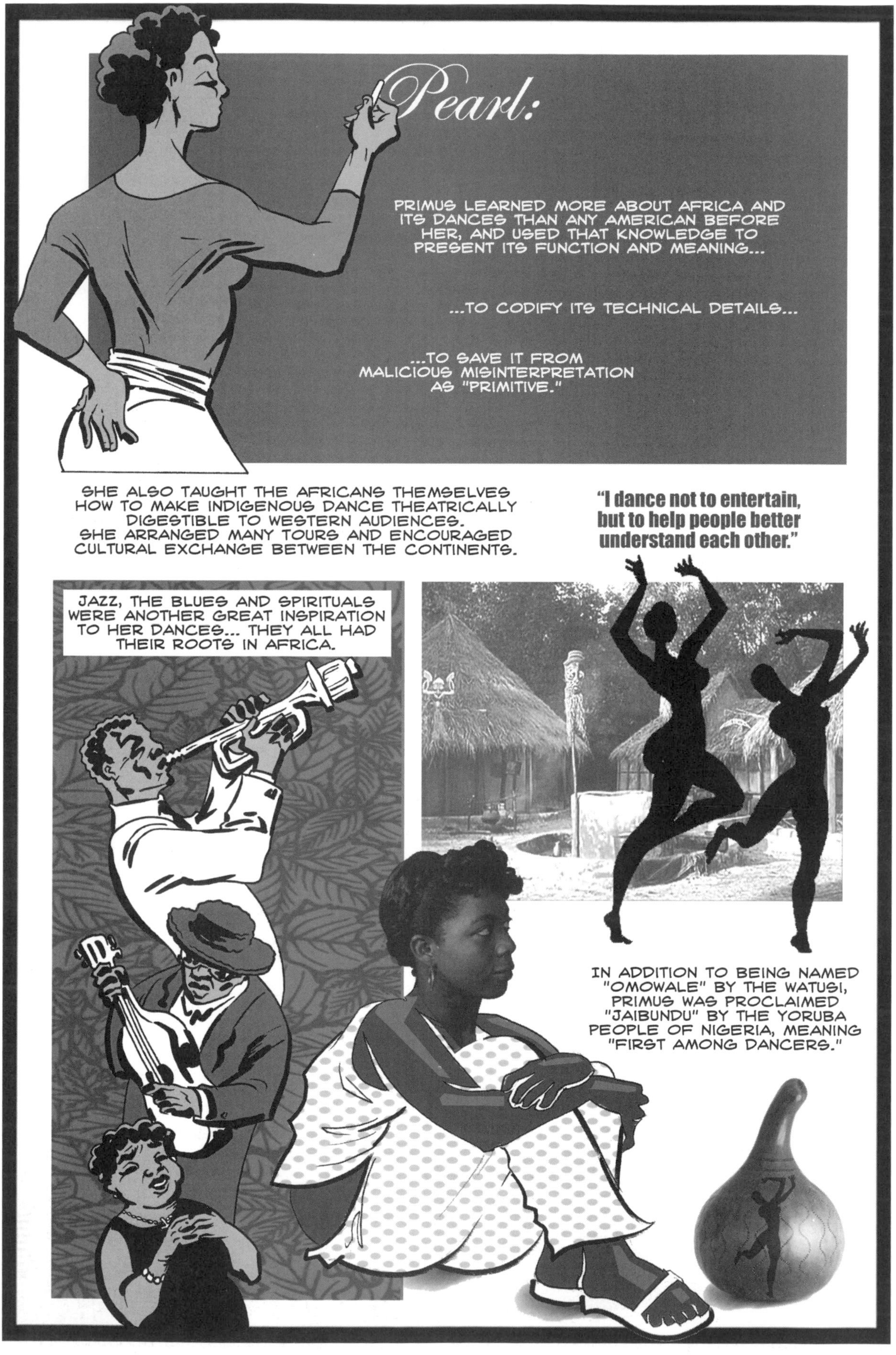
Pearl:
PRIMUS LEARNED MORE ABOUT AFRICA AND ITS DANCES THAN ANY AMERICAN BEFORE HER, AND USED THAT KNOWLEDGE TO PRESENT ITS FUNCTION AND MEANING...
...TO CODIFY ITS TECHNICAL DETAILS...
...TO SAVE IT FROM MALICIOUS MISINTERPRETATION AS "PRIMITIVE."
SHE ALSO TAUGHT THE AFRICANS THEMSELVES HOW TO MAKE INDIGENOUS DANCE THEATRICALLY DIGESTIBLE TO WESTERN AUDIENCES. SHE ARRANGED MANY TOURS AND ENCOURAGED CULTURAL EXCHANGE BETWEEN THE CONTINENTS.
"I dance not to entertain, but to help people better understand each other."
JAZZ, THE BLUES AND SPIRITUALS WERE ANOTHER GREAT INSPIRATION TO HER DANCES... THEY ALL HAD THEIR ROOTS IN AFRICA.
IN ADDITION TO BEING NAMED "OMOWALE" BY THE WATUSI, PRIMUS WAS PROCLAIMED "JAIBUNDU" BY THE YORUBA PEOPLE OF NIGERIA, MEANING "FIRST AMONG DANCERS."

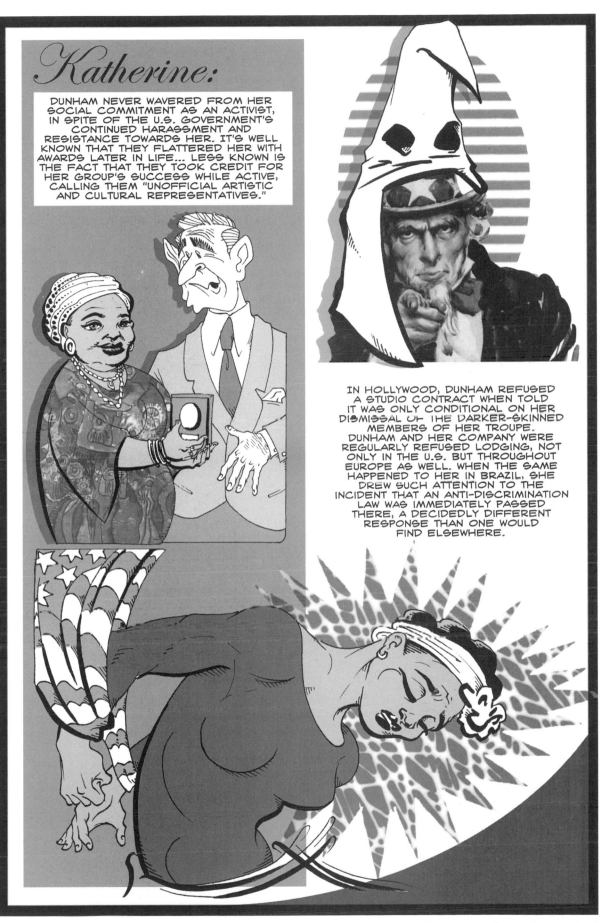

Katherine:

DUNHAM NEVER WAVERED FROM HER SOCIAL COMMITMENT AS AN ACTIVIST, IN SPITE OF THE U.S. GOVERNMENT'S CONTINUED HARASSMENT AND RESISTANCE TOWARDS HER. IT'S WELL KNOWN THAT THEY FLATTERED HER WITH AWARDS LATER IN LIFE... LESS KNOWN IS THE FACT THAT THEY TOOK CREDIT FOR HER GROUP'S SUCCESS WHILE ACTIVE, CALLING THEM "UNOFFICIAL ARTISTIC AND CULTURAL REPRESENTATIVES."

IN HOLLYWOOD, DUNHAM REFUSED A STUDIO CONTRACT WHEN TOLD IT WAS ONLY CONDITIONAL ON HER DISMISSAL OF THE DARKER-SKINNED MEMBERS OF HER TROUPE. DUNHAM AND HER COMPANY WERE REGULARLY REFUSED LODGING, NOT ONLY IN THE U.S. BUT THROUGHOUT EUROPE AS WELL. WHEN THE SAME HAPPENED TO HER IN BRAZIL, SHE DREW SUCH ATTENTION TO THE INCIDENT THAT AN ANTI-DISCRIMINATION LAW WAS IMMEDIATELY PASSED THERE, A DECIDEDLY DIFFERENT RESPONSE THAN ONE WOULD FIND ELSEWHERE.

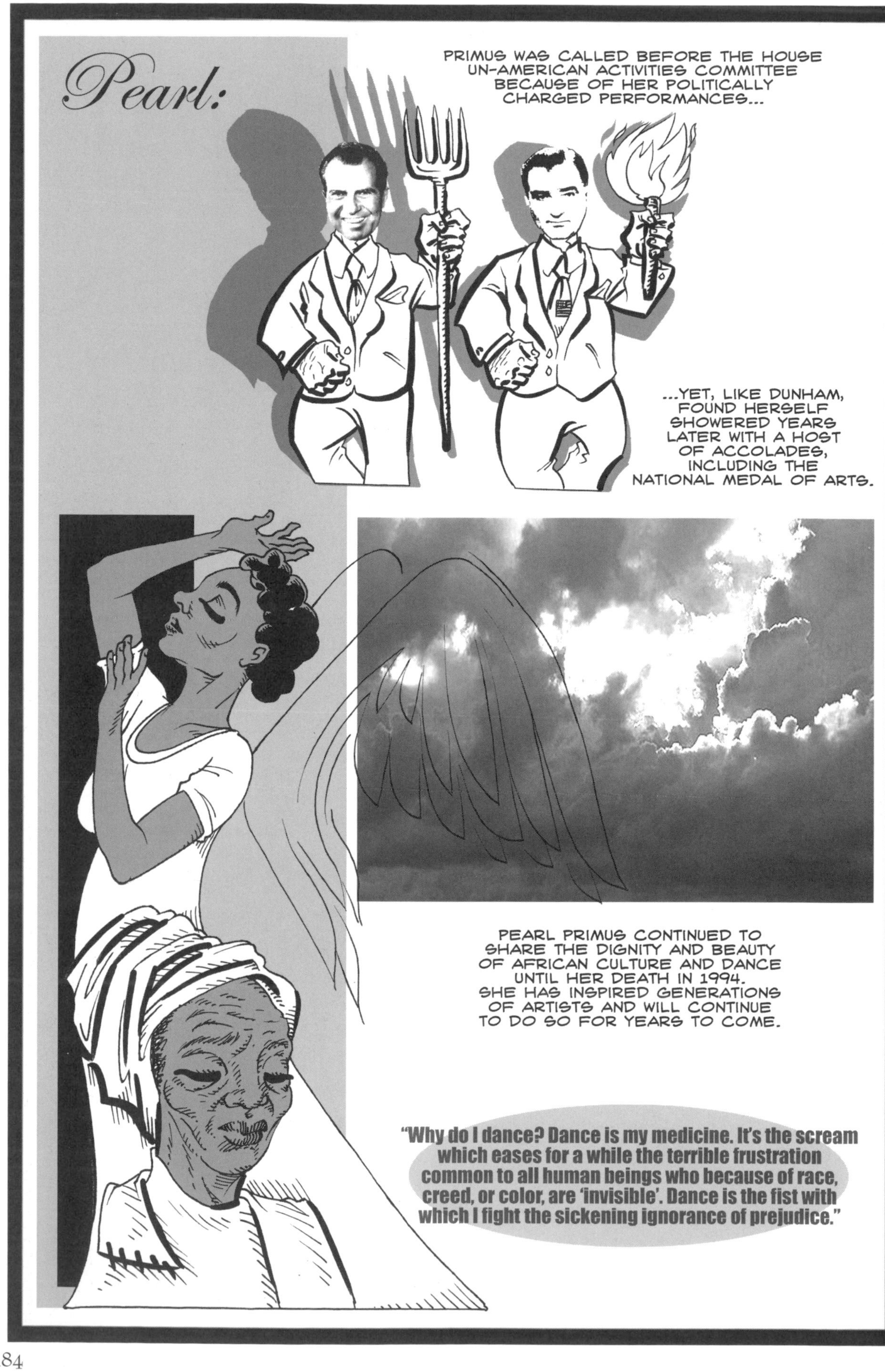
Pearl:
PRIMUS WAS CALLED BEFORE THE HOUSE UN-AMERICAN ACTIVITIES COMMITTEE BECAUSE OF HER POLITICALLY CHARGED PERFORMANCES...
...YET, LIKE DUNHAM, FOUND HERSELF SHOWERED YEARS LATER WITH A HOST OF ACCOLADES, INCLUDING THE NATIONAL MEDAL OF ARTS.
PEARL PRIMUS CONTINUED TO SHARE THE DIGNITY AND BEAUTY OF AFRICAN CULTURE AND DANCE UNTIL HER DEATH IN 1994. SHE HAS INSPIRED GENERATIONS OF ARTISTS AND WILL CONTINUE TO DO SO FOR YEARS TO COME.
"Why do I dance? Dance is my medicine. It's the scream which eases for a while the terrible frustration common to all human beings who because of race, creed, or color, are 'invisible'. Dance is the fist with which I fight the sickening ignorance of prejudice."

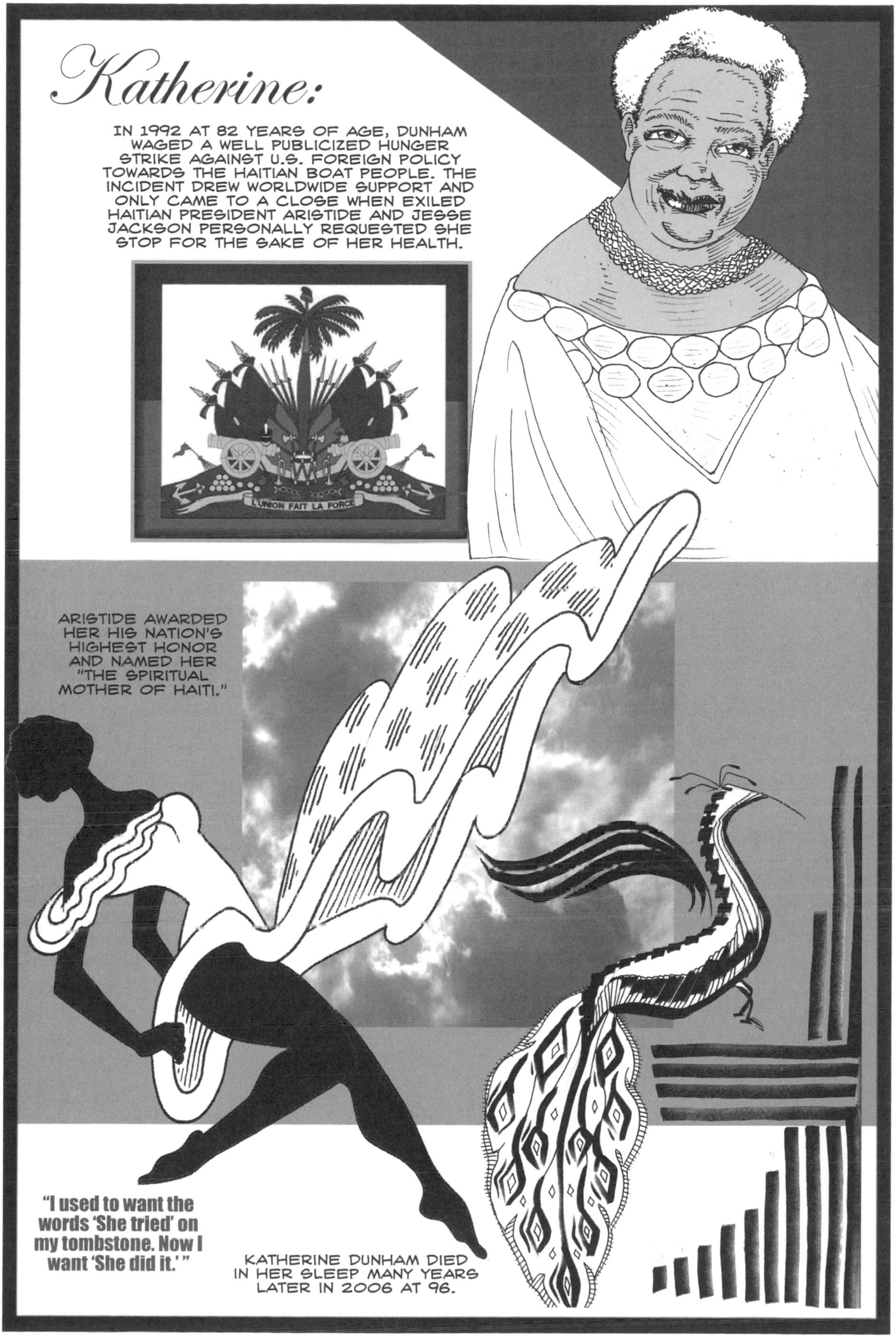
Katherine:
IN 1992 AT 82 YEARS OF AGE, DUNHAM WAGED A WELL PUBLICIZED HUNGER STRIKE AGAINST U.S. FOREIGN POLICY TOWARDS THE HAITIAN BOAT PEOPLE. THE INCIDENT DREW WORLDWIDE SUPPORT AND ONLY CAME TO A CLOSE WHEN EXILED HAITIAN PRESIDENT ARISTIDE AND JESSE JACKSON PERSONALLY REQUESTED SHE STOP FOR THE SAKE OF HER HEALTH.
L'UNION FAIT LA FORCE
ARISTIDE AWARDED HER HIS NATION'S HIGHEST HONOR AND NAMED HER "THE SPIRITUAL MOTHER OF HAITI."
"I used to want the words 'She tried' on my tombstone. Now I want 'She did it.'"
KATHERINE DUNHAM DIED IN HER SLEEP MANY YEARS LATER IN 2006 AT 96.

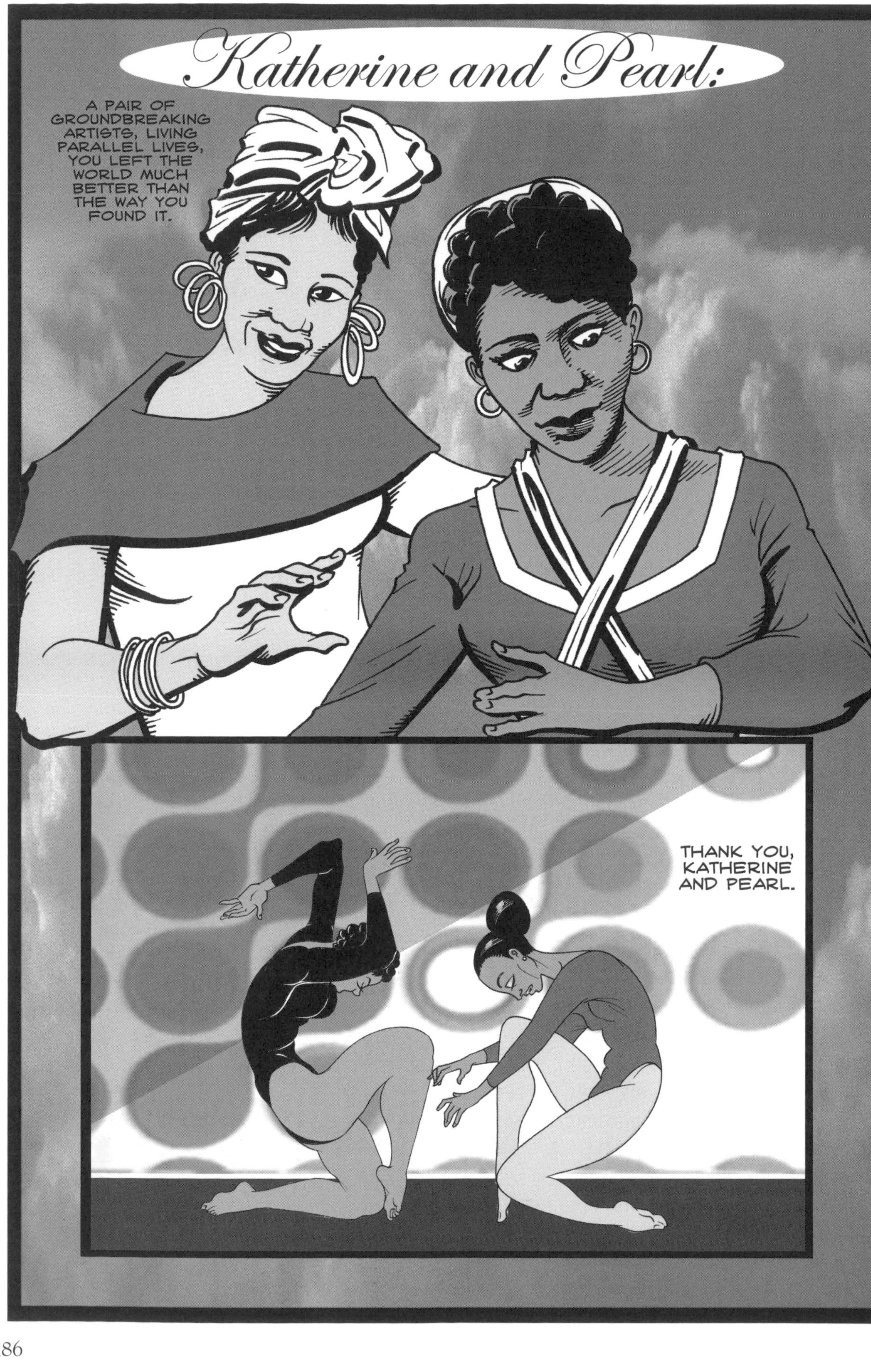
Katherine and Pearl:
A PAIR OF GROUNDBREAKING ARTISTS, LIVING PARALLEL LIVES, YOU LEFT THE WORLD MUCH BETTER THAN THE WAY YOU FOUND IT.
THANK YOU, KATHERINE AND PEARL.

Chapter Eight

Bohemians and Hipsters

The transformation of American dance (both popular dance styles and modern dance) together with improvisation in the world of jazz fairly symbolized an increasingly diverse and democratic cultural life of the 1940s. The hopes for a different kind of society remained unfulfilled, but the art forms suggested that universal human freedoms might someday be realized.

Bohemianism of the 1940s, as with the Beats to follow, looked toward black culture as a resource of cultural history but also as a center of innovation. According to the widely held truism, the two inventions of American popular culture have been comics and jazz. Equally global in their reach, appealing as much in their form as in anything that can be described as "content," they have their own rich and complex histories. Emerging more or less simultaneously in the 1890s, each had reached a crisis of sorts by the 1940s, and moved decisively forward with the cash in the hands of new customers thanks to wartime prosperity.

If comics were nearly all white (with some non-white characters drawn in mostly minstrelsy-inspired caricatures), jazz drew droves of whites onto the dance floors and to join audiences among the nightclub devotees and record-buyers. Modern dance may have been one of the few racially egalitarian realms, or rather one of the few with artists reaching for that realm. African-inspired forms, including Afro-Caribbean, took flight here, as they did in Bebop. Something new to the world was being invented and bohemians of almost every kind craved more of it.

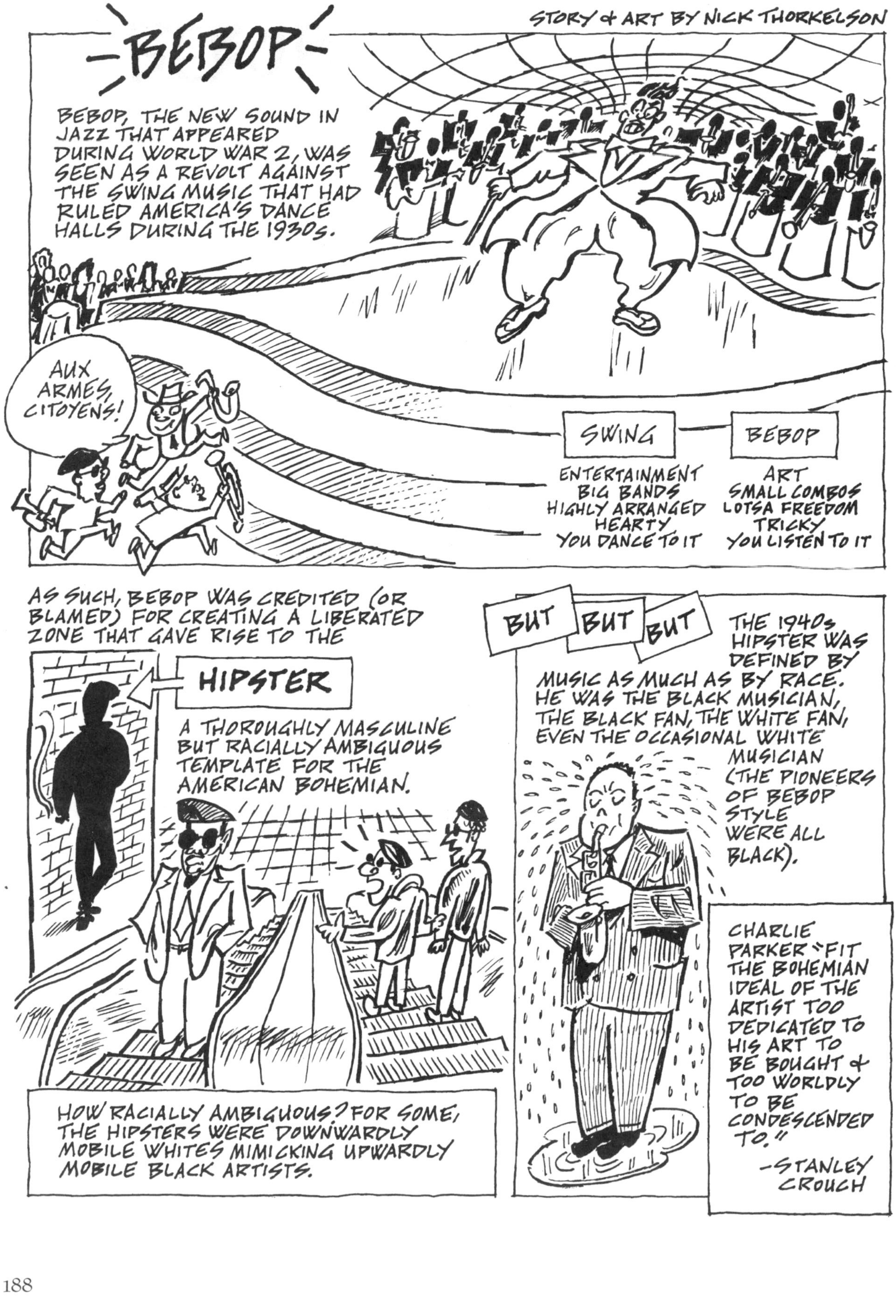
BEBOP
STORY & ART BY NICK THORKELSON
BEBOP, THE NEW SOUND IN JAZZ THAT APPEARED DURING WORLD WAR 2, WAS SEEN AS A REVOLT AGAINST THE SWING MUSIC THAT HAD RULED AMERICA'S DANCE HALLS DURING THE 1930s.
AUX ARMES, CITOYENS!
SWING
ENTERTAINMENT
BIG BANDS
HIGHLY ARRANGED
HEARTY
YOU DANCE TO IT
BEBOP
ART
SMALL COMBOS
LOTSA FREEDOM
TRICKY
YOU LISTEN TO IT
AS SUCH, BEBOP WAS CREDITED (OR BLAMED) FOR CREATING A LIBERATED ZONE THAT GAVE RISE TO THE
HIPSTER
A THOROUGHLY MASCULINE BUT RACIALLY AMBIGUOUS TEMPLATE FOR THE AMERICAN BOHEMIAN.
HOW RACIALLY AMBIGUOUS? FOR SOME, THE HIPSTERS WERE DOWNWARDLY MOBILE WHITES MIMICKING UPWARDLY MOBILE BLACK ARTISTS.
BUT
BUT
BUT
THE 1940s HIPSTER WAS DEFINED BY MUSIC AS MUCH AS BY RACE. HE WAS THE BLACK MUSICIAN, THE BLACK FAN, THE WHITE FAN, EVEN THE OCCASIONAL WHITE MUSICIAN (THE PIONEERS OF BEBOP STYLE WERE ALL BLACK).
CHARLIE PARKER "FIT THE BOHEMIAN IDEAL OF THE ARTIST TOO DEDICATED TO HIS ART TO BE BOUGHT & TOO WORLDLY TO BE CONDESCENDED TO."
-STANLEY CROUCH

AND HERE'S SOME MORE BUTS:

BUT BUT BUT

HONOR THY FATHER
AND THY MOTHER *
AND THY MUSE

BEBOP WAS NOT A REVOLUTION!

WHILE SOME OF THE OLD GUARD DID NOT CARE FOR BEBOP (FATS WALLER CALLED IT "BOPPIN' AND STOPPIN'"), THE BEBOPPERS REVERED THEIR ELDERS.

THE BEBOP PIONEERS

FELT THEY WERE SIMPLY MOVING JAZZ FORWARD. LIKE YOUNG ARTISTS OF ANY GENERATION, THEY WERE QUICK TO ADAPT TO CHANGED CIRCUMSTANCES &

AN EVOLVING ZEITGEIST, BUT ALWAYS WITH RESPECT FOR THE OLDER ARTISTS WHO HAD DONE THE SAME IN THEIR TIME.

CHARLIE PARKER BORN 1920

DIZZY GILLESPIE BORN 1917

THELONIOUS MONK BORN 1917

BUD POWELL BORN 1924

KENNY CLARKE BORN 1914

MAX ROACH BORN 1924

WHY DID THE WIDER PUBLIC EXPERIENCE BEBOP AS A REVOLUTION? ONE BIG REASON:

THE 1942-44 MUSICIANS' STRIKE

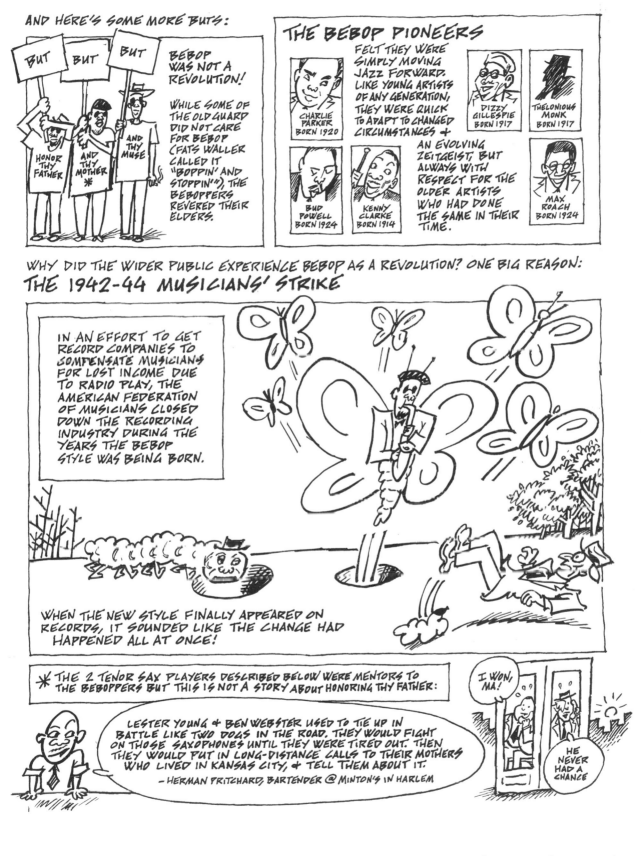

IN AN EFFORT TO GET RECORD COMPANIES TO COMPENSATE MUSICIANS FOR LOST INCOME DUE TO RADIO PLAY, THE AMERICAN FEDERATION OF MUSICIANS CLOSED DOWN THE RECORDING INDUSTRY DURING THE YEARS THE BEBOP STYLE WAS BEING BORN.

WHEN THE NEW STYLE FINALLY APPEARED ON RECORDS, IT SOUNDED LIKE THE CHANGE HAD HAPPENED ALL AT ONCE!

* THE 2 TENOR SAX PLAYERS DESCRIBED BELOW WERE MENTORS TO THE BEBOPPERS BUT THIS IS NOT A STORY ABOUT HONORING THY FATHER:

LESTER YOUNG & BEN WEBSTER USED TO TIE UP IN BATTLE LIKE TWO DOGS IN THE ROAD. THEY WOULD FIGHT ON THOSE SAXOPHONES UNTIL THEY WERE TIRED OUT. THEN THEY WOULD PUT IN LONG-DISTANCE CALLS TO THEIR MOTHERS WHO LIVED IN KANSAS CITY, & TELL THEM ABOUT IT.
— HERMAN PRITCHARD, BARTENDER @ MINTON'S IN HARLEM

I WON, MA!

HE NEVER HAD A CHANCE

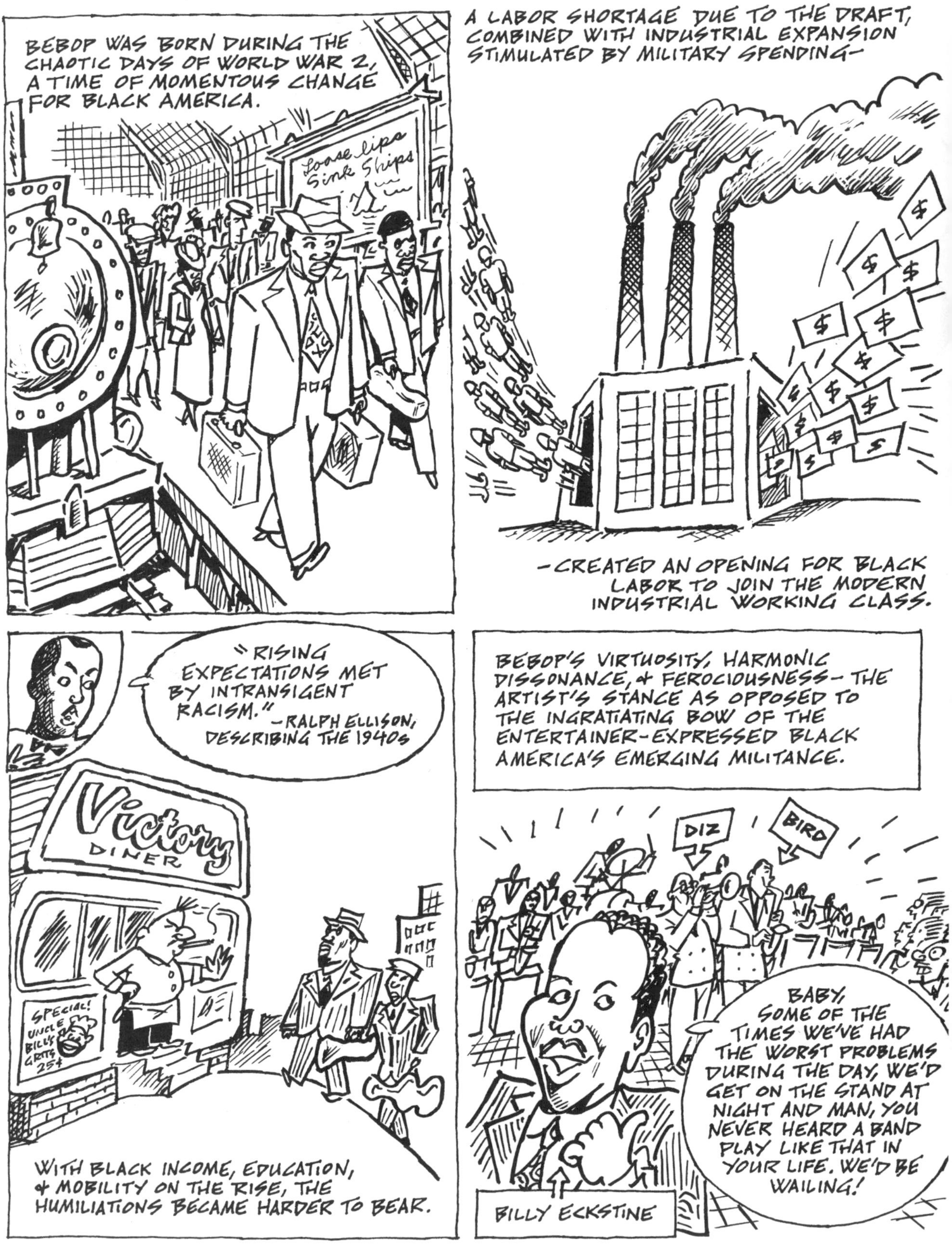
BEBOP WAS BORN DURING THE CHAOTIC DAYS OF WORLD WAR 2, A TIME OF MOMENTOUS CHANGE FOR BLACK AMERICA.
Loose lips Sink Ships
A LABOR SHORTAGE DUE TO THE DRAFT, COMBINED WITH INDUSTRIAL EXPANSION STIMULATED BY MILITARY SPENDING—
—CREATED AN OPENING FOR BLACK LABOR TO JOIN THE MODERN INDUSTRIAL WORKING CLASS.
"RISING EXPECTATIONS MET BY INTRANSIGENT RACISM." —RALPH ELLISON, DESCRIBING THE 1940s
Victory DINER
SPECIAL! UNCLE BILL'S GRITS 25¢
WITH BLACK INCOME, EDUCATION, & MOBILITY ON THE RISE, THE HUMILIATIONS BECAME HARDER TO BEAR.
BEBOP'S VIRTUOSITY, HARMONIC DISSONANCE, & FEROCIOUSNESS—THE ARTIST'S STANCE AS OPPOSED TO THE INGRATIATING BOW OF THE ENTERTAINER—EXPRESSED BLACK AMERICA'S EMERGING MILITANCE.
DIZ
BIRD
BABY, SOME OF THE TIMES WE'VE HAD THE WORST PROBLEMS DURING THE DAY, WE'D GET ON THE STAND AT NIGHT AND MAN, YOU NEVER HEARD A BAND PLAY LIKE THAT IN YOUR LIFE. WE'D BE WAILING!
BILLY ECKSTINE

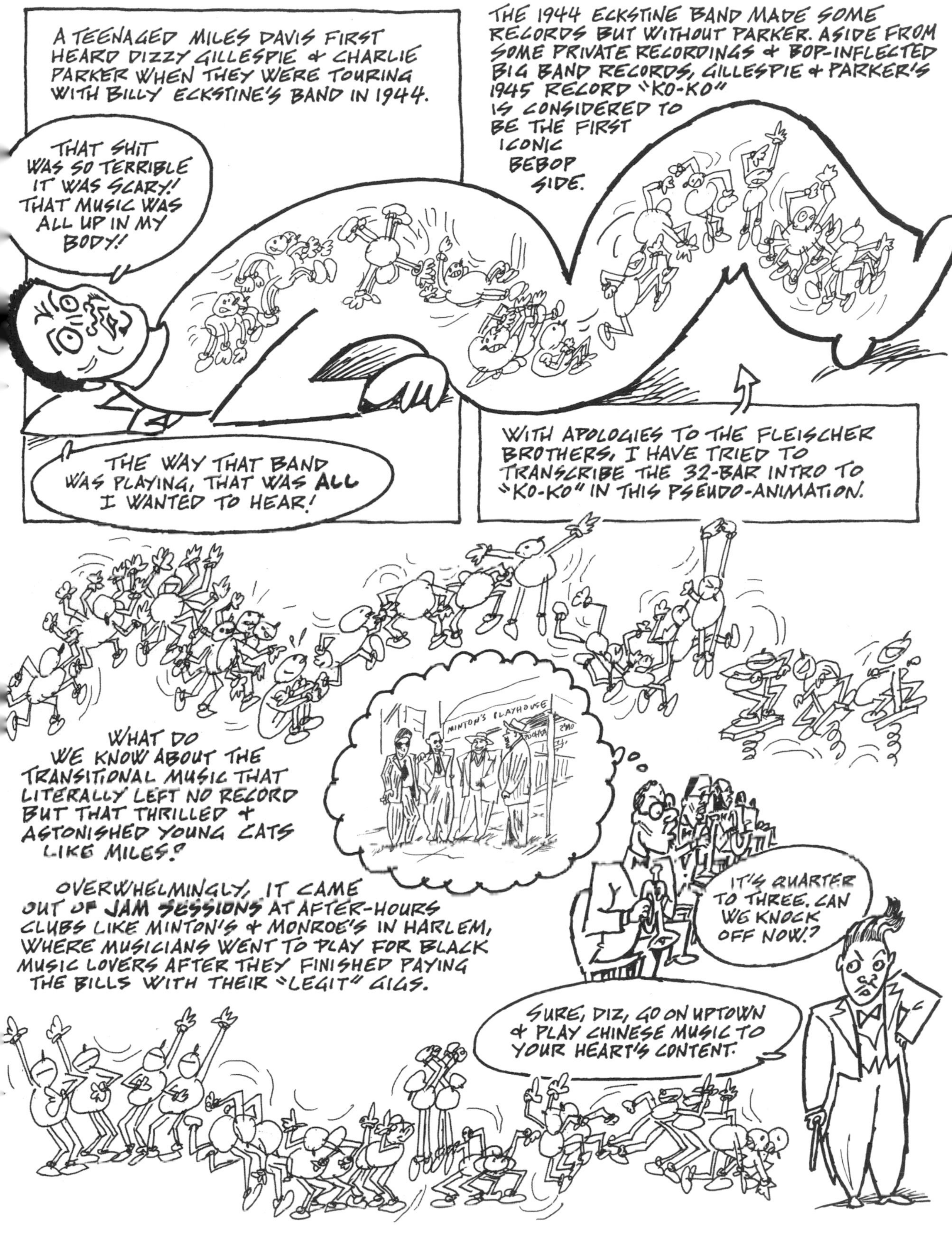
A TEENAGED MILES DAVIS FIRST HEARD DIZZY GILLESPIE & CHARLIE PARKER WHEN THEY WERE TOURING WITH BILLY ECKSTINE'S BAND IN 1944.
THAT SHIT WAS SO TERRIBLE IT WAS SCARY! THAT MUSIC WAS ALL UP IN MY BODY!
THE WAY THAT BAND WAS PLAYING, THAT WAS ALL I WANTED TO HEAR!
THE 1944 ECKSTINE BAND MADE SOME RECORDS BUT WITHOUT PARKER. ASIDE FROM SOME PRIVATE RECORDINGS & BOP-INFLECTED BIG BAND RECORDS, GILLESPIE & PARKER'S 1945 RECORD "KO-KO" IS CONSIDERED TO BE THE FIRST ICONIC BEBOP SIDE.
WITH APOLOGIES TO THE FLEISCHER BROTHERS, I HAVE TRIED TO TRANSCRIBE THE 32-BAR INTRO TO "KO-KO" IN THIS PSEUDO-ANIMATION.
MINTON'S PLAYHOUSE
WHAT DO WE KNOW ABOUT THE TRANSITIONAL MUSIC THAT LITERALLY LEFT NO RECORD BUT THAT THRILLED & ASTONISHED YOUNG CATS LIKE MILES?
OVERWHELMINGLY, IT CAME OUT OF JAM SESSIONS AT AFTER-HOURS CLUBS LIKE MINTON'S & MONROE'S IN HARLEM, WHERE MUSICIANS WENT TO PLAY FOR BLACK MUSIC LOVERS AFTER THEY FINISHED PAYING THE BILLS WITH THEIR "LEGIT" GIGS.
IT'S QUARTER TO THREE. CAN WE KNOCK OFF NOW?
SURE, DIZ, GO ON UPTOWN & PLAY CHINESE MUSIC TO YOUR HEART'S CONTENT.

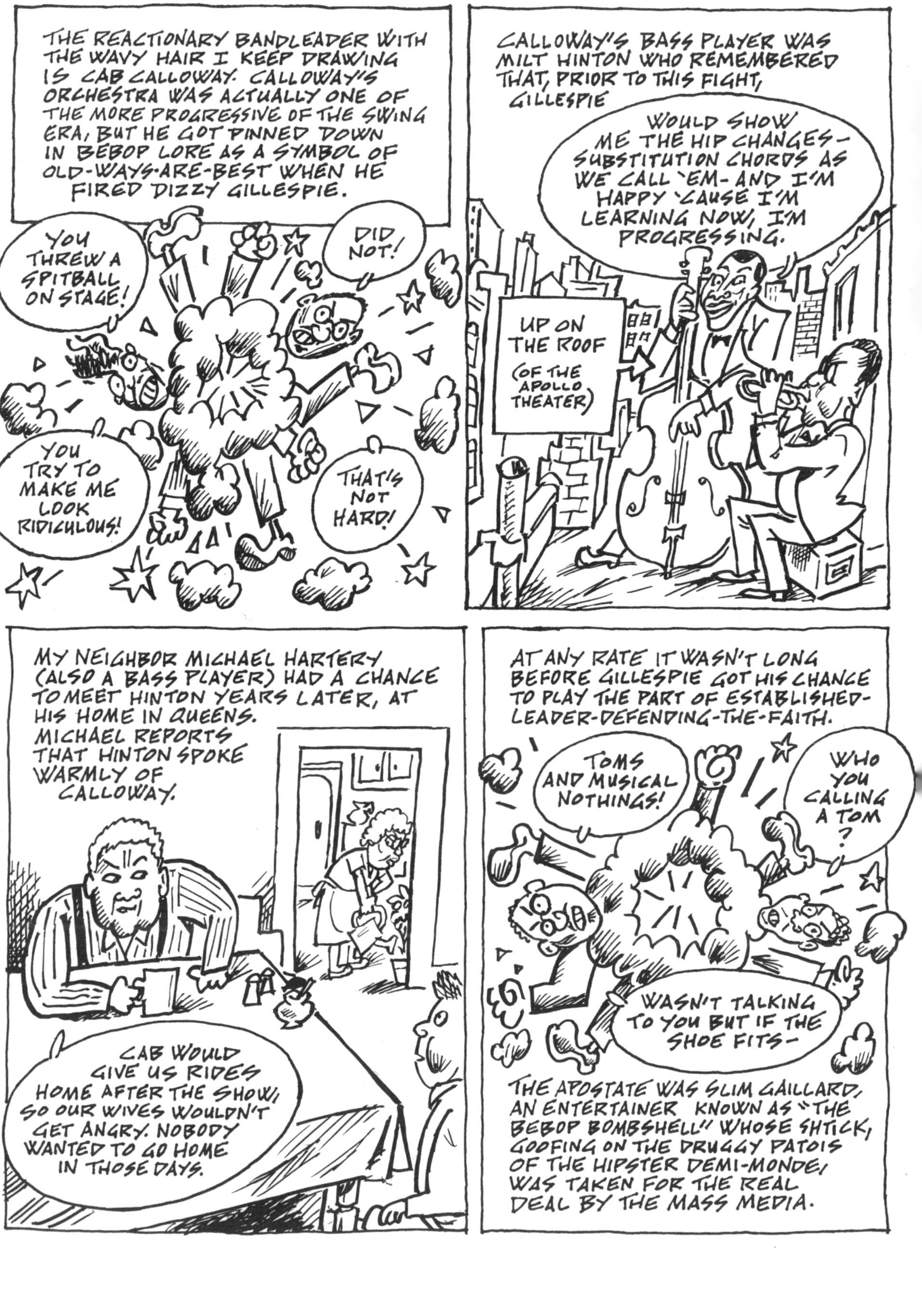

THE REACTIONARY BANDLEADER WITH THE WAVY HAIR I KEEP DRAWING IS CAB CALLOWAY. CALLOWAY'S ORCHESTRA WAS ACTUALLY ONE OF THE MORE PROGRESSIVE OF THE SWING ERA, BUT HE GOT PINNED DOWN IN BEBOP LORE AS A SYMBOL OF OLD-WAYS-ARE-BEST WHEN HE FIRED DIZZY GILLESPIE.
YOU THREW A SPITBALL ON STAGE!
DID NOT!
YOU TRY TO MAKE ME LOOK RIDICULOUS!
THAT'S NOT HARD!
CALLOWAY'S BASS PLAYER WAS MILT HINTON WHO REMEMBERED THAT, PRIOR TO THIS FIGHT, GILLESPIE
WOULD SHOW ME THE HIP CHANGES-SUBSTITUTION CHORDS AS WE CALL 'EM- AND I'M HAPPY 'CAUSE I'M LEARNING NOW, I'M PROGRESSING.
UP ON THE ROOF (OF THE APOLLO THEATER)
MY NEIGHBOR MICHAEL HARTERY (ALSO A BASS PLAYER) HAD A CHANCE TO MEET HINTON YEARS LATER, AT HIS HOME IN QUEENS.
MICHAEL REPORTS THAT HINTON SPOKE WARMLY OF CALLOWAY.
CAB WOULD GIVE US RIDES HOME AFTER THE SHOW, SO OUR WIVES WOULDN'T GET ANGRY. NOBODY WANTED TO GO HOME IN THOSE DAYS.
AT ANY RATE IT WASN'T LONG BEFORE GILLESPIE GOT HIS CHANCE TO PLAY THE PART OF ESTABLISHED-LEADER-DEFENDING-THE-FAITH.
TOMS AND MUSICAL NOTHINGS!
WHO YOU CALLING A TOM?
WASN'T TALKING TO YOU BUT IF THE SHOE FITS-
THE APOSTATE WAS SLIM GAILLARD, AN ENTERTAINER KNOWN AS "THE BEBOP BOMBSHELL" WHOSE SHTICK, GOOFING ON THE DRUGGY PATOIS OF THE HIPSTER DEMI-MONDE, WAS TAKEN FOR THE REAL DEAL BY THE MASS MEDIA.

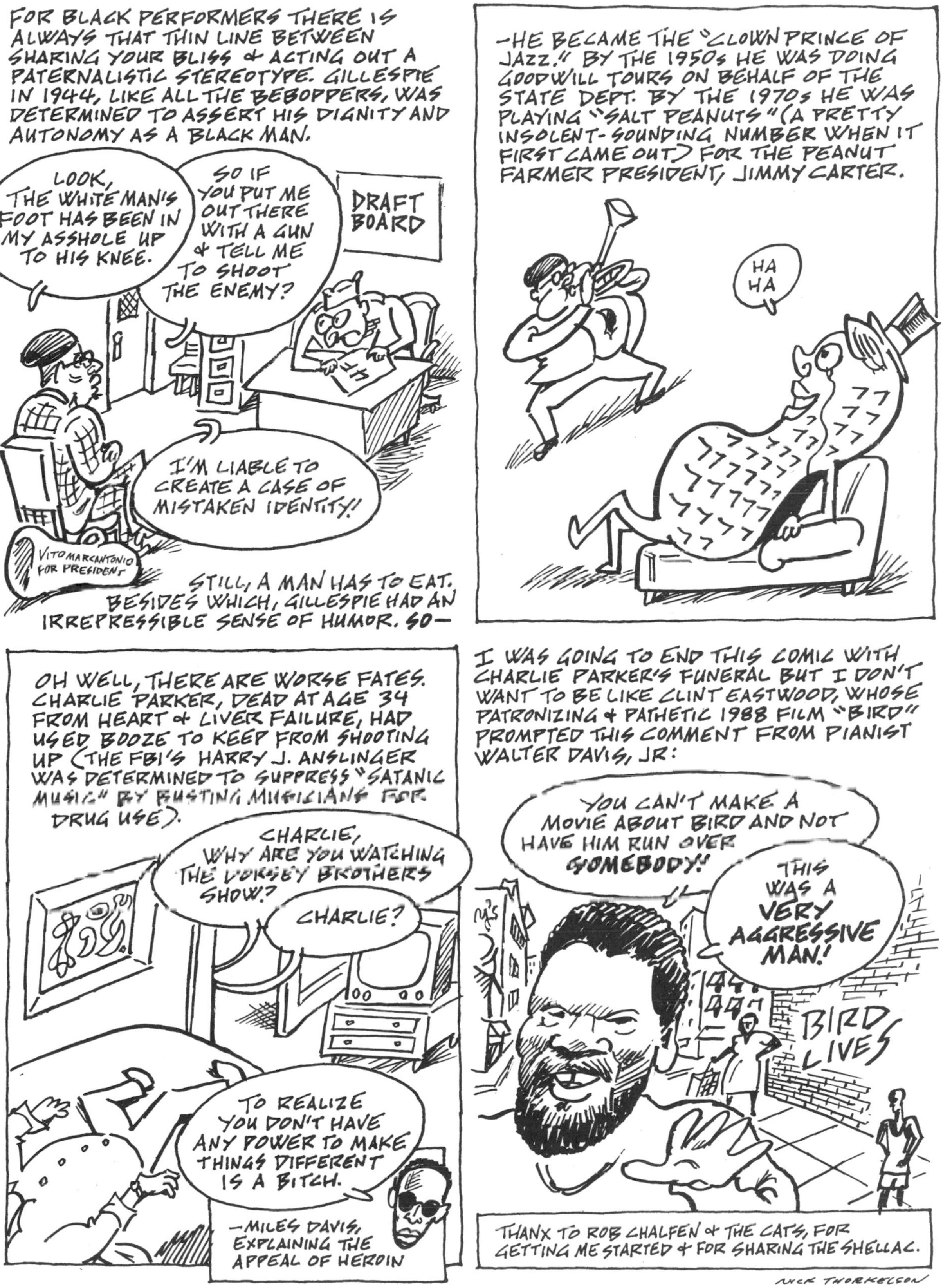
FOR BLACK PERFORMERS THERE IS ALWAYS THAT THIN LINE BETWEEN SHARING YOUR BLISS & ACTING OUT A PATERNALISTIC STEREOTYPE. GILLESPIE IN 1944, LIKE ALL THE BEBOPPERS, WAS DETERMINED TO ASSERT HIS DIGNITY AND AUTONOMY AS A BLACK MAN.
LOOK, THE WHITE MAN'S FOOT HAS BEEN IN MY ASSHOLE UP TO HIS KNEE.
SO IF YOU PUT ME OUT THERE WITH A GUN & TELL ME TO SHOOT THE ENEMY?
DRAFT BOARD
I'M LIABLE TO CREATE A CASE OF MISTAKEN IDENTITY!
VITO MARCANTONIO FOR PRESIDENT
STILL, A MAN HAS TO EAT. BESIDES WHICH, GILLESPIE HAD AN IRREPRESSIBLE SENSE OF HUMOR. SO—
—HE BECAME THE "CLOWN PRINCE OF JAZZ." BY THE 1950s HE WAS DOING GOODWILL TOURS ON BEHALF OF THE STATE DEPT. BY THE 1970s HE WAS PLAYING "SALT PEANUTS" (A PRETTY INSOLENT-SOUNDING NUMBER WHEN IT FIRST CAME OUT) FOR THE PEANUT FARMER PRESIDENT, JIMMY CARTER.
HA HA
OH WELL, THERE ARE WORSE FATES. CHARLIE PARKER, DEAD AT AGE 34 FROM HEART & LIVER FAILURE, HAD USED BOOZE TO KEEP FROM SHOOTING UP (THE FBI'S HARRY J. ANSLINGER WAS DETERMINED TO SUPPRESS "SATANIC MUSIC" BY BUSTING MUSICIANS FOR DRUG USE).
CHARLIE, WHY ARE YOU WATCHING THE DORSEY BROTHERS SHOW?
CHARLIE?
TO REALIZE YOU DON'T HAVE ANY POWER TO MAKE THINGS DIFFERENT IS A BITCH.
—MILES DAVIS, EXPLAINING THE APPEAL OF HEROIN
I WAS GOING TO END THIS COMIC WITH CHARLIE PARKER'S FUNERAL BUT I DON'T WANT TO BE LIKE CLINT EASTWOOD, WHOSE PATRONIZING & PATHETIC 1988 FILM "BIRD" PROMPTED THIS COMMENT FROM PIANIST WALTER DAVIS, JR:
YOU CAN'T MAKE A MOVIE ABOUT BIRD AND NOT HAVE HIM RUN OVER SOMEBODY!
THIS WAS A VERY AGGRESSIVE MAN!
BIRD LIVES
THANX TO ROB CHALFEN & THE CATS, FOR GETTING ME STARTED & FOR SHARING THE SHELLAC.
NICK THORKELSON

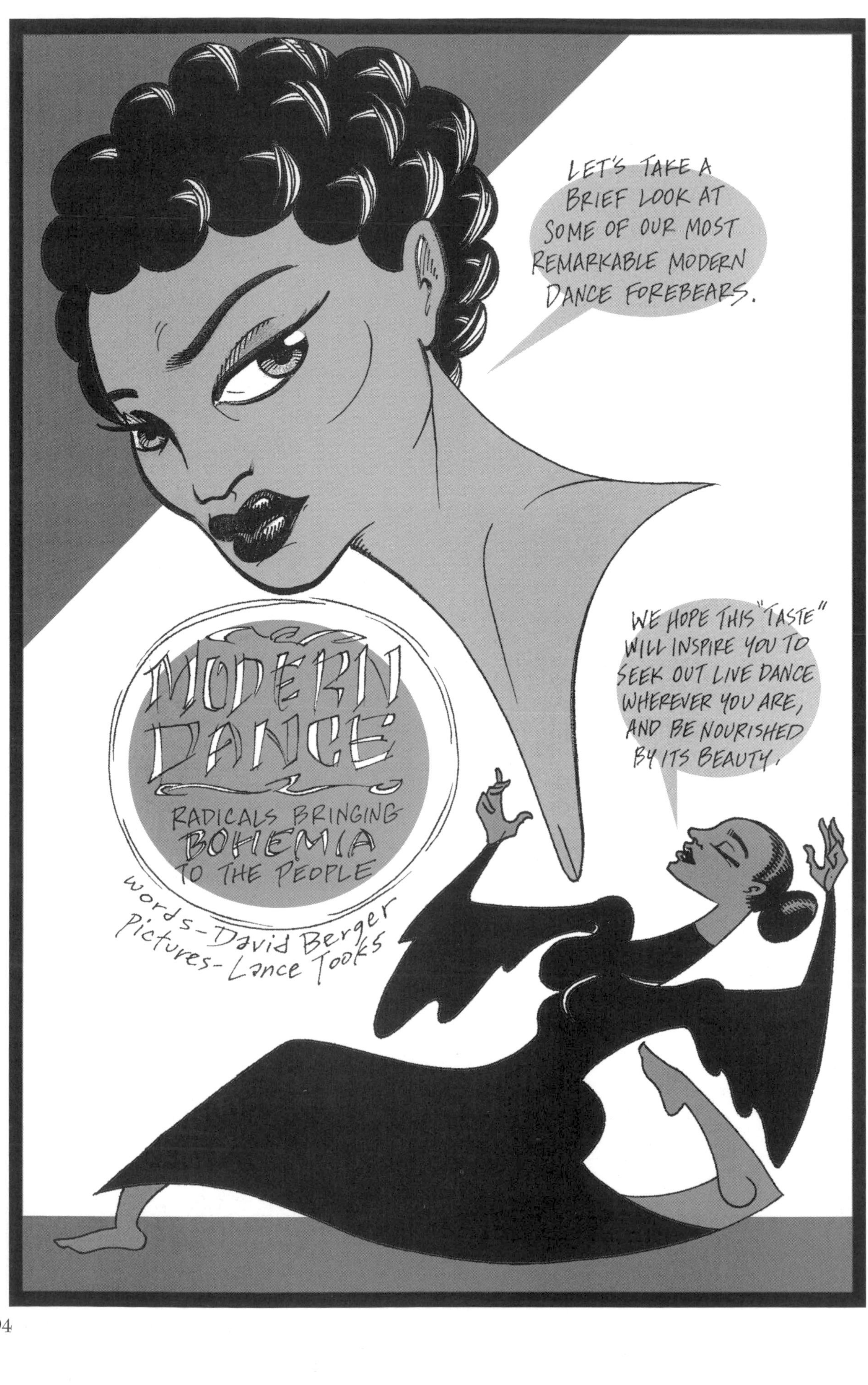
LET'S TAKE A BRIEF LOOK AT SOME OF OUR MOST REMARKABLE MODERN DANCE FOREBEARS.
MODERN DANCE
RADICALS BRINGING BOHEMIA TO THE PEOPLE
words-David Berger
Pictures-Lance Tooks
WE HOPE THIS "TASTE" WILL INSPIRE YOU TO SEEK OUT LIVE DANCE WHEREVER YOU ARE, AND BE NOURISHED BY ITS BEAUTY.

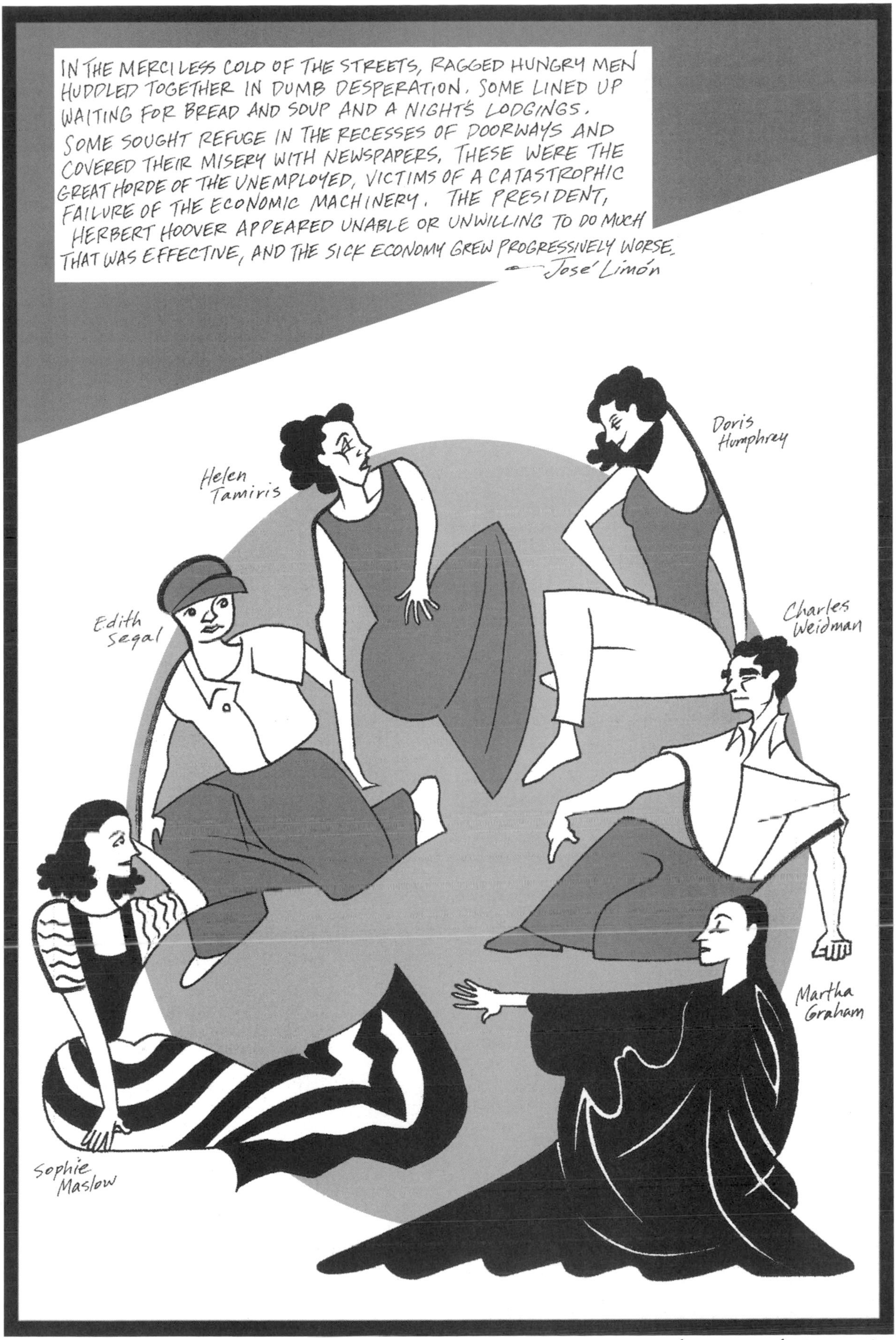
IN THE MERCILESS COLD OF THE STREETS, RAGGED HUNGRY MEN HUDDLED TOGETHER IN DUMB DESPERATION. SOME LINED UP WAITING FOR BREAD AND SOUP AND A NIGHT'S LODGINGS. SOME SOUGHT REFUGE IN THE RECESSES OF DOORWAYS AND COVERED THEIR MISERY WITH NEWSPAPERS. THESE WERE THE GREAT HORDE OF THE UNEMPLOYED, VICTIMS OF A CATASTROPHIC FAILURE OF THE ECONOMIC MACHINERY. THE PRESIDENT, HERBERT HOOVER APPEARED UNABLE OR UNWILLING TO DO MUCH THAT WAS EFFECTIVE, AND THE SICK ECONOMY GREW PROGRESSIVELY WORSE.
— José Limón
Helen Tamiris
Doris Humphrey
Edith Segal
Charles Weidman
Martha Graham
Sophie Maslow

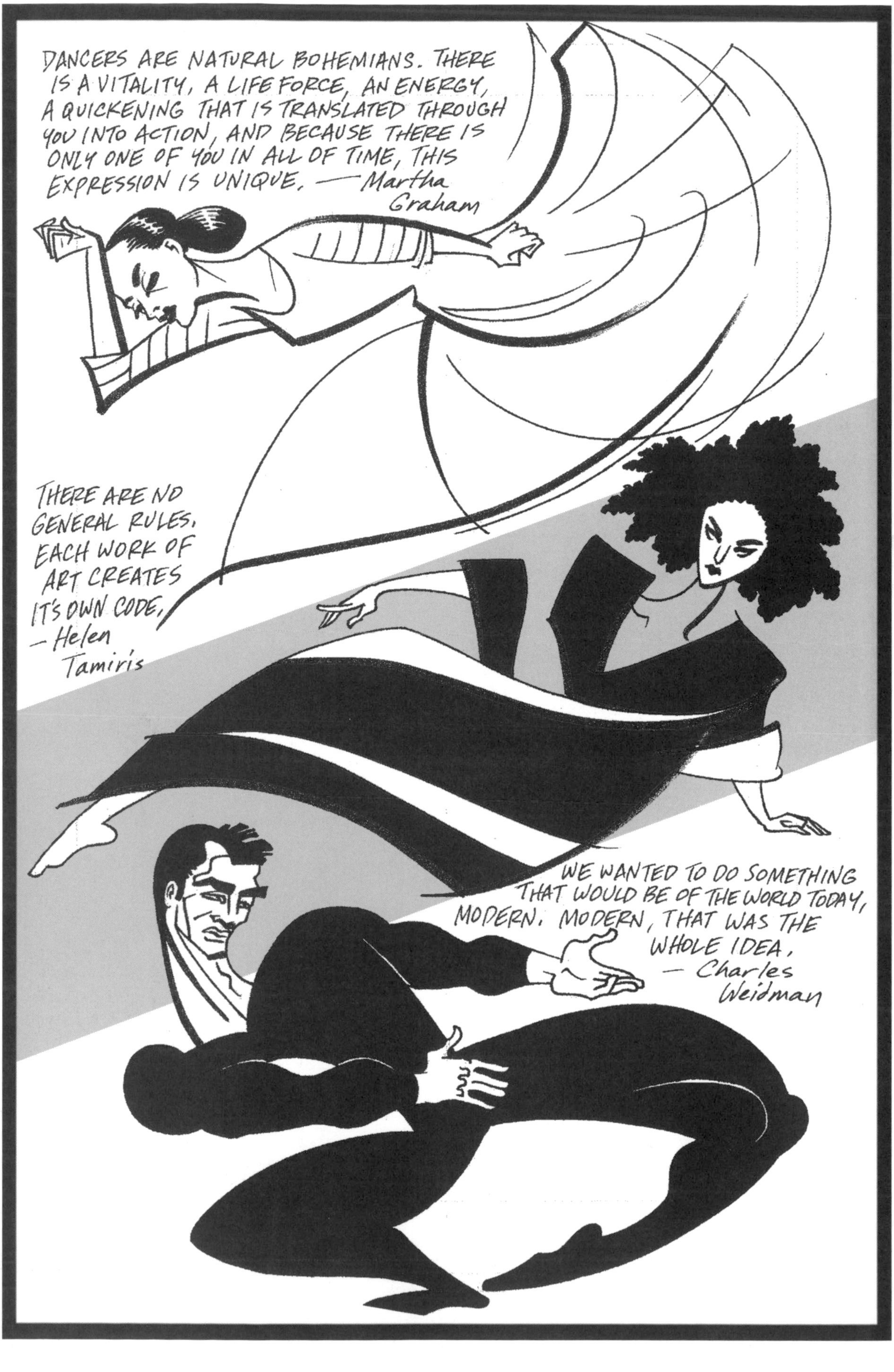
DANCERS ARE NATURAL BOHEMIANS. THERE IS A VITALITY, A LIFE FORCE, AN ENERGY, A QUICKENING THAT IS TRANSLATED THROUGH YOU INTO ACTION, AND BECAUSE THERE IS ONLY ONE OF YOU IN ALL OF TIME, THIS EXPRESSION IS UNIQUE. — Martha Graham
THERE ARE NO GENERAL RULES. EACH WORK OF ART CREATES IT'S OWN CODE. — Helen Tamiris
WE WANTED TO DO SOMETHING THAT WOULD BE OF THE WORLD TODAY, MODERN. MODERN, THAT WAS THE WHOLE IDEA. — Charles Weidman

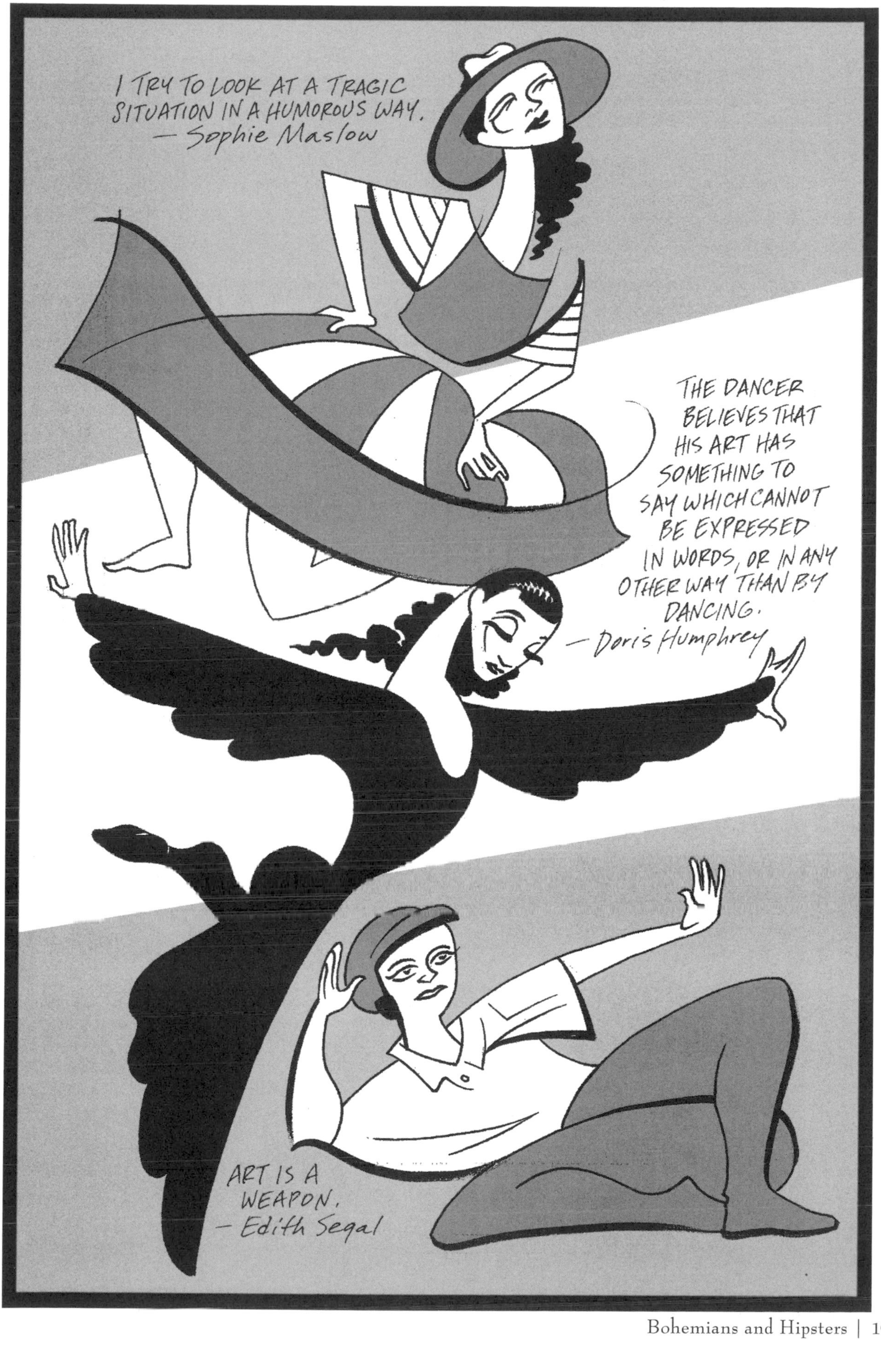
I TRY TO LOOK AT A TRAGIC SITUATION IN A HUMOROUS WAY.
— Sophie Maslow
THE DANCER BELIEVES THAT HIS ART HAS SOMETHING TO SAY WHICH CANNOT BE EXPRESSED IN WORDS, OR IN ANY OTHER WAY THAN BY DANCING.
— Doris Humphrey
ART IS A WEAPON.
— Edith Segal

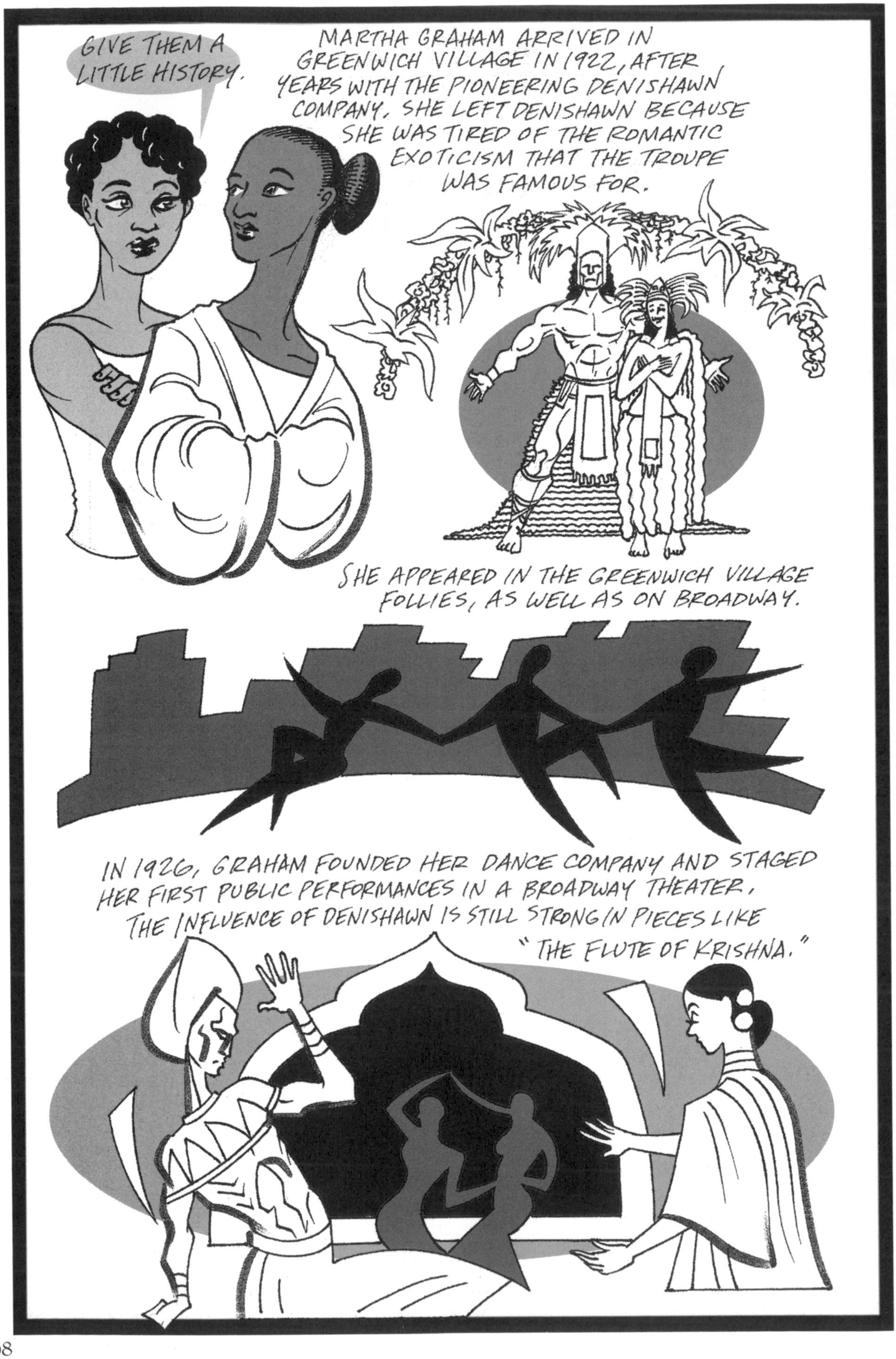
GIVE THEM A LITTLE HISTORY.
MARTHA GRAHAM ARRIVED IN GREENWICH VILLAGE IN 1922, AFTER YEARS WITH THE PIONEERING DENISHAWN COMPANY. SHE LEFT DENISHAWN BECAUSE SHE WAS TIRED OF THE ROMANTIC EXOTICISM THAT THE TROUPE WAS FAMOUS FOR.
SHE APPEARED IN THE GREENWICH VILLAGE FOLLIES, AS WELL AS ON BROADWAY.
IN 1926, GRAHAM FOUNDED HER DANCE COMPANY AND STAGED HER FIRST PUBLIC PERFORMANCES IN A BROADWAY THEATER. THE INFLUENCE OF DENISHAWN IS STILL STRONG IN PIECES LIKE "THE FLUTE OF KRISHNA."

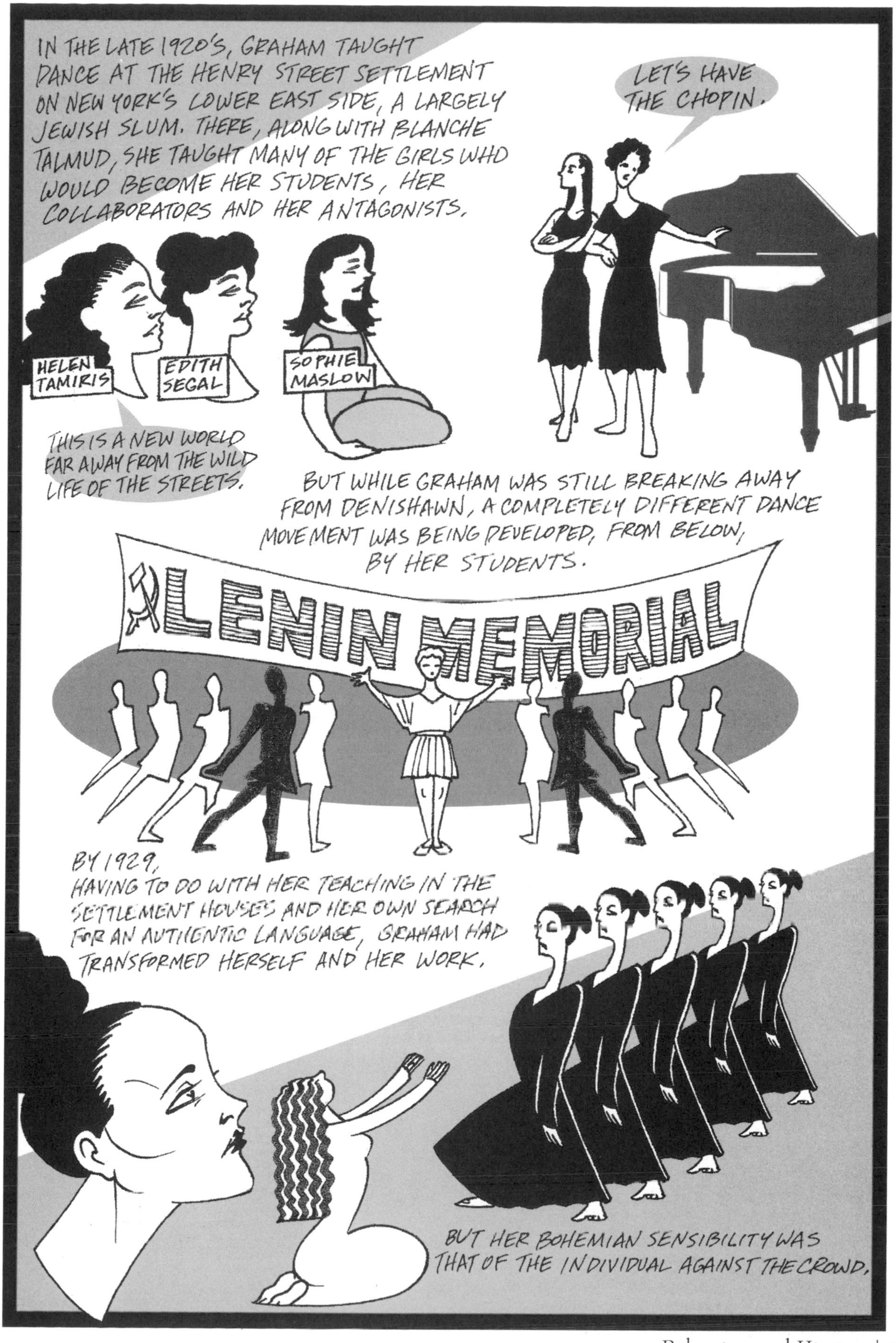
IN THE LATE 1920'S, GRAHAM TAUGHT DANCE AT THE HENRY STREET SETTLEMENT ON NEW YORK'S LOWER EAST SIDE, A LARGELY JEWISH SLUM. THERE, ALONG WITH BLANCHE TALMUD, SHE TAUGHT MANY OF THE GIRLS WHO WOULD BECOME HER STUDENTS, HER COLLABORATORS AND HER ANTAGONISTS.
LET'S HAVE THE CHOPIN.
HELEN TAMIRIS
EDITH SEGAL
SOPHIE MASLOW
THIS IS A NEW WORLD FAR AWAY FROM THE WILD LIFE OF THE STREETS.
BUT WHILE GRAHAM WAS STILL BREAKING AWAY FROM DENISHAWN, A COMPLETELY DIFFERENT DANCE MOVEMENT WAS BEING DEVELOPED, FROM BELOW, BY HER STUDENTS.
LENIN MEMORIAL
BY 1929, HAVING TO DO WITH HER TEACHING IN THE SETTLEMENT HOUSES AND HER OWN SEARCH FOR AN AUTHENTIC LANGUAGE, GRAHAM HAD TRANSFORMED HERSELF AND HER WORK.
BUT HER BOHEMIAN SENSIBILITY WAS THAT OF THE INDIVIDUAL AGAINST THE CROWD.

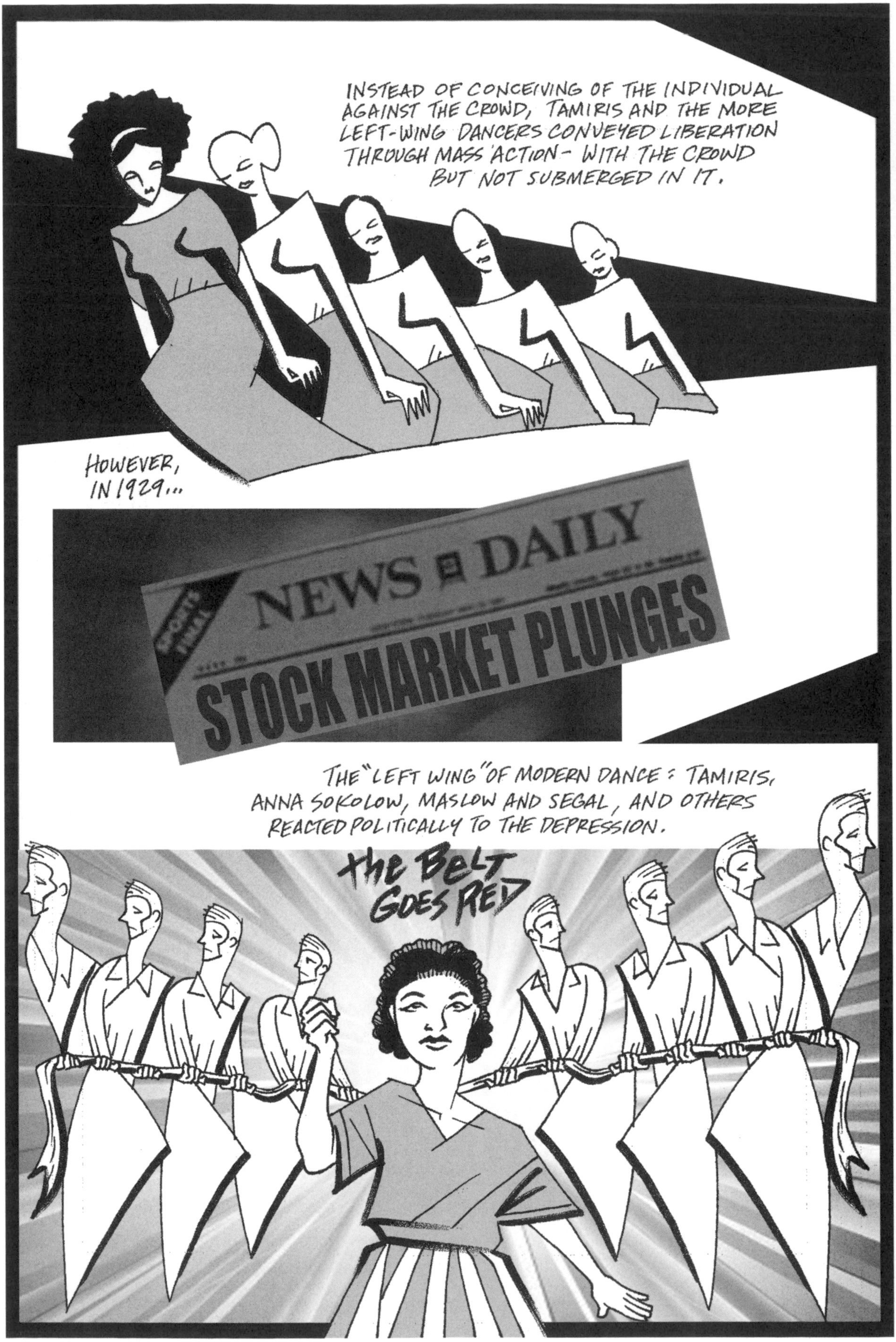
INSTEAD OF CONCEIVING OF THE INDIVIDUAL AGAINST THE CROWD, TAMIRIS AND THE MORE LEFT-WING DANCERS CONVEYED LIBERATION THROUGH MASS 'ACTION - WITH THE CROWD BUT NOT SUBMERGED IN IT.
HOWEVER, IN 1929...
NEWS DAILY
STOCK MARKET PLUNGES
THE "LEFT WING" OF MODERN DANCE: TAMIRIS, ANNA SOKOLOW, MASLOW AND SEGAL, AND OTHERS REACTED POLITICALLY TO THE DEPRESSION.
the BELT GOES RED

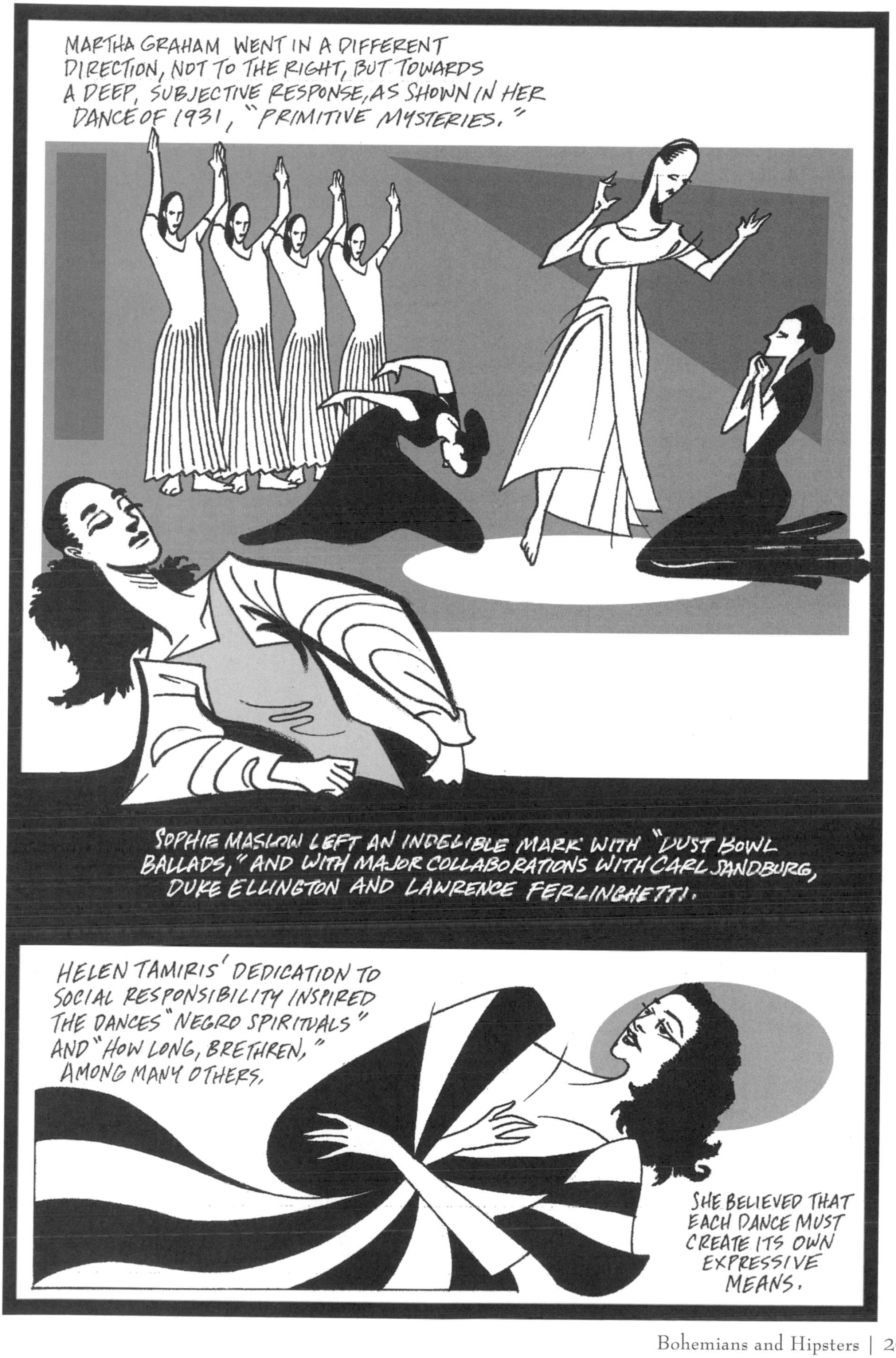
MARTHA GRAHAM WENT IN A DIFFERENT DIRECTION, NOT TO THE RIGHT, BUT TOWARDS A DEEP, SUBJECTIVE RESPONSE, AS SHOWN IN HER DANCE OF 1931, "PRIMITIVE MYSTERIES."
SOPHIE MASLOW LEFT AN INDELIBLE MARK WITH "DUST BOWL BALLADS," AND WITH MAJOR COLLABORATIONS WITH CARL SANDBURG, DUKE ELLINGTON AND LAWRENCE FERLINGHETTI.
HELEN TAMIRIS' DEDICATION TO SOCIAL RESPONSIBILITY INSPIRED THE DANCES "NEGRO SPIRITUALS" AND "HOW LONG, BRETHREN," AMONG MANY OTHERS.
SHE BELIEVED THAT EACH DANCE MUST CREATE ITS OWN EXPRESSIVE MEANS.

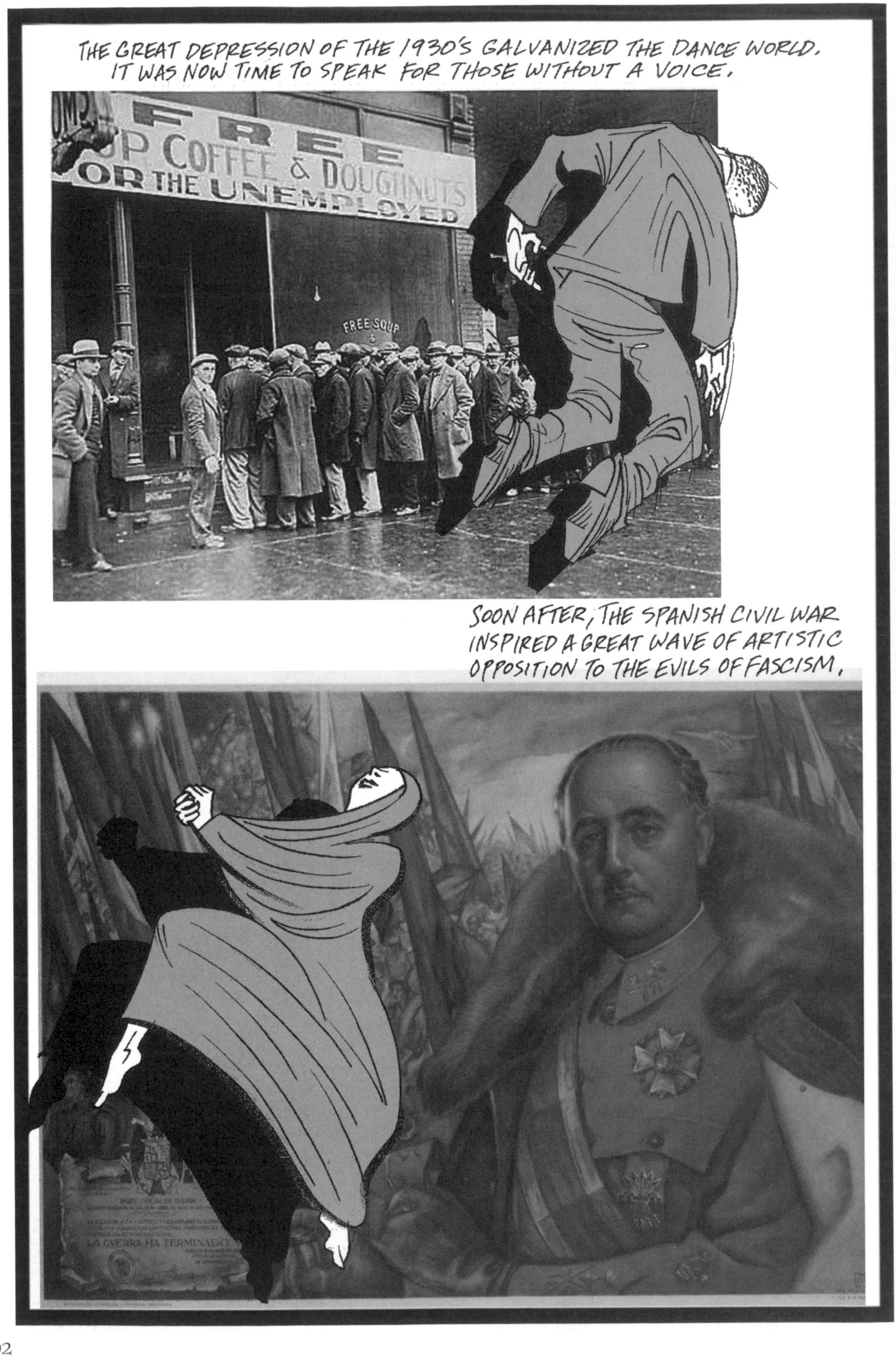
THE GREAT DEPRESSION OF THE 1930'S GALVANIZED THE DANCE WORLD. IT WAS NOW TIME TO SPEAK FOR THOSE WITHOUT A VOICE.
FREE
COFFEE & DOUGHNUTS
THE UNEMPLOYED
FREE SOUP
SOON AFTER, THE SPANISH CIVIL WAR INSPIRED A GREAT WAVE OF ARTISTIC OPPOSITION TO THE EVILS OF FASCISM.
LA GVERRA HA TERMINADO

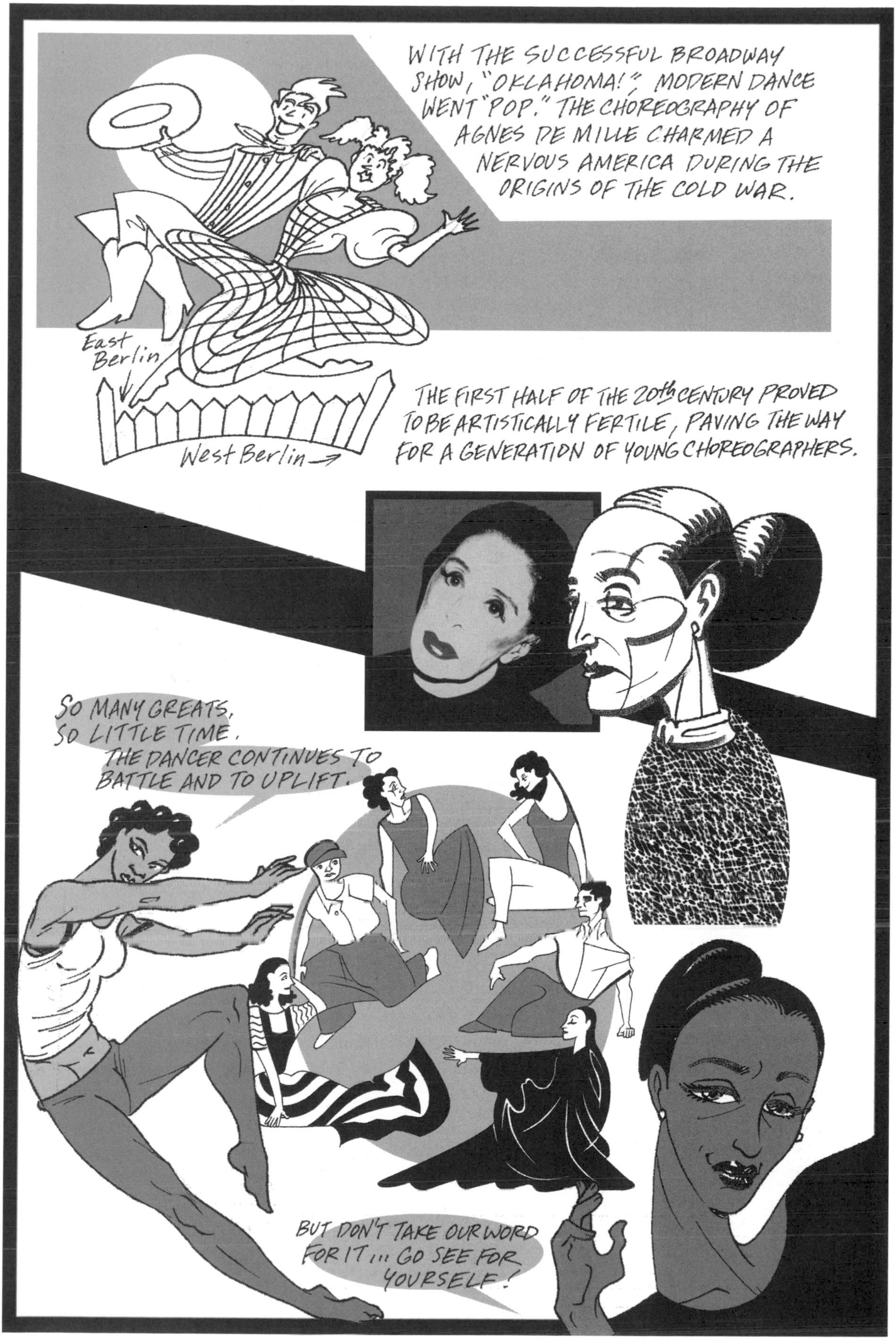
WITH THE SUCCESSFUL BROADWAY SHOW, "OKLAHOMA!," MODERN DANCE WENT "POP." THE CHOREOGRAPHY OF AGNES DE MILLE CHARMED A NERVOUS AMERICA DURING THE ORIGINS OF THE COLD WAR.
East Berlin
West Berlin
THE FIRST HALF OF THE 20th CENTURY PROVED TO BE ARTISTICALLY FERTILE, PAVING THE WAY FOR A GENERATION OF YOUNG CHOREOGRAPHERS.
SO MANY GREATS, SO LITTLE TIME.
THE DANCER CONTINUES TO BATTLE AND TO UPLIFT.
BUT DON'T TAKE OUR WORD FOR IT... GO SEE FOR YOURSELF!

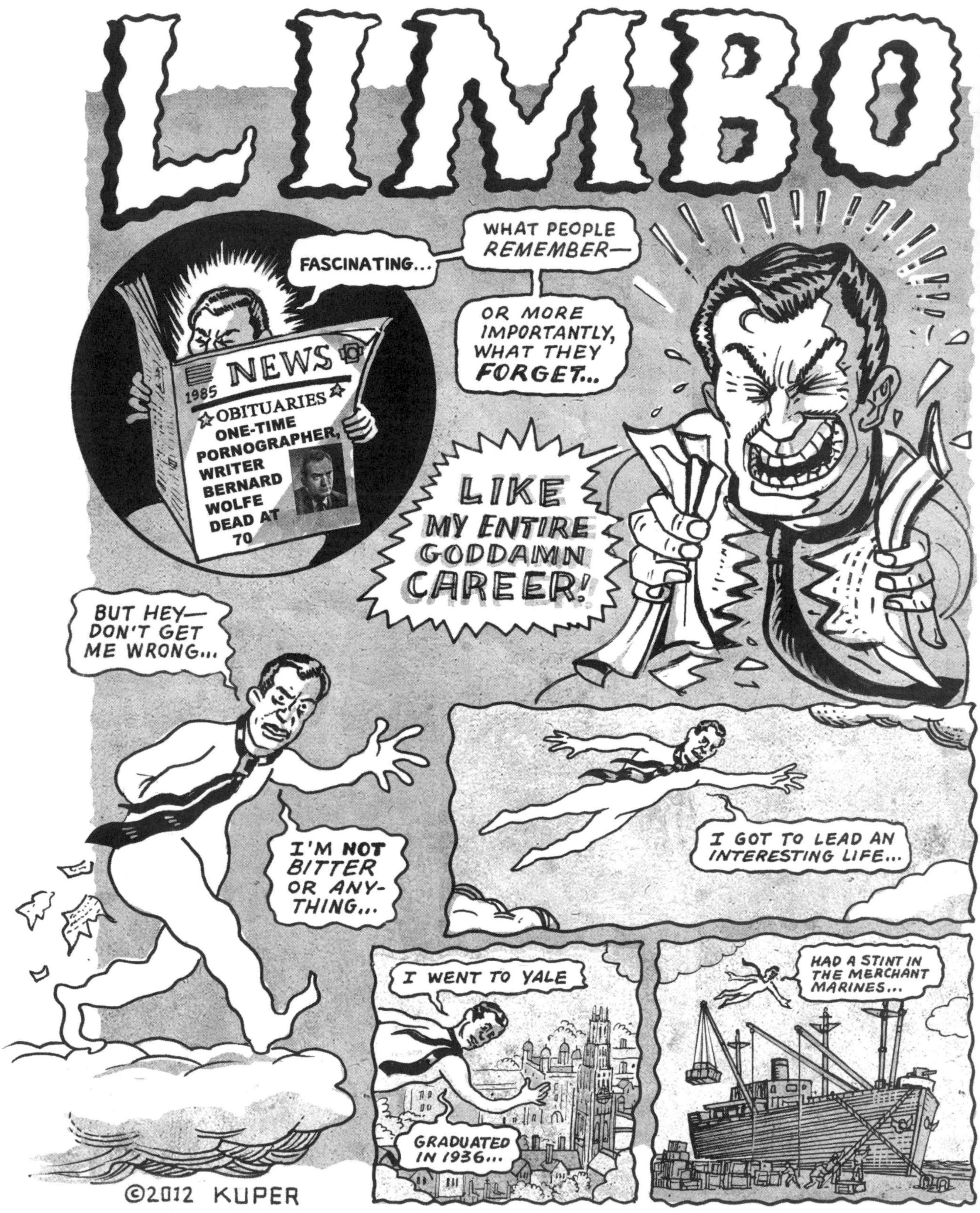
LIMBO
FASCINATING...
NEWS
1985
OBITUARIES
ONE-TIME PORNOGRAPHER, WRITER BERNARD WOLFE DEAD AT 70
WHAT PEOPLE REMEMBER—
OR MORE IMPORTANTLY, WHAT THEY FORGET...
LIKE MY ENTIRE GODDAMN CAREER!
BUT HEY— DON'T GET ME WRONG...
I'M NOT BITTER OR ANY-THING...
I GOT TO LEAD AN INTERESTING LIFE...
I WENT TO YALE
GRADUATED IN 1936...
HAD A STINT IN THE MERCHANT MARINES...
©2012 KUPER

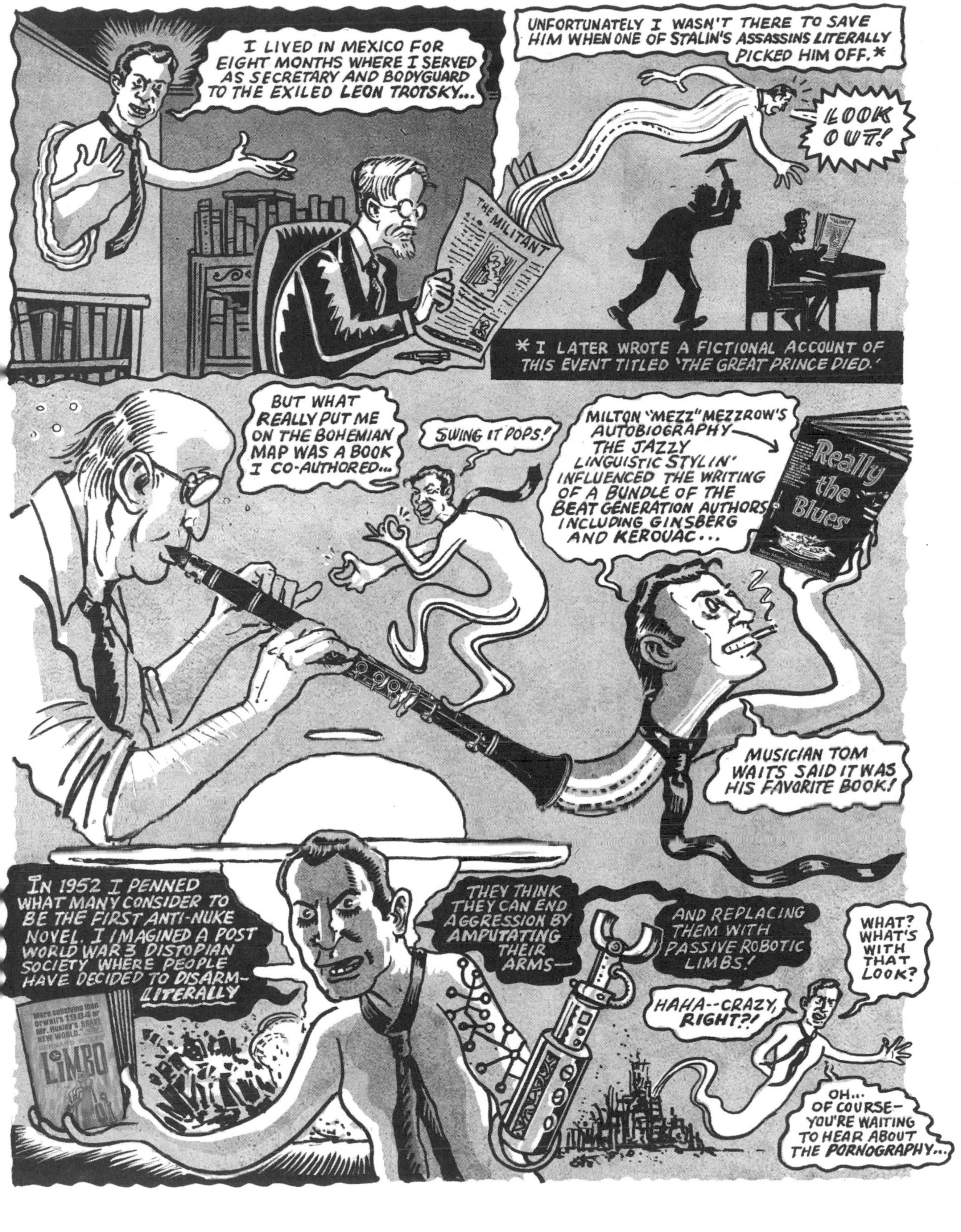
I LIVED IN MEXICO FOR EIGHT MONTHS WHERE I SERVED AS SECRETARY AND BODYGUARD TO THE EXILED LEON TROTSKY...
THE MILITANT
UNFORTUNATELY I WASN'T THERE TO SAVE HIM WHEN ONE OF STALIN'S ASSASSINS LITERALLY PICKED HIM OFF.*
LOOK OUT!
* I LATER WROTE A FICTIONAL ACCOUNT OF THIS EVENT TITLED 'THE GREAT PRINCE DIED.'
BUT WHAT REALLY PUT ME ON THE BOHEMIAN MAP WAS A BOOK I CO-AUTHORED...
SWING IT POPS!
MILTON "MEZZ" MEZZROW'S AUTOBIOGRAPHY THE JAZZY LINGUISTIC STYLIN' INFLUENCED THE WRITING OF A BUNDLE OF THE BEAT GENERATION AUTHORS INCLUDING GINSBERG AND KEROUAC...
Really the Blues
MUSICIAN TOM WAITS SAID IT WAS HIS FAVORITE BOOK!
IN 1952 I PENNED WHAT MANY CONSIDER TO BE THE FIRST ANTI-NUKE NOVEL. I IMAGINED A POST WORLD WAR 3 DISTOPIAN SOCIETY WHERE PEOPLE HAVE DECIDED TO DISARM-LITERALLY
"More satisfying than Orwell's 1984 or Mr. Huxley's BRAVE NEW WORLD."
LIMBO
THEY THINK THEY CAN END AGGRESSION BY AMPUTATING THEIR ARMS—
AND REPLACING THEM WITH PASSIVE ROBOTIC LIMBS!
HAHA--CRAZY, RIGHT?!
WHAT? WHAT'S WITH THAT LOOK?
OH... OF COURSE- YOU'RE WAITING TO HEAR ABOUT THE PORNOGRAPHY...

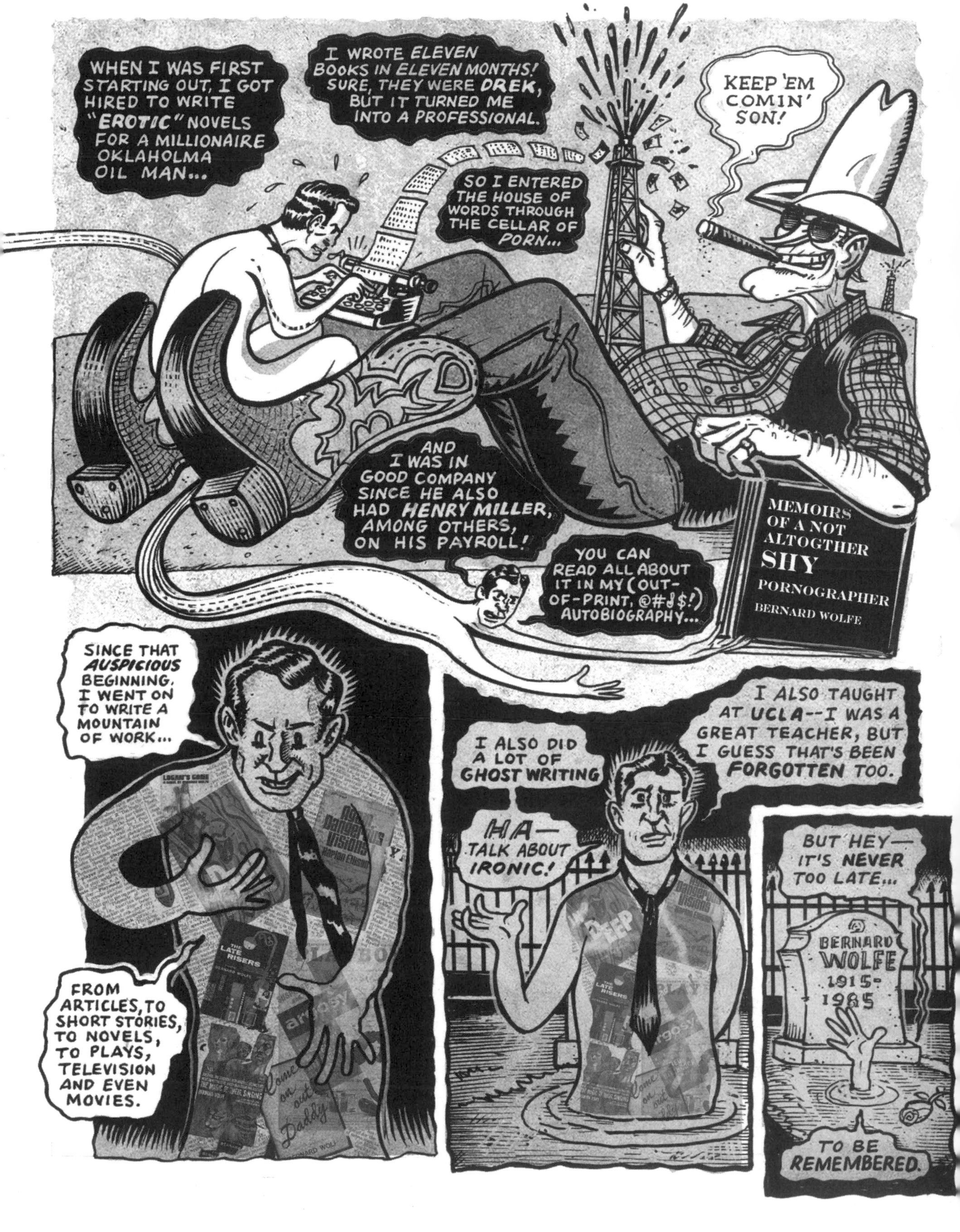
WHEN I WAS FIRST STARTING OUT, I GOT HIRED TO WRITE "EROTIC" NOVELS FOR A MILLIONAIRE OKLAHOLMA OIL MAN...
I WROTE ELEVEN BOOKS IN ELEVEN MONTHS! SURE, THEY WERE DREK, BUT IT TURNED ME INTO A PROFESSIONAL.
KEEP 'EM COMIN' SON!
SO I ENTERED THE HOUSE OF WORDS THROUGH THE CELLAR OF PORN...
AND I WAS IN GOOD COMPANY SINCE HE ALSO HAD HENRY MILLER, AMONG OTHERS, ON HIS PAYROLL!
YOU CAN READ ALL ABOUT IT IN MY (OUT-OF-PRINT, @#$!) AUTOBIOGRAPHY...
MEMOIRS OF A NOT ALTOGTHER SHY PORNOGRAPHER
BERNARD WOLFE
SINCE THAT AUSPICIOUS BEGINNING, I WENT ON TO WRITE A MOUNTAIN OF WORK...
FROM ARTICLES, TO SHORT STORIES, TO NOVELS, TO PLAYS, TELEVISION AND EVEN MOVIES.
I ALSO DID A LOT OF GHOST WRITING
I ALSO TAUGHT AT UCLA--I WAS A GREAT TEACHER, BUT I GUESS THAT'S BEEN FORGOTTEN TOO.
HA— TALK ABOUT IRONIC!
BUT HEY— IT'S NEVER TOO LATE...
BERNARD WOLFE 1915-1985
TO BE REMEMBERED.

Chapter Nine

The Look Back

In the early 1960s, Bohemia was about to be rediscovered. This is not properly part of our story. We nevertheless recall here two young, seemingly oddball characters contemplating together the leavings of a cultural history that was growing practically anonymous as the suburbs blossomed and the old cities staggered downward. It is valuable to note that Harvey Pekar, older by a half-dozen years than Robert Crumb, grew up in a triple decker tenement, speaking Yiddish with his grandfather. He tapped the experiences and memories of pre–World War II ethnic communities without knowing it, and grew toward the creation of a new kind of comic art as he surveyed his own life, as comics self-publisher and Veterans Administration clerk, homeboy hipster, and visionary. Robert Crumb had literally just escaped a brutal and alienating home for the aging metropolis and a hack job at a greeting card company. Crumb's LSD experiences, triggering a memory of street signage, animated films and more, coincided with Pekar's real life experiences extended backward through family, or accumulated firsthand as the traces remained around him. There are ample other personal stories in the remaking of comic art. None are more poignant.

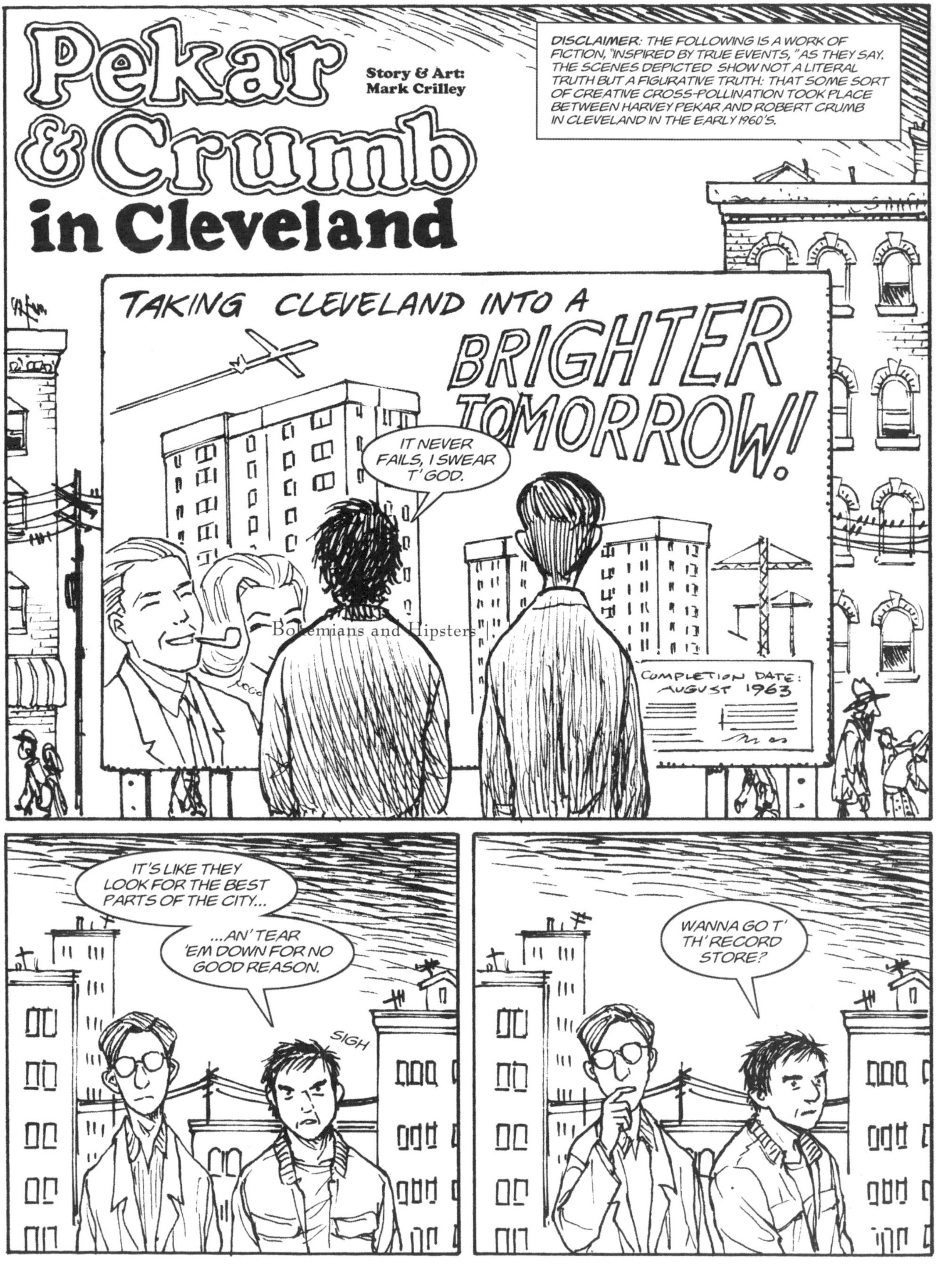
Pekar & Crumb in Cleveland
Story & Art: Mark Crilley
DISCLAIMER: THE FOLLOWING IS A WORK OF FICTION, "INSPIRED BY TRUE EVENTS," AS THEY SAY. THE SCENES DEPICTED SHOW NOT A LITERAL TRUTH BUT A FIGURATIVE TRUTH: THAT SOME SORT OF CREATIVE CROSS-POLLINATION TOOK PLACE BETWEEN HARVEY PEKAR AND ROBERT CRUMB IN CLEVELAND IN THE EARLY 1960'S.
TAKING CLEVELAND INTO A BRIGHTER TOMORROW!
COMPLETION DATE: AUGUST 1963
IT NEVER FAILS, I SWEAR T'GOD.
IT'S LIKE THEY LOOK FOR THE BEST PARTS OF THE CITY...
...AN' TEAR 'EM DOWN FOR NO GOOD REASON.
SIGH
WANNA GO T' TH' RECORD STORE?

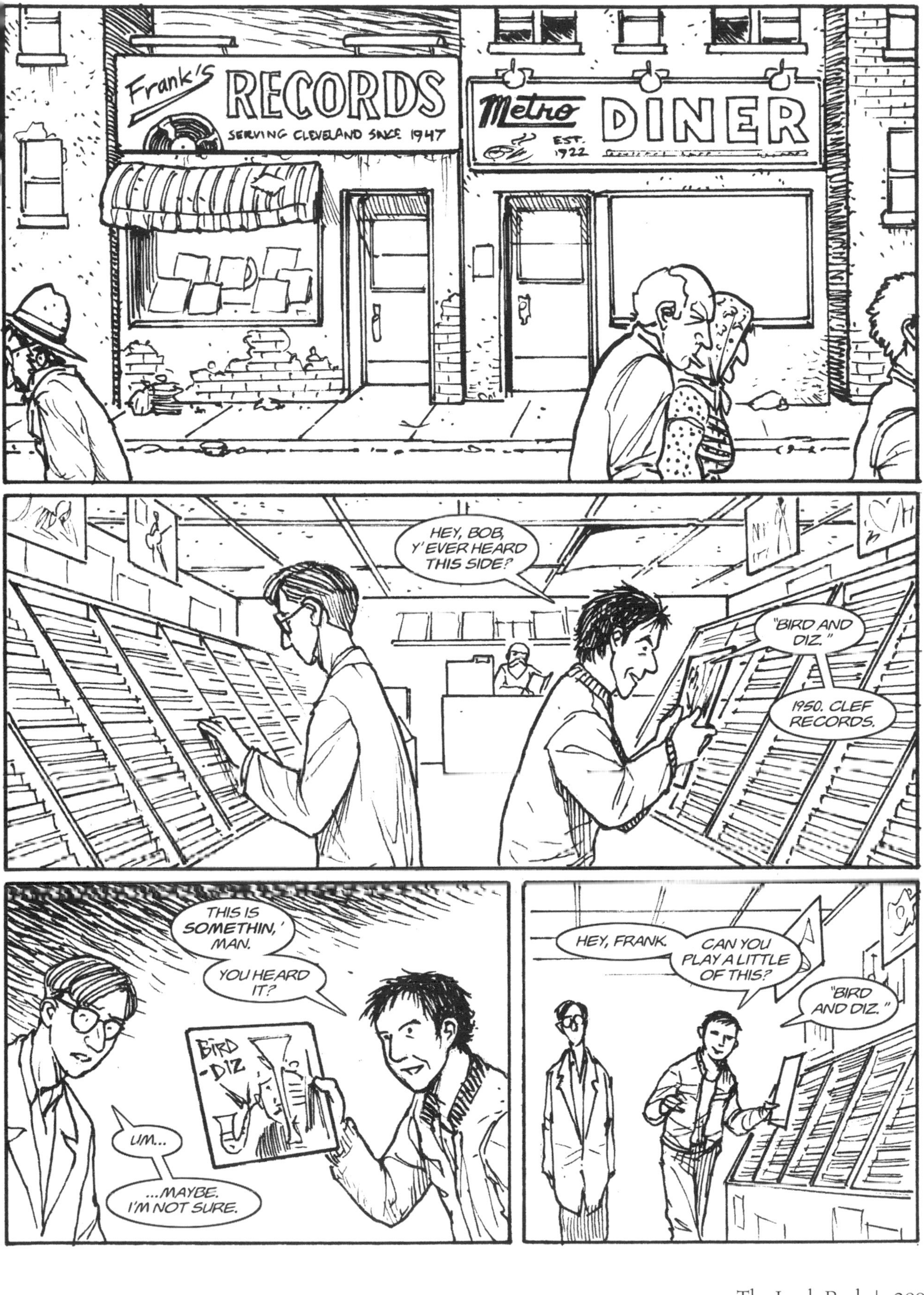
Frank's RECORDS
SERVING CLEVELAND SINCE 1947
Metro DINER
EST. 1922
HEY, BOB, Y' EVER HEARD THIS SIDE?
"BIRD AND DIZ."
1950. CLEF RECORDS.
THIS IS SOMETHIN,' MAN.
YOU HEARD IT?
BIRD -DIZ
UM...
...MAYBE. I'M NOT SURE.
HEY, FRANK.
CAN YOU PLAY A LITTLE OF THIS?
"BIRD AND DIZ."

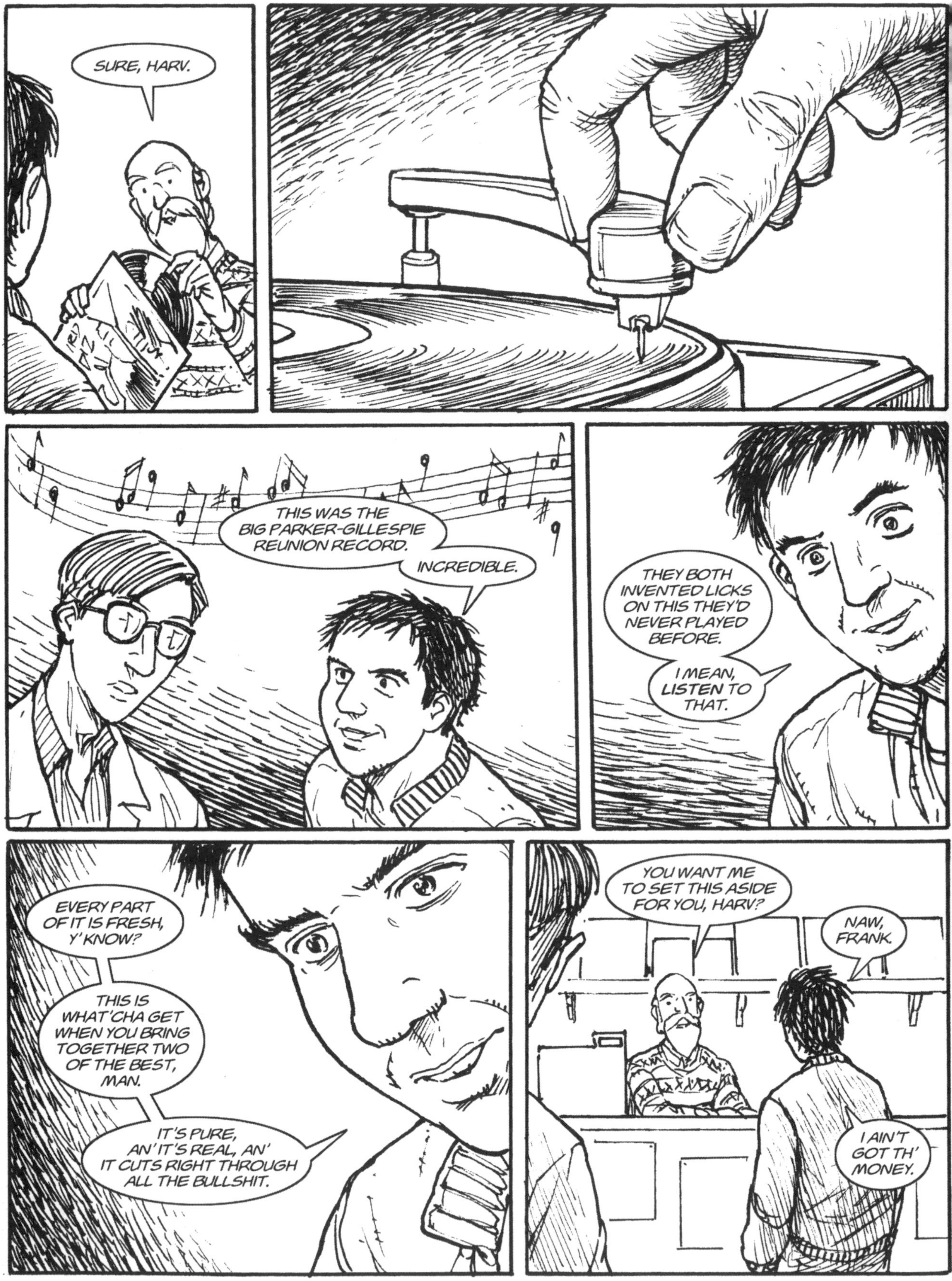
SURE, HARV.
THIS WAS THE BIG PARKER-GILLESPIE REUNION RECORD.
INCREDIBLE.
THEY BOTH INVENTED LICKS ON THIS THEY'D NEVER PLAYED BEFORE.
I MEAN, LISTEN TO THAT.
EVERY PART OF IT IS FRESH, Y'KNOW?
THIS IS WHAT'CHA GET WHEN YOU BRING TOGETHER TWO OF THE BEST, MAN.
IT'S PURE, AN' IT'S REAL, AN' IT CUTS RIGHT THROUGH ALL THE BULLSHIT.
YOU WANT ME TO SET THIS ASIDE FOR YOU, HARV?
NAW, FRANK.
I AIN'T GOT TH' MONEY.

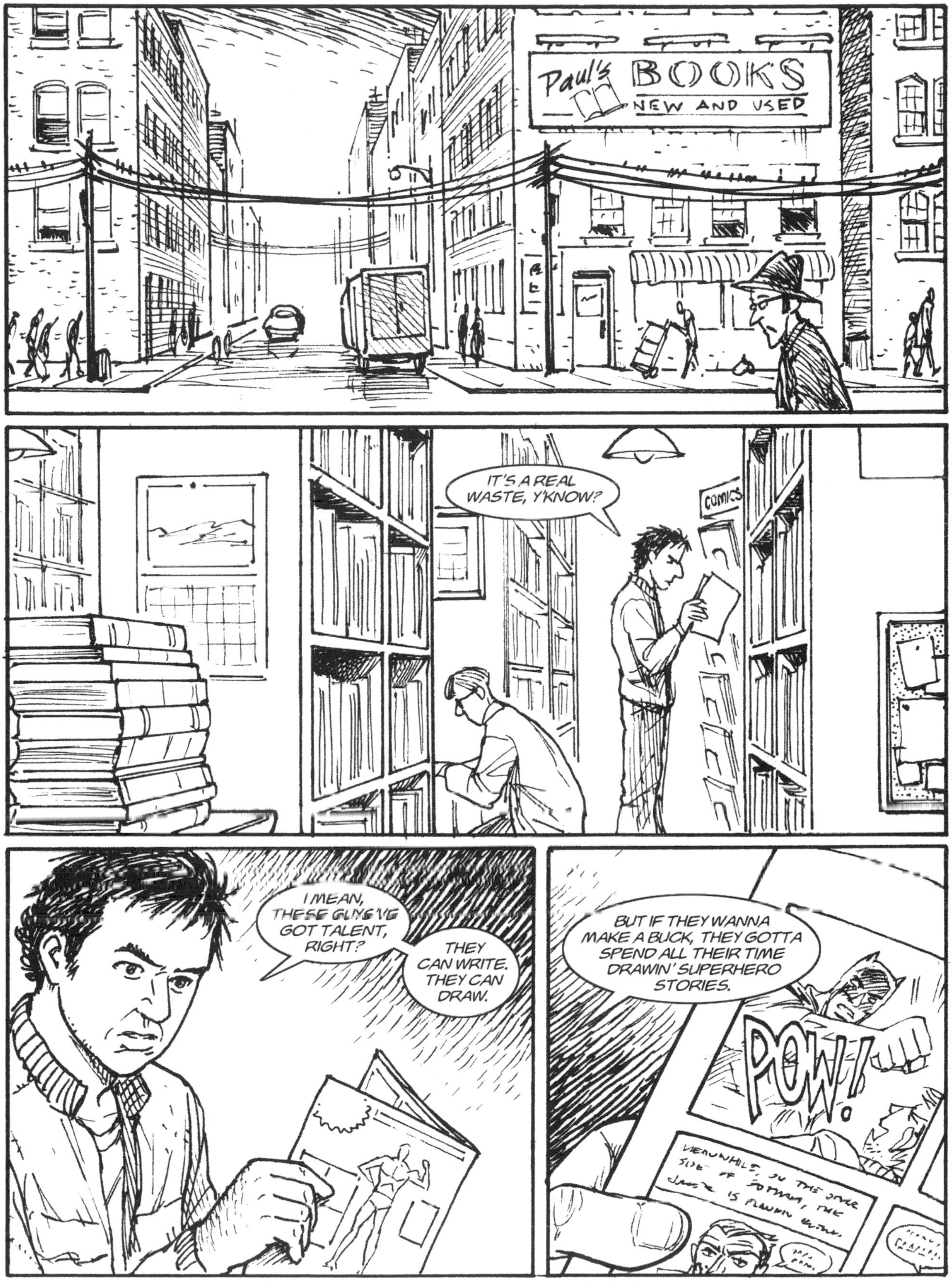
Paul's BOOKS
NEW AND USED
COMICS
IT'S A REAL WASTE, Y'KNOW?
I MEAN, THESE GUYS'VE GOT TALENT, RIGHT?
THEY CAN WRITE. THEY CAN DRAW.
BUT IF THEY WANNA MAKE A BUCK, THEY GOTTA SPEND ALL THEIR TIME DRAWIN' SUPERHERO STORIES.
POW!

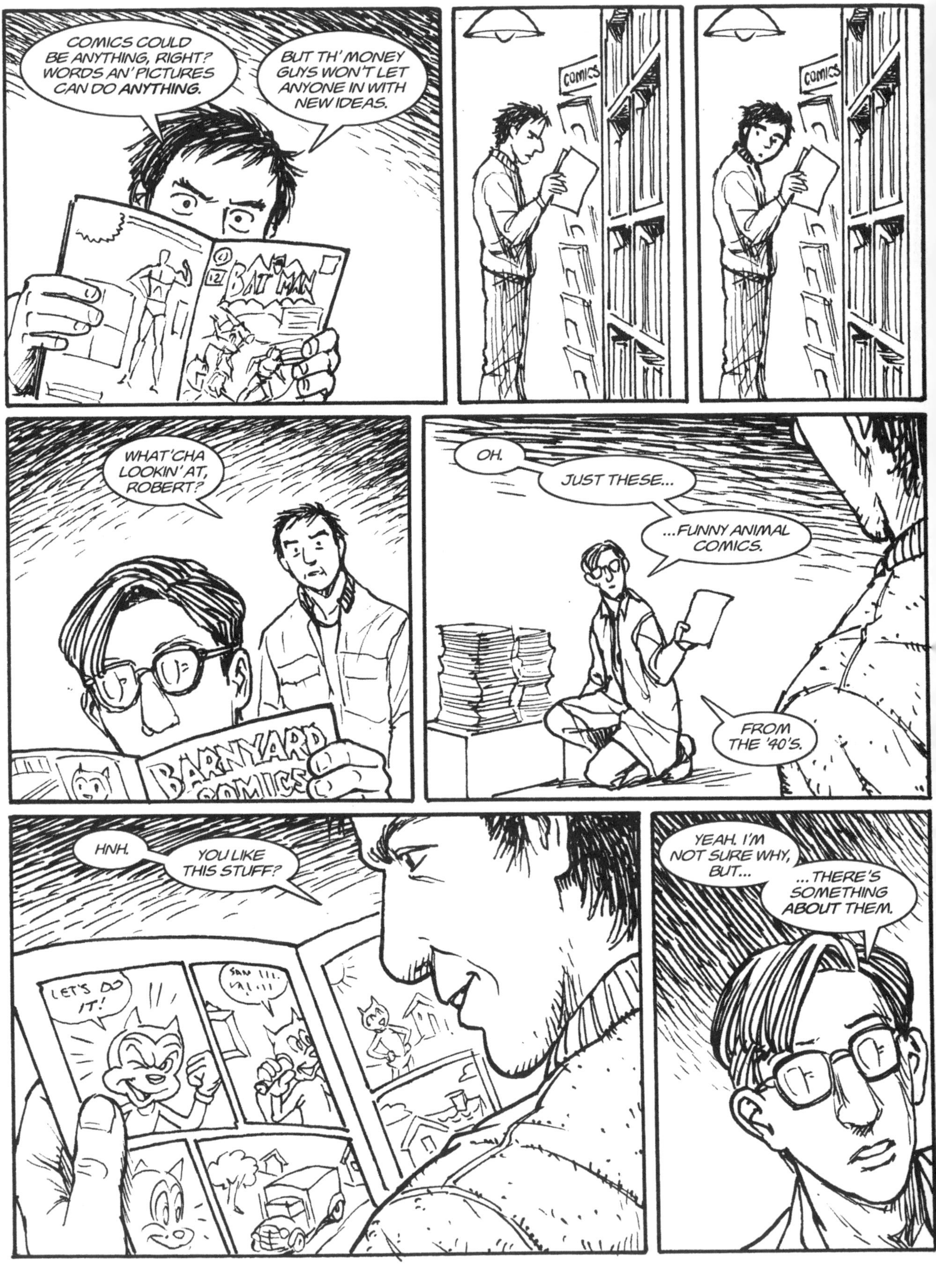
COMICS COULD BE ANYTHING, RIGHT? WORDS AN' PICTURES CAN DO **ANYTHING**.
BUT TH' MONEY GUYS WON'T LET ANYONE IN WITH NEW IDEAS.
BATMAN
COMICS
COMICS
WHAT'CHA LOOKIN' AT, ROBERT?
BARNYARD COMICS
OH.
JUST THESE...
...FUNNY ANIMAL COMICS.
FROM THE '40'S.
HNH.
YOU LIKE THIS STUFF?
LET'S DO IT!
YEAH. I'M NOT SURE WHY, BUT...
...THERE'S SOMETHING ABOUT THEM.

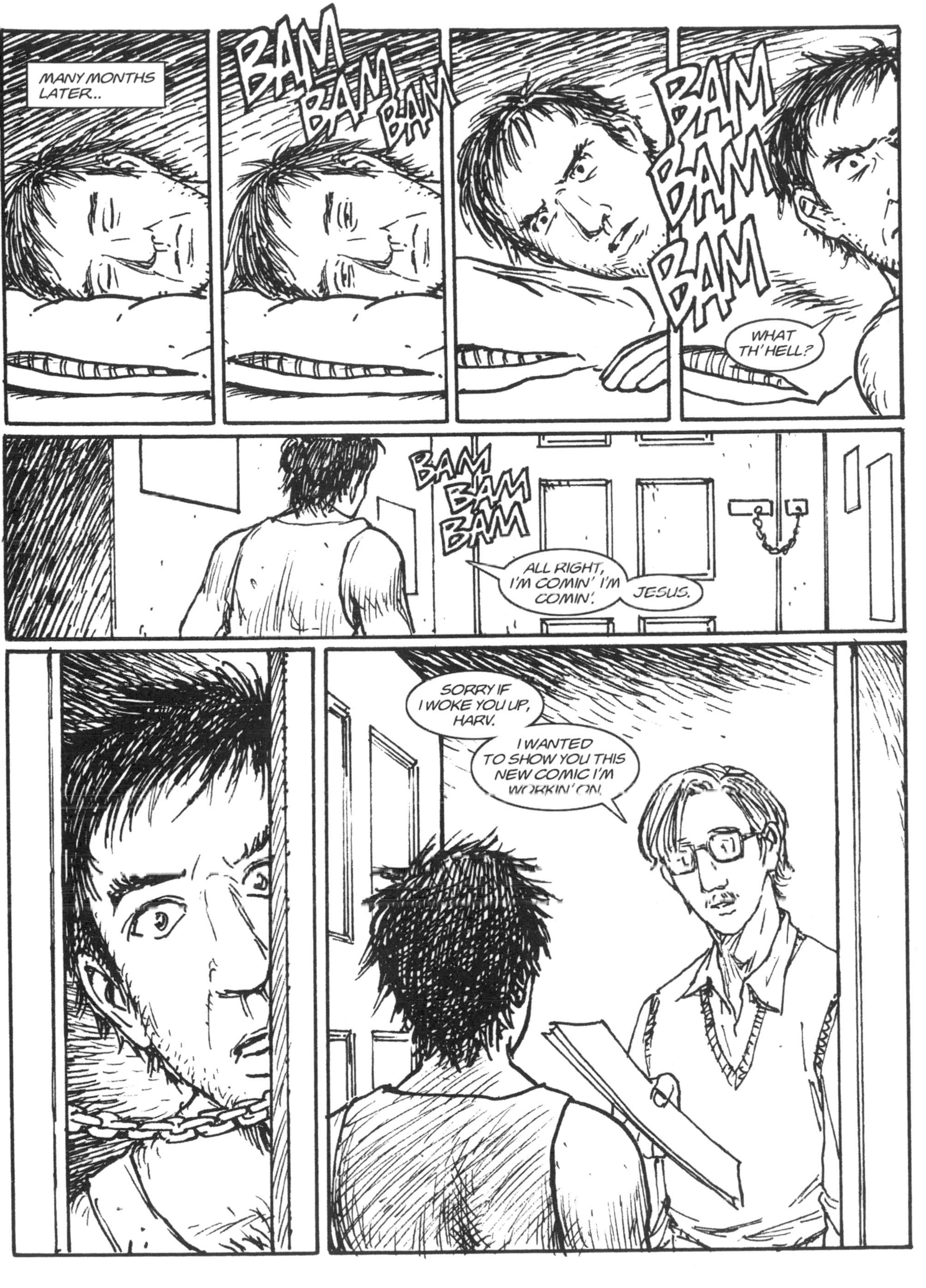
MANY MONTHS LATER...
BAM BAM BAM
BAM BAM BAM
WHAT TH' HELL?
BAM BAM BAM
ALL RIGHT, I'M COMIN' I'M COMIN'.
JESUS.
SORRY IF I WOKE YOU UP, HARV.
I WANTED TO SHOW YOU THIS NEW COMIC I'M WORKIN' ON.

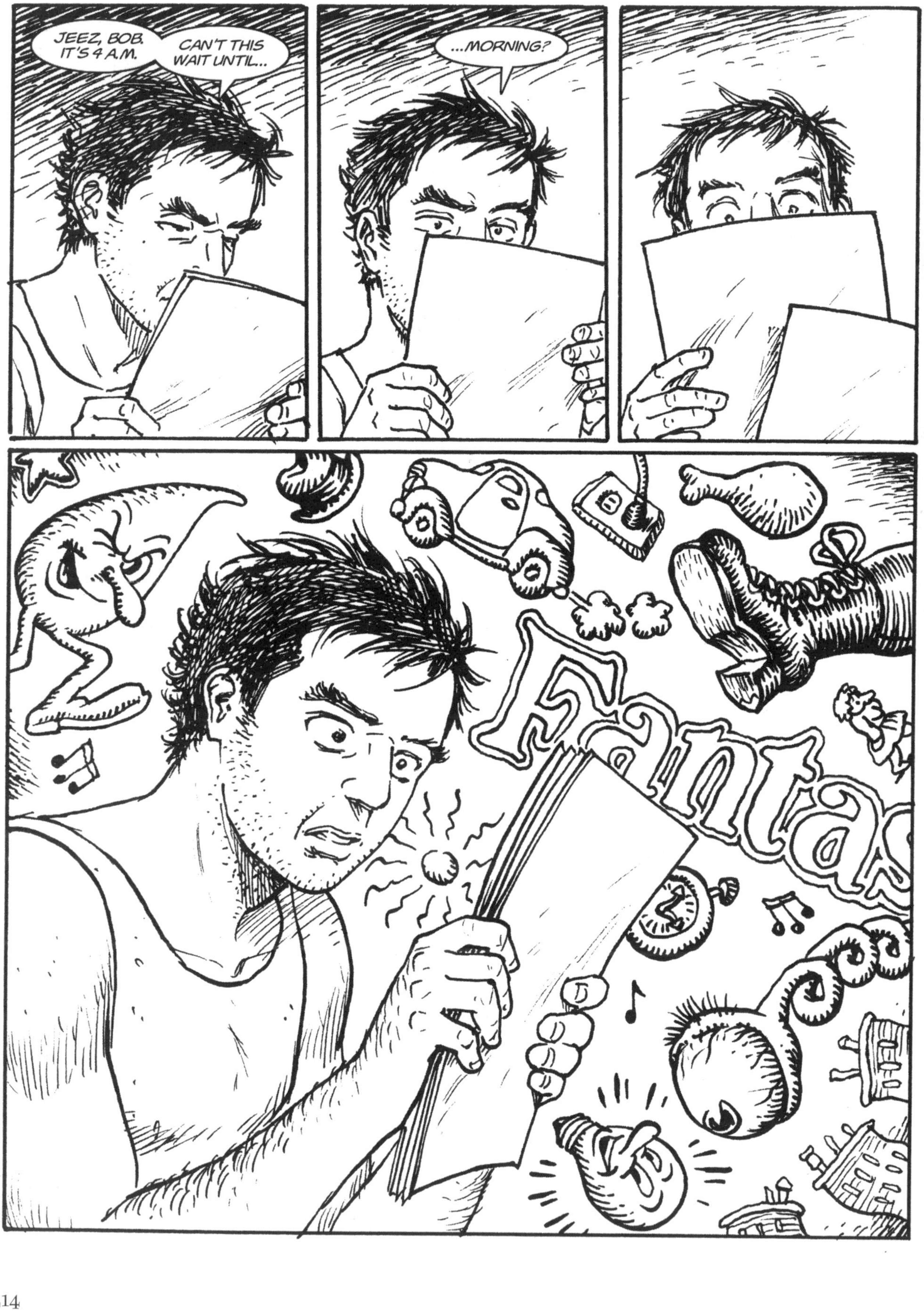
JEEZ, BOB. IT'S 4 A.M.
CAN'T THIS WAIT UNTIL...
...MORNING?
Fantas

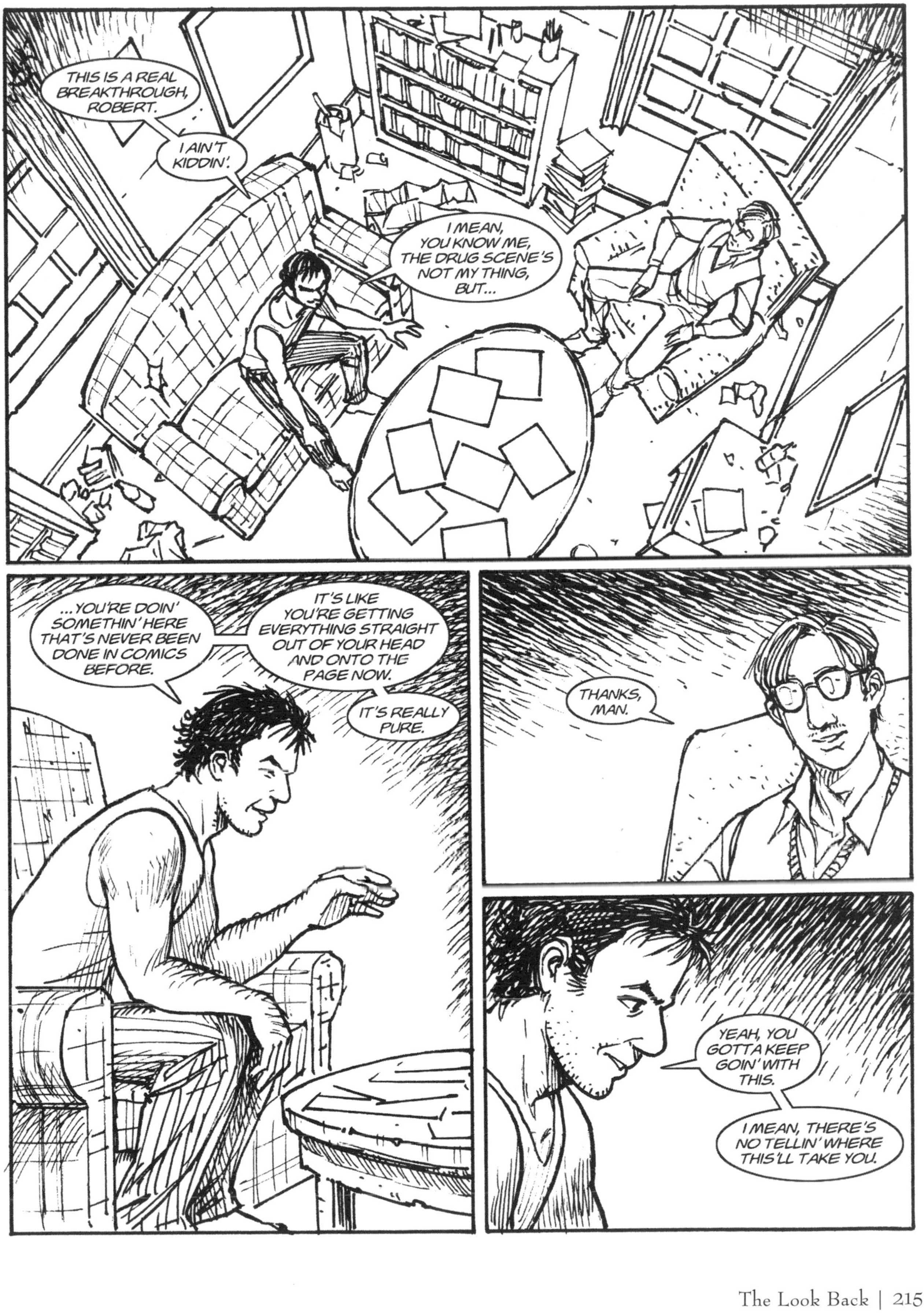
THIS IS A REAL BREAKTHROUGH, ROBERT.
I AIN'T KIDDIN'.
I MEAN, YOU KNOW ME, THE DRUG SCENE'S NOT MY THING, BUT...
...YOU'RE DOIN' SOMETHIN' HERE THAT'S NEVER BEEN DONE IN COMICS BEFORE.
IT'S LIKE YOU'RE GETTING EVERYTHING STRAIGHT OUT OF YOUR HEAD AND ONTO THE PAGE NOW.
IT'S REALLY PURE.
THANKS, MAN.
YEAH, YOU GOTTA KEEP GOIN' WITH THIS.
I MEAN, THERE'S NO TELLIN' WHERE THIS'LL TAKE YOU.

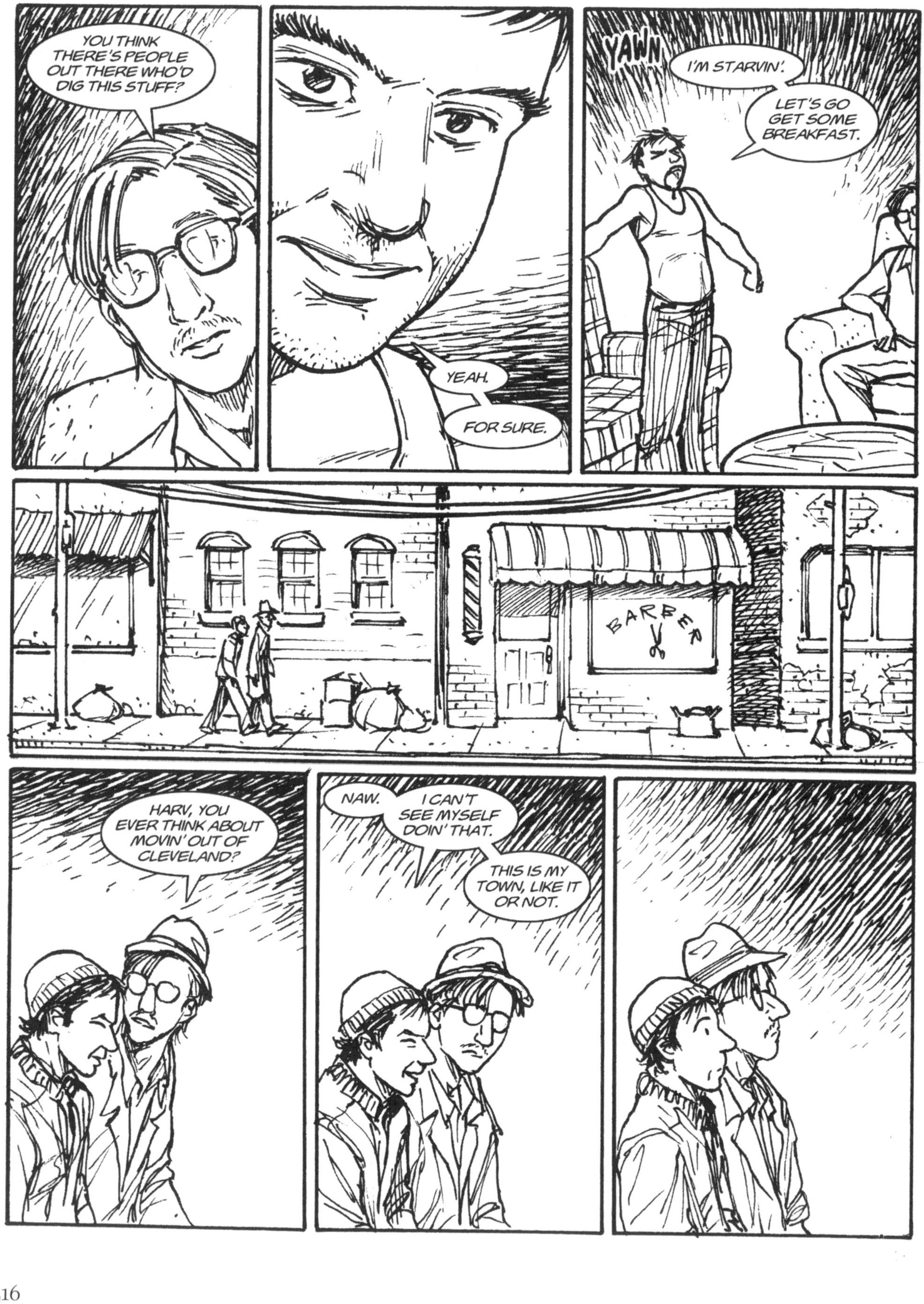
YOU THINK THERE'S PEOPLE OUT THERE WHO'D DIG THIS STUFF?
YEAH.
FOR SURE.
YAWN
I'M STARVIN'.
LET'S GO GET SOME BREAKFAST.
BARBER
HARV, YOU EVER THINK ABOUT MOVIN' OUT OF CLEVELAND?
NAW.
I CAN'T SEE MYSELF DOIN' THAT.
THIS IS MY TOWN, LIKE IT OR NOT.

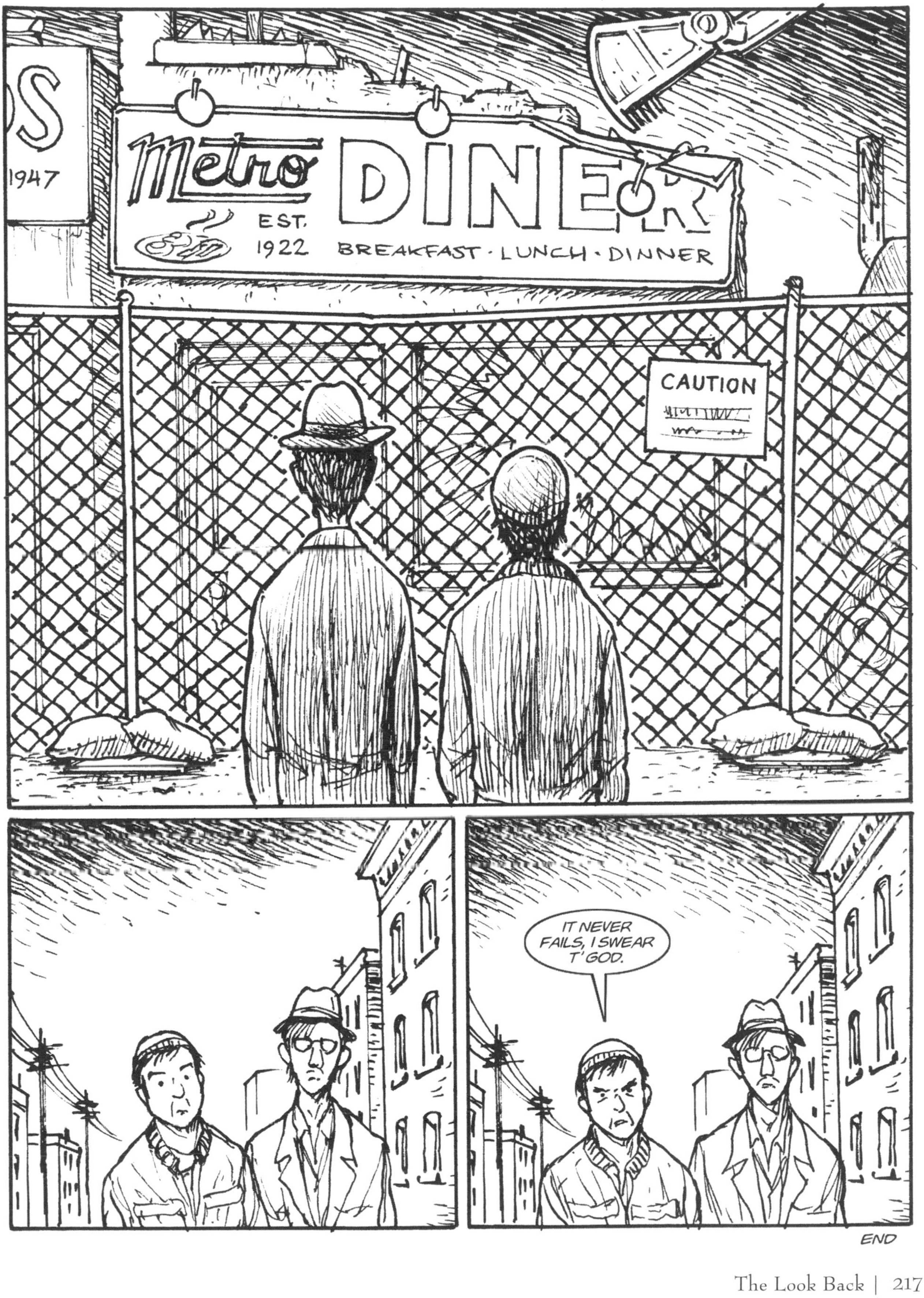
1947
Metro DINER
EST. 1922
BREAKFAST · LUNCH · DINNER
CAUTION
IT NEVER FAILS, I SWEAR T'GOD.
END

Where does bohemia end, and for that matter, where does it stand in the twenty-first century?

Jerrold Siegel, one of the architects of modern scholarship on the subject, ends his classic volume by observing that if bohemia seems in the past, new spaces will be discovered, new styles "appropriated or invented."* Obituaries for bohemia have, in short, always been premature.

*Jerrold Siegel, *Bohemian Paris: Culture, Politics, and the Boundaries of Bourgeois Life, 1830–1930* (Baltimore: Johns Hopkins University Press, 1999 ed.), p. 397.

The Editors

Paul Buhle retired from Brown University and Providence, Rhode Island in 2009, to Madison, Wisconsin and full-time work editing comics. His many books include the Verso volumes *Marxism in the United States* (third edition, 2013), *Wobblies!* (2005), and the authorized biography *C.L.R. James: The Artist as Revolutionary* (1988).

David Berger was born and raised first in Brooklyn and then in that most bohemian of suburbs Croton-on-Hudson. He currently writes and teaches and sometimes occupies Wall Street while residing in Chelsea with his wife, the singer/songwriter Audra "MsBlu" Berger.

The Contributors

Hilary Allison is a young comicstripper and freelance illustrator, as well as an editor at *World War 3 Illustrated*. Her comics can be read online at HilaryAllison.com.

Luisa Cetti, a translator and independent scholar, has written various essays on women's experiences in nineteenth-century utopian experiments. She lives in Milan, Italy.

Perhaps best known as the writer/artist of the Those Annoying Post Bros. comic book series, **Matt Howarth**'s creative outlets span numerous genres and modes—science fiction, fantasy, horror, electronic music—and all of them are notoriously strange. For more info, visit MattHowarth.com.

Sabrina Jones rediscovered Walt Whitman while creating a graphic biography of his fan Isadora Duncan. Sabrina is a longtime contributor and editor of *World War 3 Illustrated*. She has created comics on social justice and radical history for *Wobblies!*, Studs Terkel's *Working*, *Yiddishkeit*, *The Real Cost of Prisons*, *FDR and the New Deal for Beginners*, and *Radical Jesus*. She adapted Marc Mauer's *Race to Incarcerate: A Graphic Retelling*.

Jay Kinney is an editor, author and former underground cartoonist. A member—along with Skip Williamson, Jay Lynch and Robert Crumb—of the original Bijou Funnies crew, he also edited, with Bill Griffith, the romance comic satire *Young Lust*. He later founded the political comic *Anarchy Comics*, which has been recently anthologized in its entirety by PM Press. He has also written two books and published *Gnosis Magazine* (1985–99), focused on aspects of Western esoteric traditions.

Milton Knight, born in 1962 in Mineola, NY, and graduated from BOCES Cultural Arts Center (Syosset, NY). His work has appeared in *Heavy Metal*, *High Times*, *National Lampoon* and *Nickelodeon Magazine*, as well as a long, current series of fiction adaptations for *Graphic Classics*. His own comics titles include *Hugo*, *Midnite the Rebel Skunk* and *Slug and Ginger*. MiltonKnight.net.

Peter Kuper grew up in Cleveland, where he met Harvey Pekar and a visiting Robert Crumb, moved to New York in 1977 where his first job (ironically) was inking *Richie Rich* comics. In 1979 (not ironically) he co-founded *World War 3 Illustrated* with Seth Tobocman, and since 1997 has drawn the "Spy vs. Spy" feature for *Mad Magazine*. He has done comic adaptations of Franz Kafka and Upton Sinclair as well as dozens of his own graphic novels. He lives in New York when he is not gallivanting around Mexico.

David Lasky has created a number of critically acclaimed comic books, including a nine-page mini-adaptation of Joyce's *Ulysses*, eight issues of *Boom Boom Comics*, two issues of the award-nominated *Urban Hipster* and numerous short comics for anthologies including *The Best American Comics 2011*. His collaboration with writer Frank Young, *The Carter Family: Don't Forget This Song* was released in October 2012.

Jeffrey Lewis, based in New York City for thirty-six years, is the writer/artist/publisher of the comic book series Fuff. He tours the world with his band *Jeffrey Lewis and the Junkyard*, releasing albums on Rough Trade Records as well as doing occasional art, writing, working on songs and/or comic books for the History Channel, the *New York Times*, the *Guardian*, and others. His most recent illustration work includes the book *Gender and Sexuality for Beginners*.

Born on Long Island, illustrator and writer **Ellen Lindner** is the author of *Undertow*, a graphic novel about Coney Island in the early sixties, and edits the *Strumpet*, a transatlantic comics magazine showcasing work by up and coming women cartoonists. littlewhitebird.com.

Lisa Lyons and her husband live a life of bohemian abandon in a utopian community of two in a small town on the ocean in Maine. In the '60s and '70s Lisa lived in Berkeley, Oakland, and Detroit, and drew for a wide range of radical and movement organizations, including the Peace and Freedom Party, SDS, the Farm Workers, and the Black Panther Party. Her work appeared in

Workers Power and *Liberation News Service*, and she illustrated *MacBird* and was published in *It Ain't Me Babe*. Today, Lisa contributes art to *New Politics*, and is writing a utopian novel.

Summer McClinton studied printmaking at the University of Wisconsin, co-published her own comic *Thread: The Unraveling*, contributed to *The Beats*, drew for a script by Harvey Pekar—a still-unpublished biography of an American radical—and has completed a full-length comic on Shelley and labor activist Pauline Newman, *Masks of Anarchy* (Verso: 2013). She lives in Harlem.

Rebecca Migdal is a graphic journalist/novelist and a contributing editor at *World War 3 Illustrated*, a cooperatively run magazine featuring political comics from some of the world's top editorial artists. She is a member of the Lower East Side Printshop, and is also currently writing and performing puppet plays at Bank Street Bookstore in New York City.

Afua Richardson is a self-taught comic book creator, and winner of the 2011 Nina Simone Artistic Achievement Award for being one of the few African-American female comic book creators to have worked for all the comic book giants: Marvel, DC and Image Comics. She is also a political activist, a classical flautist, a professional singer, songwriter, and voice actress. AfuaRichardson.com

Award-winning herstorian and writer **Trina Robbins** has been writing books, comics and graphic novels for over forty years. Her 2009 book, *The Brinkley Girls: The Best of Nell Brinkley's Cartoons from 1913–1940* (Fantagraphics), and her 2011 book, *Tarpe Mills and Miss Fury*, were nominated for Eisner awards and Harvey awards. Her all-ages graphic novel, *Chicagoland Detective Agency: The Drained Brains Caper*, the first in a six-book series, was a Junior Library Guild Selection. Her most recent graphic novel, *Lily Renee: Escape Artist*, was awarded a gold medal from Moonbeam Children's Books and a silver medal from Sydney Taylor Awards.

The late **Spain Rodriguez** (1940–2012), one of the founders of the underground press movement, created the first underground tabloid, *Zodiac Mindwarp*. Many of his strips have offered intense historical views of social and cultural conflicts, including wars and uprisings. His Verso book *Che: A Graphic Biography* (2008) has been published in nine languages.

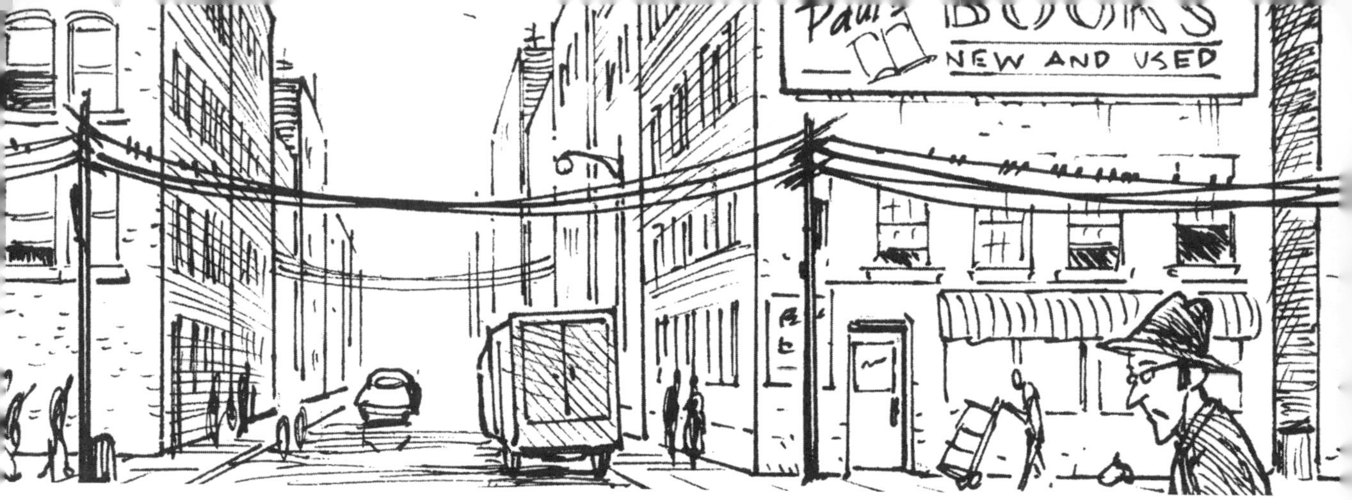
NEW AND USED

Sharon Rudahl, born in Virginia, was a civil rights activist, an artist for anti–Vietnam War underground newspapers and the feminist *Wimmen's Comix*. She will be remembered for her 2007 book *A Dangerous Woman: The Graphic Biography of Emma Goldman*. She has contributed to many anthologies and is now working, in collaboration with Paul Buhle, on *Abraham Lincoln for Beginners*. She lives in Los Angeles.

Joel Schechter teaches courses in theatre history, dramatic literature and popular theatre at San Francisco State University. Books he wrote about political satirists and circus clowns include the titles *Durov's Pig*, *The Congress of Clowns*, *The Pickle Clowns*, and *Messiahs of 1933*. His stories illustrated by Spain Rodriguez have appeared in *Jewish Currents* and *Yiddishkeit*.

Dan Steffan has occupied all of the jobs in publishing that any lifelong fanboy could imagine. He's been an illustrator, cartoonist, writer, letterer, editor, designer, art director and retailer. Now in his olden-timey years he's returned to his first love, comics—it is undoubtedly a sign of his declining mental health. He lives in Portland, OR.

Steve Stiles's first cartoon sale was to Paul Krassner's *The Realist*. Since then he's appeared in numerous underground and mainstream comics. He cocreated the first steampunk graphic novel, *The Adventures of Professor Thintwhistle*, with Richard Lupoff.

Nick Thorkelson has created comics stories for many of Paul Buhle's anthologies. His other comics include "The Underhanded History of the USA," "Economic Meltdown Funnies," "Fortune Cookies" and "The Comic Strip of Neoliberalism." Recently he completed a twenty-three-minute animation, *Où est Fleuri Rose?*, in collaboration with composer Mark Warhol and animator Amy MacDonald.

A former Marvel Comics Assistant Editor, Madrid-based cartoonist **Lance Tooks** has contributed to over 100 films, commercials and music videos as an animator. He has created the original graphic novel *Narcissa*, *The Black Panthers for Beginners* and the four-volume Lucifer's Garden of Verses series; in addition, he regularly adapts legendary authors for Eureka's Graphic Classics series, for whom he coedited their landmark volume, *African-American Classics*.

Acknowledgments

This project, a thematic successor to *The Beats* (2007, edited by Harvey Pekar and Paul Buhle, including an overlap of artists with the present volume), began with a new, Dover Books edition (2012) of the classic text by Albert Parry, *Garrets and Pretenders*, thanks to the publisher's request that Paul Buhle write a preface.

Thanks also to Wendy Johnson for providing us her uncle's memoir, *A Dancer in the Revolution* (2014), for adaptation.

Many people have been helpful through the years and along the way, helping to make this volume possible and even interesting. Our editor at Verso, Andrew Hsiao, would top that list, followed by Mark Martin, who led the difficult process of transferring many software files of comic art into a single text. Audrea Lim and Angelica Sgouros have added much in their editorial work. For the contributors and editors of this volume, Harvey Pekar and his fascination with bohemianism have been and remain an inspiration.

Bibliography

Bronson Alcott, Louisa May Alcott, and Clara Endicott Sears, *Bronson Alcott's Fruitlands: With Transcendental Wild Oats (1915)*. Whitefish, MT: Kessinger Publishing, 2010.

Sarane Alexandrian, *Marcel Duchamp*. New York: Crown Publishing, 1977

Deborah Bricker Balken, *Debating American Modernism: Stieglitz, Duchamp and the New York Avant-Garde*. New York: American Federation of the Arts, 2003

Marcella Bencivenni, *Italian Immigrant Radical Culture: The Idealism of the Sovversivi in the United States, 1890–1940*. New York: New York University Press, 2011.

Emily Bernard, *Carl Van Vechten and the Harlem Renaissance: A Portrait in Black and White*. New Haven, CT: Yale University Press, 2012.

Shari Benstock, *Women of the Left Bank: Paris, 1900–1940*. Austin, TX: University of Texas Press, 1986.

Luisa Cetti, *Un falansterio a New York: l'Unitary Household (1858–1860) e il riformismo prebellico americano*. Palermo, Italy: Sellerio Editore, 1992.

Stanley Crouch, *Considering Genius: Writings on Jazz*. Boston: Perseus Books, 2006.

Michael Denning, *The Cultural Front: The Laboring of American Culture in the Twentieth Century*. New York: Verso Books, 1997.

Scott DeVeaux, *The Birth of Bebop: A Social and Musical History*. Berkeley, CA: University of California Press, 1997.

John Egerton, *Visions of Utopia: Nashoba, Rugby, Ruskin, and the "New Communities" in Tennessee's Past*. Knoxville, TN: University of Tennessee Press, 1977.

Ralph Ellison, *Living with Music: Ralph Ellison's Jazz Writings*. New York: Modern Library, 2002.

Stephen C. Foster and Rudolf E. Kuenzli, *Dada Spectrum: The Dialectics of Revolt*. Iowa City: University of Iowa, 1979.

Ira Gitler, *Swing to Bop: An Oral History of the Transition in Jazz in the 1940s*. New York: Oxford University Press, 1985.

Woody Guthrie, *Bound for Glory: The Hard-Driving, Truth-Telling Autobiography of America's Great Poet–Folk Singer*. New York: Penguin Books, 1983

David Hajdu, *Positively 4th Street: The Lives and Times of Joan Baez, Bob Dylan, Mimi Baez Fariña, and Richard Fariña*. New York: North Point Press, 2011.

Hutchins Hapgood, *An Anarchist Woman*. New York: Duffield and Company, 1909.

Hutchins Hapgood, *The Spirit of the Ghetto: Studies of the Jewish Quarter in New York*. New York: Funk & Wagnalls, 1902.

Howard Eugene Johnson and Wendy Johnson, *A Dancer in the Revolution: Stretch Johnson, Harlem Communist of the Cotton Club*. New York: Fordham University Press, 2014.

Robin D.G. Kelley, *Thelonious Monk: The Life and Times of an American Original*. New York: Free Press, 2009.

Bruce Kellner, *Carl Van Vechten and the Irreverent Decades*. Norman, OK: University of Oklahoma Press, 1968.

Joe Klein, *Woody Guthrie: A Life*. New York: Ballantine Books, 1980.

Harriet Lane Levy, *Paris Portraits: Stories of Picasso, Mattisse, Gertrude Stein, and Their Circle*. Berkeley, CA: Heyday Books, 2011.

Mark A. Lause, *The Antebellum Crisis and America's First Bohemians*. Kent, OH: Kent State University Press, 2009.

Claude McKay, *A Long Way from Home*. New York: Arno Press, 1969 reprint.

Albert Parry, *Garrets and Pretenders: Bohemian Life in America from Poe to Kerouac*. Minneola, FL: Dover Press, 2012.

Edward Portnoy, "Modicut Puppet Theatre: Modernism, Satire, and Yiddish Culture," in John Bell, ed., *Puppets, Masks, Performing Objects*. Cambridge, MA: Massachusetts Institute of Technology 01.

Hans Richter, *Dada: Art and Anti-Art*, New York: Thames and Hudson, 1997.

Judith Schwartz, *Radical Feminists of Heterodoxy: Greenwich Village 1912–1940*. Lebanon, NH: New Victoria Publishers, 1982.

Karl Shapiro, "The Greatest Living Author," in Henry Miller, *Tropic of Cancer*, New York: Grove Press, 1961.

Tamara Stevens and Erin Stevens, *Swing Dancing*. Santa Barbara, CA: Greenwood Publishing, 2011.

Alice B. Toklas, *What Is Remembered*. San Francisco: North Point Press, 1985.

Carl Van Vechten, *Peter Whiffle: His Life and Works*. New York: Alfred A. Knopf, 1922.

Alan M. Wald, *The New York Intellectuals: The Rise and Decline of the Anti-Stalinist Left from the 1930s to the 1980s*. Chapel Hill, CA: University of North Carolina Press, 1987.

Andrea Weiss, *Paris Was a Woman: Portraits from the Left Bank*, San Francisco: Harper Collins, 1995.

Ross Wetzsteon, *Republic of Dreams: Greenwich Village, the American Bohemia, 1910–1960*. New York: Simon and Schuster, 2002.

Rebecca Zurier, *Picturing the City: Urban Vision and the Ashcan School*. Berkeley, CA: University of California Press, 2006.